Guidebook for Directors of Nonprofit Corporations

FOURTH EDITION

Nonprofit Organizations Committee

Willard L. Boyd III
Lisa A. Runquist
Editors

ABA
AMERICAN BAR ASSOCIATION
Business Law Section

Cover design by Catherine Zaccarine.

Boyd, Willard L., and Lisa A. Runquist, editors
Guidebook for directors of nonprofit corporations / Edited by Willard L. Boyd III and Lisa A. Runquist.—4th ed.

Printed in the United States of America.

28 27 26 25   5 4 3 2

ISBN: 978-1-63905-469-5

Discounts are available for books ordered in bulk. Special consideration is given to state bars, CLE programs, and other bar-related organizations. Inquire at Book Publishing, ABA Publishing, American Bar Association, 321 N. Clark Street, Chicago, Illinois 60654-7598.

www.shopABA.org

Summary of Chapters

Table of Contents

Preface

This fourth edition of the *Guidebook for Directors of Nonprofit Corporations* has been prepared by the Committee on Nonprofit Organizations of the Business Law Section of the American Bar Association. The purpose of the *Guidebook* is to assist directors of a nonprofit corporation in performing their duties. Primarily designed for the lay reader, the *Guidebook* provides a description of general legal principles as they apply to nonprofit corporations. On a more practical level, the *Guidebook* offers what is intended to be useful suggestions and procedures for both the individual directors and the corporation they serve.

The *Guidebook* is designed to serve as a useful reference book for directors and prospective directors of the thousands of nonprofit corporations in the United States—from the smallest corporation that operates principally at a local or even neighborhood level to the largest nonprofit corporation having operations that extend not only across this country but internationally as well. Nonprofit corporations have always played a large role in American life; they play a bigger role today than most people realize. In the future, it is likely that even more people will look to nonprofit corporations to help address issues and solve problems.

In general, the *Guidebook* addresses general legal principles and broad areas of concern and is not intended to be a source of specific legal advice or solutions to particular problems. Rather, its goal is to provide nonprofit corporation directors with an overall understanding of their role. It is designed to help directors identify the information they need in certain areas, and to suggest methods for obtaining this information within the framework of the corporation's particular circumstances.

This fourth edition of the *Guidebook* attempts to reflect the issues that affect directors of nonprofit corporations today. In many respects, the issues facing nonprofits now are unchanged from what they were when the previous editions came out: What does a director do? What is the scope of the director's duties? Although these questions may be timeless, the answers necessarily reflect today's realities and legal developments. We also attempted to identify developing trends and legal issues that are likely to affect nonprofit corporations and their directors in the future.

It has been said that those who select directors of nonprofit boards should look for the following qualities: "wealth, wisdom, and work—never settle for less than two."[1] Through this *Guidebook*, the Nonprofit Organizations Committee hopes to add to your wisdom, and make your work as a nonprofit director more effective; as for wealth, we can't do much for you. But if all who care for the nonprofits that they direct are wise and dedicated, there will be wealth, in many forms, for all.

The principal authors and editors of this edition are Willard L. Boyd III and Lisa A. Runquist. Jeannie Carmedelle Frey of Irving, Texas and Willard Boyd were the principal authors and editors of the third edition. George W. Overton of Chicago and Jeannie Frey were the principal authors and editors of the second edition. George Overton was the principal author of the first edition, together with Lisa Runquist, William Humenuk of Philadelphia, and other members of the Committee on Nonprofit Organizations (then known as the Committee on Nonprofit Corporations) of the ABA Business Law Section.

In addition, the following individuals provided editorial assistance for specific chapters and subject matter in the fourth edition:

- William M. Klimon of Washington, D.C. (*The Nonprofit Corporation and its Directors; What They Do, How They Do It, and for Whom*, Chapter 1; *Duties and Rights of Nonprofit Corporation Directors*, Chapter 2)
- William D. Fournier of Washington, D.C., William Klimon, and Patrick Sternal of Washington, D.C. (*Taxation*, Chapter 5)
- Myron Steeves of Newport Beach, California (*Creating For-Profit Subsidiaries and Joint Ventures*, Chapter 6)
- Frank Boyd Harty of Des Moines, Iowa (*Employees*, Chapter 8)
- Samuel R. Maizel of Los Angeles and Roy R. Leaf of Cedar Rapids, Iowa (*Bankruptcy Section*, Chapter 11)
- Cynthia R. Rowland of San Francisco and William Klimon (*Investments and Expenditures of Endowment Funds*, Chapter 12)

Special thanks and appreciation also are owed to Jeannie Frey for her overall guidance on this edition, Megan Christensen for being instrumental in initiating the work on this edition, and William Klimon for his editing and shaping the overall content.

WILLARD L. BOYD III
Des Moines, Iowa

LISA A. RUNQUIST
Los Angeles, California

1. A common variant of this qualification standard is "time, treasure, and talent." The originators of the sayings are unknown.

Introduction

Who Should Read This Guidebook?

This *Guidebook* was prepared to aid directors of a nonprofit corporation in performing their duties.[1] It is written for anyone presently serving as such a director, as well as anyone contemplating such service.

There are a wide variety of nonprofit corporations: Art museums, health care providers, social clubs, trade associations, foundations, and homeowners' associations, just to name a few, and this *Guidebook* is written for the directors of all of them. You may ask how this *Guidebook* can address the needs of directors of all nonprofit corporations, given the vast range of nonprofit activities. Despite their variety of purposes, nonprofit corporations have many things in common. For instance, most nonprofit corporations are organized and maintained pursuant to a single state statute and are managed by a single governing board. Although the size of the resources managed by nonprofit boards varies widely, their fundamental responsibilities are the same.

The rights and duties of directors of nonprofit corporations are in many respects similar to those imposed on directors of for-profit or business corporations. In a large number of states, the statute governing nonprofit corporations has been modeled at least to some degree on the statute governing business corporations. Further, the legal analysis of many corporate governance issues in the nonprofit context often draws on the lessons learned from the law applied to business corporations. A new or prospective director of a nonprofit corporation who is familiar with the working of business corporation boards is therefore likely to feel comfortable that the director understands the basic requirements of this new role. Still, nonprofit directors need to be aware that, because of the unique nature of nonprofit organizations, in some circumstances, both state and federal law may impose additional or different duties on directors of these organizations—especially directors of tax-exempt corporations and corporations deemed to be public charities.

Nonprofits play an important and sometimes irreplaceable role, not only in this country but throughout the world. The conduct of all nonprofit boards is important not only to their organizations but also to the constituencies they serve. To help effectively direct these organizations, directors need two things: an informed understanding of their role and effective procedures for making decisions and taking action.

Directors of smaller nonprofit organizations may feel that some of the suggestions in this *Guidebook* only apply to larger entities with bigger staffs and greater resources. Although there are practical limitations imposed on directors of many nonprofits, consistency and regularity in board procedures typically found in established, well-managed corporations (whether for-profit or nonprofit) are not accidental. This *Guidebook* aims to help directors of all nonprofit corporations, big and small, to use their resources to the greatest effect.

A Few Definitions

Nonprofit corporation. A nonprofit corporation is an artificial creation of a government—usually a state. Corporations do not exist simply by mutual agreement of members or directors but come into being only by specific actions of a state or federal government and are kept in existence only by compliance with the regular requirements of that government.

Articles of incorporation. As part of the creation of the corporation, the articles of incorporation are filed with the government. These articles are sometimes referred to as a charter, certificate of incorporation, or constitution. The *Guidebook* uses the term "articles of incorporation."

Bylaws. The detailed rules of the corporation's governance of the corporation, as adopted by the directors, are usually referred to as the bylaws but sometimes are labeled with other names, such as standing rules or constitution. The *Guidebook* uses the term "bylaws."

Board of directors. Every nonprofit corporation statute provides for a board of directors; however, in a given corporation, the name of this body varies with the history, tradition—and whim—of the organization involved. It may be called a board of trustees, a board of overseers, a governing committee, or any one of a dozen other names.[2] This *Guidebook* will use the terms the "board of directors" or "board," and refers to the board's members also as "directors." Throughout this *Guidebook,* the term "director" is used to denote a member of the governing body of a nonprofit corporation. Any other type of director will be qualified in the text.

Officers. There is similar variety in the titles of officers. The individual who is responsible for overseeing the day-to-day operations of the corporation may be referred to as the president, CEO, executive director, executive officer, or other title. In this *Guidebook*, the term "chief executive" is used to describe the principal executive officer of the corporation, and "chair" to describe the individual who presides over the board of directors.

Members. In the nonprofit world, the term "member" may refer to an individual or entity having the power to elect one or more of the corporation's directors and/or having other voting rights that are similar to, or even greater than, those of a stockholder of a business corporation. On the other hand, a nonprofit corporation may use the term "members" for supporters who have no voting rights, with the term member being mostly an acknowledgment of such support, used by a charitable corporation to express appreciation (and sometimes offer special benefits or discounts) to its donors. Although numerous nonprofit corporations have different categories of members, with differing rights and powers, many nonprofit corporations have no members at all. In some organizations, the term "delegate" identifies individuals, such as persons participating in conventions or other representative assemblies, who may have some of the attributes of members but whose rights may be limited to the context of a specific assembly or gathering.[3] In this *Guidebook*, the term "member" is used only to refer to a person or entity with rights to vote for directors or to vote on any type of fundamental transaction.

Focus of this guidebook. This *Guidebook* deals only with nonprofit entities that are organized as corporations. Other nonprofit entities, such as unincorporated associations, charitable trusts, or limited liability companies are outside the scope of this book.[4]

Legal Requirements vs. Good Corporate Practice

Throughout this *Guidebook*, we seek to answer two principal questions:

- What does the law require?
- What is good corporate practice, as shaped by the needs of the particular corporation involved and the practical limitations of the director's service?

Neither of these questions has a simple answer. Much of the law concerning a director's responsibility is derived from practices in business corporations where the accountability of a director may differ from that arising in a nonprofit context. What constitutes good corporate practice also will vary with the nature and resources of the corporation, its purposes, and the nature of its exposures. The practical expectations of nonprofit directors are shaped in part by the needs and resources of each corporation involved. Nonetheless, there are significant areas of common ground that apply to all nonprofit corporation directors.

The Law's Commands

In writing for directors we must first, as lawyers, alert our readers to the commands and prohibitions imposed by the law. All legal systems necessarily deal with minimum requirements of behavior: "You must do at least X" or "No matter what the circumstances, you must not do Y." This *Guidebook* indicates legal requirements by the use of imperative verbs such as *must, must not, shall, shall not, is required to,* and the like.

Our statements of the law's commands are sometimes a summary of a specific statute or regulation—such as the Internal Revenue Code and the related regulations—and sometimes a reference to the body of judge-made law concerning corporations. The Model Nonprofit Corporation Act, Fourth Edition (Model Act) is used in this *Guidebook* as the prototype or presumptive guide to issues of statutory corporate law.[5] Still, directors should be aware that state statutes and legal precedent applicable to specific nonprofit corporations may differ from the Model Act in various respects.

Good Corporate Practice

Equally important is the *Guidebook's* advice—based on experiences of lawyers for nonprofit corporations—outlining what a director should, is expected to, may, or should not do.

The *Guidebook's* statements as to what a director *should* do reflect: (a) policies underlying legal requirements; and (b) general standards of corporate management evolved from the experience of both business and nonprofit corporations.

With respect to good corporate practice, this *Guidebook* describes in part what a director is generally expected to do today and in part what a director may be expected to do in the future. Good corporate practice also describes the behavior dedicated directors will want to see from their fellow directors, and hence from themselves.

Limitations of Time vs. the Corporation's Needs

The most important practical limitation on a director's service is time. Each individual director should determine how much time the director can devote to the corporation's affairs. The board of directors as a whole should organize its affairs on a shared assumption as to the time all directors can give. Given that most directors are chosen on the basis of their experiences and activities, director time constraints are an ever-present issue. The board needs to determine how much time directors should spend to appropriately carry out their duties, and make sure that each director is willing and able to do so.

In many of the areas examined in this *Guidebook*, there are no ready-made answers to the conflict of needs versus resources; it will be up to the directors to evaluate how to mediate between these conflicts, and to reassess these decisions periodically in the light of current circumstances. Directors need to be aware of changes in the legal and business climate that affect their corporation, and that may change the determination of what is "enough" time to fulfill their individual duties to the corporation and their fellow board members.

The Organization of This Guidebook

This *Guidebook* is organized as follows:

Chapters 1 through 3 discuss matters of concern to all directors of all corporations: how a board works, the directors' rights and duties, and the functions of committees, advisory bodies, and officers.

Chapter 4 discusses officers of a nonprofit corporation.

Chapter 5, on taxation, surveys tax-exemption issues, an area of concern for most nonprofit corporations and their directors.

Chapter 6 discusses the tax-exemption issues that arise when tax-exempt nonprofit organizations create for-profit subsidiaries or contemplate joint ventures with for-profit entities.

Chapter 7 discusses a host of potential legal issues that may be relevant to a nonprofit organization's Internet activities.

Chapters 8 and 9 discuss legal issues relating to use of a nonprofit corporation's human resources, and suggest standards and procedures for the effective use of volunteers and employees.

Chapter 10 discusses considerations for directors with regard to mergers, sale of assets, affiliations, and other combinations.

Chapter 11 notes some of the general legal issues that arise in fundamental change events, such as sale of unique assets, bankruptcy, and dissolution.

Chapter 12 discusses issues relating to the investment of institutional funds and expenditures from endowment funds.

Chapter 13 covers issues relating to insurance and other liability protection for nonprofit corporation directors.

Chapter 14 offers suggestions on the steps that a nonprofit's directors can take to understand the legal environment in which the organization operates, and on how to select and use legal counsel.

Chapter 15 discusses best practices for orientation of new board members, and ways to revitalize existing board members and the board as a whole.

At the end of each chapter, the reader will find questions that we suggest each individual director review concerning the issues relevant to the subject matter of the chapter. Following the questions in each chapter is a checklist that board members may find helpful to review in light of their organization's specific circumstances.

Endnotes

1. This *Guidebook* is the work of the Committee on Nonprofit Organizations of the Business Law Section of the American Bar Association (ABA).
2. The Model Nonprofit Corporation Act, Fourth Edition (Model Act) and most state laws specifically reject the trust law standard for the conduct of nonprofit directors. *See* Model Act § 830(g). Thus, the use of the term "trustee" does not connote duties different from or additional to those of a director. In some states and in certain circumstances, however, nonprofit directors may be considered trustees of charitable assets and thereby subject to duties beyond those generally applicable to nonprofit directors. *See Chapter 2, Duties and Rights of Nonprofit Corporation Directors.*
3. *See, e.g.,* Colorado Revised Nonprofit Corporation Act, COLO. REV. STAT. § 7-121-401(1); Indiana Nonprofit Corporation Act, IND. CODE §§ 23-17-2-8 and 23-17-9-1.
4. For a discussion regarding other types of nonprofit entities, *see* Willard L. Boyd III, Ed., *Nonprofit Law: A Practical Guide to Legal Issues for Nonprofit Organizations* (American Bar Association 2017);

Lisa A. Runquist, *The ABCs of Nonprofits* (2nd ed., American Bar Association 2015) (also available in Spanish).

5. The Model Act was approved by the Committee on Nonprofit Organizations of the Business Law Section of the ABA in 2021. It was published by the Business Law Section of the ABA in 2022. It is based in large part on the ABA Model Business Corporation Act developed by the Corporate Laws Committee of the Business Law Section. For an overview of the Model Act, see Lawrence J. Beaser and William H. Clark, Jr., *Forward to the Fourth Edition* in *Model Nonprofit Corporation Act* (4th ed., American Bar Association 2022), at xvii.

Chapter 1:
The Nonprofit Corporation and Its Directors: What They Do, How They Do It, and for Whom

Chapter 1
The Nonprofit Corporation and Its Directors: What They Do, How They Do It, and for Whom

There are many types of nonprofits with some created for a charitable or public purpose, some created for a religious purpose, and some created for the benefit of the nonprofit corporation's membership. Regardless of the type, it is important that the nonprofit corporation have governance documents—typically in the form of articles of incorporation and bylaws—that accurately describe the purposes and governance structure of the corporation. In addition, a nonprofit corporation—regardless of its purpose—is generally required to have a board of directors that has the ultimate legal authority and accountability for the management of the affairs of the corporation. The composition and election of boards vary among nonprofits. Still, a common rule for all nonprofits is that the members of the board act as a collective body and not individually when acting on behalf of the corporation.

The Taxonomy of the Nonprofit World

Basic Concepts

Nonprofit corporations are corporations organized under the laws of a state and have as their objective something other than enriching shareholders. (References to "state laws" also include the laws of the District of Columbia,

U.S. territories, Native American tribes, and other U.S. jurisdictions.) The laws of each state vary, of course, so this section describes a few basic nonprofit corporate law concepts in very general terms. As noted below, nonprofits can be generally characterized as being one of three major categories: public benefit, religious, or mutual benefit.

"Public benefit" corporations

Most highly visible nonprofit corporations (e.g., educational institutions, art museums) are sometimes referred to as *"public benefit" corporations.* These corporations exist to benefit the public rather than members by engaging in a purpose that historically has been viewed as primarily "charitable" in nature. Public benefit corporations may or may not have members. And members may have important rights or no rights at all depending on how the corporation's articles of incorporation or bylaws define those rights. Members also may have rights set forth in the applicable state nonprofit corporation statute. For example, members may be entitled to vote only on a proposed merger or sale of the corporation's assets or they also may be entitled to elect some or all of the directors. Still, members of a public benefit corporation have no ownership or franchise interest in the nonprofit. Public benefit corporations are typically eligible to be exempt from federal taxation under Internal Revenue Code (Tax Code) Section 501(c)(3), which is described in more detail later, as well as other sections of the Tax Code, such as 501(c)(4). See *Chapter 5, Taxation.*

Public benefit (nonprofit) corporations are distinguishable from "benefit corporations" or "public benefit (for profit) corporations," which are for-profit corporations that have elected benefit-corporation status that usually includes the duty to consider the interests of constituencies other than shareholders, as well as some reporting and certification obligations. A benefit corporation has owners (shareholders) whereas a nonprofit corporation has no owners. In addition, a benefit corporation is taxed like any other "C" corporation or "S" corporation whereas most nonprofits are eligible for tax-exempt status.[1]

A "religious" corporation

A "religious" corporation is similar to a public benefit corporation in many respects but is established for religious purposes. Some state nonprofit corporation acts distinguish between public benefit corporations and religious corporations. Some of the older states retain separate religious corporation statutes, some regarding specific denominations.[2] Organizations that meet the Internal Revenue Service (IRS) definition of churches (which includes synagogues, mosques, and temples), conventions or associations of churches, and integrated auxiliaries of churches are automatically considered to be exempt under Section 501(c)(3), whether or not they file with the IRS to establish their exempt purposes but are otherwise still subject to most of the same legal requirements. Religious organizations that are not churches or the church-related entities as listed above remain subject to the same federal tax filing requirements to establish their exempt status as other nonprofits.[3]

A "mutual benefit" corporation

A *"mutual benefit" corporation,* in contrast to a public benefit or religious corporation, is operated to benefit its members. Its members will generally be a well-defined group, such as members of a trade association, homeowners' association, or country club. The rights of the members of a mutual benefit corporation are defined in its organizing documents. A mutual benefit corporation does not qualify for federal tax exemption under 501(c)(3) although it may qualify for exemption under another Tax Code section, such as 501(c)(6) or (c)(7).

Other classifications

California and the states that have adopted the Revised Model Nonprofit Corporation Act follow the tripartite scheme described above. But other state nonprofit corporation statutes do not use those classifications. For example, the Model Nonprofit Corporation Act, Fourth Edition (Model Act) as well as the Model Act's Third Edition recognize certain differences between charitable corporations and other types of nonprofit corporations but do not use the "public benefit," "mutual benefit," and "religious" classifications.[4] And in the last decade, Delaware, Kansas, New York, and Oklahoma each amended their corporation laws to enshrine a simple two-class distinction between charitable and noncharitable nonprofit corporations.[5]

"Articles of incorporation" and "bylaws"

As noted in the Introduction, the organizing or governing documents of a corporation are often referred to as the *"articles of incorporation"* and *"bylaws."* The articles of incorporation is a public document filed with the secretary of state or another state governmental office and available to the public. The document generally provides basic information, such as the name of the corporation, its purpose, and any special restrictions related to its status. It may include provisions such as identifying the organizers, initial board of directors, and other required or optional provisions. The bylaws set out in detail how the corporation is governed: requirements for members, if any, member voting rights, and procedures for member action (i.e., notice of meetings, quorum, voting); number, qualification, and responsibilities of directors; committees of the board; and designation, qualifications, and responsibilities of officers. The bylaws may also address other topics such as conflict of interest. In addition, the articles of incorporation or the bylaws might address other special provisions, such as indemnification and limitation of liability of directors.

The Director's Role

A director acts as a part of a board

Anyone serving as a director of a nonprofit corporation must be aware of what a director is—and isn't. As a body, a board of directors has considerable powers. In most nonprofit corporations the board plays a substantial part in the beginning or end of any corporate activity, and the board appoints or removes corporate officers and agents.

In contrast, an individual director, acting alone, has no power; rather, each director exerts any power as one participating element in the board of directors.[6] Nonetheless, the individual director is still legally accountable for corporate actions in certain circumstances and has legally protected rights and duties to participate in the board's decisions and to access all information related to them.[7]

The directors direct, but do not perform, the corporation's activities

The corporate structure contemplates that corporate actions, as determined by the board, will be carried out by officers, employees, and agents—persons chosen, directly or indirectly, by the board of directors. Often a person serving as a director also may wear another hat, such as that of an officer or agent, but corporate theory assumes that neither the board itself nor any individual director, acting solely as a director, carries out day-to-day activities.

The directors act on behalf of one or more constituencies

In a business corporation, the director's constituents are, by and large, the stockholders. The stockholders elect the directors. The directors understand that their primary function is to advance the stockholders' wealth, and it is the stockholders, in most instances, who may call the director to account.

In the nonprofit world, identifying a director's constituencies is often not so simple. The persons or entities electing or appointing nonprofit directors, the interests they serve, and those who may call the director to account can be and often are, separate parties.

Director Selection

Directors of nonprofit corporations can be selected in three ways.

Election or appointment by members or others

Membership corporations, including generally speaking all mutual benefit corporations, elect directors somewhat as stockholders elect business corporation directors. Each member has one vote, and the candidate or candidates having the most votes win. Often the members are presented with a slate of candidates for election or reelection at an annual meeting, which they are required to vote up or down. The same basic structure is used where the members are institutions or even one single person or entity. For instance, a hospital may create a subsidiary nonprofit corporation for a particular purpose, with the hospital corporation as the sole voting member electing the subsidiary's directors.

In some cases, the corporation's articles of incorporation or bylaws may provide that a person, entity, or group that is not a member of the corporation may appoint one or more of the corporation's directors.[8] For instance, some states permit bondholders or other creditors to vote for directors under certain circumstances.[9] In addition, a nonprofit that has been established to benefit a city-sponsored project might provide that a city official will appoint one or more of the directors.

Self-perpetuating boards

Many public benefit and religious corporations have self-perpetuating boards of directors in which the existing board elects—or reelects—the persons who serve as directors.

Ex officio

A director may serve ex officio by virtue of holding another position, such as chief executive of the corporation, or officer of an affiliate organization or constituency group. As noted below, ex officio directors have the same voting rights as other directors unless the articles of incorporation or bylaws specify that the ex officio directors have no voting rights.

Special Categories of Directors

Frequently, a nonprofit board will describe some person as an *honorary or emeritus, life,* or *ex officio* director. These designations often cause confusion.

Honorary directors

An honorary or emeritus director is, almost by definition, not a true director. If a nonprofit corporation's member or board wishes to recognize someone—usually a longtime member of the board—as deserving of special respect, but to be relieved of regular duties as a board member, they are free to do so.[10] Still, referring to such a person by the term "director" raises three legal issues.

Status should be provided for in the bylaws. It is helpful to have both the method of designating and the status of honorary directors described in the bylaws. Otherwise, the distinction between "regular" and honorary directors can be confusing for the board as well as for staff and other persons who deal with the board. Especially where the honorary director has recently served as a regular director (such as a board chair who has been bumped to honorary status), these bylaw clarifications are helpful for all concerned. Among other things, it is important to address voting and other rights, duties, terms, and removal of honorary directors in the bylaws.

No voting rights. Although a board may at any time invite any person, including honorary or emeritus directors, to attend any board meeting, that person's presence may not be counted for a necessary quorum, and that person may not vote, even if the person is allowed to participate in discussion at the meeting (unless the articles or bylaws provide otherwise). The invitation to attend the meeting confers no voting rights.

Attorney-client privilege issues. The board, in consulting legal counsel concerning matters that the corporation may wish to consider in confidence, must realize that *the presence at a meeting of nondirectors (including persons referred to as honorary directors), or their receipt of confidential documents, may jeopardize the attorney-client privilege*—the corporation's right to communicate with counsel while keeping that communication secret even in court.[11]

Life directors

Life directors usually occupy much the same position as honorary directors and use of that category merits the same cautions set forth above. Still, if a corporation intends to create one or more full voting directorships with a lifetime term, the board must first examine the applicable nonprofit corporation statute—as some will not permit it. The bylaws then must clearly define the status of a life director and address the rights that are associated with that position.

Ex officio directors

Ex officio is the term commonly used to describe a person whose status as a director is tied to the holding of some other office or position (inside or outside the corporation). For example, a hospital may designate whoever is chief of the medical staff as an ex officio director, to serve as long as, and only as long as, the individual is chief of staff. A museum, as a condition of its using park district land, may be required to include the park superintendent as an ex officio director. Ex officio directors may be voting or nonvoting, as specified in the articles or bylaws. If the articles and bylaws are silent on voting rights, it is likely that an ex officio director will be deemed to have voting rights. If an ex officio director has voting rights, the director is considered a regular director, with the same rights and duties as other directors.

Sometimes, however, the term ex officio is used to describe someone who needs to be recognized (or appeased) but who is *not* regarded as a fully participating director. For example, the individual may not only be nonvoting but the individual's presence at every meeting may neither be expected nor counted for purposes of determining a quorum. All the cautions mentioned with regard to honorary directors (particularly with regard to the attorney-client privilege) apply in these situations, and the ambiguity that has attached to the term ex officio dictates that its use should be limited to the situation outlined in the preceding paragraph. It is particularly important, in these cases, that the bylaws define the rights and duties of any ex officio directors, including whether or not they have any voting rights.

The Corporation's Purpose and How It Affects a Director

Defining the Corporation's Purpose and the Persons or Interests It Serves

Any person serving or asked to serve as a director must ask: For what purpose is the corporation maintained? What is the constituency that it is serving? It has been said that all organizations exist to maximize something for somebody; the nonprofit corporation is no exception. Defining the something and the somebody is the duty of every nonprofit board and every director. Once it has been determined what the corporation is maximizing and for whom, all persons serving or asked to serve as directors should determine if these aims are compatible with their reasons for serving on the board.

Statements of the Corporation's Purpose and Its Constituencies Should Be Consistent with the Corporation's Activities

Statements of corporate purposes

In all nonprofit corporations, the corporate purposes should be stated, at least in general terms, in the articles of incorporation and, if desired, the bylaws. The corporate purposes may also be reflected in a mission statement adopted by the board. Unfortunately, the foregoing documents often give inconsistent statements. To the extent the corporate purpose is described in more than one document, it is important that these descriptions be consistent. For that reason, some nonprofits do not include a description of the corporate purpose in the bylaws. Moreover, although the articles of incorporation will legally control in the event of conflicts, the purposes stated in the articles are often as broad as legally allowable and the bylaws may be equally vague.

Use of mission statements

Especially if a nonprofit corporation has no governance instrument that clearly details its present purposes, a director should urge the adoption of a mission statement. Even where a nonprofit corporation is conducting a specific program or activity, with a clear consensus among its directors, it may be beneficial to describe that activity and its purpose in a brief mission statement. The articles of incorporation and bylaws will generally define the broad general purposes of the corporation; however, the mission statement should be more specific, for example, how the purpose is being carried out today. As a practical matter, confusion over mission impairs the efficiency of the board in the discharge of its duties. On the other hand, the adoption or renewal (such as at an annual board retreat) of a corporate mission statement can rekindle the energies and help focus the attention of the board members, both individually and collectively.

Mission statements come in varying styles and shapes. An effective mission statement succinctly reflects the board's agreement regarding the corporation's purposes and constituencies. It is very important that the mission statement is consistent with any purposes statement set forth in the articles of incorporation or bylaws. Three examples of how a mission statement may help focus the activities of a nonprofit corporation are described below:

- The board of a condominium association usually operates within a fairly tight structure dictated by its declaration and statutory law, but clear choices may have to be made as to the constituency served (all owners? only owner-occupants?) or the corporate purpose (bare structural maintenance? enhanced value through annual improvements?). A mission statement enables the board to reach these decisions with minimum—or greatly lessened—interpersonal controversy.
- A local community organization—no matter how small—may have to make choices concerning the constituency served (all residents? only merchants? only youth?) or purposes (all welfare? specific social services?).
- The parent corporation of a regional healthcare system may use a mission statement to help guide its planning and strategic decisions, as well as to communicate its commitments to its employees, medical staff, and the community in which it provides services.

The board should reexamine its mission statement on a regular basis. Any vigorous nonprofit corporation will find that demands and opportunities will continually shape and alter what the corporation actually does; the environment in which it acts will change as well. Regular consideration of a mission statement also helps ensure that newer directors both understand the corporation's mission and are able to participate in the articulation of the mission. Further, a periodic examination will reveal whether the current mission statement is consistent with the purposes statement and other provisions of the articles and bylaws, and if not, what changes in these documents may be required. Tax-exempt nonprofit corporations should also evaluate whether any variations between the corporation's current activities and the statements in its articles or bylaws necessitate a filing with the IRS to confirm the organization's tax-exempt status.

Vision and values statements

Directors should be aware of two other kinds of corporate statements of more recent vintage that may also serve as statements of corporate purpose: the vision and values statements. The vision statement is a succinct summation of a corporation's aspirations for the future. The vision statement is often a product of an organization's strategic planning process. The values statement is a brief summary of a corporation's guiding philosophy. The same cautions and guidance about mission statements given above also apply to vision and values statements.

Accountability of Directors

Accountability of Directors to Defined Classes of Persons or Entities

All nonprofit directors are legally responsible to certain parties. In other words, some classes of persons or entities have the right to question a director's conduct, and even, in extreme cases, to bring the director into court. By implication, there are others who do not have that right.[12]

Accountability of Directors of Mutual Benefit Corporations Is Similar to That of Business Corporation Directors

It has been emphasized that the nonprofit corporation serves to maximize something for somebody, and the director must be able to identify the something and the somebody. In mutual benefit corporations, the somebody involved will often be the party or parties who control the tenure of the directors—for example, in a trade association the members usually elect the directors—and those same persons will be the parties who may, in appropriate circumstances, call the board of directors to account.

Thus, the directors of most mutual benefit corporations hold a relationship to their members similar to that held by the directors of business corporations to stockholders. Nevertheless, in some circumstances (such as when a mutual benefit corporation holds some assets in trust or considers merging with or selling its assets to a business corporation), the directors of a mutual benefit corporation may be called to account by the state attorney general, or other community representatives, on the basis that those assets are charitable assets that may not be disposed of without state approval.[13]

Accountability of Directors of Public Benefit and Religious Corporations

Direct beneficiaries generally have no legal oversight power over nonprofit corporation directors

From the beginning of public charities, there was a class of beneficiaries of the charitable corporation (e.g., the poor of a parish) who were not the parties appointing the director or trustee to office. Further, those beneficiaries were generally deemed incapable of enforcing the director's obligations or were persons who, it was felt, should not have that power. In some cases, moreover, the direct beneficiaries of a nonprofit organization are not people—for example, nonprofits devoted to animal welfare or preserving natural resources. The absence of a mechanism for direct action and oversight by beneficiaries of nonprofit organizations leaves an accountability vacuum. In the United States, this vacuum is often filled by the state, generally represented by the state attorney general.

Attorney general oversight

In many states, a state attorney general is generally deemed to speak for the beneficiaries of any entity, such as a public benefit corporation, which has assets that are considered to be held in a charitable trust. In effect, the attorney general becomes the voice of the constituency for whom a charitable corporation was organized.[14] In comparison, except in unusual circumstances, the attorney general does not assert a right to scrutinize activities of noncharitable corporations, such as mutual benefit corporations.

Traditionally, the attorney general's authority has been understood as giving the attorney general the power to enforce the public's interest in the maintenance of property and funds for the original charitable purpose: to prevent divergence of these funds for improper purposes and intervene if the persons holding this property attempted to change the purpose, even if the new purpose was a proper charitable activity. As a result, a public benefit corporation planning a major change in the use of its assets may be required to consult the attorney general or join the attorney general in a so-called *cy pres* proceeding in a court. Statutory provisions have broadened the power of the attorney general in most states to include a general supervision over the solicitation of monies for charitable purposes.[15]

States vary in the degree to which the attorney general is specifically empowered to investigate transactions of nonprofit corporations, such as public charities, which are deemed to hold some or all of their assets in a charitable trust.[16] Many states have adopted laws affirmatively requiring some or all nonprofit corporations to give the state attorney general prior notice and the opportunity to review transactions involving the disposition of substantially all of the corporation's charitable assets, particularly in the case of a merger or sale of assets to a for-profit institution.[17]

In recent years, nonprofit organizations, especially nonprofit healthcare entities, have experienced increased state attorney general scrutiny of their activities.[18] This has resulted in high-profile enforcement actions and legislation enhancing the enforcement authority of the attorney general around the country.[19]

Directors Are Generally Not Accountable to Donors

A director of a public benefit corporation, such as a conventional charity, will note an omission from the list of the persons to whom directors of a nonprofit corporation may be accountable: donors are not listed as a party with whom the director has a legal relationship. In general, the omission is correct, although obviously the corporation will be sensitive to the concerns of its principal donors. While there are exceptions, as a general rule, assets acquired by a charitable corporation are no longer subject to the donors' control, unless the donors have specified restrictions in the gift instrument that the assets be used or invested in a specific manner.[20]

The corporation's board of directors may use the donated assets in whatever way the board believes appropriate, consistent with the corporation's purpose and the terms of any gift instrument. If donors or others believe these uses are not appropriate, they may be able to petition the state attorney general to review the matter.[21] In some circumstances, donors may bring an action against the nonprofit corporation for enforcement of restrictions on a gift.[22] A donor also may have a contract action available based on the written instrument that sets forth the term of the gift.[23]

Accountability to Members Responsible for Appointing Directors

Although the attorney general's powers may extend to all public benefit corporations within a given state, some of these corporations also have a membership to whom the director may be accountable, to the extent this membership has the power to remove or fail to reelect the director, to sue directors directly, or to bring a derivative action on the corporation's behalf.[24] If a director is elected by one or more members, the director may have—or feel—an obligation to the member or members electing the director to make sure that their viewpoint is represented on the board. Still, that obligation to articulate member perspective does not change the director's obligation to make decisions and take other actions in accordance with the *corporation's* best interest irrespective of any member interests. Generally, the nonprofit corporation law does not recognize constituency directors. The only exception to this rule occurs when the corporation's articles and bylaws specify that certain member interests should be taken into account, such as a requirement that no action be taken that would result in the corporation losing its tax-exempt status.

Constitutional Considerations Limiting Public Accountability of Religious Corporations

The directors of religious corporations are generally subject to the foregoing considerations. Still, because U.S. constitutional law restricts the role of the government in dealing with religious corporations to a minimum enforcement of basic fiscal integrity, oversight is more limited, lest the government intrude on freedom of religion.[25]

See the Suggested Questions and Checklist following the Endnotes below to review the issues discussed in this chapter.

Endnotes

1. For further discussion on benefit corporations, *see Chapter 6, Creating For-Profit Subsidiaries and Joint Ventures.*
2. *See, e.g.*, Md. Code, Corps. & Ass'ns §§ 5-301 to 5-338; N.Y. Relig. Corp. Law §§ 1-489.
3. *See* Lisa A. Runquist and Jeannie Carmedelle Frey, Eds., *Guide to Representing Religious Organizations 55* (American Bar Association 2009).
4. The classification system was eliminated in the Third Edition of the Model Act because of the lack of uniform acceptance by states adopting the Revised Model Nonprofit Corporation Act. *See* Lizabeth A. Moody, Foreword to Model Act, at xxii (American Bar Association 2009).
5. Del. Code tit. 8, § 114(d); Kan. Stat. § 17-6014(d); N.Y. Not-for-Prof. Corp. Law § 201; Okla. Stat. tit. 18, § 1004.1.D.

6. A good analogy is that of a representative in Congress, who may, on the floor or through committee, exert immense influence on the actions of government, but is given no function, under the Constitution, when acting alone. But (again paralleling a member of Congress) the individual director has legally protected rights to participate in corporate decisions and has legally recognized rights and duties to be informed concerning corporate transactions.

   A one-person board of directors is permitted under some state statutes; where such a board exists, the single director's act is an exercise of the board's powers. The Model Act § 803 (and various state statutes) requires a minimum of three directors.
7. *See* Model Act § 801, cmt. (describing rights and duties of directors). *See also Chapter 2, Duties and Rights of Nonprofit Corporation Directors* in this *Guidebook.*
8. *See* CAL. CORP. CODE § 5220.
9. *See, e.g.,* DEL. CODE tit. 8 § 221.
10. *See* CAL. CORP. CODE § 5047.
11. *See generally* John William Gergacz, *Attorney-Corporate Client Privilege* (2024) at § 5.10 (discussing factors to be considered in determining whether attorney-client confidentiality applies); *see also id.* at § 2.5 (using Kirby v. Kirby, 1987 WL 14862 (Del. Ch. July 29, 1987) to explain why in nonprofit corporations the privilege is considered to attach to directors as part of the corporate entity).
12. *See, e.g.,* Cook v. The Lloyd Noland Foundation, Inc. & Tenet Healthcare, Inc., 825 So. 2d 83 (Ala. 2001) (holding that under the state Alabama Nonprofit Corporation Act, the only persons authorized to bring a legal proceeding to challenge an act, conveyance, or transfer of property by a nonprofit corporation were members or directors of the corporation, representatives of the corporation, and the state attorney general, and that the local district attorney and other community representatives therefore lacked standing to challenge the corporation's actions); RESTATEMENT OF THE LAW, CHARITABLE NONPROFIT ORGANIZATIONS §§ 6.01–6.05.
13. *See* James K. Orlikoff and Mary K. Totten, *Governing Conversion Foundations: A Practical Guide for Trustees,* TRUSTEE 51, no. 4 (April 1998), at T1–T4; Gary Claxton, Judith Feder, David Shactman, and Stuart Altaian, *Public Policy Issues in Nonprofit Conversions: An Overview,* HEALTH AFFAIRS 16, no. 2 (March/April 1997), at 9–28.
14. *See, e.g.,* CONN. GEN. STAT. § 3-125; MASS. ANN. LAWS ch. 12 § 8.
15. *See, e.g.,* MO. REV. STAT. § 407.450, et seq.; N.Y. EXECUTIVE LAW § 171-a, et seq.
16. *See, e.g.,* OHIO REV. CODE § 109.24 (giving the state attorney general the power to "investigate transactions and relationships of trustees of a charitable trust for the purpose of determining whether the property held for charitable, religious, or educational purposes

has been and is being properly administered in accordance with fiduciary principles..." and providing that the attorney general "shall institute and prosecute a proper action to enforce the performance of any charitable trust, and to restrain the abuse of it whenever he considers such action advisable..."). *See also* RESTATEMENT OF THE LAW, CHARITABLE NONPROFIT ORGANIZATIONS § 5.01(e). The State Attorney General has the authority to protect charitable assets and interests within the jurisdiction of the State and to seek judicial relief to protect the public's interests in those assets and interests.

17. *See* TENN. CODE ANN. § 48-62-102(g); *see also* OHIO REV. CODE ANN. § 109.34 (referring solely to nonprofit healthcare entities); Uniform Laws Commission, Model Protection of Charitable Assets Act; J.J. Leitner & Leanne C. McGrory, *The Delaware Advantage Applies to Nonprofits, Too*, ABA BUSINESS LAW TODAY (November 2016).
18. *See, e.g.*, People ex rel. Spitzer v. Grasso, 893 N.E.2d 105 (N.Y. 2008); Michael W. Peregrine and Ralph E. DeJong, *State AGs' Powers Over Nonprofits after Spitzer v. Grasso*, NATIONAL LAW JOURNAL (June 18, 2007).
19. *See, e.g.*, California Nonprofit Integrity Act of 2004, CAL. GOV'T CODE § 12585. The Uniform Laws Commission developed the "Model Protection of Charitable Assets Act," which articulates the state attorney general's protection authority over charitable assets.
20. *See* Newman v. Forward Lands, Inc., 430 F. Supp. 1320, 1324 (E.D. Pa. 1977) (holding that "only the Attorney General, a co-trustee, or someone with a special interest may sue to enforce a charitable trust"), citing RESTATEMENT (SECOND) OF TRUSTS § 391. The RESTATEMENT OF THE LAW, CHARITABLE NONPROFIT ORGANIZATIONS in §§ 6.02 and 6.05 addresses standing issues relating to gift-enforcement suits. *See also* Uniform Prudent Management of Institutional Funds Act ("UPMIFA"), § 106.
21. *See* Linda Grant, *Acts of Charity: Furious Donors Blame a Lax Board after a Fund's Scandal Toppled the Lavish-Living Hand of the United Way*, LOS ANGELES TIMES MAGAZINE, September 13, 1992, at 39; *see also* Aramony v. United Way, 28 F. Supp. 2d 147 (S.D.N.Y. 1998), *reversed on other grounds*, 254 F.3d 403 (2d Cir. 2001).
22. For example, in Iowa, a donor of a gift in excess of $100,000 may be able to bring an action against the nonprofit corporation to enforce the restrictions placed on the gift. *See* IOWA CODE § 540A.106.
23. *See, e.g.*, RESTATEMENT OF THE LAW, CHARITABLE NONPROFIT ORGANIZATIONS § 6.03, cmt. b.
24. *See, e.g.*, CAL. CORP. CODE §§ 5710; 7710; N.Y. NOT-FOR-PROFIT CORP. LAW § 623; *see also* Model Act, § 501; DEL. CODE ANN. Tit. 8 § 141(k).
25. See Model Act § 130, cmt.; Runquist and Frey, *supra* note 3, at 6–7.

Suggested Questions for Directors Regarding the Nonprofit Corporation and Its Directors

(1) Who elected me? If I wasn't elected by a voting membership, how was I elected?
(2) If I was elected by a voting membership, how is that membership defined?
(3) Where can I find: The bylaws? The articles of incorporation? Are the records of voting membership kept in good order? By whom?
(4) When does my term of office expire? Can I be reelected? Does my term run until a specific date, or until my successor is chosen?
(5) Can I be removed from my position as director? By whom? On what basis?
(6) Was I selected by some group of members or some entity in such a way that my term differs from that of the other directors?
(7) Is the nonprofit corporation in good standing under the laws of state in which it was incorporated. (This usually can be confirmed by an online search of the website for the Secretary of State's office and possibly the Attorney General's office in that state. In some states, such as California, it is important to also check with the taxing authority.).
(8) What is our corporation supposed to do and for whom? Is our purpose expressed in the articles of incorporation, bylaws, and/or a separate mission statement?
(9) Does the corporation have a mission statement? If not, why not? If so, when was the mission statement last reviewed? Is it consistent with the "purposes" of the corporation as described in the articles of incorporation or bylaws?
(10) What parties or officials can question what we do as directors of the corporation?

Checklist: The Nonprofit Corporation and Its Directors

Note: For simplicity, these checklists describe a corporation having a chair, who presides over the board of directors; a chief executive, who may be a staff person; an executive committee; a governance/nominating committee; and an audit committee. (We recognize, however, that in many smaller and other nonprofits, these committee functions may be performed by either the executive committee or the board as a whole.) We also assume a legal counsel—someone, paid or unpaid, having primary responsibility for the corporation's legal affairs. Many corporations, especially larger nonprofits, may have other committees established for specific purposes, such as establishing executive compensation; overseeing personnel matters; monitoring compliance with legal requirements; and overseeing investments and other financial matters.

Subject	Review By	How Often	Comment
1. Review the articles of incorporation	(a) Full board or governance/ nominating committee, with legal counsel (b) By new directors	(a) Periodic review, probably every three years (b) Upon joining board	Review should include: conformity to corporate purpose/mission; compliance with tax and corporate laws; any explicit provisions relating to directors and officers, including indemnification and availability of limitations on liability.
2. Review the bylaws	In general, (a) Full board or governance/ nominating other committee, with legal counsel (b) By new directors	In general, (a) Periodic review, probably every three years (b) Upon joining board	Review should include conformity to articles of incorporation, corporate purpose/ mission; problems possibly arising from changes in program; compliance with tax and corporate laws; any explicit provisions relating to directors and officers, including indemnification, insurance, and availability of limitations on liability.

Subject	Review By	How Often	Comment
(a) Does the number of directors stated in the bylaws conform to the number actually serving (or the size the board will reach if new directors are elected)? If the corporation has a rotating board with a percentage elected each year, is the percentage being elected correct? Are the directors being chosen as provided in the bylaws?	Chair or chief executive; governance/ nominating committee	Annually in all cases; always before notice goes out for meeting to elect directors	Consistency of actual board composition with articles or bylaw requirements is a frequent problem, particularly in smaller public benefit corporations.
(b) Do the bylaws have a statement of corporate mission or purpose consistent with the articles of incorporation, or other mission statement?	Chair or chief executive; governance/ nominating or other committee	Annually and every time either of these documents is changed	Bylaws may have no statement of mission or purpose and there does not have to be one; but if there is one, it should be consistent with other documents, especially the articles of incorporation.
(c) Are there, or should there be honorary directors?	Chair and chief executive	Probably every three or four years	Voting rights (or lack thereof) should be clearly defined and understood.

Subject	Review By	How Often	Comment
(d) If the corporation has members with voting rights, is there an accurate list of the members consistent with whatever definition of eligibility is contained in the bylaws?	Chief executive, governance/ nominating or other committee	At least annually, and before notice goes out for any meeting where elections are to be held	There is probably no area with greater record-keeping problems than this. Nonprofits, particularly public benefit and religious corporations, will often designate as "members" persons who are simply donors or friends, keeping no accurate membership records. The rights (or lack thereof) of these persons to vote should be clearly defined and any problems reviewed with legal counsel.
3. Review of a corporate mission statement	Chief executive reporting to board	Probably every three or four years	If there is no mission statement, a board should consider creating one.
(a) Is there a single mission statement; is it consistent with the purposes of the corporation as set forth in the articles of incorporation and/or bylaws; in what document is it embodied?	Chief executive reporting to board	Probably every three or four years	There should be a single overall mission statement; separate statements for individual programs may be in order, but they should be consistent.

Subject	Review By	How Often	Comment
(b) Are the corporation's public statements (e.g., brochures, press releases, etc.) as issued during the last year consistent with the stated purpose/mission statement?	Chief executive	Annually, and as each brochure or press release is issued	Nonprofits dealing with public controversies will often find problems here.
(c) Has the board reviewed the mission statement and understood the constituency served by the corporation? Should there be a change in the mission statement to correspond to a modification of the constituency served?	Chair, bringing issue to board	Probably every three or four years	Board should always understand the fundamental focus of the nonprofit corporation's work, such as the specific constituency served or services provided.

Chapter 2:
Duties and Rights of Nonprofit Corporation Directors

Chapter 2

Duties and Rights of Nonprofit Corporation Directors

In carrying out their functions for the corporation, directors are subject to two primary obligations: a duty of care and a duty of loyalty.

The duty of care and the duty of loyalty are the common terms for the standards that guide all actions a director takes. These standards are derived from litigation principally involving business corporations but are equally applicable to nonprofit corporations.[1]

In recent years, there has been an increased focus on the fiduciary duties of nonprofit corporation directors as a result of closer scrutiny being placed on nonprofits by both the government and the public. The IRS Form 990 requires a significant level of disclosure about exempt operations and governance issues.

State attorneys general have conducted high-profile investigations of nonprofit organizations (and their boards), which have resulted in various enforcement actions as well as legislation around the country.[2] *The Sarbanes-Oxley Act, which focused on publicly traded companies, affected views of best practices and recommended standards for the governance of nonprofit organizations. Such developments have not resulted in any fundamental change in the standards to which nonprofit directors are held but rather made clear the importance of a director fulfilling the duty of care and duty of loyalty.*

The Duty of Care

The duty of care calls upon directors to act in a reasonable and informed manner when participating in the board's decisions and its oversight of the corporation's management.

The duty of care requires that first, directors be informed; and second, that they discharge their duties in good faith, with the care that a person in a like position would reasonably believe appropriate under similar circumstances.[3]

Each of the tasks outlined below requires the director's efficient allocation of time. The appropriate amount of time required to satisfy a director's duty of care must be decided by the director in the director's reasonable judgment, under the circumstances. Nonetheless, substantial compliance with the elements of care discussed below is commonly expected of the nonprofit director and may be required by law.

Elements of the Duty of Care

The duty of care requires that a director be informed and exercise independent judgment. Satisfying the duty of care may be accomplished in part by the following activities:

Attending meetings and proxy voting limitations

Regular attendance at meetings of the board of directors is a basic requirement of director service. Generally, directors may not vote by proxy.

Importance of regular attendance. All directors must remember that they act as a group, and therefore regular board meeting attendance is essential. Continuous or repeated absence may expose the director to the risk of not satisfying the duty of care. Moreover, sporadic board attendance by a director may be grounds for the director's removal. Most states permit directors to "attend" a meeting by telephone or use other mechanisms that allow all directors to hear or communicate with each other simultaneously, such as a virtual meeting platform. Therefore, even directors with busy schedules should be able to comply with the regular attendance standard.

Attendance at committee meetings. As discussed in *Chapter 3, Committees and Advisory Bodies*, boards typically delegate many important functions to board committees. A director appointed to serve on a committee of the board is expected to regularly attend such committee meetings and to be active in the committee's deliberations and other activities. A director must satisfy the duty of care in discharging his duties as a committee member.

Limits on attendance or voting by proxy. Generally, directors cannot designate another person as the director's proxy, to attend or vote at board or committee meetings in the director's place unless expressly permitted by statute.[4] All directors should understand the reasons for this rule. First of all, whatever reasons a director's constituency (if the director was elected or appointed by members or a third party) may have had for choosing the director, that choice was the selection of a specific person to perform a duty, not the grant of a transferable privilege. Second, all the other directors, as well as the nonprofit organization itself, are entitled to demand the director's own wisdom and judgment, not that of such surrogate as the director may choose. Third, such deference and accommodation the directors themselves may give to each other in the course of their work usually cannot, as a practical matter, be transferred to purely personal appointees and it is important for directors to be present, prepared, and engaged in discussion regarding the activities of the organization where often the viewpoints of directors might change based on the discussion.

If a board of directors encounters significant problems concerning the frequency of a director's attendance, it should consider adopting or recommending bylaws or policies permitting or requiring the removal of directors who regularly miss meetings or attend only portions of meetings.[5] As an alternative, the board could consider creating honorary directorships or advisory councils for these individuals.

Exercising independent judgment

The duty of care requires that each director, no matter how selected, share *equally* in the responsibility of the board to act in the best interests of the corporation. Each director should exercise the director's independent and informed judgment on all corporate decisions. While such judgment may be informed by the director's individual expertise, experience, and affiliations, and even knowledge of the viewpoints of any entity that contributed to the director's appointment, the director's decision must be based only on what is in the corporation's best interest. No director should vote solely on the basis of what another director thinks, even if that director has special expertise; each director must use the director's independent judgment to evaluate any position taken by another director, the corporation's staff, or an outside expert.

Each director must judge what is in the corporation's best interest, irrespective of other entities with which the director is affiliated or sympathetic, or to which the director owes to the director's board appointment. The law conceives of a board of directors as an entity: each member shares the same rights and the same duties and is accountable to the same constituency. Even if a director is specifically nominated or appointed by a particular group, or is chosen in part because of an association with a certain subset of the organization's members or beneficiaries, each director shares the same fiduciary duty to act in the best interest of the entire organization.

There are situations in which a board of directors may be explicitly structured to provide for representation of certain interests. For example, a trade association may have a board of directors composed of individuals who are selected by separate regions or states. A university alumni association may have a board on which each of the schools of the university is represented by one or more directors who are alumni of that particular school. Directors may be confused about how to address situations in which the interests of their constituency and the interests of the corporation are actually or potentially in conflict. In bringing to the attention of the board, the particular sensitivities and concerns of their constituency, directors may aid the whole board in fulfilling its duty of care, and add wisdom to the whole board's deliberations. Nonetheless, the director's duty of loyalty lies with the interests of the corporation, not with any constituent group. (See the discussion in the section *"The Duty of Loyalty"* below.)

Directors may give weight to the views of directors or others having special expertise but must make an independent decision on any questions presented for board or committee determination. The reason for having more than one director is to ensure that differing viewpoints have the opportunity to be heard and that directors with different talents, expertise, experiences, and perspectives share their views and together decide on what course of action is in the corporation's best interests. To this end, it is important that each director use any expertise the director may have when serving in the role of a board member. In other words, it is important that directors not "check" their talents at the door of the boardroom.

At the same time, although it is natural, and often appropriate, for a director to seriously consider the viewpoints of another director who has special expertise or knowledge on a matter being discussed, it is part of each director's duty of care to evaluate all views and information presented to the board or board committee, and to make an independent judgment regarding the proper course of action.

The need for independent members of the board. Since the passage of the Sarbanes-Oxley Act and of the resulting greater scrutiny of tax-exempt organization operations by Congress and many state attorneys general, the concept of independent directors for a nonprofit has received increased attention. Some states place limitations on the number or percentage of directors who can be "interested" directors.[6] In addition, some states require an organization to have specific committees, like an audit committee, to be comprised of only independent directors.[7]

In the context of nonprofits, an independent director generally means a director who is not employed by the corporation and does not receive compensation from the corporation other than as a director. There is a concern that directors who are not independent might give too much deference to management, or that conflicts of interest may not be appropriately recognized and avoided, resulting in actions that are not in the best interest of the organization.[8] Commentators have noted that independent and nonmanagement board members are an organizational resource that should be used to assure the exercise of independent judgment in key committees and general board decision-making.[9]

The IRS requires nonprofits that file Form 990 to make certain disclosures about board member independence. In Form 990, the IRS defines "independence" differently than other legal sources and even from its own pronouncements in other contexts. For purposes of Form 990, a director who receives compensation from the organization as an officer or other employee or as an independent contractor exceeding $10,000, or a director involved in any disclosable interested persons transaction is considered to lack independence. Still, unless the state law limits the number or percentage of interested directors, the IRS has no power to limit the number.

In comparison, for determining whether a tax-exempt health care corporation would be considered to have a "community board," the IRS has indicated that practicing physicians "affiliated" with a hospital—such as medical staff members—are not considered independent, based on their "close and continuing connection" to the hospital, without regard to whether the nonprofit hospital compensates the physicians in any amount.[10] See also *Chapter 5, Taxation*, for more information on Form 990 requirements as it relates to the governance.

Having adequate information

To function effectively, a director needs to be adequately informed.

Assuring the adequacy and clarity of information. To satisfy the duty of care effectively, directors need to have an adequate source of information flow. This information is generally supplied by the corporation's management and other staff. To the extent that it is not adequate, a board or an individual director will have to determine what additional information is needed. The directors should carefully read the information supplied. If the information is highly technical, lengthy, or otherwise difficult to comprehend, the board may find it helpful to request an executive summary or other version of the information that is in a more understandable form. It is also important that these materials be furnished far enough in advance that the directors have sufficient time to review and analyze the information.

In addition, a director should ask questions at (or before or after) the board meeting as necessary to clarify the information or help assure that the director has fully understood it. If a director has a special expertise with respect to a certain kind of information, the director may assist the other directors by asking clarifying questions, or in pointing out specific items to the rest of the board. (But that director should try to avoid stating opinions in such a way that other directors are tempted or pressured to "rely" on the director's opinion without engaging in independent analysis.) (See the discussion in the section *"Directors may give weight to the views of directors..."* above.)

Sources of board information. In some small nonprofit entities, such as neighborhood improvement bodies or condominium associations, the board itself may be its own primary source of information. With larger organizations, however, the board will inevitably use and rely on information prepared by the corporation's officers and agents. This means that the corporation's staff will inevitably have a significant effect on the board's decisions since the staff will select much of the information the directors receive. Even when a director has total and justified confidence in the suppliers of information, the director should be at least aware that for every piece of information received, other information may have been determined to be not necessary for the board's consideration.

Especially in heavily regulated areas or other areas that are significant to the organization's existence and purpose, the director should evaluate whether the additional information is necessary to fulfill the director's duty and to best serve the organization. If for any reason any director thinks that the information provided to the directors is inadequate in any respect, the director should not hesitate to request further information from the staff or other sources. Since boards tend to become accustomed to the status quo, new board members can often serve a valuable function by calling the board's attention to the question of whether the board should be receiving different or additional information in certain areas. It is also important that any director disclose information to other directors that is not already known to the other directors when this information is material to the discharge of the board's decision-making and oversight functions.[11]

Duty to inform other Directors or Committee members. Under the Model Act, a director must disclose, or cause to be disclosed, to the other Directors or Committee members information not already known by them but known by the director to be material to the discharge of their decision-making or oversight functions, except that disclosure is not required to the extent the director reasonably believes that doing so would violate a duty imposed under law, a legally enforceable obligation of confidentiality, or a professional ethics rule.[12]

Reliance

In the ordinary course of business, a director may act in reliance on information and reports received from regular sources that the director reasonably regards as trustworthy.

A director may rely on the reports, communications, and information received from a committee or from any officer, employee, or agent, if the director reasonably believes the source to be reliable and competent. The Model Act, as well as many state nonprofit codes, expressly recognizes the concept of reliance on others. A director is entitled to rely on information, opinions, reports, or statements, including financial statements and other financial data if prepared or presented by the persons or bodies referenced below:

Officers and employees

A director may rely on information provided by officers or employees of the corporation whom the director reasonably believes to be reliable and competent in the matters presented. If the information is provided in written form, it is expected that the director would have independently reviewed or evaluated the information, or received a sufficiently detailed summary from a reliable source, before relying on it.[13]

Experts retained by the corporation

A director may rely on legal counsel, public accountants, or other persons retained by the corporation as to matters the director reasonably believes are within the person's professional or expert competence.

Board committees

A director may rely on information provided by a committee of the board of which the director is not a member as to matters within the committee's jurisdiction if the director reasonably believes the committee merits confidence.

Religious authorities presenting information to religious corporations

A director of a religious corporation may rely on information provided by religious authorities and ministers, priests, rabbis, imams, or other persons whose position or duties in the religious organization the director reasonably believes justify reliance and confidence and whom the director believes to be reliable and competent in the matters presented.[14]

Inappropriate director reliance

These general rules of reliance *never* apply if the director has personal knowledge that would make reliance on the information provided by any of the above persons unwarranted.[15] In those circumstances, relying on that information would not constitute "reasonableness" or good faith on the part of the director. Moreover, a director having knowledge that brings into question the reliability of any information presented to the board may have a duty to share this knowledge with the other board members.

Delegation

The board of directors, as such, does not operate the day-to-day business of the corporation. In delegating that function to others, it must adopt appropriate policies and procedures that ensure effective oversight of the actions of the corporation's management and other corporate agents.

General rule: the directors oversee but do not directly engage in the corporation's day-to-day operations

The board of directors is generally not expected to operate the corporation on a day-to-day basis. Even under statutes providing that the business and affairs of a corporation shall be "managed" by the board of directors, it is recognized that actual operation is a function of management, that is, the officers and agents of the corporation.[16] In conventional corporate theory, the responsibility of the board is limited to overseeing corporate operations. This principle does not relieve the board of its monitoring responsibilities; however, it does mean that directors are not personally responsible for actions or omissions of officers, employees, or agents of the corporation as long as these persons have been prudently selected and the directors have relied reasonably upon those officers, employees, or agents.

Adoption of appropriate monitoring and control procedures

It is the board's responsibility to oversee the implementation of a compliance program that helps assure the corporation's compliance with legal requirements that are applicable to the nonprofit corporation. Compliance programs are extremely important for mitigating risks of potential legal and operational problems for the nonprofit corporation. These programs also are important if a problem ever arises in operations. Under the Federal Sentencing Guidelines, a corporation can receive significant fine reductions if it has an effective compliance program in place.[17]

As part of their oversight responsibilities, directors and prospective directors of nonprofit corporations should be aware of the kind of legal claims and operational risks to which the corporation may be vulnerable, based on, among other things, trends in government enforcement actions or private litigation involving similar organizations. Directors should regularly evaluate whether the corporation has appropriate policies and procedures in place to ensure that the corporation complies with applicable laws.[18] (For a more detailed discussion of how a board can become aware of the legal environment of its corporation, see *Chapter 14, The Legal Environment of the Nonprofit Corporation.*)

Evidencing specific delegations of authority to officers

While in the for-profit world, a corporation's board often makes clear written delegations of authority to the chief executive and other officers, this is often not the case in the nonprofit world. The board may wish to adopt bylaw provisions, or a general resolution or policy, setting forth the scope of management authority delegated to the chief executive (who may then be free to subdelegate portions of this authority). Formalizing the scope of delegated authority may be particularly useful in small nonprofit corporations, where lines of responsibility may be easily blurred. For example, a bylaw provision addressing the responsibility of an executive officer may specify that the officer has the authority to execute contracts on behalf of the corporation within the scope of the corporation's ordinary conduct of business, and otherwise as specified by board resolution.

Directors with multiple "hats"

When a director occupies both the role of a director and that of an officer, employee, or other agent, corporate law treats that person, while acting in such capacity as an agent, just as the law would treat a person who is not serving on the board. It is therefore essential that this person (and the other directors) always be aware of which "hat" the director is wearing at any particular time.

Assignment of authority to members or other persons

The Model Act, as well as many state laws, permits a nonprofit corporation's articles of incorporation to specify exceptions to the general management authority of the board.[19] In those cases, the articles or bylaws may name other parties, such as the corporation's members, a representative assembly, or a board-appointed committee, or other designated body, who are specifically responsible for certain corporate governance decisions that would ordinarily fall to the board of directors. Depending on the jurisdiction and the nature of the delegation, the directors of those corporations may be partially or wholly relieved of their fiduciary responsibilities in such specified areas (while the alternate decision-maker may become correspondingly subject to fiduciary obligations to the extent of its specified authority). It is incumbent upon any director to make sure that the director clearly understands the extent to which the article or bylaw provisions serve to release the director of the fiduciary duties that would ordinarily apply.

Delegation to an executive committee

Many nonprofit corporations make extensive use of an executive committee to make board-level management decisions. Delegation of board authority may be both appropriate and practical, especially if the size of the board is very large or if it meets only a few times a year. Even fairly active boards may appropriately make use of an executive committee. The scope of delegations of board authority to an executive committee, however, should be clearly set forth in the corporation's bylaws or in board resolutions, and state nonprofit corporation statutes almost always place some limitations on what can be assigned to a committee, including an executive committee.

In addition, directors who do not sit on the executive committee should understand the extent to which the board has (and has not) delegated its authority to the executive committee. These directors should understand that they still retain a duty of oversight over the executive committee. The executive committee is accountable to the board, and the board members should receive sufficient information regarding executive committee decisions to be able to evaluate whether delegations of authority to the committee are appropriate and whether the decisions made should stand or should be modified or overridden. (See further discussion in the section *"Descriptions of Common Standing Committees"* in *Chapter 3, Committees and Advisory Bodies.*) One important way of making sure the entire board is aware of the executive committee's action is to distribute minutes of executive committee meetings to the entire board.

Discharging the Duty of Care: Some Practical Suggestions

In all but the smallest and simplest corporations, the corporation's needs for the board's attention will often exceed the time the board has to furnish this resource. Hence, well-run nonprofit corporations will adopt certain procedures, including those set forth below, to enable the board and its individual members to use their time efficiently.

Regular Schedule of Meetings

The board of directors should meet on a regular basis. The schedule of board meetings should be fixed at the beginning of each year, so that board members can place the meetings on their calendars well in advance, and thus assure attendance. While the appropriate frequency (monthly, quarterly, etc.) of scheduled board meetings will depend on the size of the corporation, the geographic nature of its constituency, budgetary considerations, the decisions to be made, and other considerations unique to each corporation, the need for a regular schedule of meetings applies to all nonprofit corporations. Without a regular schedule (with typically a minimum of 2 to 3 meetings per year), the board is more vulnerable to claims that it has not adequately fulfilled its duties of oversight of the corporation. Because decisions regarding the corporation's management occur on a regular basis, some person or body other than the board is likely making management decisions in the board's absence. By allowing this situation to occur, directors may have effectively, and inappropriately, transferred board power to persons other than the board.

Executive Sessions

Many boards meet in executive sessions where the chief executive and other staff members are absent. These sessions can be helpful to the board in discussing sensitive issues outside the presence of the staff. As a result, a board can benefit from having executive sessions as part of its regular meetings. Regular executive sessions serve the dual purposes of encouraging candid discussions of issues among board members and avoiding management anxiety if it appears that the executive sessions are only called when major concerns have been raised.

Meeting Agenda and Committee Reports

Although the items discussed will vary, most boards find it helpful to have a standard form of meeting agenda, to ensure the board routinely addresses issues important to the corporation. The agenda should include reports from the executive committee (if any), and from all other active committees, regarding significant actions taken and issues addressed since the last board meeting and the financial condition of the corporation.

Action by Written Consent

The Model Act and many state statutes permit directors to act without a meeting by unanimous written consent.[20] A small number of states permit general flexibility in governing documents that could include action by less than unanimous written consent.[21] For purposes of such authorization, many states through their nonprofit statute and/or Uniform Electronic Transactions Act and the Model Act permit "written" consents to be in electronic form if certain electronic transmission and signature requirements are met. A small number of state nonprofit corporation statutes expressly provide for the ability to take action by email.[22]

A procedure involving action by written consent may frequently be appropriate in transacting routine business or for approving specific actions that have already been fully discussed at prior board meetings. Directors should, however, be cautious about the ratification or authorization of major activities or decisions without a meeting or other opportunity for the board as a whole to raise questions and fully evaluate the ramifications of the action. Ideally, the use of consent should not be a substitute for regular meetings. Moreover, a director should never sign a written consent if the director has questions or concerns about the matter, and if the questions or concerns cannot be answered by others, a request for a meeting of the board of directors would be appropriate.

Board Voting via Email

Many nonprofit boards will communicate via email and seek to take action by an email vote. As noted above, a small number of state nonprofit corporation statutes expressly provide for the ability to take action by e-mail. Most states, however, do not have statutory provisions that expressly address board action by email, even if members vote through electronic means. As a result, any board "voting" via email likely will need to comply with the state's requirements for action by written consent (discussed above). This means, among other things, that unanimous consent may be required in order for an action to become effective. Similar to written consents, voting by email should not be a substitute for regular meetings. Moreover, the documentation of a written consent obtained via email is important. An email trail is not sufficient. There should be a formal resolution included in the email that is then approved by the directors.

Regular Schedule of Information

As much information as practical should be provided to the directors on a regular schedule.

Schedule of reports to be provided to the board

Information should be provided to the board of directors in a regular and timely manner so that the board will have a realistic opportunity to review and consider it. The board's information needs will be more easily and efficiently satisfied if the directors establish a regularly scheduled system of reports and data for those corporate activities that are sufficiently repetitive to be predictable to all parties. This information will include financial reports, program reports, and the like. Just as with infrequent board meetings, when information is provided only sporadically, directors will find it much more difficult to satisfy their duty of care on the corporation's behalf. Furthermore, in almost all those situations, *some but not all* directors are receiving more timely information, and thus inequalities within the board's knowledge base may be created. Regularity of information distribution is important for the entire board to be informed regarding significant corporate matters.

Distribution of information in advance of board meetings

Directors should require the distribution of as much material as possible in advance of a board meeting (preferably at least a week before the meeting). As noted above, certain types of reports—particularly financial reports—should be furnished on a regular schedule, whether monthly, quarterly, or semiannually.

Practical limitations on staff time to prepare required reports and other information

The board's need for regular reports and other information must necessarily be balanced by its recognition of limitations on staff time to prepare the information. The preparation of meaningful data for a board meeting consumes significant amounts of time, and particularly in small organizations, may take away from the time needed for operational activities. The board should be mindful of this in defining the information it requires. The board—as a whole or through its chair or other representative—should discuss with the staff the most efficient way to provide the board with necessary information while not impeding the staff's operational responsibilities.

Asking questions, getting answers, and taking action whenever there is a concern identified by a director

It is incumbent upon each director to ask questions and raise concerns whenever there is a "red flag" or other concern or question identified by the director with regard to any information provided to the directors or any aspect of the nonprofit corporation's operations. Asking questions is a hallmark of the kind of active engagement that is necessary to meet the duty of care. Therefore, a director should not be shy about raising questions or concerns and the board, as a whole, should make sure that whatever questions or concerns are raised receive adequate and acceptable responses.

In addition, it is important that the board of directors, upon becoming aware of any possible unethical or illegal acts of the corporation, its officers, or employees, investigate the matter and take appropriate corrective action.

Rules of Procedure and Minutes

The board should adopt rules of procedure appropriate to its size, the constituencies represented on the board, and the diversity of its membership. Minutes of the board and committee meetings also should be prepared regularly.

Any working board will determine its own standard procedures for board meetings and the degree of formality, or lack thereof, used in submitting motions, amendments to resolutions, recording votes, etc. Although the law almost never requires board action to be in any particular written form, matters of importance should always be acted on by formal resolution. Sometimes, formal procedural rules, such as Robert's Rules of Order or the Association of International Parliamentarian's Standard Code of Parliamentary Code, will be noted by a director for the proper procedure on a matter. Formal rules are not applicable until the organization adopts them for use. Formal procedural rules can be very helpful to organizations that often have issues debated. On the other hand, because those rules can be complicated, they can cause confusion for those who are not thoroughly familiar with them. Since those rules are generally intended for use by large membership organizations or delegated assemblies rather than small boards, many nonprofits opt to follow simpler rules of procedure, often based on general meeting conventions with which the directors are familiar.

The corporation's minutes should be prepared on a regular basis by a corporate secretary with the ability to accurately record and produce in a timely manner the minutes of each meeting. At a minimum, minutes of board meetings should note the names of all directors and other persons who attended each meeting, that appropriate notice was given or waived, that quorum was present, and the outcome of each vote taken (specifically noting the names of the directors who voted for, against, or abstained). Further, when the board or committee is acting on a matter involving a conflict of interest for, or compensation or other benefit to, a director or executive officer, the minutes should recite the documentation and information relied on by the board or committee in making its decision. The minutes also should reflect the vote by the board (or committee) that indicates if a director did not vote and whether or not the director was present at or participated in the discussion.

For tax-exempt corporations, the minutes and related documentation can be used to establish a rebuttable presumption of reasonableness for transactions covered by the IRS's "excess benefit" rule (including compensation decisions). (See the discussion of the excess benefits rules in the section *"Intermediate Sanctions: Excise Tax on Public Charities' Excess Benefit Transactions"* in *Chapter 5, Taxation.*) As noted above, the IRS has made clear through Form 990 that it prefers that governing bodies and committees take steps to ensure that minutes of their meetings, and actions taken by written actions or outside of meetings, are contemporaneously documented.

Board committees also should prepare minutes, particularly when acting pursuant to authority delegated by the full board. These minutes should be furnished to the full board.

Questions can arise with regard to the handling of minutes for that portion of a board meeting that is conducted in "executive session." It is important that some form of record of the executive session be maintained. If no action is taken during the executive session, there does not need to be separate executive session minutes and the "regular" meeting minutes can simply note when the board went into and came out of executive session and that no action was taken during such session. If specific action is taken, or it is desirable to note some general or specific items discussed, the specific issues discussed can be described in the regular meeting minutes or, alternatively, in a separate set of minutes for the executive session. To the extent the minutes contain sensitive information, they should be maintained in a secure location within the organization or by another party, such as the attorney for the organization, and distributed only to board members.

It is important for each board member to review minutes carefully to ensure their accuracy. If there is ever a challenge to board action, the minutes will be an extremely important document in addressing a challenge. As a result, draft minutes should be sent out soon after the meeting while the meeting is still fresh in directors' minds. It is also good practice for minutes to be approved no later than the next board meeting.[23]

The Business Judgment Rule

Even where a corporate action has proven to be unwise or unsuccessful, a director will generally be protected from liability arising from it if the director acted in good faith and in a manner reasonably believed to be in the corporation's best interest, and with independent and informed judgment.[24]

Availability of the business judgment rule to prevent second-guessing of board decisions

A director exercising good faith judgment will usually be protected from liability to the corporation or to its membership under the Business Judgment Rule. Under the Business Judgment Rule, a court, in an action brought by the corporation or its internal constituency, is not to reexamine the actions of a director in authorizing or permitting a corporate action if the director's action was undertaken in good faith, in a manner reasonably believed to be in the best interests of the corporation, based on the director's independent and informed judgment, and the director is disinterested. The doctrine basically is a statement by the courts that it is inappropriate for them to second-guess corporate management decisions barring gross negligence or self-interested action by the board. This legal concept is well established in the case law applying to business corporations. It also has been recognized as applicable to the directors of nonprofit corporations.[25] The Model Act and some state nonprofit statutes have incorporated the Business Judgment Rule concept.[26] Still, in states where the Business Judgment Rule concept has not been incorporated in the nonprofit statutes, courts may be less willing to afford directors protection of the Business Judgment Rule when individuals are harmed, or other "bad facts" are present.[27]

Following good governance practices can help establish the Business Judgment Rule protection. In this regard, the Delaware Supreme Court has indicated that although aspirational ideals of corporate good governance practices do not define the standards of liability, following good governance practices can help directors avoid liability.[28]

Exceptions to the availability of the rule

The Business Judgment Rule defense is generally not available in situations in which basic breaches of duty by the director (such as criminal activity, self-dealing, fraud, bad faith, willful and wanton misconduct) are present.[29] In addition, for public charities, business decisions that would result in significant reduction or cessation of operations (such as the decision of a nonprofit health system to close down a money-losing hospital) may be challenged by the state attorney general on grounds that the action would violate the directors' duties to maintain the functions of the charity[30]

Form 990 Governance Focus Areas

The IRS Form 990 asks certain questions regarding the governance of the tax-exempt organization, including whether certain policies relating to key governance or operational issues have been adopted. The IRS also has provided guidance regarding the content of certain governance-related policies and procedures for nonprofit organizations, such as in the areas of conflicts of interest, executive compensation, joint ventures, and fundraising. Although there is no specific law or provision of the Code mandating the adoption of many of these policies and procedures and some commentators have questioned the IRS's authority to address governance issues, the IRS focus and Form 990 questions have resulted in many nonprofit corporations adopting new or updated policies and procedures covering the topics identified in Form 990.[31] Directors should know whether the nonprofit corporation has not only adopted but also in fact implemented and complies with policies and procedures relating to the following areas:

Conflict of interest. Form 990 questions in this area focus on financial conflicts and ask if the nonprofit's conflicts policy applies to key employees as well as directors and officers. Issues regarding conflicts of interest are discussed in more detail later in this chapter, in *"Conflicts of Interest: General Principles."*

Joint ventures. A policy on this topic may not be necessary or appropriate if the organization does not engage in joint ventures. If a joint venture policy is to be adopted, consideration should be given to the type of joint ventures that are expected and the specific issues that might arise for joint ventures. If a policy is needed, it should address how it ensures that any joint venture is structured and operated consistently with the organization's tax-exempt status. Issues for directors to consider in connection with a nonprofit's participation in a joint venture with individuals or for-profit companies are discussed in more detail in *Chapter 6, Creating For-Profit Subsidiaries and Joint Ventures.*

Document retention and destruction. The Sarbanes-Oxley Act, which focuses on publicly traded companies, has certain provisions that apply to any type of entity, including a nonprofit corporation. One provision prohibits the destruction of documents pertaining to a matter under investigation.[32] If a policy is established in advance and followed, it can be used as a defense to a claim. An effective document retention and destruction policy is an important way to ensure that documents considered to be legal records or other documents that pertain to or provide detail regarding the organization's operations are retained for the period required by law, if any, or which would be useful for the nonprofit's functioning. Typically, document retention policies will include a retention schedule, organized by kind of document and specifying how long documents in specific categories should be retained; depending on the type of document a retention period may be fairly short (e.g., one year) or long (e.g., ten years after a contract termination, or indefinitely for organizational documents and amendments).

An equally important function of a document retention policy is to establish guidelines for appropriate destructions of documents when their retention is no longer needed or legally required. Directors should expect that a document retention policy will provide guidelines regarding the storage of documents in electronic form, including backup procedures, and permissible destruction periods and protocols. All document retention policies also should specify when and how routine document destruction standards for both paper and e-documents must be suspended, such as on the instruction of legal counsel in the light of actual or anticipated lawsuits or governmental investigations.

Whistleblower protection. Another Sarbanes-Oxley Act provision applicable to nonprofit corporations prohibits retaliating against someone for reporting a violation of federal law.[33] A whistleblower policy should specify a simple process (such as an anonymous telephonic or electronic "hotline") for confidentially reporting any potential wrongdoing. That process gives the organization the opportunity to investigate and, if necessary, to correct any problems. An essential part of any whistleblower policy is a prohibition on retaliation against any whistleblower based on the reporting of possible wrongdoing or noncompliance with the law, whether the report was made internally or externally, such as to a government agency.

Chapter, affiliates, and branches. Form 990 asks if nonprofit organizations with extended operations through chapters, affiliates, and branches that are controlled by a parent organization have written policies and procedures governing the activities of those affiliated organizations, to assure that the activities are consistent with the nonprofit organization's exempt purposes.

Fundraising. A fundraising policy typically describes applicable federal and state requirements, such as registration requirements and donor acknowledgements, relating to the organization's fundraising activities.

Investments. An investment policy will describe the corporation's short-term, mid-term, and long-term financial needs, its tolerance for risk, asset allocation, and application of the Uniform Prudent Management of Institutional Funds Act. Investment policies and related issues for nonprofits are discussed in *Chapter 12, Investments and Expenditure of Endowment Funds.*

Executive compensation. Form 990 asks about the process for determining executive compensation. It is recommended that a process be described in a policy that incorporates the steps required for the application of the safe harbor under the IRS's intermediate sanctions (also known as the "excess benefits") rules. Standards for setting and approving executive compensation are discussed in more detail in *Chapter 5, Taxation.*

Documenting governance decisions. Form 990 includes questions regarding the nonprofit organization's process for documenting governance decisions. Specifically, it asks if the organization contemporaneously documents the meetings held or written actions taken during the year by the nonprofit's governing board, and each committee that has authority to act on behalf of the governing board. The Form 990 instructions state that "contemporaneous" means the later of (1) the next meeting of the governing body or committee or (2) sixty days after the date of the meeting or written action.

Governance documents availability. Form 990 asks whether, and if so, how, an organization makes certain documents available to the public. The organization should consider what documents it determines are appropriate for public disclosure and adopt a policy it deems appropriate. Form 990 asks whether Form 1023, Form 990, and Form 990-T, all of which are required to be made available to the public, are in fact made available—by request, on the organization's website, or another organization's website (e.g., GuideStar) or the IRS' website. Nonprofit practice varies regarding whether these documents are posted on the organization's website; this question should be periodically reviewed by the board or a board committee, such as when Form 990 is distributed each year. In addition, board members should be aware that some states require other documents, such as audited financial statements, to be made available to the public.[34]

Form 990 also asks whether and how any of the following documents are made available to the public, although none of these documents (with the exception of the articles of incorporation, which are available from the state) are required to be made publicly available: the organization's governing documents (e.g., articles of incorporation and bylaws); conflict of interest policy; and financial statements.

Form 990 review. Form 990 requires information on the board's receipt of the Form 990 in advance of its filing. It also asks about the process for reviewing Form 990 but does not require the full board to review. The board may delegate responsibilities for an in-depth review to a committee; however, it is important that Form 990 be distributed to all board members for review prior to filing with the IRS. In addition, directors should be aware that Form 990 is not only an important regulatory document but, due to its public availability, it is also important for public relations purposes.[35]

Policies in general. Although most of the policies and procedures referenced above are not specifically required by the Code or other laws, most nonprofits will want to ensure that they can answer "yes" to any questions regarding the existence of specific policies and procedures as posed in the Form 990, both to avoid unwanted attention from the IRS and to not appear out of step on good-governance practices to the public (including potential donors and grant-makers). It is essential that directors be aware that adopting these policies and procedures is not sufficient; it is also extremely important that the corporation follow them. The only thing worse than having no policies is having a set of policies that are not followed. Accordingly, it is appropriate for the board or a board committee to ask management to report periodically on the effectiveness of these policies. This can be done annually in connection with the review of Form 990 or at other appropriate times for each applicable policy.

The list of governance policies and procedures above is not exhaustive. A nonprofit corporation likely will need other policies to assure its compliance with legal requirements.

Internet Discussions by Board Members

Some nonprofit boards use email, Internet chat rooms, discussion boards, or other designated Internet-based sites for board members to discuss issues. This may be a very helpful tool for board members to communicate between meetings. Board members should recognize that there can be issues relating to the use of these tools, including security breaches. In addition, to the extent that the subject matter relates to actual or potential litigation matters, the substance of the discussion may be discoverable and the corporation may have duties imposed on it with regard to not destroying those communications. Directors using social media should take care to avoid inadvertently communicating confidential organizational information through this media.

Satisfying Other Legal Requirements

In discharging the duty of care, a nonprofit director should be mindful of the variety of legal requirements to which the corporation may be subject. For example, organizations that use volunteers should be aware of the variety of legal issues that can arise in connection with volunteers. See *Chapter 9, Employees.* (As noted in *Chapter 14, The Legal Environment of the Nonprofit Corporation,* an awareness of the corporation's particular legal environment and risk areas gives the board the opportunity to ensure that there are appropriate policies and procedures in place to avoid or address legal problems.)

The Duty of Loyalty

The duty of loyalty requires directors to exercise their powers in good faith and in the best interests of the corporation, rather than in their own interests or the interests of another entity or person.

By assuming office, the director must understand with regard to any corporate activity, the best interests of the corporation must prevail over the director's individual interests or the particular interests of the constituency selecting the director. The basic legal principle to be observed here may also be formulated as a negative one: *The director shall not use a corporate position for individual personal advantage.* The duty of loyalty primarily relates to:

- conflicts of interest;
- corporate opportunity; and
- confidentiality.

Conflicts of Interest: General Principles

Directors of nonprofit corporations may have interests that conflict with those of the corporation. The duty of loyalty requires that a director be conscious of the potential for those conflicts and act with candor and care in dealing with those situations.

Conflicts of interest involving a director are not inherently illegal nor are they to be regarded as a reflection of the integrity of the board or of the director. It is the manner in which the director and the board deal with a conflict that determines the propriety of the transaction. In other words, a conflict is not necessarily bad, it just needs to be managed through a process that provides complete disclosure, is transparent, and helps prevent the organization from being harmed.

Conflicts of interest are not unusual

Since nonprofit corporations generally look to populate their boards with civic, business, and community leaders, it is to be expected that from time to time a director of a nonprofit corporation will encounter situations in which a proposed corporate action will in some way relate to or affect the director's other activities and affiliations. In a situation where a conflict transaction is present, the board should document that it followed an appropriate procedure, consistent with its policies, to ensure that the decision made was in the best interest of the nonprofit and not based on any influence from the conflict holder.

When is a conflict of interest present?

A conflict of interest is present whenever a director has a material personal interest in a proposed contract or transaction to which the corporation may be a party. This interest can occur either directly or indirectly. The director may be personally involved with the transaction, have an employment or investment relationship with an entity with which the corporation is dealing, or have a family member who is either personally involved with the transaction or has a relationship with an entity that is involved in the transaction. A conflict of interest may result from a director performing professional services for the organization. For example, a banker, insurance agent, attorney, or real estate broker may benefit from employment by the organization.

The board should understand that a conflict can still exist even when a director receives no direct monetary or other tangible benefit from a transaction with the corporation. As discussed below, some personal interests of directors may result in the directors experiencing a conflict between their own interests and those of the corporation. In the nonprofit world, there also are common possible conflicts of interest arising from a director's simultaneous service on the boards of other (for-profit or nonprofit) corporations; it is, therefore, important that a director disclose the director's affiliations in general, as well as any specific circumstances in which a conflict between a role as a director for one corporation creates a conflict with respect to a director position with another corporation.

Determining whether a personal interest is a conflict of interest

It is improper for a director to use the director's position to advance a personal interest. At the same time, the very reasons why a particular director is selected may relate to that director's concern for, and knowledge of, the particular business of the corporation. The following examples of personal interests illustrate that these interests may or may not be considered a conflict of interest, based on the circumstances:

- A director of an art museum may have—and probably should have—definite opinions as to the priority, in new purchases, of contemporary American painting versus Old Masters. The director's opinion and preferences present no conflict.
- If the art museum director was generally a collector of contemporary painting and the museum was faced with a particular possible acquisition in that field of art (which acquisition might then increase the recognition or value of pieces in the director's own collection), the director's personal interests might require disclosure. Also, if the director wishes to add that particular piece of art to the director's own collection, this would clearly be a conflict that would require waiver by the corporation.
- A director of a trade association might have been selected because of her familiarity with the impact of Pacific Rim competition on the products of the association's members. The director's urging, based on the director's experience, that the association advocates a particular tariff bill would present no problem even if the director's own company would benefit along with others.
- Still, if that trade association director's own company was one of the relatively small groups of manufacturers affected by Pacific imports, but most of the association's members were unaffected, a decision to use association assets and influence to advocate legislation benefiting the director's company on behalf of that minority might present a material conflict.

- A director who sits on a foundation board, as well as a community service agency board, would need to disclose the director's role with the service agency and then be recused from a discussion by the foundation board of a grant to the community service agency.

Dealing with conflicts: disclosure and approval requirements under nonprofit corporation laws and IRS rules

The law recognizes that conflicts of interest will occur. It deals with conflicts not by treating them as inherently immoral or illegal, but rather by prescribing the methods whereby affected directors should disclose conflicts and how a board of directors should proceed in the face of those situations. Under the Model Act, as well as many state nonprofit corporation laws, a director's conflict will not result in a deemed breach of the director's duty of loyalty, or render void the transaction under which the conflict arose, if the corporation can show that certain requirements were met, such as:

(1) the transaction was approved by a disinterested majority of the board (or by another disinterested party as specified by the statute including a board committee, the membership, or others), after full disclosure by the affected director of the material facts regarding the transaction and the director's interest therein; or

(2) the transaction was fair to the corporation at the time entered into or when authorized, approved, or ratified by the board of directors.[36]

IRS Form 990 includes specific questions regarding conflict-of-interest management and related governance policies. It also requires disclosure of interested-party transactions as well as director and officer relationships with the corporation and with each other. Form 990 requirements, which are further described in *Chapter 5, Taxation,* effectively require officers and directors to make fairly extensive disclosures to a nonprofit corporation of personal and professional relationships to enable the corporation to comply with new disclosure requirements on independence and interested-party transactions. Form 990 requires disclosure of any family relationships or business relationships among the directors, trustees, officers, and key employees (which includes the organization's officers and other employees who meet certain income and responsibility tests).

In addition, as discussed in the section *"Intermediate Sanctions: Excise Tax on Public Charities' Excess Benefit Transactions"* in *Chapter 5, Taxation,* the IRS has specified certain procedures for approving transactions with a corporation's "insiders" that must be followed to establish a rebuttable presumption of reasonableness under the IRS's excess benefits/intermediate sanctions rules. Failure to follow these procedures changes the burden of proving reasonableness back to the taxpayer. This can ultimately result in liability for an insider who is found to be the beneficiary of an excess benefit transaction, as well as for organization leaders who approved the transaction.

When is it appropriate to approve a transaction in which a director is interested? Provided there has been appropriate disclosure and evaluation of transactions involving a conflict of interest, there are many situations in which such a transaction not only *can* but also, in the best interests of the corporation, probably *should* be approved. For instance, a board may legitimately choose to deal with a company affiliated with a director or other insider because of greater familiarity with the supplier's reliability or the supplier's favorable pricing. In some cases, a company's affiliation with a director may result in the corporation receiving better service or prices than can be obtained from other commercial sources. Nonetheless, the corporate records must still show that the affiliation was appropriately disclosed and that the board made its decision to do business with the director's affiliated company based on the fairness of the transaction and the best interests of the corporation.

In addition, the board should be aware that all interested-party transactions have to be disclosed in Form 990, Schedule L. Finally, regardless of how beneficial the transaction is to the organization, it is important to recognize that third parties, including the press, may view the transaction as improper given the existence of a conflict. Therefore, thorough documentation of fair value and a robust process for disclosure and management of conflicts have become an important aspect of board decision-making.

Conflicts of interest policies and disclosure statements. In light of state and other laws that relate to how a board should handle the identification and evaluation of conflicts of interest involving directors and other insiders, it is good corporate practice for nonprofit corporations to adopt and adhere to a written conflict of interest policy. For instance, as noted in *Chapter 5, Taxation*, the IRS strongly encourages a nonprofit to have a conflict of interest policy. The IRS form also requests that directors and other persons having potential influence over the corporation fill out annual statements disclosing all of their significant affiliations, as well as contacts with entities doing business with the corporation. In other contexts, the presence of and adherence to a conflict of interest policy can serve as evidence that it was the corporation's regular practice to seek to identify and resolve potential conflicts. For instance, adherence to a conflict of interest policy could make the difference in a court determining whether the Business Judgment Rule defense was available to a corporate decision involving an insider since the Business Judgment Rule protection is not available to the interested director where the conflict was not properly managed in accordance with the state nonprofit corporation law and the corporation's conflict of interest policy.

Making a record of conflict disclosures and related party transactions. Whenever a conflict-of-interest situation arises, the corporate minutes or other records should document the nature of the disclosure given regarding the conflict, as well as the board's proceedings to evaluate the relevant transaction in light of the conflict. In addition, related-party transactions (such as purchase of property from a director or an officer) may have to be disclosed in the notes to the corporation's audited financial statements, and in its annual tax filing (such as Form 990) to the IRS.

Duty of disclosure. The corporation should have a formal policy that requires its board members to annually disclose relationships that may present a conflict of interest or that take them out of the category of "independent" directors. The directors also should be required to update annual disclosures as changes occur during the year. Equally important is having a process whereby the board reviews and evaluates these disclosures so that board members are aware of relationships that may affect action taken by the board. Whenever a conflict of interest policy exists that includes a formal recurring disclosure process, it is now to be described on Form 990. Nonprofits also are required to disclose whether the board closely monitors these disclosures (*see Chapter 5, Taxation*). This process is also of growing importance under state law, and nonprofit corporations are subject to increasing scrutiny regarding their attention to potential conflicts.[37]

As noted above, many state nonprofit corporation statutes uphold the validity of a transaction authorized even when a director had an undisclosed interest, as long as the transaction was "fair" to the corporation. (Note, however, that in some states, such as California, fairness is only one of several factors—including disclosure—that must be satisfied in conflict situations.[38]) Nonetheless, directors should be aware that *lack of disclosure of a conflict exposes both the affected director and the rest of the board, to greater risk.* In the event of litigation, the nondisclosing director and, in some instances, even the disinterested directors who supported the transaction will have the burden of proving after the fact that the transaction was fair. Disclosure also enables the other members of the board to evaluate the proposed transaction not merely in terms of fairness, but also for its impact on the public image of the corporation.[39] Even if a matter involving a conflict does not result in litigation, in some cases, if the conflict is disclosed publicly, it may be a source of embarrassment due to the appearance of impropriety.

Content of disclosure and participation in board discussions by interested directors. Generally, the disclosure of a conflict of interest should include the existence of the interest and its nature (e.g., those arising from financial or family relationships, or professional or business affiliations, etc.) and should be made in advance, before any action is taken by the board concerning the matter. It is generally prudent—and may be required by state law or the corporation's conflicts policy—that the interested director be absent from that part of the meeting when the matter is being discussed except when the director's information may be needed. A director having a conflict should make sure that in the director's absence from discussion and abstention from a vote relating to it is duly noted in the meeting minutes.

In some cases, a director may have an interest in a transaction but be unable, because of duties running to others, to disclose the nature of the interest. In that case, the director should at least state that the interest exists, consider leaving the meeting, or at least abstain from the discussion and not vote on the matter. When the conflicting interest presents so difficult a problem that even the above measures are impossible, the director should consider resigning.

Quorum and voting requirements. State law and other applicable laws (as well as the corporation's bylaws or conflict of interest policy) may specify whether an interested director can be counted in determining whether a quorum exists at a meeting at which the board considers the conflict of interest transaction. Legal standards and corporate procedures may also address whether an interested director may vote on the transaction in which the director has an interest. Generally, a director, even if interested, may be counted for the purpose of determining the presence of a quorum. Still, this director may not be permitted to vote, or the director's vote may not be allowed to be counted in determining whether there were sufficient votes to approve the transaction.

In some states, a transaction may not be approved by the board if too many directors have a conflict. For instance, some state nonprofit corporation laws do not recognize board approval as providing liability protection if there is only one noninterested director voting on the matter.[40] In this situation, the corporation needs to consider other alternatives, such as obtaining an outside opinion that the transaction is fair to the corporation. Given the uniqueness of how state law applies in this situation, it is advisable to consult with counsel on the matter.

In addition, the use of written consent to approve board action can present a problem when there is a conflict of interest transaction, given that states generally require unanimous consent of the directors.[41] In some states, however, the written consent does not require the signature of the interested director.[42]

Action by the board after discovering an undisclosed conflict. A board of directors that discovers that it has acted on a proposal in ignorance of an undisclosed interest should promptly reexamine the issue, with an appropriate record of its scrutiny.

Corporate Opportunity

In certain circumstances, a director is obliged to treat a business opportunity as a "corporate opportunity" that must first be offered to the corporation before the director can take advantage of it outside of his role as a corporate director. This situation could arise where, for example, a member of the board of directors of an art institute is interested in purchasing a painting for the director's own personal collection that the art institute could be interested in acquiring. The duty to treat a potential transaction as a corporate opportunity arises when a director, because of the director's position with the organization, learns of a prospective transaction or business opportunity that would be attractive to the director or the director's business apart from his role as a director, but that is also a transaction that would plausibly fall within the corporation's present or future activities. The duty of loyalty generally requires that the director affirmatively present the opportunity to the board (and for the board to decline the opportunity) before participating in the transaction outside the corporation.[43]

Although legal requirements as to these transactions vary from state to state, directors should, for their self-protection, and as a matter of good corporate practice, make a clear record of this disclosure and request that the board's abstention (if any) from the exercise of the opportunity be explicit and on the record. Further, even if entering into the transaction would not breach the director's duty of loyalty, the applicable director should consider any appearance of impropriety that could be created.

Confidentiality

A director should not, in the regular course of business, disclose information about the corporation's legitimate activities unless they are already known by the public or are of public record.

In the normal course of business, a director should treat as confidential all matters involving the corporation until there has been general public disclosure or unless the information is a matter of public record or common knowledge. The individual director is not a spokesperson for the corporation and, thus, disclosure to the public (including the press) of corporate activities should be made only through the corporation's designated spokesperson, usually the chief executive or the board chair or, in large organizations, a public relations officer. The presumption of confidential treatment should apply to all current information about legitimate board or corporate activities.[44] This includes information about board deliberations that have taken place. In addition, a director cannot use any confidential information the director may obtain through the corporation for the director's own private benefit unless the process for corporate opportunity discussed above is followed. Some nonprofit organizations will require directors to sign an agreement in which the directors acknowledge their obligations to keep matters confidential.

Directors' Rights

As a corollary to all the previously described director duties, the director has rights appropriate to the discharge of duties.

Management Access

Within the bounds of reason, board members should feel free to contact the chief executive, the board secretary, or a similar staff person, to obtain information needed to fulfill the director's duties. Board members should be more restrained in contacting other members of management and should be cognizant of management's role, of not interfering with it, and of not undercutting the chief executive or other officers. Requests for access to information or management staff are most effective (for both management and the board) if requested through the board chair, at board meetings, or for committee work or under other delegations of authority from the board. If directors also serve as volunteers or receive services from the organization, they should be especially careful when in those other roles to not make demands or requests of staff that would be inappropriate for other volunteers or clients of the organization. All board members should benefit from equal access to management staff and the information management can provide.

Books and Records

A director has a right to inspect the corporation's books and records and to be provided with requested data derived from them.[45] A director may reasonably require that the director's accountant or attorney have access to the data. Requests for information should be handled in a manner that does not unduly disrupt normal business operations.

Notice of Meetings

All directors should be given ample advance notice of all board and committee meetings that they are expected to attend. At a minimum, the corporation should comply with any notice requirements imposed by the applicable nonprofit corporation statute as well as its bylaws.

Right to Dissent and to Have Dissent Recorded

There are two circumstances in which a director may register dissent regarding actions to be taken at a board meeting. First, any director may dissent from the holding of a board meeting for which the proper notice has not been given or other procedural requirements have not been satisfied. In this circumstance, the board member should state either upon arriving or prior to voting on a specific matter that the director objects to the transaction of some or all business at the meeting, because of noncompliance with notice or other applicable procedures. If the director does not object, the director's presence at the meeting is deemed to be a waiver of any improper notice or other procedural requirement.[46]

Second, a director has the right not only to vote against any matter put forth for a vote at a board meeting but also to have the minutes of the meeting record that the director dissented from the action approved by other members of the board.[47] This right is important if the action is ever challenged. A director who voted against an action later found to be improper will not generally be subject to liability relating to this action, assuming no separate violation of fiduciary duty on the director's part (such as failure to disclose material information relating to the proposed matter to the other members of the board). But, the dissenting director needs to be able to prove, through the voting detail recorded in the meeting minutes, that the director did, in fact, dissent.

Minutes

All directors should be provided a copy of the minutes of all meetings of the full board and any committee exercising board powers as soon as possible after each meeting. Except for the minutes of the executive committee, which generally acts in place of the whole board, and for the minutes of committees of which the director is a member, a director usually will be satisfied with a review of the summarized reports of committees that are submitted to the whole board. A review of other minutes, however, can be a useful way of keeping informed, and a director has a right to receive them on request. As noted above, a director should carefully review minutes as they become available to confirm their accuracy. The minutes are important for recording board and committee action. In addition, the minutes become an important document if there is ever a question raised as to whether the directors carried out their fiduciary duties.

When a Special Duty Applies: The Director with Knowledge of Illegal Activities

A director may not ignore what the director believes or suspects to be illegal activity. When a director believes that an activity being engaged in by or on behalf of the corporation (whether or not clearly approved by the board of directors) may be illegal, the director should proceed as follows:

First, contact the chief executive or board chair. If the subject activity is ongoing or is about to take place, the board member should bring the issue to the attention of the chief executive or board chair with a demand for action or investigation; if the chief executive or board chair fails to respond, the issue should go to the full board.

Second, dissent and consult with personal counsel. If, after a board discussion, an activity that appears to a director to be illegal is not repudiated, or if the activity is a past event that the director was previously unaware of, the director's dissent should be clearly recorded in the minutes. In addition, the director may wish to consult the director's own counsel to determine if further disclosure outside the corporation is required, or if the director should resign.

Ethics and Business Conduct Codes

Current views of good governance practice recommend that in addition to a conflict of interest policy, a nonprofit corporation should consider the development and implementation of an ethics and business conduct code. An ethics code would normally be applicable to directors, senior management, agents, and employees and should require a commitment to operating the entity in the best interests of the organization and in compliance with applicable law, ethical business standards, and the organization's governing documents. There is no standard form for an ethics code. Depending on the nature of the nonprofit, it may look to the type of code adopted by its for-profit counterparts in preparing its own code.[48]

The Duty of Obedience

Courts occasionally have determined that there is an additional fiduciary duty—the duty of obedience—imposed on directors of nonprofit corporations. This "duty" carves out the requirement that directors take action in a manner consistent with the purpose of the organization, as set forth in the corporation's organizational documents, such as the articles of incorporation. The duty of obedience also has been interpreted to require directors to comply with applicable state and federal laws that relate to the organization and the manner in which it conducts its business. This duty is more frequently viewed as being encompassed under the duty of care and the duty of loyalty.[49]

When Is a Director of a Nonprofit Corporation Considered to Be a "Trustee" with Duties beyond Those Normally Attributed to Directors?

Even if the governing members of a nonprofit corporation are referred to as a board of trustees, they are not subject to a different or higher standard of care compared to nonprofit boards of directors. The use of the word *trustee* to refer to a member of a nonprofit corporation's governing board does not in and of itself change the duties of the members of the board, which are the same as those described above for directors. Still, as noted below, in certain circumstances, a member of a nonprofit board (whether called a director, trustee, or other term) may legally be required to comply with the higher standards of a trustee.

When a Director May Be Considered a Trustee

Persons who are considered trustees of a trust are traditionally subject to stringent standards of conduct. For instance, whereas most state nonprofit corporation laws treat director conflicts of interest as an issue to be dealt with by following certain guidelines and disclosures, the law of trusts generally regards a trustee's self-dealing as inherently voidable, regardless of motives or objective fairness. Furthermore, the trustee's power to delegate may be narrowly limited, much more so than a corporate director. Although the law does not consider a director of a nonprofit corporation to be a trustee in most situations, in some circumstances directors may be held to the generally higher trustee standards, such as in the following situations:

- An employer corporation maintains employee benefit plans, thereby triggering, in certain circumstances under both state and federal law, obligations analogous to those of a trustee with respect to those plans.
- A public benefit or religious corporation seeks to change its purpose or function, but members or public or community representatives challenge this action on the basis that the assets of these corporations are generally deemed to be held in trust for the purposes set forth in the corporation's governing documents, and that the proposed change is inconsistent with these purposes. In some states, the directors may not be permitted to effect the change in corporate purpose or use of corporate assets until approved by the attorney general or by a court in a cy pres proceeding.[50]

When a Director or Trustee Is Not a Trustee under the Law

Some nonprofit corporations, particularly in the public benefit field, may call their directors *trustees* without intending to confer any special powers or impose any special duties in doing so. Directors of public benefit and religious corporations (this issue rarely arises for mutual benefit corporations) should make sure they understand under what circumstances they could legally be considered to be trustees. For example, funds held by a corporation in acknowledged trusts must be identified and treated separately on the corporation's balance sheets, and the board must see to it that an appropriate officer (and counsel and the corporation's accountant) is acquainted with the terms of the relevant trust instrument. In any other circumstance in which a board is faced with an assertion that it should be held to a trusteeship standard with respect to a certain matter, the matter should be discussed with the corporation's counsel, in order to give the board clarification of its role under the specific circumstances.

The Impact of the Sarbanes-Oxley Act

In an attempt to prevent further erosion in investor confidence in the markets after the Enron and WorldCom scandals, Congress enacted the Sarbanes-Oxley Act of 2002. Only two provisions of Sarbanes-Oxley directly apply to nonprofit organizations. They relate to the penalties for obstruction of justice, including document destruction, and a prohibition on retaliation against whistleblowers.[51] Nevertheless, the concerns giving rise to Sarbanes-Oxley have some application in the nonprofit sector. This has resulted in recommendations relating to various "best practices" for nonprofit organizations. These recommendations are very similar to the recommendations set forth in this chapter and include the need for an independent board, certain committees (such as compensation committees, governance committees, and audit committees), and the need to have compliance programs and policies addressing such matters as whistleblower protection, document retention and destruction, conflicts of interest, and ethics.[52]

Panel on the Nonprofit Sector

In 2004, the Independent Sector established the Panel on the Nonprofit Sector to address various proposals that were being considered by the Senate Finance

Committee. The Panel subsequently issued several reports that contain recommendations for improving government oversight, including new rules to prevent unscrupulous individuals from abusing charitable organizations for personal gain. The Pension Protection Act of 2006 enacted many of these recommendations into law. The Panel has also focused on recommendations relating to self-regulation. In 2007 and then again in 2015, the Panel issued the *Principles for Good Governance in Ethical Practice: A Guide for Charities and Foundations.* The document sets forth 33 principles of sound practice that the Panel recommended should be considered by every charitable organization as a guide in determining how to strengthen its effectiveness and accountability. The 33 principles are organized under four main categories: (1) legal compliance in public disclosure; (2) effective governance; (3) strong financial oversight; and (4) responsible fundraising.[53]

See the Suggested Questions and Checklist following the Endnotes below to review the issues discussed in this chapter.

ESG Considerations

The concept of ESG—environmental, social, and governance—has become an important subject for the board of directors of publicly traded corporations. The concept of ESG is fairly new and continues to evolve. For-profit companies are considering their activities in terms of societal impact and sustainability. Consideration of stakeholders other than shareholders is also part of the ESG discussion. The SEC and NASDAQ have become interested in how companies are addressing ESG in their operations.

Since nonprofit corporations often have a purpose that seems more aligned with ESG factors, there may be a question as to whether (or how much) ESG needs to become a focus for boards. Still, for some nonprofits – such as nonprofit health organizations, the concept is being discussed by boards, particularly as it relates to environmental factors. Concepts such as social determinants of health have become an important topic. The U.S. Department of Health and Human Services' interest in environmental health has made it important for healthcare nonprofits to be considering ESG.

As nonprofit boards embark on ESG, it is vital that they consider the purpose or mission of the organization and how it relates to any ESG considerations. The purpose of the organization may be enhanced or expanded by ESG considerations or the board may determine that the corporation's purpose and activities do not need further modification in this area. In addition, it is important any ESG goals be measurable.

Endnotes

1. *See generally*, Model Act § 830; RESTATEMENT OF THE LAW, CHARITABLE NONPROFIT ORGANIZATIONS, § 2.02 cmt. b.
2. *See, e.g.*, People ex rel. Spitzer v. Grasso, 893 N.E.2d 105 (N.Y. 2008); New York Non-Profit Revitalization Act of 2013; California Nonprofit Integrity Act, CAL. GOV'T CODE §§ 12585, et al.
3. In determining the degree of care that a director should exhibit, the law generally sets forth an ideal, such as the care of "an ordinarily prudent person in a like position under similar circumstances" or "the care that a person in a like position would reasonably believe appropriate under similar circumstances." *See* Model Act, § 830(b). In describing a director's standard of care, the Model Act eliminated the reference to an "ordinarily prudent person," a phrase that has a special meaning under tort law but may have a different meaning in the context of a director's duty of care.
4. *See, e.g.*, 18B Am. Jur. 2d Corporations § 1285; In re Acadia Dairies, Inc., 135 A. 846 (Del. Ch. 1927). Nonetheless, a few nonprofit corporation statutes allow a director to advance written consents or opposition to an action to be considered at a board meeting or vote by proxy in certain circumstances. *See* N.D. CENT. CODE § 10-33-40; VA CODE § 13.1-852.1.
5. Under the Model Act, the board of directors may remove a director who has missed the number of board meetings specified in the articles of incorporation or bylaws, if the articles or bylaws at the beginning of the director's current term provided that a director may be removed for missing the specified number of board meetings. § 808(c)(4).
6. *See* CAL. CORP. CODE. § 5227 (no more than 49 percent of the board can be "interested persons" (i.e., any person compensated by the corporation within the past twelve months and any member of such person's family)). (Requirement does not apply to mutual benefit or religious corporations.)
7. See NEW YORK NOT-FOR-PROFIT CORPORATION LAW § 712-A.
8. *See* ABA Coordinating Committee on Nonprofit Governance, *Guide to Nonprofit Corporate Governance in the Wake of Sarbanes-Oxley* 26–28 (American Bar Association 2005).
9. *See Guide to Nonprofit Corporate Governance in the Wake of Sarbanes-Oxley, supra note 8*, at 23–28.
10. *See* Lawrence M. Braver and Charles F. Kaiser, *Tax-Exempt Health Care Organizations Community Board and Conflict of Interest Policy*, 1997 EO CPE Text (*available at* www.irs.gov/pub/irs-tege/eotopiccc97.pdf).
11. *See* Model Act § 830(c).
12. See Model Act § 830(b).

13. Comment 4 to the Model Act § 830 provides that, reliance on "a report, statement, opinion, or other information is permitted only if the director has read or heard orally presented the report, statement, opinion, or other information in question, or took other steps to become generally familiar with it."
14. *See* Model Act § 830(e)(4).
15. *See* Model Act § 830(d).
16. *See* Comment to Model Act § 801, (stating "In some corporations, the Board of Directors may be involved in the day-to-day activities and affairs and it may be reasonable to describe management as being 'by' the Board of Directors. In many other corporations, the activities and affairs are managed 'under the direction, and subject to the oversight, of' the Board of Directors, and operational management is delegated to officers and other professional manager.").
17. *See* U.S. Sentencing Commission, Federal Sentencing Guidelines, §§ 8B2.1 (Effective Compliance and Ethics Program), 8C2.5(Culpability Score).
18. In *In Re* Caremark International Inc. Derivative Litigation, 698 A.2d 959 (Del. Ch. 1996), the Delaware Chancery noted that a board's failure to assure that there was an adequate information and reporting system to provide senior management and the board with timely and accurate information regarding legal compliance might, in some circumstances, be viewed as a violation of a director's duty of care. See *also* Stone ex rel. AmSouth Bancorporation v. Ritter, 911 A.2d 362, 365 (Del. 2006), Corporate Laws Committee of the ABA Business Law Section, CORPORATE DIRECTOR'S GUIDEBOOK, 7th ed. (American Bar Association 2020), at 41.
19. *See* Model Act § 812 (permitting resting of powers in a designated body); COLO. REV. STAT. § 7-128-101; GA. CODE ANN. § 14-3-801.
20. *See* Model Act § 821; D.C. CODE § 29-406.21. Sometimes a director needs to abstain, be recused, or withhold consent of an action. The Model Act in a comment provides that in such situations, the action may not be authorized by written consent because it is not unanimous.
21. *See, e.g.,* GA. CODE ANN. § 14-3-821 (written consent by less than unanimous consent permissible if articles of incorporation or bylaws expressly permit such action); WIS. STAT. § 181.0821 (written consent by less than two-thirds of the directors then in office is permissible if the articles or bylaws so provide and if all directors receive notice of the text of the consent and its effective date and time); MINN. STAT. § 317A.239 (written consent by less than unanimous consent permissible if articles of incorporation expressly permit such action).
22. *See, e.g.,* COLO. REV. STAT. § 7-128-202 (unless bylaws provide otherwise, consent may be transmitted or received by facsimile, e-mail, or other form of wire or wireless communication that provides the nonprofit with a complete copy of the document, including a copy

of the director's signature); New York Not-For-Profit Corporation Law § 708(b).

23. In addition, Form 990 asks the organization a question about the timing of the approval of minutes.
24. Directors also may have protection under state immunity statutes. *See Chapter 13, Director Liability: Risks and Protections.*
25. *See* Oberly v. Kirby, 592 A.2d 445, 462 (Del. 1991) ("A court cannot second-guess the wisdom of facially valid decisions made by charitable fiduciaries, any more than it can question the business judgment of the directors of a for-profit corporation."). Although cases explicitly mentioning the Business Judgment Rule in a nonprofit context are few, the standards used by the courts in nonprofit cases are often clearly derived from the business context. *See, e.g.,* Oberbillig v. West Grand Towers Condominium Assoc., 807 N.W.2d 143, 155 (Iowa 2011); Beard v. Achenbach Mem. Hosp. Ass'n., 170 F.2d 859 (10th Cir. 1948).
26. *See, e.g.,* Model Act §§ 830 and 831; D.C. CODE §§ 29-406.30 and 29-406.31. The Business Judgment Rule, as applied to business corporations, is discussed in detail in Stephen A. Radin, *The Business Judgment Rule*, 6th ed. (Aspen Law & Business 2009). *See also* discussion in Jack B. Siegel, *A Desktop Guide for Nonprofit Directors, Officers, and Advisors*, 85 (John Wiley & Sons, Inc. 2006); RESTATEMENT OF THE LAW, CHARITABLE NONPROFIT CORPORATIONS, §2.03.
27. *See* Lisa A. Runquist, *The Night the Sky Fell: Directors of Nonprofits Continue at Risk*, 15 BUS. L. NEWS 15 (Spring 1994) (available at runquist.com), discussing the California Supreme Court's decision in *Francis T. v. Village Green Owners Association,* 42 Cal. 3d 490 (1986), holding that the Business Judgment Rule protection provided for under the California Corporations Code is not a bar to individual director liability for action taken as a board member if the action created an unreasonable risk of personal injury to third parties. The case was brought by the owner of a condominium who was assaulted and robbed by an intruder after the condominium board ordered the owner to stop using exterior lights she had installed outside her unit following numerous burglaries in the complex.
28. *See* In re Walt Disney Derivative Litig., 906 A.2d 27, 56 (Del. 2006).
29. *See* Stern v. Lucy Webb Hayes Nat'l Training Sch. for Deaconesses & Missionaries, 381 F. Supp. 1003, 1012-1014 (D.D.C. 1974).
30. *See* Manhattan Eye, Ear & Throat Hosp. v. Spitzer, 715 N.Y.S.2d 575 (N.Y. Sup. Ct. 1999); *see also* RESTATEMENT OF THE LAW, CHARITABLE NONPROFIT ORGANIZATIONS, § 2.02, Note 25.
31. *See* B. Hopkins and Shane T. Hamilton, THE LAW OF TAX-EXEMPT ORGANIZATIONS, § 5.7, (12th ed., John Wiley & Sons, Inc. 2019).
32. *See* 18 U.S.C. § 1519.

33. *See* 18 U.S.C. § 1514A.
34. *See* California Nonprofit Integrity Act, CAL. GOV'T CODE §§ 12585, et al., which requires audited financial statements of certain charitable organizations with certain levels of assets or gross revenues to be made available for inspection by the public and the State Attorney General in the same manner as Form 990.
35. *See* IRS, *Governance and Related Topics - 501(c)(3) Organizations,* http://www.irs.gov/pub/irs-tege/governance_practices.pdf
36. *See* Model Act § 860. Under the laws of many states, a conflict of interest transaction need only be fair to the corporation at the time it was authorized or approved to avoid treatment of the transaction as void or a potential breach of the duty of loyalty by the conflicted director. *See, e.g.,* OHIO REV. CODE ANN., § 1702.301; KY. REV. STAT. ANN. § 273.219. Some state nonprofit laws, however, are more stringent, with fairness to the corporation being only one of several elements necessary to avoid the characterization of a conflict of interest transaction as void and one that may subject the interested director to liability. *See, e.g.,* CAL. CORP. CODE, § 5233(d)(2). In addition to the need for fairness, under California law, if the director is interested, the transaction must be approved by the entire board and not just a committee of the board prior to the transaction being consummated. *Id.*
37. For example, in 2012, the Montana attorney general announced a settlement agreement with the Central Asia Institute and its founder concluding a year-long investigation into allegations of mismanagement of assets by the founder and the charity. Based on the results of the investigation, the attorney general concluded that the nonprofit's board of directors failed to fulfill some of its duties. https://dojmt.gov/campaigns/investigative-report-of-greg-mortenson-and-central-asia-institute/
38. See CAL. CORP. CODE § 5233.
39. *See* Linda Grant, *Acts of Charity: Furious Donors Blame a Lax Board after a Fund's Scandal Toppled the Lavish-Living Hand of the United Way,* LOS ANGELES TIMES MAGAZINE 39 (September 13, 1992).
40. *See* IOWA CODE § 504.833(4). The Model Act does not contain this limitation. *See* Model Act § 860.
41. *See* Model Act § 821 cmt.
42. *See, e.g.,* CAL. CORP. CODE §§ 5211 and 7211.
43. *See* Model Act § 870; Valle v. N. Jersey Auto. Club, 359 A.2d 504 (N.J. Super. Ct. App. Div. 1976).
44. Some public benefit corporations face demands for open meetings of their boards; in some cases, mixed public-private activities may impose that duty. Those practices are infrequently required as a matter of law; however, if open meetings are adopted as a practice, specific rules as to confidentiality, whether or not legally mandated, should be developed.

A somewhat different issue is raised by the many statutes governing condominiums, which require that all board meetings (with narrowly defined exceptions) be open to owners. *See, e.g.*, 765 ILL. COMP. STAT. 605/18.5(c)(4). In those cases, of course, the board meets in the presence of those to whom it is accountable.

45. *See* Model Act § 405; D.C. CODE § 29-413.05.
46. *See* Model Act § 823.
47. Otherwise, a director who is present at a board meeting at which action is taken may be presumed to have assented to the action. *See, e.g., Model Act § 824(d)* Ill. General Not For Profit Corporation Act of 1986, 805 ILL. COMP. STAT. 105/108.65(b).
48. *See Guide to Nonprofit Corporate Governance in the Wake of Sarbanes-Oxley, supra* note 8, at 41–42.
49. *See* RESTATEMENT OF THE LAW, CHARITABLE NONPROFIT ORGANIZATIONS, § 2.02, note 25.
50. *See* W.H. Hurd, et al., *The Will to Prevail: Inside the Legal Battle to Save Sweet Briar*, 51 U. RICH. L. REV. 227 (2016).
51. *See* 18 U.S.C. §§ 1514A and 1519.
52. *See Guide to Nonprofit Corporate Governance in the Wake of Sarbanes-Oxley, supra* 8, at 17–18.
53. Panel on the Nonprofit Sector, *Principles for Good Governance and Ethical Practice: A Guide for Charities and Foundations* (2nd ed. 2015).

Suggested Questions for Directors Regarding Director Duties and Rights

(1) How often does our board meet? Is this according to a regular schedule?

(2) How frequently do I attend regular board meetings?

(3) What information is given to me in advance of each board meeting? Is it relevant to decisions to be reached at the meeting?

(4) Does the corporation make board materials available via a secure board governance website?

(5) Am I satisfied with the information I have received? As to quantity? As to the subject? As to timeliness? As to reliability? Is it too little? Is it more than I can really analyze between my receipt of it and the board meeting?

(6) Is there any information submitted to me that I feel is incomplete or untrustworthy? How do I deal with this problem?

(7) Who manages, in the day-to-day sense, the business of the corporation?
(8) Is there any information that I know the other Board members do not have that is important for them to know as members of the Board?
(9) Do I have an interest—personal or business—that conflicts with the interests of the corporation?
(10) Has a situation arisen under which I should disclose that interest?
(11) Do I know of a conflict involving another director? Did the director disclose that problem?
(12) Does our corporation have a policy on conflict disclosure? Is it in writing? Do we annually sign a disclosure statement relating to this subject?
(13) Does the corporation have other policies and procedures that the Form 990 asks about?
(14) What contact do I have with the chief executive of the corporation? Is it primarily at board meetings or do I have a close personal relationship that may affect my objectivity?
(15) What contact do I have with subordinate staff members? Am I interfering in operations?
(16) What notice is given as to board meetings? How and when is such notice given?
(17) When do I receive the agenda and materials for board meetings? Do I have time to examine and consider them before voting on them? Do I, in fact, read them?
(18) When do I receive minutes of prior board meetings? Do I read them? Do I communicate any corrections needed? Do I see minutes or reports of committee meetings? When?
(19) Do I know of illegitimate or illegal acts of the corporation or its officers? What should I do if I know of or suspect such acts have occurred or are occurring?
(20) Was I chosen to serve on the board as a representative or delegate of a particular constituency? What am I expected to do for that constituency?

Checklist: Duties and Rights of Nonprofit Corporation Directors

Note: For simplicity, these and other chapter checklists describe a corporation having a chair, who presides over the board of directors; a chief executive, who may be a staff person; an executive committee; a governance/nominating committee; and an audit committee. (We recognize, however, that in many smaller and other nonprofits, these committee functions may be performed by either the executive committee or the board as a whole.) We also assume a legal counsel—someone, paid or unpaid, having primary responsibility for the corporation's legal affairs. Many corporations, especially larger nonprofits, may have other committees established for specific purposes, such as establishing executive compensation; monitoring compliance with legal requirements; and overseeing investments and other financial matters.

Subject	Review By	How Often	Comment
The Board's Record of Service			
1. What is the record of each director's attendance at board meetings?	Chair, chief executive, governance/ nominating committee	Before submission of nominations for election; from time to time during the year	Regular attendance serves to maintain an active board of high morale.
2. What members of the board have missed half the meetings during the last twelve months?	Chair, chief executive and governance/ nominating committee	Before submission of nominations for election; from time to time during the year	If the number is large, see below.
3. Does the corporation have, or should the board consider a provision in the bylaws or a written board policy for the removal of a director who fails (without adequate excuse) to reach a minimum record of attendance?	Chair, chief executive, and governance/ nominating committee	Whenever there is a review of bylaws	Sometimes the simple proposal of such a bylaw or bylaw provision will trigger appropriate resignations. Even if actual removals are accomplished by requested resignations, a bylaw provision or a director's signed acknowledgement of attendance and other expectations may be desirable, and in some states, required if a director is to be removed for attendance reasons.

Subject	Review By	How Often	Comment
4. How many board meetings took place in the last twelve months? Were all the meetings called for in the bylaws actually held?	Chair and chief executive	At least annually	The optimum number of board meetings is to be determined by needs, but a quarterly meeting schedule is often appropriate for an operating organization.
5. Is there any feeling on the part of the members of the board that the number of meetings is inadequate for effective oversight of the corporation's business?	Chair and board	Annually	This question is closely related to the committee structure of the corporation.
6. Should the number of regular board meetings be increased or reduced?	Chair and board	Annually	It is good practice to periodically evaluate if the board's meeting schedule, agenda structure, length, and location are most conducive for effective board deliberations.
7. Would more adequate oversight be obtained by delegating more duties to committees?	Chair and board	Annually	*See Chapter 3, Committees and Advisory Bodies.*

Subject	Review By	How Often	Comment
8. How many directors have contributed funds to the corporation? Have all done so? What is the average?	Chief executive and governance/ nominating committee	Annually, and before any reelection or renomination of directors	It is recommended that a charitable nonprofit corporation be explicit with board members and board candidates regarding any expectations for director philanthropy supporting the corporation.
9. What has been the attendance record of the members of the corporation's committees?	Chief executive and governance/ nominating committee	Annually, if committees are elected or appointed on a schedule, before such election or appointment	Attendance records at committee meetings should be part of director's record reviewed for any reelection decision.
The Board's Procedures			
1. What material is distributed *in advance* of board meetings?	Chair and chief executive	As a general matter, periodically by chair; as to particular meetings, chief executive	Materials should include at minimum the certain standard items, such as financial statements, prior board and committee minutes, and summary data on company operations.
Does it include:			
(a) Minutes of the last meeting and committee meetings?	Full board	All regular meetings	Always

Subject	Review By	How Often	Comment
(b) Current financial statements?	Full board and audit committee	All regular meetings	Always
(c) Current reports of committees?	Full board	At each meeting of board	Committees should report in writing, as well as orally, the committee's prior meeting minutes may suffice as the written portion of the report.
(d) Summaries of board actions or decisions that will be requested?	Full board	Before each meeting	All directors should be urged to consider identified board actions prior to the meeting. In addition to this summary, relevant documents should be provided for the directors' advance review to the extent practicable.
(e) Copies of resolutions proposed for adoption?	Full board	Before each meeting	Having resolutions distributed in advance enables the board to focus on the precise matters to be considered by the board and results in increased efficiency.

Subject	Review By	How Often	Comment
The Corporation's Policies on Conflicts			
1. Do we have a conflicts policy that requires all directors and officers to execute an annual disclosure?	Full board	Annually	IRS Form 990 and governance authorities indicate an expectation that directors and officers are subject to conflicts disclosure requirements.
(a) Has the corporation's conflict of interest policy been recently reviewed for substantive content and compliance with current governance standards?	Legal counsel and audit committee; then full board	Annually	Periodic review by the full board is recommended.
(b) Were board disclosure statements in fact provided to all directors?	Audit committee	Annually and at point at which each new director joins board	Disclosure statements should be made every year.
(c) How does the corporation deal with conflicts that arise between the execution dates of a regular conflicts disclosure?	Chief executive reporting to board	As often as conflicts arise; review of totality annually	Full and prompt reporting is essential when the conflict applies to a specific matter before the board or a board committee, or may create an appearance of impropriety.

Subject	Review By	How Often	Comment
2. Was there a meeting at which a director disclosed a potential conflict of interest regarding a decision?	Legal counsel and audit committee	The disclosure should precede or be simultaneous with the decision	Corporate minutes should record the disclosure and whether the board determined there was a conflict and how the conflict was handled.
(a) Was there a vote by disinterested directors on the issue about which the director had a conflict?	Legal counsel and audit committee	As often as this disclosure occurs	Corporate minutes should record whether the subject director voted or recused himself from voting or discussion.
(b) If so, was there a quorum (as defined by the statute of incorporation) for this vote?	Legal counsel and audit committee	At meeting in question	State statutes vary as to whether a recused director is counted for purposes of quorum and voting.
(c) Was there a vote of an adequate number of disinterested directors with the requisite quorum?	Chair, legal counsel	At meeting in question	The conflicted director should not vote on the subject transaction or decision.

Chapter 3:
Committees and Advisory Bodies

Chapter 3

Committees and Advisory Bodies

The directors of a nonprofit corporation will frequently discharge their duties through committees composed, wholly or in part, of members of the board. The directors should understand what functions can be delegated to committees, what responsibilities the board has concerning committee activities, and the degree to which directors can rely on information provided by committees. The directors should understand the difference between committees of directors and certain kinds of advisory or auxiliary boards or other bodies composed of nondirectors.

Board Committees: Introduction

Committees are usually necessary for the efficient discharge of the board's work.[1] Indeed, many boards would find it impossible to discharge their responsibilities without the use of committees. A director should understand the different types of committees available to the corporation and the extent to which the board may delegate authority to committees to act on behalf of the board. For example, in most states, only board members may serve on a committee that exercises the powers of the board. The purpose, powers, and limitations of any committee should be clearly stated in the corporation's bylaws or by resolution recorded in the minutes of the board. These documents should define the membership, term of office, and method of appointment.

The Types of Board Committees

For analysis in this *Guidebook*, we divide board committees into two categories: standing or permanent and special or ad hoc committees.

Standing or Permanent Committees

These committees are permanent and may be described or provided for in the corporation's bylaws board charters, or board resolutions. Standing committees may make recommendations, oversee operations, and study-specific areas of activity. Depending on the bylaws, charters, or resolutions creating them, they may have the power to bind the corporation. This power may be extensive (as in the case of many (or most) executive committees) or fairly limited. Still, even when a board committee is given the power to bind the corporation, the board will always have the ultimate authority and can personally override a decision of the committee.

A common standing committee is the executive committee, which generally has extensive power to act on behalf of the corporation between board meetings. Other common standing committees include a governance/nominating committee; finance committee; audit committee; compensation committee; compliance committee; investment committee; personnel/human resources committee; planning committee; public relations committee; programming committee; and capital campaigns and grants committee. Although the circumstances of each nonprofit will dictate what kinds of standing committees are appropriate, most nonprofit corporations should, at a minimum, consider the merits of a governance/nominating committee and an audit committee. (For further discussion of common standing committees, see the section *"Descriptions of Common Standing Committees"* below.)

Special Committees

Special committees are temporary or *ad hoc* groups established for a limited purpose. Most special committees will be created by board resolution as the need arises, and are often limited in their duration.

Standing Committees: General Issues

Most nonprofit corporations find it necessary, in order to fulfill their duties, to have permanent standing committees of the board.

Board Use of and Reliance on Committees

The board of directors may discharge its duties for a particular class of issues through a committee created to assemble information and make decisions or recommendations concerning a specific corporate activity. A board member who does not serve on a specific committee is entitled to rely on the committee in the normal course of business unless the director has some reason to know that the committee's action is deficient.[2]

Committee Creation: Bylaw Provision, Committee Charter, or Board Resolution

The committee's formation, purpose, and authority to act on behalf of the corporation should be stated in detail in the bylaws or in the board resolution creating the committee. In addition, the bylaws or resolution should describe the process for appointing committee members and the committee chairs. Often, these appointments occur by board action. Most states prohibit committees from appointing their own members.[3] Directors should recognize that in a dispute concerning a committee's purpose and the scope of its duties, the resolutions and minutes recording the committee's creation may be examined long after their adoption. If the board determines that a modification is necessary, it may have to amend the bylaws before the modification becomes effective.

Committee Exercise of Board Authority

Committees empowered to exercise board authority in a wide scope of activities must, first of all, be formed consistent with applicable provisions of the applicable state nonprofit corporation statute and the corporation's articles of incorporation and bylaws. Under the Model Act, executive or other committees may be authorized to exercise the board's authority in general or specific respects, except that the board may not delegate to committees the authority to take certain actions defined by law, such as approving the distribution of assets or amending the corporation's bylaws.[4]

Committee Size

As with the board itself, committees should be selected and managed to maximize the efficiency of the directors in discharging their duties. In general, smaller groups are more efficient—three to seven is an optimal size—and large committees can be unwieldy. Awarding committee memberships as "perks" or to assuage egos is a sure prescription for poor performance. Still, the committee must have enough people to carry out its purpose and to provide representation for all whose concerns are to be examined in the committee's work. As is frequently the case in the nonprofit field, there may be a conflict between the corporation's need for diversity in committee membership and its need for efficiency in its operations. The bylaws or the resolution appointing the committee should specify the size of the committee, by requiring a particular number or by setting forth a permissible range. The state laws vary on the minimum number of committee members, but the Model Act and states that follow it allow committees of one director.[5]

Conflicts of Interest

All standards regarding directors' duty of loyalty and conflicts of interest apply to members of board committees (see the section *"Conflict of Interest: General Principles"* in *Chapter 2, Duties and Rights of Nonprofit Corporation Directors*). Indeed, they apply with even greater force, since a conflict involving a single member of a small committee may have a larger adverse impact on the decisions, and ultimately affect whether a director not serving on that committee may reasonably determine that the committee's recommendations merit confidence.

Special Committees

Special committees are typically created by a board of directors to perform limited functions.

Purposes of Special Committees

Special committees can be either advisory—with no power to bind or act for the corporation—or created for a certain purpose with limited powers. The board of directors may, from time to time, create committees to investigate or recommend actions of a special nature. Special committees may be formed to negotiate the purchase of a building, plan a reception, approve drafts of documents, evaluate a major transaction, assess the fairness to the corporation of a transaction between the corporation and a director or officer, conduct a search for a new CEO, oversee a litigation matter for the corporation, or for some similar purpose. They also may be asked to represent the corporation with another group or at a meeting.

Special committees also can be delegated special powers to act as agents or to act in place of the board in appropriate situations. For instance, the applicable law or the corporation's bylaws may require the delegation of decision-making authority to a committee of "disinterested directors" to decide sensitive issues involving other board members or key management, such as indemnification, compensation arrangements, or conflict of interest transactions.

Descriptions of Common Standing Committees

Executive Committee

Many nonprofit corporations will find that the efficient discharge of their work requires the creation of an executive committee able to exercise, between board meetings, most of the power the board would otherwise exercise.

Most executive committees are composed of directors of the corporation who also are officers, and perhaps also a small number of other directors. The purpose of an executive committee is to create a group that is able to act for the board between its regular meetings and in situations in which an assembly of a quorum of the board would be impractical or impossible. An executive committee, in an organization, is not purely local in nature, and should generally consist of directors who are able to participate regularly and effectively either in person or by virtual means, including telephone. At each board meeting, the board should be informed of any actions taken by the executive committee since the last board meeting.

If the executive committee exercises a substantial amount of the power of the board, the board as a whole should periodically evaluate whether the board is meeting its fiduciary obligations through delegations to the executive committee and whether the board effectively oversees and has the opportunity to provide input regarding executive committee decisions. The board should also review the amount of board-level power that the executive committee may be delegated to the corporation's chief executive or other officers (apart from any officer's role as a director or executive committee member) to ensure that board power is not routinely exercised by officers rather than the board and its committees. As noted in the section *"Committee Exercise of Board Authority"* above, the board should be aware that state law generally places limits on the powers that a nonprofit board may delegate to an executive or other committee.

A large board that delegates a significant amount of power to its executive committee should also periodically evaluate whether the corporation would benefit from having a smaller board that meets more frequently, thereby enabling the full board to participate in many decisions being handled by the executive committee. Nonetheless, for many nonprofits, the use of the executive committee mechanism may be an appropriate and efficient use of board resources by identifying board representatives who are able to make decisions when needed on the board's behalf.

An executive committee should never be a "super" board. As with all committees, the executive committee reports to the board; the board does not report to the executive committee. Assigning duties regarding matters to be approved by the executive committee before being brought to the full board can disenfranchise the rest of the board.

In recent years, there has been decreased reliance on an executive committee by some nonprofits. This may be due to the enhanced ability to communicate offered by the Internet and the ubiquity of cell phones, which make it easier than in the past to obtain participation from the full board on matters needing to be addressed between board meetings. Still, an executive committee can be useful for some nonprofit organizations, especially those with large boards. In addition, nonprofits may find executive committees useful to make final decisions on matters previously approved by the board subject to the final determination of certain issues (such as final terms on a large transaction) or to handle matters when it is not feasible to convene all of the board in person, by phone or web access.

Governance/Nominating Committee

Good corporate practice suggests the appointment of a governance/nominating committee to strengthen the corporate mission, increase board effectiveness, and identify board candidates having the range of qualities desired for an effective board.

Importance of governance/nominating committees

A governance/nominating committee is almost always a standing committee, yet is rarely regarded as a body whose diligence or negligence is legally reviewed because final action on nominations is almost always referred back to the board of directors. Nevertheless, the process used to determine board nominations obviously is of great importance to the corporation's future and its ability to carry out the corporation's mission. The board of directors has a duty to ensure that a governance/nominating committee is organized and operated in a manner that is likely to generate quality candidates for open board positions.

A nonprofit corporation's mission may require racial and gender diversity or other specific qualifications in the corporation's governing body. Similarly, certain diversity, qualifications, or status among the corporation's board may be necessary in order to be considered for government and other funding. Even apart from those specific demands, the governance/nominating committee should formalize and develop procedures for determining who should have positions on the board itself and on committees. The presence of a governance/nominating committee also helps to ensure that important board decisions regarding the selection of directors (and perhaps also officers and committee members) will not be handled on a default basis by management alone.

Developing criteria for board nominees

The governance/nominating committee should define explicit criteria and qualities for board membership and have the full board approve the list. The criteria may include knowledge of the corporation's business or industry and purpose or mission; skills needed on the board (e.g., legal, financial, managerial, technology, fundraising); association or familiarity with the corporation's constituencies; demographic factors; prior successful board experience; evidence of commitment to the corporation's mission; experience with facing similar challenges as those currently facing the corporation; and the ability to satisfy the time commitment required for board service. The development and use of a board matrix can be helpful in identifying and tracking backgrounds, expertise, diversity characteristics, and other demographic or skillset desired for a board. The governance/nominating committee also may identify personal qualities desirable for board members, such as good listening skills, the ability to effectively (and diplomatically) articulate views contrary to those of other board members, and willingness to support board decisions in which their views are in the minority.

Other powers: recommendations for removal of directors, board size, and composition and functions

The governance/nominating committee may also have responsibility for recommending the removal of a director prior to the expiration of a director's term of office, based on inappropriate acts or the director's inattention to the director's duty.

The committee should also have other functions, including reviewing the board structure and operations to determine their effectiveness. This review should include a determination of whether there is a culture that supports collegiality, civility, openness, and respect for the board's decisions. In addition, the committee should be involved in evaluating the optimum size of the board, the age profile of board members, the merits of inclusion (or exclusion) of management officers on the board, and the types and functions of board committees, as well as reviewing and making recommendations on the corporation's governing documents. The results of that review and recommendations should be presented to the full board for consideration and action.[6]

The committee also should have responsibility for evaluating current directors to ensure the board is functioning properly, and for providing regular education.

Composition

Ideally, the governance/nominating committee should be composed of directors who do not participate in management and are free of relationships, both business and personal, that could interfere with their exercise of independent judgment. This will help provide both the appearance and the reality of objectivity. In addition, it may be prudent to rotate the members of the committee from time to time. A compromise should be reached between the need to draw on the corporation's present activities, history, and experience, and the need for fresh insights into the corporation's present and future mission.

Audit Committee

Good corporate practice and some state laws require an organization with significant financial resources to have a committee to review and guide accounting and audit practices.[7] Such a committee should be comprised solely of nonmanagement directors. An independent audit committee can help ensure the financial integrity of the corporation and strengthen the board's ability to exercise its oversight function by reviewing the audited financial statements and hearing reports from auditors firsthand, rather than simply reviewing digested material prepared by management.[8] Some nonprofit organizations maintain a finance committee and an audit committee that does not have overlapping membership. In California, the audit committee must not have a complete overlap with the finance committee, which would generally be the committee regularly reviewing the draft financial statements throughout the year and providing regular guidance.[9]

An audit committee has responsibilities concerning the corporation's auditing, accounting, and control functions. Depending on the size and activities of the nonprofit, the organization may hire an outside auditing firm to compile, review, or audit the corporation's financial books and records. Federal and state laws or regulations may require a formal audit by a certified public accountant.[10]

The audit committee serves as a liaison between the corporation and the outside auditors. In order to retain objectivity of the audit process, employees of the corporation, even if serving on the board of directors, should not be members of the audit committee. Thus, it is optimal, and in some states required, for the audit committee to be composed entirely of independent directors.[11] In addition, to be able to evaluate the financial matters related to the corporation effectively, each audit committee member should be, or be willing to become, financially literate, including the ability to read and understand the corporation's financial statements and the kind of financial issues the corporation typically faces.[12]

The audit committee's duties usually include choosing services needed in financial management, reviewing reports and determining adequate procedures and controls, reviewing financial performance, and approving the annual budget for submission to the board (unless there is a separate finance committee, in which case the finance committee may have some of these duties). Sometimes a review of legal compliance is included within the duties of an audit committee. Any additional duties should be undertaken with caution, for if the committee becomes involved in operational matters, it may jeopardize its essential independence from management. In order to adhere to the proper limits, the duties delegated to the committee should be spelled out very specifically, after consultation with and the concurrence of the outside accountant. This definition of duties can be accomplished either by bylaw provisions, committee charter, or board resolution.

With the need of the board of directors to review Form 990 prior to filing, the audit committee might be an appropriate committee to be delegated the responsibility for an in-depth review (with the full board being given an opportunity to review Form 990 after the audit committee's review). See the section "*Discharging the Duty of Care: Some Practical Suggestions: Form 990 Governance Focus Areas*" in *Chapter 2, Duties and Rights of Nonprofit Corporation Directors.*

Compensation Committee

It is useful for many nonprofit corporations to establish compensation committees to evaluate the appropriateness of compensation for the chief executive and other key individuals and to ensure that compensation decisions are tied to the executives' performance in meeting predetermined goals and objectives.[13]

A nonprofit board should consider whether it should have a standing compensation committee and whether the committee will determine the compensation or make recommendations to the board on compensation. Whether a separate committee is formed for this function or it is assigned to another committee, it is recommended that the committee be composed solely of independent persons. In addition, the corporation should clearly organize the review of staff qualifications and compensation and, in particular, the compensation of the chief executive and other key employees. Since that task involves the receipt and evaluation of confidential and sensitive data, it should be assigned to a separate standing committee if the size of the board is large enough to make this possible.

The entire board should be aware of the total compensation package for the chief executive and for other key individuals. In order to avoid conflicts of interest, however, approval of compensation may need to be delegated to a committee. (As noted in the section *"Procedures for Establishing Reasonableness"* in *Chapter 5, Taxation,* the IRS's excess benefit rules provide a presumption of reasonableness if certain financial transactions with insiders (known as "disqualified persons") are approved by disinterested members of a board or board committee, and certain other procedures are followed.) Still, in at least one state, conflicts of interest involving the board must be approved by the full board and not just a committee of the board.[14]

Investment Committee

For nonprofit corporations that maintain an endowment or significant cash reserves, good corporate practice (and the demands of the Uniform Prudent Management of Institutional Funds Act (UPMIFA)) suggests appointing an investment committee.

UPMIFA, which has been adopted in all states but Pennsylvania, provides rules governing the investment of a charity's assets. UPMIFA, which replaced the Uniform Management of Institutional Funds Act (UMIFA), provides more specific guidance than UMIFA with regard to prudence in investments and the expenditure of endowment funds. UPMIFA also eliminated a floor on spending by providing that an institution may appropriate for expenditure or accumulate so much of an endowment fund as the institution determines to be prudent for the uses, benefits, purposes, and duration for which the endowment fund is established. A more detailed discussion regarding the standards under UPMIFA is described in *Chapter 12, Investments and Expenditure of Endowment Funds.*

Compliance Committee

Nonprofit corporations also may need a committee that is assigned compliance oversight. This responsibility might be delegated to a nominating/governance committee, an audit committee, an executive committee, or a separate compliance committee. The committee with the compliance responsibility should regularly review the compliance programs established for the corporation, which should include policies aimed at mitigating legal and operational risks. It is important that any staff assigned compliance responsibilities in the corporation have direct access to the committee that is assigned compliance oversight. Where the corporation uses a committee to oversee compliance, it is still important for the full board to be involved in compliance matters. As a result, there should be regular reporting to the full board regarding compliance matters.

The Composition of a Committee

The appropriate composition of a committee will depend on the type of committee involved and any requirements set forth in the applicable state nonprofit corporation act. Executive committees may be composed primarily of directors who are also officers; in contrast, governance/nominating and audit committees should consist primarily or entirely of nonofficer directors.

The Model Act requires that all members of committees exercising board authority be members of the board of directors and they be appointed by a greater majority of the directors in office or a number of directors required in the articles of incorporation or bylaws.[15] The rationale for this requirement is that it is inappropriate to delegate board-level power to non-board members.[16] In addition, it may be difficult to hold committee members liable for breaches of fiduciary duties if not all of the voting members are directors.[17] Some state statutes permit nondirectors to serve on committees, including committees that exercise board-delegated authority; however, board members must still comprise a majority of on those committees.[18] The extent to which a committee should consist solely or predominantly of directors, or may be appointed without any directors at all, depends on the purpose of the committee and the authority given it. Advisory committees may be comprised of few, if any, board members, if appropriate under the circumstances.

Committee Procedures, Minutes, and Reports

The procedures, records, and operations of committees should be as clearly defined as those of the board itself.

The distinction between the board of directors' procedures and those of a committee will depend somewhat on the size of the corporation and the individual committee. The committees of large nonprofit boards may be of substantial size and therefore require, for orderly and efficient procedure, a degree of formality that would be inefficient (and possibly ridiculous) in smaller committees. The need for formality is increased if the directors are not routinely acquainted with each other, and the board or committee meetings may be the only occasion when any interpersonal contact is achieved. In these situations, meetings conducted according to fairly structured rules may be necessary. Nonetheless, committees may provide a more flexible way for the board to fulfill specific functions.

Committee members are entitled to notices of meetings, quorum requirements, access to records, clear resolutions in the event of controversy, and a right to record dissent. Under the Model Act, and most state laws, the procedural rules that apply to the board also apply to committees.[19] Informality of discussions should not amount to or imply an infringement of the committee members' rights in this regard.

All committees should maintain minutes of meetings and other records appropriate to their purposes. The more a board relies on a committee in the discharge of the board's duty of care as in reliance on the judgment and actions of an investment committee the more this committee should maintain fully detailed minutes and records and make regular reports to the board. Executive committees and other standing committees should submit minutes to the board in detail roughly comparable to those of the board itself. On the other hand, it may be sufficient for the board to require that a special committee prepare only a report.

Advisory and Auxiliary Bodies: Introduction

In contrast to board committees, advisory or auxiliary boards, councils, or other bodies will often include nondirectors (they may also include former directors) and largely work independently of the board. These boards may provide additional support to the corporation's mission and provide useful insight to the corporation's board. Directors should be aware, however, that such advisory boards and auxiliary groups may be regarded by the public as agents of the corporation. Board members should make sure there are effective procedures both for exercising oversight for advisory and auxiliary boards and for directing these boards to report back periodically to the corporation's board concerning their activities and recommendations.

Use of Advisory and Auxiliary Bodies

A frequent device used in nonprofit corporations is to appoint one or more advisory or auxiliary boards, councils, or committees, composed of community leaders, former directors, volunteers, other supporters, and community representatives. These bodies differ from board committees in general including in their membership nondirectors and in lacking the ability to exercise power on behalf of the board. These advisory and auxiliary bodies also are distinguished from board committees in that they may be more involved in activities supporting the organization and less involved in governance matters.

Establishing advisory and auxiliary bodies may be useful in enabling a nonprofit board to enlist the interest and input of individuals who would be too numerous or too busy to serve on the board directly. For example, a public benefit corporation may use an advisory council as a mechanism for involving the community leaders who are unable to give the time commitments necessary for board service, but whose insights and names will aid the organization in fundraising or political arenas. In some cases, an advisory board may be advantageous for a start-up nonprofit, as a means to assure donors and the community that the actions of the new organization are subject to some form of independent review. Advisory boards also may be established in connection with a merger or consolidation of nonprofit organizations, allowing the new organization to take advantage of the continued contributions and insight of persons who formerly served as directors of the merged organizations while keeping the consolidated board to a manageable size. Advisory or auxiliary bodies having either indefinite or limited duration may prove useful in a variety of other circumstances. Despite the usefulness of advisory or auxiliary groups, the board should be aware of the legal implications of creating and maintaining these groups.

Special Committees of Nonboard Members

Of course, a board of directors may, at any time, retain persons, entities, or organizations to investigate a problem and report on it, or to serve as agents of the corporation in some matter. Thus, even a committee of total outsiders, named to perform some specific function, can be formed at the discretion of the board of directors, except that in most states, the board may not delegate any board-level power to nondirector committees.

The board should note, however, that even when a special committee has either no authority, or strictly limited authority to bind the corporation, parties outside the corporation may be entitled to rely on the *apparent* authority of the committee, and both the committee and the board should be alert to this risk.

Legal Status of Advisory and Auxiliary Bodies

First of all, corporate law, in general, recognizes advisory and ancillary bodies but does not give them any particular status (unless it is a separately incorporated auxiliary) and its members do not have the same legal duties, responsibilities, and powers that have been outlined in this *Guidebook* as applicable to the board of directors.[20] For that reason, the board of directors should make sure there exists some document (whether titled charter, bylaws, regulations, or other name) describing the purposes and powers of the advisory or auxiliary group, and indicating the group's legal relationship to the establishing organization.

At the same time, any group or individual publicly acknowledged to be connected with the corporation in some manner can, in some circumstances, be considered an agent of the corporation. Thus, the advisory or auxiliary group's actions, even if unauthorized, could be found to be binding against the corporation. Because the group's advisory or unofficial status may not be clear to the public, statements or actions of an advisory group or individual may, at least in the public's eye, be attributed to the board of directors or the corporation. In addition, members of an advisory group may face the same kinds of conflicts of interest experienced by directors. None of these problems are insoluble, but they do call for scrutiny and attention.

Relationship of Board to Advisory Bodies

With respect to advisory bodies, the board should recognize that, having purported to seek advice, the board then has at least a moral obligation to give this advice some measure of consideration, perhaps through a formal process followed at the board or committee level. Directors should further recognize that, unlike the regular committees of the board whose efficient functioning may lessen the burdens of the board, an advisory body may increase those burdens by placing on the board an obligation to review and perhaps respond to its recommendations.

Relationship of Board to Auxiliary Bodies

With respect to auxiliary bodies, the board should exercise some level of oversight, since the auxiliary will be acting publicly in the name of the corporation or the institutions it operates. If the auxiliary functions as a division of the nonprofit, the chief executive or other corporate officer should oversee the auxiliary and report to the board regarding auxiliary operations. In addition, the corporation should establish a mechanism for periodically recognizing the contributions made by the auxiliary group. The board or a committee should also afford the auxiliary periodic opportunities to report on its activities and give or seek advice relating to the operations of the corporation or the auxiliary.

Scope of Activity of Advisory and Auxiliary Bodies

When creating an advisory or auxiliary body, the board must first define the purposes of the group and determine how the board of directors will exercise oversight of the group's activities. Second, the role of the group in relation to the corporation's staff should be defined in the same documents and decisions that create the group. Advisory and auxiliary board or committee members should not be allowed to demand more staff time than is appropriate to the group's role. Moreover, particularly when the advisory or auxiliary group relates to a successful or growing function, the board should be alert to the danger that the group and its related staff may develop a level of independence that fails to recognize that the group is still ultimately subject to the board's control. While developments like that are not unknown, they can be avoided through appropriate structuring of the group at the outset and continued oversight thereafter.

Limitations on Rights of Members of Advisory and Auxiliary Bodies and Liability Protection

The bylaw or board resolution creating the advisory or auxiliary body should designate the criteria for membership, the term for which such members are appointed, and the power of a corporate officer or the board itself to remove members of the advisory or auxiliary group. In general, the members of an advisory or auxiliary group have no vested right to serve, no immunity from removal, and no right to renewal of appointment. The board should be careful, however, to make sure that no resolutions or communications imply the creation of those rights. It is also prudent for the board to address whether (and the extent to which) conflicts of interest policies apply to members of advisory and auxiliary bodies. In addition, as part of the board's review of its directors and officers (D&O) insurance, indemnification rights, and other liability protections (see the discussion in *Chapter 13, Director Liability Risks and Protections*), the board should determine what protections can and should be afforded to advisory and auxiliary group members. Assuming that advisory and auxiliary bodies have no delegated board authority, members of those bodies should not be subject to the fiduciary duties imposed on the nonprofit corporation's board of directors.

Designated Bodies

For some nonprofits, certain of the responsibilities normally vested with the board of directors or the members may be vested with a different person or group. Such a person or group is sometimes referred to as a "designated body." The Model Act defines a "designated body" broadly to include a person or group (other than a committee of the board of directors) that has been vested by the articles of incorporation or bylaws with powers that otherwise would be required to be exercised by the board or the members.[21] This can arise, for instance, with a religious organization where a church authority has defined approval requirements relating to the operations of the organization.

Under the Model Act, if a designated body is created, to the extent the powers of a board of directors are vested with the designated body, the rights, duties, and liabilities of the board of directors or directors individually also apply to the designated body and to the members of the designated body individually. In addition, to the extent that the powers, authority, or functions of the board of directors have been vested with a designated body, the directors are relieved from their duties and liabilities with respect to such powers, authority, and functions.[22] Similarly, to the extent the rights of members have been vested with a designated body, the members are relieved from responsibility with respect to those rights and obligations.[23]

See the Suggested Questions and Checklist following the Endnotes below to review the issues discussed in this chapter.

Endnotes

1. *See* Jack B. Siegel, *A Desktop Guide for Nonprofit Directors, Officers, and Advisors: Avoiding Trouble While Doing Good* 31 (John Wiley & Sons 2006).
2. *See* Model Act §§ 830 (e) and (f). *See also* the section *"Reliance"* in *Chapter 2, "Duties and Rights of Nonprofit Corporation Directors."*
3. *See, e.g.*, Illinois General Not for Profit Corporation Act of 1986, 805 ILL. COMP. STAT. 105/108.40. See also Model Act § 825(b) ("Unless this Act, the articles of incorporation, or the bylaws provide otherwise, the establishment of a committee and appointment of directors to it must be approved by the greater of (1) a majority of all directors in office when the action is taken; or (2) the number of directors required by the articles of incorporation or bylaws to take action under Section 824 (quorum and voting)").
4. *See* Model Act § 825 cmt.
5. *See* Model Act § 825(a).

6. Some state statutes specifically provide for a governance/nominating committee. *See* 15 Pa. Cons. Stat. § 5725(e). *See also* ABA Coordinating Committee on Nonprofit Governance, *Guide to Nonprofit Corporate Governance in the Wake of Sarbanes-Oxley* 28–34 (American Bar Association 2005).
7. *See, e.g.,* California Nonprofit Integrity Act of 2004, Cal. Gov't. Code §§ 12585–12589.
8. Under the California Nonprofit Integrity Act of 2004, audited financial statements are required of nonprofit organizations that receive or accrue gross revenues of $2 million in any fiscal year.
9. *See* California Nonprofit Integrity Act of 2004, *supra* note 7.
10. *See Guide to Nonprofit Corporation Governance in the Wake of Sarbanes-Oxley, supra* note 6 at 28–34.
11. *See* New York Not-For-Profit Corporation Law § 712-a(a).
12. *See Guide to Nonprofit Corporation Governance in the Wake of Sarbanes-Oxley, supra* note 6 at 31.
13. *See Guide to Nonprofit Corporate Governance in the Wake of Sarbanes-Oxley, supra* note 6 at 35–37.
14. *See* California Nonprofit Integrity Act of 2004, *supra* note 7.
15. *See* Model Act § 825. (Still, nondirectors may serve on advisory committees under the Model Act.)
16. *See* Restatement of the Law, Charitable Nonprofit Organizations, § 2.06(d)(2).
17. *Id.*
18. *See, e.g.,* 805 ILCS § 105/108.40.
19. *See, e.g.,* Model Act § 825(c).
20. *See, e.g.,* Model Act § 825(h).
21. *See* Lawrence J. Beaser and William H. Clark, Jr., *Forward to the Fourth Edition* in *Model Nonprofit Corporation Act* (4th ed., American Bar Association 2022), at xxiii.
22. *See* Model Act § 812(a).
23. *Id.*

Suggested Questions for Directors Regarding Committees, Advisory Bodies, and Officers

(1) What committees does our board have? What powers does each committee have?

(2) Is there an executive committee? What are the limitations on its power to act?

(3) Do we have a governance/nominating committee? If not, how are nominations made? How is the board evaluated?

(4) Who monitors the corporation's accounting and financial reports? Is there an audit committee or a finance committee? Who serves on it?

(5) Is there a committee that reviews executive performance and compensation?

(6) If the corporation has investments, does it have or need an investment committee?

(7) Is there a committee responsible for legal compliance? If not, how does the corporation address compliance matters?

(8) How do committees report to the board?

(9) What auxiliary groups or advisory boards are associated with the corporation? What are their relationship to the corporation? How does the board monitor and recognize the activities of these groups?

(10) Is there a person or group that has been vested with the rights and responsibilities of the board of directors or members under the articles and bylaws? If so, what are these rights and responsibilities?

Checklist: Committees and Advisory Bodies

Note: For purposes of simplicity in these checklists, we describe a corporation with a chair, who presides over the board of directors; a chief executive, who may be a staff person; an executive committee; a governance/nominating committee; and an audit committee. (We recognize, however, that in many smaller and other nonprofits, these committee functions may be performed by either the executive committee or the board as a whole.) We also assume a legal counsel—someone, paid or unpaid, having primary responsibility for the corporation's legal affairs. Many corporations, especially larger nonprofits, may have other committees established for specific purposes, such as reviewing staff performance, fixing compensation, monitoring compliance with legal requirements, and periodic review of bylaws.

Subject	Review By	How Often	Comment
1. What are the committees of the corporation?	Chair, chief executive, full board	Annually	A review of bylaw provisions relating to committees should be performed simultaneously.
2. Which committees have the power to bind the corporation?	Chair, chief executive, full board	Annually	The board should periodically review whether it is delegating too much, or too little, authority to committees.
3. Which committees, with or without power to bind the corporation, deal with major parties or interests outside the corporation?	Chair, chief executive, full board	Annually	Even committees or committee members without *actual* authority to bind the corporation could have *apparent* authority in the view of outside parties.
4. Which committees simply report or advise the board?	Chair, chief executive, full board	Annually	The board should periodically review the use and usefulness of advisory committees.
5. Do we have a governance/ nominating committee? If not, how are nominations made? How is the board evaluated?	Chair, chief executive, full board	Annually, in preparation for the annual meeting; before each meeting at which a vacancy is to be filled	An effective governance/ nominating committee must discuss board evaluation and board needs with the full board prior to its annual meeting.

Subject	Review By	How Often	Comment
6. Do we have a compensation committee? If not, who determines compensation?	Chair/chief executive/full board	Annually	Compensation committee or other committee or full board should review executive compensation annually.
7. Should there be provisions limiting the number of consecutive terms a director may serve? Or a maximum age for directors?	Governance/ nominating committee, reviewing proposed changes with legal counsel, and reporting to the board	Probably every three or four years	Governance/ nominating committee should, as a regular function, analyze years of service of each director, maximum age, and average age of board. No bright-line tests apply to all cases, but decisions on these issues (including the decision to make no changes) should be conscious.
8. What committee reviews staff compensation?	Chair, chief executive, full board	Annually	This function should be formally assigned even if no separate compensation committee is created.

Subject	Review By	How Often	Comment
9. Does the committee that decides compensation matters report to the board in executive session?	Chair, chief executive, full board	Annually	Discussion of staff salaries should always be held outside of the presence of staff, without need for a special resolution to that effect.
10. Does the corporation have or need an investment committee? Is the corporation subject to the Uniform Prudent Management of Institutional Funds Act?	Chair, chief executive, chief financial officer, and full board	Every two or three years	The board should periodically review and assure that investment committee members understand their responsibilities.
11. Does the corporation have a committee responsible for oversight of legal and operational compliance matters?	Chair, chief executive, and full board	Every two or three years	Even where there is a committee assigned the responsibility of overseeing compliance matters, there should be regular reporting to the full board on these matters.

Chapter 4: Officers

Chapter 4
Officers

The board of directors is responsible for setting the direction of the nonprofit corporation while the officers are responsible for implementing such direction and managing the day-to-day affairs of the corporation. In general, there is no specific requirement to have a particular "named" officer; however, most organizations typically have, at a minimum, a president and/or chair, secretary, and treasurer. The particular officers of the nonprofit corporation should be described in the bylaws along with their rights and responsibilities.

Officers: Introduction

Nonprofit corporations typically have officers who are delegated responsibilities by the board of directors either through the articles of incorporation, bylaws, or board resolution. The officers are selected in accordance with the terms of the articles of incorporation and bylaws. Normally, the board of directors elects the officers, but in some nonprofit organizations, especially trade organizations, the members will elect certain of the officers.

Most nonprofit corporation statutes do not mandate that there be any particular officer positions; however, some statutes require the position of a president, secretary, or treasurer and such other offices as are appointed by the board if the governance documents are silent.[1]

Smaller nonprofit corporations often have a president, treasurer, and a secretary and directors may serve in these officer roles. Larger nonprofit corporations typically have board officers that might include a chair, a vice-chair, secretary, and treasurer as well as staff (nondirector) officers of the corporation who serve in the role of the chief executive officer (CEO), president, and/or executive director as well as other officers, such as one or more vice presidents, a chief financial officer, a chief operations officer, and/or a chief investment officer. Employees of the nonprofit may also serve in other roles including treasurer and secretary and so an employed chief financial officer might also serve the treasurer.

The names of the officer positions are generally not mandated by law, so, for example, a chair might also be referred to as chairperson, chairwoman, chairman, or some other title.

For some nonprofit corporations, "principal officers" are distinguishable from other officers.[2]

Some state nonprofit corporation statutes allow an individual to hold more than one officer position; however, except in the situation with small nonprofits, it is not advisable to have an individual serve in more than one officer position.[3]

Board Officers vs. Staff Officers

Nonprofit corporations may distinguish between the officer positions filled by board members versus officer positions filled by employees of the nonprofit corporation who are employed by the nonprofit. Often board members serving in the role as chair, vice chair, secretary, and treasurer are referred to as "board officers." The Model Act provides that an individual who holds a title with reference to the board (such as a chair of the board or secretary of the board) is a person with a leadership position on the board. The Model Act also provides that an individual with such a title is not an officer of the nonprofit corporation unless the articles, bylaws, or an action by the board treats an individual with that title as an officer of the corporation.[4] Staff officers, on the other hand, are typically employees of the nonprofit. This distinction is important because a board officer is typically not expected to be involved in the day-to-day activities of the nonprofit corporation where a staff officer has such responsibility.

In the for-profit context, it is not unusual for the CEO to also be the chair of the Board. This is especially true with public companies.[5] While not prohibited for nonprofit corporations, such dual roles are less common. This is due in part to the nature of a nonprofit corporation and the importance of independence of nonprofit boards.[6]

Officer Responsibilities

In general, the officers have the responsibility for implementing the directives of the board of directors. Still, as noted above, board officers usually are not involved in the day-to-day operations of the organization where there is a staff with a chief executive (who is generally an officer) who assumes this responsibility. Nevertheless, officers are accountable to the board of directors, which requires regular reporting to the directors on the activities of the organization.[7]

An individual may be both an officer and a director; however, it is important to identify the capacity in which the individual is acting at any given time. In the role of an officer, the individual typically has some role in implementing the activities approved by the board of directors and reports to the board of directors. In the role as a director, the individual, along with the rest of the board, supervises the entire operation of the corporation.[8]

Officer Positions

Chair and Vice Chair

The chair of the board (also called the "chair") is often delegated the responsibility of chairing or running the meetings of the board of directors. A chair also can be given the responsibility of chairing any meeting of the members. In addition, the chair, in some states, has signing authority on behalf of the organization and can be given authority to appoint committees as while in other states only the board can appoint committees. Although the bylaws should provide a description of the responsibilities of the chair, some of the duties of the chair may not be specified. In this situation, it is prudent for the board to consider amending its bylaws to reflect the chair's actual responsibilities. Also, a position description for the board chair can be very helpful to ensure that this role is filled appropriately and expectations are met.

Although not addressed in the articles of incorporation or bylaws, the chair plays an extremely important role in institutional dynamics. A chair needs to take a leadership role in the organization and understand and be responsive to the views and expectations of other board members and to work with them to enhance their effectiveness.[9] The chair, in conjunction with the chief executive, must establish the direction of the board's work. The chair also must take steps to ensure that the board is functioning properly in a collegial atmosphere. The chair is a team builder. It is important that the chair and chief executive regularly communicate regarding matters affecting the organization.

As noted above, in the situation where there is a chief executive, it is not expected that the chair will be involved in the day-to-day operations of the organization and the chair can be criticized for micromanaging if attempts are made to have this involvement. If the chief executive is not performing satisfactorily, the board should replace the chief executive rather than cross the line from policy making into policy administration.

A vice chair position often exists in order that there is an individual available to act as the chair in the event the chair is unavailable or becomes unable to serve. Organizations differ on whether a vice chair will automatically ascend to the chair position. The key is that this individual is able and willing to serve in the chair role if necessary.

Treasurer

A treasurer is often delegated various responsibilities relating to the financial affairs of a nonprofit corporation. This can include responsibility for maintaining all monies and securities of the corporation, keeping full and accurate records and accounts in books belonging to the corporation, depositing funds in the name of the corporation with banks designated by the corporation, and preparing the corporation's financial statements.

Nonprofit organizations may often have a board member serve as treasurer, even if the actual financial functions are handled by a staff member. Some commentators recommend that the treasurer be a director for ease in obtaining bank records when necessary. It also can be helpful to have someone on the board with check signing authority for the same reason. For nonprofit corporations with large budgets, it is generally not feasible for a board member serving in the treasurer role to be able to perform all of the designated functions of treasurer. Nonprofit organizations with a full-time chief financial officer or controller often designate this person as the organization's treasurer or, in some cases, the assistant treasurer.

Some nonprofit corporations provide in their bylaws that the treasurer is required to post bond. Depending on whether the treasurer actually handles any funds, such a requirement may be unnecessary. The corporation should, however, carefully evaluate how funds are handled within an organization, institute processes to protect against mismanagement or diversion of funds, and ensure the organization has sufficient insurance coverage to protect against diversion of funds.

Secretary

Like the other positions, most nonprofit corporation acts do not require that there be an officer called a "secretary"; however, state nonprofit corporation acts do impose requirements that often are assumed by the secretary.[10] The position of secretary typically includes the responsibilities of keeping and maintaining minutes of meetings and maintaining the corporate records for the organization. Similar to the situation with the treasurer, in smaller nonprofit organizations—and some larger organizations—a board member may serve in the secretary role. In these cases, it is often beneficial to have a staff member serve as assistant secretary to perform certain of the duties relating to the secretary. In larger nonprofit organizations, an executive such as the chief governance officer or the general counsel may serve as secretary of the organization. This individual has the responsibility not only to maintain the corporation's minutes and other governance books and records, but also to attest to board and corporate authority matters for governmental filings, banking resolutions, and secretary's certificates required in connection with transactions with third parties.

Chief Executive Officer/President/Executive Director

The CEO (or President or Executive Director) is responsible for the operations of the nonprofit. As a result, the CEO has the day-to-day administrative responsibility for achieving the organizational mission and assuring the efficient and effective operation of the organization. The CEO is generally tasked with the responsibility of implementing any decisions of the Board of Directors, which might be in the form of policies, procedures, and a strategic plan. The CEO is also responsible for assuring compliance with legal, financial, accounting, and ethical requirements.

The relationship flowing from the board to the CEO is straightforward in that the CEO is appointed, evaluated, and, if necessary, terminated by the board. As noted above in the discussion about the board chair, it is important that there is a good relationship between the CEO and the board chair. It is optimal if the relationship is one of candor and mutual respect in that these individuals are the intersection between the board and the staff. The board needs to function as the board and convey information through the board chair to the CEO. The CEO then conveys information to the staff. The staff should convey information through the CEO to the board chair.

For nonprofit corporations with employed staff besides the CEO, the CEO is able to delegate responsibilities to other employed officers as well as other employees. Some state nonprofit corporation acts allow the board to designate certain officers, such as the CEO, to appoint additional officers.[11]

In some nonprofit corporations, the CEO will be an *ex-officio* member of the board of directors.

Compensation of Chief Executive Officer

An important role of the Board of Directors is to determine the compensation of the CEO. For larger nonprofit corporations, this responsibility may be delegated to a compensation committee or executive committee. Still, the Board remains ultimately responsible and there should be a regular review of the compensation and expenses of the CEO and other senior management members in accordance with policies established in advance. The process for determining compensation for the CEO and other senior officers is described in more detail in *Chapter 9, Employees.*

Relationship between Chief Executive Officer and Board Chair

An important responsibility of the CEO is to work closely through the Board of Directors primarily through the board chair. The CEO and the board chair should work together to plan the course of the board's work along with the executive committee. This includes developing board meeting agendas, recommending to the board committee membership and policies.

Resignation and Removal of Officers

The process for resignation or removal of an officer is typically addressed in the bylaws of the nonprofit corporation. To the extent the bylaws are silent, the state nonprofit corporation act may address the process to be followed for resignations or removals.[12] Typically, a resignation requires the delivery of a notice to the board of directors, the chair of the board, the appointing officer, or the secretary.

The articles of incorporation or bylaws also typically address the process for removing officers. Similar to the situation with resignations, a nonprofit corporation statute will often have default rules for handling removals if the governance documents are silent. These rules permit removal of an officer at any time with or without cause by the board of directors, the appointing officer, or any other officer authorized in the governing documents or the board.[13]

Contract Rights of Officers

Most state nonprofit corporation acts expressly provide that the election or appointment of an officer does not, by itself, create contract rights.[14] As a result, a nonprofit corporation is able to elect or appoint an officer for a term without such election or appointment, by itself, creating any contractual obligation on the part of either the corporation or the officer.

Often employed officers will have employment agreements with the nonprofit corporations that address termination of employment. Even if there is an employment agreement, however, a person may be removed from office irrespective of any contract rights or the presence or absence of "cause" in a legal sense. Also, it is possible that an officer who prematurely resigns from an officer position will be deemed in breach of an employment agreement.[15]

Standards of Conduct for Officers

A principal officer or manager who has significant, discretionary authority over a nonprofit corporation's activities has fiduciary duties regardless of whether the officer is also a member of the board.[16] Other employees typically are not fiduciaries or may hold limited fiduciary duties to the nonprofit.[17]

The standard of conduct for officers is similar to the conduct imposed on directors discussed in *Chapter 2, Duties and Rights of Nonprofit Corporation Directors*; however, the application of this standard in the role of a director serving as an officer can differ. For instance, an officer's ability to rely on others in meeting the duty of care may be more limited, depending on the circumstances of the particular case, than the scope of reliance permitted for a director. This is because of the obligation the officer may have to be more familiar with the affairs of the nonprofit corporation.[18] In addition, officers have a duty to inform a superior officer, the board of directors, or a committee regarding information they know about the affairs of the nonprofit corporation that are material to the superior officer, board, or committee.[19] The liability protections that are available to directors (described in *Chapter 13, Director Liability Risks and Protections*) also generally apply to officers; however, they can be more limited in nature given the officer's greater involvement in the affairs of a nonprofit corporation.[20]

See the Suggested Questions and Checklist following the Endnotes below to review the issues discussed in this chapter.

Endnotes

1. *See* Wash. Rev. Code § 24.03A.585; Iowa Code § 504.841(1).
2. *See* Model Act § 421(a), cmt.
3. See Model Act § 840(d).
4. *See* Model Act § 840, cmt.
5. *See* Committee of Corporate Laws, *Corporate Director's Guidebook* (7th ed., American Bar Association 2021), at 48.
6. *See* Independent Sector, *Principles for Good Governance and Ethical Practice: A Guide for Charities and Foundations* (2nd ed. 2015), at 24.
7. *See* Lisa A. Runquist, *The ABCs of Nonprofits* (2nd ed., American Bar Association 2015) (Spanish version available), at 24.
8. *See* Runquist, *The ABCs of Nonprofits, supra* note 7, at 25–27.
9. *See* Cheryl Sorokin, Judith A. Cion, Jeannie Carmedelle Frey and Richard Sevcik, Eds., *Nonprofit Governance and Management* (American Bar Association 2011), at 18.

10. *See* Model Act § 102, cmt. 16, § 840(c).
11. *See* Model Act § 840(b).
12. *See* Model Act § 843(a).
13. *See* Model Act § 843(b).
14. *See* Model Act § 844(a).
15. *See* Model Act § 844(b).
16. *See* Restatement of the Law, Charitable Nonprofit Organizations, Section 2.01, cmt. e.
17. *Id.*
18. *See* Model Act § 842(a) and Comment to Model Act § 842.
19. *See* Model Act § 842(b).
20. *See* Model Act § 842(d), cmt.

Suggested Questions for Directors Regarding Officers

(1) What are the officer positions in the organization and what are the responsibilities of the officers?
(2) Are any of the officer positions to be held by nonboard members?
(3) What authority has been delegated to each of the officers?
(4) Can nonboard members who are officers sign documents on behalf of the nonprofit corporation?

Checklist: Officers

Note: For purposes of simplicity in these checklists, we describe a corporation with a chair, who presides over the board of directors; a chief executive, who may be a staff person; an executive committee; a governance/nominating committee; and an audit committee. (We recognize, however, that in many smaller and other nonprofits, these committee functions may be performed by either the executive committee or the board as a whole.) We also assume a legal counsel—someone, paid or unpaid, having primary responsibility for the corporation's legal affairs. Many corporations, especially larger nonprofits, may have other committees established for specific purposes, such as reviewing staff performance, fixing compensation, monitoring compliance with legal requirements, and periodic review of bylaws.

Subject	Review By	How Often	Comment
1. Do the responsibilities of the officers as described in the articles of incorporation or bylaws accurately reflect the responsibilities being carried out by the officers?	Chair or chief executive; governance/ nominating committee	Annually in all cases; always before notice goes out of meeting to elect officers	Many public benefit corporations have bylaws describing as "chair" an uncompensated person who presides over the board. In many nonprofits, the chief executive's functions are not described in bylaws if the chief executive is not the president or other corporate officer. If the chief executive is not described in the bylaws, this person may not be an officer. There should be a description either in the bylaws or some other corporate governance document.

Chapter 5:
Taxation

Chapter 5

Taxation

A director should understand the basic application of federal, state, and local tax law to the corporation. This chapter outlines the principal federal income tax issues of the more common types of nonprofit corporations.

Introduction

A director should have a general understanding of the tax status of the corporation. The director should know, for example, if the corporation is exempt from federal income tax, and if so, under what section of the Internal Revenue Code (the Tax Code); if the corporation is exempt from state taxation; if the corporation is exempt from local real estate or other taxes; and, in a general way, what is required to maintain these exemptions.

Taxation is a technical field, and a director's obligations do not require a detailed knowledge of the various tax statutes and regulations. Most nonprofit corporations have, or should consider having, their tax reporting handled by outside professionals, either accountants or attorneys. The function of the board, in oversight of these persons, is part of the oversight that the board exercises generally. Moreover, the reader should be aware that federal tax law and the interpretation of its provisions are subject to change; therefore, while the issues discussed here are areas requiring a director's attention and are likely to remain relevant to the operations of tax-exempt corporations, specific rules may change over time.[1]

The subject is a broad one, but this chapter will outline only the principal federal income tax issues of the more common nonprofit corporations. And, despite the importance of state and local tax issues, space constrains us from addressing state and local tax law. Still, directors must understand that federal tax-exempt status does not automatically confer exemption from state and local taxes.[2]

Qualifying for Exemption from Federal Income Tax

Most nonprofit corporations are exempt from the federal income taxes applicable to corporations. Still, corporations do not automatically qualify for exemption from federal income taxation simply because they are nonprofit. Although nonprofit organization status is primarily based on state law; federal tax exemption is based on federal law.

A director should not assume that because the corporation is a nonprofit that is exempt from any income tax. Tax-exempt status is a benefit that is conferred on an organization that meets and continues to meet certain requirements set out by the Tax Code. Other than churches, certain church-related entities, and very small organizations, organizations seeking exemption under Tax Code § 501(c)(3), described in this chapter, must obtain IRS approval of their applications for exemption. The IRS lists a series of tax-exempt organizations in IRS Publication 557, *Tax-Exempt Status for Your Organization,* along with brief descriptions defining their activities.[3] This list is set forth in *Appendix A* of this *Guidebook.*

A director should understand that exemption from federal income tax does not necessarily permit donors to the corporation to deduct gifts to it. The Tax Code generally permits donors to deduct gifts to tax-exempt corporations *only* if the corporation qualifies under § 501(c)(3). Payments to other types of tax-exempt corporations may be deductible by the donor only if the payment qualifies as a trade or business expense. Although the ability to attract tax-deductible charitable contributions is essential for many organizations, it is not a primary or significant source of income for others. Directors should periodically evaluate whether the corporation is qualified under the appropriate category, or whether conversion to a different category or creation of an affiliate of a different category should be considered.

Corporations Exempt from Tax under § 501(c)(3)

Most public benefit and religious corporations, and any such corporation wishing deductibility of gifts as charitable contributions, will seek exemption under § 501(c)(3).

For a corporation to be exempt under § 501(c)(3), it must be organized and operated exclusively for charitable, religious, educational, literary, or scientific purposes and other specific purposes that are normally included in the general definition of charity.[4] These general categories conform roughly to traditional common law, state law trust, and corporate definitions of "charity." Tax Code § 501 also contains additional specific requirements for certain types of § 501(c)(3) organizations, such as hospitals, child care providers, and credit counseling organizations.

Particular Advantages of § 501(c)(3) Status

In addition to exemption of the corporation itself from most federal income taxes, § 501(c)(3) organizations enjoy certain unique advantages. Contributions made to them are tax-deductible by the contributors, up to the limits imposed by Tax Code § 170(b).[5] In addition, some § 501(c)(3) corporations may finance their exempt activities by issuing tax-exempt bonds, enabling these organizations to lower their borrowing costs. Other benefits may include exemption from state real property and sales and use taxes and reduced postal rates for mailings.

General Requirements

To achieve and maintain exemption under § 501(c)(3), the corporation must comply with explicit requirements. As noted above, with limited exceptions, the IRS must issue a determination that the organization qualifies as exempt, as described in more detail in the section *"Obtaining Tax-Exempt Status"* below.

To be tax-exempt under § 501(c)(3), a corporation must be *organized and operated* exclusively for exempt purposes. The requirement that the corporation be "organized" exclusively for exempt purposes means that the articles of incorporation (and any amendments thereto) must contain appropriate restrictions on the corporation's purposes, activities, and use of assets, including ultimate disposition of assets upon a dissolution of the corporation. A director should bear this in mind in considering any amendments to the articles. It is not sufficient that the corporation merely operate in an appropriate manner. An organization is "operated" exclusively for exempt purposes if it engages primarily in activities that accomplish one or more of the exempt purposes specified in section 501(c)(3).

In addition, in order to maintain tax-exempt status, an organization must not allow any net earnings to inure to private individuals, as described in the section *"Limitations on Private Benefit and Private Inurement"* below. It also must not carry on substantial activities to influence legislation and must not participate, *in any way,* in any political campaign, as described in the sections *"Limitations on Lobbying"* and *"The Absolute Prohibition on Political Campaign Activities"* below.[6]

Limitations on Unrelated Business Activities

The conduct of unrelated business activities may not disqualify an otherwise exempt § 501(c)(3) corporation if the unrelated activities do not constitute a substantial non-exempt activity; however, the corporation may be taxed on income from the unrelated activity.

A § 501(c)(3) corporation may engage in some activities that are not related to its exempt purposes. For example, the corporation may own property that it leases to commercial tenants when the property is not needed by the corporation, or it may use its staff and resources to provide for-profit consulting services to generate income. Such activities will not disqualify the corporation from tax-exempt status so long as the corporation's unrelated activities do not constitute a substantial non-exempt activity.

Income derived from certain unrelated activities may be subject to federal tax. See the discussion in the section *"Unrelated Business Income"* below.

Limitations on Private Benefit and Private Inurement

A § 501(c)(3) corporation must not be operated for the benefit of any private individual. A § 501(c)(3) corporation is not operated for charitable purposes if it serves a private interest. This is the general standard applicable to all charitable corporations and simply incorporates into the Tax Code the trust law standards of a charity. Further, in order for the corporation to be recognized as a § 501(c)(3) organization "no part of the net earnings of" a corporation may inure "to the benefit of any private shareholder or individual."

Private benefit or private inurement may also occur, for example, when a § 501(c)(3) corporation pays more for goods or services than their fair market value, when assets of a corporation are given to or used for the benefit of an individual who gave less than fair consideration for the same, or when an individual or corporation is paid by the exempt organization in excess of reasonable compensation or on a percentage of the tax-exempt organization's net income. Private inurement relates to a benefit conferred on an "insider" of the organization, such as a director or officer. A director should understand that a non-fair-market-value transaction with such a person may jeopardize the continuing tax-exempt status of the organization. As discussed below in the section *"Intermediate Sanctions: Excise Tax on Public Charities' Excess*

Benefit Transactions," the payment of more than fair market value for items or services may also raise excise tax issues.

Limitations on Lobbying

A corporation will not qualify as a § 501(c)(3) organization if it devotes a substantial part of its activities to lobbying, propaganda, or attempting to influence legislation. "Legislation" generally refers to acts, bills, resolutions, or similar items passed or proposed to be passed or acted on by a legislative body, including treaties. In contrast, regulations adopted or other actions taken by executive or judicial or administrative bodies (e.g., school boards, zoning boards, housing authority, and water districts) are not considered legislation and therefore not subject to the lobbying limits. This includes lobbying certain government officials and grass roots lobbying. Section 501(h) of the Tax Code (discussed below) provides a helpful elective safe harbor for certain corporations (excluding churches) that wish to regularly engage in some lobbying. Although § 501(h) clarifies the scope of permitted activities, it can impose strict penalties on the corporation and its directors if these safe harbor dollar limits are exceeded.

Lobbying means attempting to influence legislation, not political campaign activity. A common (but not absolute) rule of thumb is that a nonprofit corporation will not be considered to be engaging in substantial lobbying if *less than 5 percent* of its activities are devoted to this activity. Whether or not more than 5 percent constitutes a substantial amount of activities is determined based on all the facts and circumstances.

Certain qualifying organizations may file a special election under § 501(h) of the Tax Code to allow them to spend up to a specified dollar amount (which may represent a larger percentage of total activities than would be allowed without the election) for lobbying without fear of adverse tax consequences from such activities. Organizations are advised to consider whether the § 501(h) election makes sense in their particular circumstance. While persistent lobbying in excess of that permitted by § 501(h) will lead to a loss of both the protection of the § 501(h) safe harbor and a loss of the corporation's basic tax exemption, isolated instances of lobbying in excess of permissible amounts will not cost the organization its tax-exemption. Instead, an excise tax will be applied against the organization. *In addition, penalty taxes may be imposed on any officer, director, or responsible employee of the organization* involved in the excessive lobbying activities. In some cases, the definition and measurement of lobbying activities will be easier than in others; for instance, as discussed in *Chapter 7, Nonprofits on the Internet: Fundraising, Selling Goods and Services, Lobbying, and Other Activities,* lobbying activities on the Internet pose challenging questions both for tax-exempt organizations trying to comply with § 501(h).

The Absolute Prohibition on Political Campaign Activities

A § 501(c)(3) corporation is strictly prohibited from supporting, participating in, or intervening in any election for public office.

A § 501(c)(3) corporation will lose its tax-exempt status if it participates or intervenes in a political campaign on behalf of, or in opposition to, a candidate for public office, through financial support, endorsements, or other actions directly or indirectly advocating the election or defeat of a candidate. In addition, it will be subject to an excise tax of 10 percent of the political expenditures. Unlike the restrictions on lobbying, the prohibition on political activities is absolute, and applies to any such activities, no matter how small. There are *severe penalties imposed on the corporation and, in some instances, its directors,* if prohibited political activities continue.[7]

Special Rules Relating to Public Charities and Private Foundations

The Tax Code classifies certain § 501(c)(3) organizations as "private foundations," in contrast to "public charities," the latter being the term commonly used to refer to those § 501(c)(3) organizations that are publicly supported, although this term does not appear in the Tax Code. A director should understand that all § 501(c)(3) corporations are treated as private foundations unless they can demonstrate that they meet one of the definitions of a public charity, as described below. The principal difference is that private foundations receive most, if not all, of their support from one or a few persons whereas most public charities have a broad base of support.

Private foundations are subject to various restrictions and excise taxes not applicable to other § 501(c)(3) corporations (public charities). Unlike most public charities, private foundations are subject to a requirement to distribute a minimum annual amount of funds. Since private foundations are subject to greater restrictions and certain excise taxes not applicable to public charities, a § 501(c)(3) corporation should make sure that the classification of the organization as a public charity or private foundation is properly determined and maintained. This issue is generally addressed when the public charity or private foundation is organized and during the IRS exemption application process and can be updated with the IRS as necessary. This *Guidebook* gives this question only a brief overview.

Definition of Public Charity

A corporation can avoid the additional taxes and restrictions imposed on private foundations if it falls within one of the enumerated types of organizations classified as public charities as listed in IRS Publication 557. Typical public charities include churches, schools, and hospitals. A corporation not falling within one of the categories listed in IRS Publication 557 may still avoid classification as a private foundation if it qualifies as a "publicly supported" charity or a "supporting organization" (e.g., it has a broad base of public support or provided support to another public charity). To qualify as either type of organization, certain specific tests must be met.

An organization is considered a publicly supported charity if it meets one of two tests: (1) a substantial part of the support the organization receives is in the form of contributions from publicly supported organizations, governmental units, or the general public (e.g., a human services organization whose revenue is generated through widespread public fundraising campaigns); or (2) no more than one-third of the support received by the organization is from gross investment income and more than one-third of the organization's support is received from contributions, membership fees, and gross receipts from activities related to its exempt functions (e.g., a membership-fee organization, such as a parent-teacher organization).

Supporting organizations are charities that carry out their exempt purposes by supporting other exempt organizations, usually other public charities, such as "friends of" organization. An important aspect of a supporting organization is the strong relationship with an organization it supports, which enables the supported organization to oversee the operations of the supporting organization. The supporting organization is classified as a public charity, and may be funded by a small number of persons in a manner similar to a private foundation. An example of a supporting organization is an organization that provides essential services for hospital systems. Similar to other charitable organizations, a supporting organization needs to be organized and operated exclusively for purposes described in § 501(c)(3).

A supporting organization must have one of three kinds of relationships with the supported organization(s), identified by the IRS as "Type I, Type II, or Type III" relationships. Type I supporting organizations are operated, supervised, or controlled by the supported organization. Type II supporting organizations are supervised or controlled in connection with the supported organization. Type III supporting organizations are operated in connection with the supported organization. Given that the Type III relationships are less formal than a Type I or Type II relationship, Type III organizations also need to meet other requirements (known as the responsiveness and integral part tests) that are designed to ensure that the supporting organization is responsive to the needs of a public charity and that the public charity oversees the operations of the supporting organization. Finally, the supporting organization may not be controlled directly or indirectly by disqualified persons. Additional information discussion can be found in IRS Publication 557 and the IRS's website, www.irs.gov.

Restrictions and Taxes on Private Foundations

"Private foundations" refer to organizations that are tax-exempt under § 501(c)(3) and characterized under § 509(a) of the Tax Code as a private foundation, rather than a public charity. In general, a nonprofit will be considered a private foundation if it does not meet a test for a "public charity." Private foundations generally are subject to a 2 percent excise tax on their net investment income (including capital gains). Private foundations are also subject to several other restrictions that may result in various taxes and penalties, including:

- restrictions on self-dealing between private foundations and their substantial contributors and other individuals described as "disqualified persons," including their directors and trustees (and directors' or trustees' family members and owned entities);
- minimum requirements for distribution of income and principal for charitable purposes, as described below;
- a potential tax upon termination of private foundation status;
- a potential excise tax on noncharitable grants;
- a potential excise tax on jeopardy investments;
- restrictions on excess business holdings;
- restrictions on lobbying and political activities; and
- restrictions on grants to individuals or entities that are not public charities.

Self-dealing rules

The prohibitions on self-dealing reach a broad range of transactions between a private foundation and a "disqualified person," including:

- the sale, exchange, or leasing of property;
- the lending of money or other extensions of credit;
- the furnishing of goods, services, or facilities;
- the payment of unreasonable compensation or expenses;
- the transfer to, or use by or for the benefit of, a disqualified person of the private foundation's income or assets; and
- payments to government officials.

In determining whether a transaction is restricted or prohibited by the self-dealing rules, it does not matter whether the transaction results in a benefit or a detriment to the private foundation or whether the transaction is "fair." (In this respect, the self-dealing prohibitions differ from the intermediate sanctions imposed on public charities.) An act of self-dealing includes both direct and indirect transactions between a private foundation and a disqualified person. The Tax Code does, however, permit certain exceptions to the self-dealing rules, including, for example, the payment of reasonable compensation. *Any transaction between a private foundation and a disqualified person should be reviewed by counsel or an appropriate committee to ensure the self-dealing rules are not violated.* Violations of the self-dealing restrictions may result in severe penalties on disqualified persons and foundation managers who approved the transaction.

Distribution requirements

A private foundation must distribute annually a minimum amount for charitable purposes, which is roughly 5 percent of the fair market value of its noncharitable (e.g., investment) assets. The required distribution may take the form of a direct payment for charitable purposes, such as payment of expenses incurred in conducting a charitable activity, an acquisition of assets to be used in performing the organization's exempt purposes, or a contribution to another charitable organization.

If a private foundation satisfies its distribution requirements by making charitable contributions to other § 501(c)(3) exempt organizations, the foundation's responsibilities may not end at the time the contribution is made. Except where the contribution is made to a public charity or to certain operating foundations, the private foundation must take steps to ensure that the contribution is, in fact, subsequently used by the receiving organization to accomplish exempt purposes. Some private foundations, in very limited circumstances, may avoid this requirement.

Limitation on excess business holdings

The Tax Code imposes limitations on the ability of a private foundation to hold an ownership interest in another business entity, such as a corporation or a partnership.

Liability of foundation managers

Excise taxes generally are imposed against a private foundation that violates any of the private foundation rules. In some cases, moreover, excise taxes may be imposed against "foundation managers," substantial contributors to the foundations, and, with respect to self-dealing, other "disqualified persons." Persons considered foundation managers include officers, directors, or trustees of a private foundation, and employees of the foundation who have authority or responsibility over the matter resulting in the tax.

Section 501(c)(4) Organizations: Civic Leagues and Social Welfare Organizations

A nonprofit corporation operated exclusively for the promotion of social welfare may seek exemption under § 501(c)(4). Exemption under this section will not confer charitable contributions deductibility for donors to the corporation. However, an exemption under § 501(c)(4) will enable the organization to avoid the restrictions of private foundation status, and the restrictions on lobbying and political activity.

A nonprofit corporation that is operated exclusively for the promotion of social welfare may qualify as a § 501(c)(4) organization and thus be exempt from federal income tax. In addition to the lack of deductibility as charitable contributions, contributions or dues paid to a § 501(c)(4) corporation are subject to the same tax treatment limitations as discussed with respect to trade organizations in the section "*Tax Treatment of Contributions or Dues to a § 501(c)(6) Corporation*" below.

Definition of Social Welfare

A corporation is operated exclusively for the promotion of social welfare if it is operated primarily to further the common good and general welfare of the people of a community, such as by bringing about civic betterment and social improvement, and no part of its net earnings inures to the benefit of any private shareholder or individual. In addition, a § 501(c)(4) corporation must benefit the community as a whole. Thus, a corporation will not qualify under § 501(c)(4) if its activities benefit only its membership or a select group of individuals. Still, the group benefitted may be a smaller segment of the public than is required for exemption under § 501(c)(3). Examples of the types of organizations that may qualify for § 501(c)(4) status are civic associations, advocacy organizations, and volunteer fire companies, or organizations engaged in crime prevention.

A § 501(c)(4) corporation may not, as its primary activity, conduct business with the general public in a commercial manner or engage in political campaign activities.

Comparison of § 501(c)(3) and § 501(c)(4) Exemption Status

Although the requirements for § 501(c)(3) and § 501(c)(4) appear to be similar, a corporation may more easily satisfy the requirements of § 501(c)

(4). First, it may benefit a smaller or more specific group or community than would qualify a corporation for charitable status under § 501(c)(3). Second, a § 501(c)(4) organization may engage in a greater amount of social activities, a greater amount of lobbying activities, and some, as opposed to no, political activities.

Note, however, that § 501(c)(3) status is preferable to § 501(c)(4) status if tax-deductible contributions or tax-exempt financing is important to the organization. Still, § 501(c)(4) status may be more advantageous if:

- lobbying will be a substantial part of the corporation's activities;
- freedom to support or oppose candidates for public office is sought; or
- the organization would be subject to the restrictions imposed on a private foundation (as discussed above) if the organization were exempt under § 501(c)(3).

Still, if an organization was once exempt as a § 501(c)(3) organization, but has lost its exemption because of lobbying or political campaign activities, it cannot then convert into a § 501(c)(4) organization.[8]

Section 501(c)(6) Organizations

Nonprofit business leagues, chambers of commerce, trade associations, boards of trade, and professional football leagues may qualify as § 501(c)(6) organizations.

Requirements for Exemption

A § 501(c)(6) corporation is an association of persons having a common business interest. Its purpose is to promote this interest; therefore, no part of the net earnings may inure to the benefit of any private shareholder or individual (such as members). These corporations must improve the business condition of the industry in general, rather than benefiting individual members by supplying these members with such things as management services, or improving the economy and convenience of conducting individual businesses. The corporation may satisfy this requirement if, as a whole, it represents all components of an industry or line of business within a particular geographic area. The corporation generally may not, however, be in competition with another group within the same industry or line of business, although members within the corporation may compete with each other.

Certain examples of common activities that may affect a corporation's compliance with § 501(c)(6) are worth noting. On the one hand, activities such as conducting an advertising campaign to promote an industry (rather than particular individuals) and publishing a trade publication for the benefit of an industry generally are considered activities that promote a particular line of business and, hence, are permissible activities. On the other hand, activities such as operating a real estate multiple-listing service and supplying management services and supplies to members have been found to benefit the members individually, rather than promote the industry or line of business as a whole. A § 501(c)(6) corporation may engage in some business activities that do not promote an industry or line of business, subject to the rules relating to unrelated business income (UBI) discussed in the section "*Unrelated Business Income*" below, so long as these activities are not substantial.

Tax Treatment of Contributions or Dues to a § 501(c)(6) Corporation

As a general rule, contributions or dues payable to a § 501(c)(6) organization may be deductible as trade or business expenses except to the extent they are used to:

(a) participate in a political campaign on behalf of any candidate for public office;
(b) engage in certain types of lobbying; or
(c) attempt to influence legislation that is not of direct interest to the taxpayer's business.

A § 501(c)(6) organization that incurs lobbying or political expenditures is required to notify its members of a reasonable estimate of the portion of their dues allocable to those expenditures, which are nondeductible to the members. If the organization fails to provide this notice, or otherwise elects not to provide it, the organization is required to pay a proxy tax based on the amount of the expenditures.

Contributions to § 501(c)(6) organizations cannot be deducted as charitable contributions.

Obtaining Tax-Exempt Status

With few exceptions, most § 501(c)(3) corporations must obtain IRS recognition of tax-exempt status; they hold this status only when and if such recognition is valid and applicable. Other tax-exempt organizations (i.e., § 501(c)(4), § 501(c)(6) and other corporations qualifying for exemption under § 501(c) of the Tax Code) should consider obtaining IRS recognition to ensure their tax-exempt status, but generally are not required to do so. New § 501(c)(4) corporations must notify the IRS of their intention to operate as a § 501(c)(4) corporation by filing Form 8976 within 60 days of formation.

If a corporation is, in fact, organized and operated in accordance with the applicable requirements to qualify for tax exemption under § 501(c) of the Tax Code, the corporation may claim tax-exempt status without the need for an IRS ruling to that effect, *unless* exemption under § 501(c)(3) is sought. Section 501(c)(3) corporations generally are required to obtain recognition of their tax-exempt status from the IRS as a condition to the tax exemption.

Organizations apply for tax-exempt status under Section 501(c)(3) by submitting an application on IRS Form 1023. Certain small organizations may be eligible to file a shorter application using Form 1023EZ. Section 501(c)(3) corporations that are not subject to the application requirement are (1) churches and certain other church-related corporations; (2) corporations (other than private foundations) normally having annual gross receipts of not more than $5,000; and (3) foreign corporations that receive all of their funds from foreign sources. In addition, certain corporations do not have to apply directly to the IRS for recognition of exemption under § 501(c)(3), because they are covered by a group exemption letter issued to a central organization. Other corporations should apply to obtain IRS recognition to ensure their tax-exempt status.

Unrelated Business Income (UBI)

Any exempt corporation may be subject to a tax on UBI, if it regularly carries on a trade or business that is unrelated to its exempt purpose. If its unrelated business activities are more than insubstantial, the corporation may lose its tax exemption.

The Tax Code permits an exempt organization to engage in some activities that are not related to its exempt purposes. These activities are permissible so long as the exempt corporation's unrelated activities remain insubstantial when compared to the corporation's exempt activities. Whether an activity is considered substantial is based on all the facts and circumstances, including the amount of income derived from the activity and the expenses and staff time devoted to it. No one factor is controlling.

The Tax Code imposes a tax on income generated from the conduct of an "unrelated trade or business," generally at standard corporate tax rates, and organizations must report this income on IRS Form 990-T. Certain passive types of investment income, such as rents, royalties, dividends, and interest, are generally excluded from taxation.

If the corporation conducts unrelated activities, a director should have a basic understanding of the types of activities that produce UBI to ensure that the organization's unrelated business activities do not become substantial and that procedures are in place to monitor and properly report these activities to the IRS.

Definition of Unrelated Trade or Business

An *unrelated trade or business* is any trade or business that is *regularly carried on, the conduct of which is not substantially related to the corporation's exempt purposes.* For example, if a tax-exempt corporation sells advertising in its otherwise educational publications, this may result in unrelated business income.

An activity is *regularly carried on* if the activity is conducted with the frequency and continuity comparable to commercial activities of for-profit ventures.

An activity is *substantially related* (i.e., not unrelated) to the corporation's exempt purposes if it contributes importantly to the accomplishment of the corporation's exempt purposes other than through producing income. The need for the funds generated by the activity does not make it substantially related.

The Tax Code excludes several types of activities from the definition of *unrelated trade or business.* An activity will not be treated as an unrelated trade or business if:

- substantially all of the work is performed by volunteers;
- it is carried on primarily by a § 501(c)(3) organization for the benefit of its members, students, patients, officers, or employees;
- it consists of selling merchandise, substantially all of which has been donated;
- it relates to the distribution of low-cost articles in connection with charitable solicitations; or
- the business consists of a legal bingo game, in a state where bingo games are ordinarily not conducted on a commercial basis.

Types of Income Excluded from UBI

The Tax Code excludes the following types of income from UBI unless this income is debt-financed:

- dividends, interest, payments with respect to securities loans, and annuities;
- royalties;

- most rents from real property;
- insubstantial rents from personal property when leased with real property; and
- gain from the sale of capital assets.[9]

In addition, certain research income is excluded from UBI.

Use of a Taxable Subsidiary

As noted above, an exempt corporation may conduct an insubstantial amount of unrelated activities itself. It is not necessary to establish a separate taxable corporation for these activities. Still, an exempt corporation may choose to create a taxable subsidiary through which to conduct unrelated activities, especially if these activities would otherwise become substantial and thereby jeopardize the corporation's exempt status, or for nontax reasons, such as the desire to limit the corporation's liabilities.

If a taxable subsidiary is formed, the subsidiary itself will be taxed on the income from the activities, but dividends paid by the taxable subsidiary to the exempt parent generally will not be subject to UBI. Still, the tax-exempt parent of a taxable subsidiary should be aware that for all such subsidiaries in which the parent nonprofit holds more than a 50 percent ownership interest, the tax-exempt corporation's receipt of rent, royalties, interest, and other types of income from the subsidiary may be taxable as UBI. (This is in contrast to the usual rule, under which a tax-exempt corporation's receipt of rent, royalties, interest, and similar kinds of "passive" income is not taxable as UBI, provided that such income is received from an entity unrelated to the tax-exempt corporation.)

Another possible option for a nonprofit needing a separate business organization for liability purposes is the organization of a single member limited liability company. For tax purposes, this entity can be treated either as a corporation or a single member "disregarded entity." In most cases, the nonprofit decides to have the limited liability company treated as a "disregarded entity" with the parent being taxed as a sole proprietor for income tax purposes. The disregarded entity's activities, revenues, and expenses are treated as those of the nonprofit and reported on its Form 990. Thus, this approach does not address the issue of "too much" UBI.

The use of a subsidiary requires careful tax planning as, in general, decisions made in the process are usually irrevocable. For example, future transfers of property from a taxable subsidiary to the exempt corporation and the eventual liquidation of the subsidiary may result in certain adverse tax consequences. For further discussion of issues to be considered by tax-exempt corporation directors regarding the use of taxable subsidiaries, see *Chapter 6, Creation of For-Profit Subsidiaries and Joint Ventures.*

Advertisements vs. Sponsorship Acknowledgments

Acknowledgments vs. advertisements

Directors of tax-exempt entities should understand the difference, both in terms of donor deductibility and UBI treatment, between revenues received from sponsors for which the tax-exempt organization provides public acknowledgment and revenues received in exchange for advertising.

Revenues received from corporate sponsors who are then publicly acknowledged by the tax-exempt organization—in a statement that recites only basic and "fact neutral" information about the sponsoring organization, such as its name, contact information, logo, or slogan—are generally deductible by the sponsor as a tax-exempt contribution. Provided the event being sponsored is substantially related to the tax-exempt corporation's purposes, such revenues would not be subject to taxation as UBI. In contrast, revenues received by a tax-exempt corporation for advertisements—such as an ad for a dance apparel store in the program for the annual recital of a local ballet school—would be considered payment for advertising and not be deductible as a charitable contribution by the apparel store.[10]

Some distinguishing characteristics of advertising are that it presents advantages of a product or urges purchase of a product. In this example, if the apparel store also underwrote a portion of the recital costs, and was acknowledged as a corporate sponsor in that regard, the store could deduct the portion of its payment to the school that exceeded the regular cost of the ad. In such a case, the payment by the sponsor may not be considered fully tax-deductible as a charitable contribution. Moreover, depending on the context (e.g., was the payment made in connection with an activity that is "regularly carried on" by the organization, or was it for a discrete event, such as the annual recital?), the money the sponsor paid for advertising may be considered taxable UBI to the exempt organization.

Different treatment of advertisements in periodicals

If advertising revenue is considered taxable as UBI to the tax-exempt organization, the amount of UBI tax payable will depend on whether or not the ad revenue was generated from an advertisement in a periodical publication, such as a monthly newsletter or magazine, or in a nonperiodical publication. Ad revenue that is UBI is subject to special rules that—depending on the circumstances—may result in the revenue being taxed at a lower rate if the ad appeared in a periodical. Still, in some cases, it is difficult to determine whether a publication is a periodical for which the lower UBI tax calculation would apply. The general rule is that advertising within material that appears on a regular periodic schedule, within a standard format, is likely to be considered a periodical, whereas material that appears perennially with regular updates (like a brochure) would not.

Special Reporting Requirements

Noncharitable Contributions

The director must understand that exemption from federal income tax does not necessarily mean that donations to the corporation are deductible as charitable contributions. If deductibility is not available, the corporation must disclose this fact—including disclosures on dues statements.

Any tax-exempt corporation or political organization that is not eligible to receive charitable contributions—that is, any corporation other than a § 501(c) (3) corporation—is required to disclose to its donors "in a conspicuous and easily recognizable format" in all fundraising solicitations, whether in written or printed form, by television or radio, or by telephone, that contributions to it are not deductible as charitable contributions for federal income tax purposes.[11] A dues statement or solicitation of a § 501(c)(4) or § 501(c)(6) organization counts as a fundraising solicitation for this purpose.

Charitable Contributions

Any contribution to a charitable organization of $250 or more may only be deductible as a charitable contribution to the donor if the donor receives contemporaneous substantiation from the charitable organization as to the receipt of the donation.

While technically a charitable organization is under no requirement to provide substantiation of a charitable contribution of $250 or more to a donor, the fact that the donor will not receive a charitable contribution deduction without this substantiation imposes a practical requirement on the charity to provide the information. In general, the charity should supply the substantiation contemporaneously with the receipt of the contribution and, additionally, describe the property donated and state whether any goods or services were provided in connection with the contribution. It is also possible to provide one contemporaneous written acknowledgment, such as an annual summary, to substantiate several single contributions valued at $250 or more. Detailed guidance concerning the substantiation requirements is contained in IRS Publication 1771.

Special guidelines apply to donations of motor vehicles, boats, or airplanes if the claimed value exceeds $500.[12]

Charitable Contributions in Return for Items of Value

If a donor receives an item of value in return for a contribution to a § 501(c)(3) corporation, the Tax Code requires that the donor's deduction be limited to the difference between the amount contributed and the fair market value of the goods or services received by the donor. For example, if a donor contributes $100 and receives a ticket to a symphony concert or a dinner that would normally cost $60, the donor is entitled to deduct $40. In addition, the Tax Code requires that the charity receiving the contribution (provided the contribution is in excess of $75) provide substantiation to the donor estimating the fair market value of the goods or services received in return for the contribution.

Failure to make this disclosure could result in fines against the charity.[13]

Disclosure of Annual Returns and Exemption Applications

Both annual information returns and IRS exemption applications must be made available by the tax-exempt organizations for public inspection or in copy form.

Tax-exempt corporations must make their annual tax information returns (IRS Form 990 and, for § 501(c)(3) organizations, Form 990-T) and their IRS exemption applications (e.g., Form 1023 for § 501(c)(3) organizations), including all submissions and correspondence, available for public inspection at their principal offices and at all regional offices. (The corporation may, however, withhold the names and addresses of its contributors if it is a public charity and may also withhold any information in the exemption application relating to trade secrets, patents, processes, or styles of work if the IRS determines that public disclosure of this information would adversely affect the organization.)

These organizations also are required to provide copies of the returns to individuals requesting them but may charge the requestor reasonable copying fees. Organizations that post copies of their tax returns, exemption applications, and related documents on the Internet (whether on their own website or a compilation site such as GuideStar), are relieved of the obligation to provide physical copies of the documents to requesting individuals. See the section *"Sales of Goods and Services"* in *Chapter 7, Nonprofits on the Internet* for further discussion of Internet postings of Form 990s.

Corporation personnel who have a duty to comply with the public inspection requirements and fail to comply may be subject to penalties. Criminal penalties may be imposed on any person who willfully and knowingly furnishes false or fraudulent information.

Intermediate Sanctions: Excise Tax on Public Charities' Excess Benefit Transactions

Every member of a board of directors of a § 501(c)(3) public charity or § 501(c)(4) organization should be aware of the possibility of financial sanctions that could be imposed on board members, officers, and related persons as a result of transactions that the IRS determines provide "excess benefits" to a related ("disqualified") person.

An excess benefit transaction is a transaction, such as the payment of compensation or the transfer of property, in which a disqualified person receives more than fair market value from the exempt organization or pays the exempt organization less than fair market value for property or services received. The tax imposed on the disqualified person is 25 percent of the excess benefit amount. If the excess benefit transaction is not corrected (e.g., through repayment and payment of the excess benefit interest), a second-tier tax of 200 percent of the excess benefit amount can be imposed.

The IRS defines the term *disqualified person* as any person who, at any time during the five-year period ending on the date of the transaction, was in a position to exercise substantial influence over the organization's affairs. The term also includes family members of an individual described in the previous sentence and any entity in which disqualified persons in the aggregate control 35 percent of the voting interests. For most § 501(c)(3) and § 501(c)(4) organizations, disqualified persons includes directors/trustees, officers, and "substantial contributors" to the organization. Disqualified persons will include top-management employees. Whether a person has substantial influence over the organization's affairs, however, is a facts and circumstances test. Accordingly, the definition is potentially much broader than the aforementioned categories. For example, it may include substantial contributors, founders, and others.

Taxes on Directors, Officers, and Other Managers

In addition to imposing an excise tax on disqualified persons who receive the benefit of the excess benefit transactions, the IRS has the authority to impose excise taxes on "organization managers" who knowingly approved an excess benefit transaction. An organization manager includes any officer, director, or trustee of an applicable tax-exempt organization, or any individual having the powers or responsibilities similar to those of officers, directors, or trustees of the organization. The tax is 10 percent of the excess benefit amount, up to a collective maximum of $20,000 per transaction.

Procedures for Establishing Reasonableness

In determining whether there is an excess benefit transaction, the reasonableness of compensation and the fair market value of transactions are determined under existing tax law standards. Still, there is a rebuttable presumption of reasonableness if the transaction with a disqualified person is approved in advance by an independent board or committee, comprised of individuals without a conflict of interest, who obtained and relied on appropriate objective data as to comparability and documented the basis for their determination contemporaneously in the minutes of the relevant board or committee meeting.

If the procedures for the rebuttable presumption are met, the burden of proof is on the IRS to demonstrate unreasonableness. Even without the presumption, benefits provided to disqualified persons are not excess benefit transactions if it can be demonstrated that they are part of a fair market value exchange of goods or services. In this connection, however, payment of personal expenses and benefits and non-fair-market-value transactions benefiting disqualified persons can only be justified as reasonable compensation for services if it is clear that the organization intended and made the payments as compensation for services at the time the payments were made.

Form 990 requires information with regard to excess benefit transactions. In addition, an exempt organization's reimbursement of expenses incurred by a disqualified person paid under an arrangement that is a "nonaccountable plan" is treated as an "automatic" excess benefit transaction without regard to whether the economic benefit is reasonable, any other compensation the disqualified person may have received is reasonable, or the aggregate of the reimbursements and any other compensation the disqualified person may have received is reasonable.[14]

The enactment of intermediate sanctions does not alter the actual standards of conduct for tax-exempt organizations; instead, it simply provides another mechanism for IRS enforcement of existing standards. In particular, the intermediate sanctions legislation does not eliminate revocation of exempt status as a penalty for organizations that commit egregious or repeated violations of the laws governing exempt organizations.

A full discussion of the excess benefit transaction excise tax is beyond the scope of this publication. Nonetheless, § 501(c)(3) and § 501(c)(4) organizations are encouraged to consult with their legal advisers to establish procedures that will protect parties with whom the organization deals, and its directors/trustees, officers, and other organization managers, from the potential imposition of significant personal excise taxes.

Governance and IRS Form 990

Directors of tax-exempt organizations should know that IRS Form 990 is not just an informational return asking for financial information but is a disclosure document with extensive reporting requirements that require organizations to make more intrusive inquiries into the personal and business dealings of directors and between and among directors, their family members, and businesses. The reporting requirements are complex, and the exempt organization must spend significant time and effort to collect, review, and analyze the information and track these relationships across affiliates.

The disclosure approach of Form 990 means that a significant amount of information is made available to the public about governance operations and board relationships. Certain of the questions require disclosure of complex and indirect relationships that may not be well understood by the average reader.

Governance-related disclosures can be found on the Form and on certain of the related schedules to the Form. Part VI of the core form contains questions on the governing body and management, governance policies, and disclosure practices. (There are also questions in other parts of Form 990 that relate to governance issues, including Part VII (compensation) and Part XII (financial statements and reporting).) Questions in Part VI cover board size and structure, conflicts of interest management, trustee independence, intra board relationships, audit committee practices, conflicts of interest management, governance policies, and how key corporate and financial documents are disclosed to the public. Additional discussion of governance questions that must be addressed in Form 990 can be found in the section *"Discharging the Duty of Care: Some Practical Suggestions: Form 990 Governance Focus Areas,"* at *Chapter 2, Duties and Rights of Nonprofit Corporation Directors.*

IRS Governance Guidelines

Although the Tax Code does not itself mandate governance requirements for tax-exempt organizations, the IRS believes that well-governed organizations are more likely to be tax compliant. Therefore, the IRS has designed questions on Form 990 to elicit information about governance practices. Form 990 requests information on practices or policies that are not required by federal tax law. Still, good governance and accountability practices provide safeguards that the organization's assets will be used consistently with its exempt purposes. This is a critical tax compliance consideration, especially for organizations that are subject to private benefit, excess benefit, and private inurement prohibitions.[15]

Moreover, although there are no right or wrong answers to the questions asked in Part VI of Form 990, the responses may be significant not only to the IRS, but also to donors, grant-makers, rating agencies, state regulators, community stakeholders, and the press. Further discussion on the types of policies covered by the Form 990 is in *Chapter 2, Duties and Rights of Nonprofit Corporation Directors.*

The most current and complete explanation of the IRS position on governance of charities is evident in Form 990, as explained in more detail in the Form 990 Instructions and in the IRS's website educational materials.[16]

Conflict of Interest Disclosures

In addition to the governance-related disclosures discussed above, the specific details of interested party transactions that meet certain thresholds must be disclosed on Form 990, including the names of the interested persons (whether director, family member, or related entity, and the dollar amount and description of the relationship).

Independence

The Form 990 Instructions contain a definition of "independence" that is substantially different from prior IRS interpretations of how an exempt organization should evaluate the independence of its board members. One key difference is that Form 990 independence requires that the trustee have no "interested party transaction" (as defined under the Instructions) with the tax-exempt organization. Thus, the IRS has linked conflict of interest matters to independence for purposes of the Form 990 reporting.

"Independence" for Form 990 reporting purposes requires satisfaction of *all three* of the following during the tax year:

1. The director was not compensated as an officer by the organization or an affiliate,
2. The director was not an independent contractor who received more than $10,000 from the organization or an affiliate, and
3. Neither the director nor a family member, directly or indirectly, was involved in an interested party transaction with the organization reportable on Form 990, schedule L (which requires reporting of any excess benefit transaction with an insider (in IRS terms, a "disqualified person"); any loans to or from an interested person; grants or other assistance benefitting an interested person; or other business transactions involving any interested person).

IRS Revocation of Tax-Exempt Status

The Pension Protection Act of 2006 (PPA) imposed a requirement on most tax-exempt organizations to file an annual information return or notice (Form 990, Form 990EZ, or Form 990N) with the IRS. For small organizations, the law imposed a filing requirement for the first time in 2007. Failing to timely file a required return can result in financial penalties. In addition, under the law, tax-exempt status is now automatically revoked for any organization that fails to file the required return or notice for three consecutive years.

As a result of the PPA, thousands of organizations have automatically lost their tax-exempt status because they did not file the legally required annual returns or notices for three consecutive years. A list of the automatically revoked organizations is maintained on a searchable database maintained on the IRS website at www.irs.gov. The effective date of the automatic revocation for an organization that does not file a required annual return for three consecutive years is the filing due date of the third year's return. The consequence of loss of tax exemption is that there is income tax on earned income, there is a requirement to file a Form 1120 for a corporation or Form 1041 for a trust, no deductions are permitted for donors, and there is possible liability for sales tax, property tax and other types of taxes that were based at least in part on the organization's federal tax-exempt status.

For organizations that have had their tax-exempt status automatically revoked, the organization may seek reinstatement. An organization must apply to have its tax-exempt status reinstated even if it was not originally required to file an application for the exemption. An organization also may request reinstatement back to the date of automatic revocation by showing "reasonable cause" and filing the application for reinstatement within a certain time period.

Conclusion

It is important that a director of a nonprofit organization understand the nature of the organization's federal tax-exempt status and the fundamental limitations on these organizations. For Section 501(c)(3) organizations, this includes a basic understanding of private inurement and private benefit, intermediate sanctions, and the lobbying and campaign activity rules. It also is important that a director understand the importance of Form 990 and be involved in reviewing it annually.

See the Suggested Questions and Checklist following the Endnotes below to review the issues discussed in this chapter.

Endnotes

1. Our discussion, even of these limited areas, is based on the law as it stood when this chapter was written. The Tax Code is often amended in some manner with each session of Congress, and the IRS periodically issues new rulings and interpretations that change the general understanding of tax law provisions. As a result, some statements contained in this discussion may be incomplete or inaccurate when they meet the reader's eyes. Nonetheless, the issues addressed are permanent.
2. Although many states rely on federal tax-exempt status in determining exemption from state income tax, some require separate filings. In addition, the requirements for exemption from real property and sales taxes typically may be more stringent than those in federal tax law. Generally, only certain § 501(c)(3) organizations (and usually not all of them) will qualify for these exemptions, but the criteria vary from state to state.
3. As shown in the list provided in Appendix A, § 501(a) of the Tax Code recognizes a series of tax-exempt organizations, but the list includes some entities that are outside the focus of this *Guidebook.* Three significant types of tax-exempt organizations not included in the Appendix A are trusts held under qualified pension plans, state and local government instrumentalities, and political organizations.
4. An organization also may qualify under § 501(c)(3) if it is organized for testing for public safety; fostering national or international amateur sports competition (if no part of its activities involve providing athletic facilities or equipment); or preventing cruelty to children or animals.
5. The limits on deductibility imposed by § 170(b) range from 20 to 50 percent of an individual contributor's income (60 percent for cash contributions before 1/1/2026). A discussion of these limits is outside the scope of this *Guidebook.* See, however, *IRS Publication 526, Charitable Contributions.*
6. These requirements are set forth in detail in IRS Publication 557. The requirements are also explained on the IRS website, www.irs.gov, at the "Charities and Non-Profits" tab. The IRS has developed an educational tool called *"Life Cycle of an Exempt Organization,"* which lays out, by topic area, the regulations applicable to these organizations and other compliance matters.
7. Churches are not exempt from challenge when they engage in political activities; despite the general reluctance of most government officials to challenge actions of religious organizations, the IRS has become involved when the situation is particularly egregious. *See, e.g.,* Branch Ministries v. Rossotti, 211 F.3d 137 (D.C. Cir. 2000), *aff'g* 40 F. Supp. 2d 15 (D.D.C. 1999) (revoking the tax-exempt status of Branch Ministries, Inc. dba the Church at Pierce Creek).

8. *See* I.R.C. § 504(a).
9. I.R.C. § 514 provides a special exception for real property acquired by certain "qualified organizations," including educational institutions and pension trusts. However, interest, rents, royalties, and annuities paid by controlled for-profit subsidiaries to their exempt parent generally will not be excludable from income. To the extent that income is excluded from UBI, any related deductions also are excluded from the computation of tax.
10. *See* I.R.C. § 513(i).
11. I.R.C. § 6113. The rule does not apply to (a) organizations with annual gross receipts of $100,000 or less, or (b) any letter or telephone call if the communication is not part of a coordinated campaign soliciting more than ten persons during the calendar year.
12. *See* IRS Publication No. 4302 and IRS Publication No. 4303.
13. IRS Publication 1771 provides a good summary of the IRS position on this issue.
14. *See* Reg. 53.4958-4(c)(1).
15. IRS Training Materials. https://www.irs.gov/charities-non-profits/irs-training-materials-governance.
16. The IRS's website has extensive compliance materials for tax-exempt entities at www.irs.gov/charities.

Suggested Questions for Directors Regarding Taxation

(1) Is the corporation on whose board I serve exempt from federal income taxation?

(2) If it is, under what section of the Tax Code is it exempt?

(3) If it is exempt under § 501(c)(3), is it a private foundation?

(4) If it is a private foundation, do I understand the special limitations that status imposes? Do the board and staff understand them?

(5) If we are not exempt under § 501(c)(3), do we make clear to our donors that they cannot deduct their contributions to us?

(6) Who prepares our tax returns (Form 990)? What is the process for the board review of Form 990? Have they been filed each year?

(7) What were the corporation's activities and mission as described to the IRS in applying for an exemption ruling? Is this description still an accurate portrayal of what we do? If there has been a change, was this described in a subsequent Form 990 filing?

(8) How much lobbying activity have we engaged in? How much are we allowed under our particular exemption?

(9) Has the organization made an election with the IRS under § 501(h) for its lobbying activities? If so, are the organization's lobbying expenditures below the permitted dollar limit?
(10) If we are exempt under § 501(c)(3), do I understand the scope of activities covered by the absolute prohibition on campaign activity by the organization?
(11) Has the board put procedures in place to ensure that transactions potentially subject to intermediate sanctions are reviewed and documented to the extent it determines appropriate?
(12) What activities, if any, of our corporation may result in UBI?
(13) Who on our staff monitors UBI tax matters? Do our independent accountants do so?

Checklist: Taxation

Note: For purposes of simplicity in these checklists, we describe a corporation with a chair, who presides over the board of directors; a chief executive, who may be a staff person; an executive committee; a governance/nominating committee; and an audit committee. (However, we recognize that in many smaller and other nonprofits, these committee functions may be performed by either the executive committee or the board as a whole.) We also assume a legal counsel—someone, paid or unpaid, having primary responsibility for the corporation's legal affairs. Many corporations, especially larger nonprofits, may have other committees established for specific purposes, such as reviewing staff performance, fixing compensation, monitoring compliance with legal requirements, and periodic review of bylaws.

Subject	Review By	How Often	Comment
1. If our corporation is exempt from federal income tax, under what section of the Internal Revenue Code is it exempt?	Legal counsel	Upon organization; Annually	Whole board should understand basic nature of the corporation's specific exemption. Information on this subject should be in the director's manual.

Subject	Review By	How Often	Comment
2. If it is exempt under Section 501(c)(3), is the corporation a private foundation, a private operating foundation, or a public charity?	Legal counsel, then full board	Upon organization; Annually	Board should understand the privileges or limitations imposed by the applicable provisions of the Tax Code on the corporation's particular type of activity. Public charity boards should understand the applicable public charity test and what is required to maintain that status from year to year.
3. If the corporation is exempt under Section 501(c)(3) or Section 501(c)(4) and is not a private foundation, has the corporation established procedures to identify potential excess benefit transactions and obtain the rebuttable presumption of reasonableness where appropriate?	Chief executive, legal counsel	Annually or whenever new executive compensation decisions are made	Boards should determine the level of scrutiny that will be applied to various types of transactions depending on the likelihood that the party is a disqualified person and the significance of the transaction.

Subject	Review By	How Often	Comment
4. If the corporation is exempt under Section 501(c)(3), have we engaged in activities that are limited (lobbying) or prohibited (campaign activity) by virtue of our 501(c)(3) status? Has the organization made an election to have its lobbying activities covered by Section 501(h) of the Internal Revenue Code?	Legal counsel, then full board	Annually, and during discussion of any major change in contemplated advocacy activities	This is a field of tax law with frequent new interpretations. Section 501(c)(3) organizations should closely monitor activities to ensure compliance.
5. If the advocacy activities of the corporation are restricted but not prohibited (as in the case of lobbying), have we compared the actual activities undertaken with the restrictions of applicable tax law?	Chief executive, legal counsel	Annually	If these activities are substantial and continuing, the corporation's books should be organized to quantify them. The board should also ask the chief executive or legal counsel to determine if anyone associated with the organization is required to be registered as a lobbyist.

Subject	Review By	How Often	Comment
6. If our corporation is exempt from federal income tax, has thc board reviewed Form 990?	Legal counsel, then full board	Annually	Form 990 requires the organization to describe the board's involvcment in the review of the Form 990.
7. If our corporation is exempt from federal income tax, do we have some or all of the policies identified in Part VI of Form 990?	Legal counsel, then full board	Annually	Part VI of Form 990 asks whether the corporation has certain written policies and procedures. Although it is not a legal requirement, adoption of many of these policies may be beneficial to the organization.

Chapter 6:
Creating For-Profit Subsidiaries and Joint Ventures

Chapter 6

Creating For-Profit Subsidiaries and Joint Ventures

The board of a nonprofit corporation may decide that the corporation's mission and goals would be served by engaging in an activity that does not easily fit within the corporation's current structure. If this activity is one that is typically engaged in by nonprofit organizations, the board may establish a nonprofit subsidiary or affiliate. However, if the activity is one that will generate taxable income, or is typically conducted by for-profit rather than nonprofit organizations, the board may consider establishing a for-profit subsidiary or entering into a joint-venture arrangement with a for-profit entity. Set forth below is a summary of many of the issues that a nonprofit board should consider before establishing a for-profit subsidiary or entering into a joint venture with a for-profit organization.[1]

Engaging in New Activities

A nonprofit, tax-exempt corporation may find that in order to fulfill its corporate mission, it would be useful to engage in an activity that is outside the general range of activities for which it was organized and is operated. For example, a healthcare corporation or museum may desire to operate a wellness center or a community organization may find it has an opportunity to buy used computers and resell them to low-income residents. Similarly, a corporation that owns and operates low-income housing may desire to provide housing management services to similar corporations. The revenues derived from these activities may be of a kind not generally treated as exempt from taxation. Nevertheless, the nonprofit's board may believe that engaging in the activity will further its exempt purposes. When a corporation's board considers engaging in such a nonexempt activity, the directors should keep the following considerations in mind:

Furthering Exempt Purposes

Generally, the nonexempt activity should only be engaged in if it is consistent with the corporation's mission and exempt purposes. The organization could jeopardize its tax exemption if a substantial amount of its activity is deemed to be "unrelated" to the corporation's tax-exempt purpose. In the IRS's view, an activity is treated as unrelated to a § 501(c)(3) corporation's tax-exempt purposes unless it is "substantially related" to such exempt purposes, by "contributing importantly" to the accomplishment of the exempt purposes.

UBI

If the nonexempt activity is unrelated, in the IRS's view, to the corporation's exempt purposes, the revenue from the activity may be subject to taxation as unrelated business income (UBI) and required to be reported on Form 990-T, which is a publicly available document. However, some forms of unrelated revenue are exempted from taxation, including most forms of investment income and passive income. In addition, revenues derived from unrelated activities that are performed entirely by volunteers, are primarily conducted for the benefit of members, students, officers, or employees, or involve the resale of primarily donated items are also exempt from tax.[2]

Substantiality of Nonexempt Activity

An unrelated, nonexempt activity may be conducted within the corporation as long as it would not constitute a "substantial" part of the organization's overall activity. As a rule of thumb, an activity is likely to not be considered substantial if revenues from the activity are less than 10 percent of the organization's overall revenues—although higher percentages may be permitted in certain circumstances, and lower percentages are recommended for tax-exempt corporations classified as "supporting" organizations under § 509(a)(3) of the Internal Revenue Code (the Code).

Advantages of Establishing Separate For-Profit Subsidiaries

If a proposed nonexempt activity is of a kind that is likely to be viewed by the IRS as unrelated to the corporation's purposes, the board may decide to place the activity in a separate, for-profit subsidiary, rather than maintaining it within the corporation's structure. Some of the factors that nonprofit boards tend to weigh in favor of establishing a for-profit subsidiary include the following:

(1) The amount of the unrelated activity, or the income generated by it, could become substantial and thus threaten the corporation's tax exemption if conducted within the corporation.

(2) The nonexempt activity requires a substantial devotion of management time and attention or requires a significant number of employees.

(3) The activity entails a level of business and/or legal risk that should be segregated, to the extent possible, from the assets or endowment of the charitable organization.

(4) The management of the activity requires a kind of expertise not generally present in the corporation's management officers or board.

(5) It will be easier to recruit management staff for the nonexempt activity if the activity is contained in a separate organization rather than within the confines of the nonprofit corporation. This could include providing an ownership interest or other financial benefit to the employees.

(6) It is considered desirable or necessary to be able to offer stock or stock options to senior management or other employees associated with the nonexempt activity, in order to recruit and incentivize the performance of these employees. Still, it is important to understand that there can be private benefit concerns regarding issuing stock to insiders.

(7) The nonexempt activity is best performed in a corporate environment that is less hierarchical, or otherwise distinct from that of the nonprofit.

(8) The board prefers that the revenues and expenses of the nonexempt activity not be reflected on the income statements and balance sheet of the exempt corporation. (Note, however, that most often an organization owning a majority of the stock of a subsidiary must include the subsidiary's financial statements in its own consolidated financial statement and Form 990 requires additional disclosure of subsidiaries.)

Once the board has decided to establish a for-profit subsidiary, it will need to decide on the type of new entity, how the new entity will be organized, and the extent and nature of control that the nonprofit corporation will exert over the for-profit.

Type of Organization

A nonprofit establishing a for-profit subsidiary can choose among several different types of corporate entities. These include, among others, a business corporation, benefit corporation, limited liability company (LLC), and limited partnership. A limited liability company is often attractive because of the pass-through tax treatment given to it and the flexibility in its structure.[3]

A benefit corporation is a type of business corporation but unlike a regular business corporation, which can be viewed as having shareholder primacy as a focus, a benefit corporation must consider the interests of other stakeholders in addition to shareholders. Those who manage a benefit corporation are required to pursue the creation of a positive effect on society and the environment, taken as a whole, that is material considering the corporation's size and the nature of its business and that considers stakeholder interests separately from the interests of shareholders. Important in the analysis is not just what the corporation does but how it conducts its business and operations. In the situation where the nonprofit corporation will not be the sole owner of the subsidiary, a benefit corporation may help ensure the activities of the subsidiary will be consistent with the mission of the nonprofit corporation. The use of a benefit corporation also might be viewed more favorably by the public.[4]

While unusual, there are circumstances where it may be useful to include for-profit activities in a separate nonprofit organization that is controlled by the parent nonprofit, but which does not seek to be determined to be tax-exempt. For non-exempt activities that do not generate a significant amount of revenue, a nonprofit organization controlled by a tax-exempt nonprofit organization may find simplicity in avoiding the distribution of revenues through the issuance of dividends.

Directors or Managers

If the nonprofit owns more than 50 percent of the for-profit, it usually will have the power to elect a majority of the for-profit entity's directors or managers. The board of the nonprofit should determine who will serve as the new entity's initial board of directors or managers, and whether certain director or manager positions should be filled, *ex officio*, by persons who hold certain officer or director positions with the nonprofit. For instance, the board of the nonprofit could specify that its chair, chief executive, and/or chief financial officer will serve *ex officio* on the for-profit corporation's board, or that one or more of the nonprofit's board members also will serve on the for-profit entity's board. If the new entity is a limited liability company, it also may be member-managed, which would mean the nonprofit's board or corporate officers would, in effect, be making the management decisions for the entity.

Officers

Depending on the activities of the for-profit, the nonprofit parent may desire to have some degree of overlap between the officers of the nonprofit and its for-profit subsidiary. For instance, when organizing the for-profit subsidiary, the parent nonprofit board may require the subsidiary's bylaws, operating agreement, or other governance document to provide that the chief executive or other officer of the nonprofit will serve, *ex officio*, as the chair of the for-profit subsidiary. This will ensure that the nonprofit parent is kept informed regarding all material operational issues affecting the subsidiary. Alternatively, the nonprofit, as shareholder or member, can elect directors of the subsidiary who will appoint officers acceptable to the nonprofit.

Other Oversight Mechanisms

The parent board should evaluate what other mechanisms it will use to oversee the operation of the subsidiary. In addition to any director and officer overlap between the parent nonprofit and the for-profit subsidiary, the parent board should determine how often it wishes to receive reports on the subsidiary's operations, and then incorporate such reports on the parent board's agenda. The board also may wish to provide for member or shareholder approval or veto power over significant corporate actions—such as the adoption of budgets. The board should be aware of which corporate actions (such as mergers, substantial asset sales, and dissolution) typically require approval by a majority or higher percentage of members or shareholders.

With any subsidiary, it is important to observe certain formalities relating to the exercise of the powers or management of the subsidiary. If the parent company does not do so, the debts, obligations, or other liability of the subsidiary can become the liability of the parent company through a doctrine called "piercing the corporate veil." The doctrine of "piercing the corporate veil" is well-established. In the corporate realm, the disregard of corporate formalities can be a key factor in the piercing analysis. For LLCs, which are less formal, the failure to follow corporate formalities may not be decisive. Still, other factors allowing a piercing, such as a disregard by entity's owner of the entity's economic separateness from its owners, can lead to a piercing of the veil.

Tax Implications

Any revenue generated by the for-profit subsidiary, if it is a corporation, will be subject to taxation at the corporate level, although dividends to the tax-exempt shareholder would frequently be tax-exempt in its hands, similar to other passive income. (See the discussion in the section *"Types of Income Excluded from UBI"* in *Chapter 5, Taxation.*) Any losses experienced by the for-profit corporation may be offset by the gains from that corporation's other activities. Section 512(b)(13) of the Code provides special rules with respect to any interest, annuities, royalties, or rent paid from the for-profit subsidiary to its tax-exempt parent.

Other Organizational Issues

Nonprofits that establish a subsidiary will generally find that it is most appropriate to establish this entity under the laws of the state in which the nonprofit is itself incorporated. However, nonprofit corporations may sometimes find it useful to take advantage of favorable provisions in the business entity laws of another state, by forming the subsidiary under the laws of such other state, and registering the subsidiary as a foreign corporation, LLC, or other types of entity doing business in the nonprofit corporation's state. The nonprofit corporation's legal counsel can assist the board and officers in assessing whether the use of a foreign entity offers any significant advantages to offset the administrative inconveniences of the organization under a different state.

Creating Joint Ventures with For-Profits

Nonprofit, tax-exempt corporations may also find it useful in certain circumstances to enter into joint ventures with individuals or for-profit entities. The nonprofit board should make sure that the joint venture is not structured or operated in a manner that would constitute an undue benefit to its for-profit partner or other for-profit entities.[5] A tax-exempt corporation that is a prospective partner in a joint venture (whether organized as an LLC, partnership, or corporation) must take care to structure the joint venture, and the nonprofit's role in it, in a manner that minimizes the risk that the nonprofit's participation might put the organization's tax-exemption in jeopardy or generate unexpected UBI.

Even if the tax-exempt corporation's participation in a for-profit joint venture is only a small part of the tax-exempt's total activities, the tax-exempt should exercise a level of control over the venture's operational issues that will assure that the venture operates in furtherance of the tax-exempt organization's charitable purposes. This is particularly true in the case of joint ventures structured as partnerships or LLCs. With such "pass-through" entities, the IRS attributes the acts of the partnership (or LLC) entity as being the actions of the joint-venture partners.[6] To evaluate whether a tax-exempt corporation's participation in the joint venture is in furtherance of tax-exempt purposes, the IRS will look at such issues as:

(1) Does the nonprofit appoint a majority of the joint venture's governing body?
(2) Does the nonprofit have a veto power over significant for-profit venture actions? Does the nonprofit have the ability to affirmatively require the venture to take action?
(3) Will a for-profit entity (whether a partner, a partner's affiliate, or unrelated third party) manage the operations of the joint venture? If so, what is the term of the management contract? How are the management fees determined?
(4) Do the governing documents of the joint venture explicitly provide that the joint venture will be operated consistently for the charitable purposes of the tax-exempt partner? Does the tax-exempt partner have the ability to require the joint venture to put charitable purposes ahead of economic objectives?
(5) Will the compensation paid to the joint venture's officers and vendors (especially the for-profit partner or any affiliate) be reasonable in light of the services or goods provided?
(6) Will the joint venture use space financed by tax-exempt bonds? If so, have the implications of such "bad use" on the tax exemption of the bonds been considered?

Joint Venture Policy

Joint ventures involving tax-exempt organizations have become a focus of the IRS and information regarding joint venture activities is required to be disclosed in Form 990. Form 990 requires information with regard to whether or not a nonprofit has invested in, contributed assets to, or otherwise participated in the joint venture or similar arrangement with one or more taxable entities within the past taxable year. A "yes" response requires the organization to state whether it has adopted a written policy or procedures requiring the organization to evaluate its participation in joint venture arrangements and has taken steps to safeguard the organization's exempt status with respect to such arrangements. The type of joint venture policy contemplated by the Form 990 should describe the type of activities subject to the policy. It also should require the organization to take steps to ensure that participation in the joint venture is in furtherance of tax-exempt purposes with an evaluation of the factors described above.

In addition, a policy should require that any joint venture be in writing and include the following minimum requirements: (1) with respect to any "whole operation" joint venture (i.e., a joint venture in which the nonprofit contributes essentially all of its assets to the enterprise), the nonprofit maintains control of the joint venture through majority voting rights and/or veto powers; (2) with respect to an ancillary joint venture (i.e., a joint venture in which a portion of the nonprofit's resources are contributed), the nonprofit maintains control over tax-exempt aspects of the joint venture and voting and ownership interests in the joint venture that are consistent with contributions; (3) any dealings between the parties to the joint venture must be at arm's length and for fair market value; (4) the joint venture must give priority to the nonprofit's tax-exempt purposes over maximization of profit for the participants of the joint venture; and (5) activities that would jeopardize the nonprofit's tax-exempt status are prohibited.

Taxation of Joint Venture Revenue

Any income generated by the joint venture will be subject to tax at the joint venture level, if the joint venture is a "regular" (or C) corporation. However, joint ventures structured as tax pass-through entities—that is, partnerships and LLCs—will not be taxed at the entity level. If the joint venture is appropriately structured to further the purposes of the tax-exempt partner, the tax-exempt organization's share of joint venture revenue (i.e., LLC/partnership revenue allocations) should be exempt from taxation, and not treated as UBI. Joint venture interests in S corporations present special issues. Although S corporations are generally pass-through entities, the Code specifically provides that all of an exempt S corporation shareholder's allocated income is UBI.

The UBI rules are complex. As an illustration, joint venture income that is passive (such as rents, royalties, and interest) would not ordinarily be taxed to the nonprofit when "passed through." However, any otherwise nontaxable joint venture income will be taxed to the nonprofit (at least in part) if the venture is debt-financed or if the nonprofit acquired its joint venture interest with debt. Any nonprofit contemplating a joint venture with for-profit entities should thoroughly explore the structure with tax counsel. (See the section *"Unrelated Business Income"* in *Chapter 5, Taxation.*)

See the Suggested Questions and Checklist following the Endnotes below to review the issues discussed in this chapter.

Endnotes

1. For a detailed discussion of legal issues that arise in partnerships and joint ventures involving nonprofit corporations, *see* Michael I. Sanders, *Joint Ventures Involving Tax-Exempt Organization* (4th ed., John Wiley & Sons 2013) and Michael I. Sanders, *Joint Ventures Involving Tax-Exempt Organizations 2024 Cumulative Supplement* (John Wiley & Sons, Inc. 2024) (Cumulative Supplements are generally published annually.
2. *See* David A. Levitt and Steven R. Chiodin, *Taking Care of Business: Use of a For-Profit Subsidiary by a Nonprofit Organization,* ABA BUSINESS LAW TODAY (June 2014).
3. *Id.* For a discussion on nonprofit limited liability companies, see Cassady V. Brewer, Lisa A. Runquist, and Elizabeth C. Minnigh, *Nonprofit LLCs,* ABA BUSINESS LAW TODAY (March 2017).
4. *See* Levitt and Chiodin, *supra* note 2.
5. The IRS closely scrutinizes nonprofit joint ventures with private individuals or for-profit entities. *See* I.R.S. Rev. Rul. 98-15, 1998-1 C. B. 718; Rev. Rul. 2004-51, 2004-1 C.B. 974. While the IRS is increasingly approving variations on joint ventures, it continues to examine creative approaches to assure that the tax-exempt purpose of the organization is not compromised by the joint venture. *See, e.g.,* IRS PLR 201503018 (2014), IRS PLR 201644019 (2016).
6. *See* Redlands Surgical Servs. v. Commissioner, 113 T.C. 47 (1999), *aff'd per curiam,* 242 F.3d 904 (9th Cir. 2001).

Suggested Questions for Directors Regarding For-Profit Subsidiaries and Joint Ventures

(1) Is the corporation contemplating engaging in any new business activities or joint ventures?

(2) If so, is this activity substantially related to the corporation's nonprofit purposes?

(3) Will the new activity or joint venture generate UBI?

(4) What are the reasons for or against putting a new activity in a taxable subsidiary, or conducting it with another party through a joint venture, rather than conducting the activity through a division within the corporation?

(5) If the board wants to establish a subsidiary involved in taxable activities, what will be the form of the subsidiary? Who will serve as the subsidiary's officers and directors/managers? How will the nonprofit parent board exercise oversight of the subsidiary?

(6) In what state should a subsidiary or joint venture be established?

(7) For joint ventures to be engaged in by a tax-exempt nonprofit, what controls has the nonprofit put into place to assure that the venture operates in furtherance of the nonprofit's partner's charitable purposes?

(8) How will the joint venture be organized (general partnership, LLC, corporation, benefit corporation, etc.)? What are the advantages of this form over another alternative?

(9) Will the joint venture use space that was financed by tax-exempt bonds?

(10) Who would be part of the organization's proposed joint venture? Will this party provide goods or services to the joint venture? What controls are in place to assure that the other joint venturer does not profit from the venture at the expense of the venture or the nonprofit partner?

Checklist: For-Profit Subsidiaries and Joint Ventures

Note: For simplicity, these and other chapter checklists describe a corporation having a chair, who presides over the board of directors; a chief executive, who may be a staff person; an executive committee; a governance/nominating committee; and an audit committee. (We recognize, however, that in many smaller and other nonprofits, these committee functions may be performed by either the executive committee or the board as a whole.) We also assume a legal counsel—someone, paid or unpaid, having primary responsibility for the corporation's legal affairs. Many corporations, especially larger nonprofits, may have other committees established for specific purposes, such as establishing executive compensation; monitoring compliance with legal requirements; and overseeing investments and other financial matters.

Subject	Review By	How Often	Comment
1. Are there any new taxable activities planned by the corporation that might be best conducted through a subsidiary or joint venture?	Full board and chief executive	At least annually	The chief executive should recommend, and the board should decide, if any such activities should be kept within the corporation or placed in a separate entity.
2. For existing subsidiaries and joint ventures, how often is the board apprised of financial and business issues for these entities?	Full board and chief executive	At least quarterly, with detailed reviews at least annually	
3. Are the activities and organizational form of existing subsidiaries or joint ventures consistent with the organization's nonprofit purposes?	Full board, chief executive, legal counsel	At least annually	The board should monitor the evolution of such affiliates' activities to ensure consistency with the organization's purposes.
4. How much UBI, if any, have subsidiaries or joint ventures generated for the nonprofit?	Full board, chief financial officer	At least annually	

Subject	Review By	How Often	Comment
5. Does a joint venture partner provide management or other services or goods to the joint venture? If so, does this partner derive any revenues in excess of those that would be paid to an unrelated party on an arms'-length basis?	Full board, chief executive, chief financial officer	Quarterly, with detailed reviews annually	Management contracts with for-profit joint venture partners are subject to close scrutiny for private inurement and other tax-exemption concerns.
6. Does the corporation have a joint venture policy?	Full board, governance/nominating committee, chief executive	At least annually	Form 990 asks for information regarding joint ventures.

Chapter 7:
Nonprofits on the Internet: Fundraising, Selling Goods and Services, Lobbying, and Other Activities

Chapter 7

Nonprofits on the Internet: Fundraising, Selling Goods and Services, Lobbying, and Other Activities

Nonprofit corporations are subject to various state and federal requirements depending on their activities. These include, for example, requirements relating to fundraising, lobbying and political activity, intellectual property, sales tax, and privacy. With many of these activities being conducted through the Internet, it is necessary to not only be aware of the legal requirements relating to these activities but also to the requirements relating to the use of the Internet. Although the law generally applicable to the particular issue continues to apply, the actual application of the law to activities on the Internet continues to evolve.

Lawmakers, regulators, and judges across the country have been determining how various laws written for the traditional economy fit the virtual world of the Internet. Although this chapter is designed to alert nonprofit corporation directors to some of the major legal implications of certain activities and the involvement of the Internet in these activities, specific statements may become inaccurate, or less accurate, over time. (For instance, it can be expected that the IRS will continue to make, and periodically revise, pronouncements on many of the topics discussed below.) Nonprofit boards should make sure that their corporation's activities, including those conducted through the Internet, are reviewed by legal counsel on a regular basis, to ensure compliance with changing legal standards.

Potential Hazards and Benefits of Using the Internet

The Internet offers a highly convenient and cost-effective tool for communicating a nonprofit corporation's purposes and conducting some of its activities. Still, the use of the Internet may implicate a number of legal issues applicable to nonprofit corporations generally. Some of the more significant of these general laws are discussed below. Although it may be unlikely that any one nonprofit would simultaneously (if ever) encounter all of the issues discussed below, a broad range of potential issues is presented here to alert directors to the wide variety of legal issues that could be raised by different forms of Internet activity.

Fundraising

Charitable Solicitation Registration Requirements

General rule

Most states and many local governments require nonprofit organizations and their fundraisers to register before soliciting contributions in that jurisdiction. These jurisdictions have regulations relating to telephone, mail, and other types of solicitations from organizations that are not physically located in the solicitation area.[1] A majority of the states that require charitable solicitation registration accept the Unified Registration Statement form for charitable solicitations, which was developed to ease the burden on charitable organizations of filling out multiple different registration forms. Many of these states require state-specific appendices to be submitted with the Unified Registration Statement.

Related to state registration requirements, a number of states require certain information to be disclosed by charitable organizations on written solicitations, prior to conducting telephone solicitations, upon confirmation of a gift or pledge, and when receipting gifts.[2] These disclosure requirements are intended to protect donors from fraudulent organizations soliciting funds through the use of false or misleading information. Each state's requirements differ and the definitions of "solicitation" can be quite broad, capturing any direct or indirect request or invitation to contribute.

Application to the Internet

The question of what constitutes sufficient presence over the Internet to require registration under a jurisdiction's charitable solicitation laws continues to evolve. Any organization that raises funds over the Internet should be sure that it keeps abreast of the evolving standards that apply to such fundraising.

The Internet allows nonprofits to communicate with a large audience of potential new donors, generally at less expense than traditional fundraising methods. Many nonprofits have identified this opportunity and developed websites that describe their organizations' purposes, activities, upcoming events, contact information, and more. They also may include statements that directly solicit contributions. For example, some nonprofits provide a form on their websites that enables donors to make contributions online, using their credit cards.

It is unlikely that most jurisdictions will require registration of nonprofit organizations that only maintain a passive web page and merely provide information on the organization without requesting donations. In contrast, registration may be required if a nonprofit actively solicits donations by e-mail to persons located in the jurisdiction or permits donors to make contributions by providing their credit card numbers on the organization's website. The registration requirements are less clear for nonprofits that provide the opportunity for donations to be made over the Internet via their website, but which do not otherwise actively solicit donations in specific jurisdictions. If a donation is made by a person in a state that requires registration, the organization should determine whether it needs to register before communicating further with that person, including adding them to their mailing list.

Directors should expect both that the rules in this area will continue to be refined, and that different jurisdictions may take different approaches. Accordingly, directors should periodically check with counsel whether the organization's website or other Internet activity subjects it to the charitable solicitation laws of different jurisdictions—both in and out of the United States.

The National Association of Attorneys General (NAAG) and the National Association of State Charity Officers (NASCO) issued a set of principles relating to the regulation of charitable solicitations over the Internet called the "Charleston Principles."[3] Under these principles, an organization should register with the state if (1) it is domiciled in the state; (2) its non-Internet activities require registration; (3) it specifically targets persons physically located in the state for solicitation; or (4) it receives contributions from persons in the state on a repeated and ongoing basis or a substantial basis through its website. Although these principles are not legally mandated, they can serve as very useful guidance as to the expectations of state attorneys generals.

Questions that are likely to be relevant to the issue of whether an organization's Internet activities make it subject to regulation in a particular jurisdiction include the following:

(1) Must individuals take the initiative to go to the organization's website, or does the organization contact prospective donors (such as through e-mail) and request that they log on to the website and make a donation?

(2) Does the organization's website have a mechanism for corresponding (by e-mail or regular mail) with persons who express an interest in the organization after visiting the website?

(3) Does the organization's website have a mechanism for accepting contributions from donors who provide credit card information?

(4) How much money is raised in a particular jurisdiction through Internet activities?

It is advisable to review the applicable disclosure statement requirements to determine whether they may apply to online-giving web pages or other Internet solicitation content, even if the organization is not required to register with the state.

Acknowledging Donors' Contributions

General rule

Federal tax law requires a donor contributing $250 or more to a charitable corporation to obtain a written receipt for the contribution before filing a federal income tax return in order to claim a charitable contribution deduction for the donation.[4] Similarly, charitable organizations that receive contributions of more than $75 in connection with the provision to the donor of a certain amount of goods or services—such as a seat at a table for a charity dinner (quid pro quo contributions)—must provide the donor with a written statement estimating the deductible portion of the contribution, above the value of the goods or services the donor received.[5] These requirements apply regardless of whether the contribution is made in person, over the telephone, through traditional mail or over the Internet. See the section *"Charitable Contribution"* in *Chapter 5, Taxation.*

Application to the Internet

Charitable corporations that allow contributions to be made over the Internet should be sure the corporation has a system in place for acknowledging such contributions that comply with current IRS acknowledgment requirements. An acknowledgment provided by e-mail, or that can be provided off the organization's website, will satisfy this donation acknowledgment requirement.[6]

Allowing Other Organizations to Raise Money for the Corporation

General rules

Registration requirements. A nonprofit organization may use an individual or other organization to generate donations. Such an individual or group may need to register under the charitable solicitation rules of the jurisdiction in which donations are solicited. A nonprofit organization should ensure that any third party with which it contracts for these services is properly registered, given that the third party may create a compliance risk for the nonprofit organization. To protect against such a risk, a nonprofit organization may require in its contract with a third party that the third party indemnify the nonprofit organization for any damages (including penalties) incurred by the organization as a result of the third party's failure to comply with the applicable registration laws. The ability to terminate the contract immediately without any penalty in the event of a third party's failure to comply with the registration laws also helps protect the nonprofit organization. At least one state (California) also requires that the nonprofit have control over the representations made by the third party on its behalf.[7]

Fundraiser as the agent of the tax-exempt corporation. If the individual or group is not itself tax-exempt, the fundraiser must qualify as an agent of the tax-exempt entity in order for the donor's contribution to be tax-deductible. If the fund-raiser is considered the organization's agent, contributions to such an agent are deductible in the same way that direct contributions are deductible. In contrast, if a non-tax-exempt fundraiser is not the agent of a tax-exempt organization, contributions to the fundraiser will not be tax-deductible to the donor.

Fundraising resulting from sales by taxable entities; commercial co-ventures; and cause marketing. Another way that a tax-exempt organization may raise funds is through an arrangement to receive a percentage of the sales of goods sold by a taxable entity to supporters of the tax-exempt organization. For instance, a taxable entity may volunteer, or agree, to make donations to the tax-exempt entity based on purchases made by organization supporters on a certain day or during some other time period. Similarly, for-profit stores may sell to nonprofits coupons or "scrip" for store products, at a discount to face value.

Under such an arrangement, for example, a local grocery store may agree with a tax-exempt preschool to honor coupons for groceries bought by the school's supporters. Such coupons may be purchased at a discount by the school and resold at face value to school supporters. The net income made from the sales is generally not considered unrelated business income (UBI) if the coupon sales are not an activity "regularly carried on" by the school, or if it is carried on by volunteers. Still, the payment for such purchases or scrip is not deductible by the purchasers as tax-exempt contributions, since the purchaser is getting full value for the "purchase."

Under other arrangements between a for-profit merchant and a nonprofit corporation, a merchant (such as a credit card company) may pay to a nonprofit institution (such as a nonprofit college) a percentage of sales made by a credit card depicting the college, its name, and logo. In these cases, the percentage of sales payments may be eligible to be treated as a royalty for the use of the institution's name and image, and not taxed as UBI. As noted in the section *"Types of Income Excluded from UBI"* in *Chapter* 5, *Taxation,* royalties for use of an intangible (such as a corporation's name or logo) are generally considered exempt from treatment as UBI; however, if such payments were instead to be characterized as payment for a service (i.e., the referral of customers), then this income would be considered UBI.

These arrangements, which can benefit both the tax-exempt organization and the for-profit merchant, are commonly referred to as "commercial co-ventures," "charitable sales promotions," "cause marketing" or "cause-related marketing," and can be subject to state charitable fundraising and solicitation laws. Some of these laws require that the charitable nonprofit have control over the fundraising activity and that the agreement between the parties includes certain requirements protecting the nonprofit as well as consumers. In addition, one or both of the parties involved in the arrangement may be required to register with the states where the offers are being made.

Internet applications

The Internet has spawned a number of creative fundraising mechanisms. Directors of nonprofit organizations that receive donations through websites maintained by for-profit entities should obtain legal advice regarding whether the contributions were generated in a manner consistent with IRS rules on deductibility and state law.

Websites acting as agents of tax-exempt organizations. Some websites purport to raise funds for many charities at once. They are promoted as offering donors convenience and detailed information about potential donees. Some such donation websites are not themselves operated by tax-exempt charitable organizations, so contributions made through these sites are not deductible by donors unless the donation website operator is an agent of the nonprofit. Nonprofit boards should ensure that the terms of any agreement they enter with a donation website operator establish an appropriate agency relationship if users of the site are going to be promised deductibility for their contributions.[8]

On a more fundamental level, nonprofit boards should establish a mechanism for evaluating when and whether to allow such donation websites to serve as their fundraising agents. For instance, before granting permission to a donation website to use the corporation's name, the charity should investigate the history of the website, its operators, and its operations. Other questions to ask include:

- If the website deducts an administrative fee before passing on the donations, is the fee reasonable?
- How long does it take for the site to process donation payments and then make payments to the nonprofit?
- Does the site pass through the name and contact information of the donor so that the donation may be appropriately receipted?
- How does the website company retain and use donor information for its own or other purposes?

Fundraising through sales by for-profit entities: Internet merchant affiliation and charity malls. Certain Internet sites have programs under which a tax-exempt organization receives a payment as a result of sales made by a for-profit over the Internet. In exchange for this payment, the nonprofit generally either provides a link from its website to that of the participating for-profit, or the for-profit refers to the participating nonprofit on its own website and promises to donate money to support its mission.[9] As discussed above, the structure of these programs can have different UBI implications. Moreover, the IRS has questioned whether the payment by a vendor of a percentage of sales from customers referred by a tax-exempt organization to the vendor's website can ever be considered "substantially related" for UBI determination purposes.[10]

A unique online variant of the merchant affiliation model is a website that brings together consumers, for-profit retailers, and nonprofit corporations in a program that is similar to affinity credit cards. Visitors to such a charity mall website designate a preferred charity and then shop at affiliated online retailers through links on the charity mall's website. For each item, a shopper buys through the charity mall, the retailers donate a specified percentage of the purchase price to the shopper's preferred charity through the charity mall operator.

Because shoppers initiate these donations and charities are therefore not involved in sales that are unrelated to their exempt purposes, it is generally believed that charities can treat the money they receive through charity malls as donations and not UBI. Still, donors are generally not able to deduct donations attributable to purchases they make through charity malls because they receive items of equal value in return for their payments to retailers.

Some Internet charity mall operators claim that their programs have a special structure that allows donors to deduct donations. In these programs, when a donor makes a purchase through the charity mall, the operator offers the donor a rebate on the purchase. The operator holds the rebate in an account for the donor, and the donor has the option to either receive the money or donate it to the charity through the operator. Because the donor has the choice to keep or donate the rebate, the IRS allows the donor to claim a charitable contribution deduction.[11] Before participating in a charity mall, or if a nonprofit learns that a charity mall is making donations to its organization an option for mall-site shoppers, the nonprofit should investigate the operations and operator of the charity mall to make sure that it will not be associated with a questionable program or group.

California enacted a law that provides for oversight of charitable fundraising platforms and platform charities with an online presence. The law requires that any person or entity that holds charitable property or solicits donations for charitable purposes in California is to register with the state attorney general and to annually file disclosures and other reports with the attorney general.[12]

Corporate Sponsorship vs. Advertising

General Rules

Acknowledgments vs. advertisements

The distinction between sponsorship acknowledgments and advertisements may be subtle. Simple references to an organization sponsor by name, address, and phone number would generally be characterized as acknowledgements and the funds paid by the sponsor in connection with the activity with which the acknowledgment is associated would be considered a tax-deductible contribution. In contrast, references to a sponsor's products or services that include an endorsement or statements about the relative quality of the sponsor's goods or services would be likely treated as advertisements (at least to the extent of the fair market value of comparable ads provided by the tax-exempt organization).[13] In addition, the money paid by the for-profit may be considered taxable UBI to the nonprofit, if paid in connection with an activity that is "regularly carried on." (See the section *"Advertising vs. Sponsorship Acknowledgements"* in *Chapter 5, Taxation.*)

Different treatment of advertisements in periodicals

As noted in the section *"Advertising vs. Sponsorship Acknowledgments"* in *Chapter 5, Taxation,* payments received for an individual ad placed in a nonprofit's periodical publication will be subject to less UBI tax than an ad placed in a nonperiodical. However, it may sometimes be difficult to determine whether a publication is a periodical for which the lower UBI tax calculation would apply. The general rule is that material that appears on a regular periodic schedule, in a standard format, is likely to be considered a periodical, whereas material (such as a brochure) that is continuously available but subject to updating from time to time, is not likely to be considered a periodical.

Internet Applications

Acknowledgments vs. advertisements

For-profit companies may be interested in appearing on a nonprofit corporation's website as a sponsor or as an advertiser. As noted above, if the information about a for-profit company that appears on a nonprofit corporation's website is considered a sponsorship acknowledgment ("The maintenance of XYZ Charity's website is made possible through the support of Acme Widget and Gizmo

Corporation, located at 1200 Main Street"), payment made by the sponsor is likely deductible as a charitable contribution, and the revenue received from the for-profit corporation in connection with the posted message would not be subject to tax. However, if the information about a for-profit corporation that is posted on the nonprofit corporation's website is considered an advertisement ("Need widgets or gizmos—fast? Call Acme Widget and Gizmo Corporation, a full service provider of widget and gizmos since 1999, at area code 222-333-9999, or order on-line at www.widgetsnow.biz"), the revenues received from the for-profit corporation in connection with this information will be subject to taxation as UBI.

Because of the novel nature of certain Internet applications, the acknowledgement/advertisement distinction is not always obvious. For example, the IRS has indicated that a simple displayed link to a sponsor's website is not an advertisement, even though an individual who clicks on the link will then be presented, through the for-profit's website, with information on the company's products and services and how to purchase them. In contrast, the IRS also indicated that a banner on a nonprofit organization's website that displays a for-profit organization's website, but does not provide a link to the for-profit's website, may be considered an advertisement if the banner reference shows information about the for-profit entity's product.[14]

The regulations make clear that an acknowledgment of a sponsor may include the street address of the sponsor's place of business and telephone number.[15] A link is essentially an Internet address combined with a tool the user may employ, solely at the user's discretion, to go to the linked site. There appears to be no basis for treating the link differently than a street address or telephone number.

Internet periodicals

Whether material containing advertisements published by a nonprofit corporation on the Internet can be considered a periodical for purposes of more favorable UBI tax calculation rules can be a difficult determination. The IRS has indicated that the UBI rules for periodical advertising income will not be available for Internet advertisements run by a nonprofit unless the advertisement appears in online materials that are "prepared and distributed in substantially the same manner as a traditional periodical," with an editorial staff, marketing program, and budget that is independent of the administration of the rest of the organization's website.[16] Under these rules, an advertisement that appears on a nonprofit website apart from materials that look like a periodical (e.g., a journal that is published online, sometimes in addition to being as a hard copy) would not generally be considered to be "published in a periodical," even if the website is periodically updated.

Association (Links) with Taxable Entities

General Rule

Tax-exempt corporations may lose tax-exempt status by promoting, or appearing to promote, the private interests of individuals or taxable entities, except as incidental to the tax-exempt organization's purposes.

Internet Applications

Website links with websites of taxable organizations

The nature of the Internet is to create easy-to-use links between otherwise unrelated material. Corporate sponsors and other for-profit companies may wish to establish links with a tax-exempt corporation's website (either by placing a link on the for-profit's website to the nonprofit's site, or having the nonprofit's site contain a link to the for-profit corporation's website). While a link to a for-profit corporation on a tax-exempt corporation's website may take up very little space, the existence of the link can create the impression that the tax-exempt corporation supports or is involved with some or all of the activities described on the for-profit corporation's website. Further, links to the sites of corporate sponsors may (or may not) be deemed to be advertisements subject to taxation as UBI. (See the section *"Corporate Sponsorship vs. Advertising"* above.)

Tax-exempt organizations maintaining websites are well advised to develop a policy for determining which linkage requests it will honor and which it will reject.

A nonprofit board should consider several issues as they develop and apply their linkage policy.[17] The policy should include a procedure for screening proposed links to ensure that they further the nonprofit's charitable purposes and satisfy its requirements for exemption. For instance, tax-exempt organizations should reject requests by political candidates to establish links with particular campaign sites, to avoid the appearance of making political endorsements and protect their tax-exempt status.

When a link goes to a site maintained by another nonprofit, the linkage policy also should provide for an evaluation of the § 501(c) status of the proposed linking organization, to assess the potential for attribution of the linking organization's activities to the nonprofit. For example, if the website of a nonprofit that works to preserve wetlands contains a link to an environmental advocacy group that conducts substantial lobbying, should the existence of the link cause the advocacy group's lobbying to be attributed to the nonprofit? (See further discussion of this issue in the section *"Implication of Links to Lobbying Organization Websites"* below.)

In addition, a linkage policy should include a procedure for responding to the discovery of links on a for-profit corporation's website to the nonprofit's site that were created without the nonprofit's permission. If the linking organization would not meet the approval requirements set forth in the established policy, the nonprofit may want to have communications to record the fact that the nonprofit on the destination end of the link does not approve or condone what the linking organization is saying or doing, and, if appropriate, request that the link be removed.

Lobbying

General Rule

As noted in the section *"The Absolute Prohibition on Political Campaign Activities"* in *Chapter 5, Taxation*, organizations that are exempt from federal income taxation under § 501(c)(3) are prohibited from devoting more than an "insubstantial" part of their activities to lobbying. To avoid the subjective vagaries of what insubstantial may mean—for instance, as determined by percentage of organizational revenue, percentage of volunteer time or other resources, or the impact of the activities conducted—tax-exempt organizations (other than churches and other religious organizations) may take advantage of the election under § 501(h) of the Code. This Code section provides objective measures for determining permissible levels of lobbying, based on the organization's annual spending on its exempt purposes, and with different limits for "grassroots" and "direct" lobbying. As such, the election can be extremely beneficial to a nonprofit corporation by providing a mechanism for calculating a specific "safe harbor" maximum dollar amount that the corporation may spend on lobbying activities. (For more information about the § 501(h) election, see the discussion in the section *"Limitations on Lobbying"* in *Chapter 5, Taxation.*)

Internet Applications

Benefits of § 501(h) election

The Internet provides great potential for a nonprofit to increase the scope and effectiveness of its lobbying activity while satisfying the IRS limitations on lobbying by tax-exempt corporations. Lobbying activity can be conducted over the Internet (through websites and electronic mail) at a very low cost, especially compared to the cost of traditional mail or personal lobbying visits. For example, legislative alerts or calls to action can be posted at the organization's website, referenced by links to other sites, and/or e-mail communications can be sent directly to the nonprofit corporation's list of supporters. The time and economic costs of these communications are typically trivial compared to mail or traditional broadcast mechanisms. As noted in the section *"Lobbying: General Rule"* above, the amount that a nonprofit can spend on lobbying is limited to an insubstantial amount. Tax-exempt corporations that would like to maximize the potential for lobbying (using the Internet alone or in conjunction with more traditional lobbying activities), while not jeopardizing their tax-exempt status, may wish to make the election permitted under § 501(h). (See the section *"Limitations on Lobbying"* in *Chapter 5, Taxation.*)

Allocation of costs of e-mail and website postings

Despite the fact that lobbying through e-mail or website postings can save considerable expense over traditional mail or fax communications, it is currently unclear how costs should be allocated for such Internet lobbying activities. Making an appropriate allocation of costs of Internet lobbying is essential to ensure that the nonprofit does not exceed the applicable spending limit if a § 501(h) election has been made (or remains within the insubstantial range for organizations that have not made the § 501(h) election). Costs to be allocated may include hosting and maintaining websites. Until the IRS provides specific guidance in this area, nonprofits should consult with their accountant regarding appropriate measures of the cost of these activities.

Implications of links to lobbying organization websites

Tax-exempt nonprofits should exercise caution before creating or permitting links on the nonprofit's website to a website for a lobbying organization. It is not yet clear under what circumstances, and to what extent, a link on a nonprofit organization's website to the website of an organization that engages in lobbying would be considered lobbying by the nonprofit. It can be expected that the IRS will be taking positions on this issue in the future; therefore, directors of nonprofits for whom this issue may be relevant should make sure that the organization routinely receives updated advice in this area.

Political Activity

General Rule

As noted in *Chapter 5, Taxation*, tax-exempt organizations are prohibited from supporting or opposing candidates for political office or otherwise intervening in political campaigns. (See the section *"The Absolute Prohibition on Political Campaign Activities"* in *Chapter 5, Taxation*.)

Internet Applications

Implications of links to political campaigns or candidates' websites

Charitable tax-exempt nonprofits should not create or permit links on the nonprofit's website to websites for selected political campaigns or candidates for political office. In some instances, providing strictly nonpartisan information, including links to sites maintained by all the candidates in a race, may be consistent with federal tax law requirements, but a nonprofit should get legal advice before pursuing such an approach. The IRS has stated that a website link may violate the ban on political campaigning depending on the content of the linked site.[18]

Avoiding Copyright and Trademark Infringement and Other Claims

General Rule

Like other entities, nonprofit corporations should take appropriate steps to safeguard any intellectual property (such as copyrights, trademarks, and service marks) developed or owned by the corporation, while ensuring that its activities and those of its employees and agents do not infringe on the intellectual property of others. Thus, it should place copyright symbols and notices as appropriate on original written material, and use trade/service mark symbols and notices wherever such marks are used.

Internet Applications

Protection of the nonprofit's copyrights and trademarks on the Internet

If a nonprofit corporation intends to post material that it has developed and copyrighted on its website, it should also post notices to site visitors that inform them of the copyright status and the corporation's intent to pursue those who violate its copyright. The corporation also should consider providing copyright notices at the bottom of each screen.

The organization should take similar steps to protect its trademarked names and logos, especially if these are highly valued assets. Technological advances are likely to bring improved methods to assist a nonprofit corporation in protecting its trademarks and logos for this purpose; therefore, the nonprofit board should make sure that intellectual property protection mechanisms are periodically evaluated to take advantage of such improvements.

Avoiding infringement of the copyrights and trademarks of others

Directors of a nonprofit organization should make sure that the corporation's employees and volunteers who engage in Internet activity on behalf of the corporation understand that certain activities, when done on the Internet, may constitute infringement of another organization's copyright or trademark, although an analogous "physical world" activity does not raise infringement issues. For example, whereas clipping a newspaper article from an actual newspaper and posting it on an office bulletin board would not generally be deemed to be copyright infringement, cutting the article electronically from an electronic copy of the paper and posting it on a page of the corporation's website without proper authorization may well constitute copyright infringement.[19]

Posting pictures or videos of individuals on the nonprofit's website or social media

A nonprofit may post on its website or social media photos or videos taken of individuals participating in nonprofit-sponsored activities. An individual could object to such usage if the individual did not provide permission. This is especially problematic when children are involved. As a result, it is important to obtain consent of everyone prior to posting. Alternatively, the nonprofit should be communicating in advance of an event to the participants that pictures or videos of the event will be posted and that by attending the event the individuals consent to being included in the photos or videos to be posted. Nevertheless, depending on the activities, it may still be necessary to obtain permission, which should be in writing. To the extent that the nonprofit is providing health care services to individuals, the pictures or videos of the individuals might be further protected under federal and state privacy laws, including HIPAA.

Sales of Goods and Services

General Rules

Sales in stores or through catalogs, sales tax, and foreign business registration requirements

Some nonprofit organizations, such as museums, maintain stores in which goods related to the nonprofit corporation's activities can be purchased. Others sell products through catalogs. Whether the sale of such goods constitutes an unrelated trade or business is generally assessed on an item-by-item basis, with sales of certain items being deemed "related" (and therefore not treated as UBI) and others being "unrelated" (with revenues from such items taxable as UBI). In addition, if the nonprofit transacts business in states other than the state in which the nonprofit is incorporated, the nonprofit may be required to register in such other states as a foreign corporation doing business in the state.

In general, such stores are required to collect and remit state and local sales and use taxes on their product sales. State and local sales and use taxes also must be collected and remitted on catalog sales, *if* the seller has a physical presence in the states to which the items are shipped. As a practical matter, a catalog seller may be required to collect and remit such taxes for the states in which it or any of its property is located, and in any state in which its employees or representatives engage in business on its behalf.

Auctions and trade shows

Many § 501(c)(3) corporations raise money through annual charity auctions. Charities that conduct traditional auctions generally do not pay UBIT on the income they receive from donors, provided that the auction is not "regularly carried on" or the auctioned items are all donated. Similarly, trade organizations (such as the ABA) that are exempt from federal taxation under § 501(c)(6) of the Code may raise money through trade shows that coincide with one or more meetings of the organization's membership. The trade organization receives revenue by renting space to exhibitors and receiving underwriting contributions from corporate sponsors. As with charitable auctions, such trade show revenue is generally not treated as subject to taxation as UBI, since it is not regularly carried on.

Sales of mailing lists

In contrast to sales of goods or services to supporters and others, many nonprofits raise money through the sale of their mailing lists. The value of these lists may be enhanced if the nonprofit also collects demographic information on its membership. Nonprofits may choose to sell mailing lists only to other nonprofits, or to both nonprofit and for-profit entities. Typically, the sale of mailing and membership lists is taxable as UBI. In addition, states may impose restrictions on sales of mailing lists by nonprofit organizations. However, even if not required by law, to preserve member goodwill, many organizations give their members the opportunity to opt out by requesting that their information not be sold to other organizations.

Internet Applications

Many nonprofit corporations have begun to take advantage of the Internet's wide range of business opportunities. The descriptions that follow address some of the legal implications of several such opportunities.

Online stores

Many nonprofits have established online stores or virtual storefronts, through which they sell merchandise and services from their websites. For example, a museum that operates a physical gift shop also might operate an online store to allow visitors to its website to purchase the same merchandise over the Internet. Even a nonprofit that does *not* also operate a physical store might raise money and promote its visibility by selling books it publishes over the Internet. In comparison to the overhead needed to maintain a physical store or catalog operation, the low overhead costs of maintaining a sales location on the web will enable many more nonprofits to sell goods and services in this fashion.

UBI issues. Just as is the case for physical stores or catalog sales, a nonprofit organization's revenue from the sale of goods or services over the web will generally be determined to be (nontaxable) related revenue or (taxable) UBI, on an item-by-item basis. Directors of nonprofit corporations selling an extensive array of goods and services over the Internet should make sure that, just as for traditional store and catalog sales, the nonprofit has an accounting system that tracks sales revenue and UBI status on an item-by-item basis.

Sales tax issues. The state and local sales tax treatment of Internet sales is currently similar to that of catalog sales (described in the section "*Sales in Stores...*" above), such that sales taxes for Internet sales are generally not required to be collected and paid except in states in which the organization has some form of physical presence. Directors of nonprofit corporations that are selling goods and services over the Internet will need to stay informed as to how the sales tax debate is resolved to determine what, if any, sales taxes they may be responsible for collecting.

While the standards in this area are still evolving, directors should be aware that making Internet sales to buyers located in other states or abroad may expose the corporation to potential tax liability in these other jurisdictions. However, if an organization is otherwise subject to sales tax liability (e.g., in the jurisdictions in which it has physical locations), it cannot avoid paying taxes for Internet sales to persons residing in these areas. A good number of states have participated in the Streamlined Sales Tax Project, which has been developing uniform standards and definitions for collecting sales tax, and has approved software from certain vendors to ease the collection burdens on sellers. Information on the model statutes that have been developed and the progress in getting the statutes adopted in various states is available at www.streamlinedsalestax.org.

Whether Internet sales activity constitutes doing business in a state, requiring registration as a foreign corporation. Currently, the law is unclear as to whether reaching a state through the Internet—rather than through physical presence—will cause a nonprofit corporation to be doing business in that state. However, if a nonprofit corporation finds that it is transacting business in one or more states in which it is not incorporated or otherwise has a physical presence, it should obtain legal advice regarding whether registration is required at least in those states. Failure to register as a foreign corporation doing business in another state when required may prevent a corporation from availing itself of legal process against the state's residents and could result in the imposition of other sanctions.

Secure payment methods. In traditional store and catalog settings, most individuals assume the security of credit cards and other personal information provided in connection with a purchase. Security is still a significant issue in Internet sales transactions, given the possibilities of hacker theft of credit card numbers and other concerns regarding the transmission of one's personal information across the globally linked Internet. Accordingly, a nonprofit corporation engaging in Internet sales transactions should take care to verify that it has appropriate security measures in place to avoid liability for allowing unauthorized access to this information. These security measures should be frequently reviewed and improved as both security technology and hacker capabilities evolve.

Charity auctions

Online charity auctions are an increasingly popular means of fundraising for nonprofits. Some nonprofit organizations administer the auctions themselves, while others rely on an outside provider. As noted above, charities that conduct traditional auctions generally do not pay UBIT on the income they receive from donors, because the auction is not regularly carried on and/or involves the sale of donated items. In contrast, however, many online charity auctions may not be held only once or a few times a year; because of the ease of setting up online auctions, some nonprofit organizations may hold them frequently, such as once a month, or even maintain a continuous auction, with a differing array of products available to be bid on. Some such auctions, especially those held frequently, may be more likely to include purchased merchandise as well as donated merchandise. If both of these factors are present in online auctions conducted by a nonprofit, the revenues from such auctions may be taxable to the organization as UBI.

Even if an online auction is held only once a year, nonprofit organizations may encounter UBI issues if, due to unfamiliarity with the Internet environment, they rely on an outside provider to conduct their auctions. If the organization does not retain the primary responsibility for the publicity of the auction and otherwise maintain certain controls to ensure that the auction is properly conducted as a fundraising event for IRS purposes, the auction revenues may be treated as UBI.[20]

Virtual trade shows

Some trade associations have organized online virtual trade shows that are modeled on a traditional trade show format. The trade association may rent "display space" on its own site or may simply provide multiple links on its site to the websites of various vendors, or "virtual exhibitors." Some trade associations sponsor year-round virtual trade shows, while others plan virtual trade shows to coincide with their organizations' regular annual shows.

Directors of nonprofit corporations should be aware that although, as noted above, income from traditional trade show activities is generally not subject to tax as UBI, virtual trade shows raise a number of UBI issues. Although the IRS has not yet provided official guidance in this area, the UBI treatment of income from virtual trade shows is likely to depend on whether a trade organization can demonstrate that its online activities are substantially similar to those of a traditional trade show. For example, because a traditional trade show is a finite event, it is unlikely that income from a year-round virtual trade show would be excluded from UBI treatment.[21]

Sale of e-mail addresses and other electronically gathered information

Just as many nonprofits have found that there is a market for their member/subscriber mailing and other information, nonprofit organizations have discovered that they may earn money from the sale of e-mail addresses or other data on supporters that can be mined by other organizations. The sale of e-mail addresses and the sale and maintenance of other electronically gathered information raises donor privacy issues. Although many privacy issues also are present in the non-Internet context, individuals may have greater sensitivity about information that is gathered through Internet communications compared to more traditional means.

Local, state, and federal legislators are in the process of reviewing the need for legislation to protect individual-specific information gathered online. While federal law generally does not currently protect such information, the Federal Trade Commission (FTC) recommends that nonprofits that gather donor information using the Internet establish a policy regarding the privacy of donor information and post it on their websites. The FTC has developed four "fair information practices," which would require nonprofits to:

(1) notify donors regarding what personal information they are gathering, how it is used, and with whom it will be shared;
(2) offer donors the option of directing that their information not be shared with third parties;
(3) provide donors with information regarding the security measures that protect their information; and
(4) allow donors to access their information, to review and correct it.[22]

Since the public is increasingly concerned with consumer and donor privacy issues, legislators are likely to respond by developing new laws and regulations in this area. (See further discussion of Internet privacy issues in the section *"Protecting Electronic Records Information"* below.) Directors of nonprofit corporations should consult with legal counsel on a regular basis to ensure that their practices involving donor information are in compliance with changing legal standards.

Unsolicited commercial e-mails

Federal law sets forth specific requirements for the content of unsolicited e-mails containing a commercial message.[23] Under the CAN-SPAM Act, a commercial message is a message that has as its primary purpose a commercial advertisement or promotion of a product or service. Messages that have a primary purpose relating to a specific transaction or relationship between the sender and consumer are exempt from the CAN-SPAM Act's requirements.

In order to be a transaction or relationship message, the primary purpose of the e-mail must be to do one of the following: (1) facilitate, complete, or confirm a commercial transaction previously agreed to by the e-mail recipient; (2) provide warranty, product recall, safety, or security information for a product purchased by the e-mail recipient; (3) provide certain information regarding a subscription, membership, account, loan, or similar ongoing relationship; (4) provide information regarding an employment relationship or related benefit; or (5) deliver goods or services that the e-mail recipient is entitled to receive as a result of a previously agreed upon transaction.[24]

Any person, including nonprofit organizations, that initiates commercial e-mail messages is required to comply with the CAN-SPAM requirements. These requirements include, among other things, a prohibition on deceptive subject headings in e-mails, the need for accurate information on the sender and the subject matter of the communication, the ability of e-mail recipients to opt-out of receiving commercial e-mails, which includes a clear and conspicuous notice of a right to "opt-out" of receipt of the e-mails, clear identification of the commercial nature of the e-mail, and the sender's valid physical postal address.[25] From a compliance standpoint, a nonprofit that is sending commercial messages should limit such messages to those persons who have affirmatively agreed (or opted-in) to receive such e-mails.

Posting Information Returns and Exemption Applications on the Internet

General Rule

Federal tax law requires tax-exempt organizations to provide copies of their exemption applications and three most recent information returns (Form 990s) to anyone requesting them in person or in writing.[26]

Internet Application

Tax-exempt organizations can be relieved of the requirement to physically provide copies of their exemption applications and Form 990s if they post these documents on the organization's website or another site collecting similar applications and returns.[27] The organization must provide the web address where the documents can be found to anyone who asks for it. Organizations electing this web-posting option should be careful to post a return identical to what was filed with the IRS (although confidential information may be excluded to the same extent as for 990s provided to the public by more conventional means). Having the return available on another site, such as www.guidestar.org—which posts all Forms 990 filed with the IRS—will also meet the legal requirement for disclosure, provided that it is a complete and accurate copy of what was filed with the IRS, with the exception of certain donor information on Schedule B of Form 990, which may be kept confidential. GuideStar, which gets copies of all Form 990 from the IRS and posts them as a matter of course, redacts signatures from the documents to protect against misuse. As a technical matter, the redaction means that the GuideStar version is not a perfect copy of the return filed with the IRS. Still, as it contains all the other information someone making a legitimate request could want to see, it should be rare for a nonprofit to encounter someone wanting a return who is not satisfied with what is available on GuideStar. It is important to note, however, that there is often a significant delay in GuideStar's postings from the time of filing; therefore, someone wanting the most current filing may need to obtain it directly from the organization. In addition, GuideStar does not post the exemption applications. Form 990s filed by nonprofits also are now available on the IRS website.

Implications of Serving as an Information Exchange

Defamation and Other Torts

General rule

Any organization may be held liable for defamation or invasion of privacy, based on statements about individuals made by the organization (such as in a publication) or by persons associated with the organization (including a nonprofit's volunteers).

Internet applications

Potential organizational liability for the provision of listservs, chat rooms, and social media. A nonprofit corporation may determine that its purposes are served by the provision of listservs (electronic mailing lists), chat rooms, social media, and similar technological meeting places, available to organization members or other interested persons. Messages exchanged and information made available in these forums have the potential to reach a very large audience. Consequently, there is an increased potential for claims that the content of an individual message is defamatory, invades privacy, or constitutes impermissible political activities. Messages sent through these forums by employees and others who may be seen as agents for the corporation may be attributed to the organization for purposes of these tort claims.

A corporation offering or using listservs, chat rooms, social media, and other such services may therefore wish to incorporate online disclaimers noting that the statements made in these contexts are solely those of the participants and are not endorsed or in any way attributable to the corporation.

In addition, a nonprofit corporation needs to make sure that any information or photos it posts on its website do not raise the concerns identified above.

Potential organizational liability for e-mail messages and use of social media. Defamation, privacy, and similar concerns are also present in e-mail and social media use by an organization's employees and volunteers. The nonprofit corporation's board should therefore make sure that employees and others using the corporation's e-mail system or communicating via social media on behalf of the corporation are regularly reminded about the organization's policy of the appropriate use of e-mail and websites and social media, and to avoid making or distributing offensive or other derogatory remarks or material by e-mail.

Liability Protection Available by Registration as an Internet Service Provider

The Digital Millennium Copyright Act of 1998 (DMCA) permits organizations acting as "Internet service providers" or "ISPs" to avoid liability for copyright infringement when users post material on a website the organization maintains.[28] This law defines a "service provider" as "an entity offering the transmission, routing, or providing of connections for digital online communications, between or among points specified by a user, of material of the user's choosing, without modification to the content of the material as sent or received."[29] Operating a chat room or other interactive site may cause an organization to be treated as a service provider for purposes of this law even if it does not otherwise provide users with Internet access.

To qualify for the DMCA protections, the ISP must: (1) not receive a financial benefit directly attributable to the infringing activity, where the ISP has the right and ability to control the activity; (2) not have knowledge that the material or activity is infringing or be aware of facts or circumstances that make the infringement apparent; (3) expeditiously remove or disable access to the material if it learns of the infringement or receives a notification of infringement from a copyright holder or an agent of the owner; (4) designate an agent to receive DMCA notifications and register the agent's name and contact information with the United States Copyright Office and make this information available on its service; (5) accommodate technical measures used by copyright owners to identify or protect copyrighted works; and (6) adopt, implement, and inform subscribers and account holders of a policy and procedure for terminating a repeat infringer's subscriptions and accounts.

To invoke the liability protection available under this law, the organization must register the name of an agent with the U.S. Copyright Office, which is designated to accept complaints from those who believe their copyrights have been infringed on a website maintained by an ISP.

In addition, the Communications Decency Act of 1996, which generally imposes criminal sanctions for knowingly transmitting obscene messages or materials over the Internet, provides broad immunity for online providers, including website and forum operators, with respect to postings by third parties using their services.[30]

Tax Consequences of Providing Internet Access to Others

Providing access to the Internet in exchange for a fee constitutes a trade or business, and unless that business is substantially related to the organization's tax-exempt purpose, the income generated will be subject to federal taxation as UBI. For example, providing Internet access for a fee substantially below cost to community centers in poor neighborhoods may be considered a charitable activity for a § 501(c)(3) organization, rather than an unrelated trade or business, if the activity is related to the organization's charitable purpose.[31] If providing Internet access is the organization's only function, it may qualify for tax-exempt status as an integral part of another exempt organization. Thus, a corporation may serve as an ISP to members of a nonprofit university community and qualify as an integral part of the university, or perhaps as a § 501(c)(12) organization. (The latter category includes rural telephone cooperatives, electric cooperatives, and the like.)

Note: Trade associations should take care before offering Internet access to members. Trade associations violate the requirements for continuing federal income tax exemption if they provide "particular services" to members. The IRS has not yet ruled as to whether providing Internet access to individual account holders qualifies as a particular service. On the other hand, providing a listserv, chat room, or website for the exchange of information among association members is unlikely to run afoul of the particular service restriction.[32]

Protecting Electronic Records Information

If a nonprofit organization maintains, in electronic form, medical records, student records, or other records that it is legally bound to keep private, it should verify that effective systems are in place to assure that unauthorized users cannot obtain access to those records through the organization's Internet connections. Because hackers continually become more proficient at finding ways to breach computer-based security systems, the board should require appropriate management personnel to periodically confirm that adequate security measures have been taken to prevent unauthorized access to confidential information of others or of the corporation that is stored in electronic form or transmitted over the Internet.

Moreover, the organization should make sure that it keeps abreast of legal requirements relating to the electronic storage and transmission of different kinds of personal information relating to the organization's activities. For example, nonprofit health care providers must comply with the detailed federal rules issued under the Health Insurance Portability and Accountability Act (HIPAA) regarding the use and disclosure of electronic and other medical records. The Children's Online Privacy Protection Act of 1998 (COPPA) also provides special rules that apply to websites that attract children.[33] The rules implementing COPPA set out what a website operator must include in a privacy policy, when and how to seek variable consent from a parent, and what responsibilities an operator has to protect children's privacy and safety online.

Data Protection

The possibility of loss of or improper access to data, including data containing personally identifiable information (PII), has become a significant risk for many organizations, including nonprofits. As a result, it is important that directors are aware of various applicable federal laws (including COPPA and HIPAA) as well as comprehensive state data privacy statutes that impact website operations and other uses of PII.[34]

Similar to for profit businesses, it is incumbant upon a nonprofit to implement appropriate physical, organizational, and technical safeguards to protect against PII and other sensitive data being lost or improperly accessed. Loss of data can result in significant reputational harm, legal liability, and financial penalities and can lead to a loss of donors. Data protection and retention plans can help mitigate risks associated with data loss and improper access. Organizations should also be reviewing any contracts with service providers to ensure that they comply with applicable federal and state data protection laws and otherwise properly protect the nonprofit in case the service provider is the cause for any loss or improper access or release. In addition, nonprofits should create an incident response plan to address data breach situations. Cybersecurity insurance also has become extremely important in protecting organizations.

Identity Theft

Some nonprofits may be subject to the "Red Flags Rule" that requires them to implement a written identity theft prevention program to detect warning signs of identity theft in the day-to-day operations.[35] The rationale for such a program is that by identifying "red flags" in advance, the organization is better able to identify suspicious activity that might arise and take steps to prevent it from going further. A program requires that the organization (1) identify relevant patterns, practices, and specific forms of activity (called "red flags") that could give rise to possible identity theft; (2) incorporate business practices to detect red flags; (3) describe appropriate responses to red flags in order to prevent and mitigate identity theft, and (4) update the program periodically to reflect changes in risk from identity theft.

The Red Flags Rules apply to "financial institutions" and "creditors" that hold consumer accounts designed to permit multiple payments or transactions. Many nonprofits were subject to the Red Flags Rule by virtue of being deemed creditors; however, recent amendments to the definition of creditor significantly limited the types of parties covered. Under the amendments, a creditor must regularly and in the ordinary course of business, meet one of three general criteria: (1) obtain or use consumer reports in connection with a credit transaction; (2) furnish information to consumer reporting agencies in connection with a credit transaction; or (3) advance funds to or on behalf of someone, except for funds for expenses incidental to a service the creditor provides to that person.

See the Suggested Questions and Checklist following the Endnotes below to review the issues discussed in this chapter.

Endnotes

1. Most of the states and a relatively smaller number of cities and counties require registration of organizations that conduct charitable solicitations in that state or other jurisdiction. *See* The Unified Registration Statement, The Multi-State Filer Project, www.multistatefiling.org/#yes_states; Urban Institute, Legal Compendium, Regulation of the Charitable Sector Project, http://www.urban.org/policy-centers/center-nonprofits-and-philanthropy/projects/regulation-charitable-sector-project. For a copy of the Unified Registration Statement, *see* www.multistatefiling.org.
2. *See, e.g.*, CAL. BUS. & PROF. CODE § 17510.4; GA CODE ANN. § 43-17-8; MINN. STAT. § 309.556.
3. *The Charleston Principles: Guidelines on Charitable Solicitations Using the Internet* is available at www.nasconet.org.
4. *See* I.R.C. § 170(f)(8).
5. *See* I.R.C. § 6115.
6. *See* IRS Publication No. 1771.
7. *See* CAL. GOV. CODE §12599.6(b).
8. *See* Christina Nooney, *Tax Exempt Organizations and the Internet,* 27 EXEMPT ORGANIZATION TAX REVIEW 38, 33–39 (2000).
9. *See* Cheryl Chasin, Susan Ruth, and Robert Harper, *Tax Exempt Organizations and World Wide Web Fundraising and Advertising on the Internet, in* IRS EXEMPT ORGANIZATIONS TECHNICAL INSTRUCTION PROGRAM FOR FY 2000 139 (a good discussion of individual merchant affiliate programs). *See also* Alice Anderson and Robert Wexler, *Making Use of the Internet—Issues for Tax-Exempt Organizations,* 92 JOURNAL OF TAXATION 309 (May 2000).
10. *See* IRS Publication 598.
11. *See* Michael I. Sanders, *Joint Ventures Involving Tax-Exempt Organizations* (4th ed. John Wiley & Sons, Inc. 2013).
12. Cal. Assembly Bill No. 488 (2021).
13. *See* I.R.C. § 513(i); Reg. § 1.513-4.
14. *See* Chasin, Ruth, and Harper, *supra* note 8, at 137; Donna Moore and Robert Harper, *Internet Service Providers Exemption Issues Under*

IRC § 501(c)(3) and § 501(c)(12), in IRS EXEMPT ORGANIZATIONS TECHNICAL INSTRUCTION PROGRAM FOR FY 1999 64; *see also* PLR 200303062 (October 22, 2002).

15. *See Treas.* Reg. § 1.513-4(c)(2)(iv).
16. *See* Chasin, Ruth, and Harper, *supra* note 9, at 135.
17. *See* Anderson and Wexler, *supra* note 9, for a good discussion of issues to consider when developing a linkage policy.
18. *See* Publication 557, Ch. 3.
19. A good survey of copyright and trademark issues for nonprofits can be found in Maria Malaro, *A Legal Primer on Managing Museum Collections*, 3rd ed. (Smithsonian Institute Press 2012). *See also* Lisa A. Runquist and Jeannie Carmedelle Frey, Eds., *Guide to Representing Religious Organizations* 227 (American Bar Association 2009) (discussing copyright issues for religious organizations).
20. *See* Anderson and Wexler, *supra* note 9; Nooney, *supra* note 8, at 37.
21. *See* Anderson and Wexler, *supra* note 9; Chasin, Ruth, and Harper, *supra* note 9, at 135–137. *See* IRS Announcement 2000-84.
22. *See Privacy Online: Fair Information Practices in the Electronic Marketplace: A Report to Congress,* May 22, 2000, *available at* https://www.ftc.gov/reports/privacy-online-fair-information-practices-electronic-marketplace-federal-trade-commission-report.
23. *See* Controlling the Assault of Non-Solicited Pornography and Marketing Act (CAN-SPAM Act), 15 U.S.C. §§ 7701-13. The Federal Trade Commission has implemented regulations under the CAN-SPAM Act under 16 C.F.R. Part 316.
24. *See* 15 U.S.C. § 7702(17)(A).
25. *See* 15 U.S.C. § 7704; 16 C.F.R. § 316.5.
26. *See* I.R.C. § 6104(d)(1)-(2).
27. *See* I.R.C. § 6104(d)(4).
28. 17 U.S.C. §512.
29. 17 U.S.C. § 512(k)(1)(A).
30. *See* 47 U.S.C. § 230.
31. In a Technical Advice Memorandum, the IRS concluded that an Internet Service Provider that gave Internet access solely to low-income people and other § 501(c)(3) organizations for fees set substantially below cost qualified as a § 501(c)(3) organization. I.R.S. TECH. ADV. MEM. 200208069 (Jan. 18, 2002).
32. *See generally* Moore and Harper, *supra* note 14, at 55–66.
33. 15 U.S.C. § 6501 et. seq. Details and current releases relating to COPPA can be found at http://business.ftc.gov/privacy-and-security.
34. *See, e.g.,* Sanford P. Shatz and Paul J. Lysobey, *Privacy Laws Continue Their Spread Across the Country,* 78 Bus. Law. 551 (Spring 2023).
35. 15 U.S.C. § 1681m; 12 C.F.R. § 222.90.

Suggested Questions for Directors Regarding Supervision of Internet Activities

(1) Does the corporation currently have, or is it considering creating, a web page, or does it engage in other activities using the Internet, such as social media?

(2) If the corporation engages in fundraising over the Internet, is it required to register under the charitable solicitation rules or foreign corporation laws of any other state, locality, or non-U.S. jurisdiction?

(3) Does the corporation receive donations from the Internet sites or activities of other entities? Has the corporation's board approved these activities? If other entities are collecting donations on the organization's behalf, are those other entities properly authorized to serve as agents for the organization?

(4) If the corporation has a website, does its site contain any acknowledgments or advertisements for corporate sponsors? Does the board understand the difference? If it contains advertisements, is there a way those advertisements can be converted to acknowledgments to limit UBIT?

(5) If the corporation is making sales over the Internet, has it investigated any responsibility it has for collecting and paying over sales tax to those states where it has a physical presence or where its customers are located?

(6) If the corporation is making sales over the Internet, are the sales related to its exempt purpose? If not, are the sales regularly carried on? If so, how is the organization handling any UBIT liability?

(7) Has the board evaluated whether and in what manner it may wish to engage in lobbying activities over the Internet? If it chooses to use the Internet for lobbying, has the corporation—if it is a § 501(c)(3)—made an election under IRC § 501(h)? Has it developed policies informed by IRS definitions of lobbying that will allow for strong advocacy while limiting lobbying expenditures? If it chooses to do some lobbying over the Internet, does it have an accounting system in place to gather the data necessary to allocate common costs for things like website maintenance and website hosting?

(8) Is the board aware of the distinctions between activity that would constitute permissible public education on broad issues of public policy and democratic engagement, on the one hand, and impermissible involvement in political campaigns, on the other? If the organization intends to engage in activities that may fall into

the first category, has the board developed a website policy that will help all staff and volunteers produce website content that will not cross the line and become political campaign intervention?

(9) Has the organization reviewed the copies of its Form 990 that are available on www.guidestar.org and www.irs.gov to be sure they are accurate?

(10) If the organization uses the Internet to collect information about people, what privacy notices or protections is the organization required to place on its site?

(11) Does the organization post pictures or videos on its website or social media and, if so, is it obtaining permission from the owners or individuals in the pictures or videos?

Checklist: Internet Activities: Fundraising, Selling Goods and Services, Lobbying, and Other Activities

Note: For simplicity. these and other chapters describe a corporation having a chair, who presides over the board of directors; a chief executive, who may be a staff person; an executive committee; a governance/nominating committee; and an audit committee. (We recognize, however, that in many smaller and other nonprofits, these committee functions may be performed by either the executive committee or the board as a whole.) We also assume a legal counsel—someone, paid or unpaid, having primary responsibility for the corporation's legal affairs. Many corporations, especially larger nonprofits, may have other committees established for specific purposes, such as establishing executive compensation; monitoring compliance with legal requirements; and overseeing investments and other financial matters.

Subject	Review By	How Often	Comment
1. Does the corporation raise money through contributions solicited or received over the Internet?	Chair, chief executive, legal counsel	At least quarterly, with annual reports to the full board	There are multiple ways of fund-raising over the Internet. Despite the relative ease of doing so from a technical and resource perspective, directors need to be aware of the legal implications of this activity.
2. In what states and localities may the corporation be required to register under the charitable solicitation laws as a result of its Internet fundraising activity?	Chair, chief executive, legal counsel	At least annually	Application of the charitable solicitation laws to Internet fund-raising is not always clear, but standards are evolving. Smaller nonprofits lacking the funds to pay registration fees in multiple jurisdictions may want to take steps to limit the focus of their Internet fundraising to a few or even a single state.

Subject	Review By	How Often	Comment
3. Do individuals or entities act as fundraisers or sources of contributions to the corporation? If so, do we understand the legal implications of this activity for the corporation and donors?	Chair, chief executive, legal counsel	At least annually	If the corporation raises funds through websites or social media or the assistance of other organizations, the board should ensure that management staff and legal counsel have reviewed the arrangements for compliance with laws governing charitable solicitations, charitable fundraisers, and tax-exempt contributions.
4. Are there acknowledgements or advertisements of for-profit companies on the corporation's website?	Chair, chief executive, legal counsel	At least annually	The board may want to adopt a policy for sponsor acknowledgments and third-party advertising on the corporation's website.

Subject	Review By	How Often	Comment
5. Does the corporation provide links to the website of for-profit companies, nonprofit advocacy organizations, or candidates for political office? Or, is the nonprofit aware of any such advocacy organizations that have links to the nonprofit's website on their site? What legal issues are raised by such links?	Chief executive, chief information officer (CIO), or lead technology staff person	At least annually	If a link on a tax-exempt corporation's website is determined to constitute involvement in a political campaign or promotion of a candidate for political office, the corporation's tax-exempt status could be threatened.
6. Does the organization engage in lobbying activity over the Internet? If so, does this activity meet the general "insubstantial" test, or if applicable, the standards for organizations that have made the election to have their lobby activity covered by § 501(h) of the Internal Revenue Code?	Chief executive, legal counsel, fundraising staff	At least annually for the report to the full board, with frequent monitoring at the staff level	Internet lobbying activities may not be costly but directors should be aware that the IRS's position on the appropriate ways to measure these activities is still developing.

Subject	Review By	How Often	Comment
7. Are the corporation's copyrights, trademarks, and service marks properly protected on the corporation's website and through e-mail activities of corporation employees?	Legal counsel, consultation with lead technology staff person or chief information officer	At least annually	
8. Are copyright restrictions on works by third parties complied with before these works are posted on the corporation's website?	Legal counsel, consultation with lead technology staff person or chief information officer	At least annually, with educational reminders to staff	Staff should be educated regarding the use of copyrighted works on the corporation's website.
9. Does the corporation sell goods or services over the Internet? If so:	Chief executive		
(a) Have UBI and sales tax issues been examined?	(a) Legal counsel	(a) Upon inception of any such activity; at least annually thereafter	
(b) Does this activity require registration as a foreign corporation in any states?	(b) Legal counsel	(b) Upon inception of any such activity; at least annually thereafter	

Subject	Review By	How Often	Comment
(c) Are the names, credit card numbers, and other personal information of customers adequately protected from unauthorized disclosure, or hackers, and does the corporation otherwise comply with applicable privacy laws (and corporation privacy policies) regarding this information?	(c) Chief executive, lead technology executive, and/or technology consultant staff person	(c) Ideally, at least quarterly	
10. Does the corporation make its Form 990s available on its website or the website of a Form 990 compiler? What about its 1023 exemption application?	Chair, chief executive	At least annually	If the corporation relies on another organization to list the corporation's Form 990 on that organization's website, the corporation should periodically check the accuracy of the posted information.

Subject	Review By	How Often	Comment
11. Has the corporation taken appropriate steps to limit claims by third parties resulting from:		At least annually	Defamation claims may be made by individuals or other entities based on comments made in these electronic settings.
(a) Chat rooms, listservs, and social media either provided or used by the corporation?	(a) Technology legal counsel		
(b) Employee e-mail and social media activity?	(b) Technology legal counsel		
12. If the corporation provides chat rooms or listservs, has it registered as an Internet service provider?	Chief executive, technology counsel, or consultant	When such activities begun; at least annually thereafter	
13. Has the corporation taken appropriate steps to protect against loss of or improper access to data?	Chief executive, technology counsel, or consultant	At least annually	

Chapter 8:
Volunteers

Chapter 8
Volunteers

Many nonprofit corporations find it useful or even essential to use the services of volunteers. The nonprofit director should understand not only how volunteers can be used to enhance the corporation's mission, but also the potential legal issues relating to the use of volunteers.

There is a prevalent use of volunteers in the nonprofit sector. In some circumstances, use of volunteers is essential to implement the corporate purpose, especially when the nonprofit corporation simply does not have the resources to perform its services without volunteers. In many cases, the use of volunteers is itself demonstrative of the corporation's mission. The board should periodically evaluate what part volunteers should play in the corporation. For example, is there a role or need for volunteers in implementing a new program or service? Are there services that volunteers might provide that would enhance the corporation's fulfillment of its mission and involve more of the nonprofit's community in its activities? If so, what are the legal implications of using volunteers?

Risks Associated with Using Volunteers

Volunteers working on behalf of a nonprofit corporation are agents of the nonprofit corporation in the eyes of the law. That is, their acts or omissions and their care or negligence in performing their activities as volunteers are, within limits, considered to be the acts or omissions of the nonprofit corporation. *As a general rule, the nonprofit corporation will not be exonerated from liability arising from the conduct of the agent simply because the organization is a nonprofit corporation or because the agent was a volunteer.*

Nonprofit corporations can be and are held responsible for the actions of their volunteers and are expected, within reason, to foresee and address the risks associated with the use of volunteers. The potential risks include situations in which a volunteer is used to represent the nonprofit corporation to the public or in providing services consistent with the organization's purposes—for example, a program in which the nonprofit corporation sends volunteers into homes to provide services, uses volunteers to work in a position of trust with vulnerable individuals such as minors or the developmentally disabled, or uses volunteers to drive or to perform other potentially dangerous activities.

Minimizing the Corporation's Liability

Because of the potential for liability involved in the use of volunteers, the nonprofit corporation should develop standards, guidelines, and procedures for the use of volunteers rather than enlisting the assistance of volunteers on a random or sporadic basis. This does not mean that there must be a large number of staff devoted to developing and administering a volunteer program. Rather, the decision to use as well as the use of volunteers should include an evaluation of the requirements for each volunteer position and written standards for selection, training, and supervision.

Selection of volunteers: written standards

Nonprofit corporations should develop written standards for selecting volunteers. Depending on the nature of the volunteer position, the standards for selection may include education, experience, training requirements, consideration of the volunteer's ability to commit time to the position, and the volunteer's suitability for the particular position, such as working with children. The nonprofit corporation should then use these standards to verify a volunteer's suitability for the position. This can include requiring a written volunteer application form, personal interview, background check, driving record, reference check, and other methods to verify that the volunteer is an appropriate individual for the position. If a criminal or other background check is determined to be necessary for a volunteer position, the nonprofit corporation should obtain a signed release from the applicant authorizing the corporation to obtain the necessary information from the appropriate agencies. The board should consult with legal counsel in preparing the release form.

Oversight of volunteer activities: policies and procedures

The nonprofit corporation should develop written materials for training and supervising volunteers. These materials may include written procedures, policies, or guidelines for a volunteer to use when acting on behalf of the nonprofit corporation. The corporation should provide any volunteer with clear directions and sufficient training. Developing written policies and procedures is important because a nonprofit corporation may be directly liable for its own conduct if a volunteer injures a third party due to the corporation's inadequate training or supervision of the volunteer.

Insurance

The board should make sure that the nonprofit corporation is covered by the corporation's insurance for the activities of its volunteers. For example, if a nonprofit corporation is engaged in the distribution of goods or services involving the volunteer's use of the volunteer's own automobile, the corporation may be liable for injuries caused by the volunteer's negligent driving of that automobile, even though the nonprofit corporation does not own the automobile or pay the driver.

The nonprofit corporation's insurance policies should be reviewed and modified, if necessary, to ensure that they cover the potential liability of the nonprofit corporation due to the conduct of a volunteer. *Such coverage is not automatic* and may be an issue under several types of coverage, such as the corporation's general liability insurance and directors and officers insurance. Some insurance policies specifically address the unique organizational aspects and activities of nonprofit corporations, including volunteer activities. It is good practice to review all policies with legal counsel or an insurance broker experienced in working with nonprofit insurance issues, to confirm that the organization's activities and its agents are properly insured. In addition, before anyone is allowed to drive either using their own vehicle or a corporation's vehicle, the corporation should check the individual's driver license and driving record and obtain evidence that the person's individual insurance coverage is in effect.

Protecting the Volunteer from Individual Liability

Volunteers also may be sued individually for injuries they cause while acting in a volunteer capacity. The nonprofit corporation should consider what it should do to protect its volunteers in such situations.

Statutes Protecting Volunteers

Most states have volunteer protection statutes limiting the liability of volunteers.[1] Although the scope of the protection differs somewhat from state to state, most states provide at least some degree of immunity from civil liability for a volunteer if the volunteer acts within the scope of the volunteer's duties, in good faith, and the injury is not caused by the volunteer's willful or wanton conduct.[2] There is also a federal Volunteer Protection Act, enacted in 1997, that provides some liability protection for volunteers of a nonprofit organization or governmental agency. In general, under the federal statute, volunteers will not be held liable for the harm they caused if they were acting within the scope of their responsibilities, they were properly licensed or certified (if required), the harm was not caused by their willful or criminal conduct, gross negligence, or reckless conduct, and the harm was not caused by the volunteer operating a vehicle for which the operator must have a license or that must be insured.[3]

The federal statute preempts state law to the extent that it is inconsistent with the federal statute unless the state law provides additional protection from liability relating to volunteers. *The board of directors should make sure it understands the scope of available state and federal statutory protection for volunteers by consulting with legal counsel knowledgeable in the area.* To the extent that these statutes do not provide complete protection, the board should evaluate whether the corporation has adequate insurance coverage for volunteer activities. The board also should consider alerting volunteers to the potential need for personal insurance coverage for their own activities. (See further discussion in the section "*Insurance for Volunteers*" below.)

Insurance for Volunteers

Volunteers should examine whether their individual insurance may cover any injury with which they were involved while acting as a volunteer. The board should make sure that, if possible, the corporation's volunteers are insured under its insurance policies, that is, the policy covers not only the corporation's liability for the acts of its volunteers but also directly covers the volunteers. Special insurance riders or policies may be required to insure volunteers for a special occasion or fundraising event, such as a walkathon, run, or other event. In these circumstances, an insurer may require that the corporation obtain a waiver and release of liability from the volunteers for the event.

Indemnification of Volunteers

The board should examine whether it can, or should, provide indemnification for volunteers. The nonprofit corporation acts in some states expressly permit indemnification of agents—such as volunteers (who are not directors). In these states, the board should review its articles of incorporation and bylaws to determine whether they address the indemnification of volunteers. For instance, it is not unusual to find that the indemnification provisions of a nonprofit corporation's bylaws mandate that the corporation "shall" provide indemnification to the "fullest extent permitted by law." Although the scope of such required indemnification may be limited to the officers and directors, it also may specifically apply to the corporation's "agents"—a category within which most volunteers would presumably fit.

Before broadening the corporation's indemnification obligations to include volunteers, the board should assess the corporation's actual financial ability to indemnify volunteers and whether the corporation's obligation to indemnify its volunteers could be broader than its insurance coverage, potentially requiring the corporation to dip into its own assets to fulfill the indemnity obligations. In those states in which the nonprofit corporation act does not expressly address indemnification of volunteers, the nonprofit can still choose to indemnify its volunteers; however, in such a situation it will be important to determine the standards for determining whether a volunteer should be indemnified.[4]

Claims by Volunteers against the Corporation

The use of volunteers may expose the nonprofit corporation to claims by the volunteer against the corporation. These can include a claim that the individual is an employee, not a volunteer, and therefore is entitled to compensation and benefits. This can also include a claim for compensation for injuries suffered while acting as a volunteer.

Volunteer or Employee?

As discussed in *Chapter 9, Employees*, nonprofit corporations are subject to most state and federal statutes that address employer responsibilities and liabilities. Consequently, it is important for a nonprofit corporation to be sure it is appropriately categorizing individuals as employees or volunteers. An individual's status as a volunteer rather than an employee may sometimes be difficult to establish. If an individual volunteers on a consistent basis for a nonprofit organization in a position that is similar to a paid position at the organization, under certain circumstances that person may be considered, or claim to be, an employee of the nonprofit corporation and therefore entitled to compensation and other benefits.

To avoid this possibility, the nonprofit corporation should periodically review the activities of its volunteers and the benefits they receive to evaluate whether some volunteers might be considered employees rather than volunteers under the law. For example, under the Fair Labor Standards Act, an individual is prohibited from volunteering to do the same work that the individual is paid to do by the same employer; that is, a nonprofit corporation cannot ask its paid staff to "volunteer" part of their time to the organization.

Beyond this rule, the corporation should focus on such factors as whether the volunteer is doing the same work that some of the corporation's employees are being paid to do or that similar organizations often use paid staff to perform. If so, is the volunteer being paid or receiving other financial or other benefits, such as meals, shelter, stipends, insurance, medical benefits, a savings or retirement plan, or credit toward the volunteer's degree? Is the individual relying on these benefits for the individual's sustenance? Or is the individual volunteering solely for a civic, charitable, or humanitarian reason? If the answers to these questions raise the possibility that a volunteer may be considered an employee (i.e., one who performs work for compensation), the board or chief executive should consult with legal counsel to review the volunteer's status.

Employment Laws and the Volunteer

If volunteers are compensated for their efforts in a manner that makes them look more like employees, the nonprofit corporation may be subject to the minimum wage and overtime requirements of the Fair Labor Standards Act or a similar state law, federal or state discrimination statutes, and requirements regarding payment of employee benefits. For a discussion of issues that may arise with respect to employees of nonprofit corporations, *see Chapter 9, Employees.*

Even though equal employment opportunity laws may not apply to volunteers, the board should consider whether to adhere to the principles discussed below in the selection, supervision, and termination of its employees for its volunteers. Using a structured procedure for selecting and screening volunteers replaces a potentially arbitrary process with a fair and defensible method. Similarly, consistent application of performance and evaluation criteria for terminating volunteers will help prevent not only mistakes and hard feelings but also potential discrimination complaints (whether or not valid).

Obtaining a Waiver and Release of Liability

Many nonprofit corporations may use volunteers for events or in situations that present a particular risk of harm to the volunteer, such as volunteering for a race or other outdoor event. Volunteers also may be injured by other volunteers or employees of the nonprofit corporation. Unlike an employee covered by workers' compensation, the volunteer, if injured, may be able to sue the nonprofit corporation for injuries that occur while acting as a volunteer.

To address these risks, the nonprofit corporation should consider whether to include the volunteer in the corporation's workers' compensation insurance or other general liability insurance, if possible, or obtain a written waiver and release of liability from the volunteers before permitting them to participate in the nonprofit corporation's activities. One potential problem in seeking a waiver and release is practical, in that volunteers may not be willing to serve if required to sign a release. In addition, the fact that a release has been obtained does not guarantee liability protection for the organization. For example, some courts have found releases signed by parents on behalf of minors to be unenforceable.[5]

Workers' Compensation Insurance

Workers' compensation laws vary from state to state. In some states, particular volunteers are covered by workers' compensation by statute; for example, in Colorado, volunteer firefighters for a municipal entity are automatically covered. Some workers' compensation laws may permit a nonprofit to elect to include volunteers in its existing workers' compensation insurance. One risk of including a volunteer in the workers' compensation insurance is the possibility that the volunteer would be considered an employee for other purposes. Again, this is an area in which the board should consult legal counsel in deciding how to address the organization's potential liability to its volunteers for injuries to the volunteers.

Ownership of Materials Created by a Volunteer

To the extent that volunteers are creating written curricula, videotapes, audiotapes, printed publications, photographs, or other works for the nonprofit corporation, care should be taken to make sure that the nonprofit corporation is the owner of the work (with all rights to the work product) or that it obtains a license sufficient for its uses of the work. Therefore, *before* any works are produced, the nonprofit corporation should require any volunteer who produces work that would be protected under copyright laws to sign a statement that the work is "for hire" and owned by the nonprofit corporation or to provide a license or assignment to the organization. (See the section "*Works for Hire*" in *Chapter 9, Employees.*)

See the Suggested Questions and Checklist following the Endnotes below to review the issues discussed in this chapter.

Endnotes

1. *See* RESTATEMENT OF THE LAW, CHARITABLE NONPROFIT ORGANIZATIONS, § 2.09, cmt b.
2. For example, in Colorado, the statute does not provide protection for the negligent act of a volunteer involving the operation of a motor vehicle. COL. REV. STAT. § 13-21-115.5. In Utah, the statute does not apply if the nonprofit organization fails to provide a financially secure source of recovery for individuals injured by the volunteer. UTAH CODE ANN. § 78B-4-102.
3. The federal statute does not apply to conduct that constitutes a crime of violence, an act of international terrorism, a hate crime, a sexual offense, or a violation of a federal or state civil rights law; or that occurred when the defendant was under the influence of drugs or alcohol. 42 U.S.C. § 14501 *et seq.*
4. The Model Act does not expressly address the indemnification of employees, volunteers, and other agents. Still, a nonprofit corporation has the power to indemnify and advance expenses for employees, volunteers, and other agents under traditional contract and agency law principles. *See* Model Act, Introductory Comment, Subchapter E (Indemnification and Advance for Expenses), Chapter 8.
5. *See, e.g.*, Galloway v. State of Iowa, 790 N.W.2d 252 (Iowa 2010).

Suggested Questions for Directors Regarding Volunteers

(1) Which of the nonprofit corporation's programs use volunteers?
(2) How were the volunteers recruited?
(3) What functions do they perform?
(4) Do written guidelines, standards, or procedures exist for the nonprofit corporation's selection of volunteers?
(5) Is there a training program in place for the nonprofit corporation's volunteer programs?
(6) Do the corporation's insurance policies cover claims against the corporation based on acts of its volunteers?
(7) Do the corporation's insurance policies cover the volunteers individually?
(8) Do the corporation's insurance policies cover claims against the corporation by a volunteer?

(9) Do the corporation's articles of incorporation, bylaws, or policies require or permit indemnification of volunteers?
   a. If they do, should they?
   b. If they don't, should they?
   c. What are the standards for such indemnification?

(10) Have the corporation's volunteer positions been reviewed to evaluate whether they should be employees instead of volunteers? Are they receiving any compensation, including food, housing, and clothing?

(11) Should the corporation require that its volunteers sign a waiver and release of liability for claims arising from the volunteer's activities for the corporation?

(12) Should the corporation obtain workers' compensation insurance for its volunteers?

Checklist: Volunteers

Note: For simplicity, these and other chapter checklists describe a corporation having a chair, who presides over the board of directors; a chief executive, who may be a staff person; an executive committee; a governance/nominating committee; and an audit committee. (We recognize, however, that in many smaller and other nonprofits, these committee functions may be performed by either the executive committee or the board as a whole.) We also assume a legal counsel—someone, paid or unpaid, having primary responsibility for the corporation's legal affairs. Many corporations, especially larger nonprofits, may have other committees established for specific purposes, such as establishing executive compensation; monitoring compliance with legal requirements; and overseeing investments and other financial matters.

Subject	Review By	How Often	Comment
1. Does our corporation have a volunteer program?	Chief executive, full board	Annually, or at the inception of the new program	Volunteer programs should be formally approved by management.

Subject	Review By	How Often	Comment
2. Has the program been approved by the board? Are its functions defined in the corporate resolutions or policies?	Chief executive, full board	Annually, or at the inception of the new program	Volunteer programs should be formally approved by management.
3. Who administers the program at staff level?	Chief executive	As needed, but reviewed annually	
4. Are volunteers properly screened when selected?	Chief executive, legal counsel	As needed, but reviewed annually	
5. Is volunteer training adequate so that volunteers can competently perform their tasks?	Chief executive	As needed, but reviewed annually	
6. Are the volunteers covered by the corporation's insurance program?	Chief executive, legal counsel	Annually	Directors should understand that the inclusion of volunteers is not automatic.
7. Are volunteers subject to indemnification under the corporation's articles of incorporation, bylaws, or policies concerning indemnification?	Chief executive, legal counsel	Annually	Directors should understand that the inclusion of volunteers is not automatic.

Subject	Review By	How Often	Comment
8. Do volunteers perform functions giving rise to significant risk, such as driving automobiles on the corporation's business?	Chief executive, legal counsel	Annually	It may be prudent to examine a volunteer's driver's license, driving record, and personal auto insurance coverage.
9. Are volunteers covered by the corporation's workers' compensation insurance? Can they be? Should they be?	Chief executive, legal counsel	Annually	The corporation's insurance broker can review the available options.
10. Do any volunteers receive compensation or benefits, such that they should be classified as employees rather than as volunteers (and to whom the Fair Labor Standards Acts and other laws applicable to employees would apply)?	Legal counsel	Annually, or at inception of a new program	

Chapter 9:
Employees

Chapter 9
Employees

Most nonprofit corporations employ staff to assist in carrying out the mission and activities of the corporation. The nonprofit director should have a basic understanding of the legal risks and obligations that go with having employees.

Although some nonprofit corporations may rely solely on volunteers to accomplish their missions, most nonprofit corporations employ paid staff to carry out at least some of these activities. The size of the staff can vary from a single part-time employee in a small, grassroots organization to a staff of a hundred or a thousand full-time employees. All nonprofit corporations generally must comply with federal and state employment laws. Some legal requirements may vary depending on the number of employees and the activities of the organization.

Nonprofit corporations often have the employment relationship with the chief executive defined by a formal contract, which should be approved by the board of directors or a committee of the board. In addition to being aware of the terms of the contract, directors should be aware of the law applicable to that employment relationship. The board of directors should also approve policies and employment terms applicable to other employees which may be set forth in an employee handbook. In addition, because a significant number of the lawsuits generally brought against nonprofit directors and officers involve employment-related matters, it is important for directors to have a basic understanding of the range of legal requirements and potential liabilities that may arise in connection with employees. It is becoming more common for nonprofit corporations to obtain employment practice liability insurance. This chapter will outline some of the considerations and general legal requirements for nonprofit corporations that hire employees.

Executive Employment Relationships

Chief Executives and Other Management Employees

Nonprofit corporations commonly hire a chief executive or CEO, sometimes called an executive director, who is responsible for the day-to-day operations of the organization, including hiring and supervising other staff. The chief executive reports directly to the board of directors.

Executive Employment Agreements

The board, or a committee of the board, typically will define, negotiate, and approve the chief executive's contract. Especially if the executive works directly with clients or the public, the board may want to conduct a background check before the initial hiring of an executive or approval of the contract. The executive's employment agreement should outline job responsibilities, compensation, and benefits (including any performance incentives), and contain termination provisions.

Evaluation of Chief Executive

Performance evaluations can be a good shield against potential employment-related liability if they are done well. If they are poorly done, they can be a potent sword in the hands of a former employee. Thus, it is better to do performance evaluations correctly, or not at all.

The board should establish a process for annual performance reviews of the chief executive. This process, which may be done by a committee of the board, should be designed to give the board sufficient information to evaluate the chief executive's contribution to the organization. For instance, the evaluation process might include interviews with clients or other stakeholders served by the nonprofit corporation, interviews with other staff, and review of objective measures of the organization (e.g., budget, membership numbers, etc.).

Employment Laws Applicable to Nonprofit Corporations

Generally, nonprofit corporations are subject to the same federal and state laws as other employers. These laws include statutes regarding equal employment opportunity, wage and hour issues, employee benefits, workers' compensation, and unemployment insurance. Nonprofit corporations are also subject to common law claims such as breach of contract or negligence. Because many of these laws apply to corporations with just one employee, even the smallest nonprofit corporations should have a staff member, counsel, or another adviser who is responsible for and familiar with human resources issues. Likewise, legal counsel for the nonprofit corporation should review employment policies and practices for compliance with applicable law.

Federal Equal Employment Opportunity Laws

Several federal statutes prohibit discrimination based on a particular status. As set forth below, these statutes apply to nonprofit corporations that employ at least a specified minimum number of employees.

Statute:	*Prohibits discrimination based on:*	*This applies to corporations with at least:*
Title VII of the Civil Rights Act of 1964	Race, gender, national origin, religion[1]	15 or more employees
Americans with Disabilities Act	Disability or perceived disability	15 or more employees
Age Discrimination in Employment Act	Age (over 40)	15 or more employees
Equal Pay Act	Discrimination with regard to compensation	No minimum number employees
Immigration Reform and Control Act	National origin or citizenship	4 or more employees

Statute:	*Prohibits discrimination based on:*	*This applies to corporations with at least:*
Pregnancy Discrimination Act	Pregnancy or childbirth	15 or more employees
Genetic Information	Genetic information	15 or more employees
Nondiscrimination Act[2] Uniformed Services Employment & Reemployment Rights Act	Veterans and members of the armed forces	No minimum number of employees

Nonprofit corporations that are subject to these federal statutes may not discriminate in hiring, compensation, working conditions, promotion, discipline, termination, or other employment practices. Boards of nonprofits that are not subject to some of the above laws (at least given current employee numbers) may nevertheless choose to adopt policies that conform to these laws. Even if not legally required, such policies might serve to help prevent inadvertent violations if the number of employees increases

Reasonable Accommodation of Disabilities

The Americans with Disabilities Act (ADA) as amended by the Americans with Disabilities Amendments Act (ADAA) mandates the giving of "equal opportunity" to persons with disabilities, by requiring an employer (whether nonprofit or for-profit) to provide "reasonable accommodation" to employees with disabilities.

Reasonable accommodation under the ADA may require

(a) making existing facilities used by employees readily accessible to and usable by individuals with disabilities; and

(b) job restructuring, part-time or modified work schedules, reassignment to a vacant position, acquisition or modification of equipment or devices, appropriate adjustment or modifications of examinations, training materials or policies, the provision of qualified readers or interpreters, and other similar accommodations for individuals with disabilities.[3]

Nonprofit corporations that also serve as public accommodations (schools, theaters, libraries, hospitals, etc.) likely will have additional responsibilities to provide equal access and reasonable accommodations to members of the public with disabilities. Such nonprofit corporations should also be familiar with applicable laws governing service and companion animals.

State and Local Equal Opportunity Laws

In addition to federal law, nonprofit corporations usually are subject to state or local equal employment opportunity laws that may impose the same or additional requirements. For example, some state laws parallel the federal requirements but apply to employers of all sizes—*regardless of the number of employees.* Other state and local statutes and ordinances may prohibit discrimination based on a status, such as sexual orientation, not covered by federal law. Still, as under federal law, state laws may provide certain exemptions for religious corporations with respect to laws prohibiting employment discrimination based on religion.

Equal Opportunity Policies

To formalize commitment to equal employment opportunity and comply with relevant laws, nonprofit organizations should adopt a formal equal employment opportunity policy. This policy should be approved by the board of directors and comply with all relevant laws. The policy should state the organization's commitment to equal employment opportunity, provide a procedure for reporting any alleged discrimination, and prohibit retaliation against anyone who makes a report or complaint. Once approved, the policy should be posted publicly and distributed to staff. The board should review the policy annually, and confirm that it conforms to current legal requirements.

Antiharassment Policies

In addition to an equal employment opportunity policy, boards of directors of nonprofit corporations should adopt an antiharassment policy for the corporation. Under certain circumstances, employers that have such a policy may be able to assert an affirmative defense to liability based on the existence of a written policy and a victim's failure to make a complaint under it. This policy should contain a statement that harassment will not be permitted, a complaint procedure for victims or others to report harassment and a prohibition of retaliation. The complaint procedure should allow employees to report to their supervisor or even the CEO. The policy should be expressly applicable to both employees and volunteers.

Family and Medical Leave

Under the federal Family and Medical Leave Act of 1993 (FMLA), nonprofit corporations with fifty or more employees are required to provide twelve weeks of unpaid leave for qualified employees upon the birth or adoption of a child, or if the employee or a family member has a serious health condition. The FMLA permits a spouse, son, daughter, parent, or next of kin to take up to twenty-six work weeks of leave to care for a member of the armed forces who is undergoing medical treatment, recuperation, or therapy or is otherwise disabled. The law also permits an employee to take FMLA leave for any "qualifying exigency ... arising out of the fact that the spouse, or a son, daughter or parent of the employee is on active duty or has been notified of an impending call or order to active duty." The organization must maintain the employee's position and benefits during the leave.

Some states have their own laws regarding family and medical leave that may place additional burdens on employers, including nonprofit organizations. *Nonprofit corporations that are subject to FMLA and/or state leave statutes should enact a family and medical leave policy that complies with all applicable statutes and regulations.* In addition, if the nonprofit corporation is subject to FMLA, strict notice and recordkeeping requirements apply.

Wage and Hour Issues: Fair Labor Standards Act

Many nonprofit organizations are subject to the federal Fair Labor Standards Act (FLSA), which requires that employers pay at least the federal minimum wage and provide overtime pay (one and one-half the regular rate of pay) to nonexempt employees who work over forty hours in a single work week.

Does the FLSA apply?

FLSA applies to hospitals, schools, and other organizations engaged in interstate or foreign commerce or in the production of goods for commerce, either directly or indirectly through one or more affiliates.[4]

Nonprofit organizations are *not* exempted automatically from coverage under the FLSA, even if they have no obvious commercial activities. Moreover, some kinds of organizations, such as those that operate hospitals, schools, and similar institutions, are covered by the FLSA irrespective of whether they are "engaged in interstate commerce." Other nonprofits are subject to the FLSA if they meet two tests: first, they have two or more employees engaged in commerce or in the production of goods for commerce, or employees handling, selling, or otherwise working on materials that have been moved in or produced for commerce by any person; and second, they have an annual gross volume of sales of $500,000 or more.

Whether a nonprofit corporation is "engaged in commerce" or "the production of goods for commerce" as defined by FLSA will depend on the activities of it and its affiliates. When a nonprofit engages in a commercial activity of any kind, it is considered a business purpose, which makes it subject to the FLSA, just as a for-profit commercial entity would be. Neither tax-exempt status nor charitable purposes render an otherwise commercial activity exempt from coverage. For example, fraternal orders and country clubs are considered to be operated for a business purpose, and thereby subject to the FLSA, despite their nonprofit status. On the other hand, religious and other nonprofit corporations may escape FLSA coverage if they solely engage in nonprofit activities, or only use true volunteers for their commercial activities.

With regard to the requirement that commercial activities be "interstate," this definition has been applied broadly to a wide variety of activities, including the use of supplies produced in another state.

Because courts and the Department of Labor are likely to strain to make the FLSA apply and because it is a prudent business practice to pay minimum wage and overtime to nonexempt employees, *many nonprofit organizations may find it wise to comply with FLSA, even if a plausible argument can be made that it does not apply.* A nonprofit board should make sure that the organization has received legal advice before concluding that it need not comply with the provisions of the FLSA if it otherwise meets the coverage description set forth above.

Exempt employees under the FLSA

Even if a nonprofit corporation is subject to the FLSA, not all of its employees are covered by the act. FLSA exemptions apply to certain executive, administrative, and professional employees who are compensated on a salary basis and whose job functions and salary levels meet the tests set forth in the FLSA. Special care should be given to classifying an employee as "exempt" or "nonexempt," since a disgruntled former employee may challenge such individual's classification after the fact, demanding overtime and penalties from the nonprofit corporation.

State Wage and Hour Laws

In addition to federal law (and even if the nonprofit is not subject to FLSA), most states have wage and hour laws that apply to nonprofit organizations. These laws may impose additional burdens such as a state minimum wage, requiring overtime pay for all hours over twelve worked in a single workday, payment for unused vacation pay upon termination, compensation for on-call or sleep time (also covered by FLSA), and payment of expenses related to uniforms.

Employee Handbooks and Personnel Policies

Nonprofit boards of directors often approve employee policies that make up employee handbooks. Commonly, employee handbooks are a collection of policies ranging from attendance to benefits, to compensation, to workplace violence. An employee handbook that does not contain conspicuous disclaimer language may be considered a contract that alters the otherwise "at-will" nature of employment.[5] For example, language in a handbook regarding progressive discipline, termination procedures (e.g., defining "for cause"), or even broad promises of "fair treatment" may change this status. An employee who is terminated might use the handbook as the basis for a breach of contract claim, arguing that the organization is bound to use progressive discipline procedures outlined in the employee handbook. To avoid these results, consideration should be given to introductory language that states the purpose of the handbook. A prominent disclaimer that states that the handbook does not alter the "at-will" nature of employment should also be included. The board of directors should make sure that legal counsel familiar with employment-law issues reviews the handbook or policies before they are approved and distributed to staff.

Grievance Procedures

Some nonprofit corporations have grievance procedures (often contained in the employee handbook) in which officials in the organization (such as the chief executive) or the board may hear and rule upon employee grievances with management. These grievances most typically involve adverse actions taken against an employee such as discipline, denial of promotion, or termination. Boards should decide whether or not to have such policies—since the existence of a grievance procedure or other appeal process, like a progressive discipline policy in an employee handbook, may be deemed to alter the "at-will" status of employees. If the board decides to have a grievance procedure that includes a review of an employment action by the board, board members should make sure they understand their role in the grievance process and whether the board's decision is binding or merely advisory.

Workplace Violence

As part of an employee handbook or as a separate standalone policy, it is recommended that a nonprofit corporation have an antiviolence policy that prohibits violence and weapons on the premises or any place where activities of the corporation may be conducted. Such a policy will also assist the organization to comply with Occupational Health and Safety Administration (OSHA) rules requiring a safe workplace.

Employee Benefits

Nonprofit boards of directors often approve employee benefit plans to be offered to the organization's employees. Such plans include retirement and deferred compensation plans, welfare benefit plans (health, disability, life insurance, etc.), and various fringe benefit arrangements. Directors should make sure they are informed regarding the duties and liability exposure created by such benefit plans. Some key issues relating to employee benefit plans are discussed below.

Reasonable Compensation

The value of employee benefit plans must be considered part of an employee's overall compensation in determining whether an employee is receiving reasonable compensation for services. If the value of a key employee's total compensation package is less than what similar organizations provide, the corporation may be in danger of losing the employee. On the other hand, an overly generous benefits package may, when combined with the employee's salary, raise private benefit/inurement concerns for tax-exempt organizations (see the discussion in the section *"Limitations on Private Benefit and Private Inurement"* in *Chapter 5, Taxation*). With respect to § 501(c)(3) and § 501(c)(4) tax-exempt organizations, this is especially important in avoiding the excise tax on excess benefit transactions that can be imposed both on recipients and responsible organization managers under the IRS's intermediate sanctions powers.

The process for determining the compensation of the chief executive has become a focus for the IRS. The Form 990 requires a tax-exempt organization to state whether the process for determining compensation for the chief executive and other officers and key employees includes a review and approval by a governing body or compensation committee composed of "independent" persons, use of data as to comparable compensation for similarly qualified persons in functionally comparable positions at similarly situated organizations, and contemporaneous documentation and recordkeeping with respect to deliberations and decisions regarding the compensation arrangement. The factors are important for the purposes of establishing the reasonableness of compensation. (The intermediate sanction powers of the IRS, as well as these procedures for establishing reasonableness with compensation, are discussed further in the section *"Intermediate Sanctions: Excise Tax on Public Charities' Excess Benefit Transactions"* in *Chapter 5, Taxation*).

ERISA Requirements

Most types of employee benefit plans are subject to the requirements of the Employee Retirement Income Security Act of 1974, as amended (ERISA), unless the plan is one adopted by a church or governmental plan exempt from ERISA and, in the case of a church plan, the organization has not elected to be governed by ERISA. ERISA imposes a number of reporting and disclosure requirements, creates certain minimum rights for plan participants, and imposes numerous fiduciary responsibilities. The employer organization, and under certain circumstances one or more of its employees, officers, or board members, is typically viewed as a fiduciary with respect to the plan. In addition, for certain employee benefits that are intended to receive favorable tax treatment, there are a number of technical requirements under the Code that must be satisfied, including rules intended to prevent discrimination in favor of highly compensated employees.

Plan Documents

Most types of employee benefit plans must be maintained pursuant to written plan documents. These documents should be carefully reviewed by the human resources manager or an outside benefits expert to ensure that they reflect the actual practices for operating the employee benefit plans and that they satisfy the technical requirements of ERISA and the Code.

Special Rules for Nonprofits

Employee benefits offered by tax-exempt organizations are subject to some special rules, particularly with respect to retirement and deferred compensation plans.

Tax deferral arrangements

Unlike taxable organizations, tax-exempt organizations are somewhat more limited in the amount of tax-deferred compensation that can be offered to the organization's executives or other key employees. Although the restrictions on tax-deferred compensation arrangements were significantly loosened beginning in 2002, tax-exempt organizations are still subject to certain maximum amounts ($16,500 in 2010 and 2011, adjusted annually by the IRS based on inflation) of deferred compensation that can be provided in any year to an employee, pursuant to a nonqualified plan that is an "eligible deferred compensation plan" within the meaning of 26 U.S.C. § 457(b). The limit takes into account both employer and employee contributions. Such limits are now in addition to—and are no longer offset against—any amounts that the employee has elected to defer under the organization's 401(k) or 403(b) plan. If a tax-exempt organization desires to provide any additional deferred compensation beyond the new § 457(b) limits, this compensation must be subject to a "substantial risk of forfeiture" as determined under 26 U.S.C. § 457(f).

Directors of tax-exempt organizations should make sure that their organization has taken advantage of recent liberalizations in the tax-deferred compensation rules. These changes may make it easier for tax-exempt organizations to attract and retain qualified executives, by lessening the difference between the kind of deferred compensation arrangements that can be offered by tax-exempt corporations compared to those provided by for-profit organizations.

Section 403(b) and Section 401(k) plans

Tax-sheltered annuity or mutual fund custodial account arrangements described in § 403(b) may only be offered by tax-exempt organizations described in § 501(c)(3). Other types of nonprofit organizations cannot contribute to § 403(b) plans. Previously, nonprofit corporations were not permitted to maintain § 401(k) plans; however, nonprofits are now permitted to offer such plans to their employees.

Other Laws Relating to Employees

Background Checks

The Fair Credit Reporting Act (FCRA) requires employers who use third-party consumer reporting agencies to conduct background checks to obtain applicant authorization before conducting such checks.[6] The law also requires employers to provide prior notice to the employee before taking any adverse action against the applicant, including a decision not to hire the applicant based on the information obtained.

Employee E-mail Monitoring

The Electronic Communications Privacy Act prohibits an employer from intercepting or monitoring employee e-mail and voicemail except when such interception occurs in the ordinary course of the employer's business or the employee consents to the monitoring.[7] In certain circumstances, nonprofit employers may be allowed to monitor employee e-mail if it is stored on the employer's computer system. To avoid ambiguity, the organization should notify employees, through employee handbooks or other means, that it may monitor e-mail in the ordinary course of business and as otherwise permitted by law.

Identity Theft Protection

Many states require employers to limit access to documents containing an employee's personal information, including Social Security number.

Tax Withholding and Payroll Taxes

Nonprofit corporations are also required to comply with state and federal laws regarding tax withholding and payment of payroll taxes. Directors, especially directors/officers, may be personally liable for any unpaid taxes or penalties if they are found to be responsible for the unpaid taxes.[8] In comparison, directors who do not participate in day-to-day or financial operations, and who have no responsibility for the payment of payroll taxes and no knowledge of the failure to pay payroll taxes, would generally not be personally liable for unpaid payroll taxes and any accompanying penalty.[9]

Workers' Compensation and Unemployment Insurance

Nonprofit corporations with employees are subject to state laws regarding workers' compensation and unemployment insurance. These laws vary from state to state, but typically, a nonprofit organization, like any other employer, is responsible for obtaining insurance for on-the-job injuries (workers' compensation) or the effects of terminating employees (unemployment). In some states, nonprofit corporations may elect to self-insure for unemployment compensation claims; in that case, the nonprofit does not make standard state unemployment tax payments but pays its share of actual unemployment claims. Further, many states specifically exempt churches from unemployment insurance obligations. Board approval of workers' compensation insurance policies is recommended if the policies would be material to the corporation unless the board has delegated such approval to the corporation's chief executive or other managerial personnel.

Immigration Laws

The Immigration Reform and Control Act of 1986 (IRCA) prohibits the employment of unauthorized aliens (i.e., noncitizens who are not authorized by the Immigration and Naturalization Service to work in this country). IRCA applies to nonprofit corporations and places administrative burdens on nonprofit corporations to verify that all employees are authorized to work in the United States. IRCA also has nondiscrimination provisions that prohibit discrimination on the basis of national origin or citizenship.

Work for Hire

To the extent that employees, volunteers, or third parties are creating curricula, videotapes, audio tapes, printed publications, photographs, or other works for the nonprofit corporation, care should be taken to make sure that the nonprofit corporation is the owner (with all rights to the work product) or that it obtains a license sufficient for its uses of the work. An employee's original works of authorship are deemed to be authored and owned by the employer if the work was prepared by the employee within the scope of the employee's employment. On the other hand, work done by an independent party, including an independent contractor or volunteer, or an employee working outside the scope of the employee's employment, is deemed to be authored and owned by the original author unless the parties expressly agree, in a signed writing executed *prior* to the work's creation, that the work shall be considered a work made for hire.

Independent Contractor vs. Employee

The classification of individuals as employees or independent contractors is critical for a nonprofit corporation. A nonprofit corporation is required to withhold and deposit income taxes, social security taxes, and Medicare taxes from wages paid to an employee. In addition, a nonprofit corporation is required to pay the matching employer portion of social security and Medicare taxes as well as pay unemployment taxes on wages paid to employees. A nonprofit corporation generally does not have to withhold or pay any taxes on payments to independent contractors. The governmental agencies have developed criteria for purposes of determining whether an independent contractor arrangement exists. An incorrect classification can lead to litigation and regulatory penalties. To the extent that a nonprofit corporation is utilizing independent contractors, it is important to thoroughly analyze the arrangement, including whether an independent contractor is doing the same work as an employee, as well as the written terms of the arrangement. To the extent there is a question as to an individual's status, it is generally considered less risky to classify the individual as an employee.

Confidential Information

The nonprofit corporation should also exercise care to protect its confidential and proprietary information. Employees, volunteers, and others may have access to trade secrets or confidential information such as donor or member lists, personnel information, medical records, patient or client information, or other data or materials that must be kept confidential. The nonprofit corporation should adopt a confidentiality policy and should take reasonable precautions (such as passwords, limited distribution, and stamping materials "CONFIDENTIAL") to protect against unauthorized dissemination of the organization's confidential information.

Liability to Others for Acts of Employees

Negligent Hiring and Supervision Claims

Negligent hiring and negligent supervision claims are typically raised by clients or members of the public who allege they have been injured by an employee (such as a child who is allegedly sexually abused by a daycare worker) and claim that the corporation failed to properly screen the employee before hiring or to supervise the employee once hired. To avoid such claims, and as a prudent business practice, the corporation should screen candidates for employment, especially if they work with children or other vulnerable populations. Likewise, systems should be in place to monitor and supervise employees. (Similar issues apply to volunteers who work independently with the public or vulnerable groups; see the discussion in the section *"Risks Association with Using Volunteers"* in *Chapter 8, Volunteers.*)

Liability to Employees

Wrongful Discharge in Violation of Public Policy; Whistleblower Protection

Employees may bring a wrongful discharge claim if they believe they were terminated because they refused to participate in an illegal act on behalf of the corporation or because they asserted rights under a statute, such as filing a workers' compensation claim.

In addition, nonprofit corporations need to be mindful that many state and federal laws include whistleblower protection to individuals who report information they reasonably believe evidences a violation of law or other serious problems. Under these laws, an employer generally may not take or fail to take, or threaten to take or fail to take, any personnel action against an employee because of the employee's protected whistleblowing activity.

Right to Privacy: Disclosure and E-mail Review

Most states recognize a common law right of privacy of some kind. There are generally four types of privacy rights that may be asserted by employees: intrusion upon physical solitude, public disclosure of private facts, false light in the public eye, and appropriation of name or likeness. An employee could bring an action against the nonprofit corporation if the organization did an egregious act that violated the employee's right to nondisclosure of private facts, such as disclosing publicly that an employee had AIDS.

Privacy concerns are magnified by the employer's monitoring of electronic mail and Internet usage. As noted above, in *"Other Laws Relating to Employees: Employee E-mail and Other Monitoring,"* employers are generally permitted to conduct such monitoring in the ordinary course of business. It is good practice, and in certain circumstances legally required, to notify employees in advance that the organization's e-mail and Internet systems are subject to monitoring at any time without further notice. Such statements often are contained in a written e-mail or Internet policy that may be a freestanding policy or part of an employee handbook.

Lifestyle Discrimination

Many states prohibit discrimination against employees who use tobacco products outside of the workplace. Other states have broader language that prohibits discrimination for lawful activities carried on by employees outside the workplace.

Collective Bargaining

Nonprofit corporations of a certain size or in certain industries may face issues involving unions or unionization activities. A discussion of these issues is outside the scope of this *Guidebook.*

See the Suggested Questions and Checklist following the Endnotes below to review the issues discussed in this chapter.

Endnotes

1. In some cases, there may be exceptions for religious corporations to laws prohibiting discrimination on the basis of religion, where the religious organization employs individuals of a particular religion to perform work connected with the carrying out of the religious corporation's activities. *See* 42 U.S.C. § 2000e-1 (exemption to Title VII prohibition on discrimination on the basis of religion); Lisa A. Runquist and Jeannie Carmedelle Frey, *Guide to Representing Religious Organizations*, 127-31 (ABA 2009). In addition, the First Amendment may prohibit courts from adjudicating disputes between a religious entity and a minister of that entity. *See* Our Lady of Guadalupe v. Morrisey-Berru, 140 S.Ct. 2049 (2020).
2. 42 U.S.C. § 2000ff.
3. 42 U.S.C. § 12111(9).
4. 29 U.S.C. § 203(s)(1).
5. In most states, employment is presumed to be "at-will," meaning that either side may terminate the relationship at any time for any reason or no reason at all.
6. 15 U.S.C. § 1681.
7. 18 U.S.C. § 2510 (as amended by the Stored Communications Act and Patriot Act).
8. *See* I.R.C. § 6672(a).
9. *See* I.R.C. § 6672(e).

Suggested Questions for Directors Regarding Employees

(1) How many employees does the corporation have?
(2) Which employees report directly to the board?
(3) Are there written employment contracts with these employees?
(4) How are performance reviews conducted for the chief executive?
(5) Does the corporation have an equal opportunity policy?
(6) Does the corporation have an antiharassment policy?
(7) What kind of family and medical leave policy exists?
(8) Does the corporation follow its policies?
(9) Does the corporation pay minimum wage and overtime pay to nonexempt employees?
(10) Who classifies employees as exempt or nonexempt?
(11) Does the organization have an employee handbook?
(12) Does the employee handbook contain a disclaimer regarding employment at will?
(13) Does the organization have a grievance procedure in which employment actions may be reviewed by the board? If so, what is the board's role?
(14) Does the corporation comply with applicable laws regarding workers' compensation, unemployment insurance, and tax withholding?
(15) Does the corporation comply with relevant requirements of the Immigration and Naturalization Service?
(16) Does the corporation have "work for hire" agreements with third parties (or employees acting outside their scope of employment) who produce copyrighted works?
(17) Does the corporation take adequate precautions to protect trade secrets and confidential information?
(18) If employees work with children or other vulnerable people, does the corporation do adequate preemployment screening and background checks?

Checklist: Employees

Note: For simplicity, these and other chapter checklists describe a corporation having a chair, who presides over the board of directors; a chief executive, who may be a staff person; an executive committee;

a governance/nominating committee; a personnel committee; and an audit committee. (We recognize, however, that in many smaller and other nonprofits, these committee functions may be performed by either the executive committee or the board as a whole.) We also assume a legal counsel—someone, paid or unpaid, having primary responsibility for the corporation's legal affairs. Many corporations, especially larger nonprofits, may have other committees established for specific purposes, such as establishing executive compensation; monitoring compliance with legal requirements; and overseeing investments and other financial matters.

Subject	**Review By**	**How Often**	**Comment**
1. What employment arrangements are in place with the chief executive?	Chair, chief executive, personnel committee, or full board	Annually or when the chief executive or terms of employment change	Key terms of employment agreements with chief executives should be approved by the full board.
2. How is the performance of the chief executive evaluated?	Chair, personnel committee	Annually	The chief executive's performance should be evaluated annually by the board.
3. Does the corporation have an equal opportunity policy?	Chief executive, legal counsel, board	Annually	The board should approve an equal opportunity policy.
4. Does the corporation have an antiharassment policy as well as a whistleblower protection policy?	Chief executive, legal counsel, board	Upon adoption, then reviewed annually to keep updated	The board should approve an antiharassment policy as well as a whistleblower protection policy.
5. What kind of family and medical leave is provided to employees?	Chief executive, legal counsel	Upon adoption, then reviewed annually to keep updated	Family and medical leave policies should be in writing and comply with applicable law.

Subject	Review By	How Often	Comment
6. How are employees classified as exempt/ nonexempt?	Chief executive, legal counsel	As job descriptions and positions are created	Compliance with the Fair Labor Standards Act should be monitored by legal counsel.
7. Does the organization have an up-to-date employee handbook with appropriate disclaimers?	Chief executive, legal counsel, full board or personnel committee	Upon adoption, then reviewed annually to keep updated	Boards often review and approve employee handbooks since they often contain mission statements and broad policies. Special care should be taken to have appropriate disclaimers and that policies comply with applicable laws.
8. Does the board "hear" appeals or employee grievances?	Chief executive, full board or committee of board per policy	As grievances are filed	Most nonprofits will not have such a process. If they do, the board should be familiar with the process and its role.
9. Does the corporation have systems to comply with applicable laws regarding tax withholding, immigration, workers' compensation, and unemployment insurance?	Chief executive, legal counsel	Annually	Legal counsel and the officers of the board should make sure contracts and systems are in place to ensure compliance.

Subject	Review By	How Often	Comment
10. Does the corporation own rights protecting original materials under the Copyright Act?	Chief executive, legal counsel	As works are created or commissioned	"Work for hire" agreements should be entered into with independent contractors and volunteers.
11. Does the corporation protect its confidential information?	Chief executive, board	Upon adoption, then reviewed annually	A confidentiality policy should be adopted and other precautions taken to protect secrecy of confidential information.
12. Does the corporation adequately screen employees before hiring?	Chief executive	As employees are hired	Thorough background and reference checks should be conducted on all employees who work with children or other vulnerable populations.
13. Does the corporation have an organizational chart?	Chief executive	Annually	An organizational chart of management and management reporting relationships should assist the board in understanding the organization.

Chapter 10:
Mergers, Sale of Assets, Affiliations, and Other Combinations

Chapter 10

Mergers of Sale of Assets, Affiliations, and Other Combinations

In recent years, there has been an increase in mergers, asset transfers, and affiliations involving nonprofit organizations. These "combinations" have been necessary in an environment that has become more challenging for nonprofits to obtain financial support in the form of public and private funding and contributions. The process for pursuing a nonprofit combination, including use of letters of intent or term sheets, due diligence, and the negotiation and execution of documents to effectuate the combination, is very similar to the process used with for-profit entities. Nevertheless, combinations involving nonprofits have important differences from their for-profit counterparts because of the unique nature of nonprofits.

Introduction: Considerations for Moving Forward with Combinations Involving Nonprofits

In the course of a nonprofit corporation's existence, there may come a time when its board is faced with a traumatic decision: Will the corporation's mission be better served if the corporation merges with another entity, sells all or some of its assets, converts to for-profit status, changes its membership, or undergoes some other event that will result in a change of control over the corporation's operations? The processes that a nonprofit board uses to make a change of control decision must be sufficient to satisfy the directors' fiduciary duty obligations to the corporation and its mission, as well as other applicable legal requirements.

When faced with a prospective change of control, a nonprofit corporation director should understand what actions may be required to be taken to satisfy the director's fiduciary duties to the corporation with respect to such an event. Further, the director should ask management staff or legal counsel to determine if the state attorney general or other regulatory authorities have notice rights or approval powers over the change of control decision. In addition to regulators, community interest groups may seek to change or influence the board's decision; thus, the directors will need to evaluate to what degree and in what manner the board will provide information to or seek input from these interest groups.

An initial step in any combination is determining whether such a combination makes sense to the organization. The factors that a board of directors needs to take into consideration in such evaluation are described below and can be very similar to those factors a for-profit board considers, including synergies, cost savings, and other efficiencies to be obtained through the combination, workforce issues, and the composition of the surviving entity's board and the make-up of its officers. Moreover, as described below, the fiduciary duties imposed on nonprofit directors in acting on combinations are very similar to the fiduciary duties imposed on for-profit directors. Still, there are some important differences between for-profit and nonprofit combinations. For example, a for-profit board needs to consider the financial impact a combination will have on the entity's owners (such as shareholders in a business corporation). In the context of a charitable nonprofit corporation, the interests of members may be relevant in a board's consideration of a merger, but such interests are distinguishable because members do not have an ownership interest in the nonprofit. The differences between for-profits and nonprofits lead to other unique factors that need to be considered by a nonprofit board when evaluating a possible combination.

If the proposed combination involves a nonprofit being merged out of existence, selling substantially all of its assets, or becoming a "subsidiary" of another entity, it will result in a change in control for the organization and/or its assets. For such combinations, the main focus of the nonprofit board likely is how the mission of the entity will be carried on by the surviving entity and whether there will be adequate resources dedicated to such a mission. There will generally be a requirement by the nonprofit that the mission of the surviving entity incorporate in some respect the disappearing nonprofit's mission.

Other unique considerations include what will happen to any members of the nonprofit, as well as the proposed use of any institutional funds with donor restrictions (including endowment funds) of the nonprofit.

Similar to the situation involving a for-profit business combination, as the nonprofit commences discussions with another entity regarding a possible combination, a letter of intent or term sheet (that is often non-binding) will help to structure the proposed transaction and process for the combination. In order to protect the nonprofit, it is important to have a binding confidentiality agreement in place prior to any significant discussions between the parties.

Types of Nonprofit Combinations

Nonprofit combinations can involve different levels of integrations between two or more entities and can include mergers of the entities, sale/transfer of assets between entities, affiliation agreements that create a parent-subsidiary or similar relationship, as well as contractual joint ventures.[1]

Mergers

The Model Act, and most state nonprofit corporation acts, permit a nonprofit corporation to merge with another nonprofit corporation pursuant to a process that is very similar to the process required for business entities.[2] A state nonprofit corporation act may also allow a nonprofit to merge with a for-profit entity, such as a for-profit corporation, limited liability company, or limited partnership provided that certain steps are taken to protect the charitable assets of the nonprofit.[3] In addition, a state nonprofit corporation act may allow a nonprofit to merge with an unincorporated nonprofit association as well as with an entity that is domesticated in another state.[4] For any merger, it is important to confirm that it is permitted under both the applicable nonprofit corporation statute and the enabling statute for the other entity involved in the merger.[5]

The process for a merger involving a nonprofit corporation is very similar to a merger involving a for-profit entity. It typically includes a plan of merger or merger agreement containing the terms of the merger and any appropriate representations and warranties of the merging parties. It also involves the filing of articles or certificate of merger with the state's secretary of state. Regardless of whether the nonprofit is the surviving entity, it is generally necessary to obtain board of director approval as well as member approval if the nonprofit has members.[6]

As described below, depending on the type of entity that will be the surviving entity in the merger, there may be unique state law requirements as well as requirements imposed on the nonprofit because of its tax-exempt status. A merger involving a charitable nonprofit can be subject to additional requirements if the charitable nonprofit is being merged out of existence and the surviving entity is not a charitable nonprofit. Generally, steps must be taken to ensure that the charitable assets or the fair value of such assets of a merged out entity continue to be used for a charitable purpose. A similar requirement is imposed on entities that have tax-exempt status under Section 501(c)(3) of the Internal Revenue Code.[7] Additional requirements under the Internal Revenue Code are imposed on nonprofits that are private foundations. In addition, as discussed below, some states require a merger to be approved by a governmental body, such as the state attorney general, or a court.[8] Where action must be taken to ensure the fair value of the charitable assets continue to be dedicated to such charitable purposes, a valuation by an independent appraiser is likely necessary such as when a nonprofit's assets are purchased by a business entity.

There are significant benefits with regard to proceeding with a merger as a form of combination. Similar to state for-profit entity acts, state nonprofit corporation acts provide that all assets and rights, and liabilities of the disappearing entity are automatically transferred/assumed by the surviving entity.[9] There also is no need to dissolve the disappearing entity because it no longer exists as a legal entity. In addition, any bequest, devise, gift, grant, or promise contained in a will or other instrument of donation inures to the surviving entity unless it is made pursuant to an instrument that specifically provides otherwise.[10]

A main disadvantage to a merger for the surviving entity is that such an entity inherits all of the liabilities of the disappearing entity. As a result, it is extremely important as part of the due diligence process to determine what assets and liabilities might be assumed by the surviving entity. In addition, it is not easy to unwind the arrangement if it is later determined that the combination has not resulted in the benefits the parties expected.

Some state nonprofit corporation acts also permit the consolidation of nonprofits, which is very similar to a merger of a nonprofit with another nonprofit.[11] The main distinction between a merger and consolidation is that a consolidation results in both nonprofits effectively being merged out of existence with the creation of a new entity. A main disadvantage of proceeding with a consolidation as opposed to a merger is that in a consolidation it is necessary to make an application to the IRS if the new entity seeks to have tax-exempt status under Section 501(c)(3) of the Internal Revenue Code. Given the similar treatment of mergers and consolidations of nonprofits, more recent state nonprofit corporation acts have dropped the concept of consolidation.

A merger may result in a surviving organization and a disappearing organization or in the creation of a new organization. A surviving organization may be required to provide notice to the IRS of the material change. If the entities are merged into a new organization, the new organization may need to receive a determination from the IRS that it is tax-exempt.

Asset Acquisitions/Sales

Another form of combination involves the acquisition or sale of assets of an entity. This might be in the form of a nonprofit acquiring the assets of another nonprofit or a for-profit. Alternatively, the transaction might involve a for-profit acquiring the assets of a nonprofit. The structure of such a transaction is very similar to the structure of an acquisition of assets involving for-profit entities. In particular, the selling entity transfers certain identified assets and liabilities to the acquiring entity.

Similar to a merger, the process for the sale of all or substantially all of the assets of a nonprofit is governed by the relevant state nonprofit corporation acts. The Model Act and most nonprofit corporation statutes provide that a sale by a nonprofit of all or substantially all of its assets generally requires approval by the nonprofit corporation's board of directors as well as the members if the nonprofit has members, and in some states, approval of the attorney general or a court.[12]

Often, the form of agreement used is very similar to a form of asset purchase agreement used in for-profit transactions and will include a description of the assets being transferred, the liabilities being assumed, and appropriate representations and warranties regarding such assets and liabilities and the parties. Still, such an agreement likely will need to include provisions that are unique to a nonprofit. For instance, in the situation where a noncharitable entity is acquiring the assets of a charitable entity, the buyer may require that, as a condition of closing, the seller deliver any approvals necessary from state governmental authorities for the sale of the seller's charitable assets and that fair market value be paid for the acquired assets.

A significant difference between an acquisition of the assets and liabilities of a nonprofit versus a for-profit can relate to the purchase price. If the acquisition involves two charitable nonprofit entities, it may not be necessary for the acquiring nonprofit to pay fair market value (or anything) for the assets. Instead, the transaction can be structured as a gift of assets from the selling nonprofit to the acquiring nonprofit. Such gift should be permissible as long as the "selling" nonprofit corporation's creditors are paid in full upon liquidation of the nonprofit and the acquiring nonprofit either has a similar mission, or agrees to expend its mission to incorporate the purposes of the transferring organization.

A gift structure is not possible in the event a for-profit entity is acquiring assets from a nonprofit entity. To the extent a charitable nonprofit is selling its assets to a non-charitable entity, such as a business corporation, similar to the situation in mergers, state nonprofit corporation acts generally require that there be fair market value paid for the assets. In addition, some states impose requirements that the nonprofit obtain approval from a governmental body (such as the attorney general) or a court in order to proceed with the transaction. In such a situation, it would be important to obtain an independent valuation of the assets as part of the transaction.

A main advantage of an asset transaction for the acquiring nonprofit is that such a nonprofit is able to be selective in terms of the assets and liabilities it acquires. As a result, it can avoid being burdened with the liabilities of the other entity. A main disadvantage is that additional steps may need to be taken in order to complete the transaction. These include obtaining assignments of any relevant revenue-generating agreements including consent from the other parties to such agreements. In addition, the selling entity remains in existence and its board will need to take steps to either wind down its activities and dissolve or continue its existence. A disadvantage is that it does not get any deferred gifts.

Parent-Subsidiary Type Arrangements

Nonprofit corporations differ from for-profit entities in that nonprofits have no owners whereas for-profits have shareholders or other owners. Still, a parent-subsidiary structure can be structured with nonprofits. The main difference is that the "parent" nonprofit does not own any shares or other interests in the nonprofit. Instead, it is treated as the parent because of the control it has over the other nonprofit. This might be a result of the "parent" nonprofit becoming the sole voting member of the "subsidiary" nonprofit. It also could be accomplished by the parent nonprofit having the right to determine the directors of the subsidiary nonprofit. Another important difference between a nonprofit and for-profit parent-subsidiary structure is that nonprofits are unable to file consolidated tax returns with the IRS (unless the subsidiaries are single member limited liability companies).

The arrangement, which is sometimes referred to as an "affiliation" of nonprofits, can be accomplished by amendments to the articles of incorporation and bylaws of the "subsidiary" nonprofit. These documents would be amended to reflect that the "parent" organization is either the sole member (with sole voting rights) of the "subsidiary" or has a right to determine the board of directors of the subsidiary.[13]

Because this type of combination or affiliation is similar to a merger or acquisition of assets, parties often enter into some type of affiliation agreement that covers similar topics addressed in other business combination agreements. For instance, an affiliation agreement might address any change in activities of the subsidiary nonprofit as well as the composition of the parent's board of directors as well as certain representations and warranties about the parties and their operations.

One of the main advantages of a parent-subsidiary type structure is that the parent does not assume the liabilities of the subsidiary entity. In addition, the affiliation often can be easily accomplished by amending the governance documents of the "subsidiary" entity. This type of structure is also attractive to entities that are not certain about the "permanency" of the arrangement and would like the ability to "unwind" the combination if it is subsequently determined that the combination is not working out. The unwinding of the combination can be accomplished through amendments to the governing documents to take the "parent" organization out of the control position of the "subsidiary."

A disadvantage to this type of combination is that the parties may not achieve the efficiencies that can be obtained through a merger. In particular, there will still be two separate entities that generally need to file their own Form 990s with the IRS. There also will be a need to keep in place two separate boards of directors (although the subsidiary board can be quite small and meet infrequently assuming that the parent board is addressing issues relevant to the subsidiary). In addition, the board of the subsidiary will have to make decisions based on what is best for that entity, rather than what is important for the parent organization. Some organizations that choose to use this type of structure will—through a merger—collapse the "subsidiary" into the "parent" at some later point in time when it is determined that the combination should be permanent.

A variation of this structure is the incorporation of a third nonprofit corporation that becomes the sole member (or parent) of the existing nonprofit corporations. This may be attractive to nonprofits that see themselves as "equals" to each other. The advantages of such a structure are similar to the advantages of the "parent/subsidiary" structure. One disadvantage is that a new nonprofit corporation needs to be incorporated and likely needs to obtain tax-exempt status. In addition, the IRS has shown some disfavor to granting tax-exempt status to entities that are merely holding companies with no operations. As a result, it may be necessary to have some activities of the combined nonprofits occurring at the "parent" level.

Forms of Less Integrated Affiliations

Nonprofits can be involved in other types of arrangements that result in organizations combining their resources to a lesser extent. For instance, two nonprofits may enter into arrangements for joint funding, joint programming, combined services, or other type of joint venture. These types of arrangements allow the involved nonprofits to maintain their autonomy while achieving some efficiencies. It is also possible for nonprofits to enter into joint venture arrangements with for-profit entities. Such arrangements raise tax issues that can impact the structure of any joint venture. See *Chapter 6: Creating For-Profit Subsidiaries and Joint Ventures*.

Unique Due Diligence Considerations

Similar to business combinations involving for-profit corporations, due diligence activities are important for combinations involving nonprofit corporations. Many of the considerations for a for-profit business combination are important in due diligence reviews involving a nonprofit business combination. These include reviewing information and various documents relating to the other entity, including its governance documents (such as articles of incorporation, bylaws, and board policies), financial information (including audited financial statements and any audit reports), contractual arrangements, real and personal property, litigation, insurance coverages, and workforce/employees (and employee benefits).

Still, given the unique nature of nonprofits, there are other factors important to business combinations involving nonprofits that should be considered as part of the due diligence process. Below is a description of some of these considerations.

- The tax-exempt status of any nonprofit involved in a combination is important and should be confirmed through a review of the original exemption application, and determination letter issued by the IRS. In addition, there should be a review of recent Form 990 federal tax filings for the nonprofit.
- Many nonprofits are exempt from paying property taxes on their real estate as a result of being a nonprofit. This can mean significant savings to the nonprofit. Because exemption for property tax is not automatically determined on the basis of whether an entity is tax-exempt under the Internal Revenue Code, the parties to a combination need to consider whether the resulting transaction will jeopardize any existing property tax exemptions.
- Many nonprofits depend on public and private funding as well as bond financing. The terms of such funding and financings should be reviewed to determine whether the particular form of combination will impact the continued existence of such arrangements. In addition, many nonprofits have institutional funds that have restrictions imposed on them by their donors. As noted above, in the context of a merger, any such funds presumptively are transferred to the surviving entity unless there are restrictions that prohibit such transfer. It is important that the restrictions be considered as part of the due diligence process to ensure that a transfer is possible and that the surviving entity is able to honor such restrictions.
- As described above, a combination involving a nonprofit corporation may require approval by the nonprofit's members if it has any. For nonprofits with members, it is important to determine whether such "members" meet the state nonprofit corporation act's definition of members. Typically, such a definition focuses on individuals or entities that elect part or all of the board of directors. It is possible that a nonprofit may have a group of individuals designated as "members" who do not have such rights. In such circumstances, it may not be necessary to obtain their approval of the merger (or other business combination) unless the articles or bylaws of the organization mandate such approval.

- As described below, to the extent the combination will result in an entity, other than a charitable nonprofit, as the surviving entity, it may be necessary to obtain state attorney general or court approval. Such determination should be made as part of the due diligence process.

Application of Duties of Care and Loyalty to Combination Decisions

In General

As discussed in *Chapter 2, Duties and Rights of Nonprofit Corporation Directors,* directors of nonprofits are considered fiduciaries with duties of care and loyalty to the corporation. When a combination is contemplated, the processes used by the directors to evaluate the potential change—including decisions among various alternatives—are likely to be subject to scrutiny. Persons and groups outside the board may have reason to evaluate whether the board's decision process was handled in a manner that satisfied the directors' duties.

Nonprofit directors should be aware that they may be judged in part by standards that have developed in the for-profit world, in case law challenging the propriety of board actions in change of control situations.[14] Although some issues arising in nonprofit combination circumstances do not arise in the for-profit world (and vice versa), a number of basic guidelines drawn from the for-profit arena are equally applicable to nonprofit boards. These guidelines generally focus on what actions are necessary or sufficient to show that the directors have fulfilled their fiduciary duties of care and loyalty in connection with a combination event.

Satisfying the Duty of Care

How and when the duty of care applies

The director's duty of care requires that the process by which a combination decision is made should mirror the significance of the decision. (For further discussion of a director's duty of care, see the section "*The Duty of Care*" in *Chapter 2, Duties and Rights of Nonprofit Corporation Directors.*) Sometimes, the decision process is initiated by an external prompt—for instance, another nonprofit with a similar mission proposes a merger to maximize joint corporate resources and community support, or a nonprofit or for-profit entity approaches the corporation about purchasing some or all of the nonprofit's assets and operations. More often, the corporation's own management or board initiates an evaluation process to determine the corporation's options in light of declining revenues, an inability to garner community support for new projects, loss of a stable source of volunteers, or other factors that make it difficult to fulfill the corporation's mission. Occasionally, the need for change is not recognized until the corporation is on or near the brink of insolvency. Unless this situation was brought about precipitously by unexpected events, the late discovery of such a problem may indicate a failure by the board to properly oversee the corporation's operations. (See discussion in Chapter 11, *"Insolvency or Bankruptcy"* for other board considerations in the event of insolvency.) In most cases, however, the board is aware for some time of the factors leading up to a potential need for change.

Duty to be informed

The primary means for satisfying the director's duty of care in any situation is to be adequately informed before making a decision. The recommended information gathering and evaluation process that meets the board's duty of care in a combination event context has two main components: first, identifying the nature and quality of information that should be obtained to make an informed decision, and second, ensuring that independent consultants and/or committees composed of disinterested directors take the lead in evaluating aspects of combination decisions in which some members of the board have an interest or potential interest.

Key issues to be addressed

While each combination decision is unique, certain issues are typically present. Directors should make sure that they have thorough and reliable information on these and other material issues:

(1) What are the factors requiring or motivating the board to consider a combination?
(2) What is the current economic environment?
(3) Would a combination of the corporation be consistent with the purpose/mission of the corporation?
(4) What are the alternatives to a combination generally?
(5) What are the pros, cons, and alternatives for any considered form of combination and has an independent appraisal been obtained?
(6) Should an auction or a bidding process be used to maximize the value to be paid for the corporation's assets (if applicable), or to broaden the search for parties who may be interested in engaging

in a combination transaction with the corporation? Alternatively, will the mission of the corporation be better served by a transfer of the assets to another nonprofit organization?

(7) What is the fair market value of the corporation's assets and activities? Will or should the corporation obtain a valuation prepared by an independent valuation specialist?

(8) What nonmonetary criteria should be considered by the directors when making a combination decision?

(9) What experts and other resources are available to assist the board in analyzing the relevant issues pertaining to the combination decision?

(10) If the assets of the corporation are to be sold to another (nonprofit or for-profit) entity, what will happen to the proceeds?

(11) What governmental authorities must receive notice or give their approval for a combination transaction?

(12) When and how will beneficiary groups and other parties (including donors) be informed of a combination? Should the change of control evaluation process include a mechanism for obtaining input from any such groups?

Board evaluation process

The time available for the board to evaluate a proposed combination is dictated by the circumstances at hand. In some cases, directors have some luxury of time; in other cases, financial or other circumstances require fairly quick action. In either case, however, the board should be aware that the *process* they use to make their decision—as well as the ultimate decision itself—may be subject to a high degree of scrutiny, before or after the combination is completed. Once the board has identified the key issues to be addressed, it is faced with the decision of how to address them. The use of independent legal and financial advisers is highly recommended; in some cases, failure to obtain objective and expert opinions on certain key issues (such as the value of the corporation's assets or whether the terms of the proposed transactions are fair to the corporation) may be regarded as a breach of the directors' duty of care.

Independent board committees

For some combination decisions, certain members of the board may have a personal interest or stake in the decision. In particular, board members who are also employees of the corporation and who may lose their positions, or gain new positions with a merged or acquiring entity, have conflicts of interest that make it difficult for them to objectively evaluate combination decisions. Because of these conflicts, both for-profit and nonprofit corporations are well advised to appoint a committee consisting solely of independent (i.e., nonmanagement) directors to evaluate a combination decision and make a recommendation to the board. The independent committee may engage its own independent experts (i.e., ones not regularly employed by the corporation), including attorneys, accountants, and other consultants, to assist it in evaluating the proposed transaction.

Duty of Loyalty Issues

The duty of loyalty requires each nonprofit director to act in the best interests of the corporation, and to not make decisions that further the director's own interests at the corporation's expense. If a combination decision presents a conflict of interest for one or more directors—such as a director who is also the organization president, and whose job may depend on who acquires the corporation's assets—the entire board must take steps to make sure that this conflict of interest does not affect the board's decision as to what is in the corporation's best interest.

First, directors who have a conflict or potential conflict of interest related to a proposed combination (or relating to one of several alternatives) must disclose the conflict, and follow the board's usual procedures for handling conflicts of interest. Second, the directors should evaluate whether the nature of any conflicts suggests that a special committee of independent directors should be used to evaluate a change of control proposal.

If "insider" directors are involved in the negotiation of combination transactions, they need to be aware of both actual and perceived conflicts of interest. Such directors should make sure to document that the decisions they make and actions they take in the course of negotiations are in the best interests of the company. In addition, these directors should assure that other directors are aware of any conflicts of interest and have taken the necessary steps (such as obtaining the advice of independent consultants) to allow the board to make decisions based on objective criteria.

Role of State Attorney General

Nonprofit corporations contemplating a combination event may be required to give the state attorney general notice of the proposed change. In some states, the attorney general must approve the proposed change before it occurs. Such notice and approval requirements may be set forth in the state nonprofit code or other statute, and may apply to all public benefit corporations, or only to those in specific industries (e.g., health care).[15] Such statutes may apply even if the proposed acquiring or successor entity is another nonprofit, or only when a for-profit corporation is proposed to assume control of the nonprofit's operations. Even in states in which no statute specifically requires a nonprofit to give notice to or obtain approval from the attorney general in connection with a combination transaction, the attorney general may assert rights to notice or approve the transaction based on the doctrine of *cy pres.* In many states, a state attorney general is generally considered a necessary or appropriate representative of the public interest with the power to review and/or approve a transaction that may change the charitable purpose of a nonprofit, public benefit corporation. Directors of nonprofit corporations that are considering a combination transaction should obtain the advice of counsel as to whether and how the state attorney general may become involved in the combination decision process.

Other Regulatory Approvals

Depending on the nature of the nonprofit organization, regulatory authorities other than the state attorney general may be required to receive notice of or approve the combination, or some aspect of the change. As part of evaluating a combination proposal, the board should ensure that legal counsel has identified what governmental approvals are required to implement the combination, and at what stage. For instance, where only notice is required, should such notice be given a certain number of days before or after the change is to be effective? If approval is required before the combination is effective, how long will the approval process take? The directors should factor in regulatory approval periods when determining the date that a combination will occur. The board should also be informed as to whether the approval process would be routine or involve intensive review and potential requests for changes to the structure of the transaction.

Tax Considerations

In combinations where the surviving entity will not be a tax-exempt nonprofit corporation, it is important for the board of directors to confirm that there will not be any issues in terms of private inurement, private benefit, and excess benefit transactions.[16]

Other Interest Groups Affected by a Business Combination

A nonprofit corporation's beneficiaries, donors, funders, and employees, as well as other members of the community, may all have an interest in—or an opinion on—a nonprofit's proposed combination transaction. From a legal perspective, these groups generally lack any legal right to receive advance notice, evaluate, or comment on a nonprofit change of control (unlike the state attorney general, who may have such rights in the role as the representative of the public interest and/or a charity's beneficiaries). Nonetheless, beneficiaries and other groups who learn about a proposed combination may believe they have a right to participate in, or even to challenge, a nonprofit's proposed combination. Such groups may also animate the interests of local politicians or governmental bodies in the proposed change. As part of the board's combination planning and evaluation process, the directors should consider the likely reaction of key constituencies to the proposed combination, then decide whether any specific actions should be taken to inform these constituencies or give them opportunities to formally express their views and concerns. In some cases, professional public relations consultants may be able to assist the directors in effectively addressing community concerns. In addition, if significant funding is received from a governmental entity, approval of the combination by the entity may be required (or advisable even if not required) before the transaction is completed, to ensure that the funding will continue after the combination is completed.

Summary

It is unlikely that directors of a nonprofit corporation will enter into a combination decision lightly. Still, directors should be aware of the high level of legal and public scrutiny that may be applied both to their ultimate decision, and the process by which they arrived at the decision. In addition, directors should know that there is legal precedent (often drawn from for-profit cases) regarding what actions and procedures are and are not considered sufficient means for directors to fulfill their fiduciary duties when making a combination decision. Combination decisions present a challenge to nonprofit directors to exercise their decision-making authority consistently with their fiduciary duties. In addition, the directors must be able to justify and explain their decisions to numerous interested constituencies.

See the Suggested Questions and Checklist following the Endnotes below to review the issues discussed in this chapter.

Endnotes

1. *See* Willard L. Boyd III, *Mergers, Acquisitions, and Affiliations Involving Nonprofits: Not Typical M&A Transactions*, ABA Business Law Today (June 2014).
2. *See* Model Act §1220; Wash Rev. Code §24.03A.745(4); D.C. Code §29-409.32.
3. *See* Model Act §1220; Iowa Code §504.1101; Wash. Rev. Code §24.63A.730; Restatement of the Law, Charitable Nonprofit Organizations, §3.04(c).
4. *See* Model Act §1220.
5. *See* Restatement of the Law, Charitable Nonprofit Organizations, §3.04(a).
6. *See* Model Act §1222; Wash. Rev. Code §24.03A.737.
7. *See, e.g.*, Iowa Code §504.1102; N.C. Gen. Stat. §55A-11-02.
8. *See, e.g.*, Iowa Code §504.1101.
9. *See, e.g.*, N.C. Gen. Stat. §55A-11-05.
10. *See, e.g.*, Iowa Code §504.1107; Wash. Rev. code §24.03A.745(4).
11. *See, e.g.*, 805 ILCS 12/0.01 et seq.; Ohio Rev. Code §1702.41.
12. *See, e.g.*, Model Act §1002; Ohio Rev. Stat. §1702.39.
13. *See, e.g.*, Jennifer R. Bishop and Catherine B. Amundsen, *When Are We Going to Talk about Money? A Nonprofit M&A Primer for the Business Attorney*, ABA Business Law Today (June 2017); Boyd, *supra* note 1.
14. *See* Colin T. Moran, *Why Revlon Applies to Nonprofit Corporations,* 53 Business Law 373 (1998). *See also* Revlon, Inc. v. MacAndrews & Forbes Holding, Inc., 506 A.2d 173 (Del. 1986). Under *Revlon* and other cases, courts have found that once a board has determined that a change of control of the corporation is inevitable, the board has a duty to effect the change that best maximizes the price to be received by the company's shareholders. However, the *Revlon* maximization principle does not apply in all change of control circumstances; *see* Paramount Communications, Inc. v. Time, Inc., 571 A.2d 1140 (Del. 1989). In a nonprofit change of control transactions, the state attorney general or others may argue that the changing corporation should be sold to the highest bidder, thus maximizing the proceeds available to be transferred to a charitable foundation or to be used for other charitable purposes. Still, other considerations—such as whether to sell to a nonprofit or a for-profit—may also be valid factors for the board to evaluate, depending on the circumstances.

15. *See, e.g., A Guide to Mergers and Consolidations of Not-for-Profit Corporations under Article 9 of the New York Not-for-Profit Corporation Law* (State of New York Attorney General), *available at* www.ag.ny.gov.; CAL. CORP. CODE *§§ 5917, 5923* (giving the California Attorney General the authority to review nonprofit hospital transactions, and to decide whether to permit the transaction and, if so, on what terms); Prime Healthcare Servs., Inc. et al. v. Harris, No. 3:16-cv-00778-GPC-RBB, 2016 WL 6427924 (S.D. Cal. Oct. 31, 2016) (discussing statutory and regulatory requirements for sale of not-for-profit hospital in California).
16. *See* Meghan R. Biss and Sharon P. Want, *Mergers, Acquisitions, and Conversions in the Context of Nonprofit Organizations,* ABA BUSINESS LAW TODAY (August 2018); IRS Rev. Proc. 2018-15, 2018-9 I.R.B.376.

Suggested Questions for Directors Regarding Duties of Mergers, Sale of Assets, Affiliations, and Other Combinations

(1) What information does the board need to properly evaluate a proposed combination transition? What alternatives were considered? Has the fairness of the transaction from a financial standpoint been evaluated by an independent party?

(2) What board members, officers, or other corporate insiders may be personally affected by a combination?

(3) What processes should the board put in place to address conflict of interest issues during the consideration of a potential combination, as well as during any negotiation with third parties? Should a committee of independent board members be appointed to make recommendations to the board regarding a proposed combination, or to negotiate key deal terms?

(4) Will approval of the state attorney general or other regulators be required before a combination may be effected?

(5) How will community groups, employees, and constituencies of the corporation likely react to news of a combination proposal or event? Should such concerns be addressed as part of the board's evaluation and negotiation process? Should public relations professionals be used to help communicate information about a combination?

Checklist: Duties of Directors in Mergers, Sale of Assets, Affiliations, and Other Combinations

Note: For simplicity, these and other chapter checklists describe a corporation having a chair, who presides over the board of directors; a chief executive, who may be a staff person; an executive committee; a governance/nominating committee; and an audit committee. (We recognize, however, that in many smaller and other nonprofits, these committee functions may be performed by either the executive committee or the board as a whole.) We also assume a legal counsel—someone, paid or unpaid, having primary responsibility for the corporation's legal affairs. Many corporations, especially larger nonprofits, may have other committees established for specific purposes, such as establishing executive compensation; monitoring compliance with legal requirements; and overseeing investments and other financial matters.

Subject	Review By	How Often	Comment
1. When and how should transaction counsel, financial advisers, and other experts needed be selected to assist the board and management in evaluating and accomplishing the transaction?	Chief executive, chief counsel, and chief financial officer, in consultation with board chair	As soon as possible after the proposed transaction becomes a serious consideration	Given the significance of sales, mergers, and other change of control transactions, it is important to obtain guidance from experienced consultants and counsel.
2. What special meetings or executive sessions of board (or designated special committee) meetings will be necessary to evaluate and discuss the terms and implications of the proposed transaction?	Chief executive and board chair, in consultation with the chair of the special transaction committee, if any	At the start of the transaction and at major milestone marks (e.g., before signing a letter of intent; on completion of due diligence; before signing a definitive agreement, etc.)	Combinations often involve a host of significant considerations that must be evaluated prior to approval by the board.

Subject	Review By	How Often	Comment
3. Who will coordinate internal and external communication regarding a proposed or approved combination to assure consistent messages are being delivered?	Chief executive, marketing/ communications staff, or consultants	Prior to public announcement and ongoing until the transaction is completed	Combination transactions create significant anxiety in employees, beneficiaries, donors, and other stakeholders. It is good practice to provide board members with talking points and to designate one board member (e.g., board chair) and/ or executive as the "point person" for communications with media and key stakeholders.
13. Does the corporation have an organizational chart?	Chief executive	Annually	An organizational chart of management and management reporting relationships should assist the board in understanding the organization.

Chapter 11:
Duties of Directors under Special Circumstances: Sale of Unique Assets, Dissolution, and Bankruptcy

Chapter 11

Duties of Directors under Special Circumstances: Sale of Unique Assets, Dissolution, and Bankruptcy

In addition to combinations, which are discussed in Chapter 10, special duties of directors can arise in other circumstances. This chapter discusses the duties of a director for the following special circumstances: (1) disposition of unique assets; (2) dissolution; and (3) insolvency or bankruptcy.

Disposition of Unique Assets

Circumstances in Which Disposition Issues May Arise

Some nonprofits, particularly museums (but also a wide variety of other entities), may find that legal restraints, public perceptions, and functional necessities require the sale or other disposal of property that cannot be placed on the market in a conventional manner. Thus, an art museum may decide that a given painting lacks sufficient quality to merit a regular place in its galleries, or its original attribution to a great artist proves to be erroneous. A social service institution may find that an original settlement house, no longer practical as a center for its services, is nonetheless regarded as a symbol of the community's commitment to serving the underprivileged. A church may occupy a building that is an architectural masterpiece but the congregation that built it and supported it has moved away from the neighborhood.

There is no one-size-fits-all policy that addresses the disposition of unique property, but there are examples. In the case of art museums, the problem is both eased and made more difficult because a ready market exists for works of art, even those that a museum considers unworthy of its walls. On the other hand, the possibility, real or apparent, of an officer or trustee of such a museum exploiting a deaccessioning decision to acquire, for personal use or resale, an arguably disposable object is too obvious to be disregarded.[1]

Board Considerations in the Sale of Unique Assets

A nonprofit board finding itself with the need to dispose of unique assets should seek the aid of other organizations or individuals with expertise related to the property at issue, possibly including nonprofit organizations that have an interest in protecting the particular kind of property at issue. For example, a nonprofit organization evaluating the disposition of a landmark piece of architecture could seek advice from a nonprofit entity dedicated to such functions. Similarly, in the case of vacant land, a local conservation group would likely be delighted to work with the board to help identify options that serve both the corporation's and the community's interests. Further, if the property was donated to the organization or constitutes a significant portion of the corporation's assets, the corporation should determine whether it has an obligation under state law to either notify or receive approval for the sale from the state attorney general, with respect to change of control of a major charitable asset.

Because such dispositions are by their nature unique, the best advice for board members is to proceed with care—and consider the best way to balance any competing community interests—before making a final decision.

Dissolution

Circumstances in Which Dissolution May Arise

There may be a time where the board of directors determines that it makes no sense to continue the operation of the nonprofit. This often occurs when the organization does not have the financial support to continue its operations.

Possible alternatives for the board to consider in these situations include some type of combination described in Chapter 10 or dissolution of the organization.

Process for Dissolution

Voluntary dissolution

State nonprofit corporation acts set forth procedures for voluntary and involuntary dissolutions of nonprofit corporations that are very similar to state for-profit corporation acts. In many states, voluntary dissolution requires the filing of articles of dissolution as well as the development of a plan of dissolution. The directors, in approving a dissolution, must prepare a plan of dissolution indicating to whom the assets owned or held by the corporation will be distributed after all creditors have been paid. At any time after the dissolution is authorized, the nonprofit corporation typically may dissolve by delivering articles of dissolution to the secretary of state.

Voluntary dissolution typically may occur only if approved by the board, the members, if any, and by any person or persons whose approval is required by a provision of the articles for an amendment to the articles or bylaws. State law often will provide that to the extent a corporation has no directors and no members, the incorporator of a corporation is authorized to dissolve a corporation, and to the extent a corporation has directors but no members, the directors are able to voluntarily dissolve the corporation.

Similar to the situation for a for-profit corporation, a dissolved corporation continues its corporate existence but is not allowed to carry on any activities except those appropriate to wind up and liquidate its affairs, including all the following: (1) preserving and protecting its assets and minimizing its liabilities; (2) discharging or making provision for discharging its liabilities and obligations; (3) disposing of its properties that will not be distributed in kind; (4) returning, transferring, or conveying assets held by the corporation upon a condition requiring return, transfer, or conveyance, which condition occurs by reason of dissolution, in accordance with such condition; (5) transferring its assets, subject to any contractual or legal requirements, as provided in or authorized by its articles of incorporation or bylaws; and (6) doing every other act necessary to wind up and liquidate its assets and affairs.

In some states, there are restrictions placed on the dissolution of a public benefit or religious corporation. In particular, if the corporation is a charitable organization (including public benefit and religious corporations), the distribution of assets may need to occur in a manner in which the charitable purpose of such assets will continue. This typically requires that those corporations only distribute assets to other entities described in section 501(c)(3) of the Internal Revenue Code.

In contrast, if the nonprofit is a mutual benefit corporation which has members with an "ownership" interest and a provision has not been made in its articles or bylaws for the distribution of assets on dissolution, it may be permissible to transfer assets to the nonprofit corporation's members or, if it has no members, to those persons whom the corporation holds itself out as benefitting or serving;

Similar to the situation involving a dissolution of a for-profit corporation, dissolution of a nonprofit corporation does not do any of the following: (1) transfer title to the corporation's property; (2) subject its directors or officers to standards of conduct different than those prescribed the applicable nonprofit act; (3) change quorum or voting requirements for its board or members; (4) change provisions for selection, resignation, or removal of its directors or officers or both; (5) change provisions for amending its bylaws; (6) prevent commencement of a proceeding by or against a corporation in its corporate name; (7) abate or suspend a proceeding pending by or against the corporation on the effective date of the dissolution; or (8) terminate the authority of the registered agent.

In general, state nonprofit corporation acts set forth a process for notifying creditors of both "known claims" and "unknown claims." For "known claims" against a dissolved corporation, the dissolved corporation is generally required to notify its known claimants in writing of the dissolution at any time after the effective date of the dissolution. A claim against the dissolved corporation will be barred if either of the following occurs: (1) a claimant who was given proper written notice does not deliver the claim to the dissolved corporation by the deadline, and (2) a claimant whose claim was rejected by the dissolved corporation does not commence a proceeding to enforce the claim within a certain number of days from the effective date of the rejection notice.

For "unknown claims" against a dissolved corporation, a dissolved corporation may also publish notice of its dissolution and request the persons with claims against the corporation present them in accordance with the notice. If the dissolved corporation properly publishes a notice in a newspaper of general circulation, the claims will generally be barred if they are not brought within a certain period of time, which is generally longer than the notice period for known claims.

Similar to for-profit corporation statutes, a nonprofit corporation act often will provide that a claim may be enforced to the following extent, as applicable: (1) against the dissolved corporation, to the extent of its undistributed assets; and (2) if the assets have been distributed in liquidation, against any person, other than a creditor of the corporation, to whom the corporation distributed its property to the extent of the distributee's pro rata share of the claim or the corporate assets distributed to such person in liquidation, whichever is less, but the distributee's total liability for all claims shall not exceed the total amount of assets distributed the distributee.

Administrative dissolution

State nonprofit corporation acts also provide procedures for administrative dissolution. In general, an administrative dissolution can occur as a result of

(1) a failure of the nonprofit corporation to file its annual or biennial report with the state secretary of state's office; (2) the corporation being without a registered agent or registered office in the state for a certain period of time; (3) the corporation not notifying the Secretary of State within a certain period of time that its registered agent or registered office has been changed, that its registered agent has resigned, or that its registered office has been discontinued; and (4) the corporation's period of duration, if any, as stated in its articles of incorporation expiring.

State nonprofit corporation acts may set forth a process for reinstatement following administrative dissolution. States vary on how long a nonprofit corporation can be administratively dissolved and still be eligible for reinstatement.

From time to time, a nonprofit corporation will unknowingly be dissolved due to a failure to file a required annual report or biennial report with the secretary of state. For nonprofits, this can occur when a volunteer identified as the contact person (likely the registered agent) is no longer involved with the organization and does not respond to a request by the secretary of state to file an annual report or biennial report. As a result, it is advisable to check the secretary of state's website on a regular basis to ensure the nonprofit has not been suspended or administratively dissolved.

Judicial dissolution

State nonprofit corporation acts also provide for judicial dissolution. Under the Model Act, a state court may dissolve a corporation in a proceeding brought by the state attorney general, if any of the following is established: (1) the corporation obtained its articles of incorporation through fraud; or (2) the corporation has continued to exceed or abuse the authority conferred upon it by law.[2]

A state court also may dissolve a corporation in a proceeding brought by a certain minimum number of members, or by a director or any person specified in the articles, if any of the following is established: (1) the directors are deadlocked in the management of the corporate affairs, and the members, if any, are unable to break the deadlock; (2) the directors or those in control of the corporation have acted, are acting, or will act in a manner that is illegal, oppressive, or fraudulent; (3) the members are deadlocked in voting power and have failed, for a period that includes at least two consecutive annual meeting dates, to elect successors to directors whose terms have, or would otherwise have, expired; (4) the corporate assets are being misapplied or wasted; or (5) the corporation has insufficient assets to continue its activities and is no longer able to assemble a quorum of directors or members.[3] (Depending on the nonprofit corporation act, a religious corporation may be able to preclude such an action in its articles or bylaws.)

A state court may also dissolve a corporation in a proceeding brought by a creditor, if either of the following is established: (1) the creditor's claim has been reduced to judgment, the execution of the judgment is returned unsatisfied, and the corporation is insolvent, or (2) the corporation has admitted in writing that the creditor's claim is due and owing and the corporation is insolvent.[4]

Finally, a court may dissolve a corporation in a proceeding brought by the corporation to have its voluntary dissolution continued under court supervision.[5]

Prior to dissolving a corporation, the court generally considers whether: (1) there are reasonable alternatives to dissolutions; (2) dissolution is in the public interest, if the corporation is a corporation exempt under §501(c)(3) of the Internal Revenue Code; or (3) dissolution is the best way of protecting the interests of members, if the corporation is a mutual benefit corporation.

A court in a judicial proceeding brought to dissolve a nonprofit corporation may appoint one or more receivers to wind up and liquidate, or one or more custodians to manage, the affairs of the corporation. The court may appoint an individual, or a domestic or foreign business or nonprofit corporation authorized to transact business in the state, as a receiver or custodian. In appointing a receiver, the court is to describe the powers and duties of the receiver or custodian in its appointing order.

Generally, if after a hearing the court determines that one or more grounds for judicial dissolution exist, the court may enter a decree dissolving the corporation and specify the effective date of the dissolution. After entering the decree of dissolution, the court is to direct the winding up of the corporation's affairs and liquidation of the corporation and the notification of its claimants in accordance with the notice provisions for creditors.

Tax issues relating to dissolution

A nonprofit corporation that has tax-exempt status under Section 501(c)(3), is required to permanently dedicate its assets for a Section 501(c)(3) purpose. This means that if the organization dissolves, the assets must be distributed for an exempt purpose described in Section 501(c)(3), or to the federal government, or to a state or local government for a public purpose. As a result, if the organizing document for a nonprofit corporation that is exempt under section 501(c)(3) of the Internal Revenue Code states that the assets are to be distributed to members or private individuals or for any purpose other than those provided in section 501(c)(3), the organization must amend its organizing document to remove such statements.

Board Considerations in a Voluntary Dissolution

Similar to situations where the board of a charitable nonprofit is considering a combination transition, voluntary dissolution raises heightened risks that charitable assets will be used inappropriately. As a result, steps need to be taken to ensure that the charitable assets or the fair market value of such assets to the extent the assets exceed the liabilities will continue to be used for a charitable purpose.[6] This means that a charitable nonprofit is not able to distribute assets remaining after payment of liabilities to non-charitable parties except in limited circumstances. The board also may be required by state law or the organizational documents to consult with constituencies before dissolution or termination. For example, a chapter of a fraternal organization may be required to consult or obtain approval from the "parent" fraternal organization on how the distribution of assets will occur.

The Model Act and some nonprofit corporation act provide that directors of a dissolved nonprofit corporation that has disposed of claims in accordance with the applicable requirements are not held liable for unlawful distributions for claims against the dissolved corporation that are barred or satisfied under the act's provisions on dissolution.[7]

Insolvency and Bankruptcy

It is important that the board of directors of a nonprofit corporation facing insolvency be aware of special duties that may arise with regard to the operation of a nonprofit corporation that is in the "zone of insolvency" as well as when the nonprofit is in bankruptcy. Most of the rules and issues confronting for-profit corporations in such situations also are present for nonprofit corporations. Still, there are certain unique issues relating to insolvencies and bankruptcies of nonprofit corporations, which generally reflect their unique public interest nature, mission, and corporate structure.

The "Zone of Insolvency"

Insolvency

The law suggests two separate standards that may be applied in determining insolvency depending on the jurisdiction involved. The "equitable insolvency test" considers a corporation to be insolvent when it is unable to pay its debts as they become due. The "balance-sheet insolvency test" considers a corporation to be insolvent when its total liabilities exceed its total assets.[8] A corporation also may be considered to have entered the "zone of insolvency" if it enters into a transaction that leaves the corporation with an unreasonably small capital base, making insolvency reasonably foreseeable.

The concept of a "zone of insolvency" is important because some courts have held that in the for-profit context some of the duties of the board and officers of corporations approaching or entering insolvency shift from solely protecting stockholder interests to also considering creditors' interests, and such a view has become increasingly relevant to nonprofit corporations. As a result, if a nonprofit enters the "zone of insolvency," these courts may require that the board consider (and refrain from actions unreasonably threatening) the interests of creditors in being paid, even if those decisions limit or conflict with absolute fulfillment of the charitable purpose of the nonprofit. In other words, as the corporation approaches and even enters the zone of insolvency, the board of directors may have an increasing duty to consider the impact of its decisions on creditors and the corporate enterprise and not to just "roll the dice" so as to unreasonably sacrifice creditor recoveries.

Still, most courts hold that a board of a nonprofit has no general duty to operate a corporation in the "zone of insolvency" for the benefit of creditors, rather than its conventional duties of loyalty and due care. The applicable non-bankruptcy rules require that, even with an insolvent corporation, the board's duties are limited "to the avoidance of actions that divert, dissipate, or unduly risk corporate assets that may otherwise be used to pay creditor claims," specifically including acts of self-dealing, or giving preferential treatment to a creditor over other similarly situated creditors.[9] Further, it has been recognized that "because the existence of a zone or vicinity of insolvency is even less objectively determinable than actual insolvency, ... there is no fiduciary duty prescribed under ... law that is owed to creditors by directors of the corporation solely by virtue of its operating in the 'zone' or 'vicinity' of insolvency."[10]

Moreover, in most states, there is no change unless the corporation is actually insolvent. For example, under California law, once a corporation becomes insolvent, the "trust fund doctrine" applies, and "all of the assets of a corporation ... become a trust fund for the benefit of all of its creditors."[11] Under the trust fund doctrine, recovery for breaches of fiduciary duties "generally pertain[s] to cases where the directors or officers of an insolvent corporation have diverted assets of the corporation 'for the benefit of insiders or preferred creditors.'"[12] No California cases "expressly limit the fiduciary duty under the trust fund doctrine to the prohibition of self-dealing or the preferential treatment of creditors, [but] the scope of the trust fund doctrine in California is reasonably limited to cases where directors or officers have diverted, dissipated, or unduly risked the insolvent corporation's assets."[13] In sum, for creditors to recover under the trust fund doctrine for breaches of fiduciary duties, directors must have engaged in self-dealing, favored certain creditors, or engaged in conduct that has diverted, dissipated, or unduly risked the insolvent corporation's assets. Thus, California law does not impose duties to creditors solely due to a state of corporate insolvency; before liability will be imposed under California law, directors must have engaged in some type of misconduct.

What should boards do differently if the organization is insolvent or nearly insolvent?

When in the zone of insolvency, the nonprofit board may wish to consider the financial impact of proposed corporate transactions and may choose to refrain from funding programs even if consistent with its mission where the expenditure threatens ultimate payment to creditors. In this regard, the board may consider retaining a financial adviser to advise on whether insolvency is being approached and the appropriateness of such material expenditures. Boards of nonprofit corporations approaching or within the "zone" also may consider protections that may have been or should be undertaken to assure that donor-restricted funds are held in trust or will not be used in an inappropriate manner (e.g., used in an unrestricted manner for general operations).

In situations where a nonprofit board is faced with a zone of insolvency tension between financial interests and charitable purpose duties (e.g., where a business decision might benefit or be protective of financial or creditor interests, but not strictly adhere to the charitable mission), it may even be appropriate to consult the state attorney general before such a decision is finalized. A nonprofit corporation must be aware of the position being taken by the courts in its location before taking action that might infringe on creditors' rights.

Finally, a nonprofit board on the precipice of insolvency should be aware that large transactions with creditors—and particularly creditors who are "insiders" of the nonprofit corporation—may be subject to additional scrutiny as voidable transfers under applicable state law and bankruptcy law or as preferences under bankruptcy law. Nonprofit corporate boards considering making large payments to creditors that are outside of the ordinary course of business should consult with counsel to determine whether those payments create a litigation risk both under state law and bankruptcy law.

Interests of Creditors vs. the Charitable Mission

Tax-exempt nonprofits may be subject to more limits than for-profits in taking actions to limit expenditures or to sell and turn assets into cash that can be used for overall operations and debt service. Nonprofits may be subject to criticism as well as public or attorney general scrutiny of transactions such as the sales of facilities and use of their proceeds, even if those transactions were designed to and would ultimately benefit the overall financial viability of the nonprofit.

State attorney general review of corporate transactions in many states generally has been limited to nonprofit to for-profit asset sales (or "conversions") or transactions involving outright self-dealing or *ultra vires* conduct. In some cases, however, the nonprofit transactions that have drawn fire from state officials have involved straightforward asset transfers to other nonprofit corporations and, in particular, transactions in which a financially strained nonprofit corporation seeks to sell or close a struggling facility, exit a community, or entirely divest itself of a portfolio of in-state holdings, with the goal of using the proceeds to fund other of its charitable facilities at different locations.[14] State attorneys general similarly have objected to specific expenditures by some financially challenged nonprofit corporations (including fees for hiring restructuring or bankruptcy professionals) and have suggested that nonprofit corporation funds can be viewed as held in a constructive or implied charitable trust and may only be expended in accordance with charitable mission objectives rather than made available for creditor recoveries or other purposes that might facilitate a restructuring.[15]

To the extent that attorneys general have advanced the argument that the assets of a nonprofit system are held pursuant to a constructive or implied charitable trust for the benefit of the community, the assets of a nonprofit organization may be viewed as less committed or available to fund the ongoing operations of the nonprofit organization or to pay creditors and, instead, as designated for the support of underperforming nonprofit assets or for furthering local community enterprises. Such a position creates potential problems and concerns for parties attempting to effect restructurings and other transactions involving entities, as well as creditors seeking recoveries from the assets of nonprofit organizations.

Restricted gifts

Directors of tax-exempt nonprofits that hold restricted gifts and are in or near the zone of insolvency should assume that no restricted funds are to be used (or "borrowed" with the intent to repay) to cover general operation expenses including restructuring costs, even if done with the intent to preserve the organization and its ability to continue to serve its charitable mission. If the organization's directors determine that, in order to survive, the organization must change its mission or purpose, it may be necessary to proceed through a *cy pres* proceeding to permit use of restricted funds for a new purpose or to change the nature of its charitable activities.

In the insolvency context, application of the "charitable trust" theory could be used to severely limit the ability of creditors, including tax-exempt bondholders, to recover against system assets that are deemed to be encumbered by trust obligations. Such assets could be deemed only available for designated charitable purposes and thereby excluded from a bankruptcy estate.

Loan/Bond Defaults and Out-of-Court Restructurings

Loan/bond debt

In addition to commercial lending resources that may be available, one of the significant advantages enjoyed by certain kinds of operating or revenue-producing nonprofits is the ability to secure long-term financing at lower market interest rates through the issuance of state authorized tax-exempt bonds.

Still, such nonprofits are not always able to service that debt or to avoid the incurrence of other defaults on the bonds and under the bond indenture. This and other cash flow problems may force the nonprofit to attempt to restructure its bond debt or secure other accommodations from the bondholders (or in the case of insured bonds, the bond insurers) and the indenture trustee that represents the bondholders.

Negotiations with bondholders or bond insurers and their indenture trustees may include a range of options to address debt payment concerns, such as: (1) agreeing to a temporary forbearance agreement not to exercise remedies; (2) restructuring the debt in or out of bankruptcy by changing its terms including reduction of debt, reduction of interest rate, stretching of payments, extension of maturity, and waiving or eliminating covenants; or (3) exchange offers or buy-outs where new debt or cash consideration is given to reduce the debt burden or even extinguish some of the bond debt.

For organizations with tax-exempt debt, restructurings may be subject to particular tax and other rules that control tax-exempt financings, including the requirements to maintain the tax-exempt status. For example, interest payments may only be deferrable or accrued for a limited time. Certain restructuring terms may need to be approved by the state agency which authorized the bond issuance.

Operational and trade debt

If the nonprofit's financial issues extend to difficulties or an inability to pay more currently owed debts—whether to suppliers, employees, or other service providers—the board may need to assure that the appropriate attention is given to, first, cash management, and then to the possibility of negotiating a stretch-out or discounting of current debt obligations. Such accommodations may even be included in a more global out-of-court restructuring or can be incorporated in a bankruptcy plan.

Bankruptcies

Bankruptcy is a method of dealing with and ultimately discharging (forgiving) unpaid debts either through the liquidation of assets or the reorganization of the debtor's financial affairs. Bankruptcy is authorized under the Bankruptcy Code—a uniform federal law administered by bankruptcy judges who serve as units of the United States district courts.[16] Bankruptcy may be necessary or advisable if an out-of-court restructuring cannot be achieved or to bind all creditors to a restructuring of their debt negotiated with some creditors prior to bankruptcy. Bankruptcy is also used as an interim strategy to stay collection actions or foreclosure, or to allow for rejection of disadvantageous contracts or leases.

There are two types of bankruptcy applicable to private nonprofit entities—Chapters 7 and 11. Chapter 7 bankruptcy involves liquidation of the assets of the debtor administered by a trustee appointed by the court or elected by the creditors. The debtor's operations are wound down and the assets are disposed. After the assets are converted to cash, the trustee distributes the proceeds to creditors on a pro-rata basis according to priorities established by the Bankruptcy Code.

In Chapter 11 bankruptcy, the debtor's management ordinarily remains in control and possession of the assets and continues operations (as a so-called "debtor-in-possession"), although, in cases of fraud, dishonesty, incompetence, or gross mismanagement, the bankruptcy court may appoint a Chapter 11 trustee to manage the affairs of the debtor during the reorganization process.[17] The ultimate goal is typically for the debtor to reorganize and continue its operations pursuant to a plan approved by a majority of creditors and the court. However, the debtor-in-possession can conduct a sale of its assets pursuant to Bankruptcy Code Section 363 and distribute the proceeds pursuant to a bankruptcy plan to eventually effectuate an orderly liquidation, much as in Chapter 7.

A debtor's access to its cash is crucially and dramatically altered by a bankruptcy filing. It is common for secured lenders and bondholders to have a security interest in a debtor's cash or cash equivalents (defined by the Bankruptcy Code as "cash collateral"). A trustee or debtor-in-possession may not make use of such cash, even in the ordinary course of the debtor's business, without court approval (upon a finding that the security interest is "adequately protected") or consent by the creditor(s) whose interest is secured by the cash collateral.[18]

Unique aspects of nonprofits in bankruptcy

Reflecting the public interest mission of many nonprofits, there are at least two significant procedural differences in bankruptcy law applicable to insolvent nonprofit organizations, as compared to for-profit entities: First, nonprofit entities generally cannot be forced into involuntary bankruptcy by their creditors.[19] Second, nonprofit entities cannot be converted from a Chapter 11 reorganization to a Chapter 7 liquidation by a third-party motion.[20]

Nonetheless, creditors of a financially distressed nonprofit may have other leverage (such as threats to foreclose on collateral or cease providing needed supplies) to force the nonprofit to declare bankruptcy or take other significant action to protect creditors' interests.

The Bankruptcy Abuse Prevention and Consumer Protection Act (BAPCPA), which was enacted in 2005, included three amendments that treat nonprofits differently as it relates to the transfer of nonprofit assets. Section 363(d)(1) of the Bankruptcy Code requires the trustee to comply with all applicable non-bankruptcy laws governing the transfer, sale, or lease of a nonprofit's property. Section 1129(a)(16) of the Bankruptcy Code provides that the court cannot confirm a plan of reorganization without a finding that all transfers of a nonprofit's assets comply with applicable non-bankruptcy law. Similarly, section 541(f) of the Bankruptcy Code allows a nonprofit's business to transfer property to a for-profit entity, but only under the same conditions that would apply if the debtor were not in bankruptcy.

It is important to note two sections of BAPCPA that were not codified into the U.S. Code but that are still binding and relate to the sale of a nonprofit's assets in bankruptcy. First, BAPCPA section 1221(d) states that "the court shall not confirm a plan ... without considering whether this section would substantially affect the rights of a party in interest.... The parties who may appear and be heard in a proceeding under this section include the attorney general of the State in which the debtor is incorporated, was formed, or does business." Second, BAPCPA section 1221(e) states that "[n]othing in this section [which is now Section 363(d)(1)] shall be construed to require the [bankruptcy] court in which a case under [the Bankruptcy Code] is pending to remand or refer any proceeding, issue, or controversy to any other court or to require the approval of any other court for the transfer of property." These provisions make clear both that the state Attorney General has standing to appear on issues related to the sale of nonprofit's assets and that the bankruptcy court need not defer to a state court to decide issues related to the transfer of those assets.[21]

Role of State Attorney General in Bankruptcy

When a nonprofit corporation becomes a debtor under the Bankruptcy Code, the state attorney general may exercise an oversight role, in bankruptcy court (as noted above) or outside bankruptcy court. The attorney general may participate in the bankruptcy case as a party in interest and may be able to engage in enforcement action outside the bankruptcy court, if that action falls within the state's police powers, which are not stayed by the Bankruptcy Code.[22] Still, the attorney general may be subject to the bankruptcy court's jurisdiction in areas traditionally governed by bankruptcy law.[23]

General Bankruptcy Process

Retention of professionals and appointment of creditors' committee

A trustee or debtor-in-possession generally will retain restructuring counsel, consultants, and financial advisers to provide assistance in managing or liquidating its business in Chapter 7 or 11. These professionals, in addition to playing a critical role in operations and liquidating assets, may also pursue litigation, assist in formulating and implementing a debtor's reorganization plan, or assist in marketing a debtor's assets for sale. As a debtor-in-possession, a debtor has duties to creditors (and in the case of for-profits, stockholders) and is obligated to protect and conserve its property for the benefit of all parties in interest. The interests of unsecured creditors in a Chapter 11 will generally be represented by a creditors' committee, the members of which are appointed by the United States Trustee. Both the creditors' committee and Trustee generally will be active participants in a Chapter 11 case. If the nonprofit corporation is a health care business, a "patient care ombudsman" will likely be appointed to monitor patient care issues and provide reports to the bankruptcy court about the quality of patient care being delivered during the Chapter 11 or Chapter 7 case (if the debtor is still operating).

Creation of the bankruptcy estate

Upon the filing of a bankruptcy petition, a bankruptcy estate is created by operation of law and all property of the debtor, including any legal or equitable interest of the debtor, becomes "property of the estate."[24] One of the unique issues that may arise in a case in which there are *donor-restricted funds* is whether those funds, regardless of intent, can be found to be part of the debtor's estate available for general operating expenses or to pay general creditors instead of remaining segregated and restricted for specified purposes. (The answer ultimately may turn on how well the organization has previously identified which funds provided by donors are restricted, how a court resolves the tension between charitable mission and creditor rights, and applicable state law.)

The automatic stay

Also upon the filing of a bankruptcy petition, Section 362(a) of the Bankruptcy Code operates automatically to enjoin, or "stay," all actions by creditors against both the property of the estate and the debtor, with certain limited exceptions. Prohibited actions include not only direct acts to collect on a prepetition obligation of the debtor or obtain possession of property of the estate, but any action affecting the debtor and its property, including the commencement or continuation of litigation proceedings against the debtor relating to enforcement of debt or the creation or perfection of liens on the debtor's property. The automatic stay affords the debtor a reasonable opportunity to reorganize its affairs or proceed with an orderly liquidation.

Operation of the debtor's business while in bankruptcy

A trustee, debtor-in-possession, or municipal debtor may continue to undertake transactions that are in the "ordinary course" of a debtor's normal, day-to-day business actions—without bankruptcy court approval. Any extraordinary policy or business decisions outside the "ordinary course," however, are subject to court approval. A health care or other nonprofit corporation, for example, would need to obtain bankruptcy court approval to consummate any significant asset sale or to obtain secured credit, among other things.[25]

Assumption and rejection of executory contracts and unexpired leases

Section 365 of the Bankruptcy Code allows a trustee or debtor-in-possession, in its business judgment and estimation of economic sense, to either (a) assume (in conjunction with curing any defaults) and continue to be bound by an "executory contract" (generally defined as a contract under which performance remains due on both sides) or unexpired lease or (b) reject and free itself from such agreements. It is often crucial to a debtor's operational reorganization that while certain agreements need to be kept current and in place, other agreements will no longer be necessary or economically beneficial to its business and should therefore be rejected. The debtor may also assume and assign executory contracts and leases to a third party (subject to certain conditions and exceptions), which is a beneficial tool for maximizing value for the bankruptcy estate, particularly in the case of a sale pursuant to Section 363 of the Bankruptcy Code.

Avoiding preferences and fraudulent conveyances to increase the general estate available for distribution to creditors

The Bankruptcy Code allows a trustee, debtor-in-possession, or municipal debtor to seek to unwind or avoid certain transactions that occurred during the months and years prior to the filing which may have unreasonably reduced the estate available to pay general creditors. In addition, a trustee or debtor-in-possession may unwind so-called "fraudulent transfers"—transactions relating to, among other things, transfers made within two years of the commencement of the bankruptcy case (or, if applicable, a longer statutory period under state law) on the grounds that the transfer was actually or constructively fraudulent. In proving a fraudulent transfer, a debtor must demonstrate, among other things, that the transfer was intended to hinder, delay, or defraud other creditors, or that the debtor did not receive reasonably equivalent value in exchange for the transfer, and was either (a) insolvent at the time of the transfer, (b) rendered insolvent as a result of the transfer, (c) left with an unreasonably small amount of capital as a result of the transfer, or (d) incurred debts beyond its ability to pay when due. In some cases, preferential payments to vendors connected to an officer or director of a financially distressed organization will be subject to challenge as a preferential transfer.

Reorganization plan issues for nonprofit debtors exclusivity

Initially, the debtor-in-possession in a Chapter 11 case has 120 days (extendable by the bankruptcy court to 180 days) from the date of the filing in which to prepare and file a "plan or reorganization" and "disclosure statement" containing information about the plan sufficient to allow creditors to vote on its acceptance or rejection. This "exclusive period" can be extended by the bankruptcy court "for cause" to up to 18 months after the filing date.

Plan terms. In a typical Chapter 11 plan, a debtor proposes to extend maturities of outstanding debt, reduce or extinguish the amount of principal or interest payable on debts, convert debt to other debt and/or equity, or any combination of the foregoing. It is also not uncommon for a plan to provide for the sale of certain of the debtor's assets.

Creditor approval. Each creditor whose legal or contractual rights are altered by the proposed plan is entitled to vote on the plan. If the plan is accepted by at least one class of impaired creditors, it can be "crammed down" against the remaining nonapproving classes as long as their treatment under the plan is "fair and equitable," consistent with the "best interests of creditors test" and the other confirmation requirements.

If, during the course of a Chapter 11 case, the court determines that rehabilitation is not possible or there is no feasible plan of reorganization, the case can be converted to a Chapter 7 and the debtor's assets liquidated for the benefit of creditors.

Special nonprofit plan issues. To the extent the assets of a nonprofit may be single purpose or have little alternative value, they may have limited liquidation value and be particularly difficult to value.

In some cases, however, there may be an alternative value to nonprofit property that may exceed its value in the context of use for a specified charitable mission—such as an aged hospital in an urban area in which real estate values are high. In these situations, meeting the *best interest of creditors test* (requiring receipt of no less than Chapter 7 liquidation value to a dissenting creditor) can be a particular problem in a nonprofit case, requiring a balancing of the public interest argument against strict adherence to the test.

Application of the *absolute priority rule* to nonprofits that have members as opposed to shareholders can also be complicated, although courts have generally found that the absolute priority rule allows confirmation of Chapter 11 plans for nonprofits that retain or continue the control of members even if creditors are not paid in full.[26]

Summary

The board of a financially strained or insolvent nonprofit may need to take action to more strictly control its cash and assets. Alternatively, the board may wish to attempt an out-of-court restructuring, including Chapter 11 reorganization. Although most of the rules and issues confronting for-profit corporations in these situations also apply to nonprofits, certain unique protections and issues arise with nonprofits, of which not-for-profit directors and officers should be advised and aware.

See the suggested Questions and Checklist following the Endnotes below to review the issues discussed in this chapter.

Endnotes

1. The American Association of Museums, Code of Ethics-Collections sets forth policies with regard to deaccession. (www.aam-us.org/

museumresources/ethics/coe.cfm.) Similarly, the Association of Art Museum Directors has a policy on deaccessioning. (www.aamd.org/papers/documents/FinalDeaccessioning_Report_6_25_10.pdf.)

2. Model Act § 1120(1).
3. Model Act § 1120(2).
4. Model Act § 1120(3).
5. Model Act § 1120 (4).
6. RESTATEMENT OF THE LAW, CHARITABLE NONPROFIT ORGANIZATIONS, § 3.06, cmt.
7. *See* Model Act §1109; WASH. REV. CODE §24.03A.926.
8. *See, e.g.*, Geyer v. Ingersoll Publications Co., 621 A.2d 784 (Del. Ch. 1992).
9. See Berg & Berg Enterprises, LLC v. Boyle, 178 Cal. App. 4th 1020 (2009).
10. *Id.* North Am. Catholic Educ. Programming Foundation, Inc. v. Gheewalla, 2007 WL 1453705 (Del. May 18, 2007) (directors in the "zone of insolvency" do not owe fiduciary duty to creditors); *See also* In re Healthco Int'l, Inc., 208 B.R. 288, 302 (Bankr. D. Mass. 1997).
11. Berg. 178 Cal. App. 4th at 1040.
12. Berg. 178 Cal. App. 4th at 1040–1041.
13. *Id.*
14. *See* Manhattan Eye, Ear & Throat Hosp. v. Spitzer, 715 N.Y.S.2d 575 (N.Y. Sup. Ct. 1999) where the New York Attorney General successfully blocked the sale of an acute care facility on very valuable central New York City real estate, where the proceeds would have been used to fund the operations of diagnostic and treatment centers in medically underserved areas of New York City, as changing or refocusing the original charitable mission.
15. *See* In re Nat'l. Benevolent Ass'n. of the Christian Church (Disciples of Christ), et al., Case No. 04-50948-RBK (Bankr. W.D. Tex.).
16. The Bankruptcy Code is contained in Title 11, United States Code.
17. 11 U.S.C. § 1104(a)(1). Bankruptcy courts recognize a duty of obedience applies to bankruptcy trustees. In re Chapell, No. 09-31411, 2010 WL 986400 at *6 (Bankr. S.D. Tex. 2010); In Re White, 429 B.R. 201, 213 (Bankr. S.D. Tex. 2010) (quoting Loy v. Harter, 128 S.W.3d 397, 407 (Tex. Ct. App. 2004) which held that "three broad duties stem from the fiduciary status of corporate officers and directors; namely, the duties of obedience, loyalty, and due care"); In Re Novak, 383 B.R. 660, 671 (Bankr. W.D. Mich. 2008).
18. 11 U.S.C. § 363(a).
19. 11 U.S.C. § 303(a).
20. 11 U.S.C. § 1112(c).
21. For a more detailed discussion of the sale of nonprofit healthcare assets in bankruptcy proceedings, see Samuel R. Maizel & Mary D. Lane, *The Sale of Nonprofit Hospitals through Bankruptcy: What BAPCPA Wrought*, 30(5) AM. BANKR. INST. J. (June 2011).

22. 11 U.S.C. § 362(b)(4).
23. Bankruptcy Code Section 363(d)(1) was amended in 2005 to require that any nonprofit asset sale in bankruptcy must comply with applicable nonbankruptcy law governing nonprofit assets transfers. 11 U.S.C. § 363(d)(1).
24. 11 U.S.C. § 541.
25. 11 U.S.C. §§ 363, 364.
26. *In re* Wabash Valley Power, Inc., 72 F.3d 1305, 1320 (7th Cir. 1995); *In re* Whittaker Memorial Hospital Association, Inc., 149 B.R. 812, 816 (Bankr. E.D.Va. 1993); *In re* Corcoran Hospital District; 233 B.R. 449, 458 (Bankr. E.D.Cal. 1999).

Suggested Questions for Directors Regarding Duties of Directors under Special Circumstances

Disposition of Unique Assets

(1) Why is a unique corporate asset being considered for sale?
(2) Could any directors, officers, or other corporate insiders personally benefit in any way from the sale?
(3) What other organizations, such as specialized nonprofits, appraiser agencies, or other groups, could assist the corporation in maximizing the benefits of a sale, while minimizing concerns of the community or other interested groups?
(4) Are there any organization stakeholders, such as donors, community members, or state or local officials, who may be concerned about such disposition or with whom the organization should consult or inform prior to the disposition becoming effective?

Dissolution

(1) Why is the board considering a voluntary dissolution of the nonprofit corporation?
(2) Are there alternatives to a voluntary dissolution, such as merging with another nonprofit corporation?
(3) What steps will be taken to ensure that the charitable assets of the nonprofit corporation continue to be used for a charitable purpose?

Insolvency or Bankruptcy

(1) Is our organization in a "zone of insolvency"? Are we able to pay our debts as they come due? Can we foresee a day in the near future when that will not be true?
(2) What actions can our various creditors take if we default on our obligations or fail to make required debt covenants?
(3) Is our organization eligible to file for bankruptcy?
(4) Are there any organization stakeholders, such as donors, community members, or state or local officials, who may be concerned about such disposition or with whom the organization should consult or inform prior to the disposition becoming effective?
(5) What are the potential benefits and disadvantages of declaring bankruptcy, as opposed to trying to work out a debt restructuring directly with one or more major creditors?
(6) Have steps been taken to protect restricted funds from inappropriate use?
(7) Have any payments been made that could be challenged as fraudulent transfers?
(8) If the corporation is or becomes insolvent, do we want to reorganize and continue, or liquidate and "close up shop"?
(9) Are there members or others affiliated with our organization who derive economic benefit from its activities who might be considered its "owners"? If yes, should they be asked to contribute to a reorganization effort? Can we legally require them to do so?
(10) What is the fair value of our corporate assets? What would they realize in a forced liquidation?

Checklist: Duties of Directors under Special Circumstances

Note: For simplicity, these and other chapter checklists describe a corporation having a chair, who presides over the board of directors; a chief executive, who may be a staff person; an executive committee; a governance/nominating committee; and an audit committee. (We recognize, however, that in many smaller and other nonprofits, these committee functions may be performed by either the executive committee or the board as a whole.) We also assume a legal counsel—someone, paid or unpaid, having primary responsibility for the corporation's legal affairs. Many corporations, especially larger nonprofits, may have other committees established for specific purposes, such as establishing executive compensation; monitoring compliance with legal requirements; and overseeing investments and other financial matters.

Subject	**Review By**	**How Often**	**Comment**
1. Disposition of unique assets			
(a) How will need for and alternatives to disposition be evaluated, approved, and documented?	Chief executive, legal counsel	Promptly after disposition is identified as a possible option to address the relevant organizational concerns	Evidence of a reasonable evaluation process to support a board decision to sell or dispose of a unique asset helps avoid potential challenges to the decision and may result in a smoother disposition process.
(b) What legal and other requirements (including stakeholder communications) must be met before completing the asset disposition?	Chief executive, board chair, legal counsel	Prior to or immediately after board disposition decision	By definition, disposition of unique assets are uncommon events. Board members should be assured that a thorough review of legal and other considerations has been conducted prior to approval or closing of the sale.

Subject	Review By	How Often	Comment
2. Dissolution			
(a) What process should the board follow to evaluate the options and implications for dissolution	Chief executive, board chair, legal counsel	Prior to the decision to voluntarily dissolve	Board members should consider alternatives to voluntary dissolution including a business combination transition.
(b) What steps has the board taken to ensure that the charitable assets will continue to be used for a charitable purposes?	Chief executive, board chair, legal counsel	Prior to the decision to voluntarily dissolve	Board members of a public benefit/charitable nonprofit should consider how the assets of nonprofit may continue to be used for a charitable purpose.
3. Insolvency and bankruptcy			
(a) What process should the board follow to evaluate the options and implications for an organization that is or may soon be insolvent?	Chief executive, chief financial officer, legal counsel, followed by discussion with full board	As soon as possible after the chief financial officer identifies a possible or actual insolvency condition for the organization	Because some board duties may change for insolvent organizations, it is important for the board to engage qualified financial and legal advisers to avoid inadvertently taking actions that could later be challenged by creditors.

Subject	Review By	How Often	Comment
(b) What actions may the board need to take to assure creditors in the course of restructuring debt or other workouts needed to maintain the organization's ability to continue operations?	Chief financial officer, finance committee chair, followed by discussion with full board	After discussions with creditors and prior to board approval of debt restructure or work-out arrangement	The board should be assured that constraints imposed by lenders are feasible before approving a debt restructuring.
(c) If bankruptcy, dissolution or similar actions become necessary, what is the board's role after approval of the action? What preapproval steps should be taken to avoid director liability and to satisfy the concerns of key stakeholders?	Special bankruptcy counsel, in consultation with chief executive and board chair, followed by discussion with full board	Shortly before or in conjunction with determination to pursue Chapter 7 or Chapter 11 bankruptcy or a similar process	Bankruptcy and similar proceedings (including dissolution) involve technical legal rules, and will require the board and management to obtain special bankruptcy or other legal counsel and accounting or other financial experts.

Chapter 12: Investments and Expenditure of Endowment Funds

Chapter 12

Investments and Expenditure of Endowment Funds

Many nonprofit organizations benefit from large gifts from donors that are intended to be maintained as an "endowment fund" and invested with only a portion expended on an annual basis. With limited revenue resources, many nonprofits actively seek these types of gifts. Although these gifts are extremely important to the vitality of the nonprofits, in every economic cycle, there is a period of economic turmoil—where many nonprofits would like to include the principal to cover costs and also the endowments and other funds plummet in value. This often results in questions being raised as to how much the organization can spend each year, whether the proper type of investments were made and whether the boards of directors of these nonprofits are properly managing their investments.

Gifts

Nonprofit corporations can receive various forms of financial support, including gifts from donors. These gifts can be "unrestricted," meaning they can be invested, managed, and used in a manner deemed appropriate by the corporation, or "restricted," meaning that the gift is to be used in a manner specified by the donor. Many nonprofits receive gifts in the form of what were traditionally called "endowments" under which the growth and income of the gift may be used for various purposes but the "corpus" of the gift is to remain intact. As is described below, the legal nature of endowments has changed significantly in recent years.

Potential Liability and Other Issues

Directors and officers of nonprofit corporations can be held liable when they improperly use funds through extravagant spending, negligent management, or outright misdirection of funds.[1] In addition, the failure to fulfill a donor's specified gift intent can result in adverse publicity, donor challenge, and state attorney general review.[2] Liability also can arise when the organization fails to invest the donated funds prudently or uses the funds in a manner that is inconsistent with the donor's intent.

Standards for Investment of Institutional Funds

Every state (except Pennsylvania), as well as the District of Columbia and the U.S. Virgin Islands, has adopted a uniform law that creates a standard of conduct for managing and investing institutional funds. Replacing an older law known as the Uniform Management of Institutional Funds Act (UMIFA), the Uniform Prudent Management of Institutional Funds Act (UPMIFA) sets out, among other things, the standards for the investment of institutional funds.[3] An "institutional fund" is a fund held by an institution but does not include program-related assets or assets held by an institution primarily to accomplish a charitable purpose of the institution but not primarily for investment.[4] An "institution" is a charity, a government agency holding exclusively charitable funds, or a split-interest trust in which all the noncharitable interests are extinguished.[5]

UPMIFA sets out modern articulations of two general principles: (1) that assets of charitable organizations are to be invested prudently in diversified investments that seek growth as well as income, and (2) that appreciation of assets can prudently be spent for the purposes of any endowment fund held by a charitable institution.[6]

In terms of investments, UPMIFA recognizes the application of the duty of care and duty of loyalty imposed on directors (discussed in *Chapter 2, Duties and Rights of Nonprofit Corporation Directors*) and requires investment "in good faith and with the care an ordinarily prudent person in a like position would exercise under similar circumstances."[7] It requires prudence in incurring investment costs, authorizing "only costs that are appropriate and reasonable."[8]

UPMIFA provides specific factors for investing in a prudent manner. When making investments, boards are required to consider the following factors:

- the charitable purposes of the institution and the purposes of the fund;
- general economic conditions;
- the possible effect of inflation or deflation;
- the expected tax consequences, if any, of investment decisions or strategies;
- the role that each investment or course of action plays within the overall investment portfolio of the fund;
- the expected total return from the income and appreciation of investments;
- other resources of the organization;
- the needs of the organization and the fund to make distributions and preserve capital; and
- an asset's special relationship or special value, if any, to the organization's purposes.[9]

UPMIFA adopts modern portfolio investment theory, emphasizing that investment decisions must be made in relation to the overall resources of the institution and its charitable purposes.[10] In other words, decisions on fund management and investment decisions cannot be made in isolation. UPMIFA also requires that a fund's investments be diversified unless the governing board can justify nondiversification under special circumstances.[11] A decision for nondiversification should be reviewed at least annually.

Investment Committee

Organizations with large endowments should have investment committees that may be delegated duties with regard to development of an investment policy, proposing amendments to the policy, oversight of the investment performance, and delegating investment authority to others, including third parties. It is extremely important that an investment committee be composed of directors with expertise of relevance to investments made by the organization. Alternatively, an investment committee may be configured as a designed body, so that it may include nondirector financial experts while still retaining its board-level authority, or as an advisory committee with nondirector members. As noted below, it is permissible to delegate duties with regard to investments to others; however, an investment committee should be responsible for overseeing any delegation and the performance of the organization's investments.

Investment Policy

A nonprofit corporation that intends to satisfy the UPMIFA standard of care should develop an investment policy that considers the corporation's short-term, mid-term, and long-term financial needs, and its tolerance for risk. One state, New York, requires that nonprofit corporations adopt an investment policy setting forth investment delegation and management guidelines in accord with UPMIFA.[12] The policy should be reviewed regularly, at least annually, by the investment committee in light of the changing needs of the organization, economic conditions, and any other factors that may affect the corporation's tolerance of risk and need for income. The investment committee should more fully reassess the policy from time to time with appropriate professional counsel. Any changes to the investment policy should be approved by the full board.

Following the development of an investment policy, the investment committee should determine appropriate asset-class allocations needed to satisfy the policy objectives. Here again, the committee should consult with professional investment experts in determining proper allocations of the corporation's investments. After determining appropriate asset-class allocations, the individual asset decisions should be made. Consistent with UPMIFA, it is important that the decisions regarding the assets to be acquired, retained, or sold should not be made in a vacuum. Instead, the investment committee should make each of these determinations in light of its other investments and the total portfolio's consonance with the standards of the investment policy. Particular attention should be paid to the portfolio's overall level of compensated risk.

Delegation of Duties

It is permissible to delegate management and investment functions to external agents, such as investment managers, as long as certain requirements are met. In particular, delegation, which generally would be done by either the board of directors or an investment committee, requires meeting the fiduciary duties that apply to the Board and committee members, namely that they act in good faith and with the care that an ordinarily prudent person in a like position would exercise under similar circumstances with regard to selecting an agent, establishing scope and terms of delegation, and requiring periodic reviews and supervision of the agent.[13] This means that the board or investment committee members should thoroughly investigate the proposed external agent and take care to see that they enter into an appropriate written agreement with regard to the scope of the external agent's duties and compensation. UPMIFA provides that an agent has a duty of reasonable care in performing the delegated functions.[14]

In recent years, many nonprofits have come to rely substantially on the recommendations of professional money managers, and the law generally permits the board to rely on professional investment counsel's advice.[15]

Standards for Expenditure of Endowment Funds

Various restrictions are imposed on nonprofits that maintain permanently and temporarily restricted funds. Under UPMIFA, an "endowment fund" is an institutional fund not expendable, in whole or in part, on a current basis under the terms of a gift instrument.[16] UPMIFA imposes special rules on expenditures from endowment funds. A fund from which spending is restricted by the board or management itself is not an endowment fund within the meaning of UPMIFA.

Under the predecessor uniform law, UMIFA, there was a requirement that asset growth and income could be appropriated for program purposes, subject to the rule that a fund that was intended to be held in perpetuity could not be spent below its "historic dollar value."[17] This meant that the corporation was not permitted to spend any amounts, regardless of whether they constituted income from the fund, when the total amount held in the fund was less than the amount of the original gift at the time of the gift—regardless of whether that decline in value occurred following a loss of market value or excessive expenditures.

UPMIFA provides more flexible guidance on prudence and eliminates the absolute prohibition on spending from an underwater fund. UPMIFA states that, subject to the donor's intent as expressed in a gift instrument, an institution may "appropriate for expenditure or accumulate as much of an endowment fund as the institution determines is prudent for the uses, benefits, purposes, and duration for which the endowment fund is established."[18] Notwithstanding that general rule, if the gift instrument states a particular spending rate or formula, that rate or formula will apply and the board has no discretion in determining the spending policy with respect to the particular fund.[19] In the case of an endowment fund without specific donor spending rate or formula instructions, the prudent person standard is applied, which involves consideration of the following seven criteria to guide an institution in its expenditure decisions:

- the duration and preservation of the endowment fund;
- purposes of the organization and the fund;
- general economic conditions;
- possible effect of inflation or deflation;
- expected total return from income and appreciation of investments;
- other resources of the organization; and
- the organization's investment policy.[20]

UPMIFA includes an optional provision that a minority of states have adopted that provides that spending in excess of 7 percent of the fair market value of the fund in one year creates a presumption of imprudence in spending.[21] This does not mean that spending in excess of 7 percent is in violation of the law; however, in those states, the board—if challenged—would have the burden to show that the expenditure was "prudent."

It is important that directors understand the prudence standard for spending. The board should require that clear and accurate meeting minutes detail how the above-described factors were considered when making a spending decision or adopting a policy for expenditures from endowment funds.

In addition, to prevent problems from occurring, the organization should be involved in assisting donors in articulating any gift intent in advance or in connection with making the gift and ascertaining the donor gift intent upon receipt of the gift. Directors also should carefully consider any proposed restrictions placed on gifts to the organization. To the extent the proposed restrictions are inconsistent with the organization's purposes or mission, the board should seriously consider declining the gift.

The organization should also have one or more spending policies in place that help ensure the implementation of the donor gift intent as well as monitoring the administration of the gift to make sure the donor gift intent has been implemented.

To the extent a nonprofit corporation has an investment committee responsible for the corporation's investments and a finance committee responsible for preparing the budget, it is important that these two committees coordinate to ensure that there is a common understanding with regard to issues of common concern, such as liquidity of assets for purposes of program operations.

Out-of-Date or Impractical Restrictions on Gifts

A restriction on a gift can, after time, become outdated or impractical. For example, a gift made to a nonprofit college in the form of a scholarship fund that was limited by its terms to scholarships of $50 a year would probably cost more to administer than the benefits paid out. So that kind of restriction is impractical today. In the past, the laws of many states required that the nonprofit obtain the consent of the donor to any modification to the restriction if the donor was still living. If not living, the organization often had to seek judicial relief by filing a petition with the court to change the purpose or release the restriction, a time consuming and expensive process known as a *cy pres* proceeding.

In addition to codifying *cy pres,*[22] UPMIFA recognizes and protects donor intent broadly by providing a comprehensive treatment of the modification of restrictions on charitable funds. Among other things, UPMIFA provides that a court may release or modify a restriction where the restriction is, among other things, impracticable or wasteful, or the purpose is unlawful, impracticable, impossible to achieve, or wasteful.[23] UPMIFA also established a kind of self-help modification process for small funds with a value of less than $25,000 and where more than 20 years has elapsed since their establishment, under which the institution may institute a release or modification without court approval.[24]

Accounting Treatment of Institutional Funds

For nonprofit organizations that have a donor-restricted endowment fund or board-designated endowment fund, there are special accounting rules for the treatment of these funds. In particular, the Financial Accounting Standards Board (FASB) issued FASB-No. FAS 117-1 with the dual objective of providing guidance on net asset classification of donor-restricted endowment funds for nonprofits subject to UPMIFA and providing increased disclosures about an organization's endowment funds, whether or not the organization is subject to UPMIFA.

Under this accounting rule, the assets in these endowment funds are to be classified as "temporarily restricted," "permanently restricted," or "unrestricted." A temporarily restricted asset refers to an asset that is subject to donor-imposed restriction that permits the organization to use up or expend the donated assets only as specified in the gift instrument and which restrictions may be satisfied either by passage of time or by actions of the organization. A permanently restricted asset is created when the gift instrument requires that the asset be maintained permanently. That amount must be kept permanently in accordance with explicit donor restrictions, or if no restrictions are specified, the organization's governing board determines the amount that must be retained permanently consistent with relevant law. An unrestricted asset is an asset that has no restrictions imposed by the donors. Under the accounting guidelines, investment income (including appreciation) is to be treated as temporarily restricted until appropriated for expenditure. This creates a time restriction that must first be satisfied in addition to any purpose restriction.[25]

Donor-Advised Funds

The many types of possible funds that can be maintained by a nonprofit corporation are outside the scope of this book. Still, it is worth providing a brief description of one type of fund that has received significant attention from both nonprofits and regulators.

Donor-advised funds have become a popular means for managing charitable donations on behalf of an organization, family, or individual. A donor-advised fund is maintained by a sponsoring public charity, such as a community foundation. Generally, a donor to a donor-advised fund is able to claim a charitable contribution deduction when applicable criteria are met for a contribution to a public charity, while avoiding some of the excise taxes and other restrictions imposed on private foundations. Donors may periodically advise (but not direct) the sponsoring charity on how it should invest the assets, within the prudent constraints adopted by the Board of the sponsoring organization. More commonly, donors have the right to recommend grants to charitable organizations from the donor-advised fund to which they made a contribution, also within constraints imposed by the sponsoring organization and prohibitions that the Internal Revenue Code imposes on certain types of expenditures from donor-advised funds. The sponsoring charity may accept donations of almost any asset including cash, stock, and real estate, although many do have limitations on the types of assets they will accept.

In 2006, Congress adopted legislation to regulate donor-advised funds. This legislation resulted in, among other things, the imposition of excise taxes for distributions that do not meet a charitable purpose or for certain distributions where the expenditure responsibility is not exercised.[26] The IRS has established procedures for processing applications of organizations that are applying for exemption and are planning to maintain donor-advised funds. Among other things, the IRS will determine whether the organization is in a position to ensure that accomplishing the charitable purposes through the distribution can occur.[27] The IRS has been working on additional regulations with regard to donor-advised funds for many years.[28]

See the Suggested Questions and Checklist following the Endnotes below to review the issues discussed in this chapter.

Endnotes

1. *See* Lisa A. Runquist and Jeannie Carmedelle Frey, Eds., *Guide to Representing Religious Organizations* (American Bar Association 2009), at 96.
2. *See* discussion on donors in *Chapter 1, The Nonprofit Corporation and Its Directors, What They Do, How They Do It, and for Whom.*
3. Uniform Prudent Management of Institutional Funds Act (https://www.uniformlaws.org).
4. UPMIFA § 2(5).
5. UPMIFA § 2(4).
6. UPMIFA prefatory note.
7. UPMIFA § 3(b).
8. UPMIFA § 3(c)(1).
9. UPMIFA § 3(e)(1).

10. UPMIFA § 3(e)(2).
11. UPMIFA § 3(e)(4).
12. N.Y. Not-for-Profit Corp. Law § 552(f).
13. UPMIFA § 5(a); *see also* Model Act, §§ 801(b), 830(c).
14. UPMIFA § 5(b).
15. *See* Cynthia R. Rowland, *UPMIFA, Three Years Later: What's a Prudent Director to Do?*, ABA Business Law Today, 18(6) (July/August 2009).
16. UPMIFA § 2(2).
17. UMIFA § 2.
18. UPMIFA § 4(a).
19. UPMIFA § 4(a); *see also* Rowland, *supra* note 15.
20. UPMIFA § 4(a).
21. UPMIFA § 4(d).
22. UPMIFA § 6(b).
23. UPMIFA § 6(c); *see also* Matter of Coe College, 935 N.W. 2d 581 (Iowa 2019).
24. UPMIFA § 6(d).
25. *See, e.g.*, Kelly Thornton, *FSP No. FAS 117-1, Endowments of Not-for-Profit Organizations: Net Asset Classifications of Funds Subject to Unenacted Version of the Uniform Prudent Management of Institutional Funds Act, and Enhanced Disclosures for all Endowment Funds* (ABA Section of Taxation September 12, 2008).
26. *See* Pension Protection Act of 2006, Pub. L. No. 109-208; IRS Notice 2006-109 (Interim Guidance Regarding Supporting Organizations and Donor Advised Funds).
27. *See* Runquist & Frey, *supra* note 1, at 101–102.
28. *See, e.g.*, IRS Notice 2017-73.

Suggested Questions for Directors Regarding Investments and Expenditure of Endowment Funds

(1) Does the corporation receive gifts in the form of endowments?

(2) Does the corporation have a gift policy?

(3) Does the corporation have an investment policy?

(4) What has been the experience (in terms of rate of return) of the corporation's investments? How does such experience compare to other similar entities?

(5) Does the corporation utilize the services of an external party with regard to its investments? If so, has the term of the agreement with

the agent been recently reviewed? Also, what is the experience (in terms of rate of return) with the external agent?

(6) Does the corporation have a spending policy?

(7) Does the corporation allow donors to advise on the use or expenditure of their contributions?

Checklist: Investments and Expenditure of Endowment Funds

Note: For simplicity, these and other chapter checklists describe a corporation having a chair, who presides over the board of directors; a chief executive, who may be a staff person; an executive committee; a governance/nominating committee; and an audit committee. (We recognize, however, that in many smaller and other nonprofits, these committee functions may be performed by either the executive committee or the board as a whole.) We also assume a legal counsel—someone, paid or unpaid, having primary responsibility for the corporation's legal affairs. Many corporations, especially larger nonprofits, may have other committees established for specific purposes, such as establishing executive compensation; monitoring compliance with legal requirements; and overseeing investments and other financial matters.

Subject	Review By	How Often	Comment
1. Does the corporation actively seek to obtain gifts from donors that may be subject to donor restrictions?	Chair, chief executive	At least annually	
2. If the corporation seeks gifts in the form of endowments, does the corporation have in place a gift policy?	Chair, chief executive, legal counsel	At least annually	A gift policy can be important in assisting the organization in making sure that, among other things, any restrictions placed on a gift to the organization are manageable by the organization.

Subject	Review By	How Often	Comment
3. Does the corporation have any permanent or temporarily restricted funds?	Chair, chief executive	At least annually	
4. What type of restricted funds does the corporation have? Donor-created or board-created? What are the restrictions?	Chair, chief executive, legal counsel	At least annually	
5. Does the corporation have an investment policy?	Chair, chief executive, legal counsel, investment committee	At least annually	An investment policy should comply with the terms of UPMIFA.
6. Does the corporation utilize the services of an investment manager or other third party with regard to the management of its investments pursuant to the terms of a written agreement?	Chair, chief executive, legal counsel, investment committee	At least annually	Any delegation of investment management duties should be pursuant to a written agreement between the corporation and third party.
7. Does the corporation review the performance of the investment portfolio and the performance of the investment manager?	Chair, chief executive, investment committee	At least quarterly	

Subject	Review By	How Often	Comment
8. Does the corporation comply with applicable requirements relating to the spending of any donor-restricted or board-restricted funds?	Chief executive, legal counsel	At least annually for the report to the full board, with frequent monitoring at the staff level	
9. Does the corporation allow donors to advise on investment or expenditure decisions?	Chief executive, legal counsel, tax return preparer	Annually	Special tax return reporting is required for Donor-Advised Funds.

Chapter 13: Director Liability Risks and Protections

Chapter 13
Director Liability Risks and Protections

The failure (or alleged failure) of directors of nonprofit corporations to fulfill their duties may expose them to liability to third parties, or to the corporation. Directors should therefore be aware of protections that may be available against such liability.

Litigation against directors of many varieties of nonprofits continues to increase in frequency.[1] *The demise of the charitable immunity exemption that was previously available to many kinds of nonprofit corporations has increased the frequency of suits against directors and officers of public benefit and religious corporations.*[2] *(Mutual benefit corporations and their directors have never enjoyed the protection of the charitable exemption.) Regardless of the size of the nonprofit or its activities, all directors need to understand the actions that may be taken to protect them against liability claims related to their service on a nonprofit corporation's board.*

A nonprofit corporation director should understand what the corporation's basic documents provide as to indemnification and what directors and officers liability insurance coverage the corporation maintains, and know if there are any statutory exemptions or other legal provisions that may limit the director's liability.

The Director's Exposure to Liability

A director's possible liability in litigation does not arise simply because the corporation may be liable for a matter. It arises because the director is charged with some breach of duty or other harm done to the corporation or to a specific party. A director should understand that the corporation itself may be the party asserting a claim.

A director's liability does not automatically arise from corporate liability. For directors to be exposed to liability through litigation, they must hold a duty to or have directly harmed, some party entitled—or allegedly entitled—to sue the director. Suits against directors are typically brought in one of three ways:

(1) An outside party may attempt to sue a member of the board directly, in a suit alleging some injury done *by* the corporation, but claiming the director to be a principal or implied coconspirator in connection with the injury.

(2) An aggrieved party may assert some right of the corporation against the director, suing to remedy claimed harm done to the corporation; lawsuits of this type are referred to as "derivative actions."[3] In effect, someone is suing the director on behalf of the corporation, generally because of the director's breach of the duty of care or the duty of loyalty. (See the discussion of director duties in *Chapter 2, Duties and Rights of Nonprofit Corporation Directors.*)

(3) The director may be held *personally* liable under various federal and state laws dealing with issues such as environmental claims, tax delinquencies (e.g., failure to pay sales taxes, payroll taxes, or make proper withholding), excess benefit transactions, antitrust claims, or employment claims.[4]

Although a director's exposure to potential liability claims may vary according to the size of the entity, the nature and degree of exposure will be determined more by the type of nonprofit corporation than by its size. Generally, liability exposure is based on allegations of negligence or failure to oversee.

Avoiding Liability Risks

Some litigation risks may be avoided. As discussed in *Chapter 10, Mergers, Sale of Assets, Affiliations, and Other Combinations, and Chapter 11, Duties of Directors under Special Circumstances: Sale of Unique Assets, Dissolution, and Bankruptcy,* the board should identify areas in which the corporation is vulnerable to litigation or potential legal liability, and then make sure that appropriate procedures and reporting mechanisms are put in place to avoid or minimize these risks. In some cases, the directors may wish to employ advisers and consultants to aid in decisions that are of a kind likely to be scrutinized by regulators or others. Use of outside advisers may help the board demonstrate that it satisfied its duty of care when it made a particular decision.

Similarly, in situations in which duty of loyalty issues are present, the use of an outside opinion, even to verify what seems obvious, may be prudent, and offer legal protections not otherwise available. For example, under the IRS's excess benefit rules, transactions with insiders that are approved by the board or a disinterested committee may be afforded a presumption of reasonableness if the transaction is ever challenged as involving an excess benefit (see discussion of excess benefits liability in *Chapter 5, Taxation*).

Director Indemnification

In general, the directors should seek corporate indemnification to the maximum extent permitted by applicable corporation law and the corporation's articles and bylaws. Such a program of indemnification should be sought even if the corporation's liquid net worth may make the protection limited in value.

Although the value of indemnification depends on both the legal and financial ability of the corporation to pay, the legal right of the director to be indemnified in connection with a lawsuit or other proceeding depends on the type of loss the director has incurred. In some instances, the corporation is required to indemnify a director, while in other cases, the corporation is permitted to indemnify, if the board chooses to do so. A corporation also may advance certain litigation expenses to the director in certain circumstances.

Discretionary Indemnification

Initially, it should be noted that even if the board of directors wants to indemnify a director, such an indemnification must be consistent with state law and the corporation's articles and bylaws. Mere goodwill of the board is not sufficient to authorize indemnification.

It is unclear whether there exists a common law right of indemnification; however, most, if not all, states provide for indemnification rights of nonprofit officers and directors by statute. The Model Act gives the corporation discretion to indemnify the director if the director has acted in good faith and with the reasonable belief, in the case of conduct in an official capacity, that the individual's actions were in the best interests of the corporation, and, in all other cases, that the individual's conduct was at least not opposed to the best interests of the corporation.[5] Indemnification may include sums due under a settlement agreement. Indemnification for proceedings by the corporation against the director (whether direct or derivative) is generally limited under the

Model Act to the reasonable expenses the director incurred in connection with the proceeding.[6] Indemnification may be made mandatory in most situations by appropriate provisions in the corporation's articles of incorporation or bylaws.[7]

Mandatory Indemnification

Under the Model Act as well as most state laws, directors have the *right* to indemnification from the corporation under certain circumstances.[8] Although individual state statutes may differ from the Model Act, the issues treated by the Model Act are ones that the director must face in any event. Under the Model Act, a corporation is required to indemnify a director for reasonable expenses if the director is "wholly successful" in the director's defense of any proceeding of which the director is a party as a result of being a director of the corporation.[9]

Note, however, that such mandatory indemnification is contingent on a director's being deemed wholly successful in defense of the matter for which indemnification is sought. Such success seems clear when there is a verdict or final ruling in the director's favor (including dismissal with prejudice) in a lawsuit, arbitration, or other legal proceeding. Still, depending on the facts and the applicable state, a settlement of a proceeding may or may not trigger a director's mandatory indemnification.[10] The director generally wants to have corporate indemnification to the fullest extent permitted by applicable law. This means that the corporate obligation should be set forth in the articles of incorporation or bylaws, in language as broad as the applicable statute permits. In some cases, a director also may wish to have a separate contract with the corporation providing for indemnification.

Despite the indemnification protections that might exist, directors must recognize that the corporation's uninsured obligation to indemnify may be of little value, if the corporation's net worth is insufficient to cover the directors' expenses or their exposure.

Advancement of Expenses

A director should know what specific measures the corporation has adopted to provide for the advancement of legal expenses. A director will want the corporation to have taken actions that will maximize the corporation's ability to advance the expenses of directors who are made parties to proceedings because of their director status. In some states, the ability to advance expenses is allowed under state law but may be contingent upon certain affirmative statements by the director.[11] In other states, advancement of expenses is explicitly permitted by a court (or required) if provided for in the corporation's articles or bylaws or if the court determines it is fair and reasonable to do so in light of all relevant circumstances.[12]

The director should not underestimate the importance of a procedure permitting the corporation to advance expenses, since having a right of indemnification does not mean that the director can require the corporation to immediately assume the costs of litigation or other proceeding while the matter is being pursued. Rather, indemnification rights are generally triggered only at the end of a litigation or similar proceeding, and result in reimbursement for expenses already incurred. The right of indemnification is therefore of limited help to the director without an advance for expenses. Thus, directors should know whether the corporate documents require the corporation to advance expenses to the maximum extent permitted by the state's indemnification laws.

The Model Act sets forth conditions upon which such advances may be made. Most states have similar conditions, although certain specifics may vary. Under the Model Act, a nonprofit corporation may only advance expenses to a director if the director furnishes a written undertaking to repay any sums advanced if it is ultimately determined that the director did not meet the applicable standard.[13]

The undertaking must be an unlimited general obligation of the director, but need not be secured and may be accepted without reference to the director's financial ability to make repayment. In addition, authorizations under the Model Act must be made by a disinterested body or their members, if any.[14] Still, not all state laws require such determination before advances may be made.[15]

Third-Party Indemnification

In addition, indemnification for directors may be sought from any third party who may agree to indemnify the corporation on a related matter. For instance, the owners of a group of assets sold to the corporation may agree to indemnify the corporation—and, if specified, its officers and directors—against any liability relating to periods prior to the corporation's purchase. Directors should ascertain whether such third-party indemnification runs directly to the directors, or runs only to the corporation. Directors should further ascertain at what point this protection becomes available.

Attorney General Notice

In some states, indemnification of a director of a public benefit corporation may not occur until a certain period of time after the corporation has given written notice of the proposed indemnification to the state attorney general.[16]

Protecting Directors through Insurance

A nonprofit corporation should obtain insurance to protect its directors and officers. A directors and officers (D&O) insurance policy *may,* subject to the applicable corporation act, provide coverage that is broader than any indemnification permitted or required by the Model Act or by relevant state law. Under the Model Act, a corporation can protect a director by insurance, even if the insurance coverage extends protection to situations in which the corporation is otherwise prohibited by applicable law from providing indemnification.[17] Some state statutes prohibit indemnification against settlements and judgments in derivative actions (i.e., lawsuits asserting the corporation's rights against the director) if a director is found liable unless the court determines that special circumstances entitle the director to indemnity despite that judgment.[18] Still, most, but not all, nonprofit corporation statutes *permit* the corporation to procure insurance for the director for such events, even though the corporation could not directly indemnify from its own funds.[19]

Directors and Officers (D&O) Insurance

Directors should expect the corporation to provide D&O insurance (or properly funded self-insurance) protecting them from liability. If no D&O insurance is provided, directors should examine the risks of serving without it.

Even if a nonprofit corporation has expansive indemnification provisions in its articles of incorporation or bylaws, these assurances must be considered in light of the financial strength of the corporation offering them. To the extent that qualified board members may be deterred from participating because of inadequate financial reserves to pay such claims, D&O insurance may be the most viable method of providing both the perception and reality of adequate protection for both current and prospective board members. On the other hand, nonprofit corporations with good financial resources may determine that it is more cost-effective to self-insure against director and officer litigation expenses by maintaining a self-insured fund. Such a fund gives the corporation more control over the cost of director and officer protection. It also allows the corporation to more closely tailor protection to the needs of the corporation, its officers, and directors. Nonprofit corporations should not ask directors to serve without insurance coverage if adequate insurance is available to the corporation at a reasonable cost.[20]

D&O Policy Coverage Review to Determine Who and What Is Covered

At least annually, the corporation's management or staff should review what individuals and entities are covered by its D&O policy. Where a corporation has (or has recently acquired) affiliates or subsidiaries, the extension of the insurance coverage to these entities should be verified. If the policy provides coverage to directors and officers specified by name, rather than position, the policy may need to be updated whenever new officers or directors are selected. The D&O policy also should be examined to determine if it covers the activities of nondirector members of committees, or other persons (such as volunteers) who may be subject to liability due to their activities on the corporation's behalf, including employment matters.

Impact of Dual Roles of a Director on D&O Coverage

Many typical D&O policies do not cover the activities of directors or officers when they are acting in other capacities. For example, when a board member who is an attorney is acting in the capacity of counsel, whether paid or volunteer, the board member's conduct is likely not included in the corporation's D&O protection. Such dual roles can give rise to difficult questions concerning coverage. For example, legal malpractice insurers may specifically exclude claims that arise if the attorney was acting as an officer or director of an organization. The D&O policy may have a similar provision excluding work performed as a lawyer unless the attorney is specifically named in the policy. Thus, there may be a gray area in which neither coverage applies, especially if the attorney or the attorney's law firm is also legal counsel to the corporation.[21] Similar problems can arise in other dual roles. These problems may be addressed by obtaining special riders or endorsements on policies; however, the need for clarification should be recognized by those individuals wearing multiple corporate hats.

The Nature of "Claims-Made" Policies

Most D&O policies are written on a "claims-made" basis; thus, a director should understand the limits of this type of coverage.

The claims-made type of policy contrasts with an "occurrence" policy. Occurrence policies cover all claims arising out of incidents occurring during the policy period, regardless of whether the insurance policy is still in effect at the time the claim is made. Most insurance policies with which a director will be individually familiar—for example, automobile liability, fire, and extended coverage—are occurrence policies. Thus, it is important to understand the nature and limits of claims-made coverage.

Policy coverage on a claims-made basis means that a claim is covered by insurance only if the policy is in effect at the time that the claim is made, regardless of when the event causing the claim occurred. For instance, suppose that a corporation had coverage for the past ten years, but because of a changeover in clerical staff, the policy lapsed for a month before being renewed. The corporation would not be covered for any claim made during the one month of noncoverage, even though the claim related to corporate action during the prior period in which the corporation's policy had been in effect. Furthermore, some D&O policies will limit the coverage of prior events to those arising in a specified number of years prior to the inception of the policy with that particular carrier. As can be seen, claims-made coverage may offer a very limited protection. Directors should further understand that if the corporation discontinues a D&O policy after they cease to be a director, they may be uninsured even as to acts occurring during their term of office, if the claim is made after the policy is discontinued and no "tail" policy is obtained.

In addition to the requirement that the D&O policy be in effect as of the date a claim is made, D&O policies have other requirements that must be adhered to in order to ensure that coverage is available. For instance, D&O policies typically require the corporation to advise the insurer promptly of facts that could trigger claims, and delicate issues arise as to what constitutes adequate notice of a claim. When making a D&O claim, the corporation should make sure that the form of notice conforms to the policy requirements.

Policy Coverage

D&O policies are typically divided into two parts. The first part covers reimbursement of individual directors and officers for losses for which they are not indemnified by the corporation. The second part provides reimbursement to the corporation for amounts that it has paid or is required to expend, in indemnifying its directors and officers. In other words, it provides the funds that enable the corporation to discharge its obligation to indemnify.[22]

The type of coverage, retentions, exclusions, and other aspects of the policies are sufficiently complex as to require study by the corporation's insurance committee, an insurance consultant, and possibly by legal counsel experienced in this area. The corporation also should review the issues whenever insurance carriers are changed.

Types of Coverage

When a director reviews a D&O policy, it is important to understand whether the policy covers the directors and officers (A-side coverage), the organization's obligation to indemnify its directors and officers (B-side coverage), or the entity for its own liability (C-side coverage).[23] A-side coverage can require a director who is entitled to indemnification to look first to the nonprofit rather than the insured for protection against loss. B-side coverage covers the institution regarding reimbursement for amounts advanced to satisfy indemnification claims that the directors and officers may make against the institution or entity under corporate law or organizing documents of the institution.[24] C-side coverage provides insurance for an entity itself for its own wrongful acts and to avoid an allocation of benefits between the entity and the officers and directors.[25]

Losses Covered

The D&O policy should be analyzed to determine whether the duty to defend and the cost of defense are covered. The corporation should provide the director with a memorandum on this subject as well as the losses covered or not covered. For example, usually, there is no duty to provide attorneys to defend a lawsuit; nor do typical D&O policies provide for the payment of legal expenses, except after a final determination of liability under the policy.[26] Thus, technically, a D&O policy is an *indemnity* policy, as distinguished from a *liability* policy.

Under an indemnity policy, such as the typical D&O policy, the insurer is not required to make any payments until the insured has suffered an actual loss (as defined in the policy). In comparison, a liability policy, such as the typical automobile insurance policy, requires the insurer to make certain payments even though the insured has not yet incurred a loss or paid any out-of-pocket money.[27] It is because of the nature of a D&O policy that the advances for expenses mentioned above are so crucial for the director's protection.

A director will also want to know:

- the limits of coverage of the D&O policy (i.e., the highest amount of money the insurer will pay for each loss);
- the retention level imposed on the insureds, more commonly known as the deductible (i.e., how much of the loss must be borne by the director before the insurer will begin to provide payment for the loss); and
- the amount of coinsurance, if any (i.e., the percentage that the insured continues to be responsible for paying, even when deductibles have been satisfied and the insurance is providing coverage for a loss).

Policy Exclusions

Virtually all D&O policies have substantial exclusions that must be fully understood.

In addition to the scope of coverage, directors should understand their D&O policy's exclusions. The excluded risks are not just limited to the exclusions section but occur throughout the policy. For example, the term "loss" may be defined to exclude fines or penalties imposed by law for matters uninsurable under applicable law, such as punitive damages. Other definitions and terms also set forth exclusions.[28]

The standard exclusions often involve some types of risks that could produce sizable claims against directors and officers. Often excluded are the following liabilities: losses covered by other insurance; sickness or death resulting from pollution; ERISA claims; fair employment claims; libel or slander actions; and liabilities arising from intentional conduct, including fraud, dishonesty, and criminal conduct. Most policies also will not cover fines, penalties, or punitive damages.

Just because an area of risk is excluded from a standard D&O policy, however, does not mean that coverage for such risk cannot be obtained. Many exclusions may be deleted by negotiation and payment of a separate premium. A few specialized exposures (such as ERISA claims) may be covered by specific policies. While a request for additional coverage may constitute the "red-flagging" of a problem, the disclosure of potential claims is required in the application in any event. Thus, it is in the interests of the corporation and its officers and directors to identify whether the corporation's activities result in a significant risk of liability for a type of claim excluded by its D&O policy. The corporation can then determine whether the exclusion can be eliminated, or if coverage for such claims can be obtained by other means.

The Application

All applications for D&O insurance should be carefully prepared and reviewed for accuracy.

The application for D&O insurance and the statements made in it are part of the insurance contract and may be relied on by the insurer when an issue is raised as to the policy's coverage. Because of the peculiar importance of D&O insurance, all directors should be sure that not only the policy itself but also the application for it has been reviewed with particular care since a misstatement in the application (even if the director is unaware of it) may result in a denial of coverage.

Cost

The cost of D&O insurance coverage depends on various factors, including the size of the nonprofit corporation and the risks associated with its activities. It may be possible to reduce the cost of the premium by reducing certain risks. This usually requires communication with the broker and carrier on possible ways to reduce the risks/premiums.

Statutory Protections for Directors

Many state statutes limit the liability of directors of certain kinds of nonprofit corporations.

Eliminating Liability to Third Parties

As a partial response to the increased exposure of directors and the possible unavailability of insurance, the Model Act and many states' nonprofit corporation statutes limit a director's liability except in special situations such as those involving gross negligence, recklessness, or willful misconduct.[29] An example of such a provision is § 831(d) of the Model Act, which provides that a director of a charitable corporation shall not be liable to the corporation or its members for money damages for any action taken, or any failure to take any action, as a director, except liability for (1) the amount of a financial benefit received by the director to which the director is not entitled; (2) an intentional infliction of harm; (3) an unlawful distribution; or (4) an intentional violation of criminal law.

In some states, these liability-elimination provisions apply only to directors of public benefit corporations or corporations exempt from taxation under § 501(c) of the Internal Revenue Code,[30] or to directors who serve without compensation.[31] In addition, under some state statutes, such liability-elimination only applies if the corporation has satisfied certain requirements, such as including a liability-elimination provision in its articles of incorporation or obtaining a certain level of insurance coverage.[32] Directors should make sure that the corporation has taken all actions needed to make this protection available.

Eliminating Liability for Monetary Damages to the Corporation or Its Members

Even if protection under a liability shield statute is not available, there are often other protections available under a state's nonprofit corporation statute.

Some states provide protection to directors from claims by the corporation or its members through the business judgment rule statutes. The rule provides that board members acting in good faith and the reasonable belief that their actions are in the best interests of the organization are protected from liability for erroneous judgments. *See* discussion in *Chapter 2, Duties and Rights of Nonprofit Corporation Directors.*

Some states also allow nonprofit corporations to eliminate or limit the personal liability of a director to the corporation or its members for monetary damages resulting from the breach of the director's duty of care owed to the corporation or its members.[33] Some state statutes will require such liability elimination to be set forth in the corporation's articles of incorporation. In addition, as noted above, such statutes generally do not permit the elimination of liability for intentional infliction of harm on the corporation or its members, intentional violation of criminal law, any transaction in which the director derived an improper personal economic benefit, loans to the director by the corporation, or unlawful distributions approved by the director.

Limitations of Liability Protection Statutes

The director should be aware of several fundamental weaknesses in statutes purporting to eliminate the liability of directors. First, many plaintiffs will predictably assert in the initial complaint that the act or omission involved falls within the exception to the applicable statute, that is, that the director *was* grossly negligent or willful, or that the matter involved breach of the director's duty of loyalty. Therefore, the director may still have to defend himself or herself in a court proceeding. Hence, once again, the need for advances of expenses (see discussion in the section "*Advancement of Expenses*" above). Second, whether or not these state statutes protect against director liability for claims arising under federal law is unclear. (Although the federal Volunteer Protection Act of 1997 may provide a similar level of protection, at least to uncompensated directors, it is subject to the same fundamental weaknesses.[34]) Third, immunity from liability is not automatic under these statutes; directors must *prove* that they met the due care, good faith, and other statutory requirements for elimination of liability. Therefore, even directors who are eligible to rely on these liability-elimination statutes should still request the corporation to maximize director indemnification rights available under state law and supplement these statutory protections with a D&O policy if possible.[35]

Protection against Certain Kinds of Claims

Other statutes limit the liability of corporations, or of volunteers other than directors, for certain types of claims. For instance, in New Jersey, nonprofit corporations are not liable for negligently causing injury to a beneficiary of the corporation.[36] To the extent these statutes effectively block claims to which the corporation (and potentially its directors and officers) are subject, they provide an added level of protection against litigation risks.

Conflicting Interests: The Director and Legal Counsel

In general, the board of directors is the highest authority of the corporation, and, in matters concerning the entire board, the corporation and the board are roughly identical in their legal exposure. But in some instances, the members of the board and the corporation may have conflicting interests. If the corporation and members of the board are both defendants in a proceeding, the corporation may wish (or be forced for its own protection) to assert cross claims against all or some of its directors. Further, individual directors may, through their own acts or omissions, find that they have different potential liability compared to other members of the board.

With respect to the role of legal counsel in claims made both against the corporation and some or all of the directors, the director should recognize the following:

(1) The legal positions of the board of directors and that of the corporation are not necessarily identical; in some situations the board or a portion of the board needs to seek counsel of its own, since the corporate general counsel may be obligated to pursue or assert claims against the directors in order to avoid liability of the corporation.

(2) An individual director may need independent counsel if the director finds that the director's situation differs markedly from that of other members of the board.

Summary

Directors and prospective directors will benefit from a thorough understanding of the protections against liability afforded them under state law, the corporation's articles of incorporation and bylaws, and the corporation's D&O policy or self-insurance fund. Directors may wish to require that senior management, board officers, or a committee conduct an annual review of the scope and limitations of these protections and evaluate whether it is feasible to take any actions to enhance them. The persons who conduct this review should report their conclusions to the full board.

See the Suggested Questions and Checklist following the Endnotes below to review the issues discussed in this chapter.

Endnotes

1. Individuals working in the nonprofit sector have faced an increased risk in personal liability. Since the 1980s, there has been a marked increase in the number of suits filed against individuals acting for nonprofit organizations. *See Developments in the Law—Nonprofit Corporations*, 105 Harvard Law Review 1578 (1992); *see also* D&O Liability Survey: 2021 (Willis Towers Watson); Stephen M. Foxman, *Directors and Officers Liability Insurance for Nonprofits*, 18 ABA Business Law Today 35 (July/August 2009).
2. In the past, many states held that charities were immune from lawsuits arising from injuries caused by employees or agents. This immunity has virtually disappeared through legislation and judicial decision. *See* President and Directors of Georgetown College v. Hughes, 130 F.2d 810 (D.C. Cir. 1942). *See also* Sanner v. Trustees of Sheppard and Enoch Pratt Hospital, 278 F. Supp. 138 (D. Md. 1968), *aff'd*, 398 F.2d 226 (4th Cir. 1968).
3. Derivative suits may be brought in some states by a corporation's members. *See, e.g.*, S.C. Code Ann. § 33-31-304. In many states, the attorney general may bring a derivative suit against a director. *See, e.g.*, S.C. Code Ann. § 33-31-304(b); Restatement of the Law, Charitable Nonprofit Organizations, § 6.02.
4. *See* W. Va. Code § 11-15-17 (tax delinquencies); Conn. Gen. Stat. § 42-110b (antitrust liability); 26 U.S.C. § 4958 (excess benefit transactions). See also John F. Olson, Josiah Hatch III, and Ty R. Saglow, Director and Officer Liability: Indemnification and Insurance, §§ 13.2–13:11.
5. *See* Model Act § 851(a).

6. *See* Model Act § 851(d).
7. For example, Model Act § 202(b)(8) permits a nonprofit corporation to include in its articles of incorporation a provision authorizing permissible or mandatory indemnification of a director. Such section specifically excepts liability arising out of improper financial benefit received by a director, an intentional infliction of harm on the corporation or the members, an unlawful distribution, or an intentional violation of criminal law. *See also* D.C. Code §§ 29-402.02(b)(7).
8. *See* Model Act § 8.52.
9. *See* Model Act § 852. Model Act § 102 defines "proceeding" broadly, to include a threatened, pending, or completed proceeding. Some state statutes may have different and more limited definitions. *See* Ga. Code Ann. § 14-3-140(26); N.C. Gen. Stat. § 55A-8-52; Ark. Stat. Ann. § 4-33-850(7).
10. Settlement amounts paid in connection with derivative suits may not be considered liabilities payable under the indemnification provision of the Model Act. *See* Comment 4, § 8.50.
11. *See, e.g.*, Colo. Rev. Stat. § 7-129-104.
12. *See* Restatement of the Law, Charitable Nonprofit Organizations, § 2.09, n. 45; D.C. Code § 29-406.54; Iowa Code § 504.855.
13. Model Act § 853.
14. Model Act § 853(c).
15. See, *e.g.*, Ariz. Rev. Stat. § 10-3853.
16. *See, e.g.*, Ark. Stat. Ann. § 4-33-855.
17. Model Act § 857.
18. *See e.g.*, Miss. Code Ann. § 79-11-281.
19. Restatement of the Law, Charitable Nonprofit Organizations, §2.09, cmt 37.
20. In the past, some homeowners' policies contained coverage for specific nonprofit civic activities of the insured. These provisions have largely been eliminated. Moreover, although some corporate general liability and individual personal liability policies will cover an individual's service as a director, this coverage is rarely complete.
21. *See* Willard L. Boyd III, *Lawyers' Service on Nonprofit Boards: Managing the Risks of an Important Community Activity*, 18 ABA Bus. L. Today 35, 39 (November/December 2008). A board member serving as the attorney for the corporation is discussed in more detail in *Chapter 14, The Legal Environment of the Nonprofit Corporation*—Choice of Counsel.
22. *See* Jack B. Siegel, A Desktop Guide for Nonprofit Directors, Officers, and Advisors: Avoiding Trouble While Doing Good, 614–617 (John Wiley & Sons 2006), Martin J. O'Leary,

Directors & Officers Liability Insurance Deskbook, 5th ed., 30–31 (American Bar Association 2020).

23. *See* Siegel, A Desktop Guide for Nonprofit Directors, Officers, and Advisors, *supra note 22, at* 614.
24. *See* Foxman, *Directors and Officers Liability Insurance for Nonprofits, supra* note 1.
25. *Id.*
26. *See* Zaborac v. American Casualty Co., 663 F. Supp. 330 (C.D. Ill. 1987). *But see* Okada v. MGIC Indemnity Corp. 823 F.2d 276 (9th Cir. 1986), which held to the contrary. There is considerable dispute among courts as to when legal fees would be payable. Some courts require legal fees to be paid as they are billed and payable. *See, e.g.*, Pepsico, Inc. v. Continental Casualty Corp., 640 F. Supp. 656 (S.D. N.Y. 1986).
27. In addition, an insured can be liable for legal defense costs as well as for damages on the claim itself when they exceed policy limits. A large deductible can subject a corporate insured to paying a significant portion of the initial defense costs. *See* Siegel, *supra* note 22, at 610–611. Thus, many nonprofit corporations may be underinsured.
28. Siegel, *supra* note 22, at 609–610.
29. *See* Ind. Code Ann. § 23-1-35-1; Iowa Code § 504.901; Tenn. Code Ann. § 48-58-601; Cal. Corp. Code §§ 5239 and 5047.5.
30. *See* N.J. Stat. § 2A: 53A-7.
31. *See* 805 Ill. Comp. Stat. 105/108.70(a) of the Illinois General Not for Profit Corporation Act of 1986, as amended (in addition, the elimination of liability provision only applies to directors and officers of tax-exempt corporations); Cal. Corp. Code § 5239.
32. *See State Liability Laws for Charitable Organizations and Volunteers* (Nonprofit Risk Management Center).
33. *See* Model Act, Section 202(c). *See also* Tenn. Code Ann. § 48-52-102; Ala. Code § 10A-3A-2.02(b)(4).
34. *See* Volunteer Protection Act of 1997, 42 U.S.C. §§ 14501-14505; *see also* Lisa A. Runquist and Judy F. Zybach, *Volunteer Protection Act of 1997: An Imperfect Solution* (available at www.runquist.com).
35. For a discussion of state laws providing for limited liability of nonprofit organizations' directors and officers, *see* Olson et. al., Director and Officer Liability, *supra* note 4, at § 13.12.
36. *See* N.J. Stat. Ann. §§ 2A:53A-7 and 2A:53A-8 (immunity for claim made by the hospital's intended beneficiaries for damages in excess of $250,000); *referenced in State Liability Laws for Charitable Organizations and Volunteers, supra* note 32, at 8, 72–76.

Suggested Questions for Directors Regarding Director Liability

(1) What exposure do the directors have to claims or litigation that may be brought? Who could potentially assert such claims and for what reasons?
(2) Have the directors of the corporation, past or present, been subject to litigation or threats of it? Why, and with what result?
(3) Are there similar corporations in which the directors have been sued?
(4) What provisions in the corporation's articles and bylaws address the director's risk, indemnification, and insurance?
(5) Of those provisions, which ones are mandatory upon which I can insist, and that require some approval or ratification? By whom? According to what standard?
(6) Do the mandatory provisions include the advance of expenses?
(7) Do I know what our corporation's D&O policy provides? What is not covered by it?
(8) What is the earliest date for which a matter would be covered even if a claim comes within the policy period?
(9) Who has read or examined the corporation's D&O policy, and how recently?
(10) Have I been provided with a memorandum describing our D&O coverage, available indemnification, and statutory protections available?
(11) Have I been informed of the interrelationship of the corporation's D&O coverage and other policies insuring me, such as professional malpractice or umbrella liability policies? Are there gaps in my protection?
(12) If I cease to be a director, for how long a period, if any, will the corporation's D&O policy cover me?
(13) If I have D&O coverage supplied in connection with another corporation, does it cover me as a director of this nonprofit corporation?
(14) Do applicable statutes limit my liability or exonerate me? Has the corporation taken all steps necessary to make those limitations or exonerations effective?

Checklist: Director Liability

Note: For simplicity, these and other chapter checklists describe a corporation having a chair, who presides over the board of directors; a chief executive, who may be a staff person; an executive committee; a governance/nominating committee; and an audit committee. (We recognize, however, that in many smaller and other nonprofits, these committee functions may be performed by either the executive committee or the board as a whole.) We also assume a legal counsel—someone, paid or unpaid, having primary responsibility for the corporation's legal affairs. Many corporations, especially larger nonprofits, may have other committees established for specific purposes, such as establishing executive compensation; monitoring compliance with legal requirements; and overseeing investments and other financial matters.

Subject	Review By	How Often	Comment
1. Does the organization have D&O insurance? What events does it cover?	Legal counsel, chief executive or board chair; prospective board members; risk manager/risk management committee (if any)	Perform evaluation and update all directors, at least annually	Review and evaluation of the adequacy of D&O coverage may also be merited at each change in corporate activities or structure, as well as at each change of insurer or alteration in policy coverage.
(a) What event dates are covered by D&O insurance?	Legal counsel, chief executive or board chair; risk manager/risk management committee (if any)	At least annually	This is not just an analysis of dates of policy itself, but an analysis of how far it covers prior events.
(b) Is the policy providing coverage on a "claims made" basis?	Legal counsel, chief executive or board chair; risk manager/risk management committee (if any)	At least annually	The board should understand what event constitutes a claim, and the nature of a claims-made policy. A memorandum to the directors should cover this issue.

Subject	Review By	How Often	Comment
(c) What events are not covered? Are special riders or policies available to cover specific excluded risks?	Legal counsel, chief executive or board chair; risk manager/ risk management committee (if any)	At least annually	The board should understand what event constitutes an insurable event, and what events are not covered. A memorandum to the directors should cover this issue.
(d) What are the deductibles? What coinsurance is required?	Legal counsel, chief executive or board chair; risk manager/ risk management committee (if any)	At least annually	A memorandum to the directors should cover this issue.
3. Does the organization's D&O policy exclude coverage when an otherwise insured person is covered by another liability policy—for example, an attorney's malpractice policy?	Legal counsel, chief executive or board chair; risk manager/ risk management committee (if any)	At least annually	Directors having dual coverage should inform audit committee and counsel.
4. Has the organization reviewed how possible gaps in coverage can be plugged?	Legal counsel, chief executive or board chair; risk manager/ risk management committee (if any)	At least annually	Larger corporations may use professional risk consultants in this task.

Chapter 14:
The Legal Environment of the Nonprofit Corporation

Chapter 14

The Legal Environment of the Nonprofit Corporation

Directors need to understand the corporation's legal environment in order to ensure the corporation acts within the bounds of the law and maximizes its performance for its constituency of service.

The Board's Responsibility

Understanding the Corporation's Legal Environment

To fully understand the scope of their duties, directors should have a clear picture of the corporation's legal environment, that is, the substantive law governing all the things the corporation is organized to do. *The directors must understand that this environment of laws and regulations surrounds the corporation at all times,* regardless of whether the corporation employs a lawyer, whether or not it is involved in a lawsuit, or whether some license or permit is required for the corporation's operations. Parts of this same legal landscape surround each of us individually; for the most part, we adjust to it unconsciously, without any need for professional help or guidance. The corporate director, however, must be more conscious of the corporation's legal environment, since it affects what the corporation can or cannot do.

For an analogy, think of driving a car. It is sitting in the garage; someone enters it to drive it. The law defines who that driver may be, on what side of the street the driver will drive, when the car must stop, when and where it cannot turn, and how fast it may go. The law imposes conditions of insurance, and requires pollution-free status. In some states, the law governs how many people may be in the car, or whether or not the driver must be wearing a seat belt, and other matters.

And yet, of course, no one of us gives any of this a moment's thought. Driving a car is such a normal part of our lives that we take for granted the commands of the law in doing so. If we were to drive a car from here to Mexico City, we might have different thoughts. We might find it necessary to inquire somewhere of the Mexican requirements for a permit to drive, how fast we may drive, and what we should if we had an accident. And then, if we went further and decided we wanted to take a passenger for hire to Mexico, we might see some complex legal problems emerge.

Role of Legal Counsel

Helping the corporation to navigate safely through its legal environment is a responsibility primarily of legal counsel for the corporation—whether a volunteer or paid—but that responsibility is most effectively assigned when the board of directors understands how the corporation faces the legal landscape surrounding it. On the one hand, legal counsel does not advise the board of directors to try to resolve legal problems themselves on a do-it-yourself basis, but on the other hand, legal counsel advises against the other extreme: assuming that the problem is entirely one to be assigned to legal counsel, and if legal counsel is not available, it is a problem that somehow ceases to exist. Legal counsel (whether internal or external, paid or volunteer) is a means to be used. It is the job of the board to use such means appropriately and effectively.

What We Mean by Law

In determining a corporation's legal environment, a director should first understand what the "law" is. This question is answered in three parts:

Predictable Acts by Authorities

The law is a question of how people holding power over the corporation—legislators, regulators, officials of various kinds, judges, and the like—will behave in certain situations. A distinguished jurist once said that the object of the study of law is prediction, "the prediction of the incidence of the public force through the instrumentality of the courts,"[1] and we adopt basically this view. A large part of the corporation's legal environment is the predictable behavior of power: power held by legislatures, by the administrators, by the judges, etc.

Private Acts (Contracts) That Bind the Corporation

Corporations through their own voluntary actions are frequently making law: by contracts, agreements, leases, etc. These private actions, which are part of the daily business of the corporation, create a set of legal restraints that are as effective within their limited sphere as any statute or regulation. Yet no business could survive if every contract or every purchase of goods, required the services of a lawyer. The prudent board attempting to control its legal environment will expect management to separate those contracts that require the assistance of outside legal counsel from those that can be handled by the corporation's staff (including any in-house attorneys) as part of its day-to-day business.

Litigation

The determination of law applicable to the corporation must include an understanding of the impact of litigation involving the corporation either as a plaintiff or a defendant. This *Guidebook* does not elaborate on this particular aspect of legal activity because in most situations if the corporation is entering the courtroom voluntarily, or forced into it involuntarily, the corporation must employ legal counsel.

Analysis of the Corporation's Legal Environment

Identifying Potential Areas of Legal Exposure

To understand the corporation's legal environment, directors should make the following inquiries:

(a) Does the corporation's activity require that it have relatively long-term contracts or agreements with other entities or persons?

(b) Are any activities of the corporation similar to those of other corporations that have faced litigation in connection with such activities—whether brought by a government entity or by some private entity or individual?

(c) Do any of the corporation's activities require the concurrent expenditure of money or provision of effort by another party—such as a joint venture partner?

(d) Do any of the corporation's activities require a license or permit? Is there a government body that can require reports or make inspections?

From a list such as that set forth above, the directors can note those issues where the expectations of the corporation (or the party contracting with the corporation) may not be met and where a failure to meet expectations would seriously impact the corporation. These are the areas in which the board should probably consult legal counsel. The board's recognition of the corporation's potential legal exposures will help the directors determine what actions may be taken in advance to minimize the likelihood that the corporation would suffer any damage in connection with any particular relationship or activity.

Annual Review

A general review of the corporation's legal environment should be conducted once a year. This review serves in part to promote consciousness-raising, to help make the board aware of its potential problems and legal vulnerabilities, even though no immediate solution may be needed. *This* Guidebook *does not assume that the answer to all of the demands of the corporation's legal environment is, automatically, the employment of a lawyer.* Still, once the board has performed a review of its legal vulnerabilities and needs, it will be in a better position to determine when legal counsel is and is not appropriate.

The Corporation's Contractual Environment

When to involve outside legal counsel in the contracting process

The section "*Private Acts (Contracts) That Bind the Corporation*" above refers to the private law-making function of the corporation, that is, the drafting and execution of contracts and agreements. The board should establish, or request management staff to propose guidelines regarding when outside legal counsel should be retained, in connection with a contractual matter, such as the following:

- The moneys to be committed by the corporation, or to the corporation, are a significant fraction of its budget.
- The contract involves more than two parties.
- The proposed contract involves the employment of a key person.
- The agreement is material to the corporation's activities.
- The performance to be promised (by either party) requires clear definition to avoid potential misunderstandings (such as for certain consulting or management services).
- The terms of the contract extend beyond one year.
- The activity touches on controversial issues such as fair employment, public health disputes, etc.
- The activity exposes the corporation to substantial risks, even if indemnification and insurance are available.

Use of in-house attorneys

Nonprofit organizations of sufficient size and resources may hire one or more in-house attorneys to draft and review contracts or provide other legal services. In some cases, the executive officer or other senior manager may be an attorney or otherwise capable of reviewing basic contracts without engaging outside legal counsel. To the extent such individual is not licensed to practice in the jurisdiction where the nonprofit is located, such review should not be treated as a formal legal review.

Board members may volunteer to review contracts; however, this practice raises a variety of legal and role-definition issues and should be done cautiously if at all. See "*Special Issues of the Board Member as Legal Counsel*" below.

The Litigation Environment

Litigation differs from other aspects of the legal landscape in its potential expense, the necessity of the use of legal counsel, and its unpredictable outcome.

Insurance and indemnification to limit litigation risk

The possibility that the corporation may be exposed to litigation is a risk of loss against that the board should shield the organization by insurance or indemnification if it is feasible.

Any exposure to litigation generally means an exposure to costs of significant size. Litigation requires the use of paid legal counsel, with substantial uncertainty as to cost. Even if a lawsuit against the corporation is frivolous, and the corporation may be awarded its attorneys' fees by a court or its costs are covered by insurance, by the time all expenses, including diversions of staff time and lost opportunities have been totaled up, the corporation will still have been adversely affected. If the corporation finds that other corporations having similar activities have been exposed to litigation, directors should examine why this has been so, and what differences, if any, exist between their corporation and the other corporations.

If litigation on behalf of the corporation seems essential to protect the corporation or to fulfill its purpose, it must be budgeted as best can be done. Still, in a lawsuit of anything more than routine nature, such budgeting is extremely difficult; this is an occasion on which the board may benefit from receiving advice *regarding* legal counsel, from attorney board members or trusted attorney volunteers. A board contemplating engaging an attorney for a litigation matter should recognize the following:

- No lawyer can totally control, and hence no lawyer can guarantee, the time that a lawsuit may consume. Tactics of the opponent, unforeseen developments, and congestion in the courts all add to the unmanageable character of litigation.
- Although some lawyers may undertake to handle a lawsuit for a fixed maximum fee, in doing so the lawyer may be either including a substantial contingency allowance in that quotation, or counting on readjusting the fee in some manner if the litigation proceeds in an unexpected fashion.
- No corporation should enter the courtroom on its own behalf on the assumption that it can withdraw at will; it may be subject to a counterclaim that holds it in the courthouse, or to substantial penalties imposed by the court.

The Corporation's Political/Legal Environment

Restrictions on Involvement in Political Arena

Nonprofit corporations that are tax-exempt under § 501(c)(3) of the Internal Revenue Code (Code) are prohibited from using the organization's resources on behalf of a candidate in a political campaign. (See the discussion in the section *"The Absolute Prohibition on Political Campaign Activities"* in *Chapter 5, Taxation."*) Such tax-exempt corporations may, however, engage in lobbying in connection with an issue of concern to the organization, provided that such lobbying activities are limited to an "insubstantial" amount (generally 5 percent of its total activities, or other amount if the corporation elects to rely on the safe harbor under Code § 501(h)). (See the discussion in the section *"Limitations on Lobbying"* in *Chapter 5, Taxation.*) Nonprofits that engage in lobbying also must comply with federal, state, and local lobbying regulations, such as the federal Lobbying Disclosure Act and the Honest Leadership and

Open Government Act of 2007.[2] Despite these restrictions and limitations on a tax-exempt corporation's involvement in the political arena, directors of § 501(c)(3) corporations and other nonprofits should still be aware of the legal/political environment in which their organization operates.

How Nonprofits Are Affected by the Legal/Political Environment

As discussed earlier in this chapter, all nonprofits are affected by laws and regulations relating to one or more of the organization's activities. In some cases, nonprofits look to governmental sources for grants or other revenues. In all cases, the activities of nonprofits—including hiring employees and providing services to the public—are subject to various legal requirements and restrictions.

Changes in the political environment relating to a nonprofit corporation's activities can have a significant effect on the nonprofit's ability to fulfill its mission, or even to survive. For example, an arts organization that sees its public funding diminish, or another organization suddenly faced with burdensome governmental record-keeping requirements, may need to reassess a significant portion of its operations. Similarly, any changes in the Internal Revenue Code that affect the deductibility of certain kinds of gifts—whether artwork, appreciated stock, or other assets—may have substantial consequences for nonprofit organizations. For this reason, it is important that directors have a clear understanding of the regulatory environment under which the nonprofit operates, including its public funding sources.

Keeping the Board and Others Aware of the Impact of Proposed Legal Changes

Since many nonprofits operate on slim profit margins, directors of nonprofit corporations should stay informed regarding what impact proposed legislative and regulatory changes could have on the organization. Nonprofit boards may request that their staff or outside advisers periodically review pending legislative activity relating to the nonprofit's operations, as well as identify opportunities for the organization to receive assistance from governmental bodies in connection with the organization's mission.

Some organizations may wish to adopt a lobbying plan, to ensure that their voices are appropriately heard on issues of importance to the organization or its beneficiaries. On significant topical issues, the organization may effectively pool its resources with similar nonprofits or other groups with like concerns. Even without adopting a formal lobbying plan, a nonprofit may benefit from surveying its board members and any significant donors, to identify those with connections to legislators who are active in areas of interest to the organization, or who may otherwise be willing to listen to the organization's concerns. Nonprofits should be aware that although they must at all times adhere to the legal restrictions on lobbying activity, lobbying may occasionally, or even frequently, be an important means by which they assure their continued ability to fulfill their mission.

Choice of Legal Counsel

Differences among Kinds of Nonprofit Corporations

The situation of certain nonprofit corporations should be distinguished from others with regard to employment of legal counsel. Large nonprofits will, and should, solve their needs for legal services much as a business corporation would: by the employment of professionals, either as salaried attorneys or as outside legal counsel. The considerations that lead to their choice of legal counsel remain very much those that would guide the director of a business corporation.

In comparison, the directors of small nonprofit corporations frequently have special problems and opportunities in the choice of legal counsel. First of all, some nonprofit corporations may have lawyers serving as directors. Such persons clearly offer certain benefits to the corporation, but also present certain problems, discussed below. Moreover, many such corporations have given little attention to planning or managing their legal exposures and often let them reach crisis proportions before taking action.

Budgeting for Predictable and Recurrent Legal Needs

Legal budget considerations

The first step of the board in this area is budgetary: Given the corporation's legal environment and needs, how much of its funds should the corporation set aside for predictable and recurrent needs for legal counsel? This estimate should be a part of an appropriate reserve for emergencies or other unbudgeted items.

Wise boards will choose to ignore available uncompensated legal services of volunteers or board members when preparing the corporation's legal budget.

Such a source of services, discussed later in this chapter, may on occasion be both available and appropriate; however, the corporation should not *budget* on the assumption that legal problems of serious dimensions can be so handled. If a volunteer lawyer is available and appropriate, the saving of money should be treated as an unexpected financial benefit, not as a budgetary offset.

When needs exceed capacity

If a realistic legal services budget—again, for only the predictable and recurrent legal needs—is apparently beyond the means of the corporation, it should examine, just as it would with any other excess of expected expenses over receipts, whether its resources are too small for its functional survival. The board should recognize that the risks it is unwilling to lessen or minimize here will always go somewhere: They will be borne in the disappointment of donors who see a program jeopardized or encumbered, of staff who see organizational goals unable to be achieved, or of beneficiaries who are not served. As with every other item of expense, the board must prudently provide for it, just as it must budget the corporation's income.

Making decisions within the legal budget

Given a budgetary floor, the chief executive or other appropriate officer should recommend to the board whether to:

- hire (if funds permit) one or more full-time or part-time in-house attorneys;
- budget in anticipation of retaining legal counsel on a regular basis, as a predictably necessary part of corporate existence; or
- plan to retain legal counsel to deal with particular problems as needed.

The above distinctions are inevitably one of degree: Is the predictable frequency of problems such that the services of a designated lawyer or firm that deals with all of them would be more efficient? Or is the frequency so slight or the diversity of events so great that a separate choice should be made for each case?

If a single lawyer or firm handles the bulk of the corporation's work, there are significant economies in the time necessary to initiate each engagement. If the predictable volume of work indicates continuing exposure to problems, a general retainer may be advisable.

Selecting Legal Counsel

In selecting legal counsel, the corporation should enter into a professional engagement, regardless of whether legal counsel is compensated or volunteer.

Certain generalizations can be offered about the choice of counsel, regardless of whether the lawyer is paid or unpaid.

Professional engagements

The relationship between the corporation and the lawyer serving as counsel (whether for a fee or on a volunteer basis) must be a professional engagement. It should be entered into formally, with the lawyer and the corporation each specifying (in writing) what they expect the engagement to entail.

Identifying the kind of legal counsel required

Lawyers are not one-size-fits-all products, each one of whom is capable of doing everything or being the best person available. The services needed for the particular corporation may be unique and somewhat specialized. A large professional or trade association, for example, needs regular antitrust counsel—lawyers with some experience in this area, whose work keeps them abreast of recent developments in the field that may affect the corporation. In comparison, this specialized expertise would be of little use to the board of an art museum.

On the other hand, there are a large variety of professional skills needed by a nonprofit corporation that vary little between the largest trade association and the smallest community enterprise. All these corporations need competent tax advice; all of them, from time to time, will need skill in drafting employment contracts, reviewing leases, reviewing bank loan documents, and the like. In analyzing needs, the corporation should separate its routine, legal "housekeeping" needs from its specialized needs.

With that said—and other things being equal—it is desirable to get most legal services from a single-source supplier. This will probably save money, and it enables a lawyer to have an overview of the total activities of the corporation; as a peripheral or fringe benefit of that corporation, the lawyer or she may offer an insight into some overlooked aspect of the corporation's activities. The corporation may decide that some legal housekeeping can be done by volunteer lawyers and other problems referred to paid legal counsel.

"Peacemaker" functions of legal counsel

There is another role that paid legal counsel in the proper circumstances can perform, and which may be of enormous importance. We refer to a function of an internal "peacemaker" within the corporation. Often this means simply that the lawyer conveys and certifies unwelcome truths, where other concessions to that reality may be fraught with political tensions within the board. It may be also that the lawyer, as an informed outsider, can suggest alternatives in the midst of a polarized controversy, or provide objectivity regarding certain controversial issues.

Understanding the Corporation's Rights and Obligations vis-à-vis Its Legal Counsel

Significance of client-lawyer relationship

The law regards the relationship of a lawyer and a client in a unique and peculiar way, *and does so regardless of whether the lawyer is paid or unpaid.* Still, the mere fact that a person who serves on a board of directors is a lawyer does not make the corporation that lawyer's client. If a client relationship does exist, certain consequences follow for both the lawyer and the corporation.

Authority of lawyer to bind client

The corporation must recognize that, in general, a lawyer who can describe a corporation as a client has the apparent authority to bind that client to certain kinds of commitments in certain situations. This is particularly true in the courtroom. The limits of the lawyer's apparent authority are, to some degree, discernible from common sense. Nonetheless, it is always important in engaging an attorney (again, whether volunteer or paid) to define the scope of that engagement so that any generally implied authority of an attorney can be limited to specific actions. Wherever feasible, the employment of an attorney should be defined and documented in a written letter of engagement. Such contracts of engagement are, in many states, required by the rules governing the profession. Such document can further clarify the business aspects of the arrangements such as fees, payments, advancing cash expenditures, and so on.

Standards of loyalty

When the lawyer is engaged, the client is entitled to expect certain minimum standards of loyalty. To some degree, these parallel the obligations a corporation may expect from anyone acting on its behalf, for example, a real estate broker or an executive search firm. One expects such agents to keep confidences and not to use the information obtained from the organization for the agent's advantage outside the scope of the engagement.

Confidentiality for certain client-lawyer communications

The relationship with a lawyer differs, however, in that the client can confide in the lawyer as to matters related to the professional engagement and the communications to the lawyer generally may not be disclosed by the lawyer (without a serious breach of the lawyer's obligations). A court might not require the lawyer to make that disclosure, even under a subpoena. Under the attorney-client privilege, consultations with lawyers concerning complicated and frequently delicate matters are given protections that are not available in consultations with, for example, an accountant or personnel consultant.

In dealing with controversial or sensitive matters, the protection against disclosure arising under the attorney-client privilege, this distinction may be of great importance to the corporation. In certain circumstances, however, such confidentiality protection can be lost, such as when the client (through an officer, employee, or other agent) discloses the sensitive information to a third party in addition to the lawyer. Therefore, the board should caution its members and representatives of the corporation against disclosure of such matters to persons other than the corporation's legal counsel. This includes ex officio or honorary directors who are not actual directors with a vote, but simply advisory.

Potential lawyer conflicts of interest

A cost of client confidentiality is imposed on the corporation's lawyer. The receipt of confidences from the client, whose interests may be opposed to that of another party, may prevent the lawyer from accepting certain engagements with such other parties, unless the client agrees to waive the conflict.

Use of Volunteer Lawyers

Volunteer lawyers, whether or not members of the board, may present certain opportunities to the corporation, but they should be used with caution, and with a clear understanding of their role.

Public benefit and religious corporations frequently have lawyers as board members; they also may have outside volunteer lawyers willing to serve the organization. The availability of such resources should not be overlooked, but should be approached with caution.

It should be realized that the lawyer-volunteer could be exposed to a substantial risk in undertaking a legal engagement of any significant depth. The following issues need to be considered:

- The fact that the lawyer is unpaid is immaterial in terms of professional malpractice liability of the individual involved and in terms of what the corporation is entitled to expect.[3]
- Lawyers acting in an area outside their regular experience and expertise may expose themselves to heightened risks of professional liability.

Responsibility for Monitoring the Corporation's Tax Environment

If a corporation seeks to solve most of its legal problems through the use of board members or other volunteers, at least one such volunteer should undertake to maintain regular familiarity with the tax laws affecting the corporation. A public benefit corporation should know, for example, the limits of its activities imposed by § 501(c)(3) of the Code and the distinctions between influencing legislation, where some flexibility is permitted, and engaging in political campaigns, which is absolutely prohibited. The administration of such an inquiry is time-consuming, and in fact is rarely made. Because of a director's familiarity with the ongoing activities of the corporation, this is a valuable service that may be provided by a qualified lawyer-director alone or in periodic contact with specialized tax counsel.

Special Issues of the Board Member as Legal Counsel

It is hardly uncommon for a lawyer who is a member of a nonprofit corporation's board to serve also as legal counsel for the corporation. Still, when a director serves as legal counsel for the corporation, there are special issues that both the corporation and the lawyer need to carefully consider. The practice of generally representing the corporation is frequently criticized for the following reasons:

- The lawyer's independence and objectivity in advising the corporation may be at least somewhat impaired.
- A confusion of roles may affect the lawyer's ability to assert, on behalf of the corporation, its right to confidential treatment of certain communications.
- Various types of conflicts can arise, such as when a lawyer is asked to pursue an objective that the lawyer, as a board member, opposed, when the board is taking action with regard to the law firm representing the corporation (such as voting to retain the firm) and when the lawyer is asked to opine on board actions in which the lawyer, as a board member, participated.[4]
- The lawyer's ability to negotiate on behalf of the corporation, as a professional facing another professional, is sometimes impaired by the ambiguity of roles.

A further problem arises with a board member acting as lawyer for the corporation. Effective representation of any entity—whether a hospital, school, or dance troupe—requires the full and informed confidence of the persons controlling that entity. In other words, a lawyer serving on a nonprofit board should know if the lawyer's designation as legal counsel had the active consent of all the fellow directors. Some board members who would prefer using outside legal counsel may be uncomfortable challenging a fellow director who offers legal services. A board member serving as legal counsel may be put in a difficult position if called upon to give advice regarding a matter that touches on some controversial policy or field of activity about which the board is divided. In addition, when a lawyer board member also acts as legal counsel, it may be difficult to distinguish which "hat" the director is wearing at any given time. What would otherwise be considered protectable attorney-client communication may become subject to discovery if characterized as discussion among board members.

Frequently, outside legal counsel handling a problem area is able to bring to the board an objectivity concerning a decision to be made, since the lawyer stands aside from the substantive controversy involved. This is, to a certain degree, a traditional function of lawyers serving organizations and it is a role that may be difficult for an inside lawyer to perform.

At the same time, it may be unrealistic to suggest that a small public benefit entity should avoid the use of volunteer legal services and always seek outside paid legal counsel. In fact, nonprofits often will look to their lawyer board members for assistance on certain legal matters, such as preparation of articles of incorporation, bylaws, tax returns, or employment agreements. By providing this assistance, the lawyer board member can be viewed as having established an attorney-client relationship and becoming the lawyer for the organization.

As noted above, a lawyer sitting on the nonprofit corporation's board should proceed with caution when agreeing to provide legal services to the corporation. A lawyer board member who agrees to act as legal counsel should consider and discuss with the other board members the extent of the representation and the potential hazards of serving in such dual roles. The lawyer board member also should make clear to the board when the lawyer is acting as a board member or as the attorney for the organization.[5]

Who Is the Client?

Lawyers representing nonprofit corporations owe their professional obligations to the corporation and not to the board as a whole, or to any individual director or officer.

In controversies involving corporate actions, a claimant may assert that both the corporation and one or more directors are accountable, or the corporation may wish to assert that certain directors bear the real responsibility for the controversial events. A director should understand *that in such circumstances the corporation's lawyer does not and cannot represent both the corporation and the affected directors.* Among other things, this means that the corporation's lawyer cannot receive confidences from a director that are kept from the corporation.[6]

When a situation arises that involves an actual or potential dichotomy of interest between the corporate entity and one or more directors, the affected directors should seek independent legal counsel, and the corporation's lawyer should so advise the directors.[7]

See the Suggested Questions and Checklist following the Endnotes below to review the issues discussed in this chapter.

Endnotes

1. Oliver W. Holmes, *The Path of the Law*, 10 HARVARD LAW REVIEW 557 (1896).
2. 2 U.S.C. § 1610.
3. The Model Rules of Professional Conduct, promulgated by the American Bar Association, are the basis of the professional regulation of lawyers in the vast majority of states. Rule 1.1 of the Model Rules states that "[a] lawyer shall provide competent representation to a client. Competent representation requires the legal knowledge, skill, thoroughness and preparation *reasonably necessary for the representation*" (emphasis supplied). *See also*, J.J. Leitner, *Nonprofit Organizations Need Nonprofit Lawyers*, ABA BUSINESS LAW TODAY (November 2016).
4. *See* American Bar Association, *Model Rules of Professional Conduct*, Rule 1.13, Comment 35; ABA Formal Ethics Opinion 98-410; D.C. Bar Ethics Opinion 382 (2023).
5. *See Id., See also* Willard L. Boyd III, *Lawyers' Service on Nonprofit Boards: Managing the Risks of an Important Community Activity*, 18 ABA BUSINESS LAW TODAY 35 (November/December 2008); Willard L. Boyd III, Ed., *Nonprofit Law: A Practical Guide to Legal Issues for Nonprofit Organizations*, 95-99 (American Bar Association 2017).
6. American Bar Association, *Model Rules of Professional Conduct*, Rule 1.13 states, in part:
   A lawyer employed or retained by an organization represents the organization.... In dealing with an organization's directors ... a lawyer shall explain the identity of the client when the lawyer knows or reasonably should know that the organization's interests are adverse to those of the [directors] with whom the lawyer is dealing.
7. *See* Michael W. Peregrin and James R. Schwartz, *When Does the Board Need its Own Counsel?*, 54 TRUSTEE at 23 (April 2001).

Suggested Questions for Directors Regarding the Corporation's Legal Environment and Selection of Legal Counsel

Legal Environment

(1) Do we depend on the help of another group, individual, or entity to carry out a major part of our corporate purpose or mission? Does such a party need us in a similar way?
(2) If we are in a position of dependency as described above, are the relationships clearly defined? How?
(3) Is the other party involved expending money in reliance on our activity with them? Are we devoting funds to the activity?
(4) Does the size of the undertaking or its contemplated duration suggest that the relationship be defined by a formal agreement? Do we have one?
(5) Do any such undertakings seem to be failing to achieve their purposes? Will we, or our partner in the undertaking, lose substantial funds in the event of failure?
(6) Have we ever been sued? Why? With what result?
(7) Do I know of a corporation similar to ours that was sued? Why? With what result?
(8) Is there any government agency (other than the IRS) that controls or regulates our activities? What limits does this agency place on us?
(9) Do we engage in public controversies during which we make statements attacking or criticizing some other person or entity?
(10) Do we regularly review the corporation's legal exposures?
(11) Do we review the public funding sources of the nonprofit and monitor developments in these sources?

Selection of Legal Counsel

(1) Do we include legal fees as part of our regular budget? If we do, how is the amount determined?
(2) Do other corporations with activities similar to ours find it necessary to retain legal counsel? Why? Or, if they do not, why not?
(3) Is there a lawyer, paid or unpaid, whom we generally look to for legal advice?

(4) Have we analyzed that individual's particular skills in relation to our problems?
(5) What legal skills do we need that are unique, specialized, or unusual?
(6) Is our corporation presently a plaintiff or defendant in litigation? Why? What are the prospects of a termination?
(7) If a volunteer lawyer is presently acting as legal counsel, do I feel the lawyer is qualified to serve our needs?
(8) [If I am a lawyer:] Am I asked to provide legal advice to the board of directors? Do the board and I understand when my discussion of a problem is or is not a legal opinion that is protected by the attorney-client privilege?
(9) [If I am a lawyer:] Have I considered the potential conflicts of interest that may arise from my dual role and discussed them with the board? How will they be handled when they occur?
(10) [If I am a lawyer:] If I am asked to serve as legal counsel to the corporation for some matter, am I protected under my professional malpractice policy?
(11) [If I am a lawyer:] If I am asked to provide legal advice to the corporation, has the extent of my representation been clearly defined in writing?

Checklist: The Legal Environment of the Nonprofit Corporation

Note: For simplicity, these and other chapter checklists describe a corporation having a chair, who presides over the board of directors; a chief executive, who may be a staff person; an executive committee; a governance/nominating committee; and an audit committee. (We recognize, however, that in many smaller and other nonprofits, these committee functions may be performed by either the executive committee or the board as a whole.) We also assume a legal counsel—someone, paid or unpaid, having primary responsibility for the corporation's legal affairs. Many corporations, especially larger nonprofits, may have other committees established for specific purposes, such as establishing executive compensation; monitoring compliance with legal requirements; and overseeing investments and other financial matters.

Subject	Review By	How Often	Comment
1. The Corporation's Legal Environment			
(a) Do we know in what areas our organization may be vulnerable to legal liability?	Chair, chief executive	Annually	
(b) How does the board monitor the corporation's compliance with applicable laws?	Chair, chief executive	Annually	
(c) What actions should the corporation take to minimize known legal risks?	Chair, chief executive	Annually	
2. The Selection of legal counsel			
(a) Do we need regular legal counsel?	Chair, chief executive	Annually	An analysis of how the board solves recognized legal problems should be made.
(b) Can we use volunteer legal counsel?	Chair, chief executive	Annually	Review must examine fitness of particular volunteer legal counsel's ability to meet corporation's specific needs.

Chapter 15:
Director Orientation and Revitalization

Chapter 15

Director Orientation and Revitalization

The corporation should institute formal actions and procedures to assure that all directors have received (and continue to receive) key documents and other information regarding the corporation. New directors should be given specific orientation as to the corporation's history, structure, and activities, and be encouraged to share their unique perspectives with the other directors. Board members should periodically engage in strategic planning, self-evaluation, and other analysis that show how well both the corporation and the board are fulfilling their missions.

New Director Orientation and Materials

Orientation

The corporation's board and management should organize specific events or meetings to welcome the new director. They also should make sure the director is provided with sufficient information to become an effective member of the board without a prolonged breaking-in period.

Effective use of new board members requires that they learn as much as possible about the organization, its mission, history, and hopes, as quickly as possible. Leaving the new arrivals to find this knowledge on their own, over a series of meetings, is a slow and inefficient process, and one in which the promise of many a board member can be lost to a corporation.

Set forth below is an outline of the type of reading material the corporation should provide to new board members, in the form of directors' manuals. Such information should be supplemented by site tours and specific meetings with senior staff and officers (outside of board meeting reporting sessions). Meetings of this type are very effective for new board members and may be scheduled prior to a new member's first meeting. Still, it may also be useful to schedule some meetings *after* the new member has attended a few meetings and become acquainted with the range of corporate matters within the board's purview.

Directors' Manuals or Websites

A threshold obligation of a director is to know and understand the purpose, function, and goals of the nonprofit corporation the director is serving. An invaluable tool in acclimating new directors of nonprofit corporations—as well as assisting all directors in satisfying their duties—is a manual or manuals containing important documents relating to the governance and operation of the corporation and other information that will keep the director apprised of the current state of the corporation. These may be simple loose-leaf binders, with a table of contents and a tab for each item. The use of such a binder makes updating the manual easy. As an alternative, many nonprofits have established governance sites on their websites or on another secure Internet location, in which board and committee information is maintained. This alternative allows for updates without the need to print new documents.

Increasingly, board meeting information is provided to directors of nonprofit corporations by e-mail and posted for reference on a board website, so that directors can have easy access to meeting materials and choose how much of the materials they would like to print.

The board may wish to have two board manuals, or categories of information: one containing material that a director should have ready access to at every board meeting, and a larger set of documents and information available for reference as needed. If a two-manual/category system is chosen, then the first board manual or set would include the items listed below:

Basic board reference material (first manual or information reference set)

The basic board reference material (first manual or information reference set) should contain, at a minimum, copies of the following documents:

(1) Calendar of dates and events compiled for the year, listing board, committee, and other significant meetings, activities (such as major fundraising events), and deadlines, which can be updated periodically;

(2) The corporation's articles of incorporation or charter, and any amendments;
(3) The current bylaws of the corporation;
(4) The corporate mission statement, vision statement, and any strategic plan;
(5) Board policies;
(6) Copies of all committee charters;
(7) Conflict of interest and other policies of the board or to which the board is subject;
(8) Current long-range or strategic plan; and
(9) Corporate organization chart, showing any affiliated organizations, and any departments and divisions of the corporation;
(10) Listing of names, addresses, and phone numbers of the corporation's directors and officers;
(11) List of the corporation's committees, including the name of each committee chair and all committee members; and
(12) List of key executive and administrative staff members of the corporation, including positions, addresses, and phone numbers.

Additional board reference material (second manual or information set)

The following material is recommended to be made available for a director's reference as needed:

(1) Prior minutes of board and committee meetings (these can be retained in a manual or website for one to two years, and then filed elsewhere);
(2) Financial statements of the corporation for the prior fiscal year and the operating and capital budgets for the current year;
(3) Biographical data on directors and key staff;
(4) Summary of D&O insurance, articles of incorporation and/or bylaw indemnification provisions, and statutory limitations on director liability;
(5) Current news releases by or about the corporation;
(6) Annual reports on the results of the organization's activities for the past two or three years;
(7) The last two most recent Form 990s filed by the corporation.
(8) Application for Recognition of Exemption for corporation.

As noted above, in lieu of hard-copy manuals, this information may be made available to board members via a secure governance site maintained on the nonprofit corporation's website or other secure Internet location.

New Director Review of Information

Another aspect of new director orientation (or evaluation of an invitation to become a director) requires the new or prospective director to review material on the corporation's operations and resources, as well as the operations of the board. At a minimum, the new or prospective director should review carefully the material recommended above for inclusion in the director's manuals, as well as the following materials:

Past board and committee minutes

The new director should review the minutes of the meetings of the board and its main committees for the last three years or so. Such a review is an excellent way to become knowledgeable regarding the recent history of the corporation, the issues faced by the board, and the board's methods for addressing these issues.

Past financial statements and reports

A new or prospective director should review the financial statements of the corporation for at least the last few years, noting particularly if there are any restrictions that have been placed on gifts to the corporation. For tax-exempt corporations, the director should review the corporation's annual informational returns filed with the IRS on Form 990. For corporations that acquired tax-exempt status fairly recently, a review of the corporation's Form 1023 (Application for Recognition of Exemption) also may be useful. If the corporation has issued tax-exempt bonds, the official statement related to any bond financing that is still outstanding should be reviewed; the first appendix ("Appendix A") to the official statement can provide a useful overview of the corporation and its management.

Current directors and management personnel

Ideally, before new directors join the board, they should have met the chief executive and other principal officers. The new board members also should have met the board chair and at least a few other board members—including both senior and junior members, so that the new members will not feel surrounded by strangers at their first meeting.

Compliance with law and internal control

As noted throughout this *Guidebook,* the use of assets of a nonprofit corporation is subject to certain limitations. For example, corporate assets must be used for the purpose for which they are given (generally, as stated in the corporation's articles of incorporation and bylaws and specifically as limited by agreement between a donor and corporation). The assets of tax-exempt corporations cannot be used to inure to the benefit of private individuals. (For a more in-depth discussion of limitations on tax-exempt corporations, see *Chapter 5, Taxation.*)

Prospective directors should become familiar with the role of the corporation's accountants and legal advisers in regard to matters of internal control and legal compliance. They should learn the corporation's policies and procedures regarding conflict of interest. If the corporation does not have a public accountant or regular corporate counsel, the individual should determine what steps the corporation has taken to make sure it is in compliance with any applicable limitations. In addition, some nonprofit corporations are subject to being accredited or licensed by outside agencies. Review of accrediting or survey reports, if available, can be extremely helpful in determining problem areas needing attention. (For additional suggestions for becoming familiar with the corporation's legal environment, see *Chapter 14, The Legal Environment of the Nonprofit Corporation.*)

Corporation's outlook

The new or prospective board member may find it helpful to have an in-depth discussion with the chief executive and board chair about the corporation's current plans, current prospects, critical issues being or expected to be confronted, and long-range objectives.

Board culture

Although new members are generally expected to fit into the existing board structure and culture, they also may be able to offer new perspectives and suggestions that will help the board operate more effectively. Nonetheless, prospective board members may need to think twice before agreeing to serve on a board that operates in a fashion they believe ineffective.

Board Revitalization: Retreats, Strategic Planning, and Self-Evaluation

Board Retreats

Many of the most successful nonprofit organizations have periodic board (or board/management) retreats. Retreats are used to give the board members an opportunity to conduct an assessment of the corporation and renew their individual commitment to helping the corporation satisfy its mission. A retreat may take the form of an extended board meeting or may have a different format. The agenda may focus on larger issues of mission and the future, or on particular problems facing the corporation. Retreats often include sessions designed to build relationships among board members, and thereby facilitate open discussions both then and at future board meetings. Often retreats are scheduled at locations away from the corporation's offices, where board members will be able to focus on the work at hand as well as have the opportunity to socialize and build personal rapport. Such retreats are ineffective unless all, or a very high proportion, of the board can attend. Therefore, retreats should be scheduled far in advance, and annually if possible—or at least on a regular schedule, such as every two or three years.[1]

Reviewing the Board Decision-Making Process

All directors should be aware of board discussion and decision-making style. If a director believes the current style or culture is not conducive to effective decision-making, the director should discuss the issue with the board chair or other directors, preferably apart from the boardroom. For example, are all board members given the opportunity to participate in discussions? Is adequate time allotted for questions? Do a few board members—or the board chair—tend to dominate discussions? Does the board chair give the board chair's opinion before other board members have had a chance to speak? Has the corporation had difficulty retaining chief executives? If so, could board function or board members' style be a source of the difficulty? The review of the board decision process and consideration of these questions should be conducted by the governance/nominating committee.[2]

Evaluating Whether the Board Needs to Be Restructured

Over the course of time, the board of a nonprofit corporation may require structural adjustments to enable the corporation to continue to meet its mission. For instance, the size of the board may need to be adjusted upward or downward. The resources of a large board may be more effectively channeled by using multiple committees that act in smaller groups and report back to the board. In some cases, fresh faces may be needed to help the board move away from entrenched attitudes and assumptions and to meet changing realities affecting the corporation and its mission. Again, this subject would be appropriate for the governance/nominating committee to review.[3]

Periodic review of board structure

The board should periodically provide for a process whereby the need for board structural changes can be assessed. This process may occur every three to five years at board retreats, be initiated by the board chair or chief executive, be handled by the governance/nominating committee, or consist of a report by outside advisers (in some areas, consultants or scholars in the area of nonprofit management may be available to conduct a review on a no-fee or low-cost basis). Because these reviews can be sensitive—particularly if members of the existing board feel threatened, or vulnerable to criticism for past decisions—it is recommended that such a structural review be institutionalized so that it occurs automatically every few years.

Self-evaluations of individual board members

Nonprofit corporations may benefit from board members engaging in annual or other periodic evaluations of each member's performance individually as well as the board's performance as a whole. These evaluations, or assessments, can be accomplished through the use of forms developed internally or adapted from samples developed by others, including other nonprofits, local trade associations, or writers in the area of nonprofit governance. (See discussion of information resources for nonprofit corporations in the section *"Other Sources of Information, Inspiration, and Guidance"* below, and selected titles and websites in *Appendix B*.)

Individual board members may be evaluated by the board chair and the corporation's chief executive, a governance/nominating committee, or a committee of a small number of board members or former board members. (Board members on the committee should be evaluated by a similar group.) After such evaluations, the board or committee chair should discuss the results of the evaluation with each board member. These discussion should serve as an opportunity both to acknowledge the individual director's contributions as well as to suggest ways in which the director's effectiveness could be improved.

Evaluations of the board

All board members should also complete periodic evaluations of the effectiveness of the board and the resources provided to it. Such an evaluation should include questions regarding each individual director's views on the strengths and weaknesses of the board and its committees, and provide an opportunity for directors to make suggestions for ways to improve board effectiveness. The evaluation should cover all aspects of board and committee functions, including new board member orientation, selection of future board candidates, adequacy of information provided before board meetings, conduct of board and committee meetings, effectiveness of board retreats, and opinions on future board needs. The governance/nominating committee should review the evaluations and make any recommendations to the board it believes will make the board more effective.

Board term limits

One mechanism used by nonprofit corporations to ensure they have engaged board members as well as an overall effective board involves the use of term limits. Often a nonprofit corporation will include a requirement in its bylaws that limits the number of terms an individual may serve as a director, thereby requiring the individual to be off the board for at least one year before coming back on the board.

Information-Gathering for Strategic Planning and Mission Measurement

Whether in the form of retreats or otherwise, many of the most successful nonprofit corporations require the board and staff members to engage in regular (often annual) strategic planning sessions. In order to make the most of these brainstorming and self-evaluation opportunities, the board should ask itself and its staff what information is available to determine whether the corporation has been successful in meeting its mission. For instance, are members/donors/visitors/users surveyed regarding their experiences, perceptions, and needs? Is such data available from or on comparable organizations? What other information is available quantifying the experience of the individuals who are the intended beneficiaries of the nonprofit corporation? What information *could* become available if the corporation sought to obtain it? Could volunteers be used to help gather this information? Have grant-makers required the corporation to compile information that could also be useful to review within the organization?

In general, nonprofit organizations, both big and small, tend to be much less sophisticated in terms of the information they routinely gather about their markets (both actual and potential) and market perceptions, when compared to for-profit organizations. Partly, this is a reflection of the unique nature of nonprofit corporations. A nonprofit corporation generally cannot measure the success or failure of its mission in simple monetary terms. Often, the primary mission of the nonprofit cannot be measured in amounts of X and Y calculated by an accounting firm. But this does not mean that nonprofits should not seek to count what can be counted, rather than relying on intuition or traditional assumptions. Through the use of the Internet, computer programs, interns, and volunteers, even small nonprofits with limited resources can access a wide range of information. Such data can confirm correlations between factors that an organization assumes to be relevant or reveal correlations between factors that are not intuitively obvious.

Without obtaining and analyzing available information on how well the organization is achieving its mission (and where improvement may be needed), it is very difficult for the board of a nonprofit organization to properly evaluate whether it is using its resources to their maximum potential. The organization runs the risk of becoming fixed in outdated perceptions—"this is the way things have always been"—without any mechanism to test the accuracy of these perceptions.

Although most nonprofits will not have the luxury of a full-time research department, nonprofit board members should regularly ask what information could and should be obtained in order to assist the board in evaluating whether the organization has been successful in meeting its mission. Such information can also provide board members with the tools they need to recognize when it is time to redefine the corporation's mission or make other changes to reflect new realities.

Quantifying Success for a Nonprofit Corporation

Quantification of the success or failure of a corporation is a considerably more challenging exercise in the nonprofit world compared to the for-profit business environment. While the board of directors of a for-profit must consider a large number of nonnumerical phenomena related to the operation of the corporation—legalities, risks of lawsuits, employee morale, quirks of consumer preferences, etc.—at the end of the day one factor reigns supreme: the bottom line. In the long run, no conceivable success in personnel management, marketing skills, or product development, will excuse the failure of a for-profit corporation to produce a profit, or at least break even. In the nonprofit world, in comparison, it is possible to achieve outstanding success in some missions and yet become financially insolvent.

Thus, the key challenge for any nonprofit board is both to fulfill the corporate mission and to see to it that the nonprofit survives to maximize the public benefits resulting from fulfilling its mission. A further burden on the nonprofit management is to achieve those goals with maximum efficiency. The process of assuring efficient survival will require the consideration of various numbers, including many things other than revenue dollars—such as the number of persons entering an art museum during a given month, or the increase in symphony orchestra memberships by certain minority groups and young professionals.

The subtleties of the "quantification challenge" in evaluating the success of a nonprofit corporation may be illustrated as follows: It is clear that the board of directors of an art museum must know what dollars are needed to keep the doors open and where that money can be found; it should also be able to know how many people come to the museum and when, who gives money and when, and how much a "needed" artwork will cost. All these matters are capable of being reduced to numbers. But, as an institution seeking to change a visitor's behavior and perceptions, what else does it and can it know and measure? How can it compare, numerically, one painting versus another or a visitor's different experiences after viewing those paintings—or a specific collection?

No ready answers rise to the surface, but let us examine what could be determined and counted. Probably one can learn, at relatively small cost:

- how many people come to the museum;
- on what days;
- at what hours;
- how many of those are dues-paying members;
- how many attend a given exhibit;
- how many buy books describing the exhibit;
- how many of the above are adults, children, men, or women; and
- how many live within certain zip-code areas.

In addition, for each of those questions, the organization can determine the correlation (or the lack thereof) of one classification with another. For example, do more women come on Tuesday morning than at any other time or any other day? The answers may be insignificant or mysterious, but they may, as one tracks them down, lead to other, more significant questions. All of the above data can be obtained without asking for any specific personal identification of those whose behavior is being measured, and none of it involves hidden cameras or other invasions of privacy.

But the board of a nonprofit institution, such as our hypothetical art museum, should not stop there. If it can cross the barrier that inhibits personal identification, it will want to know:

- how many of our sample live in which suburb or city area;
- how old are they;
- what is their race or ethnic identification; and
- did they come with others, and if so, who.

These last-described questions can be asked on a voluntary basis (with an increased margin of error, as many of the subjects will refuse the information, or worse, give deliberately misleading answers).

At this point our illustrative board has obtained a mass of information that can be assembled at relatively low cost—and some of it is already assembled by most museums. But at some point, it may want to go further. It will want to know:

- how would a visitor (of one of the classifications listed above) describe the motivations that brought him or her to the institution;
- were those aims satisfied;
- what other museums (of art or other purpose) does the visitor patronize; and
- what particular object or painting drew the visitor's most prolonged attention.

Once the nonprofit staff has compiled all the above answers and presented them to our board in numerical form, the board may be able to trace the correlations between trait X and trait Y, and ask if those correlations suggest management changes in the museum's programs. But such information may also lead to further questions, such as, "What is the correlation we wish to obtain? Why are we here?" Are we fulfilling our mission as effectively as possible? These are the kinds of ultimate questions that will continue to challenge the board of directors of a nonprofit corporation throughout its existence. In exercising the rights and duties described in this *Guidebook*, successive generations of a single nonprofit board will undoubtedly find different answers to these questions.

Other Sources of Information, Inspiration, and Guidance

Although this *Guidebook* has attempted to provide directors of nonprofit corporations with an overview of nonprofit corporation board service, there are a host of topics that we have not had space to address in depth or even at all. Board members seeking additional information on topics discussed in this *Guidebook*, or topics not addressed here, may take advantage of other resources available to nonprofit corporations in their community or available through the Internet.

For example, the Independent Sector and the Panel on the Nonprofit Sector, which was convened by Independent Sector (www.independentsector.org), have developed various reports and a guidebook for charities and foundations. *Principles for Good Governance and Ethical Practice: A Guide for Charities and Foundations* sets forth 33 principles of sound practice that should be considered by every charitable organization as a guide for strengthening its effectiveness and accountability. In addition, BoardSource is a national organization dedicated to advancing the public good by building exceptional nonprofit boards and inspiring service. It maintains a website (www.BoardSource.org) with information on various board governance topics. In addition, BoardSource has published numerous publications on the topic.

Similarly, the nonprofit Donor's Forum (www.donorsforum.org), an association of grant-makers, presents educational programs and maintains an extensive library of materials on nonprofit governance, financing, and operational issues. Many other communities have similar nonprofit resource organizations. College and public libraries, as well as commercial bookstores, are other resources for such materials. At *Appendix B* is a nonexhaustive sampling of publications and websites that may be of interest to nonprofit corporation directors and their advisers.

See the Suggested Questions and Checklist following the Endnotes below to review the issues discussed in this chapter.

Endnotes

1. *See* Sandra R. Hughes, *To Go Forward, Retreat!* (BoardSource EBook Series 1999).
2. *See* ABA Coordinating Committee on Nonprofit Governance, *Guide to Nonprofit Corporate Governance in the Wake of Sarbanes-Oxley* 34–35 (ABA 2005); Independent Sector, *Principles for Good Governance and Ethical Practice: A Guide for Charities and Foundations* 22–24, 2nd ed. (2015).
3. *See Guide to Nonprofit Corporate Governance in the Wake of Sarbanes-Oxley*, *supra* note 2, at 34–35.

Suggested Questions for Directors Regarding Director Orientation and Revitalization

(1) Do we have a board manual containing the corporation's basic documents?

(2) What documents does it contain?

(3) How do I keep it up to date?

(4) Are the materials maintained on a board governance website? Do I frequently access the website?

(5) What files do I keep concerning my service as a director?

(6) Does the board have an orientation program for new directors? Does the board leadership encourage new members to participate in meetings? Are the board leadership and the more experienced board members receptive to statements from (new or continuing) members questioning aspects of board culture or procedures?

(7) Do I know of practices of other corporations concerning director orientation and training that our corporation could adopt?

(8) Does the board have meetings or retreats reviewing the corporation's overall policies, mission, or specific problems?

(9) Does the board have a strategic planning process? How have past strategic plans been evaluated and updated?

(10) Does the board ask its directors to engage in annual or other periodic self-evaluations or evaluations of the board as a whole?

(11) How does the board evaluate whether the corporation is fulfilling its mission? Is there information available from or about similar corporations or grant-making agencies that could help us measure the corporation's effectiveness in meeting its mission?

Checklist: Director Orientation and Revitalization

Note: For simplicity, these and other chapter checklists describe a corporation having a chair, who pre-sides over the board of directors; a chief executive, who may be a staff person; an executive committee; a governance/nominating committee; and an audit committee. (We recognize, however, that in many smaller and other nonprofits, these committee functions may be performed by either the executive committee or the board as a whole.) We also assume a legal counsel—someone, paid or unpaid, having primary responsibility for the corporation's legal affairs. Many corporations, especially larger nonprofits, may have other committees established for specific purposes, such as establishing executive compensation; monitoring compliance with legal requirements; and overseeing investments and other financial matters.

Subject	Review By	How Often	Comment
1. Director's manual	Chair, chief executive	At least annually, and in preparation for each meeting at which directors are elected	A specific committee to undertake this task is recommended.
2. Orientation	Chair, chief executive, governance/nominating committee	At least annually, and in preparation for each meeting at which directors are elected	A successful orientation meeting will take extensive time in planning and arranging for both board and staff participation.
3. Board retreats	Chair, chief executive	Annually or at least every other year	The board may wish the retreats to be planned by staff, with input from the chief executive and a committee of junior and senior board members.

Subject	Review By	How Often	Comment
4. Self-evaluations and assessments	Chair, chief executive, governance/ nominating committee	Annually or at least every other year	Results of individual director evaluations should be discussed with that director; results of overall board assessments should be presented to and reviewed by the entire board.
5. Strategic planning	Chair, chief executive	Annually	Some nonprofit corporations of sufficient size have strategic planning committees that meet periodically through the year to assess the implementation of the corporation's current strategic plan, and report to the board on areas of shortcomings and recommendation for changes to future plans.

Appendices

Appendix A

Tax-Exempt Organization Reference Chart

Organization Reference Chart from *Tax-Exempt Status for Your Organization,* Internal Revenue Service Publication 557 (Rev. January 2024)

Section of 1986 Code	Description of organization	General nature of activities
501(c)(1)	Corporations Organized Under Act of Congress (including Federal Credit Unions)	Instrumentalities of the United States
501(c)(2)	Title Holding Corporation for Exempt Corporation	Holding title to property of an exempt organization

Section of 1986 Code	Description of organization	General nature of activities
501(c)(3)	Religious, Educational, Charitable, Scientific, Literary, Testing for Public Safety, to Foster National or International Amateur Sports Competition, or Prevention of Cruelty to Children or Animals Organizations	Activities of nature implied by description of class of organization
501(c)(4)	Civic Leagues, Social Welfare Organizations, and Local Associations of Employees	Promotion of community welfare; charitable, educational, or recreational
501(c)(5)	Labor, Agricultural, and Horticultural Organizations	Educational or instructive, the purpose being to improve conditions of work, and to improve products and efficiency
501(c)(6)	Business Leagues, Chambers of Commerce, Real Estate Boards, etc.	Improvement of business conditions of one or more lines of business
501(c)(7)	Social and Recreational Clubs	Pleasure, recreation, social activities
501(c)(8)	Fraternal Beneficiary Societies and Associations	Providing for payment of life, sickness, accident, or other benefits to members within a lodge system
501(c)(9)	Voluntary Employees' Beneficiary Associations	Employee association providing for payment of life, sickness, accident, or other benefits to members

Section of 1986 Code	Description of organization	General nature of activities
501(c)(10)	Domestic Fraternal Societies and Associations	Earnings association providing for payment of life, sickness, accident, or other benefits to members
501(c)(11)	Teachers' Retirement Fund Associations	Teachers' association for payment of retirement benefits
501(c)(12)	Benevolent Life Insurance Associations, Mutual Ditch or Irrigation Companies, Mutual or Cooperative Telephone Companies, etc.	Activities of a mutually beneficial nature similar to those implied by the description of class or organization
501(c)(13)	Cemetery Companies	Burials and incidental activities
501(c)(14)	State-Chartered Credit Unions, Mutual Reserve Funds	Loans to members
501(c)(15)	Mutual Insurance Companies or Associations	Providing insurance to members substantially at cost
501(c)(16)	Cooperative Organizations to Finance Crop Operations	Financing crop operations in conjunction with activities of a marketing or purchasing Association
501(c)(17)	Supplemental Unemployment Benefit Trusts	Provides for payment of supplemental unemployment compensation benefits
501(c)(18)	Employee-Funded Pension Trust (created before June 25, 1959)	Payment of benefits under a pension plan funded by employees

Section of 1986 Code	Description of organization	General nature of activities
501(c)(19)	Post or Organization of Past or Present Members of the Armed Forces	Activities implied by nature of organization
501(c)(21)	Black Lung Benefit Trusts	Funded by coal mine operators to satisfy their liability for disability or death due to black lung diseases
501(c)(22)	Withdrawal Liability Payment Fund	To provide funds to meet the liability of employers withdrawing from a multi-employer pension fund
501(c)(23)	Veterans Organization (created before 1880)	To provide insurance and other benefits to veterans
501(c)(25)	Title-Holding Corporations or Trusts with Multiple Parents	Holding title and paying over income from property to 35 or fewer parents or beneficiaries
501(c)(26)	State-sponsored Organization Providing Health Coverage for High-Risk Individuals	Provides health care coverage for high-risk individuals
501(c)(27)	State-Sponsored Workers' Compensation Reinsurance Organization	Reimburses members for losses under workers' compensation acts
501(c)(28)	National Railroad Retirement Investment Trust	Manages and invests railroad retirement assets
501(c)(29)	Co-op health insurance issuers	A qualified health insurance issuer that has received a loan or grant under the co-op program

Section of 1986 Code	Description of organization	General nature of activities
501(d)	Religious and Apostolic Associations	Regular business activities. Communal religious community
501(e)	Cooperative Hospital Service Organizations	Performs cooperative services for hospitals
501(f)	Cooperative Service Organizations of Operating Educational Organizations	Performs collective investment services for educational organizations
501(k)	Child Care Organization	Provides care for children
501(n)	Charitable Risk Pools	Pools certain insurance risks of § 501(c)(3) organizations
501(q)	Credit Counseling Organization	Credit Counseling services
521(a)	Farmers' Cooperative Associations	Cooperative marketing and purchasing for agricultural producers
527	Political Organizations	A party, committee, fund, association, etc., that directly or indirectly accepts contributions or makes expenditures for political campaigns

Appendix B

Suggested Publications, Periodicals, and Websites

The general literature on nonprofit boards and corporations is becoming extensive and this appendix does not purport to cover all titles, particularly in view of the uneven quality of some of the material currently offered on the market. The following, however, merit perhaps more extensive attention:

Publications

The Model Nonprofit Corporation Act, Fourth Edition (American Bar Association 2022); William H. Clark, Jr., editor, contains both the Model Act provisions and official commentary.

Nonprofit Governance And Management, 3rd ed. (American Bar Association 2011) is a practical guide for executive staff and boards of directors of nonprofit organizations. The book provides an overview of the basics of nonprofit governance as well as board structure and operations. It also provides 27 samples of important governance forms and guidelines.

For a basic understanding of nonprofits and the issues facing nonprofits, *see* Lisa A. Runquist, The ABCs of Nonprofits, 2nd ed. (American Bar Association 2015) (Spanish version available). The book describes how nonprofit corporations are formed, options for organizational structure, matters relating to the operation of the corporation, and basic tax issues for nonprofits.

The Guide to Representing Religious Organizations (American Bar Association 2009) addresses critical issues and risk factors of concern for religious organizations ranging from formation and governance to taxes, fundraising, employment issues, and property rights. It outlines the general requirements of applicable law and highlights areas in which religious organizations receive special consideration under the law.

THE GUIDE TO NONPROFIT CORPORATE GOVERNANCE IN THE WAKE OF SARBANES-OXLEY (American Bar Association 2005) provides a basic overview of the provisions of the leading Sarbanes-Oxley reforms that might be relevant to nonprofit organizations and describes governance structures, processes, and procedures that have been recognized as "good governance practices."

NONPROFIT LAW: A PRACTICAL GUIDE TO LEGAL ISSUES FOR NONPROFIT ORGANIZATIONS (American Bar Association 2017) is a publication intended for lawyers who do not represent nonprofit organizations on a regular basis. It is based on the Nonprofit Organizations Committee "Nonprofit Law for the Non-Nonprofit Lawyer" CLE Series.

Jim Collins's monograph on GOOD TO GREAT AND THE SOCIAL SECTORS: WHY BUSINESS THINKING IS NOT THE ANSWER (Jim Collins 2005) applies and reconceives Collins's core lessons in his well-known book GOOD TO GREAT: WHY SOME COMPANIES MAKE THE LEAP...AND OTHERS DON'T (Harper Collins Publishers Inc. 2001), examining how the Hedgehog Concepts of good-to-great companies work in nonprofit, mission-oriented organizations.

The late Bruce R. Hopkins wrote several excellent treatises on tax-exempt organizations, including THE LAW OF TAX-EXEMPT ORGANIZATIONS, 12th ed. (John Wiley & Sons, Inc. 2019) (with annual updates by Shane T. Hamilton).

Michael I. Sanders, JOINT VENTURES INVOLVING TAX-EXEMPT ORGANIZATIONS, 4th ed. (John Wiley & Sons, Inc. 2013) (with annual updates) provides an excellent treatise on legal issues on joint ventures involving nonprofits.

The American Law Institute has published RESTATEMENT OF THE LAW, CHARITABLE NONPROFIT ORGANIZATIONS (2021), which addresses the law for the nonprofit sector, including principles relating to governance and the duties of the governing boards. Its scope includes state, federal, and private regulation.

Periodicals

Periodicals focusing on the nonprofit sector include the following:

The Chronicle of Philanthropy, a newspaper focusing on the nonprofit world (*see* website at https://www.philanthropy.com). The *Chronicle* publishes annually its *Non-Profit Handbook,* with lists of books, periodicals, software, Internet sites, and other resources, organized by subject matter (such as "Advocacy," "Boards," and "Fundraising").

Don Kramer's Nonprofit Issues is a national newsletter reporting on tax and other legal developments affecting nonprofit organizations and is available at https://www.nonprofitissues.com.

The Nonprofit Times, a business publication directed to nonprofit management, with 12 monthly editions plus bimonthly special editions on direct marketing and financial management, and an annual nonprofit salary survey (for information and selected articles, *see* https://www.thenonprofittimes.com).

Useful Websites and Organizations

A reader interested in pursuing further material in this area may consult the following organizations and their websites:

The IRS website, https://www.irs.gov, has a section focused on charities and nonprofits that contains extensive information on compliance with tax-exempt requirements. It also includes a database of Form 990s filed by the tax-exempt organizations.

The GuideStar website, https://www.guidestar.org, is produced by Philanthropic Research, Inc., and contains a database of information from the Form 990s of over 700,000 U.S. nonprofit organizations.

Many states' secretary of state websites and attorney general websites contain useful information for nonprofit organizations. Examples include the California Attorney General Charity Portal https://oag.ca.gov/charities, the Illinois Attorney General Charity Portal https://www.illinoisattorneygeneral.gov/consumer-protection/charities/, and Iowa Secretary of State website https://www.sos.state. ia.us/business/nonprofits/faqs.html.

BoardSource, https://www.boardsource.org, which has an extended bibliography on topics relevant to nonprofit boards.

Charity Navigator, https://www.charitynavigator.org/ provides comparison information on thousands of charitable organizations and other information, including executive compensation studies.

The Uniform Law Commission (formerly the National Conference of Commissioners of Uniform State Laws (ULC) maintains a website of uniform laws, which includes the Uniform Prudent Management of Institutional Funds Act, the Uniform Unincorporated Nonprofit Association Act, and the Model Protection of Charitable Assets Act, at https://www.uniformlaws.org.

The National Council of Nonprofit Associations, www.councilofnonprofits.org, is a network of state and regional associations of nonprofit organizations, developed to provide nonprofits with services, peer support, and a mechanism for collective advocacy. Various states have nonprofit associations and resource organizations that maintain websites with resource information specific to the state. Examples include the Minnesota Nonprofit Council, https://www.minnesotanonprofits.org, the Larned A. Waterman Iowa Nonprofit Resource Center, https://inrc.law.uiowa.edu, and the New York Council on Nonprofits, https://www.nycon.org. The National Council on Nonprofits maintains a directory of state nonprofit associations.

The Nonprofit Organizations Committee of the Business Law Section of the American Bar Association maintains a website, https://www.americanbar.org/groups/business_law/about/committees/nonprofit-organizations/, that contains various materials, including links to CLE program materials and nonprofit articles.

The website for Idealist (formerly called the Internet Nonprofit Center) provides suggested book titles, practical guides, essays, and other resource information about nonprofit organizations, as well as Nonprofit FAQ, an "online encyclopedia of information" designed for use by nonprofit organizations. *See* https://www.idealist.org.

The National Center for Charitable Statistics (NCCS) is a repository of data on the nonprofit sector in the United States. The NCCS' activities include the development of uniform standards for reporting on the activities of charitable organizations. *See* https://urbaninstitute.github.io/nccs/.

The *Blue Avocado* website, https://www.blueavocado.org, is maintained by The Alliance of Nonprofits for Insurance, Risk Retention Group, Nonprofit Insurance Alliance of California, and Compasspoint Nonprofit Services, and contains links to a newsletter and practical advice on the operation of nonprofit organizations.

The Independent Sector provides information on and promotes the range of nonprofit organizations that comprise America's independent sector. *See* www. independentsector.org. In 2004, the Independent Sector convened the Panel on the Nonprofit Sector. This resulted in several publications, including the *Principles for Good Governance and Ethical Practice: A Guide for Charities and Foundations*, (2nd ed. 2015), which contains 33 practices designed to support board members and staff leaders of every charitable organization as they work to improve their own operations. This publication, as well as other related publications, are available on the Independent Sector website.

Index

A

B

C

F

J

L

M

P

T

U

V

W

$$Ib_{mask}(x, y) = \begin{cases} 0 & \text{if } std(Ib(x, y)) \leq T, \\ 1 & \text{otherwise} \end{cases} \tag{5.14}$$

where Ib contains the blocks of size 8×8 pixels. The threshold, T, is set to 0.1. Morphological operations are run on the block-wise mask image, Ib_{mask}, for filling holes and removing isolated blocks yielding Ib'_{mask}. Two different structures are used for the morphological operations: a square rotated 45° with a diagonal length of five blocks and a square with a length of three blocks. The series of open operations are conducted by alternating between the two shapes, starting with the rotated square. The close operations are executed in the same fashion, however starting with the *unrotated* square. The shapes have been set empirically. The final pixel-wise fingerprint mask, I_{mask}, is the up-scaled version of the final block-wise mask, Ib'_{mask}. This segmentation is specifically for our analysis. The strength of the approach is that it removes unclear borders which might be identified as altered while keeping low quality areas that reside within the *ROI*. Likewise, this segmentation is not ideal for fingerprint recognition purposes in general since too many foreground blocks would be removed possibly erasing important minutiae. Low quality areas within the fingerprint can also add unwanted minutia or features that can compromise the comparison algorithm whereas they will play an important part in determining if the image has been altered or not.

5.4.1.3 Rotation

Landmarks of the fingerprint image are normally used as a reference point for rotation purposes. Different approaches have been proposed for rotating a fingerprint image, such as computing the image orientation using *singular point* as reference points [28] or using the fingerprint Center Point Location (*CPL*) as a reference point [31]. Using minutia or singular points as reference points requires significant analysis of the fingerprint image and can be quite complex. The approach taken in this work is based on [31] since it is a simple and efficient approach which does not require complex computations. The approach is built on the assumption that most fingerprints have an ellipsoidal shape. The rotation method therefore uses the *mask* of the fingerprint which was constructed in the previous step. The image is shifted so that the centroid of the *ROI* is at point $(0, 0)$.

Consider the image being placed in a Cartesian coordinate system, see Fig. 5.13. Two areas, a_1 and a_2 are defined where a_1 is composed of quadrant 2 (upper left) and 4 (bottom right) while a_2 is composed of the remaining diagonal quadrants. The idea is to rotate the foreground image around the center so that the amount of foreground pixels is balanced between a_1 and a_2. This is an iterative process.

Fig. 5.13 The fingerprint mask is placed in a coordinate system and rotated. The sums of the fingerprint foreground of the quadrants with the patterned background are compared to the sums of the quadrants with a clear background

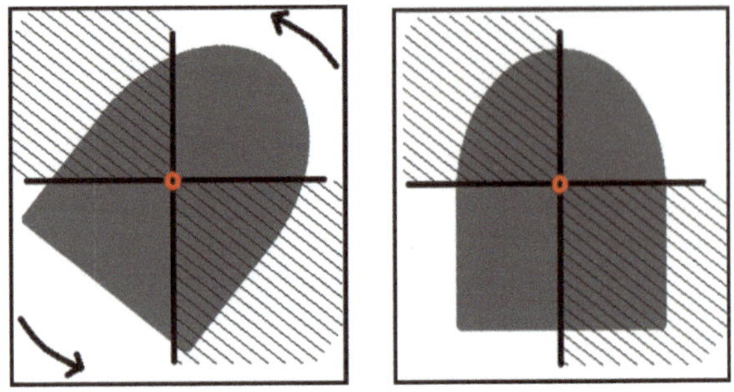

(a) Original (b) After rotation

5.4.1.4 Resizing

Before resizing, the image must be cropped again since rotation might have added additional background to the sides of the image. There are many ways that the image can be re-cropped, e.g. by using the *Nfseg* algorithm or removing columns and rows that contain only zeros. The image is resized to the closest fit for 512×480 pixels and thereafter segmented afresh.

5.4.1.5 Enhancement

The final step of the preprocessing pipeline is enhancement of the fingerprint image. The goal of fingerprint enhancement techniques are traditionally to improve the clarity of friction ridges and remove unwanted noise in order to assist the following analyses or feature extraction algorithms. Numerous fingerprint enhancement techniques have been proposed. Two processes were conducted on the image to slightly enhance it: histogram equalization in the spatial domain and a simple enhancement in the frequency domain.

Histogram equalization is a common method for enhancing the contrast of a image. The method defines a mapping of grey levels p into grey levels q which attempts to uniformly distribute the grey levels q [20]. A cumulative histogram of the enhanced image would show a relatively linear curve and the ideal mean would be right in the center of the density value. Histogram equalization is described in Eq. (5.15) where k is the greyscale level of the original image, n_j is the number of times pixel value j appears in the image, n is the total number of pixels and L is the number of grey levels (for example 256). The contrast of grey levels are stretched near the histogram maxima using histogram equalization. This improves the detectability of many image features [26].

$$\forall i \in \{1..R\}, j \in \{1..C\} : G(i,j) = H(I(i,j)) = H(k) = \sum_{j=0}^{k} \frac{n_j}{n}(L-1) \tag{5.15}$$

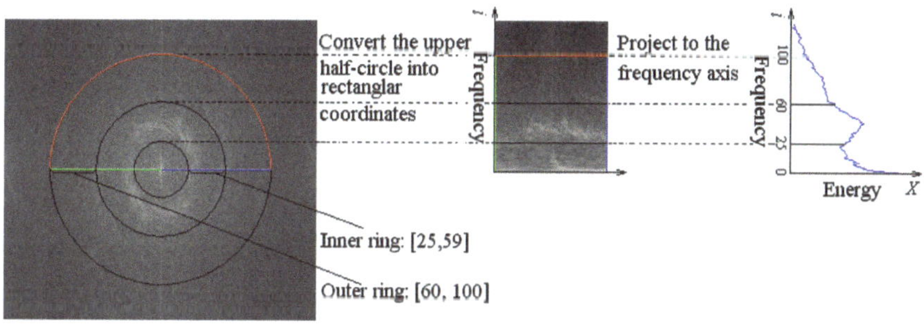

Fig. 5.14 Fingerprint images produce a ring pattern in the frequency domain. Note the spectral energy in the *inner ring*. *Source* [23]

Fingerprints can also be enhanced in the frequency domain. Ridges can be locally approximated by single sine waves. The orientation of the ridges gives frequencies in all directions. A good quality fingerprint image will therefore produce a clear ring pattern around the center in the frequency domain (see Fig. 5.14). The clearness of the ring is based on the consistency of the ridge characteristics.

The radial power spectrum is an established method to determine a quality score of the fingerprint [33]. The quality score is based on the peak of maximum energy in the *inner ring*. This can also be seen in Fig. 5.14. One method of improving the clarity of the ridge patterns could be to apply a filter which enhances the frequencies in the inner ring while minimizing or even eliminating frequencies outside of the inner ring. Altered fingerprints will have unnatural ridge properties on a global scale and—depending on the type of alteration—be of a less quality. It is desired to also enhance discrepancies since the impending analyses will be on these inconsistencies. Watson et al. [40] presented a simple enhancement method based on enhancing dominant frequencies in the frequency domain. This method concentrates on local properties and is performed using overlaying blocks. This approach will be used to enhance fingerprint images in this study (Fig. 5.15).

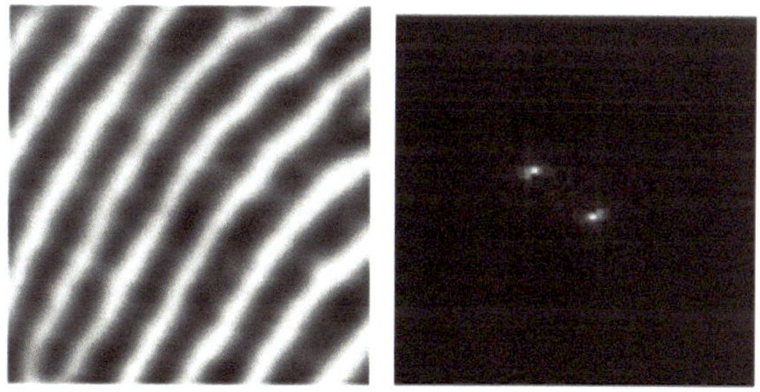

Fig. 5.15 Orientation and frequency of ridges in local area. *Source* [7]

(a) Ridges in local area (b) Frequency domain of (a)

(a) Original (I) (b) Enhanced (I_{enh}) (c) Mask (I_{mask}) (d) Final image

Fig. 5.16 Enhancement of an unaltered fingerprint. *Source* **a** [6]

This method is quite efficient in enhancing the image for the specific purpose, as it fills up small holes in ridges and also otherwise enhances the appearance of the friction ridges.

The fingerprint image is divided into blocks of size 8×8 pixel. An additional overlapping border of 8×8 pixels is added around each block such that the actual size of each block is 24×24 pixels. The *FFT* of each block is multiplied by an exponentiation of its magnitude; the exponent factor k is set to 0.45. The enhanced block $B'(x, y)$ based on the original block $B(x, y)$ is done accordingly:

$$B'(x, y) = FFT^{-1}(FFT(B(x, y)) \cdot |FFT(B(x, y))|^k) \tag{5.16}$$

Notice that in Eq. 5.16 blocks $B(x, y)$ and $B'(x, y)$ are 24×24 pixels, i.e. they are extended by the borders. The enhanced image, I_{enh}, is combined by the center 8×8 pixels in each block of B'. Examples of the resulting enhancements on altered and unaltered fingerprint images can be seen in Figs. 5.16 and 5.17, respectively. The reason for using overlapped blocks is to minimize the border effect of the block-wise *FFT*. The idea of the method is that dominant frequencies of each block correspond to the ridges, amplifying these dominant frequencies increases the ratio of ridge information to nonridge noise [40].

It is important that the choice of enhancement algorithm complements the alteration detection algorithms. As opposed to traditional minutia extraction methods used for fingerprint recognition purposes the selected algorithm should retain some local inconsistencies.

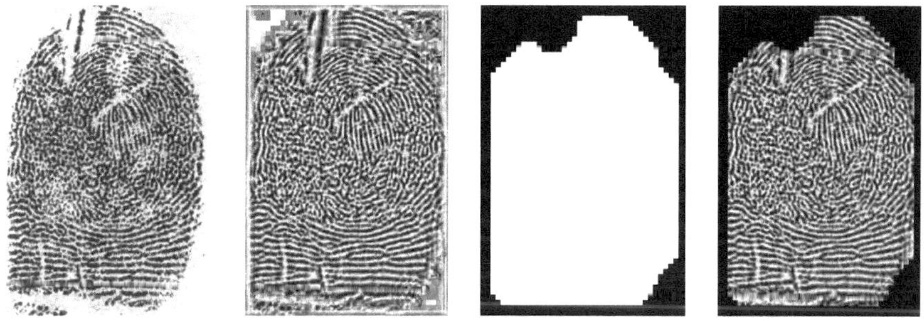

(a) Original (I) (b) Enhanced (I_{enh}) (c) Mask (I_{mask}) (d) Final image

Fig. 5.17 Enhancement of a altered fingerprint. *Source* **a** [38]

5.4.2 Singular Point Density Analysis

The proposed method, Singular Point Density Analysis (SPDA) is based on local analysis of the orientation field using the Poincaré index to detect noisy friction ridge areas. An altered fingerprint will have a higher density of such areas than an unaltered. Singular points namely *core* and *delta*, act as control points around which the ridge lines are wrapped [30]. The suggested approach is partly inspired from research done by Petrovici [35] and calculates amplitudes of singular points based on the reliability of their orientation. Before describing the actual method, a brief analysis of the characteristics of the orientation field will be conducted on altered and unaltered images.

5.4.2.1 Orientation Certainty Level

The Orientation Certainty Level (OCL) is a common analysis used as a quality measure to determine the certainty of local orientations. It measures the energy concentration along the direction of ridges [42]. In Sect. 5.3.1.2 the two intensity gradients, δ_x and δ_y, were found for each pixel using a Sobel operator. The orientation certainty can be calculated as the ratio of the two eigenvalues of the covariance matrix of the gradient vector. The covariance matrix C of the gradient vector for an N points image block is given by:

$$C = \frac{1}{N}\sum_{i=1}^{N}\left\{\begin{bmatrix}dx_i\\dy_i\end{bmatrix}\begin{bmatrix}dx_i & dy_i\end{bmatrix}\right\} = \begin{bmatrix}\frac{1}{N}\sum_{i=1}^{N}dx_i^2 & \frac{1}{N}\sum_{i=1}^{N}dx_i dy_i\\ \frac{1}{N}\sum_{i=1}^{N}dy_i dx_i & \frac{1}{N}\sum_{i=1}^{N}dy_i^2\end{bmatrix} = \begin{vmatrix}a & c\\ c & b\end{vmatrix} \tag{5.17}$$

(a) Original (b) Certainty (c) Original (d) Certainty

Fig. 5.18 Two unaltered images and their corresponding orientation certainty. Since the images are of relatively good quality, low certainty is in areas of high curvature. *Source* **a**, **c** [6]

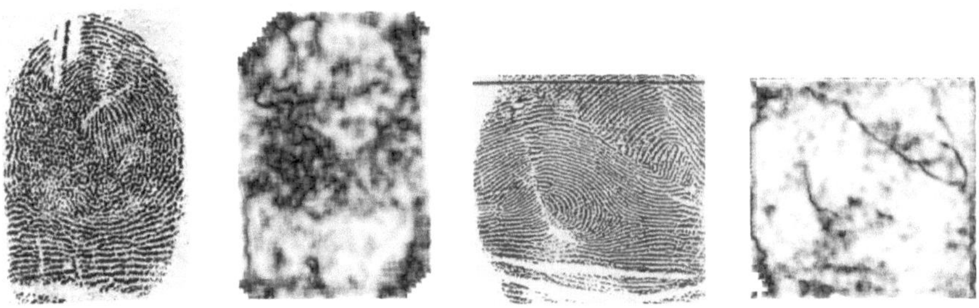

(a) Original (b) Certainty (c) Original (d) Certainty

Fig. 5.19 Two altered images and their corresponding orientation certainty. Areas with low friction ridge quality caused by scars and obliteration cause low orientation certainty. *Source* **a** [38], **c** [41]

where $dx = \delta_x$ and $dy = \delta_y$ are the gradient densities at each pixel. The eigenvalues, λ_{max} and λ_{min}, can be calculated as [27] (Figs. 5.18 and 5.19):

$$\lambda_{max} = \frac{(a+b) + \sqrt{(a-b)^2 + 4c^2}}{2} \tag{5.18}$$

$$\lambda_{min} = \frac{(a+b) - \sqrt{(a-b)^2 + 4c^2}}{2} \tag{5.19}$$

The *OCL* is defined in the range [0, 1] where a high value means good quality. The formula for calculating the *OCL* is therefore:

$$Ocl = 1 - \frac{\lambda_{min}}{\lambda_{max}} \tag{5.20}$$

5.4.2.2 Orientation Entropy

Considering the pixel-wise orientation, $\theta(x, y)$, as a random variable and using a sample rate, n, determining the amount of possible orientation values, a quantification scale $\frac{\pi}{n}$ is used to discretise the orientation field. The discrete orientation field, θ_n, with sample rate n can be computed as:

$$\forall x \in \{1..R\}, y \in \{1..C\} : \theta_n(x, y) = \frac{\pi}{n}(\frac{\theta(x, y)}{\frac{\pi}{n}} \mod n) \tag{5.21}$$

where R and C define the row count and column count of the orientation image, respectively. The entropy for each orientation is calculated according to the amount of different possibilities in the surrounding area. Blocks of size 5×5 are used in the current implementation. The discrete entropy image, E_n, can be constructed as:

$$\forall x \in \{3..R-2\}, y \in \{3..C-2\} : E_n(x, y) = -\sum_{i=1}^{n} p_{x,y}(\frac{\pi}{i}) \log_{10} p_{x,y}(\frac{\pi}{i}) \tag{5.22}$$

where $p_{x,y}(\frac{\pi}{i})$ is the probability of the discrete orientation $\frac{\pi}{i}$ in the block belonging to (x, y). Since blocks of size 5×5 are used, pixels that don't have a complete border of 2×2 surrounding pixels are not considered. Figures 5.20 and 5.21 show multiple scaled orientation entropy images of unaltered and altered fingerprint images, respectively.

The characteristics of the entropy images are very distinct. The center points in the orientation entropy images which have a constant high entropy value are points with uncertain orientations. The difference between the entropy values in the illustrated unaltered and altered images can be summarized as: Unaltered fingerprint images have a constant high entropy value in the center of singular regions. On the contrary altered fingerprint images have many spurious positions with a constant high entropy value. Scarred regions and mutilated areas add uncertainties in the pixel-wise orientations which lead to the high entropy values. From Fig. 5.20 it becomes clear that it is possible to use the entropy to locate singular points. It can be concluded that altered images have a number of positions with a high orientation uncertainty. Based on both the uncertainty and entropy analysis it seems that altered images have a higher amount of positions in a fingerprint with characteristics similar to a singular point.

5.4.2.3 Poincaré Index

Methods for detecting singular points are commonly based on the Poincaré index which in this context analyses the change of direction around a given point as proposed by Kawagoe and Tojo [25]. The Poincaré index has shown high accuracy, but low robustness [36]. The method fails to correctly localize reference points in poor

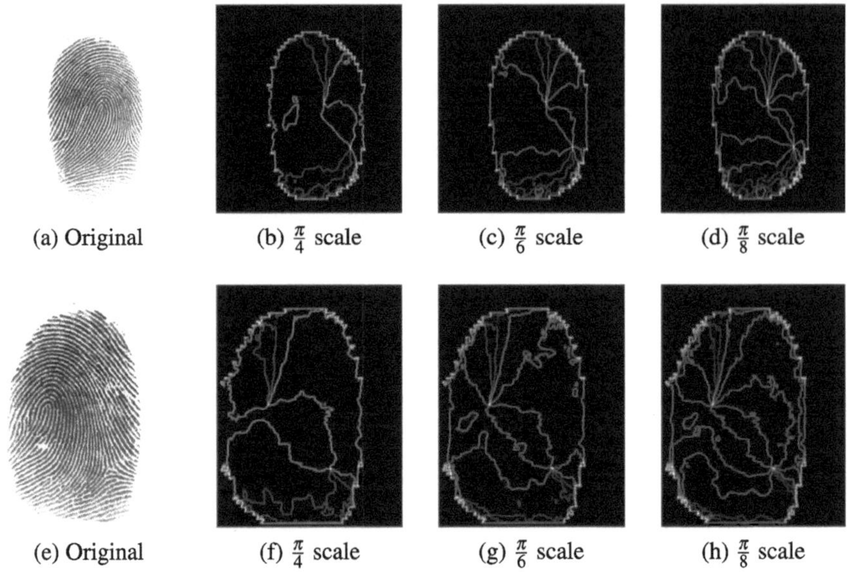

(a) Original (b) $\frac{\pi}{4}$ scale (c) $\frac{\pi}{6}$ scale (d) $\frac{\pi}{8}$ scale

(e) Original (f) $\frac{\pi}{4}$ scale (g) $\frac{\pi}{6}$ scale (h) $\frac{\pi}{8}$ scale

Fig. 5.20 Multiple scaled orientation entropy images of unaltered fingerprints. Images have sample rate $n = 4, 6$, and 8. Constant high entropy values are in singular regions where they act as center points. The entropy varies in other positions of the fingerprint according to the scale. *Source* **a**, **e** [6]

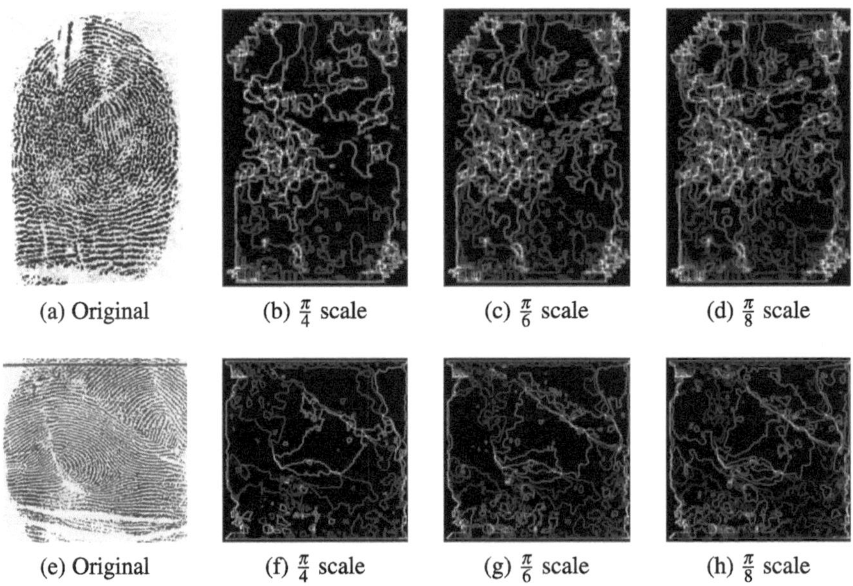

(a) Original (b) $\frac{\pi}{4}$ scale (c) $\frac{\pi}{6}$ scale (d) $\frac{\pi}{8}$ scale

(e) Original (f) $\frac{\pi}{4}$ scale (g) $\frac{\pi}{6}$ scale (h) $\frac{\pi}{8}$ scale

Fig. 5.21 Multiple scaled orientation entropy images of altered fingerprints. Images have sample rate 4, 6 and 8. Obliterated areas and scars generate high entropy readings. Even with multiple scaled entropy images, there are many central points with a constant high entropy value. *Source* **a** [38], **e** [41]

quality fingerprints with cracks and scars, dry skin or poor ridge and valley contrast [21]. Many false core and delta points can be produced when the orientation field is noisy, e.g. in low quality fingerprint areas. The proposed method takes advantage of this limitation. For correctly detecting singular points different heuristics are used to filter out false locations, e.g. iterative smoothing of the orientation field [5], using a modified gradient-based Poincaré method [3] and in combination with additional filters [4, 45]. No filtering process will be used in the current analysis which will therefore detect singular point candidates. In the current context, the Poincaré index for a given point $P(x, y)$ can be defined as the cumulative change in the orientation field traveling clockwise around the neighbouring points. The possible values of $P(x, y)$ are 0, $\pm\pi$ and $\pm 2\pi$:

$$P(x,y) = \begin{cases} 2\pi, & \text{if } (x,y) \text{ belongs to a whorl} \\ \pi, & \text{if } (x,y) \text{ belongs to a loop} \\ -\pi, & \text{if } (x,y) \text{ belongs to a delta} \\ -2\pi, & \text{if } (x,y) \text{ is in the center of a rare } \textit{diamond} \text{ shape} \\ 0, & \text{otherwise} \end{cases} \tag{5.23}$$

After calculating the Poincaré index for all pixels in the fingerprint image, the Poincaré matrix, $P_b(x, y)$, is binarised accordingly:

$$P_b(x,y) = \begin{cases} 1, & \text{if } P(x,y) \in \{\pm\pi, \pm 2\pi\} \\ 0, & \text{otherwise} \end{cases} \tag{5.24}$$

The resulting binarised Poincaré image will generally have a small cluster of one to four adjacent pixels with high values in the singular regions. However, noisy or low quality areas in unaltered images may lead to the detection of additional false singular points. The unnatural flow of friction ridges in altered fingerprints will generally result in a higher detection of false singular points. Figure 5.22 shows the resulting binarised Poincaré image, P_b, of two unaltered fingerprints. Figure 5.22d illustrates the problem with poor quality fingerprint images. Figure 5.23 shows P_b of altered images. An observation can be made on the spurious false singularities found in both altered and unaltered fingerprints that can further strengthen the analysis of singularities and help detect if a fingerprint has been altered or not. In the following section Gabor filters will be used to determine quality measures of the friction ridges with the intention to highlight *singular points* in good quality areas.

5.4.2.4 Gabor Filters

The goal is to determine the clarity of friction ridges in a fingerprint so that found singularities can be classified based on the quality score of their position. Gabor

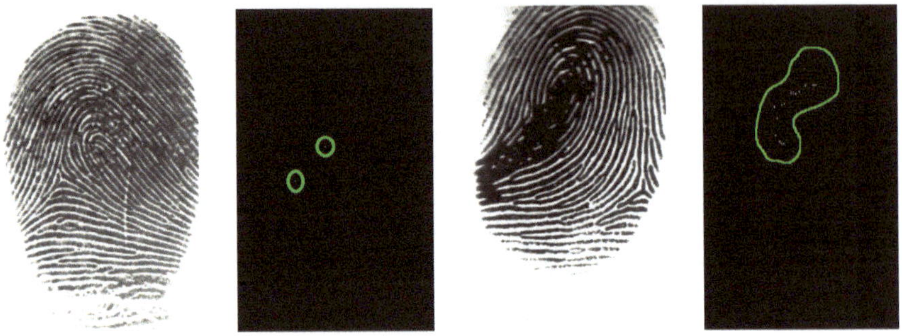

Fig. 5.22 Singular point detection of unaltered fingerprints. **a** Fingerprint image [6], **b** its corresponding binarised Poincaré image with highlighted readings, **c** Poor quality fingerprint image [6], **d** its corresponding binarised Poincaré image. Low quality images will result in spurious false singularities

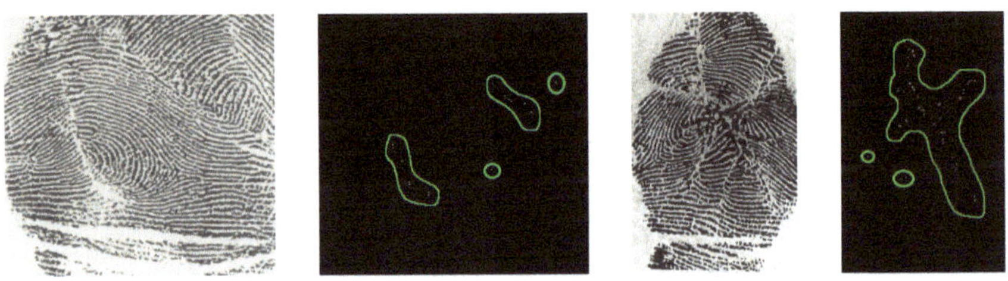

Fig. 5.23 Singular point detection of altered fingerprints. **a** Distorted fingerprint [41], **b** its corresponding binarised Poincaré image with highlighted readings, **c** Heavily damaged fingertip [38], **d** its corresponding binarised Poincaré image

filters will be used to measure the quality of friction ridges. Gabor filters are band-pass filters that have both frequency and orientation properties; they can therefore be constructed to present friction ridge frequency and orientation.

A global quality measure based on Gabor filter responses was proposed by Olsen et al. [34]. This study uses an adaptation of this approach applying different filter bank sizes. The first step is to convolve the fingerprint image, I, with a two-dimensional Gaussian with $\sigma = 1$. The convolution is subtracted from the original image to give $\bar{I}$ which is a high-pass filtered image. The quality of the ridge-valley structure of the friction ridges is found by convolving the fingerprint image, $\bar{I}$, with two-dimensional Gabor filters in n orientations ($n = 8$). The orientations θ are computed:

$$\theta = \pi \frac{k-1}{n}, \quad k = 1, \ldots, n \tag{5.25}$$

The general form of a complex two-dimensional Gabor filter in the spatial domain can be defined as:

$$h(x, y, \theta_k, f, \sigma_x, \sigma_y) = exp(-\frac{1}{2}(\frac{x_{\theta_k}^2}{\sigma_x^2} + \frac{y_{\theta_k}^2}{\sigma_y^2}))exp(j2\pi f x_{\theta_k}), \quad k = 1, \dots, n \tag{5.26}$$

where

n is the number of orientations used in the filter bank
$x_{\theta_k} = x \sin\theta_k + y \cos\theta_k$,
$y_{\theta_k} = x \cos\theta_k - y \sin\theta_k$,
f is the frequency of the sinusoidal plane wave along the orientation θ_k,
σ_x and σ_y are the parameters of the Gaussian window.

The filter frequency, f, is set to 0.1 as the average inter-ridge distance (corresponding to the wavelength) is approximately 10 pixels in a 500 dpi fingerprint image [21]. The standard deviation of the Gaussian envelope along the x and y axes are set as $\sigma_x = \sigma_y = 6.0$. The magnitude of the responses is convolved with a two-dimensional Gaussian with $\sigma = 4$ to smoothen the magnitudes. Areas containing clear ridge-valley structures will have a strong response from one or more of the filter orientations, see Fig. 5.24 while low quality areas will have low responses. A pixel-wise standard deviation of the bank of Gabor responses is calculated, G_{std}.

The resulting Gabor quality matrix, G_{std}, is transformed to the interval [0, 1] by:

$$Q_G(x, y) = \begin{cases} G_{std}(x, y)/T, & \text{if } G_{std}(x, y) \leq T \\ 1, & \text{otherwise} \end{cases} \tag{5.27}$$

where T is a given threshold ($T = 0.01$). The threshold is determined empirically.

5.4.2.5 Density Map

The quality metrics matrix, Q_G, are factors that determine the quality of friction ridges in each pixel. The quality score is defined in the interval [0, 1] where 1 is the best quality. An initial density map, P_d, is created from combining the Poincaré matrix, $P_b(x, y)$, and the normalized Gabor quality matrix, Q_G, by multiplication:

$$P_d(x, y) = P_b(x, y) \cdot Q_G(x, y) \tag{5.28}$$

P_d is a density map where singularities positioned within clear areas receive a higher value than singularities in poor quality areas. Similar to the previous minutia distribution analysis, the final density map, SP_d, is constructed by using the Parzen window method with uniform kernel function and smoothed using a low-pass

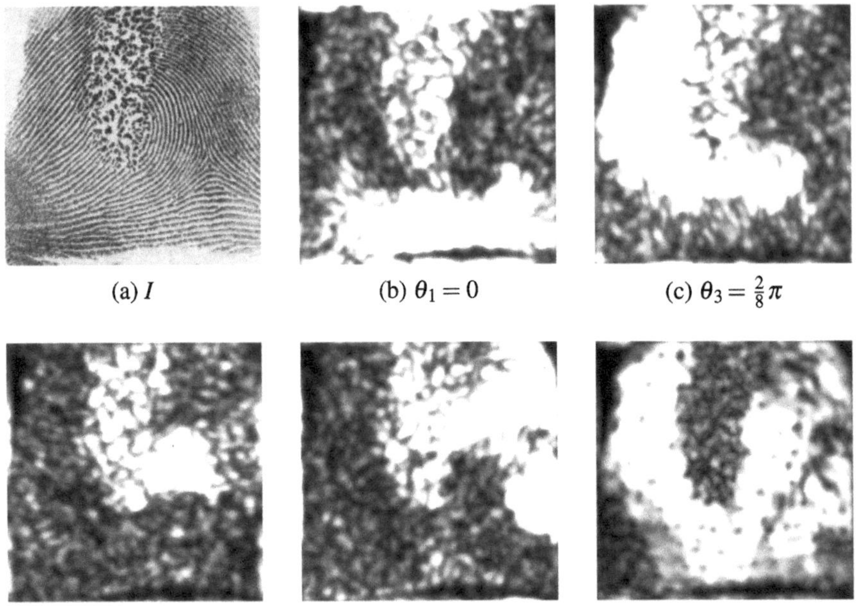

(a) I (b) $\theta_1 = 0$ (c) $\theta_3 = \frac{2}{8}\pi$

(d) $\theta_5 = \frac{4}{8}\pi$ (e) $\theta_7 = \frac{6}{8}\pi$ (f) Q_G

Fig. 5.24 Gabor filter responses of an obliterated fingerprint. **a** Input image [44], **b–e** absolute values of Gabor filter responses in different orientations after Gaussian smoothening and **f** standard deviation of the Gabor responses with different orientations

Gaussian filter. Figures 5.25 and 5.26 show examples of the final density maps of unaltered and altered fingerprints, respectively. Notice that the altered fingerprints have a higher density of singularities than the unaltered in the final density maps.

5.4.3 Minutia Orientation Analysis

The Minutia Orientation Analysis (*MOA*) takes advantage of the excessive number of minutia that appears due to alteration. Instead of relying on the actual distribution of minutia as the *MDA* does, properties of minutia in local areas will be analyzed. Altered fingerprints have an unnatural orientation flow. Likewise, the *MOA* shows that minutia distribution of altered fingerprints often differs from that of natural fingerprints. Scars will produce broken ridges which will contribute to some of the additional minutiae that is extracted from altered fingerprints. Figure 5.27 shows an example of a z-cut alteration where a relatively large portion of minutiae is concentrated around the scarred areas. The idea is to register a metric for each minutia point, which describes the change in orientation in its surroundings. There are multiple options that can be considered. Two simple approaches based on analyzing orientations in a certain radius, r, from the minutia could be:

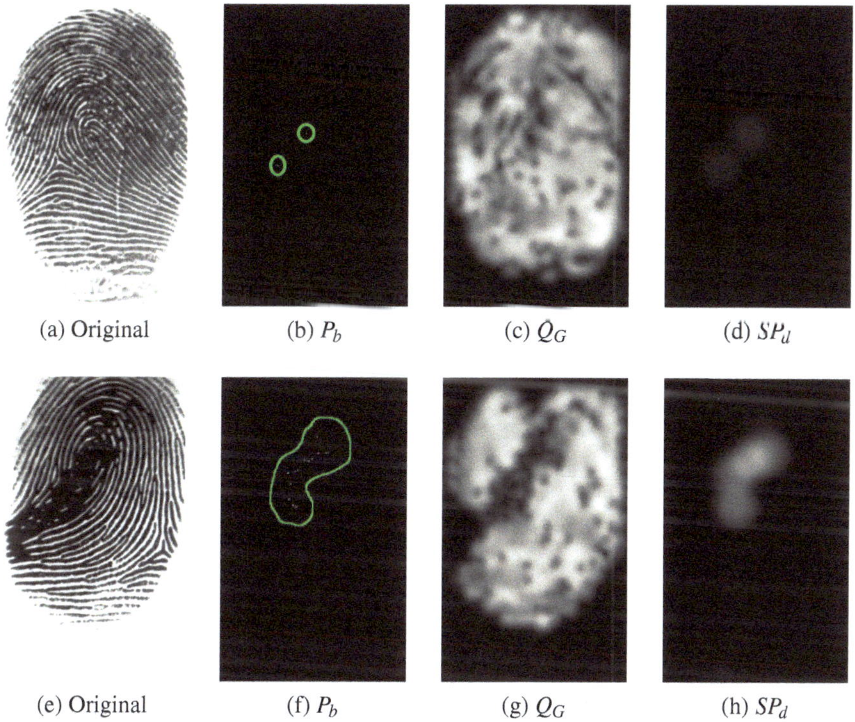

Fig. 5.25 Singular point density analysis of unaltered fingerprints. **a** Input image, **b** its corresponding binarised Poincaré image with highlighted readings, **c** quality measurement of the friction ridges, **d** the final singular point density map. **e–g** show the same as **a–d** but with a lower quality image. *Source* **a**, **e** [6]

1. Using a rotating line. A circle of radius r is considered around each minutia point. Using the computed orientation field, the maximum difference of orientation between a series of orientation pairs on opposite sides of the circle around the minutia point can be found based on Fig. 5.28. Here, steps of $\frac{\pi}{4}$ are used to find a set of 8 points around the minutia point. The minutia is assigned the maximum difference in orientation of the points on opposite sides of the minutia.
2. Based on minutia direction. The minutia extractor assigns a direction to every minutiae, normally in the range $[0, 2\pi)$, pointing towards the current friction ridge that it belongs to. Instead of analyzing multiple points around a circumference with radius r around the minutia, only the point in the given direction of the minutia and on the opposite side are measured like earlier. The minutia is assigned the orientation difference of these two points. See Fig. 5.29.

The problem with both of the above mentioned approaches is that minutia close to high curvature regions will be assigned high values. The second approach is an improvement since it takes into account the actual direction of the minutia. A sim-

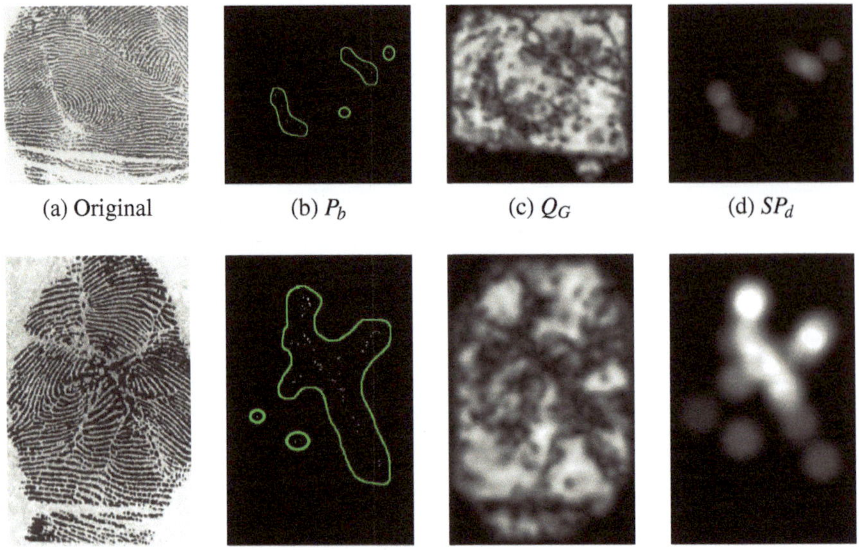

(a) Original (b) P_b (c) Q_G (d) SP_d

(e) Original (f) P_b (g) Q_G (h) SP_d

Fig. 5.26 Singular point density analysis of altered fingerprints. **a** Input image, **b** its corresponding binarised Poincaré image with highlighted readings, **c** quality measurement of the friction ridges, **d** the final singular point density map. **e–g** show the same as **a–d** with a heavily damaged fingertip. *Source* **a** [41], **e** [38]

(a) Original (b) Minutia (c) Minutia density with outline of scar

Fig. 5.27 Scars cause higher concentration of minutiae. *Source* **a** [41]

ple method is proposed comparing neighboring minutia that are closer than a given radius. To compare neighboring minutiae, it is desired that minutia are found on both sides of scars in order to analyze changes. The problem comparing minutia, is that minutia extractors generally do a lot of analyses of candidate minutiae in order to remove false minutiae. Even though the density of minutiae is higher along scars, the minutia extractor does a good job in limiting minutia with conflicting orientations. While in principle every minutia extractor could be used, we have employed the NIST MINDTCT.

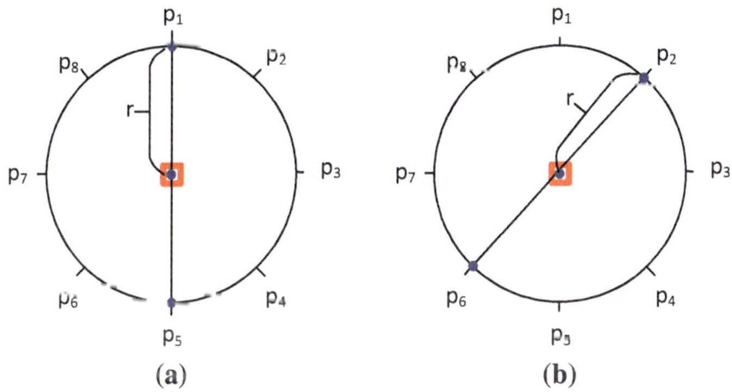

Fig. 5.28 Differences in orientations can be measured in a certain distance, r. A *line* is rotated *clockwise* in steps of $\frac{\pi}{4}$. **a** Orientation difference between points p_1 and p_5 are found, **b** the *line* is rotated and the difference between points p_2 and p_6 are found. The minutia is assigned the maximum orientation difference of the four measurements

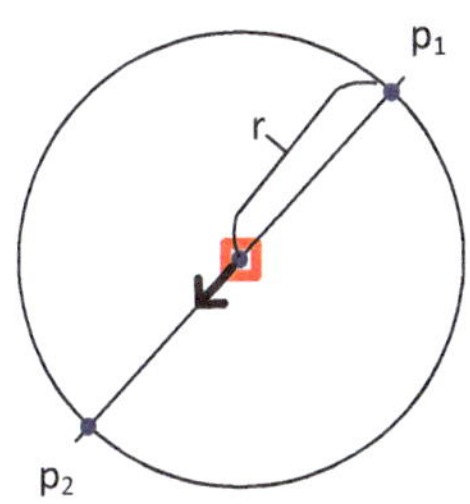

Fig. 5.29 Differences in orientations can be measured based on points in a certain distance, r, from the minutia. Points are found by the actual orientation of the minutia. The minutia is assigned the orientation difference of points p_1 and p_2

5.4.3.1 Minutia Analyses

The NIST minutia feature extractor prepares output files in multiple formats and with additional information intended for miscellaneous fingerprint comparison algorithms.

Based on the above dissection of the minutia extractor small modifications are made to the source in order to provide additional minutiae in strategic places. It is very important that the extractor still filters out minutiae; leaving out the whole filtering process would result in an excessive amount of minutiae. This would lead to large areas around singularities being identified as having unnatural changes in the flow of friction ridges based on the high curvatures. Modifications are the following:

Islands and Lakes: A pair of candidate minutia will be detected at each end of islands and lakes. If two minutiae are found to be closer than a given threshold (16 pixels) with a minimum direction angle $\geq 123.75°$, then the pair of minutiae is removed from the candidate list. An illustration of this is shown in Fig. 5.30.

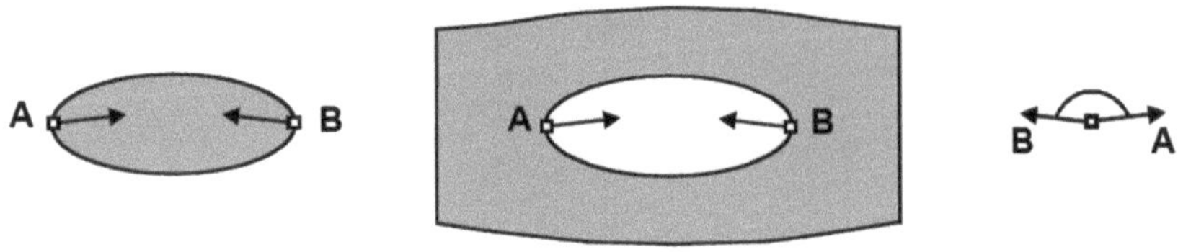

(a) Island (b) Lake (c) Direction angle

Fig. 5.30 The minimum direction angle between a pair of minutiae points is used to determine if candidate minutiae are removed or not

Fig. 5.31 Minutiae belonging to hooks have directions that differ from the friction ridge orientation

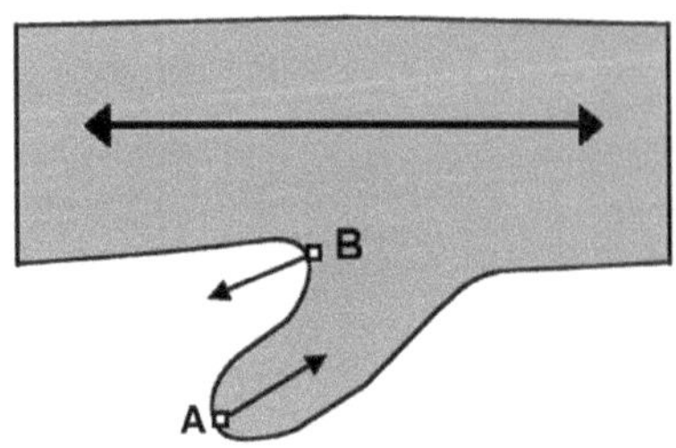

Fig. 5.32 Discontinuities in ridges or valleys has a pair of minutiae points in opposite directions

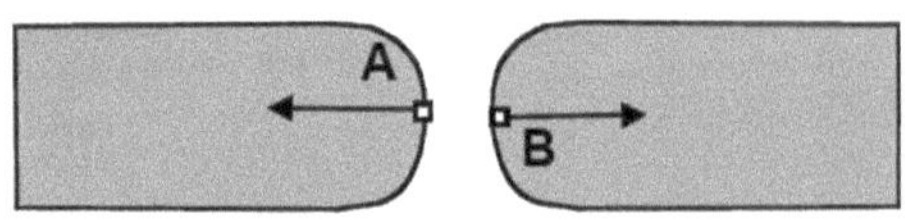

The modified version increases the threshold of the direction angle to 157.5°. This will give a larger amount of minutiae belonging to small islands and lakes.

Hooks: Scarred regions will produce hooks that protrude off the side of ridges. It would therefore seem obvious to keep candidate minutia belonging to hooks in the modified minutia extractor. The problem with hooks is that they have directions which do not correspond to the actual ridge flow in the corresponding area, see Fig. 5.31. Leaving minutiae belonging to hooks will increase the inconsistency of minutiae directions in unaltered regions of the fingerprint also. This is therefore unmodified in the current solution.

Discontinuities: Minutiae belonging to discontinuities (see Fig. 5.32) in ridges or valleys are removed in the standard feature extractor. Criteria are based on a combination of minutia distance, the difference of the directional angles between them and the direction of a line joining the two minutiae points.

Friction ridges on opposing side of scars can be considered as discontinuities. The modified feature extractor leaves out this check and does therefore not remove minutiae on the basis of discontinuities. Discontinuities in unaltered regions will not have a great impact on the analysis of minutia orientations since they generally are consistent with the local friction ridge orientation. Alterations with a sufficient amount of friction ridges will reside in a region with an orientation—it will be unreliable—and will generally belong to the *ROI* of the fingerprint. Minutiae in these areas will typically have a lower quality score. Checks dealing with unreliable/invalid orienta-

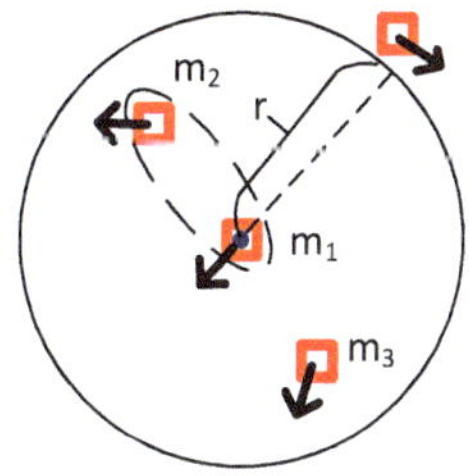

Fig. 5.33 Each minutia point finds the minutia with the largest orientation difference from its own within a given radius, r. Minutia point m_1 is being processed. Only minutia within the given radius are considered. Minutia point m_2 differs most from m_1; the minutia which is being processed is assigned the orientation difference of these two points

tions are therefore unmodified in the feature extractor. The checks that test if ridges are to wide or too narrow do not greatly affect the minutiae points around scars and obliterated regions and will therefore be unmodified in the feature extractor. Only a couple of small modifications are done to the feature extractor. To summarize the above, only the process that removes islands and lakes has been modified while the process that checks for discontinuities has been removed.

5.4.3.2 MOA Algorithm

The *MOA* is a relatively simple algorithm which analyses local orientation differences of minutiae. Each minutia point compares its orientation with every surrounding minutiae within a given radius, see Fig. 5.33. The largest orientation difference is registered and saved in a *orientation difference* map. A density map is then constructed from the orientation difference map.

Descriptions on how the orientation difference and orientation density maps are created is described below.

5.4.4 *Orientation Difference Map*

A function is introduced $\phi(\mathbf{u}, \mathbf{v}, r)$ which gives 1 if the distance between points **u** and **v** is less than a given radius (distance), r, and 0 otherwise:

$$\phi(\mathbf{u}, \mathbf{v}, r) = \begin{cases} 1 & \frac{|\mathbf{u}-\mathbf{v}|}{r} < 1, \\ 0 & otherwise \end{cases} \tag{5.29}$$

Minutia directions are in the range $[0, 2\pi)$. The directions are transformed to lie in the interval $[0, \pi)$, using modulo π, such as they now are orientations. The difference, $d(\theta_i, \theta_j)$, between two minutia orientations, θ_i and θ_j, is given as:

$$d(\theta_i, \theta_j) = \min(|\theta_i - \theta_j|, \pi - |\theta_i - \theta_j|) \tag{5.30}$$

Let $\mathbf{S_m}$ be the set of minutiae of the fingerprint containing the minutia's position and orientation, i.e.,

$$\mathbf{S_m} = \{(\mathbf{x}, \theta) \quad | \quad \mathbf{x} = (x, y) \text{ is the position and } \theta \text{ is the orientation of minutia}\}. \tag{5.31}$$

A set, $\mathbf{S_{diff}}$, containing the position of each minutia together with the largest orientation difference is given as:

$$\mathbf{S_{diff}} = \{(\mathbf{x}, \theta_{max}) \quad | \quad (\mathbf{x}, \theta) \in \mathbf{S_m} \wedge \theta_{max} = \text{Max}(\mathbf{x}, \theta, r, \mathbf{S_m})\}, \tag{5.32}$$

where $r = 30$ and $\text{Max}(\mathbf{x}, \theta, r, \mathbf{S_m})$ returns the largest orientation difference, a, between θ and any minutia within the radius r by Eq. (5.33).

$$\forall b \in \{\phi(\mathbf{x}, \mathbf{x_0}, r) \cdot d(\theta, \theta_0) \quad | \quad (\mathbf{x_0}, \theta_0) \in \mathbf{S_m}\} : (b \leq a) \tag{5.33}$$

The initial minutia orientation difference map, $M'_{diff}(x, y)$, is initiated by zeroes in the size of the fingerprint image. The minutia difference values, $\mathbf{S_{diff}}$, are plotted into M'_{diff} such that the location of each minutia is assigned the corresponding minutia orientation difference.

The values of $M'_{diff}(x, y)$ are transformed to lie in the interval [0, 1] by

$$M_{diff}(x, y) = \begin{cases} M'_{diff}(x, y)/T, & \text{if } M'_{diff}(x, y) \leq T, \\ 1, & \text{otherwise} \end{cases} \tag{5.34}$$

where T is a predetermined threshold (T is set to $\pi/4$).

M_{diff} is basically an image where each pixel $M_{diff}(x, y)$ contains a normalized orientation difference of the minutia centered at (x, y). If no minutia is in (x, y) then the value is 0.

5.4.5 *Orientation Density Map*

The final orientation density map is computed as for the other density maps:

1. An initial density map, M'_{dens}, is constructed by

$$M'_{dens}(\mathbf{x}) = \sum_{\mathbf{x_0} \in M_{diff}} K_r(\mathbf{x} - \mathbf{x_0}) \tag{5.35}$$

where $K_r(\mathbf{x} - \mathbf{x_0})$ is a kernel function centered at $\mathbf{x_0}$ with a radius r (30 pixels).

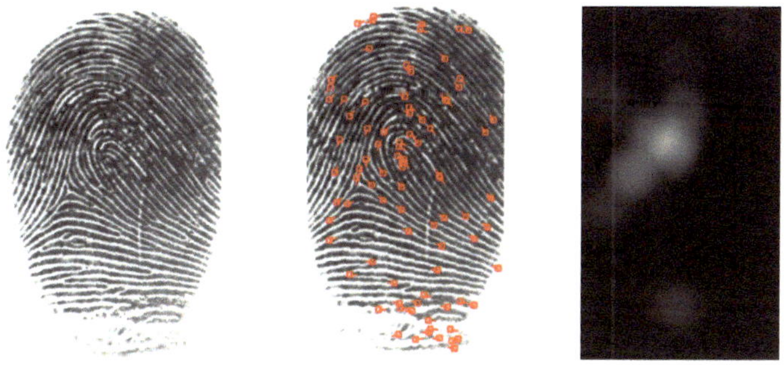
(a) Original (b) Minutia (c) MOA

Fig. 5.34 MOA of an unaltered fingerprints. Minutia points generally share similar orientations to their neighbors. Singular regions will introduce variations; the MOA will therefore have higher amplitudes around singular regions. *Source* **a** [6]

2. Smoothening. The initial density map, M'_{dens}, is smoothed by a low-pass Gaussian filter of size 30×30 with a standard deviation of 10 pixels.
3. Normalization. The values of $M'_{dens}(\mathbf{x})$ are transformed to the interval $[0, 1]$ by

$$M_{dens}(x, y) = \begin{cases} M'_{dens}(x, y)/T, & \text{if } M'_{dens}(x, y) \leq T, \\ 1, & \text{otherwise} \end{cases} \tag{5.36}$$

where T is a predetermined threshold (T is set to 6.9).

Figures 5.34 and 5.35 show the resulting density map of the *MOA*. A natural fingerprint will generally only have small peaks around singular regions. The additional minutia around scars and obliterated areas with conflicting orientations in altered fingerprint images will produce areas with higher amplitudes such that the distribution of the density image will differ from an unaltered fingerprint image.

5.4.5.1 Extraction

There are multitudes of different ways of analyzing data and extracting features to be used by an *SVM*. The feature extraction is equivalent to the previously presented state-of-the-art-method, since both of the proposed analysis algorithms are reliant on the distribution of special features across the fingerprint in a similar fashion to the predefined method. The final density maps from each analysis are images in the size of 512×480 pixels with intensity values that are normalized to the range of $[0, 1]$. The feature extraction will construct a 189-dimensional vector from each analysis. This is done as follows:

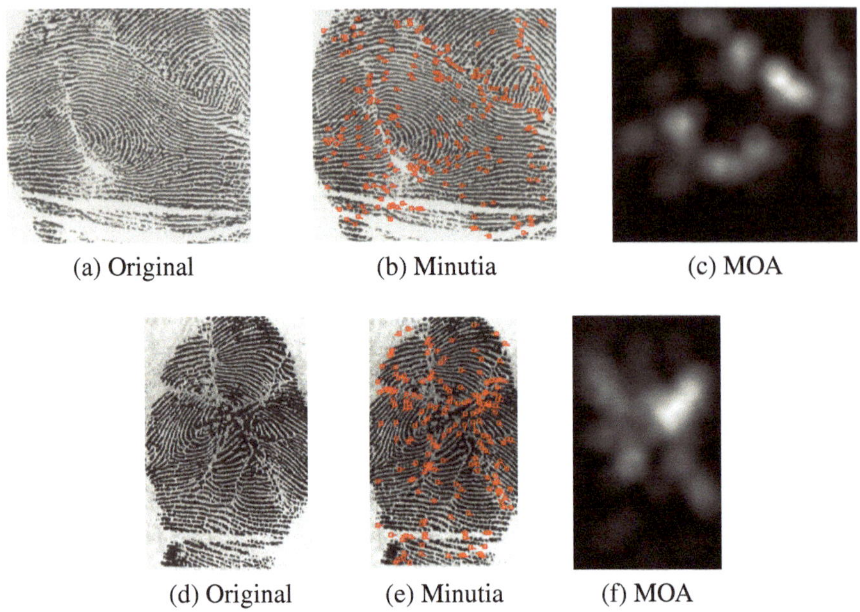

Fig. 5.35 MOA of two altered fingerprints. Regions around scars will add additional high amplitudes to the density map. *Source* **a** [41], **d** [38]

1. Columns of 16 pixel are removed from each side of the density map. This gives a density map of size 480×480 pixels.
2. In order to separate and extract features from different sections of the image it is divided into 3×3 cells. The size of each cell is thus 160×160 pixels.
3. Histograms in 21 bins in the range [0,1] are computed for each of the nine cells.
4. The nine histograms are concatenated into a 189-dimensional feature vector.

The two feature vectors are fused by concatenation which results in a 378-dimensional feature vector. The feature vector is fed into a *SVM* for classification.

5.5 Evaluation and Results

In biometric research we commonly expect that proposed methods are evaluated on publicly accessible datasets, such that research results can be reproduced. For the research addressed in this work such a public dataset does not exist. Due to the nature of the target characteristic of interest it is neither possible to ask volunteers on large numbers to alter their fingerprints and to conduct a dedicated data collection. Seemingly, a possibility would be in using the forensic and immigration control databases. However, the individuals typically seek to avoid criminal prosecution or blacklisting by immigration control authorities, and the altered fingerprints, if identified, are still subject to legal protection. This limitation forced the researchers working in this field to test their methods either using synthetically generated datasets of altered fingerprints or to benchmark them with the very few datasets that do contain altered fingerprint sample. The proposed method was tested on a dataset of altered fingerprints composed from the following sources:

- Brno [2]. A collection of fingerprints containing a wide variety of dermatological diseases.
- GUC 100 [1]. An *in-house* database from Gjøvik University College (GUC) in Norway. A few images containing dermatological diseases have been used as altered.
- Samischenko [38]. The book *Atlas of the Unusual Papilla Patterns* by S.S. Samischenko contains a large collection of fingerprint images with unusual fingerprint patterns together with some natural ones. The database contains fingerprints from fingers altered by burns, acid burns, transplantation, miscellaneous injuries, and diseases.
- NIST SD14—fingerprints that have been identified as altered in the NIST Special Database 14

Moreover we added nonaltered images from public sources [1], FVC 2004 [6]. For the FVC 2004 Images from DB1 (set A) of the public fingerprint database collected for the Fingerprint Verification Competition 2004 (FVC 2004) have been used as unaltered images. The resulting dataset contains 116 altered and 180 unaltered fingerprint images normalized to the size 512×480 pixels.

Both the resulting density maps from the Singular Point Density Analysis (SPDA) and Minutia Orientation Analysis (MOA) are classified using the approach used by Yoon et al. [43]. The density maps are cropped into a rectangular shape, normalized into the interval [0, 1] and divided into 3×3 blocks, in total 9, blocks. For each block, a 21-bin histogram is computed that represents the distribution of the density values in the interval [0, 1]. For each of the density maps, all the histograms for all of the blocks are then concatenated into a single 189-dimensional feature vector that can be used for classification. For benchmarking the approach by Yoon et al. [43] was fully reimplemented. The results as presented by Ellingsgaard in [11] are listed in Table 5.3.

Table 5.3 Initial evaluation results of Ellingsgaard [11]

Method	Analysis	Alteration Detection Rate (%)
Yoon et al. [43]	OFA	93.7
	MDA	77.5
Ellingsgaard [11]	SPDA	92.0
	MOA	81.6
Feature level fusion	**OFA/SPDA**	**94.6**

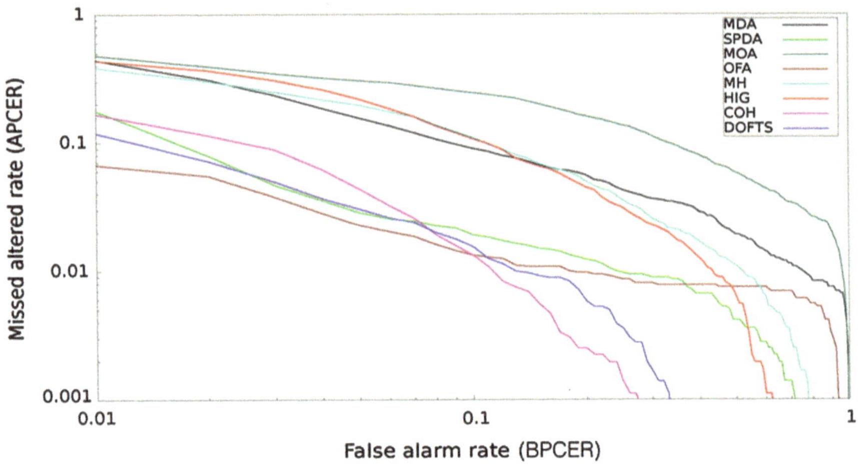

Fig. 5.36 DET curves comparing the alteration detection performance. *Source* [14]

The results demonstrate that the proposed method based on SDPA and OA perform on the same accuracy level as the method published by Yoon et al. [43]. An improvement can be achieved by feature fusion of the Orientation Field Analysis (OFA) by Yoon et al. [43] and the proposed Singular Point Density Analysis (SPDA).

A more intensive evaluation also combined with very recently proposed algorithms can be found in Gottschlich et al. [14]. The accuracy of various fingerprint alteration detection methods are illustrated in Fig. 5.36.

Those results are presented in terms of the *Attack Presentation Classification Error Rate (APCER)* and *Bona Fide Presentation Classification Error Rate (BPCER)* metrics, which are derived from the international standardization project ISO/IEC 30107-3 [19]. The APCER metric is expressing the proportion of presentations of altered fingerprints incorrectly classified as bona fide presentation (a.k.a. normal presentations). The BPCER metric is the proportion of presentation of normal fingerprints incorrectly classified as being altered (i.e. attacks).

5.6 Conclusion

A novel method for detecting altered fingerprints has been developed that performs competitively with the state-of-the-art method by Yoon et al. [43] by achieving Alteration Detection Rate of **92 %** on the evaluation dataset. In addition, the classification performance can be further improved to **94.6 %** by combining the approach of Yoon et al. [43] and the proposed method. The future work would involve testing on a larger datasets of altered fingerprints from government sources.

Acknowledgements The authors would like to thank Anil Jain (Michigan State University), Christophe Champod (Universite de Lausanne), Martin Drahansky (Brno University of Technology, Faculty of Information Technology—STRaDe) and FN Olomouc that kindly provided access to the altered fingerprint data used in this work. Also thanks to Ctirad Sousedik and Martin Olsen for fruitful discussions. This work is carried out under the funding of the EU-FP7 INGRESS project (Grant No. SEC-2012-312792).

References

1. GUC100 multisensor fingerprint database for in-house (Semipublic) performance test, January 2009. Gjøvik University College (GUC)
2. Fingerprint database. Alterations caused by diseases, March 2013. Faculty of Information Technology at Brno University of Technology and the research group STRaDe in collaboration with dermatologists from FN Olomouc
3. Bazen AM, Gerez SH (2001) Extraction of singular points from directional fields of fingerprints. In: The 7th annual CTIT workshop mobile communications in perspective workshop. Centre for Telematics and Information Technology, Enschede, pp 41–44
4. Bazen AM, Gerez SH (2002) Systematic methods for the computation of the directional fields and singular points of fingerprints. IEEE Trans Pattern Anal Mach Intell 24(7):905–919. 060.02
5. Bo J, Ping TH, Lan XM (2008) Fingerprint singular point detection algorithm by poincaré index. WTOS 7(12):1453–1462
6. Cappelli MM, Maio D, Maltoni D, Wayman JL, Jain AK (2004) FVC2004: Third fingerprint verification competition. In Proceedings of the first international conference on biometric authentication 1–7
7. Chikkerur SS, Cartwright AN, Govindaraju V (2005) Fingerprint image enhancement using STFT analysis. In IN PROC. ICAPR, pp 20–29
8. Commission, E. (2012) Visa information system—VIS. http://ec.europa.eu/dgs/home-affairs/what-we-do/policies/borders-and-visas/visa-information-system/index_en.htm
9. Cummins H (1935) Attempts to alter and obliterate finger-prints. J Crim Law Criminol 25:982–991
10. Doležel M, Drahanský M, Urbánek J (2013) Einfluss von hauterkrankungen auf den biometrischen erkennungsprozess. Datenschutz un Datensicherheit (DuD) Heft 6-2013, 358–362
11. Ellingsgaard J (2013) Fingerprint alteration detection. Master thesis, Technical University of Denmark. (June 2013)
12. Ellingsgaard J, Sousedik C, Busch C (2014) Detecting fingerprint alterations by orientation field and minutiae orientation analysis. In 2014 international workshop on biometrics and forensics (IWBF), (March 2014), pp 1–6
13. Feng J, Jain AK, Ross A (2009) Fingerprint alteration. Tech. Rep. MSU-CSE-09-30, Department of Computer Science, Michigan State University, East Lansing, Michigan. (December 2009)
14. Gottschlich C, Mikaelyan A, Olsen M, Bigun J, Busch C (2015) Improving fingerprint alteration detection. In Proceedings of 9th international symposium on image and signal processing and analysis (ISPA 2015)
15. Gu J, Zhou J (2003) A novel model for orientation field of fingerprints. In IEEE computer society conference on computer vision and pattern recognition, pp 493–498
16. Hoover JE, Collins FL (1943) The man without fingerprints. Collier's Weekly (January 1943), p 16
17. ISO/IEC JTC1 SC37 Biometrics (2009) ISO/IEC 29794-1:2009 Information Technology—Biometric Sample Quality—Part 1: Framework. International Organization for Standardization

18. ISO/IEC JTC1 SC37 Biometrics (2016) ISO/IEC 30107-1. Information Technology—Biometric presentation attack detection—Part 1: Framework. International Organization for Standardization
19. ISO/IEC JTC1 SC37 Biometrics (2016) ISO/IEC DIS 30107-3. Information Technology—Biometric presentation attack detection—Part 3: Testing and Reporting. International Organization for Standardization
20. Jain AK (1989) Fundamentals of digital image processing. Prentice-Hall Inc, Upper Saddle River, NJ
21. Jain AK, Prabhakar S, Hong L, Pankanti S (2000) Filterbank-based fingerprint matching. IEEE Trans Image Process 9:846–859
22. Jain AK, Yoon S (2012) Automatic detection of altered fingerprints. IEEE Comput 45(1):79–82
23. Jin C, Kim H, Elliott S (2007) Liveness detection of fingerprint based on band-selective fourier spectrum. In Proceedings of the 10th international conference on information security and cryptology, ICISC'07. Springer, Berlin, pp 168–179
24. Kamei T, Mizoguchi M (1995) Image filter design for fingerprint enhancement. In international symposium on computer vision, 1995. Proceedings, pp 109–114
25. Kawagoe M, Tojo A (1984) Fingerprint pattern classification. Pattern Recognit 17(3):295–303
26. Kim B-G, Park D-J (2002) Adaptive image normalisation based on block processing for enhancement of fingerprint image. Electron Lett 38(14):696–698
27. Lim E, Jiang X, Yau W-Y (2002) Fingerprint quality and validity analysis. In 2002 international conference on image processing (ICIP), vol 1, pp 469–472
28. Liu M, Jiang X, Kot AC (2005) Fingerprint reference-point detection. EURASIP J. Appl Signal Process 2005:498–509
29. MailOnline (2009) Calais migrants mutilate fingertips to hide true identity (July 2009). http://www.dailymail.co.uk/news/article-1201126/Calais-migrants-mutilate-fingertips-hide-true-identity.html
30. Maltoni D, Maio D, Jain AK, Prabhakar S (2009) Handbook of fingerprint recognition, 2nd edn. Springer Publishing Company, Incorporated
31. Merkle J, Ihmor H, Korte U, Niesing M, Schwaiger M (2010) Performance of the fuzzy vault for multiple fingerprints (extended version). arXiv:1008.0807
32. NIST (2012) Development of NFIQ 2.0—quality feature definitions. Tech. rep. (June 2012)
33. Olsen M, Smida V, Busch C (2015) Finger image quality assessment features—definitions and evaluation. IET J Biom. (December 2015)
34. Olsen MA, Xu H, Busch C (2012) Gabor filters as candidate quality measure for NFIQ 2.0. In 2012 5th IAPR international conference on biometrics (ICB), pp 158–163
35. Petrovici A, Lazar C (2010) Identifying fingerprint alteration using the reliability map of the orientation field. The Annals of the Univeristy of Craiova. Series: Automation, Computers, Electronics and Mechatronics 7(34), 45–52. (1)
36. Rajanna U, Erol A, Bebis G (2010) A comparative study on feature extraction for fingerprint classification and performance improvements using rank-level fusion. Pattern Anal Appl 13(3):263–272
37. Ravishankar RA (1990) A taxonomy for texture description and identification. Springer, New York, NY
38. Samischenko S (2001) Atlas of the unusual papilla patterns/atlas neobychnykh papilliarnykh uzorov. Urisprudentsiia, Moscow
39. Watson C, Garris M, Tabassi C, Wilson RM (2012) NIST biometric image software. (December 2012). http://www.nist.gov/itl/iad/ig/nbis.cfm
40. Watson CI, Candela G, Grother P (1994) Comparison of fft fingerprint filtering methods for neural network classification. NISTIR 5493 (1994)
41. Wertheim K (1998) An extreme case of fingerprint mutilation. J Forensic Identif 48:466–477
42. Xie SJ, Yang JC, Yoon S, Park DS (2008) An optimal orientation certainty level approach for fingerprint quality estimation. In Second international symposium on intelligent information technology application, 2008. IITA'08. (2008), vol 3, pp 722–726

43. Yoon S, Feng J, Jain AK (2012) Altered fingerprints: analysis and detection. IEEE Trans Pattern Anal Mach Intell 34(3):451–464
44. Yoon S, Feng J, Jain AK, Ross A (2009) Automatic detection of altered fingerprints. ICPR. (August 2009, Presentation)
45. Zhou J, Chen F, Gu J (2009) A novel algorithm for detecting singular points from fingerprint images. IEEE Trans Pattern Anal Mach Intell 31(7):1239–1250

Part II
Face and Video Analysis

Chapter 6
Face Sketch Recognition via Data-Driven Synthesis

Nannan Wang, Shengchuan Zhang, Chunlei Peng, Jie Li and Xinbo Gao

Abstract In some real-world scenarios, there does not always exist a normal photo for face recognition or retrieval purpose, e.g. suspect searching for law enforcement. Under the circumstances, a sketch drawn by the artist is usually taken as the substitute for matching with the mug shot photos collected by the police office. However, due to the great discrepancy of the texture presentation between sketches and photos, common face recognition methods achieve limited performance on this task. In order to shrink this gap, sketches can be transformed to photos relying on some machine learning techniques and then synthesized photos are utilized to match with mug shot photos. Alternatively, photos can also be transformed to sketches and the probe sketch drawn by the artist is matched with the transformed sketches subsequently. Existing learning-based face sketch–photo synthesis methods are grouped into two major categories: data-driven methods (example-based methods) and model-based methods. This chapter would give a comprehensive analysis and comparison to advances on this topic.

N. Wang
State Key Laboratory of Integrated Services Networks, School of Telecommunications Engineering, Xidian University, No. 2 Taibai South Road, Yanta District, Xi'an 710071, People's Republic of China
e-mail: nnwang@xidian.edu.cn

S. Zhang · C. Peng · J. Li · X. Gao (✉)
Lab of Video & Image Processing Systems, School of Electronic Engineering, Xidian University, No. 2 Taibai South Road, Yanta District, Xi'an 710071, People's Republic of China
e-mail: xbgao@mail.xidian.edu.cn

S. Zhang
e-mail: zsc_2007@163.com

C. Peng
e-mail: clp.xidian@gmail.com

M. Tistarelli and C. Champod (eds.), *Handbook of Biometrics for Forensic Science*, Advances in Computer Vision and Pattern Recognition,
DOI 10.1007/978-3-319-50673-9_6

6.1 Introduction

The intrinsic fluidity of face imaging and uncontrollable extrinsic imaging conditions (such as an intended target deliberately concealing his/her identity) means that suitable face images for processing and identifying a person cannot always be obtained [22]. For example, face images acquired by live surveillance cameras at a distance are usually in a low resolution. Though face super-resolution techniques could be utilized to enhance the resolution to some extent, there are still many limits to the problem [1]. An effective way to resolve this problem is to invite artists draw a sketch according to the surveillance video. Another case is that a photo of the culprit is not always available in suspect searching. As a substitute, face sketches are drawn by an artist based on the recollection of an eyewitness. Once a sketch is obtained in aforementioned scenarios, it can be employed to identify the suspect.

However, since face sketches and photos vary a lot in texture representation and imaging mechanism, traditional face recognition techniques perform poorly on this challenging task by matching a sketch with a mug shot database [17, 30]. In order to shrink the great gap between sketches and photos, they can be transformed to the same modality and then conventional face recognition techniques could be applied.

There have been many attempts to interactively or automatically synthesize facial sketches. For example, some commercial software designed for image processing is becoming widely popular, such as Adobe Photoshop,[1] Meitu,[2] and PaperArtist.[3] Figure 6.1 gives some generated sketches by these software and the sketch drawn by the artist. Li et al. [10] presented a simple filter-based framework for face photo–sketch synthesis. Although sketches generated by these analytic-based methods can achieve satisfying visual quality, they look more like photographs and are less stylistic. This would introduce great difficulty for face matching since these generated sketches are actually still in a heterogeneous modality with the sketch drawn by the artist. To really shrink the gap between sketches and photos, learning-based face sketch–photo synthesis methods described in this chapter have proven surprisingly successful in face identification from sketches [22]. Face sketch synthesis means transforming photos in the mug shot database to sketches and then the probe sketch can be matched with these synthesized sketches. Alternatively, face photo synthesis transform the probe sketch drawn by the artist to a photo. Indeed, these two strategies are invertible by just switching the roles of sketches and photos. Thus in following text, we would take face sketch synthesis as an example to introduce existing synthesis methods.

Learning-based methods generally synthesize a sketch relying on some sketch-photo examples through machine learning techniques. Existing learning-based methods incorporate two major categories: model-based methods and data-driven methods. Model-based methods first learn a model from training sketch-photo pairs which is then directly applied to generate sketches from input test photos.

[1] http://www.adobe.com/products/photoshop.html.

[2] http://xiuxiu.web.meitu.com/.

[3] http://paperartist.net/.

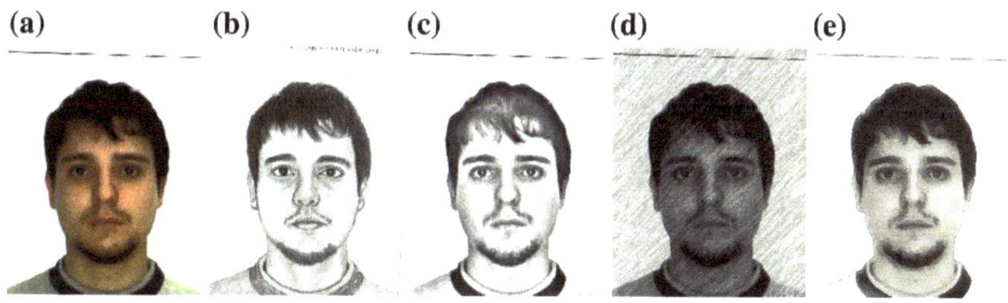

Fig. 6.1 Sketch comparison generated from different sources: (a) input photo; (b) sketch drawn by the artist; (c) sketch generated by Meitu; (d) sketch generated by Photoshop; (e) sketch generated by Paper Artist

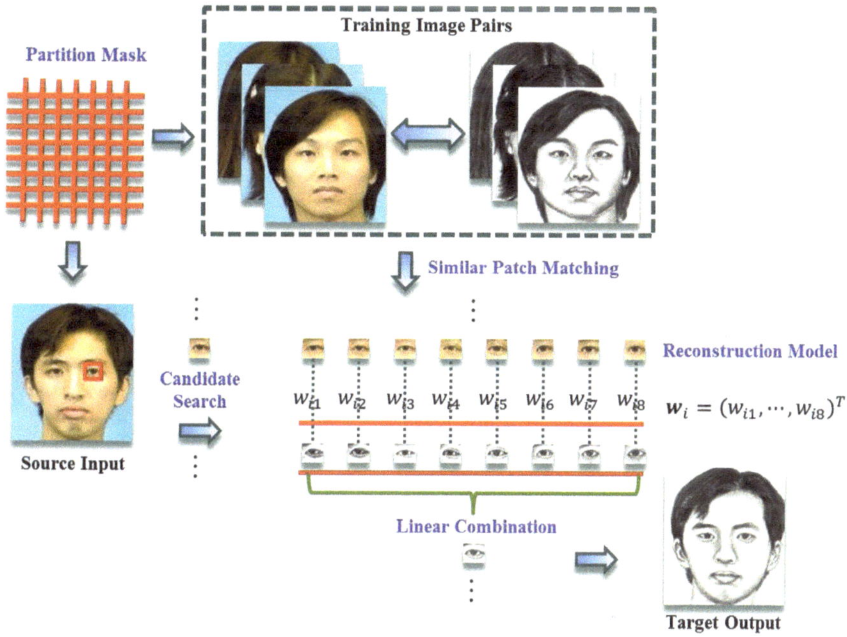

Fig. 6.2 General procedures for data-driven methods

Gao et al. [7, 8, 25, 26, 31] employed embedded hidden Markov model (E-HMM) to learn the nonlinear relationship between sketches and their counterpart photo images. A coupled sketch–photo model is trained which can be simply seen as introducing a series of hidden variables into the Markov chain to control the generation process of a photo–sketch pair (See Fig. 6.2) [22]. The photo model (separated from the coupled model) explains the face photo generation process and the sketch model (separated from the coupled model) describes the generation process of corresponding sketch. Given an input test photo, the trained photo model is first utilized to interpret the test photo to obtain the hidden states. The trained sketch model is then employed to generate the sketch corresponding to the input photo with the help of obtained hidden states. When E-HMM was first applied for face sketch synthesis [7, 31], the holistic face image is modeled as an E-HMM. Considering the fact that certain fine local features such as those associated with eyes, nose, and mouth, could not be learned, they afterwards proposed to divide each face image into some patches and each patch is taken as an E-HMM [8, 25, 26].

Chang et al. [2] proposed to explore multivariate output regression (ridge regression and relevance vector machine) to learn the mapping relation from photo patches to sketch patches. Each face image (both sketch and photo) is divided into some patches. A local regression function is learned from the training sketch–photo patch pairs corresponding to the same location. Inspired by the success application of sparse representation to image denoising [5] and image restoration [12, 27], sparse representation has been utilized to face sketch synthesis [3, 23]. Actually L1-norm constrained sparse representation relaxation is known as the Lasso, essentially a linear regression regularized with L1-norm on the coefficients [17]. Chang et al. [3] improved their previous multivariate regression method [2] by substituting the original L2-norm regularization with the L1-norm sparse constraint. Different from aforementioned sparse representation based methods, which assumed that the source input and the target output had the same sparse representation coefficients, Wang et al. [23] relaxed this assumption by supposing that they had their respective sparse representations. These two sparse representations are connected through a linear transformation. Then the objective function is composed of two sparse representation parts: one fidelity term between the sparse representation coefficients, and other the regularization term on the linear transformation matrix, under some scale constraints to each atom of dictionaries. They separated the objective function into three subproblems: sparse coding for training samples, dictionary updating and linear transformation matrix updating.

In the following text, we would review existing data-driven methods in Sect. 6.2. Our proposed two kinds of data-driven methods (sparse representation supported neighbor selection methods and graphical representation methods) are sequentially introduced in Sects. 6.3 and 6.4, respectively. Section 6.5 gives experimental results and some concluding remarks are summarized in Sect. 6.6.

6.2 Related Work

Data-driven methods synthesize a sketch by searching similar example sketches (or sketch patches) from the training dataset (see Fig. 6.2, the partition mask in this figure is utilized to divide an image into some even patches with some overlap). These selected sketches (or sketch patches) are usually linearly combined to generate the target sketch (or sketch patch) weighted by reconstruction coefficients obtained from reconstruction models. This category of methods generally assumes that a sketch and the corresponding photo share the same linear combination coefficients.

Principal component analysis (PCA) plays the role of the reconstruction model in the eigentransformation method proposed by Tang and Wang [16–18]. The eigentransformation method works on the image level rather than the image patch level. The input test photo is first projected onto the whole photo training set to obtain the linear combination coefficients. The target sketch is then synthesized by linearly combining sketches in the training set with aforementioned coefficients. Here the whole sketch training set is taken as the similar sketch candidates to the target output sketch. Since these PCA-based methods performed on a holistic face image, this may result in the loss of some critical fine details and blurring effect.

In order to overcome limitations resulted from the holistic strategy in [16–18], Liu et al. [11] proposed a patch-based method assuming that sketch patches and their corresponding photo patches are sampled from two manifolds sharing a similar geometrical structure. The input photo patch is first reconstructed in a least square manner using its K nearest neighbors selected from the patches extracted from the photo training set. The reconstruction coefficients are computed in this process. The target sketch patch is then synthesized by linearly combining candidate sketch patches corresponding to those neighbor photo patches of the test photo patch, weighted by obtained reconstruction coefficients. After fusing all obtained target sketch patches, the final target sketch is generated.

Markov random field (MRF) is explored to model the interaction between sketch–photo pairs and neighborhoods through two compatibility functions [24]: data compatibility (constraints on the fidelity between the test photo patch and the target sketch patch) and spatial compatibility (constraints on the neighboring patches of the target sketch). Considering the strong structural property of face images, the uniform scale of MRF has limited ability to address the long-range dependency among local patches. Wang and Tang [24] further proposed a multiscale MRF model which constructs a hierarchical model of several MRFs corresponding to different scales (image patch size). Their method constructs the pairwise compatibility functions through the nearest neighbors searched from a training set across different scales. Under the maximum a posterior (MAP) rule, the best matched candidate sketch patch is taken as the target output sketch patch corresponding to the input photo patch. This can be interpreted as the weight coefficient corresponding to the selected candidate sketch patch is 1 and 0 s for other candidate sketch patches in Fig. 6.2.

Zhou et al. [32] claimed that above-mentioned MRF-based method [24] had two major drawbacks: cannot synthesize new sketch patches (i.e., each patch of final target output is from the training set) and NP-hard for the optimization problem in solving the MRF model. Then they proposed a weighted MRF method to model the relation between sketch and photo patches. By a linear combination of selected candidate sketch patches, their method could synthesize new sketch patches existing not in the training sketch set. In addition, the objective function is a convex optimization problem which has the unique optimal solution.

The core distinction between different data-driven methods lies in the fact that they either employ different patch matching strategies to select candidate sketch patches or construct different reconstruction models to resolve reconstruction weights. Following we would introduce two methods for each of these two issues repectively.

6.3 Sparse Representation Supported Candidate Selection Methods

This section would introduce two sparse representation based face sketch synthesis methods. Different from aforementioned model-based face sketch synthesis methods [3, 23], the two proposed methods do not learn a coupled dictionary for face sketch synthesis. Instead, they utilize sparse representation as a tool for candidate sketch patch selection. We will introduce these two methods sequentially.

6.3.1 Sparse Feature Selection Based Face Sketch Synthesis

Aforementioned data-driven methods all search fixed number of candidate sketch (or sketch patches) to synthesize the target sketch (or sketch patch). It may result in some blurring effect or noise on the synthesized sketch. The underlying reason is that different parts of faces have different number of nearest neighbors in the training set. This can be easily understood by the following example: if the number of nearest neighbor $K = 6$ and there are actually only 5 nearest neighbors most related to the test image patch. Then K-NN based method may still choose another image patch which is in fact a mismatched (noisy) patch. Inspired by the fact that sparse representation is capable of finding the fewest closely related dictionary atoms to reconstruct the input signal, we proposed a sparse feature selection (SFS) method for face sketch synthesis based on sparse representation [6].

Given a query photo $\mathbf{P}_t$, it is first divided into M even patches with some overlap $\{\mathbf{t}_1, \ldots, \mathbf{t}_i, \ldots, \mathbf{t}_M\}$. Each patch is ordered lexicographically as a column vector. Let $\mathbf{D}_p$ denote a dictionary whose columns consist of patches sampled from the photo training set and $\mathbf{D}_s$ indicate the dictionary with the sketch patches corresponding to photo patches in $\mathbf{D}_p$ as its column vectors. Then the sparse representation of $\mathbf{t}_i$ can be represented as follows:

$$\min_{\mathbf{c}_i} \|\mathbf{c}_i\|_1, s.t. \|\mathbf{D}_p\mathbf{c}_i - \mathbf{t}_i\|_2^2 \leq \varepsilon, \tag{6.1}$$

where $\mathbf{c}_i = (c_{i1}, \ldots, c_{il})$ indicates the coefficient vector and l is the number of columns in $\mathbf{D}_p$. We can solve the above optimization problem for $\mathbf{c}_i$. Afterwards the neighborhood of photo patch $\mathbf{t}_i$ is achieved according to the following criteria:

$$\mathcal{N}(\mathbf{t}_i) = \{k | \delta(c_{ik}) \neq 0, 1 \leq k \leq l\}, \tag{6.2}$$

where $\mathcal{N}(\mathbf{t}_i)$ denotes the neighborhood for $\mathbf{t}_i$ and $\delta(\cdot)$ is a neighbor selection function:

$$\delta(c_{ik}) = \begin{cases} c_{ik}, & | c_{ik} | > \sigma \\ 0, & \text{otherwise} \end{cases} \tag{6.3}$$

where σ is a small positive real number, which is set to 0.001 in our experiments. Once the neighborhood is determined, the weight for every neighbor in $\mathcal{N}(\mathbf{t}_i)$ is calculated as follows:

$$c_{ik} = \frac{\delta(c_{ik})}{\sum_{k=1}^{l} \delta(c_{lk})}, \tag{6.4}$$

Finally, the corresponding target sketch patch can be synthesized as

$$\mathbf{s}_i = \mathbf{D}_s \mathbf{c}_i. \tag{6.5}$$

For each photo patch in the query photo, we iterate the above steps and then fuse all these synthesized patches into a whole sketch by averaging the overlapping areas. In addition, in order to compensate the high frequency or detail information filtered with overlapping areas averaged, they employed support vector regression for further improving the quality of the synthesized sketch [20].

6.3.2 *Sparse Representation Based Greedy Search for Face Sketch Synthesis*

Most existing methods cannot handle some non-facial factors, such as hair styles, hairpins, glasses and backgrounds, if these factors are excluded in the training set. The reason is that these methods directly utilize image intensities as the query feature to search nearest neighbors and restrict the search range in local region to save computational time since images have been aligned by the positions of the eyes. We proposed a face sketch synthesis method via sparse representation based greedy search by considering a tradeoff between computational time and search range to overcome aforementioned drawbacks [28]. Their method adopted sparse coefficient values and dictionary atom selection orders as the query feature to find nearest neighbors which are robust to image backgrounds. In addition, they exploited the distribution of image patches extracted from the training set. After organizing these image patches in a tree structure, each query image patch was checked for its own leaf without costing much computational time. Since the search range was extended to the whole training set, their method can synthesize non-facial factors with facial elements (e.g., glasses can be substituted by face contours).

Suppose there are N photo–sketch pairs $(\mathbf{p}_1, \mathbf{s}_1), \ldots, (\mathbf{p}_i, \mathbf{s}_i), \ldots, (\mathbf{p}_N, \mathbf{s}_N)$ in the training set (see Fig. 6.3), we divide them into overlapping photo–sketch patch pairs denoted as $\{B_\mathbf{p}, B_\mathbf{s}\}$, $B_\mathbf{p} = \{\mathbf{p}_{11}, \ldots, \mathbf{p}_{1M}, \ldots, \mathbf{p}_{ij}, \ldots, \mathbf{p}_{N1}, \ldots, \mathbf{p}_{NM}\}$ is the sampled photo patches and $B_\mathbf{s} = \{\mathbf{s}_{11}, \ldots, \mathbf{s}_{1M}, \ldots, \mathbf{s}_{ij}, \ldots \mathbf{s}_{N1}, \ldots, \mathbf{s}_{NM}\}$ is the corresponding

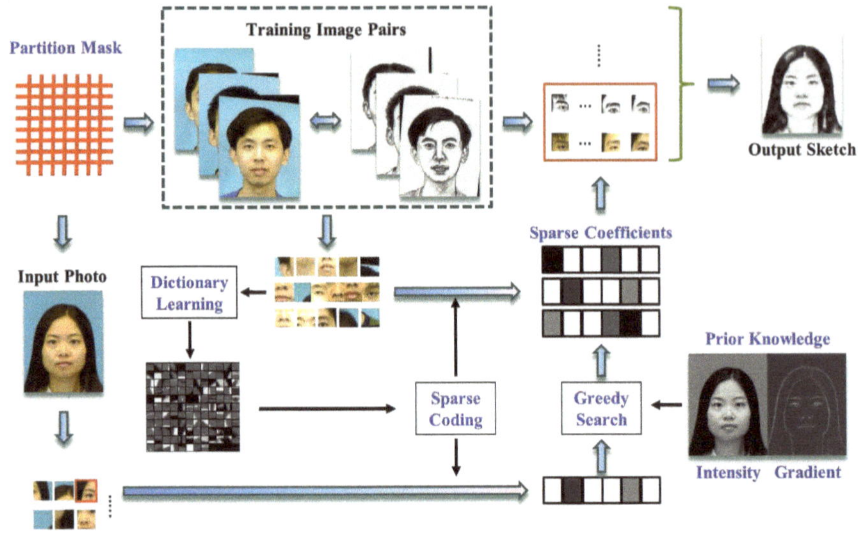

Fig. 6.3 Diagram of face sketch synthesis via sparse representation based greedy search

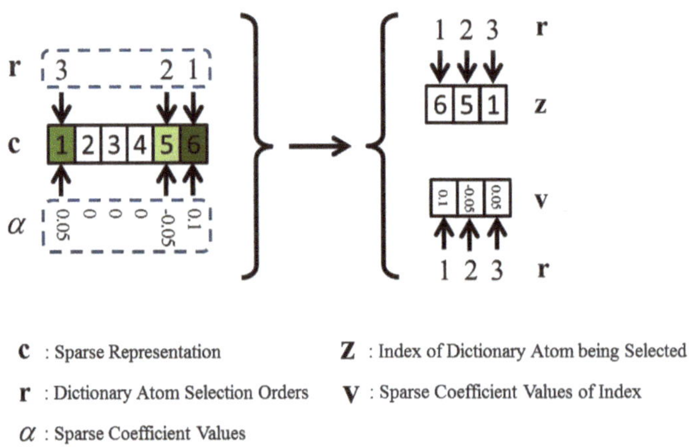

Fig. 6.4 Illustration of dictionary atom selection orders **r** and sparse coefficient values α. Here the dictionary atom selection orders **r** refers to the order of corresponding atom being selected. Given a sparse representation **c**, we can rearrange **r** and α to obtain its index of dictionary atom being selected **z** and sparse coefficient values of index **v**

sketch patches where M denotes the number of sampled patches in each image. Then a photo patch dictionary $\mathbf{D}_p$ is learnt with the randomly selected photo patches from $B_\mathbf{p}$. By sparse coding, the sparse representations $C_\mathbf{p}$ of $B_\mathbf{p}$ is obtained where $C_\mathbf{p} = \left\{\mathbf{c}_{11}, \ldots, \mathbf{c}_{1M}, \ldots, \mathbf{c}_{ij}, \ldots, \mathbf{c}_{N1}, \ldots, \mathbf{c}_{NM}\right\}$. Each sparse representation $\mathbf{c}_{ij}$ contains two variables: sparse coefficient values α_{ij} and dictionary atom selection orders $\mathbf{r}_{ij}$. As shown in Fig. 6.4, these two variables can be further arranged to obtain index of dictionary atom being selected $\mathbf{z}_{ij}$ and sparse coefficient values of index $\mathbf{v}_{ij}$. Given an input photo $\mathbf{x}$, it is divided into overlapping patches $\left\{\mathbf{x}_j\right\}_{j=1}^{M}$ in the same way as the training set. For each photo patch $\mathbf{x}_j$, its sparse representation $\mathbf{c}_j$ including sparse coefficient values α_j, dictionary atom selection orders $\mathbf{r}_j$, index of dictionary atom being selected $\mathbf{z}_j$ and sparse coefficient values of index $\mathbf{v}_j$ is first acquired by sparse coding with learnt photo patch dictionary $\mathbf{D}_p$. Then two criteria are applied to select nearest neighbors as follows.

$$\begin{gathered} \{\mathbf{c}\}_t = \left\{\mathbf{c} \,\middle|\, \mathbf{z}_q(k) = \mathbf{z}_g(k) \right\} \\ \{\mathbf{c}\}_t = \left\{\mathbf{c} \,\middle|\, \left|\mathbf{v}_q(k) - \mathbf{v}_g(k)\right| \le \varepsilon \right\} \end{gathered} \tag{6.6}$$

where symbol q represents the test image patch (query patch) and symbol g denotes the training image patches (gallery patches). ε is the threshold. k is the index of dictionary atom selection order in sparse representations $\mathbf{c}_q$ and $\mathbf{c}_g$ where $\mathbf{c}_q = \mathbf{c}_j$ and $\mathbf{c}_g \in C_\mathbf{p}$. $\{\mathbf{c}\}_t$ is the sparse representations subset after t iterations. Figure 6.5 illustrates the detail of data indexing structure. It can be seen that test patch searches through the data indexing structure until termination condition (all the nonzero coefficients in sparse representation of the test patch are traversed or the number of selected patches meets the requirement) is met. The sparse representations of final selected patches set are similar to that of test patch both in sparse coefficient values and dictionary atom selection orders directions. For each test photo patch, we can obtain its candidate sketch patches via above operations. The final sketch can be synthesized through the single-scale MRF-based model described in [24].

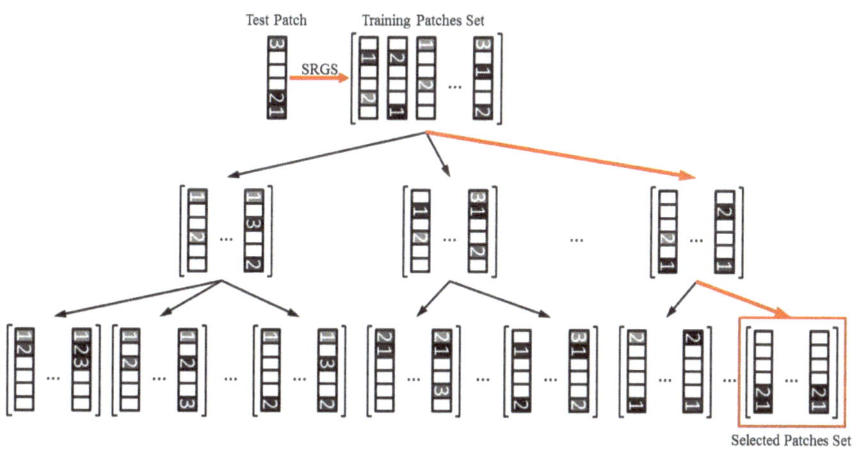

Fig. 6.5 Data indexing structure. Brackets denote selected subsets. Numbers in the squares represent the dictionary atom selection order while different levels of square transparency represent different sparse coefficient values. Each arrow represents the neighbor searching process with the assistance of dictionary atom selection orders and sparse coefficient values

6.4 Graphical Representation Based Reconstruction Models

This section would introduce two graphical model based methods: the transductive method and the multiple representation based method.

6.4.1 Transductive Face Sketch Synthesis

Above face sketch–photo synthesis methods are under the inductive learning framework which may result in high losses for test samples. The underlying cause is that inductive learning only considers the empirical loss of training samples and neglects test samples. We presented a novel transductive face sketch–photo synthesis method that incorporates both the test samples and the training samples into the learning process [21]. In particular, it defines a probabilistic model to optimize both the reconstruction fidelity (whether the generated sketches are recognized as the original person in the test photo) of the input photo and the synthesis fidelity (whether the generated sketches are as close to the ones drawn by artists as possible) of the target output sketch, and efficiently optimizes this probabilistic model by alternating optimization.

Let $\mathbf{X}$ denote the data matrix containing both training and test photo patches, $\mathbf{Y}$ represent the corresponding training sketch patches and target output sketch patches, and $\mathbf{W}$ consist of the weight vectors. They are all arranged in a row form which means each row vector in $\mathbf{X}$ denotes a photo patch and $\mathbf{Y}$ and $\mathbf{W}$ have a similar meaning:

$$\mathbf{X} = \begin{bmatrix} (\mathbf{p}_1^1)^T \\ \vdots \\ (\mathbf{p}_M^N)^T \\ \mathbf{x}_1^T \\ \vdots \\ \mathbf{x}_M^T \end{bmatrix} = \begin{bmatrix} \mathbf{X}_{1\cdot} \\ \vdots \\ \mathbf{X}_{(NM)\cdot} \\ \mathbf{X}_{(NM+1)\cdot} \\ \vdots \\ \mathbf{X}_{\left((N+1)M\right)\cdot} \end{bmatrix}$$

$$\mathbf{Y} = \begin{bmatrix} (\mathbf{s}_1^1)^T \\ \vdots \\ (\mathbf{s}_M^N)^T \\ \mathbf{y}_1^T \\ \vdots \\ \mathbf{y}_M^T \end{bmatrix} = \begin{bmatrix} \mathbf{Y}_{1\cdot} \\ \vdots \\ \mathbf{Y}_{(NM)\cdot} \\ \mathbf{Y}_{(NM+1)\cdot} \\ \vdots \\ \mathbf{Y}_{\left((N+1)M\right)\cdot} \end{bmatrix}, \mathbf{W} = \begin{bmatrix} \mathbf{W}_{1\cdot} \\ \vdots \\ \mathbf{W}_{(NM)\cdot} \\ \mathbf{W}_{(NM+1)\cdot} \\ \vdots \\ \mathbf{W}_{\left((N+1)M\right)\cdot} \end{bmatrix}$$

where $\mathbf{X}_{i\cdot}$, $\mathbf{Y}_{i\cdot}$ and $\mathbf{W}_{i\cdot}$, $i = 1, \ldots, (N+1)M$ denote the ith row vector of $\mathbf{X}$, $\mathbf{Y}$, and $\mathbf{W}$ respectively (the same meaning as the following similar representations).

Fig. 6.6 Illustration of the generative process of photo patches and sketch patches from common hidden parameters

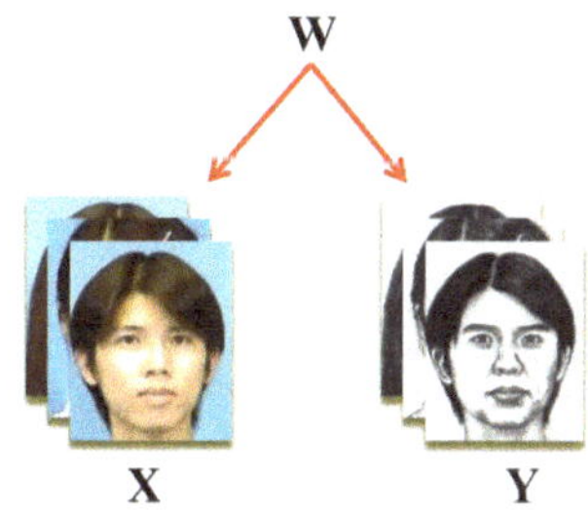

We can model the generative process of photo patches and sketch patches by their common hidden parameters **W** as shown in Fig. 6.6. Sketch–photo patch pairs are sampled from the joint distribution $P(\mathbf{X}, \mathbf{Y}, \mathbf{W})$ governed by the weight matrix **W**. We can then decompose the generative process as

$$\begin{aligned} &P(\mathbf{Y}, \mathbf{X}, \mathbf{W}) \\ &= P(\mathbf{Y}, \mathbf{X} \mid \mathbf{W})P(\mathbf{W}) \\ &= P(\mathbf{Y} \mid \mathbf{X}, \mathbf{W})P(\mathbf{X} \mid \mathbf{W})P(\mathbf{W}) \end{aligned} \tag{6.7}$$

where **W** controls the generation of sketches and photos, $P(\mathbf{W})$ denotes the prior probability of the hidden parameters **W**, $P(\mathbf{X} \mid \mathbf{W})$ is the conditional probability of generating photos **X** given **W**, and $P(\mathbf{Y} \mid \mathbf{X}, \mathbf{W})$ indicates the conditional probability of generating sketches **Y** given corresponding photos **X** and parameters **W**. The prior probability is usually treated as a regularization term on **W**. In this paper, we explore the compatibility constraint on overlapping regions between neighboring sketch patches to model $P(\mathbf{W})$

$$\begin{aligned} &P(\mathbf{W}) \propto \\ &\prod_{(i,j)\in\mathcal{E}} exp\left\{ -\frac{\| \sum_{k\in\mathcal{N}(i)} \mathbf{W}_{ik}\mathbf{Y}_k^{(i,j)} - \sum_{l\in\mathcal{N}(j)} \mathbf{W}_{il}\mathbf{Y}_l^{(j,i)} \|^2}{2\sigma_r^2} \right\} \\ &s.t. \sum_{k\in\mathcal{V}} \mathbf{W}_{ik} = 1, \mathbf{W}_{ik} \geq 0, \forall i \in \mathcal{V} \end{aligned} \tag{6.8}$$

where $\mathcal{N}(i)$ denotes the indices of neighbors of the node i, $\mathbf{W}_{ik}$ represents the element located on the ith row and the kth column of the matrix **W**, $\mathbf{Y}_k^{(i,j)}$ means the pixel intensities of the overlapping region (determined by the neighboring relation of nodes i and j) of the kth neighbor of the node i, and $\mathbf{Y}_l^{(j,i)}$ means the pixel intensities of the overlapping region (determined by the neighboring relation of nodes i and j) of the lth neighbor of the node j. Note that elements in the ith $i = 1, 2, \dots, (N+1)M$

row of the weight matrix $\mathbf{W}$ are 0 except for elements located in the neighborhood of the ith node. This prior indicates the compatibility of the overlapping regions of neighboring sketch patches.

In face sketch synthesis, $\mathbf{X}$ is observed, so $P(\mathbf{X}|\mathbf{W})$ is the likelihood function. It can be modeled as a Gaussian distribution:

$$P(\mathbf{X}|\mathbf{W}) \propto \prod_{i\in\mathcal{V}} exp\Big\{ - \frac{\|\mathbf{X}_{i\cdot} - \sum_{j\in\mathcal{N}(i)} \mathbf{W}_{ij}\mathbf{X}_{j\cdot}\|^2}{2\sigma_{dp}^2}\Big\} \tag{6.9}$$

The probability $P(\mathbf{X}|\mathbf{W})$ mainly considers the reconstruction fidelity between a photo patch $\mathbf{X}_{i\cdot}$ and its nearest neighbors $\mathbf{X}_{j\cdot}, j \in \mathcal{N}(i)$.

From Fig. 6.6, we find that given $\mathbf{W}$, $\mathbf{Y}$ is conditionally independent of $\mathbf{X}$, i.e., $P(\mathbf{X},\mathbf{Y}|\mathbf{W}) = P(\mathbf{X}|\mathbf{W})P(\mathbf{Y}|\mathbf{W})$ and then $P(\mathbf{Y}|\mathbf{X},\mathbf{W}) = P(\mathbf{Y}|\mathbf{W})$. It is straightforward that the probability $P(\mathbf{Y}|\mathbf{W})$ can be modeled as a product of a series of independent and identically distributed normal distributions:

$$\begin{aligned} P(\mathbf{Y}|\mathbf{X},\mathbf{W}) &= P(\mathbf{Y}|\mathbf{W}) \\ &\propto \prod_{i\in\mathcal{V}} P\big(\mathbf{Y}_{i\cdot} - \sum_{j\in\mathcal{N}(i)} \mathbf{W}_{ij}\mathbf{Y}_{(j\cdot)}\big) \\ &\propto \prod_{i\in\mathcal{V}} exp\Big\{ - \frac{\|\mathbf{Y}_{i\cdot} - \sum_{j\in\mathcal{N}(i)} \mathbf{W}_{ij}\mathbf{Y}_{j\cdot}\|^2}{2\sigma_{ds}^2}\Big\} \end{aligned} \tag{6.10}$$

$$\begin{aligned} P(\mathbf{X},\mathbf{Y},\mathbf{W}) &\propto \prod_{i\in\mathcal{V}} \Big\{ exp\{ - \frac{\|\mathbf{Y}_{i\cdot} - \sum_{j\in\mathcal{N}(i)} \mathbf{W}_{ij}\mathbf{Y}_{j\cdot}\|^2}{2\sigma_{ds}^2}\} exp\{ - \frac{\|\mathbf{X}_{i\cdot} - \sum_{j\in\mathcal{N}(i)} \mathbf{W}_{ij}\mathbf{X}_{j\cdot}\|^2}{2\sigma_{dp}^2}\}\Big\} \\ &\prod_{(i,j)\in\mathcal{E}} exp\{ - \frac{\| \sum_{k\in\mathcal{N}(i)} \mathbf{W}_{ik}\mathbf{Y}_k^{(i,j)} - \sum_{l\in\mathcal{N}(j)} \mathbf{W}_{il}\mathbf{Y}_l^{(j,i)}\|^2}{2\sigma_r^2}\} \\ &= exp\Big\{ - \sum_{i\in\mathcal{V}} \{ \frac{\|\mathbf{Y}_{i\cdot} - \sum_{j\in\mathcal{N}(i)} \mathbf{W}_{ij}\mathbf{Y}_{j\cdot}\|^2}{2\sigma_{ds}^2} + \frac{\|\mathbf{X}_{i\cdot} - \sum_{j\in\mathcal{N}(i)} \mathbf{W}_{ij}\mathbf{X}_{j\cdot}\|^2}{2\sigma_{dp}^2}\} \\ &\quad - \sum_{(i,j)\in\mathcal{V}} \frac{\| \sum_{k\in\mathcal{N}(i)} \mathbf{W}_{ik}\mathbf{Y}_k^{(i,j)} - \sum_{l\in\mathcal{N}(l)} \mathbf{W}_{il}\mathbf{Y}_l^{(j,i)}\|^2}{2\sigma_r^2}\Big\} \end{aligned} \tag{6.11}$$

$$\begin{aligned} &\max_{\mathbf{W},\mathbf{y}_1,\ldots,\mathbf{y}_M} P(\mathbf{W},\mathbf{y}_1,\ldots,\mathbf{y}_M|\mathbf{x}_1,\ldots,\mathbf{x}_M,\mathbf{X}_{1\cdot},\ldots,\mathbf{X}_{(NM)\cdot},\mathbf{Y}_{1\cdot},\ldots,\mathbf{Y}_{(NM)\cdot}) \\ &\Leftrightarrow \max_{\mathbf{W},\mathbf{y}_1,\ldots,\mathbf{y}_M} \frac{P(\mathbf{Y},\mathbf{X},\mathbf{W})}{P(\mathbf{X},\mathbf{Y}_{1\cdot},\ldots,\mathbf{Y}_{(NM)\cdot})} \\ &\Leftrightarrow \max_{\mathbf{W},\mathbf{y}_1,\ldots,\mathbf{y}_M} P(\mathbf{Y},\mathbf{X},\mathbf{W}) \end{aligned} \tag{6.12}$$

$$
\begin{aligned}
&\min_{\mathbf{W},\mathbf{y}_1,\ldots,\mathbf{y}_M} \sum_{i\in\mathcal{V}} \{\|\mathbf{Y}_{i\cdot} - \sum_{j\in\mathcal{N}(i)} \mathbf{W}_{ij}\mathbf{Y}_{j\cdot}\|^2 + \alpha\|\mathbf{X}_{i\cdot} - \sum_{j\in\mathcal{N}(i)} \mathbf{W}_{ij}\mathbf{X}_{j\cdot}\|^2\} \\
&\quad + \beta \sum_{(i,j)\in\mathcal{V}} \| \sum_{k\in\mathcal{N}(i)} \mathbf{W}_{ik}\mathbf{Y}_k^{(i,j)} - \sum_{l\in\mathcal{N}(j)} \mathbf{W}_{il}\mathbf{Y}_l^{(j,i)}\|^2 \\
&\quad s.t. \quad \sum_{k\in\mathcal{V}} \mathbf{W}_{ik} = 1, \mathbf{W}_{ik} \geq 0, \forall i \in \mathcal{V} \\
\Leftrightarrow &\min_{\mathbf{W},\mathbf{y}_1,\ldots,\mathbf{y}_M} \; tr(\mathbf{Y}^T\mathbf{M}\mathbf{Y}) + \alpha tr(\mathbf{X}^T\mathbf{M}\mathbf{X}) + \beta \sum_{(i,j)\in\mathcal{V}} \| \sum_{k\in\mathcal{N}(i)} \mathbf{W}_{ik}\mathbf{Y}_k^{(i,j)} - \sum_{l\in\mathcal{N}(j)} \mathbf{W}_{il}\mathbf{Y}_l^{(j,i)}\|^2 \\
&\quad s.t. \quad \sum_{k\in\mathcal{V}} \mathbf{W}_{ik} = 1, \mathbf{W}_{ik} \geq 0, \forall i \in \mathcal{V}
\end{aligned}
\tag{6.13}
$$

We can then reformulate the joint probability as in Eq. (6.11) on the next page. In face sketch synthesis, we are given an input photo as the test image and a number of sketch–photo pairs as the training set, and the objective is to infer the sketch corresponding to the input. This can be formulated as a maximum a posterior probability estimation problem (6.12). According to (6.11), the above maximization problem (6.12) is equivalent to the minimization of the objective function (6.13), where $\mathbf{M} = (\mathbf{I} - \mathbf{W})^T(\mathbf{I} - \mathbf{W})$, $\alpha = \frac{\sigma_{ds}^2}{\sigma_{dp}^2}$, $\beta = \frac{\sigma_{ds}^2}{\sigma_r^2}$, $\mathbf{I}$ is the identity matrix with the same size as $\mathbf{W}$, the superscript T is the transpose operator and $tr(\cdot)$ is the trace operator.

We apply the alternating minimization method to the above problem to obtain a local solution according to the following two steps:
(1) fixing $\mathbf{W}$, update $\mathbf{y}_1, \ldots, \mathbf{y}_M$ by solving (6.14)

$$
\min_{\mathbf{y}_1,\ldots,\mathbf{y}_M} tr(\mathbf{Y}^T\mathbf{M}\mathbf{Y}) \tag{6.14}
$$

(2) then fixing $\mathbf{y}_1, \ldots, \mathbf{y}_M$ to be the above obtained value, and update $\mathbf{W}$ by solving (6.15)

$$
\begin{aligned}
&\min_{\mathbf{W}} \|\mathbf{U} - \mathbf{W}\mathbf{U}\|^2 \\
&\quad + \beta \sum_{(i,j)\in\mathcal{V}} \| \sum_{k\in\mathcal{N}(i)} \mathbf{W}_{ik}\mathbf{Y}_k^{(i,j)} - \sum_{l\in\mathcal{N}(j)} \mathbf{W}_{il}\mathbf{Y}_l^{(j,i)}\|^2 \\
&s.t. \quad \sum_{k\in\mathcal{V}} \mathbf{W}_{ik} = 1, \mathbf{W}_{ik} \geq 0, \forall i \in \mathcal{V}
\end{aligned}
\tag{6.15}
$$

where $\mathbf{U} = [\mathbf{X} \quad \sqrt{\alpha}\mathbf{Y}]$ and we name each row of $\mathbf{U}$ a *pairwise patch* since it consists of two patches extracted from a sketch–photo pair. We alternately conduct (6.14) and (6.15) until convergence.

6.4.2 Multiple Representation Based Face Sketch Synthesis

As we know, face images can be described using features from multiple aspects. However, most existing face sketch synthesis methods simply utilize image intensities to measure the similarity of two image patches which may lead to incorrect patch matching. In order to sufficiently dig out the information in image patches to correct patch matching, we presented a novel multiple representations based face sketch–photo synthesis method that adaptively combines multiple features to represent an image patch and further conduct more reasonable patch matching which is robust to light variation [15].

In order to synthesize the sketch patch $\mathbf{y}_i$ corresponding to the input photo patch $\mathbf{x}_i$, where $i = 1, 2, \dots, N$, we find K candidate photo patches $\{\mathbf{x}_{i,1}, \mathbf{x}_{i,2}, \dots, \mathbf{x}_{i,K}\}$, where $\mathbf{x}_{i,k}$ represents the kth candidate photo patch for the ith input photo patch $\mathbf{x}_i$ within the search region around the location of $\mathbf{x}_i$. The target sketch patch $\mathbf{y}_i$ $(i = 1, 2, \dots, N)$ can then be obtained by the linear combination of the corresponding K candidate sketch patches $\{\mathbf{y}_{i,1}, \mathbf{y}_{i,2}, \dots, \mathbf{y}_{i,K}\}$ weighted by the K-dimensional vector $\mathbf{w}_i$, where $w_{i,k}$ represents the weight of the kth candidate sketch patch as follows:

$$\mathbf{y}_i = \sum_{k=1}^{K} w_{i,k} \mathbf{y}_{i,k} \tag{6.16}$$

where $\sum_{k=1}^{K} w_{i,k} = 1$.

To estimate the weights of the candidate sketch patches and generate a target sketch of high quality, we need to jointly model all the patches using the Markov network framework, similar to [21, 24, 32] and [29]. Since the target sketch patches are only dependent on the weights, as shown in Eq. (6.16), the joint probability of the input photo patches and the target sketch patches is equal to that of the input photo patches and the weights. It is defined as

$$\begin{aligned} & p(\mathbf{y}_1, \dots, \mathbf{y}_N, \mathbf{x}_1, \dots, \mathbf{x}_N) \\ = \; & p(\mathbf{w}_1, \dots, \mathbf{w}_N, \mathbf{x}_1, \dots, \mathbf{x}_N) \\ = \; & \prod_i \Phi(\mathbf{f}(\mathbf{x}_i), \mathbf{f}(\mathbf{w}_i)) \prod_{(i,j)\in \Xi} \Psi(\mathbf{w}_i, \mathbf{w}_j) \end{aligned} \tag{6.17}$$

where, $(i,j) \in \Xi$ means that the ith image patch and the jth image patch are neighbors, $\Phi(\mathbf{f}(\mathbf{x}_i), \mathbf{f}(\mathbf{w}_i))$ is the local evidence function, and $\Psi(\mathbf{w}_i, \mathbf{w}_j)$ is the neighboring compatibility function. In the local evidence function, $\mathbf{f}(\mathbf{x}_i) = [\mathbf{f}_1(\mathbf{x}_i), \mathbf{f}_2(\mathbf{x}_i), \dots, \mathbf{f}_L(\mathbf{x}_i)]$, where $\mathbf{f}_l(\mathbf{x}_i)$ means the lth representation of the photo patch $\mathbf{x}_i$, and $\mathbf{f}(\mathbf{w}_i) = [\mathbf{f}_1(\mathbf{w}_i), \mathbf{f}_2(\mathbf{w}_i), \dots, \mathbf{f}_L(\mathbf{w}_i)]$ in which $\mathbf{f}_l(\mathbf{w}_i) = \sum_{k=1}^{K} w_{i,k} \mathbf{f}_l(\mathbf{x}_{i,k})$.

$\Phi(\mathbf{f}(\mathbf{x}_i), \mathbf{f}(\mathbf{w}_i))$ can be represented as

$$\begin{aligned} & \Phi(\mathbf{f}(\mathbf{x}_i), \mathbf{f}(\mathbf{w}_i)) \\ \propto \; & exp\{-\sum_{l=1}^{L} \mu_{i,l} \|\mathbf{f}_l(\mathbf{x}_i) - \sum_{k=1}^{K} w_{i,k} \mathbf{f}_l(\mathbf{x}_{i,k})\|^2 / 2\delta_{\Phi}^2\} \end{aligned} \tag{6.18}$$

where $\mu_i = [\mu_{i,1}, \mu_{i,2}, \dots, \mu_{i,L}]$. $\mu_{i,l}$ represents the weight of the distance of the lth representation between the ith photo patch $\mathbf{f}_l(\mathbf{x}_i)$ and the combination of its candidates. The rationale behind the local evidence function is that if $\sum_{k=1}^{K} w_{i,k}\mathbf{y}_{i,k}$ is a good estimation of $\mathbf{y}_i$, $\mathbf{f}_l(\sum_{k=1}^{K} w_{i,k}\mathbf{x}_{i,k})$ should be similar to $\mathbf{f}_l(\mathbf{x}_i)$. In order to exploit the relationship between the target image patch and its candidate image patches represented by multiple representations, we simply assume that $\sum_{k=1}^{K} w_{i,k}\mathbf{f}_l(\mathbf{x}_{i,k})$ should also be similar to $\mathbf{f}_l(\mathbf{x}_i)$ here, which is easier to be optimized, too.

The neighboring compatibility function $\Psi(\mathbf{w}_i, \mathbf{w}_j)$ is defined as

$$\begin{aligned} &\Psi(\mathbf{w}_i, \mathbf{w}_j) \\ \propto \;& exp\{-\|\sum_{k=1}^{K} w_{i,k}\mathbf{o}_{i,k}^{j} - \sum_{k=1}^{K} w_{j,k}\mathbf{o}_{j,k}^{i}\|^2/2\delta_{\Psi}^2\} \end{aligned} \tag{6.19}$$

where $\mathbf{o}_{i,k}^{j}$ represents the overlapping area of the candidate sketch patch $\mathbf{y}_{i,k}$ with the jth patch. This term is utilized to guarantee that neighboring patches have compatible overlaps. In Eqs. (6.18) and (6.19), δ_{Φ} and δ_{Ψ} are two parameters balancing the local evidence function and the neighboring compatibility function separately.

To avoid the weight of multiple representations overfitting to one representation [9], a regularization term $exp\{-\lambda_i\|\mu_i\|^2\}$ is added to the joint probability in Eq. (6.17):

$$\begin{aligned} & p(\mathbf{y}_1, \dots, \mathbf{y}_N, \mathbf{x}_1, \dots, \mathbf{x}_N) \\ = \;& p(\mathbf{w}_1, \dots, \mathbf{w}_N, \mathbf{x}_1, \dots, \mathbf{x}_N) \\ = \;& \prod_{(i,j)\in\Xi} \Psi(\mathbf{w}_i, \mathbf{w}_j) \prod_i \Phi(\mathbf{f}(\mathbf{w}_i), \mathbf{f}(\mathbf{x}_i)) \prod_i exp\{-\lambda_i\|\mu_i\|^2\} \end{aligned} \tag{6.20}$$

where $\mu_i = [\mu_{i,1}, \mu_{i,2}, \dots, \mu_{i,L}]$ and λ_i balances the regularization term with the other two terms. To obtain the optimal weights for sketch synthesis, we need to maximize the joint probability in the above equation. The optimization problem could be solved in an alternative manner similar as that described in the aforementioned transductive method. The proposed approach is outlined in Fig. 6.7.

6.5 Experimental Results

We conduct experiments on the CUHK face sketch database (CUFS) [24]. The CUHK face sketch database consists of 606 sketches corresponding to 606 faces collected from the CUHK student database (including 188 photos), the AR database (including 123 photos) [13], and the XM2VTS database (including 295 photos) [14]. Examples of CUFS database are shown in Fig. 6.8.

For the synthesis purpose, in the CUHK student database, we choose 88 sketch–photo pairs for training and the rest 100 pairs for testing. In the AR database, a leave-one-out likelihood strategy is adopted in which we leave 23 out. In the XM2VTS database, 100 sketch-photo pairs are collected as the training set and the rest as the

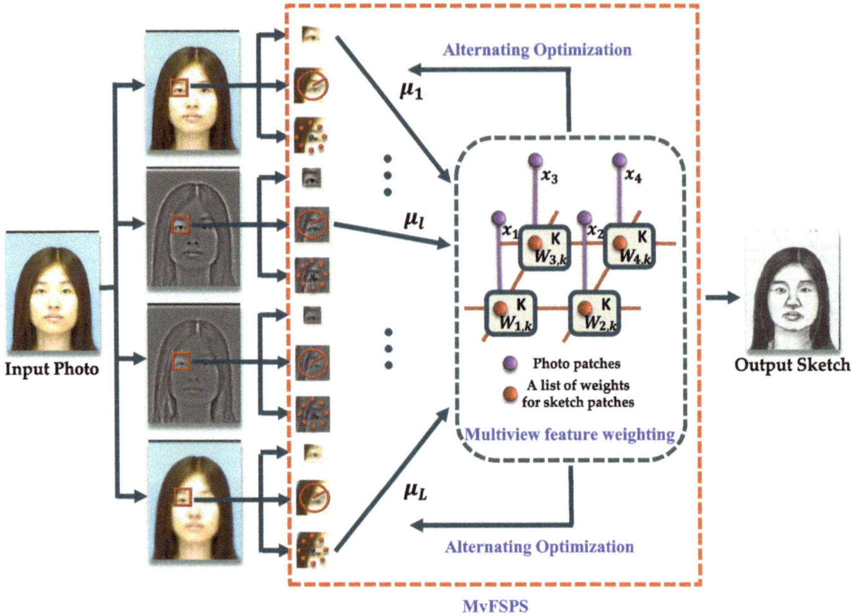

Fig. 6.7 The framework of the proposed multiple representations based face sketch synthesis

Fig. 6.8 Examples used in experiments: the two leftmost columns come from the CUHK student database, the second two columns come from the AR database, and the two rightmost columns come from XM2VTS database

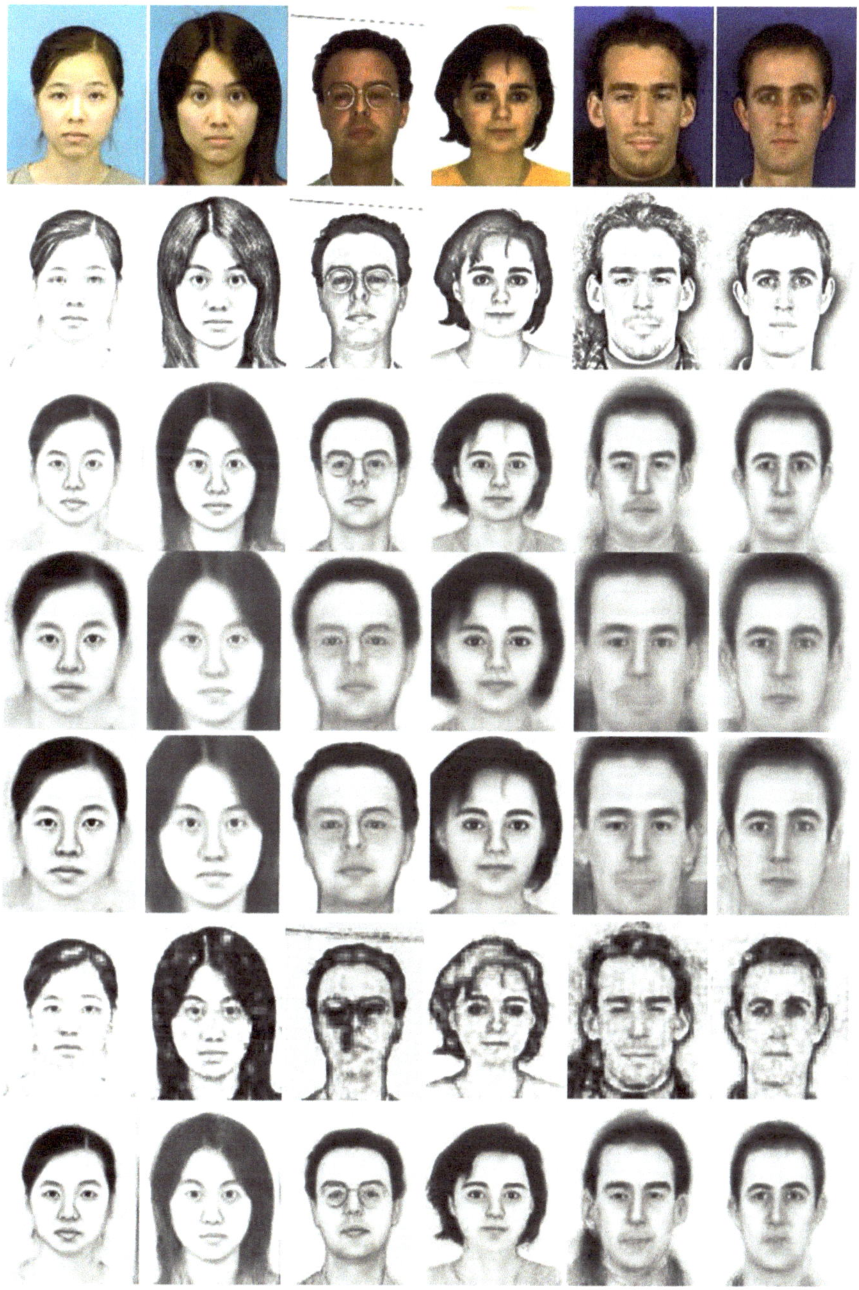

Fig. 6.9 Comparison of the Meitu software, the approaches [6, 15, 21, 28, 32]. Top row: input photos. Second row: results of Meitu software. Third row: results of method [15]. Fourth row: results of method [6]. Fifth row: results of method [20]. Sixth row: results of method [28]. Last row: results of method [21]

test set. As a result, we totally possess 418 synthesized images (photo or sketch) which include 100 from the CUHK student database, 123 from the AR database and 195 from the XM2VTS database. Some synthesized sketches and photos are shown in Figs. 6.9 and 6.10.

We performed face sketch recognition on the three databases together in the following two ways: (a) first transform all face photos in the gallery to sketches using our proposed face sketch synthesis method, and then a query sketch is identified from the synthesized gallery sketches; (b) first transform the query sketch to a photo exploiting the above synthesis method by switching the role of sketches and photos, and subsequently, match the synthesized photo to the gallery photo to identify the

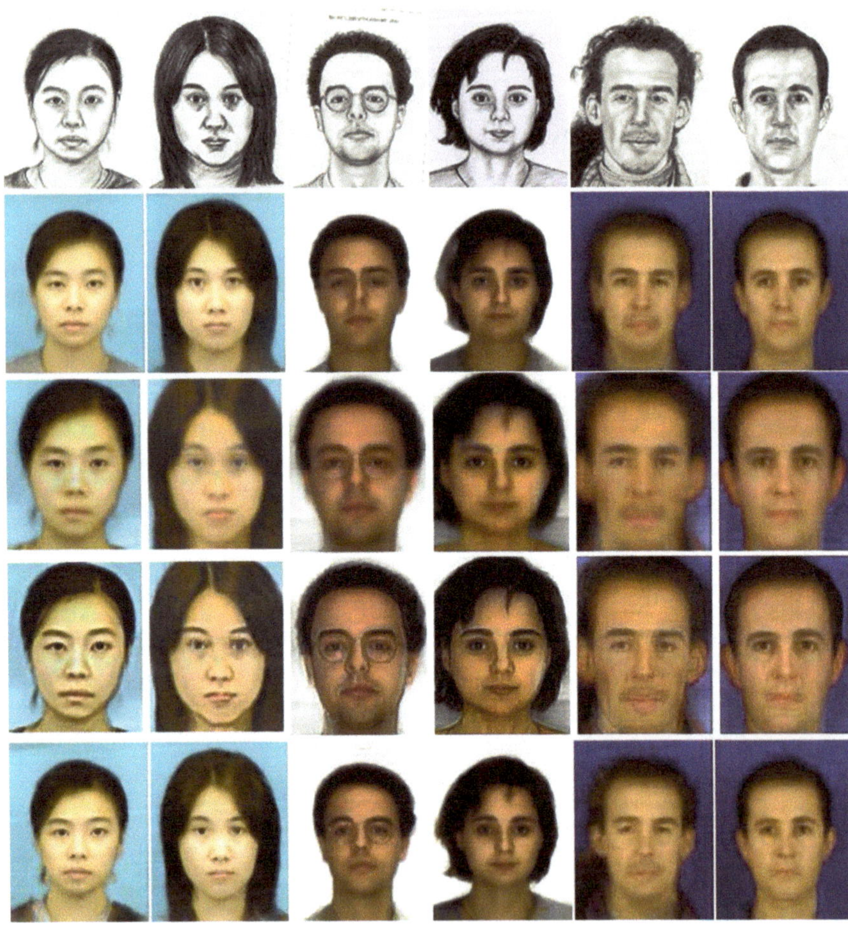

Fig. 6.10 Comparison of the approaches [6, 15, 21, 32]. Top row: input sketches. Second row: results of method [15]. Third row: results of method [6]. Fourth row: results of method [20]. Last row: results of method [21]

Table 6.1 Synthesized sketch based rank one recognition accuracy using different synthesis methods and face recognition approaches (%). The number in the bracket is the dimension at which the corresponding recognition method achieves the best recognition accuracy

	Meitu	MrFSS	SFS	SFS-SVR	SRGS	TFSPS
Eigenface [19]	40.24 (173)	74.09 (155)	68.90 (165)	70.43 (178)	46.65 (156)	69.21(123)
NLDA [4]	71.65 (88)	92.38 (86)	86.89 (89)	82.93 (73)	73.78 (86)	83.84 (74)

Table 6.2 Synthesized photo based rank one recognition accuracy using different synthesis methods and face recognition approaches (%). The number in the bracket is the dimension at which the corresponding recognition method achieves the best recognition accuracy

	MrFSS	SFS	SFS-SVR	TFSPS
Eigenface [19]	41.16 (179)	52.44 (159)	66.46 (164)	56.40 (150)
NLDA [4]	69.82 (87)	64.63 (83)	82.01 (89)	81.10 (84)

person. For strategy (a), we will obtain 418 pairs of pseudo-sketch and corresponding original sketch. These 418 pairs are separated into tow subsets. Subset 1 containing 90 pairs (30 pairs come from above three databases respectively) is used for training the classifiers. Subset 2 consists of the remaining 328 pairs and is taken as the test set. For strategy (b), we will obtain 418 pairs of pseudo-photo and corresponding original photo instead and then perform face sketch recognition similar to strategy (a). We apply two face recognition methods to perform face recognition: Eigenface [19] and Null-space LDA (NLDA) [4]. Tables 6.1 and 6.2 compare the recognition accuracies of different synthesis methods Meitu, [6, 15, 20, 21, 28].

6.6 Conclusion

This chapter mainly introduces some data-driven face sketch synthesis methods for sketch-based face recognition. Theoretically, model-based methods can possess a fast generation process because it exploits the learnt mapping function to evaluate the target sketch which inevitably looks less stylistic than the one generated by data-driven methods. Data-driven methods can preserve sketch style well since it directly applies the training samples to synthesize the target sketch. However, the computational time in synthesis- based generation model grows linearly with the amounts of training samples. Among data-driven approaches, graphical representation based methods could achieve more satisfying visual perception than other methods.

Acknowledgements This work was supported in part by the National Natural Science Foundation of China (under Grant 61501339 and 61671339).

References

1. Baker S, Kanade T (2002) Limits on super-resolution and how to break them. IEEE Trans Pattern Anal Mach Intell 24(9):1167–1183
2. Chang L, Zhou M, Deng X, Han Y (2011) Face sketch synthesis via multivariate output regression. In: Proceedings of international conference on human-computer interaction, pp 555–561
3. Chang L, Zhou M, Han Y, Deng X (2010) Face sketch synthesis via sparse representation. In: Proceedings of international conference on pattern recognition, pp 2146–2149
4. Chen L, Liao H, Ko M, Lin J, Yu G (2000) A new lda-based face recognition system which can solve the small sample size problem. Pattern Recognit 33(10):1713–1726
5. Elad M, Aharon M (2006) Image denoising via sparse and redundant representations over learned dictionaries. IEEE Trans Image Process 15(12):3736–3745
6. Gao X, Wang N, Tao D, Li X (2012) Face sketch-photo synthesis and retrieval using sparse representation. IEEE Trans Circuits Syst Video Technol 22(8):1213–1226
7. Gao X, Zhong J, Li J, Tian C (2008) Face sketch synthesis algorithm using e-hmm and selective ensemble. IEEE Trans Circuits Syst Video Technol 18(4):487–496
8. Gao X, Zhong J, Tao D, Li X (2008) Local face sketch synthesis learning. Neurocomputing 71(10–12):1921–1930
9. Geng B, Tao D, Xu C, Yang L, Hua X (2012) Ensemble manifold regularization. IEEE Trans Pattern Anal Mach Intell 34(6):1227–1233
10. Li X, Cao X (2012) A simple framework for face photo-sketch synthesis. Math Probl Eng:1–19
11. Liu Q, Tang X, Jin H, Lu H, Ma S (2005) A nonlinear approach for face sketch synthesis and recognition. In: Proceedings of IEEE conference on computer vision and pattern recognition, pp 1005–1010
12. Mairal J, Sapiro G, Elad M (2008) Learning multiscale sparse representations for image and video restoration. SIAM Multiscale Model Simul 17:214–241
13. Martinez A, Benavente R (1998) The ar face database. Technical report, CVC Technical Report #24
14. Messer K, Matas J, Kittler J, Luettin J, Maitre G (1999) Xm2vtsdb: the extended m2vts database. In: Proceedings of international conference on audio- and video-based biometric person authentication, pp 72–77
15. Peng C, Gao X, Wang N, Tao D, Li X, Li J (2015) Multiple representations based face sketch-photo synthesis. IEEE Trans Neural Netw Learn Syst:1–13
16. Tang X, Wang X (2002) Face photo recognition using sketches. In: Proceedings of IEEE international conference on image processing, pp 257–260
17. Tang X, Wang X (2003) Face sketch synthesis and recognition. In: Proceedings of IEEE international conference on computer vision, pp 687–694
18. Tang X, Wang X (2004) Face sketch recognition. IEEE Trans Circuits Syst Video Technol 14(1):1–7
19. Turk M, Pentland A (1991) Face recognition using eigenfaces. In: Proceedings of IEEE conference on computer vision and pattern recognition, pp 586–591
20. Wang N, Li J, Tao D, Li X, Gao X (2013) Heterogeneous image transformation. Pattern Recognit Lett 34(1):77–84
21. Wang N, Tao D, Gao X, Li X, Li J (2013) Transductive face sketch-photo synthesis. IEEE Trans Neural Netw Learn Syst 24(9):1364–1376
22. Wang N, Tao D, Gao X, Li X, Li J (2014) A comprehensive survey to face hallucination. Int J Comput Vision 106(1):9–30
23. Wang S, Zhang L, Liang Y, Pan Q (2012) Semi-coupled dictionary learning with applications to image super-resolution and photo-sketch synthesis. In: Proceedings of IEEE conference on computer vision and pattern recognition, pp 2216–2223
24. Wang X, Tang X (2009) Face photo-sketch synthesis and recognition. IEEE Trans Pattern Anal Mach Intell 31(11):1955–1967
25. Xiao B, Gao X, Tao D, Li X (2009) A new approach for face recognition by sketches in photos. Signal Process 89(8):1576–1588

26. Xiao B, Gao X, Tao D, Yuan Y, Li J (2010) Photo-sketch synthesis and recognition based on subspace learning. Neurocomputing 73(4–6):840–852
27. Yang J, Wright J, Huang T, Ma, Y.: Image super-resolution as sparse representation of raw image patches. In: Proceedings of IEEE conference on computer vision and pattern recognition, pp 1–8
28. Zhang S, Gao X, Wang N, Li J, Zhang M (2015) Face sketch synthesis via sparse representation-based greedy search. IEEE Trans Image Process 24(8):2466–2477
29. Zhang W, Wang X, Tang X (2010) Lighting and pose robust face sketch synthesis. In: Proceedings of European conference on computer vision, pp 420–423
30. Zhao W, Chellappa R, Phillips P, Rosenfeld A (2003) Face recognition: a literature survey. ACM Comput Surv 35(4):399–458
31. Zhong J, Gao X, Tian C (2007) Face sketch synthesis using e-hmm and selective ensemble. In: Proceedings of IEEE international conference on acoustics, speech, and signal processing, pp 485–488
32. Zhou H, Kuang Z, Wong K (2012) Markov weight fields for face sketch synthesis. In: Proceedings of IEEE conference on computer vision and pattern recognition, pp 1091–1097

Chapter 7
Recent Developments in Video-Based Face Recognition

Jingxiao Zheng, Vishal M. Patel and Rama Chellappa

Abstract Face recognition with its wide range of commercial and law enforcement applications has been one of the most active areas of research in the field of computer vision and pattern recognition. Personal identification systems based on faces have the advantage that facial images can be obtained from a distance without requiring cooperation of the subject, as compared to other biometrics such as fingerprint, iris, etc. Face recognition is concerned with identifying or verifying one or more persons from still images or video sequences using a stored database of faces. Depending on the particular application, there can be different scenarios, ranging from controlled still images to uncontrolled videos. Since face recognition is essentially the problem of recognizing a 3D object from its 2D image or a video sequence, it has to deal with significant appearance changes due to illumination and pose variations. Current algorithms perform well in controlled scenarios, but their performance is far from satisfactory in uncontrolled scenarios. Most of the current research in this area is focused toward recognizing faces in uncontrolled scenarios. This chapter presents an overview of recent video-based face recognition methods. In particular, recent sparse coding-based, manifold-based, probabilistic, geometric model-based, and dynamic model-based methods are reviewed.

J. Zheng · R. Chellappa (✉)
Center for Automation Research, University of Maryland,
College Park, MD 20742, USA
e-mail: rama@umiacs.umd.edu

J. Zheng
e-mail: jxzheng@umiacs.umd.edu

V.M. Patel
Rutgers, The State University of New Jersey,
94 Brett Road, Piscataway, NJ 08854, USA
e-mail: vishal.m.patel@rutgers.edu

M. Tistarelli and C. Champod (eds.), *Handbook of Biometrics for Forensic Science*, Advances in Computer Vision and Pattern Recognition,
DOI 10.1007/978-3-319-50673-9_7

7.1 Introduction

Video-based face recognition has received a significant amount of attention in recent years. This is mainly due to the fact that large amounts of video data are becoming available everyday. Millions of cameras have been installed in buildings, streets, and airports around the world, and people are using billions of handheld devices that are capable of capturing videos. As a result, 350 million photos are uploaded to Facebook every day and 100 h of video are uploaded to YouTube each minute.

For video-based face recognition problem, the identification and verification tasks are all based on videos rather than still images compared to the classical image-based face recognition problem. Approaches for video-based face recognition need to identify a person in a video, given some possible candidates, or to decide whether the two people in two different videos are the same person.

In most of the video-based face recognition methods, given video data, tracking algorithms like [38] are first used to detect faces in the video frames. Then fiducial extraction methods like [47] are applied to align the detected faces. After the alignment, traditional feature extraction techniques such as SIFT [30], HoG [14], LBP [31] or the very popular DCNN features [26, 35, 36] are used to extract features for matching.

In video-based face recognition, a key challenge is in exploiting the extra information available in a video, e.g., face, body, and motion identity cues. In addition, different video sequences of the same subject may contain variations in resolution, illumination, pose, and facial expressions. These variations contribute to the challenges in designing an effective video-based face recognition algorithm. Whether the temporal information is considered or not, most video-based face recognition can be divided into sequence-based methods or set-based methods. Sequence-based face recognition methods consider the video as a sequence of images and make use of the temporal information for recognition. On the other hand, set-based face recognition methods only consider the video as a set of images and ignore their order.

Besides using temporal information, video-based face recognition can also be sorted by the techniques used to model the video. These include sparse coding-based methods, manifold-based methods, probabilistic methods, geometrical model-based methods, and dynamical model-based methods. In this chapter, we give an overview of some of these modeling approaches.

7.2 Sparse Coding-Based Methods

For sparse coding-based methods, faces (or features extracted from faces) in videos are modeled as dictionaries, which are overcomplete atoms learned from the training data with sparsity constraints.

Given L video frames with faces of dimension M concatenated in a matrix $\mathbf{Y} = [\mathbf{y}_1, \dots, \mathbf{y}_L] \in \mathbb{R}^{M \times L}$, the problem of learning a dictionary, which minimizes

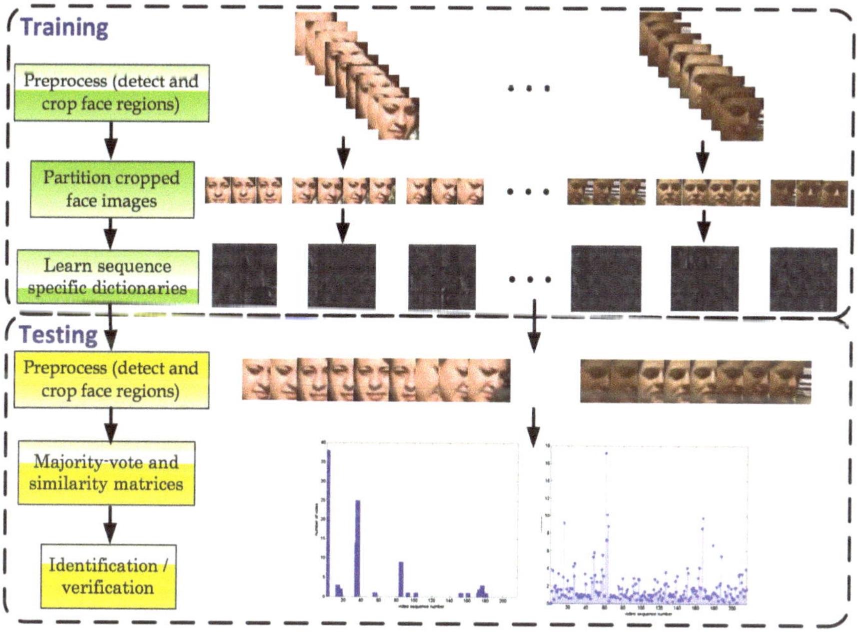

Fig. 7.1 Dictionary-based face recognition from video [12]

the representation error with a sparseness constraint is equivalent to solving the following optimization problem

$$\min_{\mathbf{D},\mathbf{X}} \|\mathbf{Y} - \mathbf{D}\mathbf{X}\|_F^2 \ \text{ s.t } \ \|\mathbf{x_i}\|_0 \leq T, \ \ \mathbf{d}_i^T\mathbf{d}_i = 1 \quad \forall i, \tag{7.1}$$

where $\|\cdot\|_F$ is the Frobenius norm, $\|\mathbf{x}\|_0$ is the ℓ_0 norm of $\mathbf{x}$ which counts the number of nonzero elements in $\mathbf{x}$, $\mathbf{D} = [\mathbf{d}_1, \ldots, \mathbf{d}_S] \in \mathbb{R}^{M\times S}$ is the dictionary, $\mathbf{X} = [\mathbf{x}_1, \ldots, \mathbf{x}_N] \in \mathbb{R}^{S\times N}$ is the corresponding collection of sparse coefficients, S is the number of atoms in the dictionary, and T is a sparsity parameter. Because of the sparsity constraint, the learned dictionaries are robust to different kinds of variations in video sequences.

[12] proposed a generative dictionary learning method for video-based face recognition. The main idea of the method is to partition the video frames into clusters with different poses and illuminations and learn a set of sub-dictionaries for each cluster. Then the concatenation of the sub-dictionaries removes the temporal redundancy in the videos and can handle large variations on poses and illumination variations. An overview of this method is shown in Fig. 7.1.

For each frame in a video sequence, the face regions are first detected and cropped. Then all the cropped face images are partitioned into K different partitions by a K-means clustering type of algorithm. For each partition, a dictionary is learned with the minimum representation error under a sparseness constraint using (7.1).

Thus, there will be K sub-dictionaries built to represent a video sequence. Then the video sequence-specific dictionary is constructed by concatenating these partition-level sub-dictionaries as $\mathbf{D}_p = [\mathbf{D}_p^1, \mathbf{D}_p^2, \ldots, \mathbf{D}_p^K]$. Due to changes in pose and lighting in a video sequence, the number of face images in a partition will vary. Those partitions with very few images will be augmented by synthesized face images. This is done by creating horizontally, vertically, or diagonally position shifted face images, or by in-plane rotated face images.

For identification task, testing videos are partitioned into K partitions as well. Given a testing frame $\mathbf{q}_{l,k}$ from the kth partition, the frame-level decision $\hat{p}_{l,k}$ is the sequence p with the minimum residual error from its projection onto the subspace spaned by $\mathbf{D}_p$ as

$$\hat{p}_{l,k} = \underset{p}{\operatorname{argmin}} \|\mathbf{q}_{l,k} - \mathbf{D}_p \mathbf{D}_p^{\dagger} \mathbf{q}_{l,k}\|_2 \tag{7.2}$$

The sequence-level decision $\hat{p}$ is then the weighted sum of votes from K partitions as

$$\hat{p} = \underset{i}{\operatorname{argmax}} \sum_{k=1}^{K} w_k \sum_{l} \mathbf{1}\{\hat{p}_{l,k} = i\} \tag{7.3}$$

For verification task, given a query video sequence m and gallery video sequence p (with learned dictionary $\mathbf{D}_p$), the similarity score is

$$\mathbf{R}^{m,p} = \min_{k} \min_{l} \|\mathbf{q}_{l,k}^{m} - \mathbf{D}_p \mathbf{D}_p^{\dagger} \mathbf{q}_{l,k}^{m}\|_2. \tag{7.4}$$

which is the minimum residual among all l and all k, between the frames from query video sequence m and gallery dictionary $\mathbf{D}_p$.

[11] further introduced the joint sparsity constraints into their dictionary learning algorithm. Given video frames sets $\{\mathbf{Y}^k\}$, instead of learning dictionaries from each frame partition independently as

$$\min_{\mathbf{D}^k, \mathbf{X}^k} \|\mathbf{Y}^k - \mathbf{D}^k \mathbf{X}^k\|_F^2 \ \text{ s.t } \ \|\mathbf{x}_\mathbf{i}^\mathbf{k}\|_0 \le T, \ \ \mathbf{d}_i^{kT} \mathbf{d}_i^k = 1 \quad \forall i \tag{7.5}$$

based on the joint sparse constraints, the dictionaries are learned jointly as

$$\min_{\{\mathbf{D}^k\}, \mathbf{X}} \frac{1}{2} \sum_{k=1}^{K} \|\mathbf{Y}^k - \mathbf{D}^k \mathbf{X}^k\|_F^2 + \lambda \|\mathbf{X}\|_{1,2} \ \text{ s.t } \ \mathbf{d}_i^{kT} \mathbf{d}_i^k = 1 \quad \forall i \tag{7.6}$$

where $\|\mathbf{X}\|_{1,2} = \sum_{i=1}^{d} \|\mathbf{x}_i\|_2$ is the sparse constraint on $\mathbf{X} = [\mathbf{X}^1, \ldots, \mathbf{X}^K]$. It enforces the sparse pattern for each column of $\mathbf{X}$ to be similar, which makes the learned dictionaries more robust to noise and occlusion. [11] also introduced a kernel version of their algorithm to deal with those non-linearly separable cases and improve the performance.

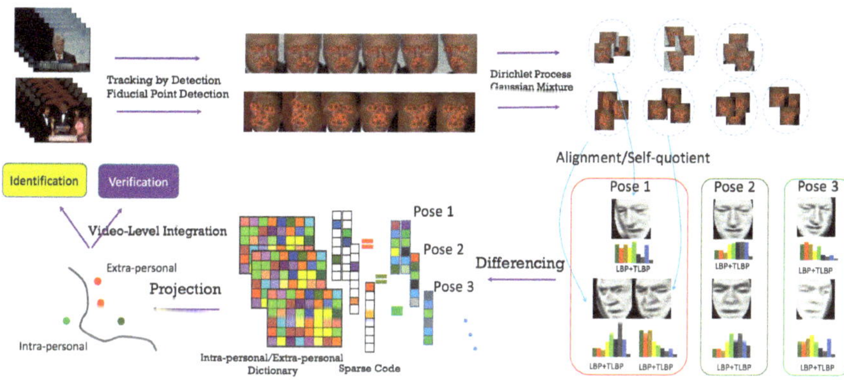

Fig. 7.2 Video-based face recognition using the intra/extrapersonal difference dictionary [16]

Du and Chellappa [16] proposed a video-based face recognition method based on intra/extrapersonal difference dictionary. Since pose variations often cause within-class variance to exceed between-class variance in face recognition, instead of learning dictionaries from the face features directly, pose-specific dictionaries are learned from those intra/extrapersonal difference features. Also, instead of learning generative dictionaries by merely minimizing the reconstruction error, it jointly learns dictionaries and discriminative projection matrices, which improves performance. The overall algorithm is shown in Fig. 7.2.

In their algorithm, given a video $\mathbf{V}$, faces are first detected and cropped from the videos by using a tracking algorithm. Fiducial points are then detected by a structural SVM approach. These cropped faces are aligned and clustered by the K-means algorithm into K clusters according to their poses. Then a given video can be characterized by its K cluster centers $\{\mathbf{v}_k, k = 1, 2, \ldots, K\}$ considered as representative images.

For the training videos, the intrapersonal difference features $\{\mathbf{x}_{In} = \mathbf{v}_i^m - \mathbf{v}_j^n, ID(\mathbf{V}_i) = ID(\mathbf{V}_j)\}$ and the extrapersonal ones $\{\mathbf{x}_{Ex} = \mathbf{v}_i^m - \mathbf{v}_j^n, ID(\mathbf{V}_i) \neq ID(\mathbf{V}_j)\}$ are employed to learn the dictionary $\mathbf{D}$ and the projection matrix $\mathbf{W}$ simultaneously for each pair of poses by solving the following Label-Consistent K-SVD problem (LC-K-SVD):

$$\min_{\mathbf{D},\mathbf{A}} \|\mathbf{X} - \mathbf{D}\mathbf{A}\|_2^2 + \mu\|\mathbf{Q} - \mathbf{B}\mathbf{A}\|_2^2 + \sigma\|\mathbf{F} - \mathbf{W}\mathbf{A}\|_2^2 + \lambda \sum_i \|\boldsymbol{\alpha}_i\|_1, \qquad (7.7)$$

where $\mathbf{X} = \left[\mathbf{X}_{In}\ \mathbf{X}_{Ex}\right]$ is the concatenation of intrapersonal and extrapersonal features. The columns of $\mathbf{F} \in \mathbb{R}^{2\times N}$ are the corresponding labels (same or different), represented using the 1-of-K coding scheme. It enforces $\mathbf{W}$ to encode discriminative information from the sparse codes. $\mathbf{B} \in \mathbb{R}^{K\times d}$ is a linear transformation that encourages the samples from the same class to be reconstructed using the entries in the sub-dictionary of that class. $\mathbf{Q} \in \mathbb{R}^{K\times N}$ has a block diagonal form: The c-th block contains entry $\mathbf{Q}_{ij}$, $i \in v_c$, $j \in h_c$, where v_c are the indices of atoms from class c

(i.e., intrapersonal or extrapersonal) and h_c are the indices of training instances from class c. All the nonzero entries in $\mathbf{Q}$ are assigned with unit value. This problem can be converted to a typical K-SVD [3] objective function and solved using the same procedure.

At the testing stage, for every probe-gallery video pair $\{\mathbf{V}_p, \mathbf{V}g\}$, feature difference vectors $\{\mathbf{x}_{p,g}^{m,n} = \mathbf{v}_p^m - \mathbf{v}_g^n\}$ from each pair of poses are calculated. The sparse representation of $\mathbf{x}_{p,g}^{m,n}$ is obtained by solving $\boldsymbol{\alpha}_{p,g}^{m,n} = \operatorname{argmin}_{\boldsymbol{\alpha}} \sum_{i=1}^{N} \frac{1}{2}\|\mathbf{x}_{p,g}^{m,n} - \mathbf{D}\boldsymbol{\alpha}\|_2^2 + \lambda\|\boldsymbol{\alpha}\|_1$ using the learned dictionary $\mathbf{D}$ in the training stage. The similarity score for this video pair is then calculated as

$$s(p,g) = \sum_{m=1}^{M}\sum_{n=1}^{N} \mathbf{1}(\mathbf{t}_1\mathbf{W}\boldsymbol{\alpha}_{p,g}^{m,n} > \mathbf{t}_0\mathbf{W}\boldsymbol{\alpha}_{p,g}^{m,n})/MN \tag{7.8}$$

where $\mathbf{t}_0 = [0, 1]^T$ and $\mathbf{t}_1 = [1, 0]^T$ are the 1-of-K coding label for intrapersonal and extrapersonal class, respectively. For video-based recognition, the decision is made by $ID(\mathbf{V}_p) = \operatorname{argmax}_g s(p, g)$.

Some of the other sparse dictionary learning-based methods for video-based face recognition include [18, 32].

7.3 Manifold-Based Methods

In manifold-based methods, videos are usually modeled as image sets. These image sets are considered as the approximation of manifolds and the problem actually turns into looking for a discriminant distance metric between manifolds. The basic idea is shown in Fig. 7.3.

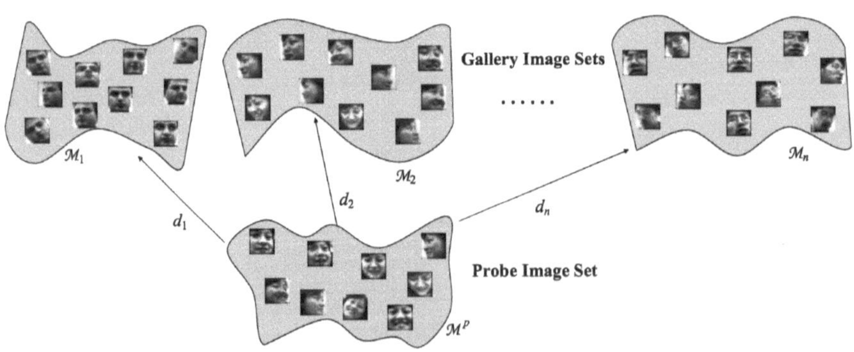

Fig. 7.3 Manifold-based face recognition [41]

In [41], the image set classification problem is based on the computation of manifold–manifold distance. It models the image sets cropped from videos as manifolds which consist of component linear subspaces. Then the manifold-to-manifold distance can be considered as the similarity between two videos.

Given face image set $X = \{\mathbf{x}_1, \mathbf{x}_2, \ldots, \mathbf{x}_N\}$ from a video, it is partitioned into a collection of disjoint Maximal Linear Patches $\{C_i\}$. Each video is considered as a manifold consisting of these local linear patches which can be obtained by Algorithm 1.

Algorithm 1 Local model construction.

1. Initialize that $i = 1, C_i = \emptyset, X_T = \emptyset, X_R = X$.
2. While($X_R \neq \emptyset$)

   2.1 Randomly select a seed point from X_R as $\mathbf{x}_1^{(i)}$, update $C_i = \{\mathbf{x}_1^{(i)}\}, X_R = X_R - \{\mathbf{x}_1^{(i)}\}$.

   2.2 For $(\forall \mathbf{x}_m^{(i)} \in C_i)$
   Identify each of its k-NNs $\mathbf{x}_c$ as *candidate*. If $\mathbf{x}_c$ satisfies simultaneously $\mathbf{x}_c \in X_R$ and

   $$D_G(\mathbf{x}_c, \mathbf{x}_n^{(i)})/D_E(\mathbf{x}_c, \mathbf{x}_n^{(i)}) < \theta, \ \forall \mathbf{x}_n^{(i)} \in C_i \tag{7.9}$$

   then update $C_i = C_i \cup \{\mathbf{x}_c\}, X_R = X_R - \{\mathbf{x}_c\}$, until no candidate point can be added into C_i.

   2.3 $X_T = \cup_{j=1}^{i} C_j, X_R = X - X_T, i = i + 1, C_i = \emptyset$.

Here, $D_E(\cdot)$ denotes the Euclidean distance and $D_G(\cdot)$ denotes the geodesic distance. Their ratio reflects the linear deviation of the local linear subspace. Threshold θ controls the degree of linear deviation. Thus larger θ implies fewer local structures but large linear deviation in each structure. After obtaining the local linear subspaces for each video, the manifold-manifold distance between two video manifolds M_1 and M_2 can be computed as

$$d(M_1, M_2) = \min_{C_i \in M_1} \min_{C_j \in M_2} d(C_i, C_j) \tag{7.10}$$

which is the distance between the closest local subspace pair.

Suppose $\mathbf{e}_i$, $\mathbf{e}_j$ and $\mathbf{P}_i \in \mathbb{R}^{D \times d_1}$, $\mathbf{P}_j \in \mathbb{R}^{D \times d_2}$ are the exemplars (means) and orthonormal bases of two subspaces C_i and C_j. $r = \min(d_i, d_j)$. The SVD of $\mathbf{P}_1^T \mathbf{P}_2$ is $\mathbf{P}_1^T \mathbf{P}_2 = \mathbf{Q}_{12} \mathbf{\Lambda} \mathbf{Q}_{21}^T$ and $\mathbf{\Lambda} = diag(\sigma_1, \ldots, \sigma_r)$. The distance between two local subspace is defined as

$$d(C_i, C_j) = (1 - \alpha) d_E(C_i, C_j) + \alpha d_V(C_i, C_j). \tag{7.11}$$

Here, $d_E(C_i, C_j) = \|\mathbf{e}_i\| \|\mathbf{e}_j\| / \mathbf{e}_i^T \mathbf{e}_j$ is called the *exemplar distance measure*, which measures how similar the two sets are. $d_V(C_i, C_j) = r / \sum_{k=1}^{r} \sigma_k$ is called the *variation distance measure* which measures how close the common variation modes of the two sets. By fusing these distance measures, the overall manifold–manifold

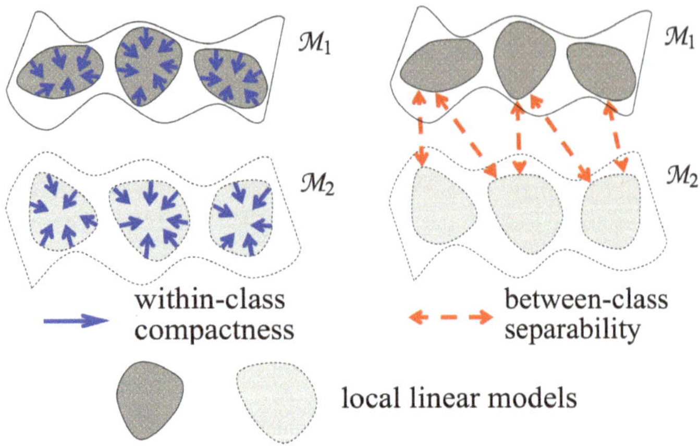

Fig. 7.4 Manifold discriminant analysis [39]

distance captures the difference of both average appearance and variation information between two sets.

Finally, for verification task, the similarity score between any gallery and probe video pair is the manifold–manifold distance between their corresponding manifolds. For identification task, decision is made by finding the video with the minimum manifold–manifold distance.

A manifold-based discriminative learning method called Manifold Discriminant Analysis for image set classification was proposed in [39]. It learns an embedding space where manifolds with different class labels are better separated and local data compactness within each manifold is enhanced. An overview of this method is shown in Fig. 7.4.

Like [41], given image sets considered as manifolds, local linear models are first extracted as $M_i = \{C_{i,k}\}$. The learning method is formulated as:

1. Two graphs are constructed, which are intrinsic graph G and penalty graph G'. In both graphs, nodes are all the images in the training set $\mathbf{X} = \{\mathbf{x}_m\}$. In G, nodes $\mathbf{x}_m$ and $\mathbf{x}_n$ are connected if $\mathbf{x}_m \in C_{i,k}$, $\mathbf{x}_n \in C_{j,l}$, $i = j$ and $k = l$, which means only the nodes come from the same local linear model are connected. In G', nodes $\mathbf{x}_m$ and $\mathbf{x}_n$ are connected if their class labels are different and $C_{i,k}$ is among the k'-nearest between-class neighbors of $C_{j,l}$.
2. The weight matrix $\mathbf{W} = \{w_{mn}\}$ for G is computed as

$$w_{mn} = \begin{cases} 1 & \text{if } \mathbf{x}_m \text{ and } \mathbf{x}_n \text{ are connected} \\ 0 & \text{otherwise} \end{cases} \tag{7.12}$$

$\mathbf{W}'$ for G' is computed in the same way. $\mathbf{D}$ and $\mathbf{D}'$ are diagonal matrices with diagonal elements $d_{mm} = \sum_n w_{mn}$ and $d'_{mm} = \sum_n w'_{mn}$. $\mathbf{L}_w = \mathbf{D} - \mathbf{W}$ and $\mathbf{L}_b = \mathbf{D}' - \mathbf{W}'$ are their Laplacian matrices, respectively.

3. A linear embedding $\mathbf{z} = \mathbf{V}^T\mathbf{x}$ based on linear projection is learned, where $\mathbf{V} \in \mathbb{R}^{d \times l}$ with $l \ll d$. For each column of $\mathbf{V}$, learning is fulfilled by maximizing the between-class scatter $S_b = \sum_{m,n} \|\mathbf{v}^T\mathbf{x}_m - \mathbf{v}^T\mathbf{x}_n\|^2 w'_{m,n} = 2\mathbf{v}^T\mathbf{X}\mathbf{L}_b\mathbf{X}^T\mathbf{v}$ and minimizing the within-class scatter $S_w = \sum_{m,n} \|\mathbf{v}^T\mathbf{x}_m - \mathbf{v}^T\mathbf{x}_n\|^2 w_{m,n} = 2\mathbf{v}^T\mathbf{X}\mathbf{L}_w\mathbf{X}^T\mathbf{v}$. This is equivalent to solving the optimization problem:

$$\underset{\mathbf{v}}{\text{maximize}} = \frac{S_b}{S_w} = \frac{\mathbf{v}^T\mathbf{X}\mathbf{L}_b\mathbf{X}^T\mathbf{v}}{\mathbf{v}^T\mathbf{X}\mathbf{L}_w\mathbf{X}^T\mathbf{v}} \tag{7.13}$$

The columns of the optimal $\mathbf{V}$ are the generalized eigenvectors corresponding to the l largest eigenvalues in

$$\mathbf{X}\mathbf{L}_b\mathbf{X}^T\mathbf{v} = \lambda\mathbf{X}\mathbf{L}_w\mathbf{X}^T\mathbf{v}. \tag{7.14}$$

Finally, for verification task, given two manifolds M_k and M_l, their distance is calculated as $d(M_k, M_l) = \min_{i,j} d(C_{i,k}, C_{j,l})$, which is same as the manifold-to-manifold distance proposed in [41]. $d(C_{i,k}, C_{j,l}) = \|\mathbf{e}_{i,k} - \mathbf{e}_{j,l}\|$ is the *empirical distance* between each pair of local linear models, where $\mathbf{e}_{i,k} = \frac{1}{N_{i,k}} \sum_{n=1}^{N_{i,k}} \mathbf{V}^T\mathbf{x}_{i,k}^n$ is the sample mean of $C_{i,k}$ and $\mathbf{e}_{j,l} = \frac{1}{N_{j,l}} \sum_{n=1}^{N_{j,l}} \mathbf{V}^T\mathbf{x}_{j,l}^n$ is the sample mean of $C_{j,l}$, both in the learned embedding space.

Similarly, Wang et al. [40] proposed a discriminative learning approach for image set classification by modeling the image set using its covariance matrix. The conceptual illustration of this method is shown in Fig. 7.5.

Given face images from a video, $\mathbf{S} = [\mathbf{s}_1, \mathbf{s}_2, \ldots \mathbf{s}_n]$, the samples covariance of this image set is

$$\mathbf{C} = \frac{1}{n-1} \sum_{i=1}^{n} (\mathbf{s}_i - \bar{\mathbf{s}})(\mathbf{s}_i - \bar{\mathbf{s}})^T \tag{7.15}$$

where $\bar{\mathbf{s}}$ is the sample mean. The video is thus characterized by its covariance matrix $\mathbf{C}$. Since $\mathbf{C}$ is an SPD matrix, it lies on a Riemannian manifold. It is not easy to train a classifier on the manifold because most of the classic classifiers are

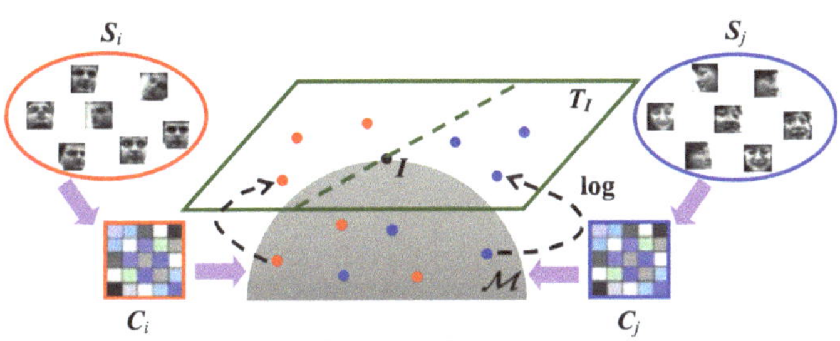

Fig. 7.5 Covariance discriminative learning [40]

designed for Euclidean metrics. In the paper, a distance metric, Log-Euclidean distance (LED) is introduced as $d_{LED}(\mathbf{C}_1, \mathbf{C}_2) = \|\log(\mathbf{C}_1) - \log(\mathbf{C}_2)\|_F$ where $\log(\cdot)$ here is the ordinary matrix logarithm operator. If $\mathbf{C} = \mathbf{U\Sigma U}^T$ is an SPD matrix, $\log(\mathbf{C}) = \mathbf{U}\log(\mathbf{\Sigma})\mathbf{U}^T$.

Given training videos $\{\mathbf{S}_i^{tr}\}$ from C different classes, first the covariance matrices $\{\mathbf{C}_i^{tr}\}$ are calculated. Then, two different learning methods are used:

1. Kernel LDA
   The KLDA optimization problem is:

$$\boldsymbol{\alpha}_{opt} = \underset{\boldsymbol{\alpha}}{\operatorname{argmax}} \frac{\boldsymbol{\alpha}^T\mathbf{KWK}\boldsymbol{\alpha}}{\boldsymbol{\alpha}^T\mathbf{KK}\boldsymbol{\alpha}}, \tag{7.16}$$

   where $\mathbf{K}_{ij} = k(\mathbf{S}_i^{tr}, \mathbf{S}_j^{tr}) = d_{LED}(\mathbf{C}_i^{tr}, \mathbf{C}_j^{tr})$. And $\mathbf{W}$ is defined as:

$$\mathbf{W}_{ij} = \begin{cases} 1/n_k & \text{if } \mathbf{S}_i^{tr}, \mathbf{S}_j^{tr} \text{ are both in the } k\text{th class} \\ 0 & \text{otherwise} \end{cases} \tag{7.17}$$

   and n_k is the number of videos in the kth class.
   The solution to (7.16) is the eigenvector corresponding to the largest eigenvalue of the problem $\mathbf{KWK}\boldsymbol{\alpha} = \lambda\mathbf{KK}\boldsymbol{\alpha}$. Then given a testing video $\mathbf{S}^{te}$ with its covariance matrix $\mathbf{S}^{te}$, its projection in the $C-1$ dimensional discriminant subspace is:

$$\mathbf{z}^{te} = \mathbf{A}^T\mathbf{K}^{te} \tag{7.18}$$

   where $\mathbf{A} = \left[\boldsymbol{\alpha}_1, \boldsymbol{\alpha}_2, \ldots, \boldsymbol{\alpha}_{C-1}\right]$ is the collection of $C-1$ largest eigenvectors and $\mathbf{K}^{te} = \left[k(\mathbf{S}_1^{tr}, \mathbf{S}^{te}), k(\mathbf{S}_2^{tr}, \mathbf{S}^{te}), \ldots\right]^T$. Nearest Neighbor classification in the discriminant subspace based on Euclidean distance is then performed.
2. Kernel PLS
   Different from KLDA, KPLS directly learns a regression model between training observations $\{\mathbf{S}_i^{tr}\}$ and their 1-of-K coding labels $\mathbf{Y}^{tr}$ (refer to [34] for more details). Then given testing video $\mathbf{S}^{te}$, its KPLS prediction is given by

$$\mathbf{y}^{te} = \mathbf{K}^{teT}\mathbf{U}(\mathbf{T}^T\mathbf{KU})^{-1}\mathbf{T}^T\mathbf{Y}^{tr} \tag{7.19}$$

   where $\mathbf{U}$ and $\mathbf{T}$ are regression parameters learned by KPLS, $\mathbf{K}$ and $\mathbf{K}^{te}$ are the same as in KLDA. The entry index with the largest response in $\mathbf{y}^{te}$ determines the label of the video.

Furthermore, [22] introduced a method that learns the projection metric directly on the Grassmann manifold rather than in Hilbert space. It performs a geometry-aware dimensionality reduction from the original Grassmann manifold to a lower dimensional, more discriminative Grassmann manifold. The method is demonstrated in Fig. 7.6.

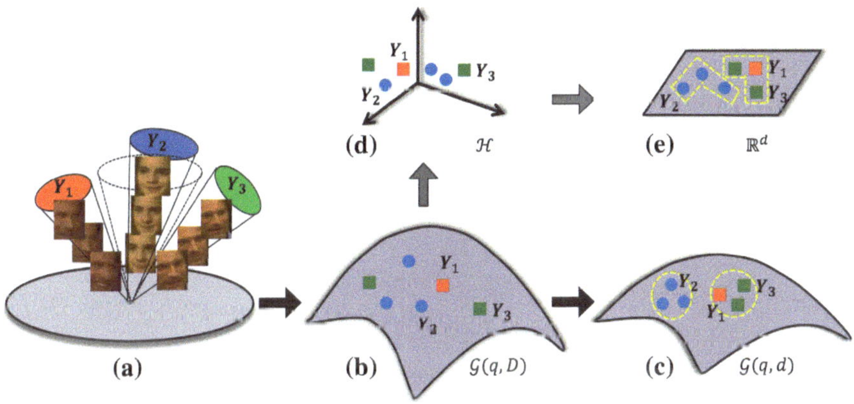

Fig. 7.6 Projection metric learning on Grassmann manifold [22]

Given face frames $\{\mathbf{X}_i\}$ from videos where $\mathbf{X}_i \in \mathbb{R}^{D\times n_i}$ describes a data matrix of the n_i frames from the ith video, $\mathbf{X}_i$ is represented by a q-dimensional linear subspace spanned by an orthonormal basis matrix $\mathbf{Y}_i \in \mathbb{R}^{D\times q}$. This is calculated by $\mathbf{X}_i\mathbf{X}_i^T \simeq \mathbf{Y}_i\mathbf{\Lambda}_i\mathbf{Y}_i^T$, $\mathbf{\Lambda}_i$ and $\mathbf{Y}_i$ correspond to the q largest eigenvalues and eigenvectors, respectively.

The linear subspace span$(\mathbf{Y}_i)$ lies on a Grassmann manifold $\mathcal{G}(q, D)$. It can be represented by the projection mapping $\Phi(\mathbf{Y}_i) = \mathbf{Y}_i\mathbf{Y}_i^T$ since there is a one-to-one mapping between each projection matrix and the point on the Grassmann manifold. The projection distance metric between $\mathbf{Y}_i\mathbf{Y}_i^T$ and $\mathbf{Y}_j\mathbf{Y}_j^T$ is defined as

$$d_p(\mathbf{Y}_i\mathbf{Y}_i^T, \mathbf{Y}_j\mathbf{Y}_j^T) = 2^{-1/2}\|\mathbf{Y}_i\mathbf{Y}_i^T - \mathbf{Y}_j\mathbf{Y}_j^T\|_F. \tag{7.20}$$

The method learns a mapping $f : \mathcal{G}(q, D) \to \mathcal{G}(q, d)$ which is defined as

$$f(\mathbf{Y}_i\mathbf{Y}_i^T) = \mathbf{W}^T\mathbf{Y}_i\mathbf{Y}_i^T\mathbf{W} = (\mathbf{W}^T\mathbf{Y}_i)(\mathbf{W}^T\mathbf{Y}_i)^T \tag{7.21}$$

where $\mathbf{W} \in \mathbb{R}^{D\times d}$ is the column full rank transformation matrix. Here, $\mathbf{W}^T\mathbf{Y}_i$ is not a orthonormal basis in general, which doesn't lie on a Grassmann manifold. Thus, $\mathbf{W}^T\mathbf{Y}_i$ is replace by $\mathbf{W}^T\mathbf{Y}_i'$, which is an orthonormal basis of $\mathbf{W}^T\mathbf{Y}_i$.

After transformation, the projection distance between $\mathbf{W}^T\mathbf{Y}_i'\mathbf{Y}_i'^T\mathbf{W}$ and $\mathbf{W}^T\mathbf{Y}_j'\mathbf{Y}_j'^T\mathbf{W}$ is

$$d_p^2(\mathbf{W}^T\mathbf{Y}_i'\mathbf{Y}_i'^T\mathbf{W}, \mathbf{W}^T\mathbf{Y}_j'\mathbf{Y}_j'^T\mathbf{W}) = \frac{1}{2}\|\mathbf{W}^T\mathbf{Y}_i'\mathbf{Y}_i'^T\mathbf{W} - \mathbf{W}^T\mathbf{Y}_j'\mathbf{Y}_j'^T\mathbf{W}\|_F^2 = \frac{1}{2}\mathrm{tr}(\mathbf{P}\mathbf{A}_{ij}\mathbf{A}_{ij}^T\mathbf{P}), \tag{7.22}$$

where $\mathbf{A}_{ij} = \mathbf{Y}_i'\mathbf{Y}_i'^T - \mathbf{Y}_j'\mathbf{Y}_j'^T$ and $\mathbf{P} = \mathbf{W}\mathbf{W}^T$, which is a rank-$d$ $D \times D$ PSD matrix.

The method learns $\mathbf{P}$ by minimizing the projection distances of any within-class subspace pairs and maximizing the projection distances of between-class subspace pairs. The corresponding objective function $J(\mathbf{P})$ is defined as

$$\mathbf{P}^* = \underset{\mathbf{P}}{\operatorname{argmin}}\, J(\mathbf{P}) = \underset{\mathbf{P}}{\operatorname{argmin}}(J_w(\mathbf{P}) - \alpha J_b(\mathbf{P})), \tag{7.23}$$

where α is the trade-off parameter between within-class scatter $J_w(\mathbf{P})$ and between-class scatter $J_b(\mathbf{P})$,

$$\begin{aligned} J_w(\mathbf{P}) &= \frac{1}{N_w} \sum_{i=1}^{m} \sum_{j:C_i=C_j} \operatorname{tr}(\mathbf{P}\mathbf{A}_{ij}\mathbf{A}_{ij}^T\mathbf{P}) = \operatorname{tr}(\mathbf{P}\mathbf{S}_w\mathbf{P}) \\ J_b(\mathbf{P}) &= \frac{1}{N_b} \sum_{i=1}^{m} \sum_{j:C_i \neq C_j} \operatorname{tr}(\mathbf{P}\mathbf{A}_{ij}\mathbf{A}_{ij}^T\mathbf{P})\operatorname{tr}(\mathbf{P}\mathbf{S}_b\mathbf{P}). \end{aligned} \tag{7.24}$$

Since $\mathbf{W}\mathbf{Y}_i'$ need to be orthogonal all the time, an algorithm is proposed to optimize $\mathbf{P}$ and solving $\mathbf{Y}_i'$ iteratively. In each iteration, $\mathbf{W}^T\mathbf{Y}_i$ is first decomposed into $\mathbf{W}^T\mathbf{Y}_i = \mathbf{Q}_i\mathbf{R}_i$ by QR-decomposition. $\mathbf{Y}_i'$ is normalized by $\mathbf{Y}_i' = \mathbf{Y}_i\mathbf{R}_i^{-1}$. Then $\mathbf{P}$ is solved using Riemannian Conjugate Gradient algorithm [1]. Finally, for verification task, given two videos, their projection distance in the low-dimensional space can be calculated using (7.22).

In [21] a hybrid metric learning method for image set-based face recognition was proposed, which is essentially an extension of [20]. The image sets are modeled simultaneously by mean, covariance matrix and Gaussian distribution and fused together for robustness. Another highlight of this paper is that the metrics are learned based on deep learning features. Combining set-based face recognition algorithm and the power of deep learning, the proposed method achieved state-of-the-art results in many challenging datasets. The conceptual illustration of the method is shown in Fig. 7.7.

Given an image set $\mathbf{X} = \{\mathbf{x}_1, \dots, \mathbf{x}_n\}$, $\mathbf{x}_i \in \mathbb{R}^d$, the DCNN features $\mathbf{Y} = \{\mathbf{y}_1, \dots, \mathbf{y}_n\}$ are first extracted. Here, according to [9], the DCNN network is trained on 256 by 256 pixel face images. The face images are normalized using detected eye positions. The network has 17 layers, including 14 convolution layers, 2 fully connected layers, and 1 soft-max layer. The training of the DCNN network consists of pretraining and fine-tuning. The pretraining is conducted on "Celebrities on the Web" (CFW) dataset [44]. The fine-tuning is carried using the training part of the given dataset. Finally, the output of the second fully connected layer of the trained DCNN network is used as the deep feature. All the network training and feature extraction are accomplished by the Caffe deep learning framework [24].

After the deep features are obtained, the first statistic, the sample mean is defined by $\mathbf{m} = \frac{1}{n}\sum_{i=1}^{n}\mathbf{y}_i$, which lies in Euclidean space $\mathbb{R}^d$. The second statistic, the covariance matrix, is defined by $\mathbf{C} = \frac{1}{n-1}\sum_{i=1}^{n}(\mathbf{y}_i - \mathbf{m})(\mathbf{y}_i - \mathbf{m})^T$, which lies on Riemannian manifold Sym_+^d. The third statistic, the Gaussian Mixture Model, is learned by Expectation Maximization algorithm. It can be written as

$$G = \sum_{i=1}^{M} w_i \mathcal{N}(\mathbf{y}|\tilde{\mathbf{m}}_i, \tilde{\mathbf{C}}_i), \tag{7.25}$$

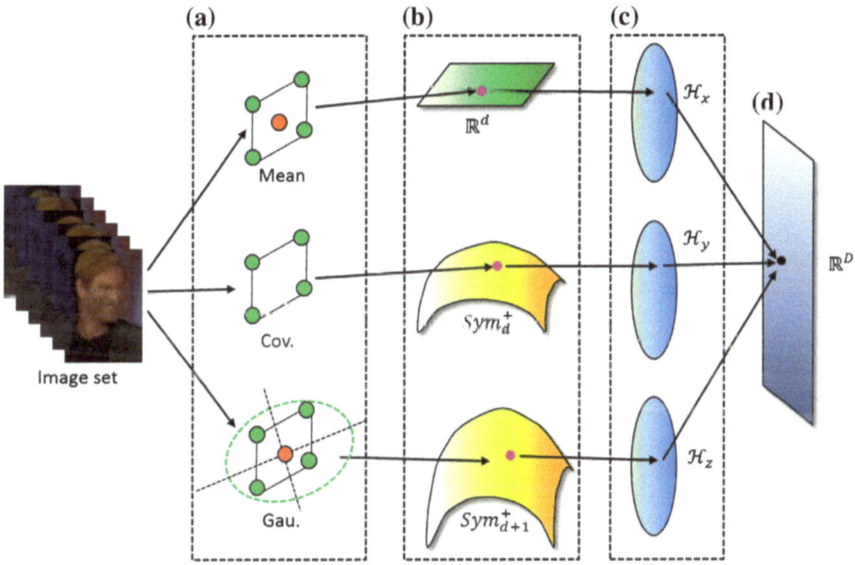

Fig. 7.7 Hybrid Euclidean-and-Riemannian metric learning [21]

where $\tilde{\mathbf{m}}_i$ and $\tilde{\mathbf{C}}_i$ are the mean and covariance matrix for the ith Gaussian component. According to the information geometry theory in [29], it can be embedded into Sym_+^{d+1} and represented by a $(d+1) \times (d+1)$-dimensional SPD matrix $\mathbf{P}$ as

$$\mathcal{N}(\tilde{\mathbf{m}}_i, \tilde{\mathbf{C}}_i) \sim \mathbf{P} = |\mathbf{Q}|^{-2/(d+1)} \begin{bmatrix} \mathbf{Q}\mathbf{Q}^T + \tilde{\mathbf{m}}_i\tilde{\mathbf{m}}_i^T & \tilde{\mathbf{m}}_i \\ \tilde{\mathbf{m}}_i^T & 1 \end{bmatrix}, \tag{7.26}$$

where $\tilde{\mathbf{C}} = \mathbf{Q}\mathbf{Q}^T$ and $|\mathbf{Q}| > 0$. For mean vectors, the linear kernel is directly used, which is

$$K_m(\mathbf{m}_i, \mathbf{m}_j) = \mathbf{m}_i^T\mathbf{m}_j. \tag{7.27}$$

For covariance matrices, the Log-Euclidean Distance is used, which is $d(\mathbf{C}_i, \mathbf{C}_j) = \| \log(\mathbf{C}_i) - \log(\mathbf{C}_j)\|_F$. It leads to the kernel

$$K_C(\mathbf{C}_i, \mathbf{C}_j) = \mathrm{tr}(\log(\mathbf{C}_i, \mathbf{C}_j)). \tag{7.28}$$

For GMMs, the LED metric is used as well. The kernel function is

$$K_G(\mathbf{G}_i, \mathbf{G}_j) = \sum_{a=1}^{M_a} \sum_{b=1}^{M_b} w_a w_b \mathrm{tr}(\log(\mathbf{P}_i^a) \log(\mathbf{P}_j^b))), \tag{7.29}$$

where $\mathbf{P}_i^a$ is the ath Gaussian component of the i th GMM.

Given training sets $\mathbf{X}_i$ and $\mathbf{X}_j$, let $\mathbf{\Phi}_i^r$ and $\mathbf{\Phi}_j^r$ be the high dimensional features in RKHS of the rth statistic feature. The distance metric is defined as

$$d_{A_r}(\mathbf{\Phi}_i^r, \mathbf{\Phi}_j^r) = \mathrm{tr}(\mathbf{A}_r(\mathbf{\Phi}_i^r - \mathbf{\Phi}_j^r)(\mathbf{\Phi}_i^r - \mathbf{\Phi}_j^r)^T), \tag{7.30}$$

where $\mathbf{A}_r$ is the learned Mahalanobis matrix for the rth statistic in the high dimensional RKHS ($r = 1, \ldots, 3$ here). Using the Information-Theoretic Metric Learning method proposed in [15], the objective function for learning $\{\mathbf{A}_r\}$ is formulated as

$$\begin{aligned} &\min_{\mathbf{A}_1 \geq 0, \ldots, \mathbf{A}_R \geq, \xi} \frac{1}{R} \sum_{r=1}^{R} D_{\ell d}(\mathbf{A}_r, \mathbf{A}_0) + \gamma D_{\ell d}(\mathrm{diag}(\xi), \mathrm{diag}(\xi_0)), \\ &s.t. \frac{\delta_{ij}}{R} \sum_{r=1}^{R} d_{\mathbf{A}_r}(\mathbf{\Phi}_i^r, \mathbf{\Phi}_j^r) \leq \xi_{ij}, \ \forall i,j \end{aligned} \tag{7.31}$$

where $D_{\ell d}(\mathbf{A}_r, \mathbf{A}_0) = \mathrm{tr}(\mathbf{A}_r \mathbf{A}_0^{-1}) - \log\det(\mathbf{A}_r \mathbf{A}_0^{-1}) - d$, d is the dimensionality of the data. ξ is a vector of slack variables and is initialized to ξ_0, where $\xi_{0ij} = \delta_{ij}\rho - \zeta\tau$, ρ is the threshold for distance comparison, τ is the margin, and ζ is the tuning scale of the margin. $\delta_{ij} = \begin{cases} 1 & \text{if } \mathbf{X}_i \text{ and } \mathbf{X}_j \text{ come from the same class} \\ -1 & \text{otherwise} \end{cases}$

Learning $\mathbf{A}_r$ is equivalent to learning $\mathbf{W}_r$ such that $\mathbf{A}_r = \mathbf{W}_r \mathbf{W}_r^T$. By applying the kernel trick, explicit computation of $\mathbf{\Phi}^r$ can be avoided. Assume that every column of $\mathbf{W}_r$ is a linear combination of all the training samples in RKHS, $\mathbf{w}_k^r$ can be expressed by $\mathbf{w}_k^r = \sum_{j=1}^{N} \mathbf{u}_j^k \mathbf{\Phi}_j^r$, $\mathbf{u}^k$ are the expansion coefficients here. Let $\mathbf{U}_r = \left[\mathbf{u}^1, \ldots, \mathbf{u}^N\right]$, $\mathbf{W}_r = \mathbf{\Phi}^r \mathbf{U}_r$, instead of learning $\mathbf{W}_r$ directly, $\mathbf{U}_r$ can be learned. Then the objective function can be rewritten as

$$\begin{aligned} &\min_{\mathbf{B}_1 \geq 0, \ldots, \mathbf{B}_R \geq, \xi} \frac{1}{R} \sum_{r=1}^{R} D_{\ell d}(\mathbf{B}_r, \mathbf{B}_0) + \gamma D_{\ell d}(\mathrm{diag}(\xi), \mathrm{diag}(\xi_0)), \\ &s.t. \frac{\delta_{ij}}{R} \sum_{r=1}^{R} d_{\mathbf{B}_r}(\mathbf{K}_{\cdot i}^r, \mathbf{K}_{\cdot j}^r) \leq \xi_{ij}, \ \forall i,j, \end{aligned} \tag{7.32}$$

where $\mathbf{B}_r = \mathbf{U}_r \mathbf{U}_r^T$ is the new Mahalanobis matrix. $d_{\mathbf{B}_r}(\mathbf{K}_{\cdot i}^r, \mathbf{K}_{\cdot j}^r) = \mathrm{tr}(\mathbf{B}_r(\mathbf{K}_{\cdot i}^r - \mathbf{K}_{\cdot j}^r)$ $(\mathbf{K}_{\cdot i}^r - \mathbf{K}_{\cdot j}^r)^T)$. $\mathbf{K}_{\cdot i}^r$ is the ith column of $\mathbf{K}^r$. The proposed method adopted the cyclic Bregman projection method [10] to solve this problem.

After $\{\mathbf{B}_r\}_{r=1}^3$ are learned for all statistics, for verification task, given two image sets $\mathbf{X}_i$ and $\mathbf{X}_j$, their corresponding DCNN features are first calculated. Means, covariance matrices and GMMs are then computed. Then the kernels between these testing samples and the training samples are computed as $\mathbf{k}_i^r$ and $\mathbf{k}_j^r$. Finally, their distance is calculated by

$$d(\mathbf{X}_1, \mathbf{X}_2) = \sum_{r=1}^{3} d_{\mathbf{B}_r}(\mathbf{k}_i^r, \mathbf{k}_j^r) = \sum_{r-1}^{3} \mathrm{tr}(\mathbf{B}_r(\mathbf{k}_i^r - \mathbf{k}_j^r)(\mathbf{k}_i^r - \mathbf{k}_j^r)^T). \tag{7.33}$$

Besides the methods mentioned above, Wang et al. [42] proposed a face recognition method for image sets using Gaussian Mixture Model which lies on specific Riemannian manifold. Huang et al. [23] provided a image set-based metric learning method using Log-Euclidean metric on SPD manifold. Arandjelovic and Cipolla [6] built a pose-wise linear illumination manifold model for video-based face recognition. Arandjelovic and Cipolla [5] modeled the video faces by shape-illumination manifolds which are robust to different variations. Kim et al. [25] introduced canonical correlations between two subspaces for image set recognition. Huang et al. [19] proposed the Euclidean-to-Riemannian Metric for Point-to-Set Classification on Riemannian manifold.

7.4 Probabilistic Methods

Probabilistic methods provide flexibility so that the similarity scores can either be modeled as "distance" or as "likelihood".

In [27], a video-based face recognition algorithm based on probablistic appearance manifolds is introduced. The image set of a given object can be treated as a low-dimensional appearance manifold M_k in the image space. Given a testing image I, identity k^* is determined by finding the manifold M_k with minimal distance to I, which is

$$k^* = \underset{k}{\mathrm{argmin}}\, d_H(I, M_k), \tag{7.34}$$

where d_H denotes the L^2-Hausdorff distance between the image I and M_k. Probabilistically, let

$$P(k|I) = \frac{1}{\Lambda} \exp(-\frac{1}{2\sigma^2} d_H^2(I, M_k)), \tag{7.35}$$

where Λ is a normalization term. Thus, (7.34) turns into

$$k^* = \underset{k}{\mathrm{argmax}}\, P(k|I). \tag{7.36}$$

Since M_k is usually not known and can only be estimated by samples, $d_H(I, M_k)$ cannot be calculated directly. Let $p_{M_k}(x|I)$ be the probability that x is the point on M_k at minimal L^2 distance to I. Also, since the appearance manifold is complex and non-linear, it is decomposed into a collection of m simpler disjoint manifolds as $M_k = C^{k1} \cup \ldots \cup C^{km}$ where C^{ki} is called a pose manifold. Each pose manifold is further approximated by an affine plane through PCA. $P(C^{ki}|I)$ denotes the probability that C^{ki} contains point x^* with minimal distance to I. Then

$$d_H(I, M_k) = \int_{M_k} d(x, I) p_{M_k}(x|I) dx = \sum_{i=1}^{m} P(C^{ki}|I) \int_{C^{ki}} d_H(x, I) p_{C^{ki}}(x|I) dx$$
$$= \sum_{i=1}^{m} P(C^{ki}|I) d_H(I, C^{ki}), \qquad (7.37)$$

which is the average expected distance between I and each pose manifold C^{ki}. This is shown in Fig. 7.8.

For video-based face recognition, the temporal coherence between consecutive image frames can be exploited. As the example shown in Fig. 7.9, $\{I_t\}$ probably originate from M_B by looking at the whole sequence. But because of the appearance variations, some of the frames are closer to M_A. By considering the temporal coherence, the image-to-manifold can be estimated more robustly.

Given previous frames $I_{0:t-1}$ at time t, assume I_t and $I_{0:t}$ are independent given C_t^{ki}, C_t^{ki} and $I_{0:t-1}$ are independent given C_{t-1}^{ki}, $P(C_t^{ki}|I_t, I_{0:t-1})$ can be calculated as

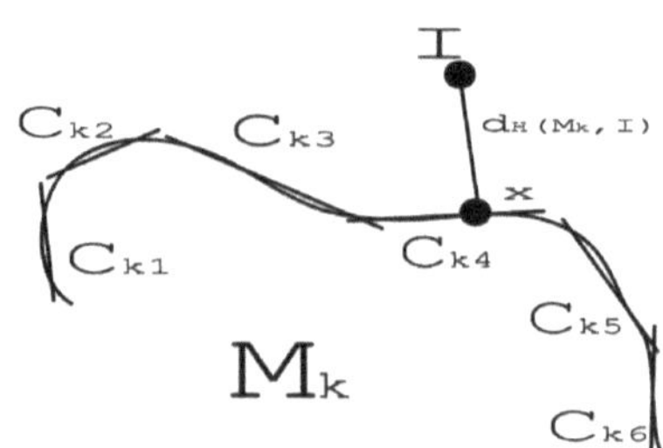

Fig. 7.8 $d_H(I, M_k)$ [27]

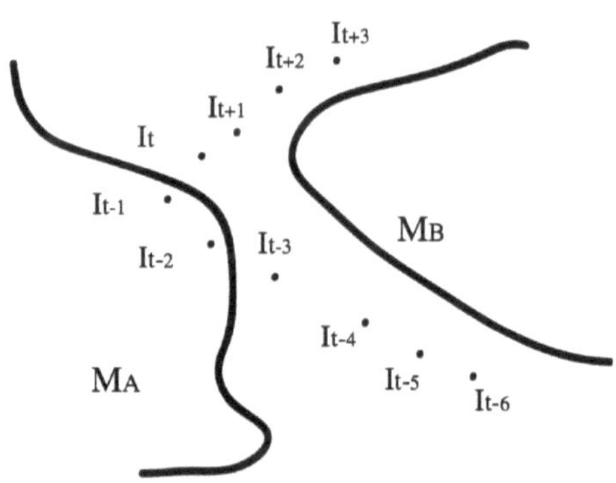

Fig. 7.9 Exploit temporal coherence [27]

$$
\begin{aligned}
P(C_t^{ki}|I_t, I_{0:t-1}) &= \alpha P(I_t|C_t^{ki}, I_{0:t-1})P(C_t^{ki}|I_{0:t-1}) \\
&= \alpha P(I_t|C_t^{ki}) \sum_{j=1}^{m} P(C_t^{ki}|C_{t-1}^{kj}, I_{0:t-1})P(C_{t-1}^{kj}|I_{0:t-1}) \\
&= \alpha P(I_t|C_t^{ki}) \sum_{j=1}^{m} P(C_t^{ki}|C_{t-1}^{kj})P(C_{t-1}^{kj}|I_{t-1}, I_{0:t-2}),
\end{aligned} \tag{7.38}
$$

where α is a normalization constant. $P(C_t^{ki}|C_{t-1}^{kj})$ is the probability of $x_t^* \in C^{ki}$ given $x_{t-1}^* \in C^{kj}$. Because of the temporal coherency between consecutive frames, x_{t-1}^* and x_t^* should have small geodesic distance on M_k. $P(C_t^{ki}|C_{t-1}^{kj})$ is thus related to their geodesic distance. Equation (7.38) can be computed recursively if $P(I_t|C_t^{ki})$ and $P(C_t^{ki}|C_{t-1}^{kj})$ $\forall i, j, t$ are known.

Given training image sets $\{S_k\}$ from videos, K-means algorithm is used to partition these sets into m disjoint subsets $\{S_{k1}, \dots, S_{km}\}$. For each S_{ki}, a linear approximation L_{ki} of local manifold C^{ki} is obtained by PCA. $P(C^{ki}|C^{kj})$ is then calculated by

$$
P(C^{ki}|C^{kj}) = \frac{1}{\Lambda_{kj}} \sum_{t=2}^{l} \delta(I_{t-1} \in S_{ki})\delta(I_t \in S_{kj}), \tag{7.39}
$$

which is counting the actual transitions in the corresponding training set. Λ_{kj} is a normalization constant. $P(I|C^{ki})$ is calculated by

$$
P(I|C^{ki}) = \frac{1}{\Lambda_{ki}} \exp(-\frac{1}{2\sigma^2} d_H(I, L_{ki})), \tag{7.40}
$$

where L_{ki} is the low-dimensional linear approximation of manifold C^{ki}. Λ_{ki} is a normalization constant. $d_H(I, L_{ki}) = d_H(I, C^{ki})$ is the distance between I and C^{ki}. Finally, for identification task, given an image I_t from a testing video sequence $\{I_t\}$, $P(C_t^{ki}|I_t, I_{0:t-1})$, $\forall k, i$ are calculated recursively by (7.38). $d_H(I, M_k)$ is then obtained by (7.37). The decision is made by (7.36).

A probability distribution-based method for video-based face recognition was proposed in [7]. The Kullback–Leibler divergence is used as the distance measure between the distributions of videos. Given image sets collected from videos, Gaussian mixture models $\hat{p}$ are learned for each image set. This is done using the Expectation Maximization algorithm. EM is initialized by K-means clustering and constrained to diagonal covariance matrices. The number of components is selected according to the minimal description length criterion [8]. Then for each training and testing video pair (Vte, V^{tr}), the KL divergence between the learned distributions $\hat{p}^{te}$ and $\hat{p}^{tr}$ is used as the distance measure, which is

$$
d(V^{te}, V^{tr}) = D_{KL}(\hat{p}^{te}||\hat{p}^{tr}) = \int \hat{p}^{te}(\mathbf{x}) \log \left(\frac{\hat{p}^{te}(\mathbf{x})}{\hat{p}^{tr}(\mathbf{x})} \right) d\mathbf{x}. \tag{7.41}
$$

The KL divergence $D_{KL}(p||q)$ quantifies how well the distribution p describes samples from q. It is nonnegative and equal to zero if $p \equiv q$. Since the calculation of the KL divergence involves integration, there is no closed form when $\hat{p}^{te}$ and $\hat{p}^{tr}$ are GMMs. However, according to the law of large numbers, the KL divergence can still be approximated by sampling using Monte-Carlo simulation:

$$D_{KL}(\hat{p}^{te}||\hat{p}^{tr}) \approx \frac{1}{N}\sum_{k=1}^{N} \log\left(\frac{\hat{p}^{te}(\mathbf{x}_k)}{\hat{p}^{tr}(\mathbf{x}_k)}\right), \tag{7.42}$$

where $\mathbf{x}_k$ are samples drawn from distribution $\hat{p}^{te}$. Then for identification task, the similarity between every training and testing video pair is computed using (7.42).

Liu and Chen [28] proposed a Hidden Markov Models based method to perform video-based face recognition. When training, the statistics and the temporal information of training videos are learned by HMMs. During the recognition phase, the temporal characteristics of the testing videos are analyzed by the HMM corresponding to each subject. The decision is made by finding the highest likelihood scores provided by the HMMs.

A continuous HMM model is defined as the triplet $\lambda = (\mathbf{A}, \mathbf{B}, \boldsymbol{\pi})$. $\mathbf{A} = \{a_{ij}\}$ is the transition probability matrix, where $a_{ij} = P(q_t = S_j | q_{t-1} = S_i)$, $1 \leq i, j \leq N$. $\mathbf{B} = \{b_i(\mathbf{o})\}$ is the observation probability density function, where $b_i(\mathbf{o}) = \sum_{k=1}^{M} c_{ik} \mathcal{N}(\mathbf{o}; \boldsymbol{\mu}_{ik}, \boldsymbol{\Sigma}_{ik})$. $\boldsymbol{\pi} = \{\pi_i\}$ is the initial state distribution, where $\pi_i = P(q_1 = S_i)$, $1 \leq i \leq N$. Here $\mathbf{S} = \{S_1, S_2, \dots, S_N\}$ is the set of states in the model. $\mathbf{O} = \{\mathbf{o}_1, \mathbf{o}_2, \dots, \mathbf{o}_T\}$ are the observations and $\mathbf{Q} = \{q_1, q_2, \dots, q_T\}$ are the corresponding hidden state variables. Given state S_i, $b_i(\mathbf{o})$ is a Gaussian Mixture Model with M Gaussians. c_{ik}, $\boldsymbol{\mu}_{ik}$ and $\boldsymbol{\Sigma}_{ik}$ are the mixture coefficient, mean and covariance for the kth Gaussian, respectively.

Given training videos, the face images are first projected to a low-dimensional space using PCA. Then each video is modeled as an HMM with these low-dimensional features as observations $\mathbf{O}$, which is shown in Fig. 7.10.

The estimation for HMM parameter $\lambda = (\mathbf{A}, \mathbf{B}, \boldsymbol{\pi})$ is as follows:

1. $\mathbf{A}$, $\mathbf{B}$, and $\boldsymbol{\pi}$ are initialized (observations are clustered into M Gaussians. c^0_{ik}, $\boldsymbol{\mu}^0_{ik}$ and $\boldsymbol{\Sigma}^0_{ik}$ are estimated for each Gaussian). $n = 0$.
2. Do.

   2.1. Reestimate λ using the expectation maximization algorithm, in order to maximize the likelihood $p(\mathbf{O}|\lambda)$. The reestimation is defined as

$$\pi_i^{n+1} = \frac{P(\mathbf{O}, q_1 = i | \lambda^n)}{p(\mathbf{O}|\lambda^n)} \tag{7.43}$$

$$a_{ij}^{n+1} = \frac{\sum_{t=1}^{T} p(\mathbf{O}, q_{t-1} = i, q_t = j | \lambda^n)}{\sum_{t=1}^{T} p(\mathbf{O}, q_{t-1} = i | \lambda^n)} \tag{7.44}$$

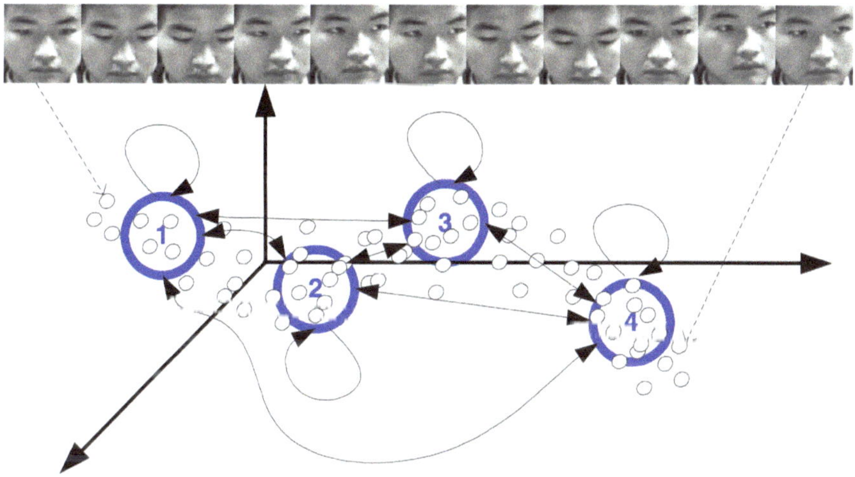

Fig. 7.10 Temporal HMM for modeling face sequences [28]

$$c_{ik}^{n+1} = \frac{\sum_{t=1}^{T} P(q_t = i, m_{q_t t} = k|\mathbf{O}, \lambda^n)}{\sum_{t=1}^{T}\sum_{k=1}^{M} P(q_t = i, m_{q_t t} = k|\mathbf{O}, \lambda^n)} \quad (7.45)$$

$$\boldsymbol{\mu}_{ik}^{n+1} = \frac{\sum_{t=1}^{T} \mathbf{o}_t P(q_t = i, m_{q_t t} = k|\mathbf{O}, \lambda^n)}{\sum_{t=1}^{T} P(q_t = i, m_{q_t t} = k|\mathbf{O}, \lambda^n)} \quad (7.46)$$

$$\boldsymbol{\Sigma}_{ik}^{n+1} = (1-\alpha)\mathbf{C} + \alpha \frac{\sum_{t=1}^{T}(\mathbf{o}_t - \boldsymbol{\mu}_{ik}^{n+1})(\mathbf{o}_t - \boldsymbol{\mu}_{ik}^{n+1})^T P(q_t = i, m_{q_t t} = k|\mathbf{O}, \lambda^n)}{P(q_t = i, m_{q_t t} = k|\mathbf{O}, \lambda^n)} \quad (7.47)$$

where $m_{q_t t}$ indicates the mixture component of state q_t and time t. $\mathbf{C}$ is a general model for the variance of all videos. α is a weighting factor, which prevents the estimated $\boldsymbol{\Sigma}$ to be singular.

2.2 $n = n + 1$

3. Until $p(\mathbf{O}|\lambda)$ converges.

For identification task, after the HMM models $\{\lambda_c^{tr}\}$ are estimated for training videos, given a testing video, the face images are projected onto the same low-dimensional space as the training samples and obtain the testing observation $\mathbf{O}^{te}$. Then the likelihood score $p(\mathbf{O}^{te}|\lambda_c^{tr})$ of the observation given the training testing HMM models are computed. The identification decision is made by $p = \text{argmax}_c\, p(\mathbf{O}^{te}|\lambda_c^{tr})$, which finds the highest likelihood score.

In addition to the methods discussed above, Zhou et al. [45] introduced an appearance-adaptive model-based on particle filter to realize robust visual tracking and recognition. Zhou et al. [46] proposed a time series based method for video-based face recognition. Arandjelovic and Cipolla [4] provided another method based on kernelized distribution-to-distribution distance. Wang et al. [43] introduced a probablistic nearest neighbor search method for image set classification.

7.5 Geometrical Model-Based Methods

Geometrical model-based methods construct certain geometrical models for faces in the videos. Then the texture map of the faces are projected on to these models and features are extracted. The recognition will based on these features. The models can vary from the simple spherical head models to the human-specific 3D head models. Geometrical model based methods are more robust to illumination and pose variations because they exploit the geometrical structures from the faces.

Sankaranarayanan and Chellappa [17] proposed a novel feature for robust video-based face recognition in camera networks. It is developed using the spherical harmonic representation of the face texture mapped onto a spherical head model. Spherical harmonics are a set of orthonormal basis functions defined over the unit sphere, and can be used to linearly expand any square-integrable function on $\mathbb{S}^2$ as

$$f(\theta, \phi) = \sum_{l=0}^{\infty} \sum_{m=-l}^{l} f_{lm} Y_{lm}(\theta, \phi), \tag{7.48}$$

where $Y_{lm}(\cdot, \cdot)$ defines the SH basis function of degree $l \geq 0$ and order $m \in (-l, -l+1, \ldots, l-1, l)$. f_{lm} is the coefficient associated with the basis function Y_{lm} for the function f. The spherical coordinate system is used here. $\theta \in (0, \pi)$ and $\phi \in (0, 2\pi)$ are the zenith and azimuth angles, respectively. There are $2l + 1$ basis functions for a given order l. The SH basis function for degree l and order m has the following form (shown in Fig. 7.11):

$$Y_{lm}(\theta, \phi) = K_{lm} P_l^m(\cos\theta) \mathbf{e}^{jm\phi}, \tag{7.49}$$

where K_{lm} denotes a normalization constant such that

$$\int_0^{\pi} \int_0^{2\pi} Y_{lm} Y_{lm}^* d\phi d\theta = 1. \tag{7.50}$$

Here, $P_{lm}(x)$ are the associated Legendre functions. As with Fourier expansion, the SH expansion coefficients f_l^m can be computed as

$$f_l^m = \int_\theta \int_\phi f(\theta, \phi) Y_l^m(\theta, \phi) d\theta d\phi. \tag{7.51}$$

Given two multiview videos, the head centers in these videos are first obtained using a multiview tracking algorithm proposed in the paper. Then a spherical head model for each head is build. The SH spectrum features are extracted from the texture map projected on the models from all views. The projection of the texture map is shown in Fig. 7.12.

These features are projected into a reproducing kernel Hilbert space (RKHS), which is performed via an Radial Basis Function (RBF) kernel. The limiting

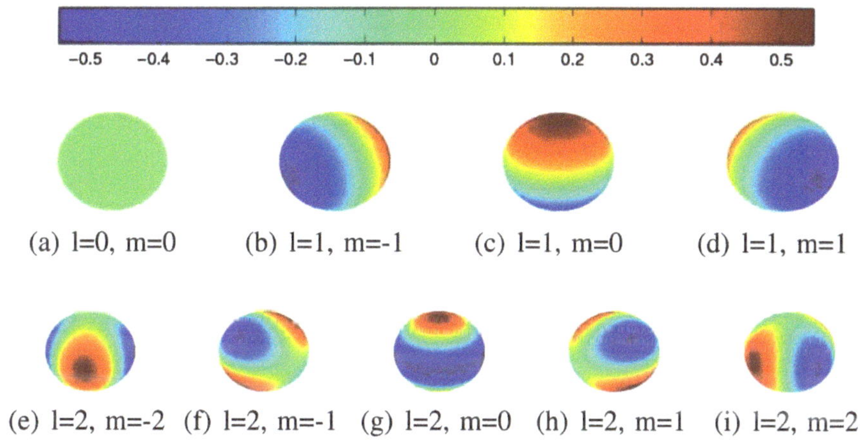

Fig. 7.11 Visualization of the first three degree of Spherical Harmonics [17]

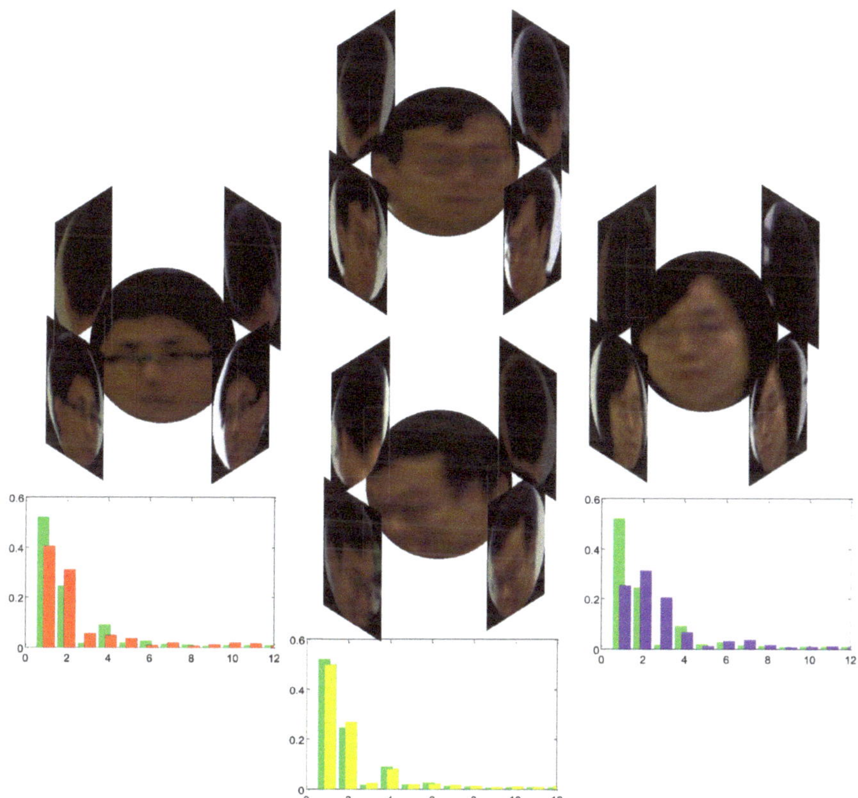

Fig. 7.12 Texture map projection [17]

Bhattacharyya distance between these probability distributions in RKHS (assume to be Gaussian) is considered as the distance measure. The limiting Bhattacharyya distance in this case is

$$D = \frac{1}{8}(\alpha_{11} + \alpha_{22} - 2\alpha_{12}), \tag{7.52}$$

where

$$\alpha_{ij} = \boldsymbol{\mu}_i^T (\frac{1}{2}\mathbf{C}_i + \frac{1}{2}\mathbf{C}_j)^{-1}\boldsymbol{\mu}_j. \tag{7.53}$$

$\boldsymbol{\mu}_i$ and $\mathbf{C}_i$ are the means and covariance matrices in RKHS which cannot be directly calculated. Denote the Gram matrix as $\mathbf{K}_{ij}$, where $i,j \in \{1,2\}$ are the indices of videos. $\mathbf{K}_{11}$ and $\mathbf{K}_{22}$ are centered by

$$\mathbf{K}'_{ii} = \mathbf{J}_i^T \mathbf{K}_{ii} \mathbf{J}_i, \mathbf{J}_i = N_i^{-\frac{1}{2}}(\mathbf{I}_N - \mathbf{s}\mathbf{1}^T), \tag{7.54}$$

where $\mathbf{s} = N_i^{-1}\mathbf{1}$, $\mathbf{1}$ is a $N_i \times 1$ vector of 1s and N_i is the number of features from video i. Then α_{ij} is calculated by

$$\alpha_{ij} = \mathbf{s}_i^T \mathbf{K}_{ij} \mathbf{s}_j - \mathbf{s}_i^T \begin{bmatrix} \mathbf{K}_{i1} & \mathbf{K}_{i2} \end{bmatrix} \mathbf{B} \begin{bmatrix} \mathbf{K}_{j1} \\ \mathbf{K}_{j2} \end{bmatrix} \mathbf{s}_j, \tag{7.55}$$

where

$$\mathbf{B} = \mathbf{P}\mathbf{L}^{-1}\mathbf{P}, \mathbf{L} = \mathbf{P}^T \begin{bmatrix} \mathbf{K}_{11} & \mathbf{K}_{12} \\ \mathbf{K}_{21} & \mathbf{K}_{22} \end{bmatrix} \mathbf{P} \tag{7.56}$$

and

$$\mathbf{P} = \begin{bmatrix} \sqrt{\frac{1}{2}}\mathbf{J}_1\mathbf{V}_1 & 0 \\ 0 & \sqrt{\frac{1}{2}}\mathbf{J}_2\mathbf{V}_2 \end{bmatrix} \tag{7.57}$$

$\mathbf{V}_i$ is the matrix which stores the first r eigenvectors of $\mathbf{K}'_{ii}$ (i.e., corresponding to the r largest eigenvalues). For identification and verification tasks, the similarity between the two set of features is measured by the computed limiting Bhattacharyya distance between them.

Park and Jain [33] also provided a video-based face recognition method which reconstructs 3D face models from the videos and recognizes faces at frontal view.

7.6 Dynamical Model-Based Methods

Dynamical model-based methods are sequence-based methods. They consider videos as dynamical systems with video frames as the observation of these systems. The advantage of these methods is that the extra temporal information is exploited.

Dynamical models are often used to represent motions or activities, but there are some publications that use dynamical models for face recognition.

In [2], the video-to-video face recognition problem is transferred into a dynamical system identification and classification problem. Videos are modeled by dynamical systems. Here, the ARMA model is used for the dynamical system. The ARMA model is defined as

$$\mathbf{x}(t+1) = \mathbf{A}\mathbf{x}(t) + \mathbf{v}(t) \tag{7.58}$$

$$\mathbf{y}(t) = \mathbf{C}\mathbf{x}(t) + \mathbf{w}(t), \tag{7.59}$$

where $\mathbf{x}(t)$ is the state vector, $\mathbf{y}(t)$ is the observation. $\mathbf{A}$ and $\mathbf{C}$ are transition matrix and observation matrix, respectively. The system is driven by the IID process $\mathbf{v}(t)$. $\mathbf{w}(t)$ is the observation noise.

Suppose $\mathbf{v}(t) \sim \mathcal{N}(0, \mathbf{Q})$ and $\mathbf{w}(t) \sim \mathcal{N}(0, \mathbf{R})$, given a video sequence $\mathbf{Y}^\tau = [\mathbf{y}(1), \ldots, \mathbf{y}(\tau)]$, (7.59) can be rewritten as

$$\mathbf{Y}^\tau = \mathbf{C}\mathbf{X}^\tau + \mathbf{W}^\tau, \tag{7.60}$$

where $\mathbf{X}$ and $\mathbf{W}$ are similarly defined. Then the model parameters can be estimated by

$$\hat{\mathbf{C}}(\tau) = \mathbf{U} \tag{7.61}$$

$$\hat{\mathbf{X}}(\tau) = \mathbf{\Sigma}\mathbf{V}^T \tag{7.62}$$

$$\hat{\mathbf{A}}(\tau) = \mathbf{\Sigma}\mathbf{V}^T\mathbf{D}_1\mathbf{V}(\mathbf{V}^T\mathbf{D}_2\mathbf{V})^{-1}\mathbf{\Sigma}^{-1} \tag{7.63}$$

$$\hat{\mathbf{Q}}(\tau) = \frac{1}{\tau}\sum_{t=1}^{\tau} \hat{\mathbf{v}}(t)\hat{\mathbf{v}}^T(t), \tag{7.64}$$

where $\mathbf{Y}^\tau = \mathbf{U}\mathbf{\Sigma}\mathbf{V}^T$ is the SVD of $\mathbf{Y}^\tau$. $\mathbf{D}_1 = \begin{bmatrix} 0 & 0 \\ \mathbf{I}_{\tau-1} & 0 \end{bmatrix}$ and $\mathbf{D}_2 = \begin{bmatrix} \mathbf{I}_{\tau-1} & 0 \\ 0 & 0 \end{bmatrix}$. $\hat{\mathbf{v}}(t) = \hat{\mathbf{x}}(t+1) - \hat{\mathbf{A}}(\tau)\hat{\mathbf{x}}(t)$.

Given video pairs $\mathbf{V}_1$ and $\mathbf{V}_2$, their model parameters M_1 and M_2 are first estimated, respectively. Then the distance between two ARMA models is calculated by

$$d_M(M_1, M_2)^2 = \ln \prod_{i=1}^{n} \frac{1}{\cos^2 \theta_i} \tag{7.65}$$

$$d_g(M_1, M_2) = \sin \theta_{max} \tag{7.66}$$

$$d_f(M_1, M_2)^2 = 2\sum_{i=1}^{n} \sin^2 \theta_i, \tag{7.67}$$

where $d_M(M_1, M_2)$ is the Martin distance, $d_g(M_1, M_2)$ is the gap distance and $d_f(M_1, M_2)$ is the distance based on Frobenius norm. θ_i's are the subspace angles between M_1

and M_2 (see [13] for more details). Different distances can be chosen for different scenarios or fused together to improve the performance.

Turaga [37] also considered videos as ARMA models and treated each video as a point on the Grassmann manifold for recognition.

7.7 Conclusion and Future Directions

As we saw in this chapter, most of the modeling approaches for video-based face recognition focus on how to define the similarity scores (or the "distances") between videos. Sparse coding-based methods model videos as dictionaries and use reconstruction error as the similarity score. Manifold-based methods use special kernels between manifolds as the similarity. Probabilistic methods are more flexible. The similarity scores can be the KL divergence between distributions, or the expected distance under some certain distributions. Dynamical model-based methods consider videos as dynamical systems. The similarity scores are the distance between two systems on a certain manifold. Geometrical model-based methods are slightly different from the others since their main objective is to construct geometrical models from videos and project texture maps onto them.

Since deep learning is becoming increasingly important recently, one of the future directions for video-based face recognition will be the classic methods combined with deep learning-based methods. The special statistical and geometrical properties of deep features will lead to new modeling techniques. Another possible direction would be to build 3D DCNN networks, where the convolutions are applied through the time-axis as well, in order to capture the temporal information between consecutive frames. Also, thanks to the fast developments in deep learning-based detection and landmark extraction techniques, face detection and alignment are becoming more and more precise, which can provide geometrical model-based methods with improved performance.

Acknowledgements This research is based upon work supported by the Office of the Director of National Intelligence (ODNI), Intelligence Advanced Research Projects Activity (IARPA), via IARPA R&D Contract No. 2014-14071600012. The views and conclusions contained herein are those of the authors and should not be interpreted as necessarily representing the official policies or endorsements, either expressed or implied, of the ODNI, IARPA, or the U.S. Government. The U.S. Government is authorized to reproduce and distribute reprints for Governmental purposes notwithstanding any copyright annotation thereon.

References

1. Absil PA, Mahony R, Sepulchre R (2007) Optimization algorithms on matrix manifolds. Princeton University Press, Princeton, NJ, USA
2. Aggarwal G, Chowdhury A, Chellappa R (2004) A system identification approach for video-based face recognition. In: Proceedings of the 17th International Conference on Pattern Recognition, ICPR 2004, vol 4, pp 175–178
3. Aharon M, Elad M, Bruckstein A (2006) K-svd: an algorithm for designing overcomplete dictionaries for sparse representation. IEEE Trans Signal Process 54(11):4311–4322
4. Arandjelovic O, Cipolla R (2004) Face recognition from face motion manifolds using robust kernel resistor-average distance. In: Conference on Computer Vision and Pattern Recognition Workshop, 2004. CVPRW '04, p 88
5. Arandjelovic O, Cipolla R (2006) Face Recognition from Video Using the Generic Shape-Illumination Manifold. In: Proceedings of Computer Vision—ECCV 2006: 9th European Conference on Computer Vision, Graz, Austria, 7–13 May 2006, Part IV. Springer, Berlin Heidelberg, pp 27–40
6. Arandjelovic O, Cipolla R (2009) A pose-wise linear illumination manifold model for face recognition using video. Comput Vis Image Underst 113(1):113–125
7. Arandjelovic O, Shakhnarovich G, Fisher J, Cipolla R, Darrell T (2005) Face recognition with image sets using manifold density divergence. In: IEEE Computer Society Conference on Computer Vision and Pattern Recognition, 2005, CVPR 2005. vol 1 (2005), pp 581–588
8. Barron A, Rissanen J, Yu B (1998) The minimum description length principle in coding and modeling. IEEE Trans Inf Theory 44(6):2743–2760
9. Beveridge J, Zhang H, Draper B, Flynn P, Feng Z, Huber P, Kittler J, Huang Z, Li S, Li Y, Kan M, Wang R, Shan S, Chen X, Li H, Hua G, Struc V, Krizaj J, Ding C, Tao D, Phillips P (2015) Report on the fg 2015 video person recognition evaluation. In: 2015 11th IEEE international conference and workshops on Automatic Face and Gesture Recognition (FG), vol 1, pp 1–8
10. Bregman L (1967) The relaxation method of finding the common point of convex sets and its application to the solution of problems in convex programming. USSR Comput Math Math Phys 7(3):200–217
11. Chen YC, Patel V, Shekhar S, Chellappa R, Phillips P (2013) Video-based face recognition via joint sparse representation. In: 2013 10th IEEE International Conference and Workshops on Automatic Face and Gesture Recognition (FG), pp 1–8
12. Chen YC, Patel VM, Phillips PJ, Chellappa R (2012) Dictionary-Based Face Recognition from Video. In: Computer Vision— ECCV 2012: 12th European Conference on Computer Vision, Florence, Italy, 7–13 Oct 2012, Proceedings. Springer, Berlin, pp 766–779
13. Cock KD, Moor BD (2002) Subspace angles between arma models. Syst Control Lett 46(4):265–270
14. Dalal N, Triggs B (2005) Histograms of oriented gradients for human detection. In: Proceedings of the 2005 IEEE Computer Society Conference on Computer Vision and Pattern Recognition (CVPR'05), CVPR '05, vol 1. IEEE Computer Society, Washington, DC, USA, pp 886–893
15. Davis JV, Kulis B, Jain P, Sra S, Dhillon IS (2007) Information-theoretic metric learning. Proceedings of the 24th International Conference on Machine Learning., ICML '07ACM, New York, NY, USA, pp 209–216
16. Du M, Chellappa R (2014) Video-based face recognition using the intra-personal/extra-personal difference dictionary. In: Proceedings of the British Machine Vision Conference. BMVA Press
17. Du M, Sankaranarayanan A, Chellappa R (2014) Robust face recognition from multi-view videos. IEEE Trans Image Process 23(3):1105–1117
18. Hu Y, Mian A, Owens R (2011) Sparse approximated nearest points for image set classification. In: 2011 IEEE Conference on Computer Vision and Pattern Recognition (CVPR), pp 121–128

19. Huang Z, Wang R, Shan S, Chen X (2014) Learning euclidean-to-riemannian metric for point-to-set classification. In: 2014 IEEE Conference on Computer Vision and Pattern Recognition (CVPR), pp 1677–1684 (2014)
20. Huang Z, Wang R, Shan S, Chen X (2015) Hybrid Euclidean-and-Riemannian Metric Learning for Image Set Classification. In: Computer Vision—ACCV 2014: 12th Asian Conference on Computer Vision, Singapore, Singapore, 1–5 Nov 2014, Revised Selected Papers, Part III. Springer International Publishing, Cham, pp 562–577
21. Huang Z, Wang R, Shan S, Chen X (2015) Face recognition on large-scale video in the wild with hybrid euclidean-and-riemannian metric learning. Patt Recogn 48(10):3113–3124
22. Huang Z, Wang R, Shan S, Chen X (2015) Projection metric learning on grassmann manifold with application to video based face recognition. In: 2015 IEEE Conference on Computer Vision and Pattern Recognition (CVPR), pp 140–149
23. Huang Z, Wang R, Shan S, Li X, Chen X (2015) Log-euclidean metric learning on symmetric positive definite manifold with application to image set classification. In: Blei D, Bach E (eds.) Proceedings of the 32nd International Conference on Machine Learning (ICML-15), JMLR Workshop and Conference Proceedings, pp 720–729
24. Jia Y, Shelhamer E, Donahue J, Karayev S, Long, J, Girshick, R, Guadarrama S, Darrell T (2014) Caffe: convolutional architecture for fast feature embedding. arXiv preprint arXiv:1408.5093
25. Kim TK, Kittler J, Cipolla R (2007) Discriminative learning and recognition of image set classes using canonical correlations. IEEE Trans Pattern Anal Mach Intell 29(6):1005–1018
26. Krizhevsky A, Sutskever I, Hinton GE (2012) Imagenet classification with deep convolutional neural networks. In: Pereira E, Burges C, Bottou L, Weinberger K (eds) Advances in neural information processing systems, vol 25. Curran Associates, Inc., pp 1097–1105
27. Lee KC, Ho J, Yang MH, Kriegman D (2003) Video-based face recognition using probabilistic appearance manifolds. Proceedings of the 2003 IEEE Computer Society Conference on Computer Vision and Pattern Recognition, CVPR'03. IEEE Computer Society, Washington, DC, USA, pp 313–320
28. Liu X, Chen T (2003) Video-based face recognition using adaptive hidden markov models. Proceedings of the 2003 IEEE Computer Society Conference on Computer Vision and Pattern Recognition, CVPR'03. IEEE Computer Society, Washington, DC, USA, pp 340–345
29. Lovri M, Min-Oo M, Ruh EA (2000) Multivariate normal distributions parametrized as a riemannian symmetric space. J Multivariate Anal 74(1):36–48
30. Lowe DG (2004) Distinctive image features from scale-invariant keypoints. Int J Comput Vision 60(2):91–110
31. Ojala T, Pietikainen M, Maenpaa T (2002) Multiresolution gray-scale and rotation invariant texture classification with local binary patterns. IEEE Trans Pattern Anal Mach Intell 24(7):971–987
32. Ortiz E, Wright A, Shah M (2013) Face recognition in movie trailers via mean sequence sparse representation-based classification. In: 2013 IEEE Conference on Computer Vision and Pattern Recognition (CVPR), pp 3531–3538
33. Park U, Jain AK (2007) 3D Model-based face recognition in video. In: Advances in Biometrics: International Conference, ICB 2007, Seoul, Korea, 27–29 Aug 2007. Proceedings. Springer, Berlin, pp 1085–1094
34. Rosipal R, Kramer N (2006) Overview and recent advances in partial least squares. In: Proceedings of the 2005 International Conference on Subspace, Latent Structure and Feature Selection, SLSFS'05. Springer, Berlin, pp 34–51
35. Simonyan K, Zisserman A (2014) Very deep convolutional networks for large-scale image recognition. CoRR **abs/1409.1556**
36. Szegedy C, Liu W, Jia Y, Sermanet P, Reed S, Anguelov D, Erhan D, Vanhoucke V, Rabinovich A (2015) Going deeper with convolutions. In: The IEEE Conference on Computer Vision and Pattern Recognition (CVPR)
37. Turaga P, Veeraraghavan A, Srivastava A, Chellappa R (2011) Statistical computations on grassmann and stiefel manifolds for image and video-based recognition. IEEE Trans Pattern Anal Mach Intell 33(11):2273–2286

38. Viola P, Jones MJ (2004) Robust real-time face detection. Int J Comput Vision 57(2):137–154
39. Wang R, Chen X (2009) Manifold discriminant analysis. In: IEEE Conference on Computer Vision and Pattern Recognition, 2009, CVPR 2009. pp 429–436
40. Wang R, Guo H, Davis L, Dai Q (2012) Covariance discriminative learning: a natural and efficient approach to image set classification. In: 2012 IEEE Conference on Computer Vision and Pattern Recognition (CVPR), pp 2496–2503
41. Wang R, Shan S, Chen X, Gao W (2008) Manifold-manifold distance with application to face recognition based on image set. In: IEEE Conference on Computer Vision and Pattern Recognition, 2008, CVPR 2008, pp 1–8
42. Wang W, Wang R, Huang Z, Shan S, Chen X (2015) Discriminant analysis on Riemannian manifold of Gaussian distributions for face recognition with image sets. In: 2015 IEEE Conference on Computer Vision and Pattern Recognition (CVPR), pp 2048–2057
43. Wang W, Wang R, Shan S, Chen X (2015) Probabilistic nearest neighbor search for robust classification of face image sets. In: 2015 11th IEEE international conference and workshops on automatic Face and Gesture Recognition (FG) (Vol. 1, pp. 1–7)
44. Zhang X, Zhang L, Wang XJ, Shum HY (2012) Finding celebrities in billions of web images. IEEE Trans Multimedia 14(4):995–1007
45. Zhou S, Chellappa R, Moghaddam B (2004) Visual tracking and recognition using appearance-adaptive models in particle filters. IEEE Trans Image Process 13(11):1491–1506
46. Zhou S, Krueger V, Chellappa R (2003) Probabilistic recognition of human faces from video. Comput Vis Image Understand 91(12):214–245. Special Issue on Face Recognition
47. Zhu X, Ramanan D (2012) Face detection, pose estimation, and landmark localization in the wild. In: 2012 IEEE Conference on Computer Vision and Pattern Recognition (CVPR), pp 2879–2886

Chapter 8
Face Recognition Technologies for Evidential Evaluation of Video Traces

Xingjie Wei and Chang-Tsun Li

Abstract Human recognition from video traces is an important task in forensic investigations and evidence evaluations. Compared with other biometric traits, face is one of the most popularly used modalities for human recognition due to the fact that its collection is non-intrusive and requires less cooperation from the subjects. Moreover, face images taken at a long distance can still provide reasonable resolution, while most biometric modalities, such as iris and fingerprint, do not have this merit. In this chapter, we discuss automatic face recognition technologies for evidential evaluations of video traces. We first introduce the general concepts in both forensic and automatic face recognition, then analyse the difficulties in face recognition from videos. We summarise and categorise the approaches for handling different uncontrollable factors in difficult recognition conditions. Finally we discuss some challenges and trends in face recognition research in both forensics and biometrics. Given its merits tested in many deployed systems and great potential in other emerging applications, considerable research and development efforts are expected to be devoted in face recognition in the near future.

8.1 Introduction

The UK currently has the most widely deployed CCTV coverage in the world. In 2013, the British Security Industry Authority (BSIA) estimated that there are up to 5.9 million CCTV in the UK equating to 1 camera for every 11 people. With increasing emphasis on national and global security, there is a growing and acute need for human recognition (e.g. identifying or searching victims/witnesses/suspects) from videos.

X. Wei (✉)
School of Computing Science, Newcastle University, Newcastle upon Tyne NE1 7RU, UK
e-mail: xingjie.wei@ncl.ac.uk

C.-T. Li
Department of Computer Science, University of Warwick, Coventry CV4 7AL, UK
e-mail: C-T.Li@warwick.ac.uk

M. Tistarelli and C. Champod (eds.), *Handbook of Biometrics for Forensic Science*, Advances in Computer Vision and Pattern Recognition,
DOI 10.1007/978-3-319-50673-9_8

Biometrics is the science of identifying an individual based on the physiological and behavioural characteristics. The physiological characteristics are related to the shape of the body including face, iris, retina, fingerprint, palmprint, palm vein, hand geometry, DNA, earlobe, etc. The behavioural characteristics are related to the pattern of behaviour of a person such as gait, signature, keystroke dynamics, voice, etc. Among these biometric traits, face is the most commonly seen and used for human recognition due to the fact that its collection is non-intrusive and requires less cooperation from the subjects. Everyone has a face and it is widely accepted as a means of recognition.

Forensic science is the scientific knowledge and technical methods in gathering and examining traces which might be useful for the investigations of crime. The biometric traces are of great interest for both biometrics and forensics research [40]. A large number of biometric applications such as fingerprint identification systems and computerised DNA databases, were implemented to serve forensic purposes. Among them, the face recognition system is becoming increasingly important due to the abundance of image and video data provided by surveillance cameras, mobile devices, Internet social networks, etc. The videos collected during an investigation needs to be evaluated by investigators throughout the forensics process. The evaluation is to explore whether additional line of questions can be identified and make sure that the current investigated actions have been completed.

There are broadly two types of evaluation during a forensics process[1]: *investigative evaluation* and *evidential evaluation*. The investigative evaluation concerns (1) *what is known* and (2) *what is unknown*, (3) *what are the consistencies* and (4) *conflicts* in the cases. On the other hand, the evidential evaluation focuses on the *relevance*, *reliability* and *admissibility* of the materials considering issues such as *the overall strength of the case* and *whether sufficient evidence exists against the offender to proceed to charge*.

In a typical forensic face recognition scenario, a forensic expert is given face images of a suspect and a person in question, who may or may not be the suspect. The forensic expert gives a value which represents the degree to which these images appear to be of the same person. When a large amount of images and videos have been gathered, identifying the possible suspects manually is extremely time consuming. Face recognition technologies can be used as a tool in the forensic scenarios for helping with queries against a large enrolled database. The query can be a *one-to-many* search, or a *one-to-one* check, as shown in Fig. 8.1. The West Yorkshire Police in UK has tested a face recognition system for matching CCTV images against a database of mugshots and they have reported that although the technology is not fully mature, it has proven to be a useful investigation tool [46]. We will introduce the face recognition technologies for forensics evaluation of video traces in the rest of this chapter.

[1] National Police Library, http://www.college.police.uk/.

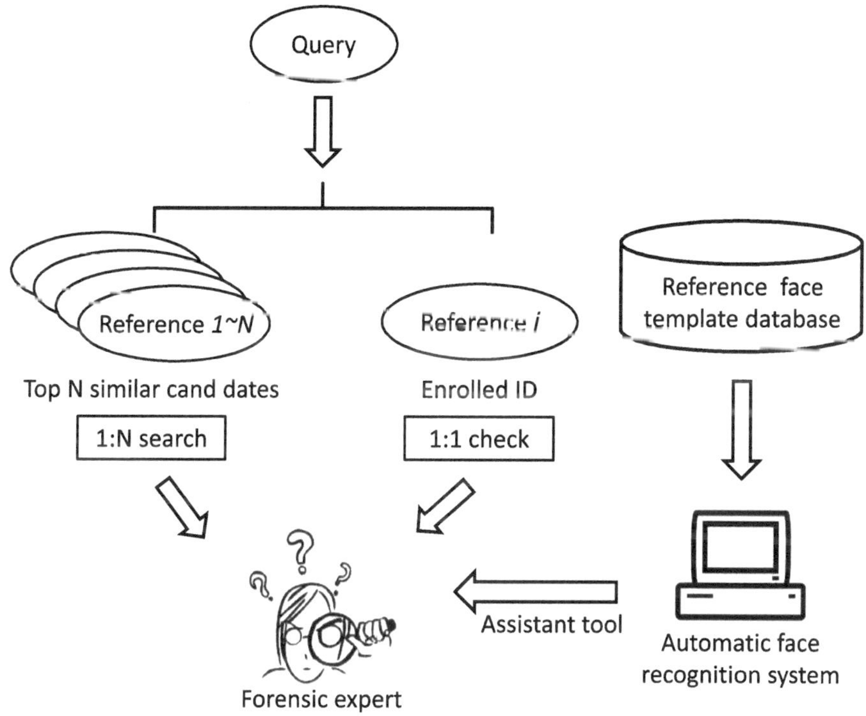

Fig. 8.1 The process of the forensic face recognition augmented with automatic face recognition system on queries against a large enrolled database. The query can be a one-to-many search or a one-to-one check

8.2 Automatic Face Recognition

A general automatic face recognition system usually consists of the following modules: a face detector, a feature extractor and a matcher, as shown in Fig. 8.2. The face detector first determines which image area contains a face. With the detected face pre-processed, facial features are extracted by the feature extractor and are fed to the matcher as input for comparison against the features of the enrolled images. A similarity score between the query face and each enrolled face is generated by the matcher and used for recognition in either identification mode or verification mode.

8.2.1 Face Detection

The face detector locates and tracks the face area from the background of an image or video frames. Facial components such as eyes, nose and mouth are located based on the facial landmarks. As shown in Fig. 8.2, this *first-detetion/tracking-then-*

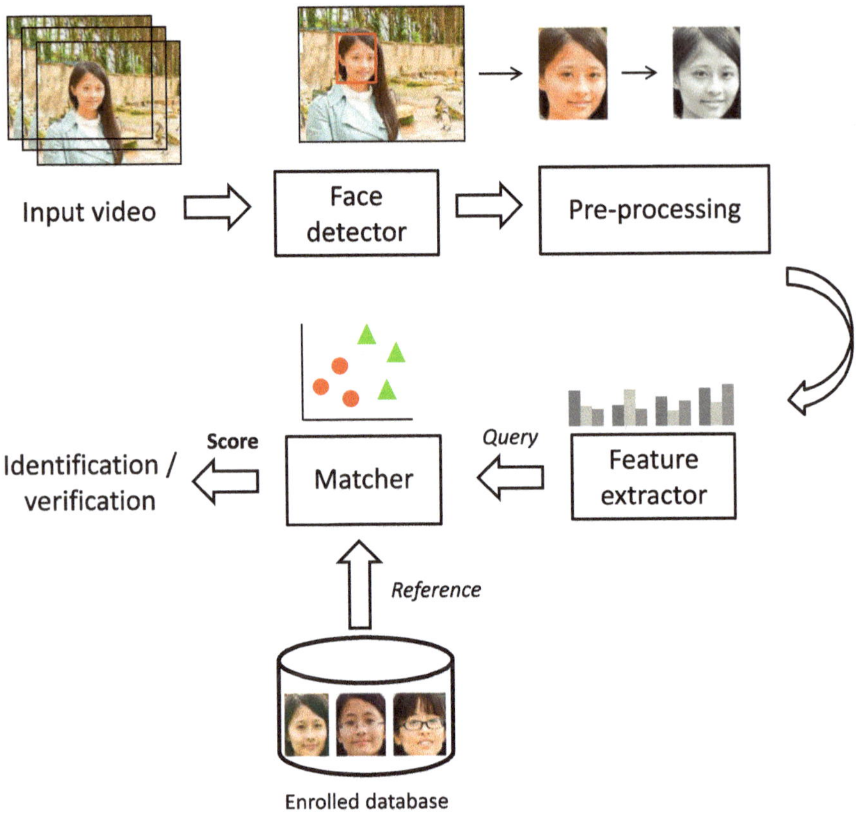

Fig. 8.2 Basic framework of the automatic face recognition. It usually consists of a face detector, a feature extractor and a matcher. Recognition typically works in identification mode or verification mode

recognition framework is applied in most image-based face recognition systems. For face recognition from videosFace recognition from videos, approaches based on this scheme first selects key frames (with good image quality, ideal face size, pose, etc.) and then perform detection/tracking and recognition sequentially. On the other hand, in order to deal with the uncertainties in tracking as well as in recognition, some methods [32, 57] perform simultaneous tracking and recognition using the temporal information in videos. Such *tracking-and-recognition* provides more flexibility for face recognition from videos. It is applicable to the *image-to-video* and *video-to-video* recognition scenarios.

8.2.2 Feature Extraction

Usually preprocessing such as face alignment and normalisation by the facial landmarks are performed before feature extraction. The face area is cropped from an image and normalised according to its geometrical properties (e.g. size and pose) using geometrical transforms or morphing. Usually a detected face area is further normalised with respect to its photometrical properties (e.g. illumination). After that, the feature extractor extracts discriminative information from the face image for distinguishing different individuals. The features can be holistic representations of the face [7, 47], or local patterns around certain salient points of the face [3, 38], depending on the methodology of the matching algorithm. Formulating an effective feature set is a nontrivial task. An effective feature set ideally should be able to characterise the discriminating features in a compact manner. Redundant features not only add little value, but also reduce the power of other useful features. An overly expressive feature set may also lead to the so-called *Curse of Dimensionality*, which requires dimension reduction in order to facilitate efficient matching.

8.2.3 Matching

The matcher compares two faces according to the extracted features producing a similarity score for the ensuing face recognition to be based on. There are two modes in face recognition: *identification* and *verification*, corresponding to the forensic tasks in Fig. 8.1. In the identification mode, the face recognition system matches the features of the query face to the features of each enrolled reference face template in the database. The templates and query sample can be still images or videos. An ordered list of the *top n* most similar candidates are returned as the possible identities of the query according to the similarity scores. The performance of the system in the identification mode is measured in terms of *rank-n* identification rate which is the rate at which the true association is included in the top n matches. The identification rate usually refers to *rank-1* identification rate where the system returns a single match (the best match), as the most probable association with the query face. This rate is also called the *recognition rate*.

On the other hand, verification is the task where the recognition system attempts to confirm an individual's claimed identity by comparing the query sample to the individual's previously enrolled reference templates. Verification is based on a decision threshold which is set by computing the similarity scores of all samples pairs in the database. The threshold is chosen to separate the genuine (i.e. match) similarity scores distribution from the impostor (i.e. non-match) similarity scores distribution and gives the best performance based on one of the following metrics. Here an impostor is a person who submits a sample attempting to claim the identity of another person.

- *False acceptance rate* (FAR) is the rate at which the comparison between two different individuals' samples is erroneously accepted by the system as the true match. In other words, FAR is the percentage of the impostor scores which are higher than the decision threshold.
- *False rejection rate* (FRR) is the percentage of times when an individual is not matched to his/her own existing reference templates. In other words, FRR is the percentage of the genuine scores which are lower than the decision threshold.
- *Equal error rate* (EER) is the rate at which both acceptance and rejection errors are equal (i.e. FAR = FRR). Generally, the lower the EER value, the higher the accuracy of the system.

The first fully automatic face recognition system was presented by Kanade [28] in 1973, which marked a milestone at that time. Over the past four decades, there has been significant progress in automatic face recognition. However, albeit the fact that some unconstrained factors have been considered in the still-image based face recognition, recognising face from videos remains a relatively less explored area due to various factors, such as low resolution, occlusions, lack of subject's cooperation, constantly changing imaging conditions, etc. In the next section we will briefly introduce the challenges in face recognition from videos in the real-world environment.

8.3 Face Recognition from Videos Traces

During the *London Riots* in 2011, the London Metropolitan Police used automatic face recognition software attempting to find the suspects from video traces, but in many cases it failed [16]. The poor quality of most CCTV footage makes it very difficult to trust standard automatic facial recognition techniques. Changes in illumination, image quality, background and orientation can easily fool the face recognition systems.

In 2013, Klontz and Jain [30] conducted a case study that used the photographs from the CCTV footage of the two suspects in the *Boston Marathon bombings* to match against a background set of mugshots. The suspects' images released by the FBI were captured in the uncontrolled environment and their faces were partially occluded by sunglasses and hats. The study showed that current commercial automatic face recognition systems have the notable potential to assist law enforcement. But the matching accuracy was not high enough, suggesting that further technical progress needs to be made in order to be able to recognise faces from CCTV footage taken from unconstrained environments.

Compared with still images, videos contain more information: e.g. multiple views of the face or different illumination conditions and temporal information. However, face recognition from CCTV footages is an even more challenging problem than recognising faces from still images taken from a short distance. First of all, there are two main difficulties for face tracking [59]: (1) real-world videos (e.g. surveillance

Table 8.1 Unconstrained variations in face recognition from video traces

Caused by users	Pose
	Facial expression
	Occlusion
Caused by environment	Illumination
	Low resolution
	Blur (motion blur and focus blur)

videos) are usually of low resolution, which contains less useful information of faces, and (2) illumination changes have a strong impacts on the accuracy of tracking.

In addition, face recognition from videos in real scenarios usually involves the remote face recognition (i.e. *face recognition at a distance* (FRAD)), which is also one of the most challenging problems in face recognition. *Remote face* usually refers to the face data captured at 10 m or further away from the cameras. FRAD is often related to the security and defense applications. Compared with the traditional face recognition (e.g. near-distance face recognition), FRAD is faced with two difficulties: (1) less or even no user-cooperation is available, and (2) the environment condition is more difficult to control. The FRAD algorithms need to consider more serious unconstrained variations in face data in the real-world scenarios. These variations are mainly due to two main factors: the user and the environment, as shown in Table 8.1.

The approaches of recognising face from videos can be divided into three categories [6, 9]: (1) *set-based approaches*, *sequence-based approaches* and *dictionary-based approaches*. The set-based approaches [49] regard a video as a set of unordered images and the recognition robustness is achieved by exploiting the multiple viewing conditions contained in the image set. Traditional still-image based methods can be extended to videos image sets. Recognition is performed by fusing the matching results from multiple frame-pairs at different levels (i.e. feature level, score level and decision level), or by measuring the similarity between the query and reference subspaces/manifolds which are learned from image sets. On the other hand, sequence-based approaches explicitly utilise the temporal information between video frames during recognition. This category of approaches exploits the appearance as well as the motion information of faces to obtain better recognition accuracy. To utilise the temporal information, time series state models such as sequential importance sampling (SIS) [56], and Hidden Markov Models [37] are used to model the video sequences. In recent years, matching face images based on sparse representation via a dictionary becomes popular [13]. *Dictionary* here is a large collection of face images where every individual has multiple images containing a wide range of variations such as poses, expressions and illumination changes. Face frames from a given query video are projected onto the subspace spanned by the atoms in the dictionary and the representation residuals are computed for matching.

8.4 Handling Uncontrollable Factors Present in Videos

Videos provide abundant information in the form of multiple frames and temporal information compared to still images. These information can be exploited for improving the performance of face recognition and provide robustness to large variations in facial poses, expressions and illumination conditions, occlusions and low image quality factors. In the following sub-sections, we introduce face recognition approaches according to the uncontrollable factors they are dealing with. Although some approaches are developed for still images, they do shed light on the new development for video-based systems.

8.4.1 Approaches for Handling Pose Variations

Forensics experts, or even ordinary people are able to recognise a person by the face from different views. However, due to the complex 3D structures of faces, the view generalisation is nontrivial and often ill-posed task for automatic face recognition systems. The main challenge of pose problem is that appearance variations caused by variable poses of the same person (i.e. intra-class variations) can be larger than those caused by identity differences (i.e. inter-class variations). The similarity between two faces from different persons in the same pose can be larger than that of the same person in different poses.

For pose-invariant face recognition, a natural solution is to collect multi-view images/videos which increase the chances of the face being captured in a favourable frontal pose. This is straight-forward and the frontal face recognition algorithms can be directly extended to solve the non-frontal pose problem. Usually pose estimation, which is the process of inferring the orientation of a head, is needed when processing the multi-view data. Then view selection is performed to select images/frames with ideal view conditions based on the pose information. Li et al. [35] estimate the head pose using the SVM regression. The pose information is used to choose the appropriate face detector for multi-view face detection which provides improved performance in terms of accuracy and speed. Only the frontal faces are retained for recognition.

Another direction is to model the pose variations. One of the popular methods is the face manifold. An image of a given size can be viewed as a high-dimensional vector in a Euclidean image space where the dimensionality equals to the number of pixels. The surface and texture of a face is mostly smooth confining it to an embedded face manifold. The basic idea of face manifold-based methods is to cluster the images of similar pose and train a linear subspace to represent each pose cluster. Face manifold is approximated by the linear subspace model. In this way, two face manifolds of similar poses can be compared under a small variation in pose parameters. Arandjelović and Cipolla [5] propose a method, which first decomposes an appearance manifold to Gaussian pose clusters then fuses the fixed-pose comparison results using a neural network for recognition. Wang et al. [49] define the manifold–manifold distance as the distance between the gallery manifold learned from the training gallery image set and the probe manifold learned from the probe image set.

The above methods deal with the pose variations by performing explicit pose estimation or model registration from the multi-view image set or videos. In a surveillance environment, these processes are still very challenging due to the fact that the image quality is poor and the calibration of cameras is not accurate. Du et al. propose a pose-insensitive feature [14] which does not require explicitly estimate the pose of the face. The proposed feature is developed using the spherical harmonic representation of the face texture-mapped onto a sphere. The texture map itself is generated by back-projecting the multi-view video data. One limitation of the method is that the pose-insensitive feature relies on the assumption that the spherical function remains unchanged other than a rotation. The assumption works in normal illumination conditions but does not hold in extreme lightings.

Another limitation for pure 2D image-based methods as described above is that they assume the pose transformation is continuous within the 2D space. On the other hand, approaches with assistance of 3D models [11, 27] which are estimated from videos achieve better performance when addressing pose variations. Compared with 2D image-based methods, 3D model-based methods usually incur a higher computational cost.

8.4.2 Approaches for Handling Occlusion Variations

In the real-world environments, faces are easily occluded by facial accessories (e.g. sunglasses, scarf, hat, veil) or objects in front of the face (e.g. hand, food, mobile phone). These occlusions can largely change the appearance of the face, which makes the face detection more difficult. In forensic investigations, although occluded faces can be manually detected and cropped, recognising partially occluded faces images is still challenging for automatic systems.

One intuitive idea is to first determine whether a face image is occluded or not [44], and then reject the occluded images in applications. This rejection mechanism is not always suitable for face recognition especially in forensic scenarios where no alternative image can be obtained due to the lack of subject cooperation. Some approaches first segment the occluded regions from face images and then perform recognition based on the remaining parts [25, 26, 41]. These models require a skin colour-based *occlusion mask* to detect the occluded areas in faces. The occlusion detectors are usually trained on specific types of occlusions (i.e. the training is data-dependent) and hence generalise poorly to various types of occlusions in real-world environments.

So performing recognition with the presence of occlusions is very challenging. There are three main categories of approaches for face recognition without detecting occlusion in advance: (1) *reconstruction-based approaches*, (2) *local matching-based approaches* and (3) *occlusion-insensitive feature-based approaches*.

The first category, reconstruction-based approaches treats occluded face recognition as a reconstruction problem [51, 53, 55]. A clean image is reconstructed from an occluded query image by a linear combination of reference images. Then the occluded image is assigned to the class with the minimal reconstruction error. A common drawback of reconstruction-based methods is that they usually require a large number of samples per subject to represent a query image. Most of them assume that the reference/training images are captured in well controlled conditions. However, this assumption does not usually hold in real-world scenarios. Another drawback is this category of approaches usually incur a high computational cost [53].

The second category is the local matching-based approaches [39, 45, 50, 52]. Facial features are extracted from local areas of a face, for example, overlapping or non-overlapping patches of an image, so the affected and unaffected parts of the face can be analysed in isolation. In order to minimise matching errors due to occluded parts, different strategies such as local space learning [39, 45], multi-task sparse representation learning [36] or voting [50] are performed. The common intuition behind the local matching-based approaches is based on that the facial appearance changes caused by occlusions are local in nature. Only part of a face is distorted by occlusions while others are less affected and reliable for recognition. So compared with the reconstruction-based methods, local matching-based methods are less likely to be able to handle the situation in which more than half of the face is occluded.

In addition to the above approaches, which focus on improving the robustness to occlusions during the matching stage, researchers also pay attention to image representation. The third category is occlusion-insensitive feature-based approaches [48, 58] which attempts to extract occlusion-insensitive features from face images. Tzimiropoulos et al. [48] pointed out that PCA learning in the gradient orientation domain with a cosine-based distance measure helps reduce the effects due to occlusions in face images. The distribution of image gradient orientation (IGO) differences and the cosine kernel provide a powerful way to measure image correlation/similarity when image data are corrupted by occlusions. The face representations learned from the image gradient orientations are relatively invariant to the occlusion effects. Inspired by their work, Zhu et al. [58] further proposed a Gabor phase difference representation for occluded face recognition. They find that the Gabor phase (GP) difference is more stable and robust than gradient orientation to occlusions.

8.4.3 Approaches for Handling Illumination Variations

Due to the 3D structure and various surface reflectance of faces, light sources can cast shading and shadows, creating nonuniform illumination on faces, which accentuates or diminishes certain facial features. The differences induced by this impact in the facial appearance can be greater than that between individuals.

There are two categories of approaches for addressing the illumination problem—*active* and *passive* ways [60]. The active approaches attempt to obtain face images which are invariant to the illumination changes. Usually specific devices such as 3D scanners, thermal cameras, infrared cameras, etc. other than the visible light cameras are required. A good survey on 3D face recognition can be found in [1]. Thermal images and near-infrared images are more insensitive to large illumination changes as compared to visible light images. Introductions to illumination invariant face recognition using thermal images and near-infrared images are presented in [17, 34], respectively.

On the other hand, the passive approaches attempt to directly deal with images which have already been affected by illuminations. There are usually three classes of approaches. (1) Illumination normalisation [12, 15], which seeks to suppress the illumination variations either by image transformations or by synthesising an unaffected image from affected ones, (2) illumination invariant representation [3, 18], which attempts to extract features invariant to illumination changes, and (3) illumination variation modelling. Illumination core [8, 20] and sparse representation [53] are based on the theoretical principle that the set of images of a convex Lambertian object [31] obtained in a wide variety of illumination conditions can be approximated by a low-dimensional linear subspace in which the recognition can be performed. These methods require well-registered face images and the availability of face images with different illumination conditions. Such requirements limit their applicability in practice, especially for videos captured in unconstrained environments. Some models for pose variations are also applicable to solving of the illumination problem. Using the manifold model introduced in Sect. 8.4.1, the illumination variation for each of the pose clusters can be modelled using a linear, pose-specific illumination subspace. Given a reference template and a novel cluster with the same pose, the illumination changes can be normalised by adding a vector from the pose illumination subspace to the frame so that its distance from the reference cluster is minimised [5].

8.4.4 Approaches for Handling Low Image Quality Variations

In security-related face recognition applications such as surveillance, usually the face images/videos captured are degraded by low resolution and blur effects. When sufficient videos are available, one simple idea is to select a set of frames which yield the best recognition accuracy by a classifier. This can help to remove or give lower weight to the poor quality frames during recognition.

For the low resolution problem, another intuitive solution is the super-resolution (SR) based method [4]. SR is a technique for synthesising high-resolution images from low resolution images for visual enhancement. After applying SR, a higher resolution image can be obtained and then used for recognition, for example, matching a face in a low resolution surveillance footage against a set of higher quality gallery sequences enrolled in a database. One common drawback of SR-based face recognition approaches is that SR does not directly contribute to recognition. The identity information may be contaminated by some artefacts attributed to the SR process.

Another category of approaches do not apply the SR preprocessing to low resolution images. Li et al. [33] proposed a method to learn coupled mappings (CMs), which minimises the difference between the low resolution image and its high-resolution counterpart. Then the low resolution image is projected onto a unified feature space where higher recognition performance can be achieved. Biswas et al. [10] proposed a method using Multidimensional Scaling (MDS) to transform the low resolution gallery and probe images into an Euclidean space such that the distances between them approximates the best distances. Shekhar et al. [43] propose a generative approach to low resolution image-based on learning class specific dictionaries, which is also robust to illumination variations.

There are two types of effect attributed to the blur problem: *focus blur* and *motion blur*. A focus is the point where lights originating from a point on the object converge. When the light from object points is not well converged, an out-of-focus image with the blur effect will be generated by the sensor (e.g. camera). The work in [24] analysed the impact of out-of-focus blur on face recognition performance. On the other hand, motion blur is due to the rapid object movement or camera shaking. Blurring affects the appearance of faces in images, causing two main problems [42]: (1) the appearance of face images from the same individual changes significantly due to blur, and (2) different individuals tend to appear more similar when blurred due to the loss of discriminative features. There are two main categories of approaches to improve the quality of the blurred face images: (1) blurred image modelling through subspace analysis [42] or sparse representation [54], and (2) blur-tolerant descriptors which attempt to extract blur insensitive features such as Local Phase Quantisation (LPQ) [2, 23] to represent the face images.

8.5 Future Trends

As introduced in the last section, the appearance variations caused by the unconstrained conditions are still challenging for face recognition from images and videos. This section will discuss several specific face recognition problems, which are the new trends of research in both biometrics and forensics communities.

8.5.1 Combining with Other Biometric Traits

When faces are heavily occluded or degraded due to extreme conditions, face recognition technologies become ineffective. In unconstrained environments, the face is not the only trait used by humans to recognise each other. It is natural to combine face and other biometric data to improve the recognition performance. These data is either from other modalities such as voice, gait [21] or soft biometric features such as height, gender, hair, skin and clothing colour. The advantages of using such features are: (1) they can be captured without constraint in uncontrollable environments, and (2) they can be captured along with the face using the same sensor such as a CCTV camera. How to represent the features from different modalities and how to fuse these features and matching scores will be the important issues for future investigations.

8.5.2 Contending with the Face Ageing Issue

Facial ageing is a complex process that affects both the shape and texture (e.g. skin tone or wrinkles) of a face. The typical scenario of face recognition across ageing is to detect if a particular person is present in a previously recorded database. Applications include missing children identification, suspect watch-list check, etc. For still-image based recognition, ageing effect has been studied in two directions: (1) developing *age estimation techniques* to classify face images-based on age [19, 22] and (2) developing *ageing robust systems* to perform recognition. However, the ageing issue are seldom considered in video-based face recognition algorithms. One most challenging aspect of face recognition involving the ageing issue is that it must address all other 'historical' unconstrained variations as well. Pose, expression, illumination changes and occlusions can occur when images are taken years apart.

Compared to still images, videos contain the temporal information which is of great value for face recognition. It is interesting to investigate into the ways of utilising the temporal information effectively to deal with the ageing issue.

8.5.3 Different Imaging Modalities

Face recognition across different imaging modalities, also called *heterogeneous face recognition* [29], is another interesting area for further explorations. It involves matching two face images from different imaging modalities, which is of great practical value in forensic scenarios. The images of suspects may come from various sources, e.g. still images captured from CCTV, footages taken by the police helicopters or images snapped by members of the public. In addition, in some extreme situations, only a particular modality of a face image is available. For example, in night-time environments, infrared imaging may be the only modality for acquiring a useful face image of a suspect. But the mug-shots held by the police are visible band images. Another example is the sketch-photograph matching. When no photograph of a suspect is available, a forensic sketch is often generated according to the description of an eye-witness. Matching sketches against face photographs is very important for forensic investigation. On the other hand, 2D-3D face matching is expected to attract intensive research efforts in the near future since face can be represented by heterogeneous features in the 3D and 2D modalities in the real-world cases.

8.5.4 Other Issues in Forensic Tasks

The face recognition technologies discussed in previous sections mainly focus on how to improve the recognition accuracy from face images and videos. This is essential in forensic investigation and case linking. Besides that, there are other requirements in other forensic tasks [40]. For example, in forensic identification, such as identifying missing people, besides recognition accuracy, the other challenges lie in the development and management of reference databases. How to increase the integrity, quality and interoperability of the template data with the help of face image processing or analysis technologies is an important issue. For forensic evidence evaluation, the challenges are not only about the development of automatic methods, but also the integration of expert-based and automatic methods into hybrid methods.

8.6 Summary

The face is one of the most popular biometric traits used in the daily life for human recognition. The widespread use of CCTV cameras for surveillance and security applications have stirred extensive research interests in video-based face recognition. Face recognition can play an important role in identifying perpetrators of crime activities as well as missing peoples. Automatic face recognition technology is becoming an indispensable tool for modern forensic investigations.

In this chapter we have introduced the advanced face recognition technologies. The past decades have seen significant progress in automatic face recognition. But the performance of the face recognition from videosFace recognition from videos taken in unconstrained environments is still unsatisfactory. Uncontrollable illumination, pose changes, low image quality and occlusions pose acute challenges to face recognition techniques. Therefore, intensive research efforts to contend with these interweaving factors are required in the years to come.

References

1. Abate AF, Nappi M, Riccio D, Sabatino G (2007) 2D and 3D face recognition: a survey. Pattern Recognit Lett 28(14):1885–1906. Image: Information and Control
2. Ahonen T, Rahtu E, Ojansivu V, Heikkila J (2008) Recognition of blurred faces using local phase quantization. In: International conference on pattern recognition (ICPR), pp 1–4
3. Ahonen T, Hadid A, Pietikainen M (2006) Face description with local binary patterns: application to face recognition. IEEE Trans Pattern Anal Mach Intell 28(12):2037–2041
4. Arandjelović O, Cipolla R (2007) A manifold approach to face recognition from low quality video across illumination and pose using implicit super-resolution. In: IEEE international conference computer vision (ICCV), pp 1–8
5. Arandjelović O, Cipolla R (2009) A pose-wise linear illumination manifold model for face recognition using video. Comput Vis Image Underst 113(1):113–125

6. Barr JR, Bowyer KW, Flynn PJ, Biswas S (2012) Face recognition from video: a review. Int J Pattern Recognit Artif Intell 26(5)
7. Belhumeur PN, Hespanha JP, Kriegman DJ (1997) Eigenfaces vs. fisherfaces: recognition using class specific linear projection. IEEE Trans Pattern Anal Mach Intell 19(7):711–720
8. Belhumeur PN, Kriegman D (1996) What is the set of images of an object under all possible lighting conditions? In: IEEE conference computer vision and pattern recognition (CVPR), pp 270–277
9. Bhatt HS, Singh R, Vatsa M (2014) On recognizing faces in videos using clustering-based re-ranking and fusion. IEEE Trans Inf Forensics Secur 9(7):1056–1068
10. Biswas S, Bowyer KW, Flynn PJ (2010) Multidimensional scaling for matching low-resolution facial images. In: IEEE international conference on biometrics: theory, applications, and systems (BTAS), pp 1–6
11. Castillo CD, Jacobs DW (2009) Using stereo matching with general epipolar geometry for 2d face recognition across pose. IEEE Trans Pattern Anal Mach Intell 31(12):2298–2304
12. Chen T, Yin W, Zhou XS, Comaniciu D, Huang TS (2006) Total variation models for variable lighting face recognition. IEEE Trans Pattern Anal Mach Intell 28(9):1519–1524
13. Chen YC, Patel VM, Phillips PJ, Chellappa R (2012) Dictionary-based face recognition from video. In: Fitzgibbon A, Lazebnik S, Perona P, Sato Y, Schmid C (eds) European conference computer vision (ECCV), vol 7577. Lecture notes in computer science. Springer, Berlin, pp 766–779
14. Du M, Sankaranarayanan AC, Chellappa R (2014) Robust face recognition from multi-view videos. IEEE Trans Image Process 23(3):1105–1117
15. Du S, Ward R (2005) Wavelet-based illumination normalization for face recognition. In: IEEE international conference on image processing (ICIP), vol 2, pp II-954-7
16. Firth N (2011) Face recognition technology fails to find UK rioters. New Sci
17. Gabriel H, del Solar JR, Verschae R, Correa M (2012) A comparative study of thermal face recognition methods in unconstrained environments. Pattern Recognit 45(7):2445–2459
18. Gao Y, Leung MKH (2002) Face recognition using line edge map. IEEE Trans Pattern Anal Mach Intell 24(6):764–779
19. Geng X, Zhou Z-H, Smith-Miles K (2007) Automatic age estimation based on facial aging patterns. IEEE Trans Pattern Anal Mach Intell 29(12):2234–2240
20. Georghiades AS, Belhumeur PN, Kriegman D (2001) From few to many: illumination cone models for face recognition under variable lighting and pose. IEEE Trans Pattern Anal Mach Intell 23(6):643–660
21. Guan Y, Wei X, Li C-T, Marcialis GL, Roli F, Tistarelli M (2013) Combining gait and face for tackling the elapsed time challenges. In: IEEE international conference on biometrics: theory, applications, and systems (BTAS), pp 1–8
22. Guodong G, Fu Y, Dyer CR, Huang TS (2008) Image-based human age estimation by manifold learning and locally adjusted robust regression. IEEE Tran Image Process 17(7):1178–1188
23. Hadid A, Nishiyama M, Sato Y (2010) Recognition of blurred faces via facial deblurring combined with blur-tolerant descriptors. In: 2010 20th international conference on pattern recognition (ICPR), pp 1160–1163
24. Hua F, Johnson P, Sazonova N, Lopez-Meyer P, Schuckers S (2012) Impact of out-of-focus blur on face recognition performance based on modular transfer function. In: IAPR international conference biometrics (ICB), pp 85–90
25. Jia H, Martínez AM (2008) Face recognition with occlusions in the training and testing sets. In: IEEE international conference automatic face and gesture recognition (FG), pp 1–6
26. Jia H, Martínez AM (2009) Support vector machines in face recognition with occlusions. In: IEEE conference computer vision and pattern recognition (CVPR), pp 136–141
27. Jiang D, Hu Y, Yan S, Zhang L, Zhang H, Gao W (2005) Efficient 3d reconstruction for face recognition. Pattern Recognit 38(6):787–798. Image Understanding for Photographs
28. Kanade T (1973) Picture processing system by computer complex and recognition of human faces. In: Doctoral dissertation, Kyoto University

29. Klare B, Jain AK (2010) Heterogeneous face recognition: matching NIR to visible light images. In: International conference on pattern recognition (ICPR), pp 1513–1516
30. Klontz JC, Jain AK (2013) A case study on unconstrained facial recognition using the Boston marathon bombings suspects. Technical Report MSU-CSE-13-4
31. Lambert J (1760) Photometria sive de mensura et gradibus luminus. Colorum et Umbrae, Eberhard Klett
32. Li B, Chellappa R (2002) A generic approach to simultaneous tracking and verification in video. IEEE Trans Image Process 11(5):530–544
33. Li B, Chang H, Shan S, Chen X (2010) Low-resolution face recognition via coupled locality preserving mappings. IEEE Signal Process Lett 17(1):20–23
34. Li SZ, Chu R, Liao S, Zhang L (2007) Illumination invariant face recognition using near-infrared images. IEEE Trans Pattern Anal Mach Intell 29(4):627–639
35. Li Y, Gong S, Sherrah J, Liddell H (2004) Support vector machine based multi-view face detection and recognition. Image Vis Comput 22(5):413–427
36. Liao S, Jain AK, Li SZ (2013) Partial face recognition: alignment-free approach. IEEE Trans Pattern Anal Mach Intell 35(5):1193–1205
37. Liu X, Chen I (2003) Video-based face recognition using adaptive hidden markov models. In: IEEE conference computer vision and pattern recognition (CVPR), vol 1, pp I–340–I–345
38. Lowe DG (2004) Distinctive image features from scale-invariant keypoints. Int J Comput Vis 60(2):91–110
39. Martínez AM (2002) Recognizing imprecisely localized, partially occluded, and expression variant faces from a single sample per class. IEEE Trans Pattern Anal Mach Intell 24(6):748–763
40. Meuwly D, Veldhuis R (2012) Forensic biometrics: from two communities to one discipline. In: International conference of the biometrics special interest group BIOSIG, Darmstadt, Germany, pp 1–12
41. Min R, Hadid A, Dugelay J-C (2011) Improving the recognition of faces occluded by facial accessories. In: IEEE international conference automatic face and gesture recognition (FG), pp 442–447
42. Nishiyama M, Hadid A, Takeshima H, Shotton J, Kozakaya T, Yamaguchi O (2011) Facial deblur inference using subspace analysis for recognition of blurred faces. IEEE Trans Pattern Anal Mach Intell 33(4):838–845
43. Shekhar S, Patel VM, Chellappa R (2011) Synthesis-based recognition of low resolution faces. In: IEEE international joint conference on biometrics (IJCB), pp 1–6
44. Storer M, Urschler M, Bischof H (2010) Occlusion detection for ICAO compliant facial photographs. In: IEEE conference computer vision and pattern recognition workshops (CVPRW), pp 122–129
45. Tan X, Chen S, Zhou Z-H, Liu J (2009) Face recognition under occlusions and variant expressions with partial similarity. IEEE Trans Inf Forensics Secur 4(2):217–230
46. Travis A (2008) Police trying out national database with 750,000 mugshots. MPs told. The guardian
47. Turk MA, Pentland AP (1991) Face recognition using eigenfaces. In: IEEE conference computer vision and pattern recognition (CVPR), pp 586–591
48. Tzimiropoulos G, Zafeiriou S, Pantic M (2012) Subspace learning from image gradient orientations. IEEE Trans Pattern Anal Mach Intell 34(12):2454–2466
49. Wang R, Shan S, Chen X, Gao W (2008) Manifold-manifold distance with application to face recognition based on image set. In: IEEE conference computer vision and pattern recognition (CVPR), pp 1–8
50. Wei X, Li C-T (2013) Fixation and saccade based face recognition from single image per person with various occlusions and expressions. In: IEEE conference computer vision and pattern recognition workshops (CVPRW), pp 70–75
51. Wei X, Li C-T, Hu Y (2012) Robust face recognition under varying illumination and occlusion considering structured sparsity. In: International conference digital image computing techniques and applications (DICTA), pp 1–7

52. Wei X, Li C-T, Lei Z, Yi D, Li SZ (2014) Dynamic image-to-class warping for occluded face recognition. IEEE Trans Inf Forensics Secur 9(12):2035–2050
53. Wright J, Yang AY, Ganesh A, Sastry SS, Ma Y (2009) Robust face recognition via sparse representation. IEEE Trans Pattern Anal Mach Intell 31(2):210–227
54. Zhang H, Yang J, Zhang Y, Nasrabadi NM, Huang TS (2011) Close the loop: joint blind image restoration and recognition with sparse representation prior. In: IEEE international conference computer vision (ICCV), pp 770–777
55. Zhang L, Yang M, Feng X (2011) Sparse representation or collaborative representation: which helps face recognition? In: IEEE international conference computer vision (ICCV), pp 471–478
56. Zhou S, Krueger V, Chellappa R (2003) Probabilistic recognition of human faces from video. Comput Vis Image Underst 91(1–2):214–245. Special issue on face recognition
57. Zhou SK, Chellappa R, Moghaddam B (2004) Visual tracking and recognition using appearance-adaptive models in particle filters. IEEE Trans Image Process 13(11):1491–1506
58. Zhu J, Cao D, Liu S, Lei Z, Li SZ (2012) Discriminant analysis with Gabor phase for robust face recognition. In: IAPR international conference biometrics (ICB), pp 13–18
59. Zou WW, Yuen PC, Chellappa R (2013) Low-resolution face tracker robust to illumination variations. IEEE Trans Image Process 22(5):1726–1739
60. Zou X, Kittler J, Messer K (2007) Illumination invariant face recognition: a survey. In: IEEE international conference on biometrics: theory, applications, and systems (BTAS), pp 1–8

Chapter 9
Human Factors in Forensic Face Identification

David White, Kristin Norell, P. Jonathon Phillips and Alice J. O'Toole

Abstract Facial identification by forensic examiners is a core component of criminal investigations and convictions. These identifications are often done in challenging circumstances that require experts to match identity across images and videos taken at a various distances, under different illumination conditions, and across a wide range of poses. Until recently, laboratory studies of human face identification have concentrated, almost exclusively, on face identification by untrained (naïve) observers, with only a handful of studies focusing directly on the accuracy of expert forensic facial examiners. Over the last two decades, DNA-based exonerations of convicted criminals in the United States have revealed weaknesses in the forensic identification process due to *human factors*. In this paper, we review and analyze the factors known to impact facial identification accuracy for both naïve participants and trained experts. Combined, these studies point to a set of challenges that impact accuracy for both groups of participants. They also lead to an understanding of the specific conditions under which forensic facial examiners can surpass naïve observers at the task of face identification. Finally, we consider the role that computer-based face recognition systems can play in the future of forensic facial identification. These systems have made remarkable strides in recent years, raising new questions about how human and machine strengths at face identification can be combined to achieve optimum accuracy.

In (Eds. M. Tistarelli, C. Champod) *Biometrics in Forensic Sciences.*

D. White
University of New South Wales, Sydney, Australia

K. Norell
Swedish National Forensic Centre, Linköping, Sweden

P.J. Phillips
National Institute of Standards and Technology, Gaithersburg, USA

A.J. O'Toole (✉)
The University of Texas at Dallas, Richardson, USA
e-mail: otoole@utdallas.edu

M. Tistarelli and C. Champod (eds.), *Handbook of Biometrics for Forensic Science*, Advances in Computer Vision and Pattern Recognition,
DOI 10.1007/978-3-319-50673-9_9

9.1 Introduction

Identification by forensic facial analysis experts contributes evidence in criminal cases in most countries that have functioning governments and court systems. Societies and individuals have a vested interest in assuring the accuracy and credibility of these identification judgments. Accurate judgments contribute to communities that are safe from dangerous criminals and also uphold the rights of innocent people from being falsely accused and convicted of crimes. What do we know *scientifically* about the accuracy of these forensic facial identification judgments? In a perfect world, forensic examiners would receive feedback on the correctness of every judgment they make in a criminal or court case. This is not possible when corroborating evidence in a case which is weak or when a suspect maintains innocence, even after conviction. Unfortunately, incorrect forensic judgments are detected only when some other form of corroborating evidence, such as a DNA test or a clear alibi, provides convincing counterevidence to the accuracy of the judgment.

In recent years, the United States has seen a disturbing number of forensic judgments, and indeed the criminal convictions supported by these decisions, set aside based on evidence from belated DNA testing of convicted felons [59]. These cases have involved forensic examiners with expertise in wide variety of evidence types (e.g., face, fingerprint, and hair). As DNA testing has became more widely available and accessible to investigators and adjudicators, a steady stream of DNA-based exonerations have come to light in the United States, bringing with them an intense public discussion about the role of forensics in the justice system. This prompted the National Academy of Sciences in the United States to issue a report aimed at strengthening forensic sciences [42]. One recommendation of the report was a call for scientific research aimed at understanding the factors that impact accuracy in forensic analysis.

The goal of this chapter is to review what we know scientifically about the accuracy of forensic facial examiners. We begin with a brief statement of the nature of the facial identification problem solved by forensic examiners. The remainder of the chapter is organized as follows. First, we discuss the factors known to affect human face recognition accuracy in laboratory studies of people without training or professional experience in forensic face recognition. Second, we will review studies that compare the accuracy of professional forensic facial examiners to that of untrained participants. This literature is sparse, but growing, with several recent studies testing professional forensic examiners. These studies have expanded our knowledge of how professionals may differ, both qualitatively and quantitatively, from untrained individuals. In the third section of the chapter, we discuss advances in computer-based face recognition software and assess their strengths and weakness in comparison to both untrained and professional populations. We conclude with a road map for a way forward. We will argue that the route forward should include strategies for retaining the advantages and skills of forensic face examiners, while understanding the inherent limits of forensic facial identification science. We will also consider the potential of combining human and computer-based biometric "systems" to their best advantage.

9.1.1 *The Problem*

The nature of the analysis presented by an expert typically involves an identity comparison made between two or more images and/or videos of faces. Often these images and videos are captured under photometric conditions (illumination, viewpoint, and distance) that vary substantially and across a variety of media types. Forensic facial examiners commonly deal with media types that include high quality passport images, drivers' license photos, surveillance video taken at the scene of a crime, and image/video data taken by bystanders using handheld mobile devices.

In a perceptual or laboratory version of the task, participants are asked to match the identity of two individuals in pairs of images, usually presented simultaneously. In casework, as in laboratory studies, the response comes in the form of a simple judgment of whether the two (or more) images depict the same person or different people. Almost always, this judgment is accompanied by a rating of confidence or certainty in the judgment. In casework, the certainty rating provides a guide as to whether the judgment can be used as evidence in a legal setting. In laboratory studies, certainty ratings make the data amenable to standard signal detection analysis and to the construction of receiver operator characteristic (ROC) measures that can be compared across perceivers and conditions [36]. This type of analysis also facilitates comparisons between expert forensic facial examiners and untrained people tested in laboratory conditions and between computer-based face recognition systems and both types of participants.

9.2 Characteristics of Human Face Recognition Relevant for Forensics

9.2.1 *Familiarity*

The most common face identification task that humans perform is not the image comparison task performed in forensic examination. Rather, in our daily lives, we recognize faces of colleagues, friends, and family by matching their face to a representation that is stored in our memory. Although an impressive computational feat, this skill does not require special training to perform accurately. Familiar face recognition is the primary route to person identification in our daily lives [75]. Indeed, through evolutionary and developmental pressures, the human brain has developed robust processes for this important task. As a result, people are excellent at identifying familiar faces, enabling them to recognize high school classmates from yearbook photographs with very high accuracy, 15 years after graduating [3].

Our impressive abilities with *familiar* faces appear to stem from a representational system that is specifically tuned to face perception. Given our highly developed perceptual apparatus, human performance in this task has been exalted as the "gold-standard" for face identification, to which machine-based systems should aspire [61]. This is a sensible aim, given that human face recognition displays many desirable properties for a recognition system. For example, we are able to accurately identify familiar faces from very low quality closed caption television (CCTV) images [12]. Importantly, memory representations supporting familiar face recognition are highly tolerant of within-identity variation caused by changes in image-specific properties. This is particularly important for face recognition because of the relatively large within-identity variation (due to image- and person-based factors; see Sect. 9.2.2) in comparison to the subtle differences between faces that are diagnostic of identity. Being able to recognize familiar faces despite this very low signal-to-noise ratio is the core computational challenge of face recognition.

Importantly, our tolerance of image variation is strongly contingent on our familiarity with the face [8, 24]. This has been demonstrated consistently in studies of face identification using *unfamiliar* faces, which we discuss in more detail in the next section. For now, to demonstrate this important distinction and the challenge presented by unfamiliar faces, we invite the reader to estimate how many people are pictured in Fig. 9.1. Jenkins et al. [24] presented student participants with a similar array (containing pictures of Dutch celebrities) and asked them to sort the images into piles by identity; such that each pile contained a single person, with a unique

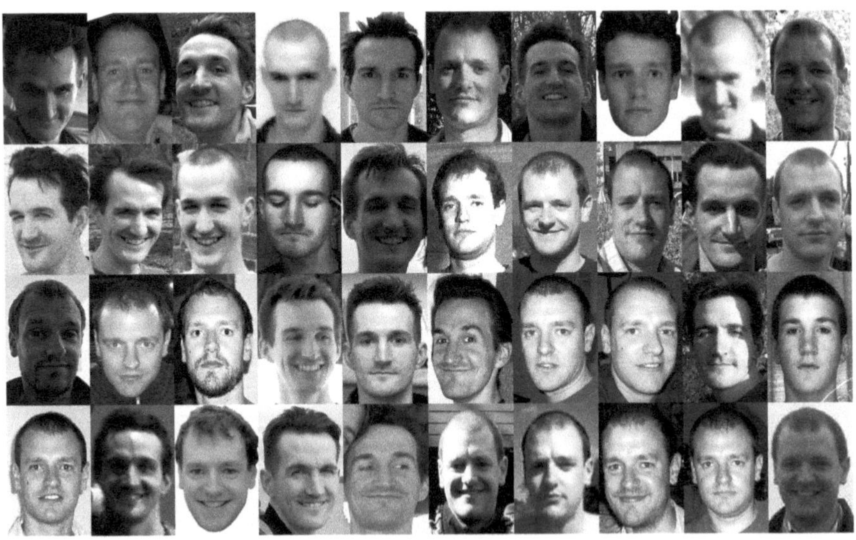

Fig. 9.1 How many people are pictured in this array? (From [24]). See text for the correct answer

pile for each person. Students from the Netherlands, who were familiar with the faces, correctly answered that there were only two people present in the array. However, students from the United Kingdom, who were unfamiliar with the faces in the array, saw many more than two identities. These British participants sorted the photographs into an average of seven piles, indicating that they believed there were seven people in the array.

The Jenkins et al. [24] study demonstrates that face identification accuracy is strongly constrained by the degree of familiarity we have with a face. This is also true of the types of decisions typically made in forensic facial comparison; where two images are presented simultaneously and participants have to decide if the images are of the same person or two different people. When matching high quality images of unfamiliar faces, taken under very similar lighting conditions and on the same day, people make a large proportion of errors on this apparently straightforward task (e.g., Megreya and Burton [39], Burton et al. [11]). However, when the faces are familiar to participants, this task becomes trivial. In a series of studies, Clutterbuck and Johnston [14–16] compared performance in this task across faces of varying levels of familiarity. Their data show a graded improvement in face matching as faces become familiar, leading the authors to suggest that performance in pairwise matching provides a sensitive index of a person's familiarity with a face [15].

These findings are consistent with earlier work by Bruck et al. [10], who tested participants' ability to match yearbook photographs of classmates taken 25 years previously. This matching ability was better for classmates than for people who were not previously classmates. Remarkably, this was true despite the fact that the classmates had not seen the people in the photographs during the intervening 25 years. When images of faces were taken from different angles, match accuracy was adversely affected for control participants, but not for classmates. Therefore, the benefit of familiarity was remarkably sensitive and long lasting. The findings are also similar to those observed by Jenkins et al. [24], in showing that participants who were familiar with the faces were able to match identity across variation in the image-level qualities (in this case, head angle). This invariance is a key characteristic of familiar face representation (see also Jiang et al. [25]).

The ability of our visual systems to produce these higher-order representations is the main source of our impressive face recognition skills. Where these representations are not available, the power of human face recognition system is not fully exploited and performance is far less impressive. Unfortunately, in forensic practice and most other applied settings, the full benefits of this expert system are not available because the faces encountered are almost always *unfamiliar*. Because of the very clear advantages of familiarity, recent work has attempted to improve the accuracy of face matching by leveraging familiarity from multiple images of an individual [2, 13, 67]. In parallel to similar work to develop methods in machine learning (see Sect. 4.3), the hope is that methods that make best use of the image data for the purpose of face learning may benefit forensic practice in future.

It is important to note that the potential for leveraging familiarity in this way is limited to cases where multiple images of an individual are available.

Unfortunately, in most instances, forensic casework is based on comparison of single images. As a result, forensic methods tend to focus on developing strategies for one-to-one image comparison of unfamiliar faces. In such cases, the research summarized in this section should serve to underline that forensic examiners should not generalize the very accurate identification performance seen with familiar faces to the task performed in their daily work.

9.2.2 *Image and Demographic Factors*

Human face recognition has been studied for decades, primarily under laboratory conditions in which participants learn the identity of an individual from a single image and are tested subsequently with a different image. In addition, there are many studies in which people compare face identity perceptually in two images that are simultaneously available. From both recognition and perceptual matching studies, much is known about the factors that impact our ability to extract and compare identity information from face images. These factors can be divided into *stimulus factors*, *subject factors,* and *interactive factors.* Interactive factors result from specific combinations of stimulus factors and subject factors.

Stimulus factors encompass all of the ways that images of individuals can vary. There are two categories of stimulus factors. *Image-based factors* are the result of the way a particular image is taken. They include illumination, viewpoint (i.e., pose), distance, resolution, and other parameters inherent to the image capture process. *Person-based* factors are changes inherent to the person's appearance. These include changes in facial expression, facial hair, accessories (e.g., glasses, tattoos, make-up, etc.), as well as changes that occur on a longer time scale (aging, facial surgery, and weight gain/loss). *Categorical factors* refer to the sex, age, and race of the person to be recognized, as well as the "typicality" of the person relative to these reference groups. *Subject factors* pertain to characteristics of the perceiver, including their sex, race, and age. The only interactive factor we will consider is the "other-race effect", which is the well-known finding that people recognize faces of their own race more accurately than faces of other races [37].

9.2.2.1 Stimulus Factors

Image-based factors. To a first approximation, the story here is simple. People recognize faces best when the image they learn is captured under photometric conditions similar to the conditions under which the test image is captured. This is true for recognition over changes in illumination (e.g., Braje et al. [7], Hill and Bruce [22]) and viewpoint [47, 65]. In general, there is no "optimal view" for recognition, although several studies indicate that recognition is best from images that show a face in three-quarter profile (e.g., Logie et al. [31], O'Toole et al. [31, 47]). Notably, face recognition is extremely difficult when face images are presented upside down [74]. It is also difficult when face images are presented in the photographic negative [20]—a manipulation that produces an image similar to what would be seen if a face were illuminated from below. The effects of image inversion and photographic negation suggest that human face processing operates in a mono-oriented fashion and with sensitivity that is not limited to the contours of the face image, but extends to the subtle shading variations that are disrupted with face inversion.

The rule that face recognition performance varies directly with the closeness of the viewing parameters between the learning and test images finds exception in the case of image resolution. Liu et al. [30] showed that identity matching is more accurate with a high-resolution and low-resolution image, than with two low-resolution images. They also showed that the recognition of high-resolution and low-resolution faces is generally equivalent when participants learned people from low-resolution gait videos. This suggests that the availability of a high-resolution image actually *improved* face-matching performance from a low-resolution image, perhaps by allowing for the creation of a more robust and generalizable representation from the high-resolution image.

Person-based Factors. It is tempting to conclude that person-based factors affect recognition in the same way as image-based factors—that is to say, when a person's appearance is similar in two images (e.g., same age, same expression, same weight, and same make-up), recognition is more accurate than when appearance has changed in some way. Although this seems intuitively likely, and even obvious, remarkably few psychological studies have tested this question formally. Although systematic evaluations of these person-based factors have not been carried out, recent work shows a substantial drop-off in face-matching accuracy across relatively modest age spans. Megreya et al. [40] show that matching performance is reduced by around 20% when matching across age-differences of between one and two years, which is consistent with a more recent study (White et al. [69]; photo-to-photo test).

The sparseness of the literature on this topic is likely due the fact that most databases available for face recognition contain only one or two images of a person. These images are often taken over a relatively short time span, ranging from a few minutes up to a few months. In the last few years, far richer face databases, collected from web crawling, have become available. These databases now contain hundreds of images of the same person, taken over years and even decades. Recent use of these database resources for testing computer-based face recognition systems has contributed to the fast pace of progress in that field. These databases will likely become more prominent in psychological studies in the years to come, enabling more systematic assessments of the impact of person- and image-based factors on the accuracy of face identification in humans. In the meantime, photographic demonstrations of the variability in facial images of a single individual (see Fig. 9.1) provide compelling anecdotal evidence that person-based appearance changes (e.g., age, expression) make face identification more difficult—at least for unfamiliar faces.

Categorical Factors. Are some categories of faces easier to recognize than others? For standard demographic categories of faces, the answer to this question, based on what is currently known, is "no." Although there have been limited tests to consider whether male versus female faces are more recognizable, findings of substantial differences in the literature are rare and inconsistent. This is also true when examining faces of different races. Faces are not differentially recognizable as a function of their race or ethnic heritage. Where age is concerned, the literature is sparse, but again, there is no indication that faces of particular age groups are more or less recognizable than faces of other-age groups [18, 71].

It would not be true, however, to say that all faces are equally recognizable. The primary face characteristic that predicts recognition success is its perceived typicality [29], such that the more similar a face is to the average, the less accurate recognition will be. This advantage for recognizing distinct or unusual faces helps to explain why face caricatures can be recognized easily. In caricatures, the distinctive or unusual features of a face are exaggerated. For instance, a large nose becomes even larger in a caricature. A paradox in understanding human face recognition abilities is that caricatures are highly recognizable, despite the degree of distortion of features and configural information introduced into the image. However, while caricatures improve familiar face recognition [57], recent attempts to improve unfamiliar face recognition have produced quite modest benefits. McIntyre et al. [38] asked if this same technique could be used to improve the veracity of photo-identification, and found evidence that participants showed enhanced ability to discriminate matching from non-matching photo-ID when images were subjected to subtle levels of caricature manipulation.

9.2.2.2 Subject Factors

The *perceiver* also introduces variability into the process of face recognition. Two effects are worth noting. First, girls and women are more accurate at face recognition than boys and men (cf. Herlitz and Lovén [21] for a review). This is not a large effect, but it is reasonably consistent. Second, and perhaps of more consequence, several studies have indicated that face recognition accuracy declines as we age [4, 18]. In particular, older people are more likely to falsely recognize an unfamiliar person as "known" than are younger people. Importantly however, this same effect of aging does not appear to hold for face identification tasks that do not involve memory, such as the image comparison tasks typical of forensic identification (see Burton et al. [11]).

9.2.2.3 Interactive Factors

In some cases, recognition accuracy varies as a combined function of the demographics of the perceiver and the person to be identified. The other-race effect—the finding that people recognize faces of their own race more accurately than faces of other races [37]—is a well-known example of this kind of interaction. The phenomenon has been documented consistently in the literature and is associated with large effects. The general nature of this effect is clear and it has been found with diverse groups of participants, stimuli, and tasks (e.g., recognition: O'Toole et al. [46]; perceptual matching Phillips et al. [24, 55], Megreya et al. [41]; and categorization: O'Toole et al. [45]). For forensic examiners, this basic finding of an own-race advantage for recognition has far-reaching consequences that have not been explored.

Although less studied, a handful of recent papers have begun to consider whether an analogous "other-age" effect exists for face recognition [21]. This type of effect would also have implications for the accuracy of forensic facial examinations in particular situations where the examiner and face-to-be-examined are diverse in age. To date, although some studies have reported other-age effects in a range of tasks [1], others have not [71]. Moreover, recent work has indicated that findings of other-age effect might be contingent on experience [34] or the type of task being performed [35]. A definitive answer to this question requires more experimental data.

In summary, the factors that affect face recognition accuracy for untrained people include the familiarity of the face, stimulus factors that stem from the conditions under which an image is captured, subject factors (e.g., age, sex), and interactions between the stimulus and subject. In the next section, we consider the skills of expert facial examiners on the task of unfamiliar face image comparison.

9.3 Are Facial Image Comparison "Experts" More Accurate at Facial Image Comparison Than Untrained People?

Despite the importance of knowing the answer to the question we pose in the heading of this section, professional facial forensic examiners have been tested directly in only a handful of scientific studies. Moreover, the few available studies have not provided converging evidence on the question of whether professionals are more accurate than naïve subjects. An early study by Wilkinson and Evans [72] (cf. also, Wilkinson and Evans [72]) tested two forensic examiners and found that they were superior to untrained participants on the task of matching identity between CCTV video and a small set of reference images. Participants in that study viewed a video showing a person's head, either with or without a baseball cap, and were asked to determine whether the person also appeared in one of the reference images. Experts were more accurate both at detecting correct matches and rejecting false ones. Notably, when the entire head was visible, experts were better on all four measures of identification: hits, false alarms, correct rejections, and misses. One limitation of this study, however, is that only two examiners were tested. These examiners, who were also authors of the study, may not be representative of the overall population of experts.

In two other studies, trained participants fared no better than naïve participants when comparing identity in across a video and still images [9, 28]. Both of these studies tested a larger number of trained subjects, although the training and experience characteristics of the subjects differed. Lee et al. [28] tested students in a forensics course and Burton et al. [12] tested police officers with an average of 13.5 years of experience. These, and other, critical differences in the methods and tasks might account for the divergence of findings between these studies and Wilkinson and Evans [72, 73]. Though seemingly a minor change in the protocol, the task used by Burton et al. [12] required participants to view a series of videos prior to the identification task. This task involves more than perceptual matching. Instead, participants had to *remember* multiple individuals across a series of videos —a more difficult task than the perceptual matching task of Wilkinson and Evans [72]. Likewise, Lee et al. [28] tested participants with very poor quality videos. This is also more challenging than the task used in Wilkinson and Evans [72], albeit for different reasons. Image quality, as we shall see, is important in predicting the relative performance of experts and naïve observers. Notwithstanding, in these earlier studies it is not possible to know whether the different findings are due to the level of difficulty, the use of different test paradigms, or the different types of experience and training of the participants.

In a more naturalistic study, White et al. [69] tested passport officers and untrained students on their ability to match photo-ID cards to the card-bearers. Comparing photos to "live" people in this way mimics a ubiquitous task performed continuously at our national borders and in numerous other applications where an identity must be verified with and ID card for access to valuable resources (e.g., bank accounts) or entrance to restricted locations (e.g., embassies). In a first experiment, thirty passport officers with an average of over eight years experience falsely accepted "fraudulent" (i.e., nonmated) photo-IDs on 14% of trials. When participants presented a matching photo, these valid IDs were falsely rejected on 6% of trials. This substantial error rate is somewhat surprising given the task and the background of the participants. Notably, White et al. [67, 69] found no relationship between performance and years on the job, despite large individual differences in accuracy and a wide spread of experience levels.

In a second experiment, White et al. [67, 69] compared passport officers to untrained students on a photo-to-photo identity comparison test. Participants in this study viewed two images and were asked to determine whether the images showed the same person or different people. White et al. [67, 69] also compared accuracy for laboratory-style images taken two years apart and for image pairs consisting of a currently valid Photo-ID (of indeterminate age) and a recent high quality photograph. There was no overall difference in accuracy for the passport officers and students, for either the matching or non-matching identity trials. However, the type of photographs used for matching affected performance, with lower accuracy when participants matched official Photo-IDs to high quality recent images than when they matched laboratory images taken two years apart. In a final experiment, passport officers were tested with the Glasgow Face Matching Test (GFMT; Burton et al. [11])—a standardized test of photo-to-photo face-matching ability. Passport officers' scores on the GFMT did not differ from existing normative scores from untrained participants.

It is worth noting, that the finding of comparable performance between passport officers and students should be considered in the context of the full range of performance duties assigned to the passport issuance officers in this study. Although clearly experienced in face matching, these face-matching tasks are performed in the context of many other eligibility checks involving biographical and other personal information in the passport application process. Thus, the primary focus of the job may not be the face identification task. Further, the training these passport officers received was limited to a short module provided as part of introductory training. This larger context issue applies also to the police officers tested by Burton et al. [12], and even more so, to the participants tested by Lee et al. [28]. It is possible, therefore, that advantages will be seen only in cases where face identification is done in a focused and deliberate way—such as in criminal investigations or for court testimony. Professionals who perform this type of task are likely to participate in intense and sustained training and to be cognizant of the importance of each and every decision.

To address this, two recent studies tested individuals who perform face identification in these more directed applications. In the first study, Norell et al. [43] tested the skills of 17 European forensic experts, using a facial image comparison task. These experts had experience in facial image comparison and have been called on to apply their knowledge to criminal casework for legal authorities. The primary goal of the study was to determine whether image quality affected the accuracy of the detectives in matching identity. Additionally, the study also included a comparison group of untrained university students, whose performance was compared with that of the experts.

For the experiment with trained examiners, Norell et al. [43] compiled a test of 30 one-to-one facial image comparisons. In each case, a reference image was paired with a test image. Reference images were high quality images taken under studio conditions, whereas test images were taken using a camera intended for surveillance video. The time lag between the reference and test images varied between several months to several years, thereby assuring some change in appearance (e.g., hair style, etc.) between two images that show the same identity. For images that showed different identities, "similar" people were paired to make the task challenging.

Image quality was varied for the test images by changing the zoom and distance parameters of the camera to blur the image. Norell et al. [43] tested identification with three image qualities, allowing the participants to directly examine the images, with no time constraints. An additional innovation of this study was to ask participants to respond on a 9-point *conclusion scale*, similar to the scales used in forensic facial image comparison casework in many European countries. This response procedure enabled participants to grade their responses according to nine levels of certainty, varying from *very strong support of the same source* (i.e., "the observations extremely strongly support that it is the same person") to *very strong support of different source* (i.e., "the observations extremely strongly support that it is not the same person"), with a mid-point indicating *no support for either conclusion* ("the observations support neither that it is the same person nor that it they are different persons").

This conclusion scale allows, not only for the standard classes of errors, but also for a noncommittal response, which is neither correct nor incorrect. By standard classes of errors, we mean the following. For pairs that show the same identity, a *false negative* is defined as failing to affirm that the images are of the same person. For pairs of images that show different people, a *false positive* is defined as falsely judging the images to be of the same person. In forensic identification, it is often not possible to make an identity judgment based on the image evidence and so an important part of an examiners' role is to assess whether the images are suitable for comparison (cf. Ulery et al. [66]).

Interestingly, Norell and colleagues found that noncommittal responses revealed differences between the experts and students. First, experts made fewer errors than students. Notably however, as image quality decreased, experts increased their use of the noncommittal response, whereas students did not. With high quality images, experts were considerably more accurate than students—more often determining that matching images depicted the same person. Students, on the other hand, may have hesitated to affirm the same identity in images that differed substantially. A particularly interesting finding was that the difference in errors for the students versus experts was smallest for the *lowest quality images*. This might suggest that experts are able to access more useful information from high quality images than untrained observers. It might also suggest that training may help experts to exercise more caution (i.e., by using the noncommittal response) when image quality is low.

Finally, the number of false positives is something that is generally seen as a serious problem in the forensics field, because in most cases, it means that an innocent person would be implicated as guilty. In Norell et al. [43], experts had fewer false positives than the untrained students, consistent with similar biases toward making "non-match" responses for fingerprint examiners [64, 66]. Interestingly, studies of radiologists screening x-ray images have shown opposite response bias in these experts, with false positive errors being made more frequently than "miss" errors (see e.g., Kundel et al. [27]). Encouragingly, this suggests that expert performance is calibrated to counteract the risk of costly errors.

A second study of face identification accuracy in forensic examiners has recently been carried out by White et al. [70]. They tested a large group of facial forensic examiners attending a Facial Identification Scientific Working Group meeting (FISWG; www.fiswg.org) in May, 2014. This meeting was hosted at the FBI Academy in Quantico, Virginia, and was attended by an international group of forensic examiners who have very rigorous training and many years of experience in facial identification (7 years on average). To test the expertise of this group, White et al. created a battery of tests of pairwise facial image comparison (see Fig. 9.2). These tests were created to model the types of challenging decisions that might be encountered by forensic facial image examiners in their daily work, by selecting image pairs that were challenging to both machine recognition systems and also to

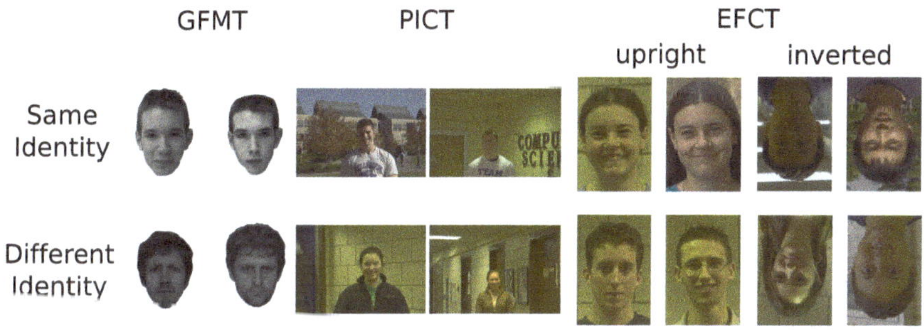

Fig. 9.2 Examples of image pairs from face-matching tests in White et al. [70]. Examiners outperformed control participants on the Glasgow Face Matching Test (GFMT), Person Identification Challenge Test (PICT), and Expertise in Facial Comparison Test (EFCT). Images in the GFMT were all taken on the same day and under very similar lighting conditions, whereas images from the PICT and EFCT were captured in diverse ambient conditions and over a longer time period. For details see text below

untrained student participants. White and his colleagues also mapped the performance of this group to established normative performance using the GFMT [11]. Examiners performance on the three tests was compared to a control group of FISWG attendees who did not perform facial identification in their daily work, and to a group of untrained student participants.

The results of these tests showed a consistent ordering of performance across three groups with examiners more accurate than controls, and controls more accurate than students. Notably however, examiner performance was not perfect for any of the tests. Moreover, performance was quite variable within the examiner group; with some examiners performing extremely well and others performing much less impressively. Following from recent work showing that matching performance is improved by aggregating the responses across individuals [44, 68], White et al. [70] "fused" responses of the examiners and other groups by averaging match score ratings across examiners, controls, and students. Consistent with previous work, combining responses in this way produced near-perfect human performance on these very challenging tasks, and far better performance than had been achieved by computer algorithms on the same image pairs. In another recent study, student participants who performed the GFMT collaboratively showed similar gains in accuracy [17]. Evidence from that study also suggests that collaboration may carry an additional training benefit, by improving performance of those who initially performed poorly in the task.

These fusion results are encouraging because in forensic practice it is common for examiners to confer when making identity judgments. Therefore, better understanding of the group decision-making process in forensic face identification promises to produce substantial gains in accuracy and can inform the design of peer review processes in forensic identification.

In their study of forensic experts, White et al. [70] were also motivated to examine the nature of examiners' perceptual expertise. They therefore tested examiners' accuracy under different exposure durations and with different image orientations (cf., Yin [74]). First, the results indicated that examiners were more accurate both when making quick decisions (with 2 s limit) and when making slower decisions (with 30 s limit). However, their superiority was greatest when they were provided with the longer exposure time to reach their decision. This is evidence that examiners' superiority relied, to some extent, on the analytic and strategic analysis of images that is taught in training. Second, the data also showed that examiners were less impaired than controls or students when the images were presented upside down. The size of the "inversion impairment"—known in face recognition research as the face inversion effect (FIE)—is an important measure in the study of human face recognition performance. This is due to the fact that inversion impairs face recognition performance far more than object recognition. As a result, the FIE has been considered as an index of human "expertise" with faces. Because of this qualitative difference in examiner performance, we suggest that their superiority on the face comparison task relies on a type of expertise that is different from standard human abilities for faces. As noted, there is evidence to suggest that human face processing is specialized to operate in a mono-oriented fashion [74].

We speculate that the smaller inversion effect for examiners, relative to controls and students, may be because the examiners are treating the face images not, as faces *per se,* but as *images*. This account would explain why the expertise of the examiner group was more pronounced when the faces were presented upside down: training in forensic examination may have caused them to rely less on the face–specific processes that govern performance in the population at large, by revealing alternative routes to identification. For example, forensic examiners are taught to compare images for "unexplainable" and "exclusionary" differences (e.g., Scientific Working Group Imaging Technology [60]), which may reveal inconsistency in local details that are missed by untrained participants. For now this account is speculative, but it is nevertheless important to develop a theoretical understanding of the underpinnings of examiners' expertise in facial image comparison to inform training and recruitment of facial examiners in the future.

The FISWG test represents the first effort to apply a broad approach to testing the state-of-the-art in forensic face identification. However, it is important to note that the study has limits in the extent to which it can be applied as a performance benchmark for practitioners. First, because this was a perceptual test, it was not designed to recreate the normal working conditions of forensic examiners. The motivation of this research was to examine perceptual expertise in this special population, rather than to provide a rigorous evaluation of their working practices. Because of this, examiners were not provided with unlimited time or allowed access to digital tools that they would use to support decisions in their daily work. In future benchmarking exercises it will be important to administer tests in a manner that is more reflective of working practice, in order to establish best working practices and the limits of identification accuracy in facial forensic examination.

9.4 Can Computer-Based Face Identification Systems Address Weaknesses of the Forensic Examiner and the Forensic Examination Process?

There has been a decade-long effort to directly compare the accuracy of human and machine performance on face identification [51]. These human–machine comparisons have been carried out in conjunction with competitions organized and implemented by the National Institute of Standards and Technology (NIST), with performance measured on identity matching for pairs of still images and videos. The still image types have varied in these competitions from high quality images taken in a studio environment to low quality images taken with handheld cameras such as those found in cell phones. These facial image comparison tasks are quite similar to those given to forensic facial examiners. Indeed, the intended applications for machine-based face recognition include tasks currently done by human face recognition experts. Thus, understanding machine performance in the context of both trained and untrained humans will facilitate the design of human–machine processes for face identification.

One of the key goals of the NIST competitions has been to facilitate the advancement of automatic face recognition technology. For all participants (i.e., algorithms) in a competition, NIST reports the accuracy on a common set of face images. The reported accuracy allows the face recognition community to assess the performance of state-of-the-art algorithms on a controlled set of images/videos. Because the human face identification studies have been conducted in conjunction with the NIST competitions, human–machine benchmarks now exist for state-of-the-art algorithms on a variety of image/video types that span high quality studio images to handheld point and shoot camera data from mobile devices.

In what follows, we will first outline some key elements of the human–machine comparisons including the definition of an "unfamiliar face recognition" task for an algorithm. We also consider some critical parameters in measurement of human performance in this task. Next, we provide a brief synopsis of where machine performance stands relative to untrained and trained human perceivers.

9.4.1 Unfamiliar Face Recognition Tasks for Machines

As noted, the task done by most automatic face recognition systems is to determine whether two images depict the same person or different people. For face recognition algorithms to model "unfamiliar" face recognition (i.e., the task assigned typically to forensic face examiners), it is necessary to define what it means for a face to be familiar to an algorithm. Indeed, the notion of familiarity is conceptually different for machines than for humans. For humans, familiarity means experience with a wide variety of diverse images of a person that span the image- and person-based variability described in Sect. 9.2.2.1. For algorithms, there are four ways to produce "familiarity effects." All of these improve the performance of an algorithm based on gains derived from the algorithm's "experience" with face identities and/or face images. In all but one case, the mechanisms behind the improvements are unrelated to the mechanism we assume for human familiarity. Notwithstanding, there is a relationship between the gains achieved with these nonhuman familiarity mechanisms and the benefits conferred by familiarity, as defined for humans.

First, an algorithm might become familiar with a person, if other images of the person are present in the database used to train the algorithm. Training is used in many face recognition algorithms to find "features" that are statistically reliable indicators of identity [19]. Training can also serve a variety of other functions involved in tuning algorithm parameters. When faces of the same identity are present in both the training and test set, there is a substantial increase in algorithm accuracy [33]. It is worth noting that this is an indirect definition of familiarity, because it does not entail providing the algorithm with additional specific and labeled information about individual people.

Second, consider the case where there are multiple images of a face in the set of images used as test images. Algorithm performance is increased in this case as well [56], because the existence of multiple test images increases the likelihood of finding a close match to the reference image.

The third way to achieve effects similar to familiarity is to "over-tune" an algorithm to a face dataset. Particular databases are often characterized by a common set of imaging parameters (viewpoints, illumination, resolution). When an algorithm is trained with a subset of images from a database, the machine becomes tuned to the characteristics of those images. This tuning can provide an accuracy advantage when the algorithm is tested with another subset of images from the same database. Importantly however, this is due to familiarity with the dataset as a whole and so nothing is learnt about individual identities. Instead, this familiarity is based on global characteristics of the training set, without propagating to the level of identity.

A careful look at the literature shows that algorithms tend to over-tune to the best available database, perhaps at the cost of thinking more generally about the problem of face identification. For publicly available datasets, there is always a competition to develop face recognition algorithms that are more accurate than the previous algorithm. As newer and more challenging databases are collected, over time, benchmark algorithm performance invariably reaches 95% or above—often crossing the 99% threshold. Although some of the progress in performance is linked to improvements in algorithmic techniques, it is likely that some progress is also due to over-tuning algorithm design to the data set. A face recognition algorithm consists of numerous components. The first part is selecting components that optimize performance on a particular data set. These components include preprocessing steps, feature extraction methods, feature normalization, and classifier selection. Another method is to select a training set tuned to the test data. For example, if a test set consists primarily of faces looking to the left, then a training set consisting of left-looking faces will optimize performance on the test set; however, the resulting algorithm will not necessarily generalize to frontal faces.

The effects of over-tuning may look like familiarity in that they improved algorithm performance via an understanding of the image variability that is present in the dataset. However, over-tuning to a single data set risks under-tuning to general image features that are not captured in that dataset. Ultimately, over-tuning is good, only if the database is highly diverse in terms of capturing image- and person-based face variability. If the database is not diverse, performance generalization to other kinds of images is typically poor.

A simple illustration of over-tuning can be seen in the other-race effect found for algorithms participating in the NIST Face Recognition Grand Challenge (FRCG) competition [52]. Algorithms from East Asian countries performed better on East Asian faces and algorithms from Western countries performed better on Caucasian faces. The likely reason for this other-race effect for algorithms is that algorithms may have over-tuned to faces from locally available data sets.

The fourth definition of algorithm familiarity is the closest to the human definition. This definition refers to the case in which an algorithm has access to multiple images and videos of a single person. This allows algorithms to use diverse images/videos to construct a unitary representation of a face that encompasses the variability of a person's appearance in different imaging conditions and under different person-based factors (aging, glasses, facial hair, etc.). The field is just beginning to go in this direction and we expect that the coming years will see computational examples that harness this variability to capture some basic elements of becoming familiar with a face. We return to this point in the Sect. 4.3.

9.4.2 Measuring Human Performance for Comparison with Machines

Measuring human performance in a way that relates to algorithm performance requires researchers to make methodological choices that have implications for estimates of human versus machine standing. As noted, human and machine comparisons have been carried out regularly in the NIST tests, starting in 2007. At that time, the task was to compare images with controlled and uncontrolled illumination [50]. In the most recent test, image comparisons are made with image/video taken from a handheld mobile device camera data (Phillips et al. in press; cf. Phillips and O'Toole, 2014 for a review of these studies). Intervening studies have provided comparisons that track the progress of face recognition algorithms [48, 49].

In all of the NIST comparisons, human performance was measured with an *aggregation* method—a standard behavioral protocol for measuring human performance. In this method, each subject rates a pair of images or videos, with a comparison scale. If a subject rates m pairs and there are n subjects, this will produce nm ratings and an ROC is computed separately from each of the nm ratings. The aggregate ROC measures are then computed to produce an estimate of average human performance over a population of image pairs.

The human–machine comparisons in the NIST tests have spurred algorithm developers to regularly include man–machine comparisons for new face recognition algorithms. As such, other studies introducing automatic face recognition algorithms have followed suit. These algorithms have operated on large-scale, publically available datasets such as Labeled Faces in the Wild (LFW) [23] and on other web-based training sets. The LFW dataset consists of still face images of celebrities and famous people downloaded from the World Wide Web. In measuring human performance on these datasets, the method applied involves an implicit fusion of human ratings that ultimately estimates human performance to be more accurate than the estimates made with the standard aggregation protocol. Generally, these methods have relied on large numbers of Amazon Mechanical Turk[1] workers who provide ratings of the likelihood that pairs of images show the same person.

More concretely, in the fusion method, all n subject ratings for each image or video pair are averaged. This results in m average ratings, one for each image or video pair. From the m average ratings a single ROC can be computed, which is used to represent human performance. In our experience, fusing human ratings in this way produces a significant increase in the estimate of performance accuracy over the aggregate method and estimates increase as the number of people rating the image pairs increases [50, 68, 70] (Phillips et al. accepted) [5]. Indeed, accuracy obtained by fusion methods often exceeds accuracy of the best performing individual in the group [68, 70].

Although both ways of estimating human performance are fundamentally sound, it is important to understand that estimates reached by the aggregate and fusion methods will not necessarily agree. Most importantly for benchmarking accuracy in forensic examination, the type of method used to compute human accuracy should correspond to the method used in practice; otherwise unrealistic estimates will be obtained. In situations where identification decisions are based on the decisions of single examiners, an aggregate method will produce most reliable measures. However, where the possibility exists for judgments to be made by multiple examiners, fusion offers a useful method for estimating the benefit of combining responses across groups of examiners (see White et al. [70]).

9.4.3 Measuring Human Performance for Comparison with Machines

How well do algorithms currently perform relative to humans? The answer to this question depends on the type or image or video available for identity matching. As of 2007, state-of-the-art systems surpassed untrained humans matching identity

[1]The identification of any commercial product or trade name does not imply endorsement or recommendation by NIST.

between high quality images, with one image taken under controlled illumination and the other taken under uncontrolled indoor illumination [50]. These image pairs varied in appearance and in facial expression. By 2012, the best algorithms surpassed humans on matching identity in images that varied also across indoor and outdoor illumination [48]. In that case, however, a stratification of the dataset base into three levels based on algorithm performance showed very strong machine advantages in the two easier partitions of the data, but equivalent performance for humans and machines on the most difficult data partition [53].

In a follow-up study, Rice et al. [58] isolated the "worst-case scenario" for the algorithms, finding a set of image pairs on which the algorithms failed 100% of the time. These image pairs showed examples of highly different images of the same person and highly similar images of different people. Humans performed quite accurately with this sample. The study demonstrated, however, that human performance was supported *entirely* by matching the identity using the body, rather than the face.

Most recently, Phillips et al. [54] replicated the Rice et al. [58] with humans and machines on images and video from the Point and Shoot Challenge (PaSC) dataset [6]. This dataset contains images and video taken by handheld cameras in unconstrained environments with both indoor and outdoor illumination. For images, human performance again was much better than the benchmark algorithm and improved as additional human rater responses were fused or averaged. For the video, beginning with the worst-case data for the benchmark algorithm, human performance again was much better than the benchmark algorithms on the most challenging cases, but was not as good as the best available algorithm on the less challenging case.

In expanding beyond the NIST tests, Kumar et al. [26] reported a human–machine comparison for a face verification algorithm based on face attributes. Both the algorithm and Mechanical Turk Workers matched image pairs from the LFW data set. The human score for each face-pair was the average of all Mechanical Turk Workers that rated the pair. Humans in this case fared better than the algorithm, though again it was clear, as in Rice et al. [58], that human performance was supported, at least in part, by information in the body and in the external face (e.g., hair, shoulders, etc.).

In 2014, the first two reports appeared showing better performance for algorithms than for people on the LFW database. The successful algorithms used deep learning [32, 62, 63]. Note that estimates of human accuracy were obtained by the fusion method, which is likely to have led to inflated estimates of human accuracy on this challenging task, pointing to an even more impressive result by the algorithm. Note also that the faces in LFW dataset are celebrities and famous people. From the human side, this takes us full circle, back to an understanding that humans in this task are doing *familiar* face identification, and so they are operating at their best. From the algorithm side, the fact that the faces are those of celebrities, (for whom diverse images are readily available), makes it possible that the algorithms may have over-tuned to the people in these images. The inclusion of multiple images of people, even as part of the training, may represent a case where algorithm results reflect critical components of the mechanisms humans employ for recognizing familiar faces. We may, therefore, be on the cusp of performance parity for humans and machines. In other words, when powerful algorithms can utilize rich and diverse training data for the identities to be recognized, they may be able to achieve the high level of perfomance shown by humans recognizing the faces of people they know well.

In summary, computer-based face recognition has been at the level of human recognition of unfamiliar faces for some years now. Progress is being made now on the greater challenge of moving machines to performance levels that are close to humans recognizing familiar faces. Some part of this progress is due to the development of more powerful algorithms than those available previously. The remainder is due to the rich datasets available from the web for training and testing these algorithms.

To return to the question of whether forensic examiners perform more accurately than algorithms, we have to ask another question first. Do forensic facial examiners perform unfamiliar face recognition at the level at which most people perform familiar face recognition? We do not yet know the answer to this question yet, but future research should make the goal of answering this question a priority.

9.5 Discussion and Future Directions

In summary, we reviewed studies that speak to the question of how accurate forensic face examiners are relative to untrained humans. We began with evidence indicating that there are substantial qualitative and quantitative differences between familiar and unfamiliar face recognition. The former represents human face recognition skills at their best and is characterized by a high degree of accuracy and an ability to generalize recognition across a wide range of image- and person-based variability. Because unfamiliar faces do not benefit from the rich memory representations that are tolerant to these sources of variability, recognizing unfamiliar faces is a far greater challenge. This leaves unfamiliar face matching "exposed to the elements" such that even small changes in facial appearance can lead to substantial decreases in matching accuracy. Although our knowledge of human performance on this task is almost entirely based on performance of untrained novices, the image-bound nature of unfamiliar face identification is also likely to place an upper bound on human accuracy in forensic face identification.

Recent studies of forensic examiners have begun to test this hypothesis empirically and as a result some characteristics of examiner performance have emerged. First, quantitative differences show that the majority of examiners tested exceed performance of untrained novices. It is also apparent from these studies that this superiority varies as a product of the nature of image evidence and test protocol. For example, although examiners outperform novices overall, their superiority is tied to image quality. When image quality is poor, examiners do not necessarily perform better than untrained novices on the task. This qualitative difference provides an interesting parallel to algorithm–novice comparisons, where algorithm superiority to humans is most pronounced in conditions with high quality image pairs. Examiners' superiority is also most apparent when they are provided with longer times to study image pairs. This suggests that their superiority is driven by a close and careful analysis of features in facial images, which is consistent with the training that these examiners receive.

Despite these indications that forensic training is driving forensic examiners' superior accuracy, it will be important in the future to establish directly the extent to which this superiority is caused by training, experience, and natural aptitude in face matching. This is important not only for developing training and recruitment of the next generation of forensic examiners, but also in courtroom settings, to inform judges and juries as to the reliability of identification evidence. To further this aim, in future benchmarking exercises, it will not only be necessary to assess the impact of these and other examiner-based factors in isolation, but also to explore their interactions with the image and subject-based factors described earlier in this chapter. Such interactions have served to reveal important differences in previous research, and have served to deepen scientific understanding of cognitive processes supporting expert forensic examination.

Finally, improved understanding of the interactions between human and machine processing perhaps hold most potential for improving forensic identification in the future. Algorithms, novices, and experts deal with the same challenges in identifying faces, but they come to the problem with different strengths and limitations. Determining optimal divisions of labor in forensic investigation and criminal trials presents an important challenge in the years ahead; we hope that computer engineers and psychologists rise to this challenge together.

References

1. Anastasi JS, Rhodes MG (2005) An own-age bias in face recognition for children and older adults. Psychon Bull Rev 12:1043–1047. doi:10.3758/BF03206441
2. Andrews S, Jenkins R, Cursiter H, Burton AM (in press) Telling faces together: learning new faces through exposure to multiple instances. Q J Exp Psychol. doi:10.1080/17470218.2014.1003949
3. Bahrick HP, Bahrick PO, Wittlinger RP (1975) Fifty years of memory for names and faces: a cross-sectional approach. J Exp Psychol Gen 104(1):54–75. doi:10.1037/0096-3445.104.1.54
4. Bartlett JC, Leslie JE (1986) Aging and memory for faces versus single views of faces. Mem Cogn 14:371–381
5. Best-Rowden L, Bisht S, Klontz JC, Jain AK (2014) Unconstrained face recognition: establishing baseline human performance via crowdsourcing. In: 2014 IEEE international joint conference on biometrics (IJCB)

6. Beveridge JR, Phillips J, Bolme DS, Draper B, Givens GH, Lui YM, Teli MN, Hao Z, Scruggs WT, Bowyer KW, Flynn PJ, Cheng S (2013) The challenge of face recognition from digital point-and-shoot cameras. In: IEEE sixth international conference on biometrics: theory, applications and systems (BTAS), 2013
7. Braje WL, Kersten DJ, Tarr MJ, Troje NF (1998) Illumination effects in face recognition. Psychobiology 26(4):371–380
8. Bruce V (1982) Changing faces: visual and non-visual coding processes in face recognition. Br J Psychol 73(1):105–116
9. Bruce V, Henderson Z, Greenwood K, Hancock PJB, Burton AM, Miller P (1999) Verification of face identities from images captured on video. J Exp Psychol Appl 5:339–360
10. Bruck M, Cavanagh P, Ceci SJ (1991) Fortysomething: recognizing faces at one's 25th reunion. Mem Cogn 19(3):221–228
11. Burton AM, White D, McNeill A (2010) The glasgow face matching test. Behav Res Methods 42:286–291
12. Burton AM, Wilson S, Cowan M, Bruce V (1999) Face recognition in poor-quality video: evidence from security surveillance. Psychol Sci 10:243–248
13. Burton AM, Kramer RS, Ritchie KL, Jenkins R (in press) Identity from variation: representations of faces derived from multiple instances. Cogn Sci. doi:10.1111/cogs.12231
14. Clutterbuck R, Johnston RA (2002) Exploring levels of face familiarity by using an indirect face-matching measure. Perception 31(8):985–994
15. Clutterbuck R, Johnston RA (2004) Matching as an index of face familiarity. Vis Cogn 11 (7):857–869
16. Clutterbuck R, Johnston RA (2005) Demonstrating how unfamiliar faces become familiar using a face matching task. Eur J Cogn Psychol 17(1):97–116
17. Dowsett AJ, Burton AM (in press) Unfamiliar face matching: pairs out-perform individuals and provide a route to training. Br J Psychol. doi:10.1111/bjop.12103
18. Fulton A, Bartlett JC (1991) Young and old faces in young and old heads: the factor of age in face recognition. Psychol Aging 6:623–630
19. Furl N, Phillips PJ, O'Toole AJ (2002) Face recognition algorithms and the other-race effect: computational mechanisms for a developmental contact hypothesis. Cogn Sci 26(6):797–815
20. Galper RE, Hochberg J (1971) Recognition memory for photographs of faces. Am J Psychol 84(3):351–354
21. Herlitz A, Lovén J (2013) Sex differences and the own-gender bias in face recognition: a meta-analytic review. Vis Cogn 2013:1. doi:10.1080/13506285.2013.823140
22. Hill H, Bruce V (1996) Effects of lighting on the perception of facial surfaces. J Exp Psychol Hum Percept Perform 22:986–1004
23. Huang GB, Ramesh M, Berg T, Learned-Miller E (2007) Labeled faces in the wild: a database for studying face recognition in unconstrained environments. Technical Report 07-49, University of Massachusetts, Amherst
24. Jenkins R, White D, Montfort XV, Burton AM (2011) Variability in photos of the same face. Cognition 121(3):313–323. doi:10.1016/j.cognition.2011.08.001
25. Jiang F, Blanz V, O'Toole AJ (2007) The role of familiarity in three-dimensional view-transferability of face identity adaptation. Vis Res 47(4):525–531
26. Kumar N, Berg AC, Belhumeur PN, Nayar SK (2009) Attribute and simile classifiers for face verification. In 2009 IEEE 12th international conference on computer vision, pp 365–372
27. Kundel HL, Nodine CF, Conant EF, Weinstein SP (2007) Holistic component of image perception in mammogram interpretation: gaze-tracking study 1. Radiology 242(2):396–402
28. Lee WJ, Wilkinson C, Memon A, Houston K, Res M (2009) Matching unfamiliar faces from poor quality closed-circuit television (CCTV) footage: an evaluation of the effect of training on facial identification ability. AXIS: Online J CAHId 1(1):19–28
29. Light LL, Kayra-Stuart F, Hollander S (1979) Recognition memory for typical and unusual faces. J Exp Psychol: Hum Learn Mem 5:212–228

30. Liu CH, Seetzen H, Burton AM, Chaudhuri A (2003) Face recognition is robust with incongruent image resolution: relationship to security video images. J Exp Psychol: Appl 9:33–44
31. Logie RH, Baddley AD, Woodhead MM (1987) Face recognition, pose and ecological validity. Appl Cogn Psychol 1(1):53–69
32. Lu C, Tang X (2014) Surpassing human-level face verification performance on LFW with GaussianFace. arXiv preprint arXiv:1404.3840
33. Lui YM, Bolme D, Phillips PJ, Beveridge JR, Draper B (2012) Preliminary studies on the good, the bad, and the ugly face recognition challenge problem. In: 2012 IEEE computer society conference computer vision and pattern recognition workshops (CVPRW), pp 9–16
34. Macchi Cassia V (2011) Age biases in face processing: the effects of experience across development. Br J Psychol 102:816–829. doi:10.1111/j.2044-8295.2011.02046.x
35. Macchi Cassia V, Proietti V, Gava L, Bricolo E (2015) Searching for faces of different ages: evidence for an experienced-based own-age detection advantage in adults. J Exp Psychol Hum Percept Perform. doi:10.1037/xhp0000057
36. Macmillan NA, Creelman D (2005) Detection theory: a user's guide. Lawrence Erlbaum Associates
37. Malpass RS, Kravitz J (1969) Recognition for faces of own and other race faces. J Pers Soc Psychol 13:330–334
38. McIntyre AH, Hancock PJ, Kittler J, Langton SR (2013) Improving discrimination and face matching with caricature. Appl Cogn Psychol 27(6):725–734
39. Megreya AM, Burton AM (2006) Unfamiliar faces are not faces: evidence from a matching task. Mem Cogn 34:865–876
40. Megreya AM, Sandford A, Burton AM (2013) Matching face images taken on the same day or months apart: the limitations of photo ID. Appl Cogn Psychol 27(6):700–706
41. Megreya AM, White D, Burton AM (2011) The other-race effect does not rely on memory: evidence from a matching task. Q J Exp Psychol 64(8):1473–1483
42. National Research Council (2009) Strengthening forensic science in the United States: a path forward. The National Academies Press, Washington, DC
43. Norell K, Lathen KB, Bergstrom P, Rice A, Natu V, O'Toole A (2015) The effect of image quality and forensic expertise in facial image comparisons. J Forensic Sci 60:331–340
44. O'Toole AJ, Abdi H, Jiang F, Phillips PJ (2007) Fusing face-verification algorithms and humans. IEEE Trans: Syst Man Cybern B 37:1149–1155
45. O'Toole AJ, Deffenbacher KA, Peterson J (1996) An "other-race effect" for classifying faces by sex. Perception 25:669–676
46. O'Toole AJ, Deffenbacher KA, Valentin D, Abdi H (1994) Structural aspects of face recognition and the other-race effect. Mem Cogn 22:208–224
47. O'Toole AJ, Edelman S, Bülthoff HH (1998) Stimulus-specific effects in face recognition over changes in viewpoint. Vis Res 38:2351–2363
48. O'Toole AJ, An X, Dunlop JP, Natu V, Phillips PJ (2012) Comparing face recognition algorithms to humans on challenging tasks. ACM Trans Appl Percept 9(4), Article 16
49. O'Toole AJ, Phillips PJ, Narvekar A (2008) Humans versus algorithms: comparisons from the face recognition vendor test 2006. In: Proceedings of the 8th IEEE international conference on automatic face and gesture recognition
50. O'Toole AJ, Phillips PJ, Jiang F, Ayyad J, Pénard N, Abdi H (2007) Face recognition algorithms surpass humans matching faces across changes in illumination. IEEE: Trans Pattern Anal Mach Intell 29(9):1642–1646
51. Phillips PJ, O'Toole AJ (2014) Comparison of human and computer performance across face recognition experiments. Image Vis Comput 32(1):74–85
52. Phillips PJ, Jiang F, Narvakar A, Ayyad J, O'Toole AJ (2011) An other-race effect for face recognition algorithms. ACM Trans Appl Percept 8(2):ART14
53. Phillips PJ, Beveridge JR, Draper BA, Givens G, O'Toole AJ, Bolme DS, Dunlop J, Lui YM, Sahibzada H, Weimer S (2011) An introduction to the good, the bad, & the ugly face

recognition challenge problem. In: IEEE international conference on automatic face and gesture recognition, pp 346–353
54. Phillips PJ, Hill MQ, Swindle JA, O'Toole AJ (2015) Human and algorithm performance on the PaSC face recognition challenge. In: IEEE seventh international conference on biometrics: theory, applications and systems (BTAS 2015)
55. Phillips PJ, Jiang F, Narvekar A, Ayyad J, O'Toole AJ (2011) An other-race effect for face recognition algorithms. ACM Trans Appl Percept 8(2), ART 14
56. Phillips PJ, Flynn PJ, Scruggs T, Bowyer KW, Chang J, Hoffman K, Marques J, Min J, Worek W (2005) Overview of the face recognition grand challenge. In IEEE computer society conference on computer vision and pattern recognition, 2005. CVPR 2005, vol 1, pp 947–954
57. Rhodes G, Brennan S, Carey S (1987) Identification and ratings of caricatures: implications for mental representations of faces. Cogn Psychol 19(4):473–497
58. Rice A, Phillips PJ, Natu V, An X, O'Toole AJ (2013) Unaware person recognition from the body when face identification fails. Psychol Sci 24(11):2235–2243
59. Sacks MJ, Koehler JJ (2005) The coming paradigm shift in forensic identification science. Science 309:892–895
60. Scientific Working Group Imaging Technology (2010) SWGIT guidelines for the forensic imaging practitioner section 6: guidelines and recommendations for training in imaging technology in the criminal justice system. Retrieved from: https://www.swgit.org/documents/Current%20Documents
61. Sinha P, Balas B, Ostrovsky Y, Russell R (2006) Face recognition by humans: nineteen results all computer vision researchers should know about. Proc IEEE 94(11):1948–1962
62. Sun Y, Wang X, Tang X (2014) Deep learning face representation from predicting 10,000 classes. In: Computer vision and pattern recognition meeting
63. Taigman Y, Yang M, Ranzato MA, Wolf L (2014) Deepface: closing the gap to human-level performance in face verification. In: 2014 IEEE conference on computer vision and pattern recognition (CVPR), pp 1701–1708
64. Tangen JM, Thompson MB, McCarthy DJ (2011) Identifying fingerprint expertise. Psychol Sci 22(8):995–997
65. Troje NF, Bülthoff HH (1996) Face recognition under varying poses: the role of texture and shape. Vis Res 36(12):1761–1771
66. Ulery BT, Hicklin RA, Buscaglia J, Roberts MA (2011) Accuracy and reliability of forensic latent fingerprint decisions. Proc Natl Acad Sci 108(19):7733–7738
67. White D, Burton AM, Jenkins R, Kemp RI (2014) Redesigning photo-ID to improve unfamiliar face matching performance. J Exp Psychol: Appl 20(2):166–173
68. White D, Burton AM, Kemp RI, Jenkins R (2013) Crowd effects in unfamiliar face matching. Appl Cogn Psychol 27(6):769–777
69. White D, Kemp RI, Jenkins R, Matheson M, Burton AM (2014) Passport officers' errors in face matching. PLoS ONE 9(8):e103510. doi:10.1371/journal.pone.0103510
70. White D, Phillips PJ, Hahn CA, Hill M, O'Toole AJ (2015) Perceptual expertise in forensic facial image comparison. In: Proc R Soc B: Biological Sciences, 282:1814–1822
71. Wild HA, Barrett SE, Spence M, O'Toole AJ, Cheng Y, Brooke J (2000) Recognition and sex categorization of adults' and children's faces: examining performance in the absence of sex stereotyped cues. J Exp Child Psychol 77:269–291
72. Wilkinson C, Evans R (2009) Are facial image analysis experts any better than the general public at identifying individuals from CCTV images? Sci Justice 49(3):191–196
73. Wilkinson C, Evans R (2011) Corrigendum to "Are facial image analysis experts any better than the general public at identifying individuals from CCTV images?" [Sci Justice 49:191–196 (2009)]. Sci Justice 51(4):218–221
74. Yin RK (1969) Looking at upside-down faces. J Exp Psychol 81(1):141–145
75. Young AW, Hay DC, Ellis AW (1985) The faces that launched a thousand slips: everyday difficulties and errors in recognizing people. Br J Psychol 76(4):495–523

Part III
Human Motion, Speech and Behavioral Analysis

Chapter 10
Biometric Evidence in Forensic Automatic Speaker Recognition

Andrzej Drygajlo and Rudolf Haraksim

Abstract The goal of this chapter is to provide a methodology for calculation and interpretation of biometric evidence in forensic automatic speaker recognition (FASR). It defines processing chains for observed biometric evidence of speech (univariate and multivariate) and for calculating a likelihood ratio as the strength of evidence in the Bayesian interpretation framework. The calculation of the strength of evidence depends on the speaker models and the similarity scoring used. A processing chain chosen for this purpose is in the close relation with the hypotheses defined in the Bayesian interpretation framework. Several processing chains are proposed corresponding to the scoring and direct method, which involve univariate and multivariate speech evidence, respectively. This chapter also establishes a methodology to evaluate performance of a chosen FASR method under operating conditions of casework.

10.1 Introduction

Biometrics is the science of establishing identity of individuals based on their biological and behavioural characteristics [30]. Speaker recognition is a biometric modality that uses an individual's speech for distinguishing one person from another [24]. Forensics means the use of scientific methods and techniques in the establishment of facts or evidence in the court of law [28]. The role of forensic expert is the provision of information (factual or opinion) to help answer questions of importance to courts of law [27].

The purpose of forensic speaker recognition (FSR) is to provide information (e.g. non-categorical opinion) of evidential weight if speech in the questioned speaker recording originates from suspected speaker or not [8, 9]. The judge or the jury in the court uses such an opinion for their deliberations and decision [39].

A. Drygajlo (✉) · R. Haraksim
Swiss Federal Institute of Technology Lausanne (EPFL), Lausanne, Switzerland
e-mail: andrzej.drygajlo@gmail.com

M. Tistarelli and C. Champod (eds.), *Handbook of Biometrics for Forensic Science*, Advances in Computer Vision and Pattern Recognition,
DOI 10.1007/978-3-319-50673-9_10

Forensic automatic speaker recognition (FASR) is an established term used when automatic speaker recognition methods are adapted to and used within a forensic application [8, 11, 31].

Best-practice FASR is associated with the Bayesian interpretation framework [2, 3, 9, 21, 35, 40, 41]. In this framework, an opinion of evidential weight, based upon case specific hypotheses (propositions) and conditioning information (framework of circumstances) should be provided for use in court [15, 17]. If there are two competing hypotheses, then the odds form of Bayes' theorem can be used:

$$\underset{\text{posterior odds}}{\frac{P(H_0|E,I)}{P(H_1|E,I}} = \underset{\text{likelihood ratio}}{\frac{p(E|H_0,I)}{p(E|H_1,I)}} \times \underset{\text{prior odds}}{\frac{P(H_0|I)}{P(H_1|I)}}$$

In FASR, the evaluative opinion of the forensic expert is a numerical statement of strength of evidence (likelihood ratio *LR*) of the observed biometric speech evidence (*E*) given two competing hypotheses H_0 and H_1 and background information *I* [9, 15].

The odds form of Bayes' theorem shows how new data, reported as likelihood ratio (*LR*) , can be combined with prior knowledge about the case in order to arrive at posterior odds. Only the *LR* is the province of the forensic expert; the prior odds and posterior odds are the province of the court.

The numerator of the *LR*, i.e. likelihood $p(E|H_0, I)$, represents the degree of similarity of the evidence with respect to the suspect and the denominator of the *LR*, i.e. likelihood $p(E|H_1, I)$, represents the degree of typicality with respect to the relevant population. The *LR* is the ratio between these two degrees corresponding to non-categorical opinion in the form of numerical statement. With *LR* values larger than unity there is stronger support for the H_0 hypothesis and with *LR* values smaller than unity there is stronger support for the H_1 hypothesis.

The value of a likelihood ratio (*LR*) critically depends on the choices one makes for stating the observed speech evidence (*E*) and the hypotheses H_0 and H_1, with corresponding models of within-speaker or same-speaker and between-speaker or different-speaker speech variability. It also depends on several aspects of the speech analysis, including the non-automatic aspects of the data pre-processing stage, the kind of features, feature models and similarity scoring used, as well as the databases employed in the process. Consequently, the methodology using the Bayesian interpretation framework concerns also performance evaluation of *LR* methods for method validation and case-specific evaluation purposes [34, 36, 42].

Therefore, in FASR three types of biometric measures should be provided:

- Observed biometric evidence of speech,
- Strength of observed biometric evidence (likelihood ratio),
- Performance evaluation measures of the strength of evidence.

10.2 Biometric Evidence in FASR

Biometric recognition has essentially the same generic processing chain common across biometric modalities (Fig. 10.1) [30].

In automatic speaker recognition (ASR), the biometric recognition methodology concerns speech feature extraction, feature modelling (to create speaker models) and comparative analysis for similarity scoring (Fig. 10.2) [15].

In FASR, the observed biometric evidence (*E*) of speech can be defined on the level of similarity scoring or feature extraction [4, 5, 16]. This chapter is focused on calculation of observed biometric evidence and its strength (likelihood ratio) using any feature extraction and feature modelling technique [29].

If the observed biometric evidence (*E*) of speech is defined on the level of similarity scoring, it consists of single score representing the degree of similarity between speaker-dependent features extracted from the questioned speaker recording and speaker-dependent features extracted from the suspected speaker reference database, represented by this speaker model (Fig. 10.3) [13, 14].

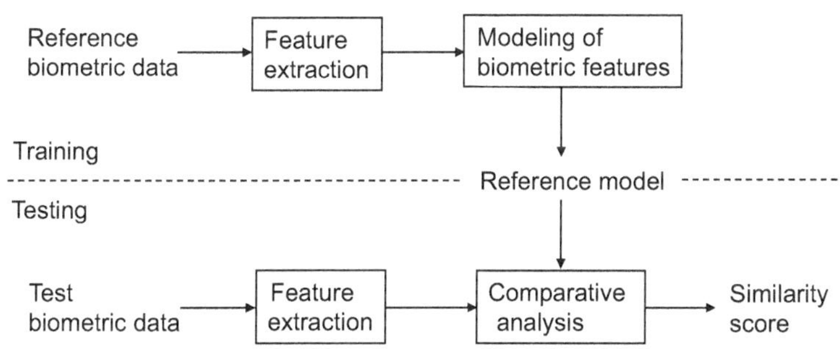

Fig. 10.1 Generic processing chain for biometric recognition

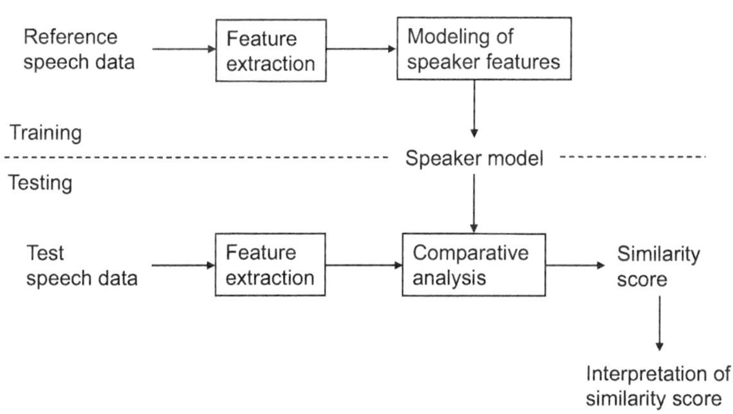

Fig. 10.2 Generic processing chain for automatic speaker recognition [15]

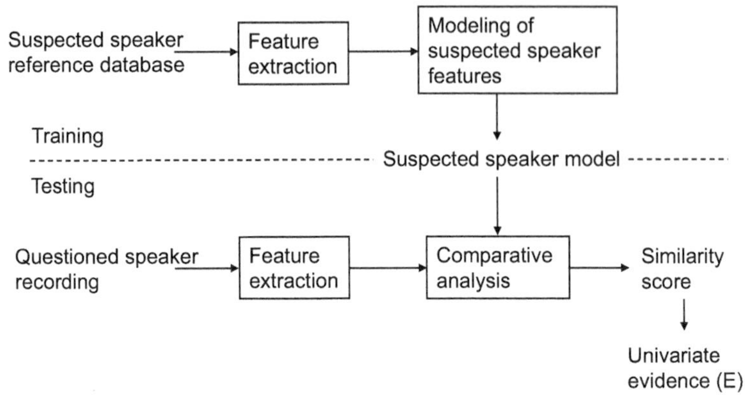

Fig. 10.3 Processing chain for calculating univariate biometric speech evidence (*E*) [15, 16]

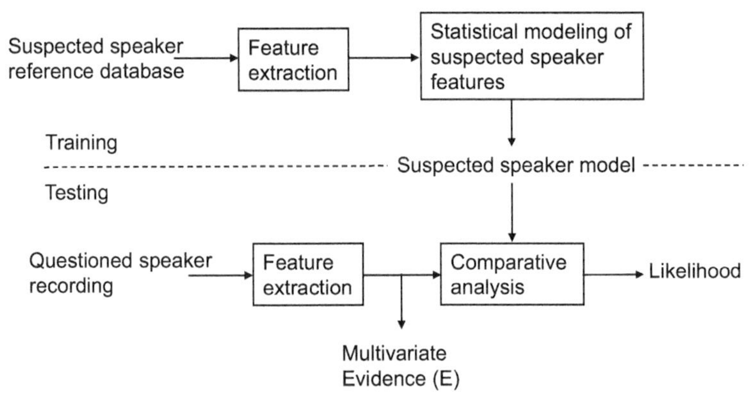

Fig. 10.4 Processing chain for calculating multivariate biometric speech evidence (*E*)

Automatic speaker recognition based on statistical modelling techniques has a useful property in that it directly returns a likelihood (as a score) of whether a speech signal (e.g. of questioned speaker recording) can correspond to the statistical model created for a speaker (e.g. suspected speaker in Fig. 10.4) [5, 16].

If statistical modelling techniques, which return likelihoods, are used in FASR, the observed biometric evidence is defined on the level of feature extraction as the ensemble of features extracted from the questioned speaker recording. Such an ensemble of features represents multivariate speech evidence (*E*) [1, 5].

10.3 Calculation of Likelihood Ratio (*LR*)

The calculation of a likelihood ratio (*LR*) depends on the speaker models and the similarity scoring used, as well as on the choice one makes for stating the hypotheses. There are two main methods commonly used for this purpose: the scoring method and the direct method [5, 12, 16].

10.3.1 Scoring Method

The methodological approach based on the scoring method is independent of the features and speaker models chosen. This methodology needs a two-stage processing. The first stage consists of calculating scores using any type of feature vectors (multivariate data) as well as any of the speaker models (e.g. vector quantization (VQ), Gaussian mixture model (GMM), i-vector) and similarity scoring (Figs. 10.5 and 10.8) [10, 18, 32, 33]. The second stage transforms the obtained similarity scores into two univariate distributions, which are represented by probability density functions (Figs. 10.9 and 10.10). The values of these

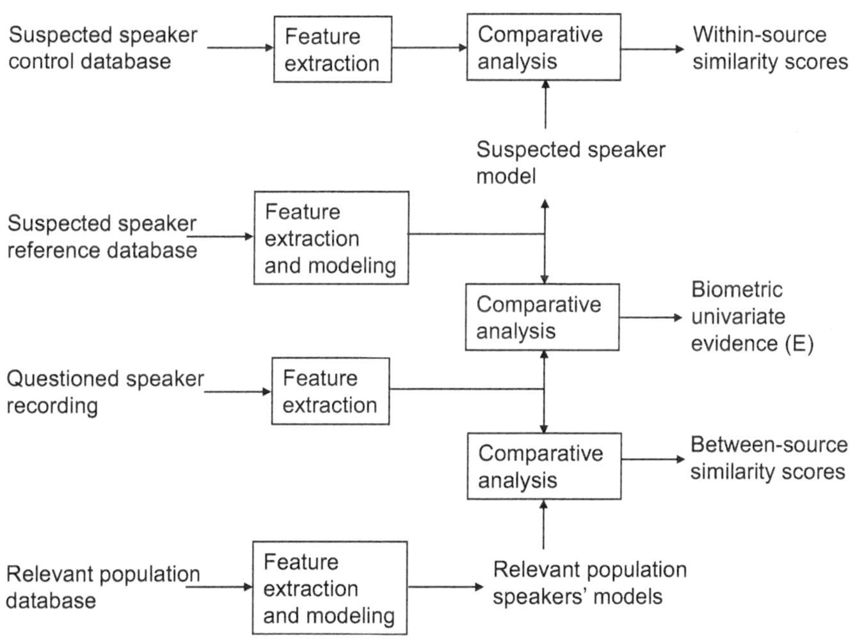

Fig. 10.5 Processing chain of feature extraction, feature modelling, comparative analysis and calculation of biometric univariate speech evidence as well as within-source and between source similarity scores for the scoring method [14, 16, 17]

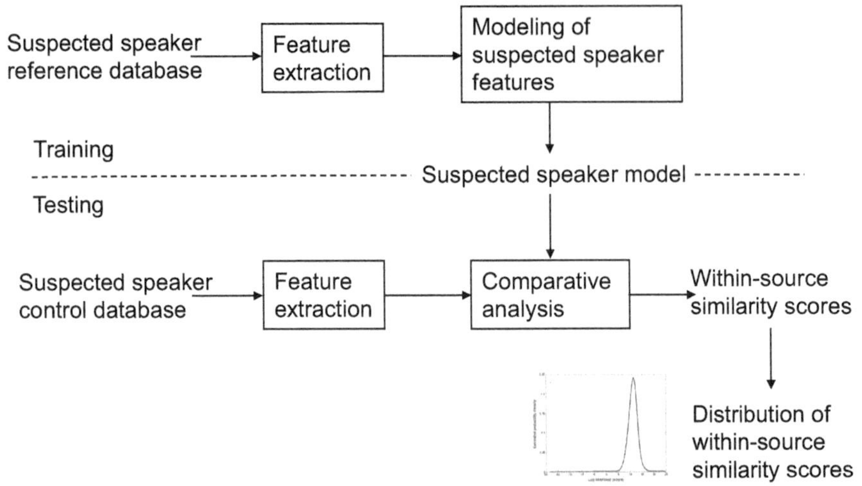

Fig. 10.6 Processing chain for calculating within-source similarity scores and their interpretation as a distribution [15, 16]

functions represent likelihoods of scores given chosen hypotheses. This two-stage processing can be done in many ways depending on the choices one makes for stating the hypotheses [4, 19, 22, 37].

If the hypotheses are stated as follows:

- H_0—the suspected speaker is the source of the questioned recording,
- H_1—the suspected speaker is not the source of the questioned recording,

the H_1 hypothesis can be represented by the distribution of between-source similarity scores, which result from comparing the feature vectors or model of the questioned speaker with the ones of several other speakers from the relevant population database, and the H_0 hypothesis can be represented by the within-source distribution of similarity scores as the result of comparing the feature vectors or model of the suspected speaker using its control database with the ones of the same speaker using its reference database (Figs. 10.5, 10.6 and 10.7) [14, 16, 17].

In this case, the strength of evidence is represented by the likelihood ratio (*LR*) calculated as the ratio of likelihoods obtained from the distributions of within-source and between-source similarity scores for the single score *E* representing the value of the observed speech evidence (Figs. 10.9 and 10.10). This score (*E*) is obtained by comparing the feature vectors or model of the questioned speaker recording with the ones of the suspected speaker using the suspected speaker reference database (Fig. 10.3).

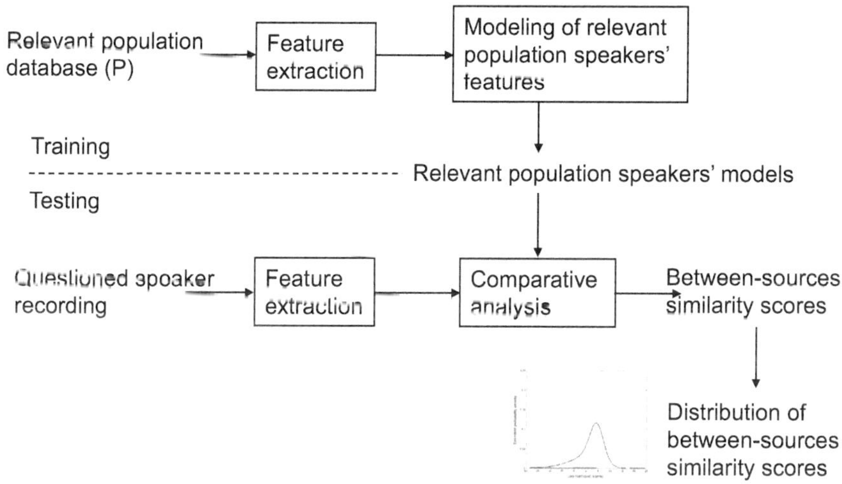

Fig. 10.7 Processing chain for calculating between-source similarity scores and their interpretation as a distribution [15, 16]

If the hypotheses are stated as follows:

- H_0—the suspected speaker recording and the questioned recording have the same source,
- H_1—the suspected speaker recording and the questioned recording have different sources,

the H_0 hypothesis can be represented by the distribution of similarity scores that result from same-speaker comparisons, and the H_1 hypothesis can be represented by the distribution of similarity scores as the result of different-speaker comparisons using the relevant population database in both cases (Fig. 10.8) [23, 37].

In this respect, the *LR*, as the strength of evidence, can be calculated by dividing the likelihoods from the distributions of the same-source and different-source similarity scores for the single score *E* representing the value of the observed speech evidence (Fig. 10.9). This score (*E*) is obtained by comparing the feature vectors or model of the questioned speaker recording with the ones of the suspected speaker (Fig. 10.3).

The scoring method is illustrated in Fig. 10.10. The distributions of the same-source (within-source or same-speaker) and different-source (between-source or different-speaker) similarity scores constitute a common representation for any pair of H_0 and H_1 hypothesis used in this method.

The conclusion that the forensic expert provides to the court shall be related to the assigned likelihood ratio *LR* (strength of evidence), the observable speech evidence *E* and the hypotheses H_0 and H_1 under consideration.

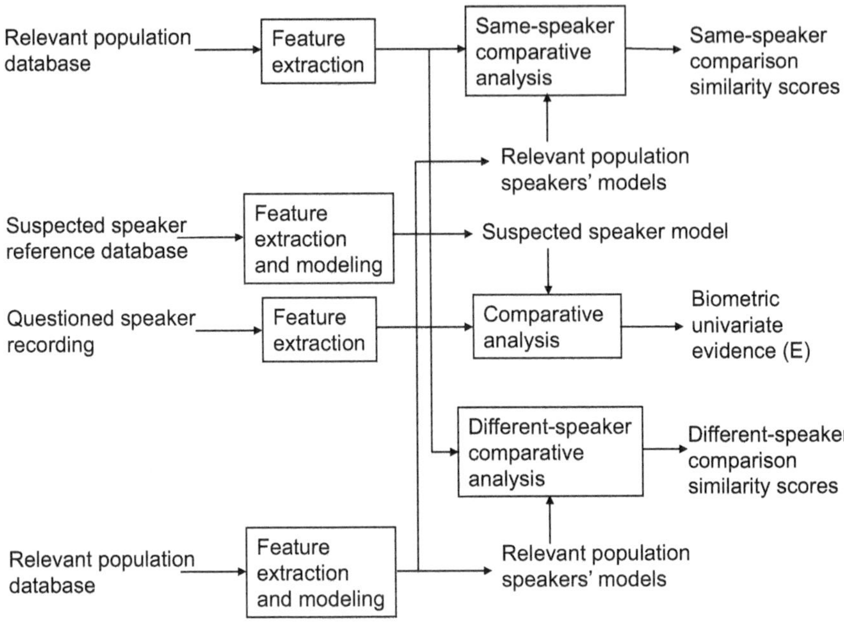

Fig. 10.8 Processing chain of feature extraction, feature modelling, comparative analysis and calculation of biometric univariate speech evidence as well as same-speaker and different-speaker comparison similarity scores for the scoring method

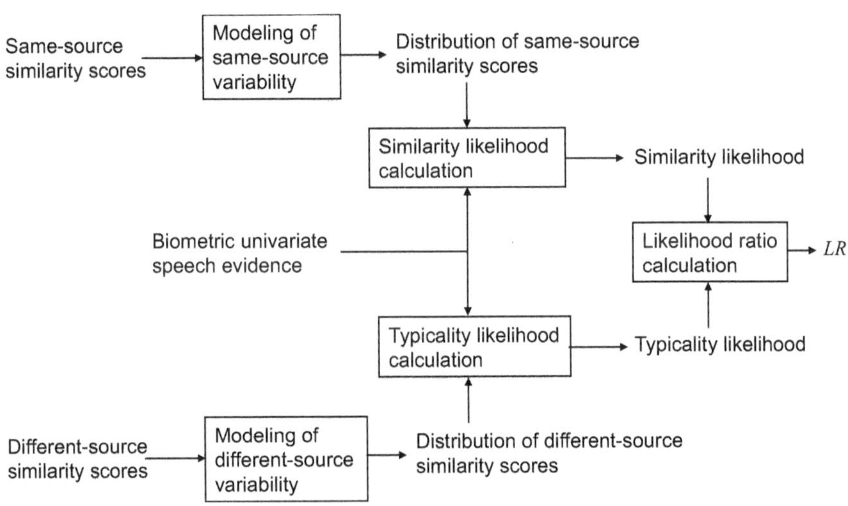

Fig. 10.9 Processing chain of the Bayesian interpretation framework of biometric univariate speech evidence for calculating the likelihood ratio (*LR*) for the scoring method using the distributions of the same-source (within-source or same-speaker) and different-source (between-source or different-speaker) similarity scores [14, 16]

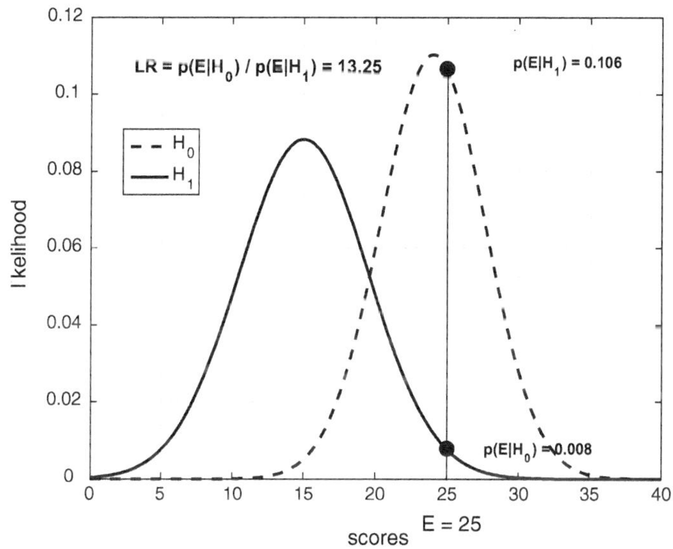

Fig. 10.10 Illustration of the scoring method. In this example, the evidence score is $E = 25$. Dividing the likelihood value of H_0 distribution (right side of figure) by the likelihood value of H_1 distribution (left side of figure) for the observed speech evidence score E results in $LR = 13.25$ [4, 31–33, 37]

Such a non-categorical opinion can be expressed, for example, as follows [19]:

A likelihood ratio of 13.25 (obtained in Fig. 10.1), means that it is 13.25 times more likely to observe the speech evidence score (E) given the hypothesis H_0 (e.g., the suspected speaker recording and the questioned recording have the same source) than given the hypothesis H_1 (e.g., the suspected speaker recording and the questioned recording have different sources).

The judge or the jury in the court uses such an opinion for their deliberation and decision.

10.3.2 Direct Method

The methodological approach based on the direct method needs a statistical model, which can compute a likelihood value when feature vectors are compared against such a model [4, 5, 7]. For example, GMMs or i-vectors combined with PLDA offer such a property [5, 6, 37, 42].

The direct method uses two databases: the suspected speaker reference database and the relevant population database. They can be used to create two statistical models, e.g., GMM 1—statistical model of the suspected speaker and GMM 2—statistical model of the relevant population. The universal background model

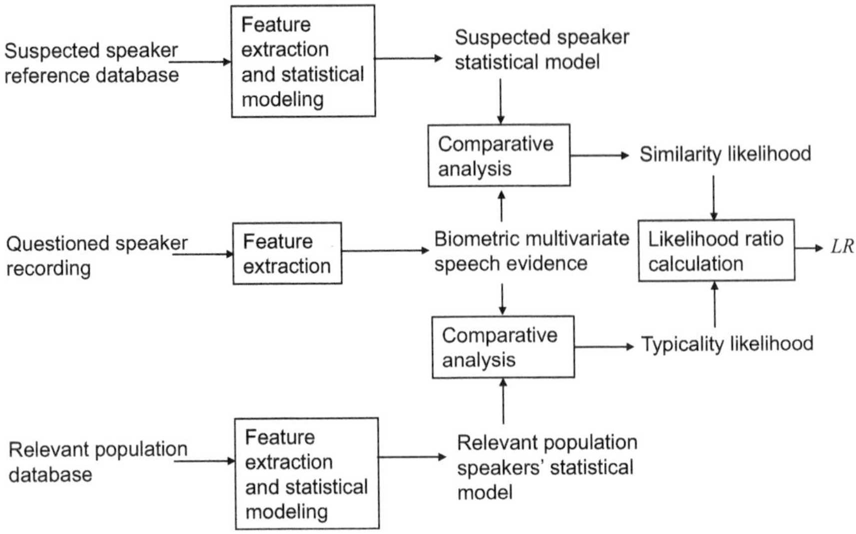

Fig. 10.11 Processing chain of feature extraction, feature modelling, comparative analysis and calculation of biometric multivariate speech evidence as well as similarity and typicality likelihoods and likelihood ratio (*LR*) for the direct method [16]

(UBM) trained with the relevant population database can also be used as GMM 2. In order to calculate the likelihood ratio, the multivariate evidence (*E*) represented by the ensemble of feature vectors extracted from the questioned recording is compared to GMM 1 and GMM 2. The first comparison gives the similarity likelihood score (numerator of *LR*) and the second one the typicality likelihood score (denominator of *LR*). The *LR*s obtained with the direct method are often not well calibrated (Fig. 10.11).

The conclusion using the direct method, to be provided to the court by the forensic expert, can be stated in a way similar to the conclusion expressed in the scoring method.

10.4 Performance Evaluation

Evaluation of specific case findings concerns the likelihood ratio (*LR*), which summarises the statement of the forensic expert in the casework, and its comparison with the likelihood ratios that can be obtained from the observed speech evidence under operating conditions of the case, on one hand when the hypothesis H_0 is true and, on the other hand, when the hypothesis H_1 is true [19].

Evaluation should be carried out using a relevant population database of the case. The intrinsic property of this database is the known ground truth regarding the source of origin of each of the recordings. When the ground truth of the recordings related to the origin of the speakers is known, there are two types of trials, e.g.:

- Same source (within-source or same-speaker) trials (SS trials)
- Different-source (between-source or different-speaker) trials (DS trials)

In the process of empirical evaluation on the relevant population database the FASR method outputs a *LR* for each of the SS and DS trials. Given the *LR*s and the ground truth regarding the SS and DS trials, it is possible to derive a number of performance characteristics and metrics. For evaluating the strength of evidence (*LR*), performance characteristics and metrics can be used together with the case-specific likelihood ratio LR_{case}.

10.4.1 Performance Characteristics and Metrics

Performance characteristics (e.g. Tippett plots I and II as well as Empirical Cross Entropy (ECE) plots) describe support for the correct hypothesis of a *LR* method [17, 20, 36, 37].

Performance metrics provide a single numerical value that describes the performance in terms of, e.g. accuracy, discriminating power and calibration of the *LR* method (probabilities of misleading evidence ($PMEH_0$ and $PMEH_1$), equal proportion probability (EPP) , log-likelihood-ratio cost (Cllr) [19, 37, 42].

A starting point for elaborating performance characteristics in FASR corresponds to histograms (count vs. *LR*) of the *LR*s for H_1 and H_0 hypotheses. In order to move from the histograms (count vs. *LR*) of the *LR*s for H_1 and H_0 hypotheses to cumulative distribution functions (probability vs. *LR*), they have to be approximated by probability density functions and normalised so that the area under each of the curves is equal to one. Following the normalisation of the *LR* distributions the cumulative distribution functions (CDFs) of the *LR*s can be computed. The cumulative distribution functions, unlike the normalised *LR* distributions are plotted as the probability on the y-axis, vs. the *LR*s on the x-axis. They represent the cumulative proportion of *LR*s less than or equal to the *LR* value on the x-axis for the H_1 and H_0 hypotheses.

10.4.1.1 Performance Characteristics—Tippett Plots

In this chapter, the case-specific evaluation is limited to Tippett plots, which correspond to cumulative distribution functions and are the most frequently used performance characteristics in FASR. There are two versions of these plots: Tippett plots I and II [17, 35].

Tippett plots I correspond to the inverse CDFs (iCDFs) of *LR*s for both H_0 and H_1 hypotheses. They represent the cumulative proportion of *LR*s greater than the *LR* value on the x-axis for the H_1 and H_0 hypotheses.

Tippett plots II are a combination of the CDF for the H_0 hypothesis and the inverse CDF (iCDF) for the H_1 hypothesis.

They represent:

- the cumulative proportion of *LR*s less than or equal to the *LR* value on the x-axis for the H_0 hypothesis; $P(LR(H_0) \leq LR)$,
- the inverse cumulative proportion of *LR*s greater than the *LR* value on the x-axis for the H_1 hypothesis; $P(LR(H_1) > LR)$.

Figures 10.12 and 10.13 show examples of Tippett plots II. In these figures, the natural logarithm transformation (log*LR*) is applied to the *LR* values. The main advantage of the log transformation is the symmetrical scale with the centre of symmetry at log*LR* = 0. The *LR*s supporting the hypothesis H_0 tend to have positive values and the *LR*s supporting the hypothesis H_1 tend to have negative values.

10.4.1.2 Performance Metrics

Performance metrics related to the Tippett plots II are Probabilities of Misleading Evidence ($PMEH_0$ and $PMEH_1$) and Equal Proportion Probability (EPP) . They are applied to measure accuracy and discriminating power of the *LR* method used in

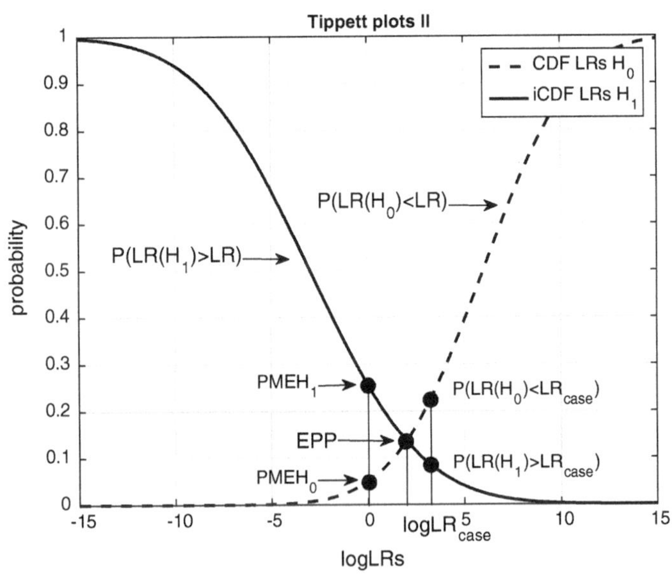

Fig. 10.12 Relation between case-specific *LR* (LR_{case}) and Tippett plots II for non-calibrated *LR*s [19]

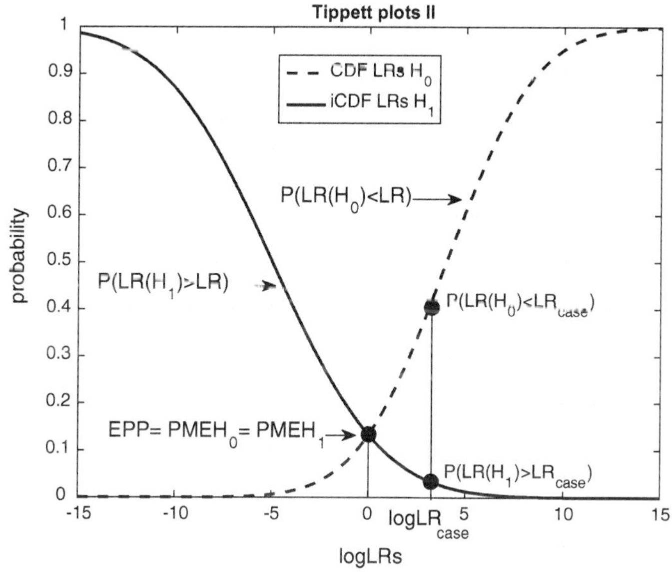

Fig. 10.13 Relation between case-specific *LR* (LR_{case}) and Tippett plots II for calibrated *LR*s [19]

casework, respectively [25]. Accuracy is a performance property, which presents the closeness of agreement between an assigned *LR* value and ground truth status of the hypothesis. Discriminating power is a performance property representing the capability of a given method to distinguish between same-source (SS) and different-source (DS) trials where different hypotheses are true.

Another metric that allows for combined measure of accuracy, discriminating power and calibration loss is the log-likelihood-ratio cost (*Cllr*) [37, 42].

Performance Metric 1—Probabilities of Misleading Evidence ($PMEH_0$ and $PMEH_1$)

Probabilities of Misleading Evidence ($PMEH_0$ and $PMEH_1$) are associated with the Tippett plots representation. They are defined in the following way [19]:

- $PMEH_0$: probability of misleading evidence in favour of the hypothesis H_1. The probability of all *LR*s that are smaller or equal to 1, knowing the H_0 hypothesis is true $PMEH_0 = P(LR(H_0) \leq 1)$.
- $PMEH_1$: probability of misleading evidence in favour of the hypothesis H_0. The probability of all the *LR*s that are bigger than 1, knowing the H_1 hypothesis is true $PMEH_1 = P(LR(H_1) > 1)$.

Based on their definitions the PMEs can be seen as a measure of accuracy of a *LR* method used in casework (Figs. 10.12 and 10.13). The PMEs in these two examples are: $PMEH_0 = 0.05$ and $PMEH_1 = 0.25$, in Fig. 10.12 and $PMEH_0 = PMEH_1 = 0.14$ in Fig. 10.13, in both examples at $\log LR = 0$.

Performance Metric 2—Equal Proportion Probability (EPP)

The advantage of Tippett plots II is that at the intersection of the CDF and iCDF we find the Equal Proportion Probability (EPP) [35]. The corresponding EPP value is EPP = 0.14 at $\log LR = 2$ in Fig. 10.12 and EPP = 0.14 at $\log LR = 0$ in Fig. 10.13.

The EPP can be seen as a metric of discriminating power. The lower the EPP the better the discriminating capabilities of a FASR system, e.g. capacity of the system to discriminate between the SS and DS trials. If comparing different FASR methods or if comparing the same method based on data recorded in various conditions, the EPPs compare the systems based on the discriminating power [7, 26].

Tippett plots II also can serve as an indicator of miscalibration. For a perfectly calibrated system the EPP is equal to both types of misleading evidence ($EPP = PMEH_0 = PMEH_1 = 0.14$) calculated for $\log LR = 0$ (Fig. 10.13).

Performance Metric 3—Log-Likelihood-Ratio Cost (*Cllr*)

Log-likelihood-ratio cost (*Cllr*) is proposed as a metric of accuracy related to the average cost of a *LR* method used [37]:

$$Cllr = \frac{1}{2 \cdot N_{SS}} \sum\nolimits_{i_{SS}} \log_2\left(1 + \frac{1}{LR_i}\right) + \frac{1}{2 \cdot N_{DS}} \sum\nolimits_{j_{DS}} \log_2\left(1 + LR_j\right),$$

where N_{SS} and N_{DS} are respectively the number of likelihood ratios in the SS and DS dataset. The indices i_{SS} and j_{DS} denote summing over the SS and DS likelihood ratios. As the accuracy of a speaker recognition system gets higher the *Cllr* tends towards zero. Following the pool-adjacent-violators (PAV) transformation of the $\log LRs$ we can obtain the parameter $Cllr^{\min}$ as discriminating power metric [42].

The calibration loss performance metric $Cllr^{\text{cal}}$ is obtained by subtracting $Cllr^{\min}$ from *Cllr*. In a well-calibrated system this difference is small [18, 37, 38, 43].

10.4.2 Evaluation of Case-Specific Strength of Evidence

When applied to specific speaker recognition based casework, a FASR method allows a numerical statement about the strength of evidence (*LR*) that the method can provide. Such casework can involve measuring calibration of likelihood ratios [38].

Tippett plots provide performance characteristics in terms of actual values of the *LR*s derived in the specific case for the relevant population of same-source and different-source trials under H_0 and H_1 hypotheses [6]. General information about the accuracy of the system used in the case can be given by probabilities of misleading evidence PMEH_0 and PMEH_1, which represent accuracy metrics. The value of the discriminating power metric EPP (Equal Proportion Probability) , corresponding to the crossing point of H_0 and H_1 plots, shows the discrimination of the system used. Misalignment of this crossing point with $\log LR = 0$ on the x-axis indicates that the system is non-calibrated.

Figure 10.12 shows an example of Tippett plots II for non-calibrated set of *LR*s. The intersection point between the plots of $P(\text{LR}(H_1) > LR)$ and $P(LR(H_0) \leq LR)$ does not occur at or near $\log LR = 0$ on the x-axis but occurs at some distance from it (2 in this example).

Cllr can be used to state the accuracy performance of the non-calibrated *LR*s. $Cllr^{\min}$ and $Cllr^{\text{cal}}$ can be used to confirm discrimination power and calibration loss of the system, respectively. Calibration loss is greater in a non-calibrated than a calibrated system.

An example of a case-specific $LR_{\text{case}} = 30$ ($\log LR_{\text{case}} = 3.4$) expressed as non-calibrated likelihood ratio is shown along with Tippett plots II in Fig. 10.12.

Calibrated *LR* is understood here as a likelihood ratio computed with a method aimed at improving the calibration metric. Some methods for calculating *LR*s produce well-calibrated results without the need for additional calibration.

Calibrated likelihood ratios are the most desirable strength-of-evidence statements and they are most compatible with the Bayesian interpretation framework. Calibrated likelihood ratios have a direct interpretation that can be reported and explained to the court. For example, (Fig. 10.13), if the likelihood ratio of a case has a value of 26.31 it is 26.31 times more likely to observe speech evidence supporting the H_0 hypothesis than the H_1 hypothesis given the questioned speaker and suspected speaker recordings, as well as the relevant population database.

An example of a case-specific LR_{case} expressed as calibrated likelihood ratio is shown along with Tippett plots II in Fig. 10.13.

Similarly to non-calibrated *LR*s, for calibrated *LR*s general information about the accuracy of the system used in the case can be given by probabilities of misleading evidence $\text{PMEH}_0 = \text{PMEH}_1$, which represent accuracy metrics. The value of discrimination power metric EPP (Equal Proportion Probability) , corresponding to the crossing point of H_0 and H_1 plots, shows the discriminating power of the system used.

Alignment of this crossing point with $\log LR = 0$ ($\text{EPP} = \text{PMEH}_0 = \text{PMEH}_1 = 0.14$) on the x-axis indicates that the system is calibrated.

As before with non-calibrated *LR*s, *Cllr* can be used to state the accuracy performance of the calibrated *LR*s. $Cllr^{\min}$ and $Cllr^{\text{cal}}$ can be used to confirm discrimination power and calibration loss of the system, respectively.

For calibrated *LR*s, if the case-specific LR_{case} falls on the right side of $\log LR = 0$, the case-specific speech evidence provides stronger support for the H_0 hypothesis than the H_1 hypothesis. In the example presented in Fig. 10.13, the reported LR_{case} value is equal to 26.31 ($\log LR_{case} = 3.27$). Such a value is reported to the court as the strength of evidence.

Within the performance characteristic (Tippett plots II) it is also possible to report what the probabilistic distance (PD) of case-specific LR_{case} is to the misleading evidence $PMEH_0$ [19]. This distance can be calculated as $P(LR(H_0) < LR_{case}) - PMEH_0$. For the example of calibrated *LR*s PD = 0.42 − 0.03 = 0.39 (Fig. 10.13) and for non-calibrated case example PD = 0.23 − 0.05 = 0.18 (Fig. 10.12). It corresponds to the proportion of likelihood ratios $LR(H_0)$ greater than $LR = 1$ and smaller than LR_{case}.

It is furthermore possible to report the case-specific probabilistic error (PE) expressed as proportion of likelihood ratios $LR(H_1)$ greater than the LR_{case} value $P(LR(H_1) > LR_{case})$. In calibrated case example (Fig. 10.13) PE = 0.03 and in non-calibrated one (Fig. 10.12) PE = 0.08.

An analogous set of values can be reported if LR_{case} falls on the left side of $\log LR = 0$.

10.5 Conclusion

In this chapter, a methodology for calculation and Bayesian interpretation of biometric evidence in forensic automatic speaker recognition (FASR) was provided. Processing chains for observed biometric evidence of speech and for calculating a likelihood ratio as the strength of this evidence were systematically developed. In FASR, the observed biometric evidence of speech can be defined on the level of similarity scoring (biometric univariate evidence) or feature extraction (biometric multivariate evidence). Based on this choice, calculation of a likelihood ratio can be performed by the "scoring method" or the "direct method", respectively. Processing chains developed for this purpose are in close relation with the hypotheses defined in the Bayesian interpretation framework. Several proposed chains correspond to the scoring and direct method, which involve univariate and multivariate biometric speech evidence.

This chapter also established a methodology to evaluate performance of a chosen FASR method under operating conditions of casework. It was possible to derive a number of performance characteristics and metrics given a relevant population database, a FASR method, which outputs the likelihood ratio value for each of the same-source and different-source trials and the ground truth regarding these trials. The performance evaluation was focused mainly on performance characteristics of Tippett plots and performance metrics such as probabilities of misleading evidence, equal proportion probability and log-likelihood-ratio cost. All these performance characteristics and metrics were combined together for evaluation of the case-specific strength of biometric evidence. Examples for non-calibrated and calibrated likelihood ratios were presented.

This chapter aimed at developing universal methodology, to be used for any specific speech data of the case, that provides a coherent way of presenting recorded speech as observed biometric evidence, calculation of its strength (likelihood ratio) and evaluation of the FASR method used for this calculation.

The methodology developed in this chapter has been adapted by the same authors to "Methodological Guidelines for Best Practice in Forensic Semiautomatic and Automatic Speaker Recognition" elaborated in the framework of ENFSI FSAAWG project "Methodological guidelines for semiautomatic and automatic speaker recognition for case assessment and interpretation", chaired by Andrzej Drygajlo.

References

1. Aitken CGG, Lucy D (2004) Evaluation of trace evidence in the form of multivariate data. Appl Stat 53:109–122
2. Aitken CGG, Taroni F (2004) Statistics and evaluation of evidence for forensic scientists, 2nd edn. Wiley, Chichester
3. Aitken CGG, Roberts P, Jackson G (2010) Fundamentals of probability and statistical evidence in criminal proceedings. Guidance for judges, lawyers, forensic scientists and expert witnesses. Practitioner guide no 1, Royal Statistical Society
4. Alexander A (2005) Forensic automatic speaker recognition using Bayesian interpretation and statistical compensation for mismatched conditions. PhD dissertation, EPFL Lausanne
5. Alexander A, Drygajlo A (2004) Scoring and direct methods for the interpretation of evidence in forensic speaker recognition. In: Proceedings of the International Conference on Spoken Language Processing (ICSLP), Jeju, Korea, pp 2397–2400
6. Alonso Moreno V, Drygajlo A (2012) A joint factor analysis model for handling mismatched recording conditions in forensic automatic speaker recognition. In: Proceedings of the International Conference on Biometrics (ICB 2012), New Delhi, pp 484–489
7. Arcienega M, Alexander A, Zimmermann P, Drygajlo A (2005) A Bayesian network approach combining pitch and spectral envelope features to reduce channel mismatch in speaker verification and forensic speaker recognition. In: Proceedings of INTERSPEECH 2005, Lisbon, pp 2009–2012
8. Campbell JP, Shen W, Campbell WM, Schwartz R, Bonastre J-F, Matrouf D (2009) Forensic speaker recognition: a need for caution. IEEE Signal Process Mag 26:95–103
9. Champod C, Meuwly D (2000) The inference of identity in forensic speaker recognition. Speech Commun 31:193–203
10. Dehak N, Kenny P, Dehak R, Dumouchel P, Ouellet P (2011) Front-end factor analysis for speaker verification. IEEE Trans Audio Speech Lang Process 19:788–798
11. Drygajlo A (2007) Forensic automatic speaker recognition. IEEE Signal Process Mag 24:132–135
12. Drygajlo A (2009) Statistical evaluation of biometric evidence in forensic automatic speaker recognition. In: Geradts ZJ, Franke KY, Veenman CJ (eds) Computational forensics. Springer, Berlin, pp 1–12
13. Drygajlo A (2009) Forensic evidence of voice. In: Li SZ (ed) Encyclopedia of biometrics. Springer, Berlin, pp 1388–1395
14. Drygajlo A (2011) Voice: Biometric analysis and interpretation of. Wiley Encyclopedia of Forensic Science. Accessed 15 Dec 2011. doi:10.1002/9780470061589.fsa1034
15. Drygajlo A (2012) Automatic speaker recognition for forensic case assessment and interpretation. In: Neustein A, Patil HA (eds) Forensic speaker recognition. Law enforcement and counter-terrorism. Springer, Berlin, pp 21–39

16. Drygajlo A, (2014) From speaker recognition to forensic speaker recognition. In: Cantoni V, Dimov D, Tistarelli M (eds) Biometric authentication: first international workshop, BIOMET 2014, Sofia, Bulgaria, Revised Selected Papers. Springer, Berlin, pp 93–104
17. Drygajlo A, Meuwly D, Alexander A (2003). Statistical methods and Bayesian interpretation of evidence in forensic automatic speaker recognition. In: Proceedings of EUROSPEECH 2003, Geneva, pp 689–692
18. Drygajlo A, Ugnat L (2012) Comparative evaluation of calibrated deterministic and statistical models for forensic automatic speaker recognition systems. Presentation at the European Academy of Forensic Science Conference (EAFS 2012), The Hague
19. Drygajlo A, Jessen M, Gfroerer S, Wagner I, Vermeulen J, Niemi T (2015) Methodological guidelines for best practice in forensic semiautomatic and automatic speaker recognition including guidance on the conduct of proficiency testing and collaborative exercises. ENFSI, Verlag für Polizeiwissenschaft, Frankfurt
20. Evett IW, Buckleton JS (1996) Statistical analysis of STR data. In: Carracedo A, Brinkmann B, Bär W (eds) Advances in forensic haemogenetics, vol 6. Springer, Berlin, pp 79–86
21. Evett IW (1998) Towards a uniform framework for reporting opinions in forensic science casework. Sci Justice 38:198–202
22. Gonzalez-Rodriguez J, Drygajlo A, Ramos-Castro D, Garcia-Gomar M, Ortega-Garcia J (2006) Robust estimation, interpretation and assessment of likelihood ratios in forensic speaker recognition. Comput Speech Lang 20:331–355
23. Gonzalez-Rodriguez J, Rose P, Ramos D, Toledano DT, Ortega-Garcia J (2007) Emulating DNA: rigorous quantification of evidential weight in transparent and testable forensic speaker recognition. IEEE Trans Audio Speech Lang Process 15:2104–2115
24. Hansen JHL, Taufiq H (2015) Speaker recognition by machines and humans. IEEE Signal Process Mag 32:74–99
25. Haraksim R (2014) Validation of likelihood ratio methods used in forensic evidence evaluation: Application in forensic fingerprints. PhD dissertation, University of Twente, Enschede
26. Haraksim R, Ramos D, Meuwly D, Berger CEH (2015) Measuring coherence of computer-assisted likelihood ratio methods. Forensic Sci Int 249:123–132
27. Jackson G, Jones S, Booth G, Champod C, Evett I (2006) The nature of forensic science opinion—a possible framework to guide thinking and practice in investigations and in court proceedings. Sci Justice 46:33–44
28. Jackson G, Aitken C, Roberts P (2015) Case assessment and interpretation of expert evidence. Guidance for judges, lawyers, forensic scientists and expert witnesses. Practitioner guide no 4
29. Kinnunen T, Li H (2010) An overview of text-independent speaker recognition: from features to supervectors. Speech Commun 52:12–40
30. Li SZ, Jain A (eds) (2015) Encyclopedia of biometrics, 2nd edn. Springer, US
31. Meuwly D (2001) Reconnaissance automatique de locuteurs en sciences forensiques: l'apport d'une approche automatique. PhD dissertation, University of Lausanne
32. Meuwly D, El-Maliki M, Drygajlo A (1998) Forensic speaker recognition using Gaussian Mixture Models and a Bayesian framework. In: COST-250 workshop on speaker recognition by man and by machine: directions for forensic applications, Ankara, pp. 52–55
33. Meuwly D, Drygajlo A (2001) Forensic speaker recognition based on a Bayesian framework and Gaussian Mixture Modelling (GMM). In: Proceedings of ODYSSEY 2001, Crete, pp 145–150
34. Meuwly D, Haraksim R, Ramos D (2016) A guideline for the validation of likelihood ratio methods used for forensic evidence evaluation. To appear in Forensic Science International
35. Morrison GS (2009) Forensic voice comparison and the paradigm shift. Sci Justice 49:298–308
36. Morrison GS (2010) Forensic voice comparison. In: Freckelton I, Selby H (eds) Expert evidence (Chapter 99). Thomson Reuters, Sydney

37. Ramos-Castro D (2007) Forensic evaluation of the evidence using automatic speaker recognition systems. PhD dissertation, Universidad Autónoma de Madrid
38. Ramos D, Gonzalez-Rodriguez J (2013) Reliable support: Measuring calibration of likelihood ratios. Forensic Sci Int 230:156–169
39. Robertson B, Vignaux GA (1995) Interpreting evidence. Evaluating forensic science in the courtroom. Wiley, Chichester etc.
40. Rose P (2002) Forensic speaker identification. Taylor & Francis, London
41. Rose P (2006) Technical forensic speaker recognition: evaluation, types and testing of evidence. Comput Speech Lang 20:159–191
42. Van Leeuwen DA, Brümmer N (2007) An introduction to application-independent evaluation of speaker recognition systems. In: Müller C (ed) Speaker classification I: fundamentals, features, and methods. Springer, Berlin, pp 330–353
43. Van Leeuwen D, Brümmer N (2013) The distribution of calibrated likelihood ratios in speaker recognition. In: Proceedings of INTERSPEECH 2013, Lyon, pp 1619–1623

Chapter 11
On Using Soft Biometrics in Forensic Investigation

Paulo Lobato Correia, Peter K. Larsen, Abdenour Hadid, Martin Sandau and Miguel Almeida

Abstract This chapter addresses the usage of biometric recognition tools in the context of forensic investigations. In particular, the authors are concerned with the extraction of evidence from video sequences captured by surveillance cameras. In such scenarios many of the biometric traits traditionally used for recognition purposes, such as fingerprints, palmprints or iris, are not available. Therefore, the focus is on the extraction of soft biometrics, which encompasses personal characteristics used by humans to recognize or help to recognize an individual. This work starts by reviewing how forensic casework relying on surveillance video information is conducted nowadays. Then, a software platform, BioFoV, is proposed to automate many of the required procedures and including some initial implementation of soft biometric extraction tools. Furthermore, novel biometric methods to analyze human gait and facial traits are described and experimentally validated as a demonstration of future perspectives in soft biometrics.

11.1 Introduction

Forensic investigations rely on the application of a broad spectrum of sciences to answer questions of interest to a legal system, eventually in relation to a crime or to a civil action. One of the main goals is often to identify people involved in some action.

P.L. Correia (✉) · M. Almeida
Instituto de Telecomunicações, Instituto Superior Técnico, Universidade de Lisboa, Torre Norte, 10-15, 1049-001 Lisbon, Portugal
e-mail: plc@lx.it.pt

P.K. Larsen
University of Copenhagen, Copenhagen, Denmark

A. Hadid
University of Oulu, Oulu, Finland

M. Sandau
Danish Institute of Fire and Security Technology, Hvidovre, Denmark

M. Tistarelli and C. Champod (eds.), *Handbook of Biometrics for Forensic Science*, Advances in Computer Vision and Pattern Recognition,
DOI 10.1007/978-3-319-50673-9_11

Biometric researchers, on the other hand, have done much research on the recognition of people, but often without targeting or having access to data from cases found in real forensic scenarios. The EU COST Action 1106 "Integrating Biometrics and Forensics for the Digital Age" was established to bring these two communities together to foster cooperation and new research, and the work reported here has been carried out in this context.

The present work addresses the analysis of surveillance videos captured in crime scenes, notably in view of the extraction of soft biometrics that can provide evidence to be used as part of a forensic investigation.

Soft biometrics can be understood as traits that can provide information useful for recognition purposes, even if in some cases it may not be enough to, on its own, establish identity [23]. Soft biometrics are also often related to traits that humans use to recognize their peers, whose degree of distinctiveness and permanence may not always be the same [8]. Examples of soft biometric traits include gender, ethnicity, age, height, weight, body geometry, gait, scars, marks, or tattoos, among others. In some contexts also the information about clothing or other accessories can be used for recognition purposes.

This chapter presents one an effort made toward easing the usage of soft biometrics in forensic investigations. It starts by overviewing some of the procedures often adopted in forensic case investigations. Then a software platform developed to support forensic investigators is proposed, into which a first set on modules requested by a law enforcement agency were included. The rest of the chapter is devoted to present further soft-biometrics research work conducted by the authors that can benefit forensic researchers.

11.2 Forensic Case Work as It Is Performed Today

11.2.1 Forensic Image Analysis at Present

Much forensic case work is based on the same methods as finger print examination, where forensic experts for many decades have examined two fingerprints for similarities and differences in the patterns of the skin, known as minutiae. The more similarities the examiner can find in the fingerprints, the more confident can the expert be in stating that the fingerprints belong to the same person.

The same principle is used in facial image comparison and as well as comparison of soft biometrics, which include bodily traits, such as birthmarks, scars, tattoos, gait, and height measurements based on pictures (known as photogrammetry—this subject will be described later in this chapter). The principle still is: the more similar traits found, the stronger is the support for perpetrator and suspect having congruent identity.

Minutiae are very characteristic traits, such as a special scar, while other traits are more general and can be said to distinguish between groups of people. Often it

Fig. 11.1 Example of real-case where ankle bending angle is used as soft biometric

is a subjective judgement of the expert how characteristic a given soft biometric trait is. An example of two traits of gait, notably bodily proportions and feet rotation angle, are illustrated in Fig. 11.1. Here it can be seen that the suspect (to the left) has similar bodily proportions as the perpetrator and also a markedly outward rotated feet. These traits can be categorized as quite common to a lot of people. Nevertheless, there will also be many subjects not sharing these traits. More notably the trait marked with "b"—an "outward bent" left ankle—indicate that both suspect and perpetrator have the same anomaly. This trait will provide strong support for perpetrator and suspect having congruent identity.

How strong support a given trait provides is often based solely on the expert experience, due to the lack of databases. A reason for this could be that it is time consuming and challenging to build up databases and forensic scientists often do not have the expertise and/or are too busy with case work.

However, the biometric is contributing in this direction with the creation of databases, for instance for tattoos, gait and facial images.

If the forensic examination can be based on empirical data, then it is possible to base the statement on uncertainty expressions such as likelihood ratios giving a statement of how likely it is that a given trace originates from the suspect rather than from any other subject in the population [34]. Likelihood ratios have been implemented in forensic courtrooms, for instance through DNA evidence.

In fact, for some traits it may be simpler to establish databases to calculate uncertainty measures, like for a DNA profile, for fingerprint minutiae or for the measurement of heights because it is quite clear how to find differences within the traits objectively. However, for some other traits, e.g., as obtained from images, it can be harder, because they depend on the perception of the observer [4]. Different observers will, for instance, have different perceptions of when and in which degree a nose seen in profile should be labeled as curved, crooked or bent.

11.2.2 Presentation of Findings in Court

All biometrics traits found to be in support or against congruent identity are summarized by the expert in a statement to court using a conclusion scale.

One of the simpler scales has been used by fingerprint experts based on the number of matching minutiae found [24]:

- Identification
- No conclusion
- Different marks

Other scales used are versions where the "no conclusion" statement has been replaced with different levels on support for congruent identity such as this one first used by the Danish police to compare tool marks and then modified by the Unit of Forensic Anthropology, University of Copenhagen to use for comparison of a given perpetrator and suspect(s):

(a) Identification
(b) Strong support for congruent identity
(c) Moderate support for congruent identity
(d) Inconclusive
(e) Limited support for congruent identity
(f) Not congruent identity

Both these scales are based on the expert knowledge. In the last decades, there has been an ongoing discussion in the forensic community whether and in which degree statements should be based on uncertainty statements or expert knowledge. "The expert knowledge side" argues that it is possible to positively identify a perpetrator and future research should point toward clarifying the error ratio associated with the identification. Contrary "the uncertainty statement side" would say that is not possible to positively identify a given suspect as being the perpetrator so research should be aimed toward expressing how probable it is that the suspect indeed is the perpetrator compared to any other subject in a relevant population.

A conclusion scale used by the Digital Image Working Group (DIWG) for proficiency tests in facial image comparison (Fig. 11.2) in the European Network of Forensic Scientists (ENFSI) tries to combine the two domains.

When using this conclusion scale, the forensic expert is encouraged to express an expert based opinion, which also can be used in the uncertainty domain. In this way, this scale can be used to express an "experience based uncertainty measure".

+5	**The results of the examination extremely strongly support that the same person is depicted in the questioned and the reference image.** *(The results are extremely more probable if the main hypothesis is true compared to if the alternative hypothesis is true. 1 000 000 ≤ V)*
+4	**The results of the examination strongly support that …** *(The results are far more probable if the main hypothesis is true compared to if the alternative hypothesis is true. 10 000 ≤ V < 1 000 000)*
+3	**The results of the examination support that …** *(The results are much more probable if the main hypothesis is true compared to if the alternative hypothesis is true. 100 ≤ V < 10 000)*
+2	**The results of the examination give moderate support that …** *(The results are more probable if the main hypothesis is true compared to if the alternative hypothesis is true. 10 ≤ V < 100)*
+1	**The results of the examination give weak support that …** *(The results are slightly more probable if the main hypothesis is true compared to if the alternative hypothesis is true. 2 ≤ V < 10)*
0	**The results of the examination support neither … nor …** *(The results are equally probable if the main hypothesis is true compared to if the alternative hypothesis is true. 1/2 < V < 2)*
-1	**The results of the examination give weak support that it is not …** *(The results are slightly more probable if the alternative hypothesis is true compared to if the main hypothesis is true. 1/10 < V ≤ 1/2)*
-2	**The results of the examination give moderate support that it is not …** *(The results are more probable if the alternative hypothesis is true compared to if the main hypothesis is true. 1/100 < V ≤ 1/10)*
-3	**The results of the examination support that it is not …** *(The results are much more probable if the alternative hypothesis is true compared to if the main hypothesis is true. 1/10 000 < V ≤ 1/100)*
-4	**The results of the examination strongly support that it is not …** *(The results are far more probable if the alternative hypothesis is true compared to if the main hypothesis is true. 1/1 000 000 < V ≤ 1/10 000)*
-5	**The results of the examination extremely strongly support that it is not …** *(The results are extremely more probable if the alternative hypothesis is true compared to if the main hypothesis is true. V ≤ 1/1 000 000)*

Fig. 11.2 Conclusion scale used in proficiency tests in facial image comparison. Note that it is possible both to give expert based opinions and uncertainty based measures with this scale

If the expert does not find he/she has the empirical data to express such a ratio, then there is the possibility to perform a one-to-one comparison between the suspect and perpetrator and then use an experience based scale to express a degree of support for or against congruent identity between perpetrator and suspect. If it is questioned in court how many other people could be the perpetrator, the answer should be that this is not known. In this context, the evidence cannot stand for itself but should be considered as a part of an evidence chain.

11.2.3 Directions of Further Research

It has been shown that, statements based on a forensic expert's experience tend to express stronger support for congruence or non-congruence for identity than statements based on empirical data [47]. This encourages the movement from forensic work based on experience to work based on the empirical data indicating that collecting and building databases must be of primary focus.

The problem of traits which are difficult to label or quantify, such as the profile of the nose, could possibly be addressed by using soft biometric pairwise comparisons where observers use pairwise comparisons to judge which of two persons, e.g., has the most crooked or straight nose, and then rank a group of people by the given trait [44]. The new challenge is to ask the right questions for each pairwise comparison.

However, methods such as pairwise comparisons still need an observer to make the judgements. Another interesting direction of research is to develop automatic recognition systems so the human bias is bypassed. There has been progress made in this direction, for instance in the field of fingerprint examination.

The field of biometrics is tailor made for research in these directions. However, there are some challenges to address before biometric research can be easily transformed into techniques for forensic casework. Some of the problems are that biometric research traditionally does not answer forensic questions and some terms are used differently in the two communities. As an example, the term "recognition rate" is widely used in biometric research to describe how good a given technique is at identifying the right subject in a database. In forensics, "recognition" is used when a witness recognizes a subject, and it is never known whether the perpetrator is present in the database used. One of the ways to bridging the gap would naturally be to find ways to express result of research as uncertainty measures instead.

11.3 A Software Platform to Support Forensic Investigations: BioFoV

A forensic expert practitioner needs to handle a diverse set of tools, often not available in the same integrated software package. BioFoV aims to provide a forensic casework tailor-made software, based on state of art knowledge in fields such as soft biometrics, gait recognition, photogrammetry, etc. Forensic experts, police officers and others working with forensic video analysis can also benefit from more "intelligent" video handling tools, such as automatic event detection, to help search the relevant video footage prior to the actual case work.

Software packages aimed at forensic video and image analysis have been developed, such as Forevid [20] or the tools developed by Ocean Systems [39], although more directed either for video capture and processing or enhancement of the material, not fully addressing the above-mentioned challenges. A tool for forensic gait analysis has recently been developed [22] and automatic facial algorithms are valuable tools for the forensic expert [27]. Including such tools into a common and extensible software platform would allow narrowing down the software tools a forensic video analyzer needs to master, and, more importantly, would support the combination of results from different algorithms to enhance overall forensic analysis results.

This book chapter proposes such a software platform, BioFoV, resulting from the cooperation between a biometrics research group and an experienced group of forensic practitioners. The objective is to provide an extensible tool, useful to forensic investigators of different backgrounds. By automating a set of time consuming and laborious tasks, it is expected to enable a deeper case analysis, requiring less effort from the investigator, while allowing to focus the effort on those case aspects that require expert insight, contributing to an overall quality increase.

Two key characteristics of this proposal are: (i) the usage of open software, to avoid complex licensing; and (ii) its extensibility, to allow the inclusion of new modules adding functionality, as well as the possibility to include alternative or improved versions for existing modules when new relevant research emerges making new developments available to the community, instead of remaining in a hard-disk once a research project is completed.

BioFoV is developed in C ++, using Qt [43] for the graphical user interface (GUI) and the OpenCV library [41] for supporting computer vision and image processing functionalities. With this option, the same software can be compiled for different platforms. It has been successfully tested on GNU/Linux (Debian and Ubuntu) and Microsoft Windows. An OS X build should also be easily compiled on the target platform. All developed software is Free and Open Source, therefore the final product can be shipped without restrictive licenses or extra fees, allowing free sharing amongst those wanting to use and improve it.

11.3.1 User Interface

The GUI allows users to take advantage of the implemented functionalities. It supports the selection of input video contents, its display, information about the current user selections and, to execute the required module functionalities.

The GUI main window—see Fig. 11.3—is organized into four main areas: (i) top menu, where all functionalities are listed in sub-menus; (ii) input and result tabs, where inputs and outputs are listed; (iii) details area, where extra information about what is selected or being played back can be shown to the user; (iv) playback area, supporting user interaction with video or still images, via mouse input, and supporting video actions like seeking, zooming, pausing, or taking snapshots.

The present GUI is structured to support improvements, as further feedback from practitioners is gathered on the best layout for user interaction.

11.3.2 Modules

The motivation behind the BioFoV software platform development is the functionality to be offered to forensic researchers. The current version includes a set of general purpose modules, expected to be used by most practitioners, such as camera calibration, or event detection. Also a couple of more specific modules have been included, notably for the computation of soft biometrics such as bodily and joint angle measurements, or facial detection, as examples of possible feature extraction modules.

A set of other useful functionalities are included such as: (i) print, to enable quick physical access to the displayed image; (ii) export, allowing extracted features to be bulk exported to separate image files; or (iii) a tool for exporting video events that were automatically detected.

To illustrate BioFoV modules' functionality, sample results are included considering input videos acquired with a Logitech c270 webcam, with 640 × 480 pixel resolution, at 10 frames per second, from which videos were captured using ffmpeg and encoded with an H.264 codec.

11.3.2.1 Camera Calibration

Even the best video cameras distort the captured images, requiring a calibration step to compensate for distortions and to support accurate measurements. By recording a video of a symmetrical chess pattern with the same camera, the calibration parameters can be calculated once and saved to a file. Later it can be imported for usage with footage captured by the same camera.

The present implementation is based on the OpenCV functions *findChessboardCorners* and *calibrateCamera*, the latter being based on [6, 51]. The

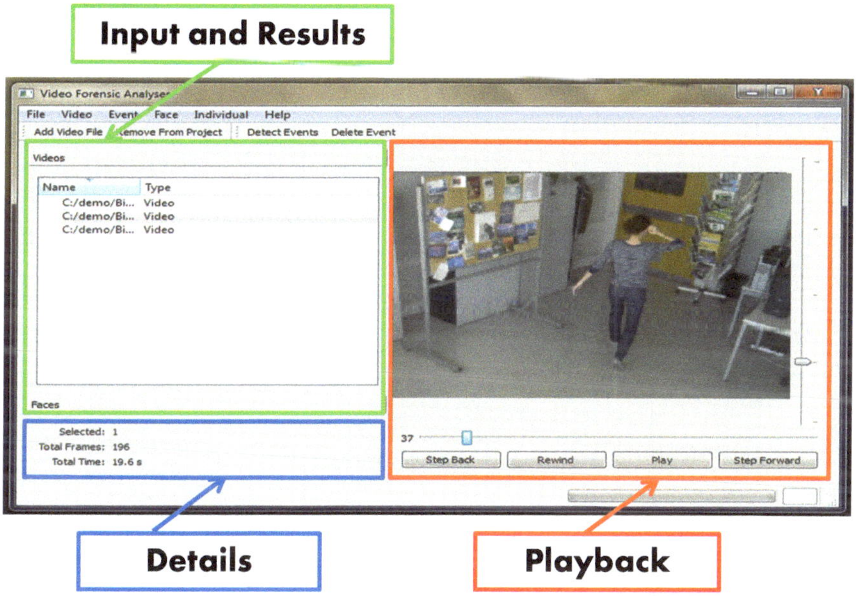

Fig. 11.3 Graphical User Interface of the proposed BioFoV platform

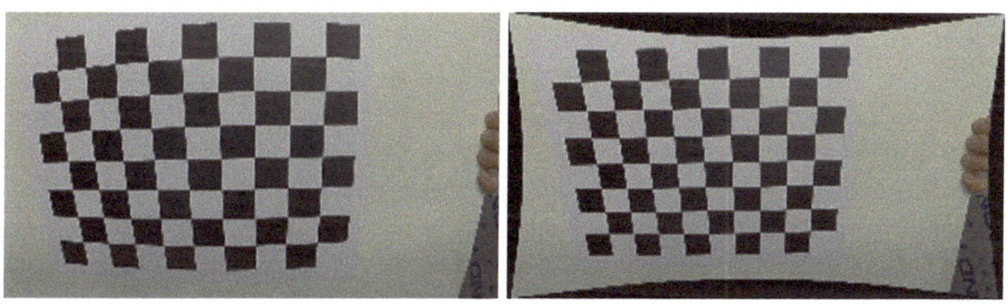

Fig. 11.4 Camera calibration example: original (*left*) and calibrated (*right*) images

algorithm is applied to patterns captured from surveillance videos, which sometimes can be blurry, affecting the precision of the calibration. For this reason, the pattern should be moved slowly and under good illumination conditions while performing the calibration. In order to capture the edge distortions properly, the pattern was moved along the areas captured near the image border. Camera calibration results are illustrated in Fig. 11.4.

11.3.2.2 Event Detection

When a surveillance video has to be analysed thoroughly, a lot of man time needs to be spent visualizing it, even if nothing relevant is happening for most of the time. This module allows a faster analysis of long videos, automatically looking for the occurrence of relevant events. The present implementation trims the video parts that show no movement, keeping the user from having to watch the entire video, which sometimes can be several days long. An adaptive background subtraction model is used, checking each video frame for significant changes [53]. The user can adjust a parameter to control the amount of change considered significant enough for selecting frames for further analysis.

As an example, a 2 days, 11 h and 30 min sample video was captured in an office environment. BioFoV identified a set of events considered relevant with a total length of 17 min (210 times shorter). These results were manually validated by an operator as not missing any of the relevant events taking place in the area under surveillance. This illustrates the saving of a considerable amount of time that the forensic expert can use to a better purpose.

11.3.2.3 Re-Projected Image Plane Measurements

BioFoV enables the computation of soft biometrics such as heights, lengths or angles, by supporting the measurement of distances in a re-projected image plane. Prior to any measurement, the camera has to be calibrated.

An image transformation tool allows an image to be re-projected to a vertical plane visible in a captured frame. This allows, for example, the comparison of heights or widths between known static planar objects and those of items of interest, or to estimate soft biometrics such as bodily measurements of individuals in the re-projected plane. The implemented tools support the measurement of: (i) linear distance between two points; (ii) vertical distance between two points; (iii) horizontal distance between two points; (iv) angles.

It should be noticed that bodily measurements of individuals computed using this tool, for instance the height, is precise only under very strict conditions, such as: (i) the individual standing straight; (ii) being in the same vertical plane as the one used for re-projection; (iii) the point on the top of the head being well defined, as well as its vertical projection on the floor. These conditions are seldom met at the same time. Alternative measurements may be considered, as the height to the eyes, the length of a limb, or the angle between leg and foot in a given part of the gait cycle. As discussed in the previous chapter, the best option can be to compare measurements obtained in similar poses.

A measurement example is presented in Fig. 11.5, where measurement conditions are close to ideal. The image is re-projected into the plane of the board, which is aligned with the person. The board height is known to be 91 cm. Using, a previously calibrated camera, a height measurement value for the person of 1.68 m was obtained, while the person height is in fact 1.72 meters. The difference is mainly due to the imprecision of manually marking the top and bottom points of the person image.

To give the user more freedom and avoid the restriction of the individual having to stand in the same plane as the referential a more complete spatial measurement module needs to be developed, notably to allow, from several post event photos of

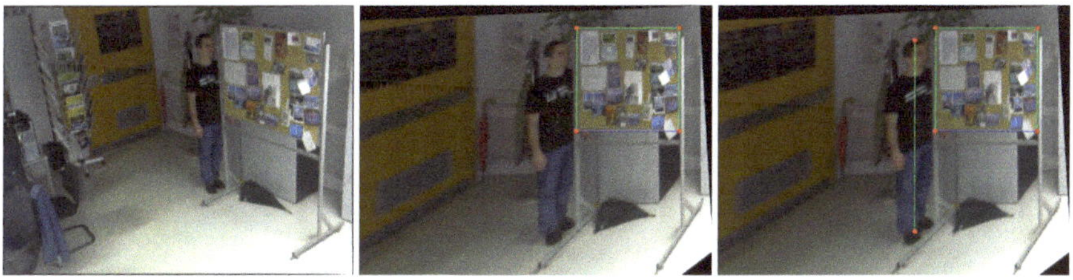

Fig. 11.5 Height measurement with a reference: calibrated frame (*left*); re-projected frame (*middle*); height measurement (*right*)

the same scene, eventually captured from different angles, to reconstruct points, edges, planes, and volumes that can be used as measurement reference. From these, virtual references can be constructed and overlaid with the video, allowing bodily measurements in arbitrary locations in the scene, thus avoiding the coplanar restriction imposed by the previously described image measurement module. A step in this direction is presented in the following chapter.

11.3.2.4 Feature Extraction—Face Detection Example

Feature extraction modules enable the automatic detection and extraction of a selected feature, from a set of videos or from previously detected events. Additional modules can be added accommodating the desired type of analysis.

In the present BioFoV version a feature extraction module dedicated to frontal face detection has been included. The feature extraction module is the implementation of a Haar Feature-based Cascade Classifier [33, 48] and implemented in OpenCV. With this module the user can easily create a facial database of people detected in the video.

11.3.3 How to Get BioFoV

A first release of the BioFoV platform code and an issue tracking tool are freely available online, open to anybody who wants to contribute or use it. The reference for the repository is https://www.github.com/BioFoV/BioFoV.

Code is documented using Doxygen and a tutorial for implementing a simple module will be made available, allowing anyone with programming knowledge to integrate new modules and share them with all BioFoV users. The management of the project, and code review of any new feature submission, as well as tracking of bug reports will be ensured by the current team to allow tight quality control on the program releases.

11.4 Applications of 3D Markerless Motion Capture in Forensic Gait Analysis

Forensic analysis of gait and bodily dimensions suffers from a high resource demand and the bias caused by the subjective judgements provided by the experts [30], as previously mentioned. Fully automatic gait recognition algorithms like [1, 13] may cope with this in the future. However, these kinds of algorithms are infeasible for forensic analysis at the current stage.

Comparison of gait and bodily dimensions obtained from different image perspectives further challenges the expert's judgement power. The BioFoV's re-projection tool can compensate for this to some extent, but no single view method has proven to be inherently view invariant and thus 3D CCTV may be a solution in the future.

3D imaging can be obtained by active or passive methods. Active methods provide depth perception using the relative position of light emitters and photo or imaging sensors, while passive methods uses the relative positions of the photo or imaging sensors exclusively. Active methods embrace Time-of-Flight (ToF) [50] and triangulation methods based on shape from shading [21], structured light or pseudo-random patterns [49], while passive methods embrace the triangulation methods based on either stereo vision or shape from silhouette (SFS) [3]. The advantages of the active systems are that they are less dependent on ambient illumination from external light sources and the texture of the object, but the emission of light limits the effective range and are often inapplicable under exposure of direct sun light. Passive methods can typically obtain a larger effective range farther out assuming the external light conditions, the focal length and the distance between the cameras are appropriately configured. However, oppose to active systems, SFS methods are highly dependent on high contrast between object and background and stereo vision methods require locally uniqueness in the texture of surfaces.

This chapter describes how 3D measurements and 3D reconstructions can be obtained with stereo vision and how this can be applied to create a laboratory setup feasible for full 3D reconstructions of human gait. The laboratory description is followed by a study demonstrating the discriminatory power of gait features conducted in the proposed 3D laboratory. Lastly, you will find a presentation of the latest work on conducting 3D CCTV for field environments.

11.4.1 Accurate 3D Imaging of Human Gait and Bodily Dimensions

To obtain measurements in 3D from images, the pin-hole model is applied to describe the geometric relations between the object and its projection into the image plane. The parameters required to use the model embrace the intrinsic camera

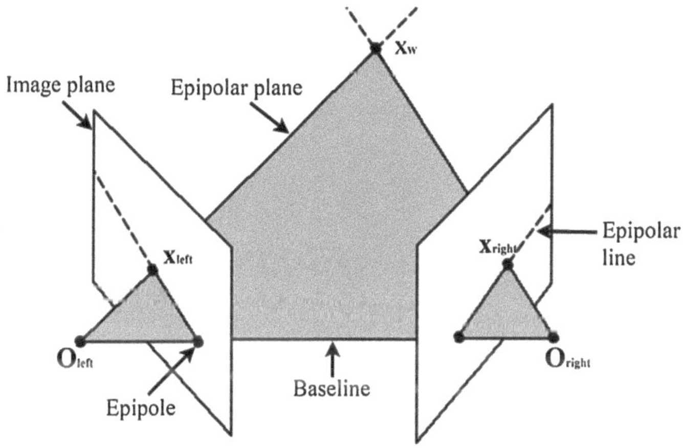

Fig. 11.6 Sketch of a point X_w in world space and its projection into the *left* and *right* image planes as the points x_{left} and x_{right}, respectively. The optical centers of the cameras are defined as O and these are separated by a baseline. Together with X_w the optical centers define the epipolar plane, which intersection with the image planes define the epipolar lines

parameters including the focal length, principal point, pixel aspect ratio, and lens distortion and the extrinsic parameters describing the location and the orientation of the cameras.

Given two cameras with different viewpoints, stereo matching algorithms can be applied to identify point correspondences between the images automatically and knowing the epipolar geometry 3D world coordinates can be computed by triangulation [19]. Point matching algorithms also reduce the search of corresponding points using the epipolar geometry as one point in one image is constrained to lie on the epipolar line in the other image, as illustrated in Fig. 11.6.

The laboratory setup was custom built and consisted of eight monochromatic 2048 × 2048 pixel cameras mounted pair wise with a vertical baseline in the corners of the laboratory. The field of view covered roughly $2.0 \times 2.0 \times 2.0$ m^3.

Point matching and triangulation was obtained using the Patch based Multi-View Stereo algorithm [11]. The PMVS algorithm finds point correspondences in a three-step procedure embracing matching, expanding and filtering. First image features based on Harris corners [18] and Difference of Gaussians (DoG) [36] are matched by a correlation along the epipolar lines, then an expansion step and a filtration step are iteratively executed to create a denser point cloud and to filter the outliers by constraining the visibility consistency and the point spread. A sequence of 3D reconstructions from a normal gait trial are illustrated in Fig. 11.7.

Fig. 11.7 *Side view* of multiple 3D point clouds from a person performing a gait cycle

11.4.2 Using Gait Kinematics and Random Forests for Recognition

Recognition based on the kinematics from the upper and lower extremities has been tested on 16 slim suited participants who were annotated by the same expert. Random forests [7] was applied for automatic recognition as this allows estimation of a certainty score for each recognition using the distribution of the votes among the trees and the importance of the parameters can be quantified by the out-of-bag variable importance [7], which provides substantial information for the decision maker. Five trials from two different days were applied as test and training data, respectively. The training data were applied to train the random forest, whereas recognition was performed on the test data. The random forest was built with 250 trees as the out-of-bag recognition error hereby reached convergence.

The ranking of the parameter importance listed in Fig. 11.8 shows that shoulder-to-shoulder angles, shoulder joint angles and the knee joint angles were among the most important parameters and both the frontal and the sagittal parameters seemed equally important for recognition. However, the importance of

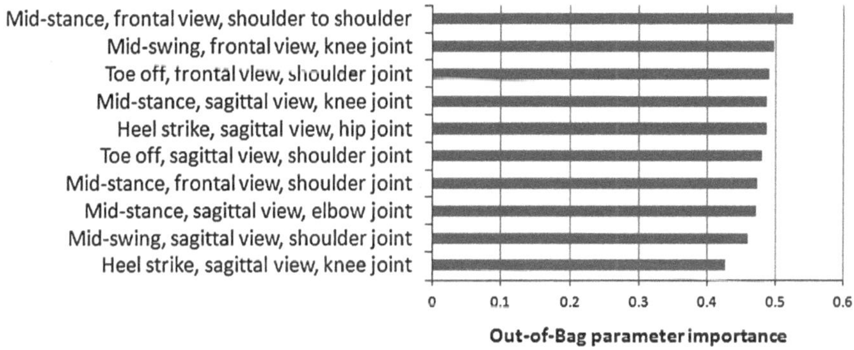

Fig. 11.8 The top 10 of out-of-bag parameter importance (i.e., the out-of-bag error increase as a fraction of the error before the parameter was randomly permuted)

the kinematic parameters and the view angle depended highly on the phase in the gait cycle, which should be considered during comparisons of gait patterns.

The correct recognition rate as a function of the number of parameters included in the recognition is illustrated in Fig. 11.9. Parameters were included according to the ranking of the parameter importance listed in Fig. 11.8 in decreasing order. The results show that single parameters have a relatively weak discriminatory power with 13% to 17% correct recognitions. With inclusion of six parameters, all participants were correctly recognized based on five trials and the correct recognition rate for one gait trial converged around 27 parameters with over 96% correct recognitions.

The results of the study emphasize the importance of considering a series of gait trials rather than a single trial and to consider the kinematics of both the upper and lower extremities.

Current study was conducted with a controlled experimental setup and a group of participants with limited variations in terms of bodily dimensions. Challenges related to gender, adiposity, race, clothing, lighting conditions, etc. were therefore not considered in the study and these parameters have to be addressed in future studies to reflect the practical issues regarding surveillance.

11.4.3 3D Surveillance and Future Perspectives in Gait Recognition

In the previous sections, we have shown the discriminatory power of gait and bodily dimensions and how 3D imaging can provide an improved alternative for biometric measurements compared to 2D images. However, the 3D imaging method presented so far is only feasible for laboratory environments. Therefore, the research community is currently testing other 3D acquisition systems suited for

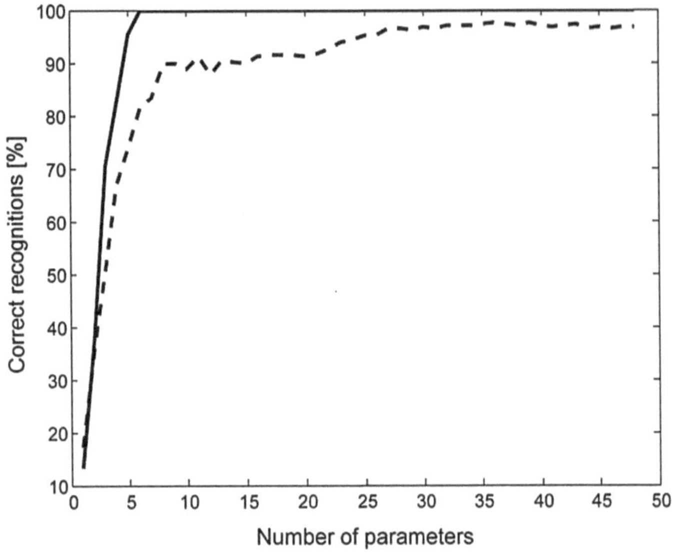

Fig. 11.9 Correct recognition rate as function of number of random forest parameters. Parameters were included according to their importance in decreasing order. The *dashed line* and the *solid line* are recognition based on one and five gait trials, respectively

biometric analysis in field environments. So far, a low cost system consisting of a Kinect v2,[1] a mini computer and a NAS server, which enables acquisition of 3D point clouds with an effective range between 2 and 5 m. The Kinect obtains 3D reconstructions using the ToF technology and thus it is less sensitive to textures on clothes and skin but suffers from the exposure of direct sunlight. Nevertheless, the Kinect v2 has several advantages as it is already calibrated such that the 3D point cloud is scaled in known metrics and is capable of capturing RGB images so the 3D point cloud can be textured with 'true' colors, which may be helpful for the forensic expert. Proof of concept experiments are currently in progress in various indoor environments as illustrated in Fig. 11.10. However, further scientific work should also validate the accuracy of the 3D reconstructions obtained with the system.

[1]Microsoft, Redmond, Washington, USA.

(a) (b)

Fig. 11.10 **a** RGB image obtained from the Kinect and **b** body height measurement obtained from the corresponding 3D point cloud rotated to side view

11.5 Extraction of Soft Biometrics from Facial Images

A significant number of soft biometric traits can be extracted from face images and facial movements. This generally includes gender recognition (i.e., man vs. woman), age categorization (e.g., child, youth, adult, middle-age, and elderly) and ethnicity classification (e.g., Asian, Caucasian and African). Other soft biometric traits that can be extracted from faces include eye movements, kinship information (i.e., verifying whether two persons are from the same family or not), skin and eye color, the periocular region of a face image, facial tattoo, facial scars and moles, etc.

Though there has been a great deal of progress in face analysis in the last two decades, most of the work has mainly focused on face detection and recognition problems, rather than on soft biometrics. Consequently, the design of algorithms that are effective in discriminating between males and females, or classifying faces into different age and ethnic categories remain open areas of research. Findings from human perception studies, suggested that peculiar texture patterns, sparsely located on the face image, are often used by humans for a rapid identification of faces. The same approach demonstrated to be applicable in forensic cases, as well as other applications. Such isolated patterns, which may correspond either to a skin defect (such as a scar or a mole), or to a specific facial area (eyebrow, chin) with a distinctive appearance, often do not allow for an accurate classification but can be exploited in conjunction with other techniques to improve the recognition performance. For instance, Klare et al. [26] proposed an approach, where human describable face attributes are exploited to perform face identification in criminal investigations. The extracted facial attributes, such as eyebrows, chin, and eyes shape are compared with the same attributes encoded in hand drawn police sketches. The experimental analysis demonstrated its applicability in forensic identification of suspects.

11.5.1 Extracting Gender from Face Images

First attempts of using computer vision based techniques to gender classification started in early 1990s. Since then, a significant progress has been made and several approaches have been reported in literature. Fundamentally, the proposed techniques differ in (i) the choice of the facial representation, ranging from the use of simple raw pixels to more complex features, such as Gabor responses, and in (ii) the design of the classifier, ranging from the use of nearest neighbor (NN) and fisher linear discriminant (FLD) classifiers to artificial neural networks (ANN), support vector machines (SVM), and boosting schemes. For instance, Moghaddam and Yang [37] used raw pixels as inputs to SVMs while Baluja and Rowley [2] adopted AdaBoost to combine weak classifiers, constructed using simple pixel comparisons, into a single strong classifier. Both systems showed good classification rates of above 90% but under controlled settings. An empirical comparative analysis on gender classification approaches can be found in [35] whereas a recent survey on the topic can be found in [38]. Note that there is no public database specifically designed for gender recognition evaluation. Most of the recent works have been evaluated on the Images of Groups database [12], which is a collection of face images of groups of people from Flickr. This database has been mainly designed for unconstrained demographic classification (age and gender).

11.5.2 Age Classification from Facial Images

Automatic age classification aims to assign a label to a face regarding the exact age (age estimation) or the age category (age classification) it belongs to. This is challenging problem because the appearance of a particular face varies due to changes in pose, expressions, illumination, and other factors such as make-up, occlusions, image degradations caused by blur and noise, etc. In addition to these difficulties, which are shared with the standard problems of face recognition, aging is a very complex process that is extremely difficult to model: a group of people of the same age may look very different depending on, for example, environment, lifestyle, genes, etc. Thus, deriving a universal age classification model is troublesome. Many face image representations for age estimation have been studied, such as anthropometric models, active appearance models (AAM), aging pattern subspace, and age manifold. An extensive review of age representation methods can be found in [9]. Regarding age classification schemes, the existing methods are based on either pure classification or regression analysis. Perhaps, among the pioneering studies on age classification are those proposed by Kwon and da Vitoria Lobo [28], Lanitis et al. [29], and Guo et al. [14]. Although relatively successful in some scenarios (e.g., high-quality and occlusion-free images, neutral facial expression), most existing methods tend to suffer under uncontrolled settings as noted in [9]. The most commonly used public face databases for evaluating age classification are MORPH [45] and FG-NET [42] databases and the more challenging Images of Groups [12] database.

11.5.3 Ethnicity Classification from Facial Images

While gender and age recognition have been explored by many other researchers, automatic ethnicity classification problem has received relatively far less attention despite the potential applications. This is perhaps due to the ambiguity and complexity in defining and describing different ethnic groups. The terms "race" and "ethnicity" are sometimes used interchangeably although they refer to biological and sociological factors, respectively. Generally, race refers to a person's physical appearance or characteristics, while ethnicity is more viewed as a culture concept, relating to nationality, rituals and cultural heritages, or even ideology [10]. The most commonly encountered and accepted racial groups are African/African American, Caucasian, East Asian, Native American/American Indian, Pacific Islander, Asian Indian, and Hispanic/Latino. A very recent survey on extracting race from face images can be found in [10]. Most of the proposed methods are evaluated on general face databases, which are not intentionally designed for race classification.

11.5.4 Experimental Analysis on Extracting Facial Soft Biometrics from Videos

The way a person is moving his/her head and facial parts (such as the movements of the mouth when a person is talking) defines so called facial dynamics and characterizes personal behaviors. In this section, we provide an experimental analysis on the use of facial dynamics for extracting soft biometrics from video sequences. Two baseline approaches based on LBP features [40] and support vector machines (SVM) are implemented and discussed. The first approach is using only static images and thus ignoring the facial dynamics while the second approach uses spatiotemporal representation thus combining facial structure and dynamics. The aim of the experiments is to evaluate the benefit of incorporating the facial dynamics. The choice of adopting the LBP approach [40] is motivated by the recent success of using it for combining appearance and motion for face and facial expression recognition [15] and for dynamic texture recognition [52]. We describe below the two experimental approaches and then report the results on gender classification, age estimation and ethnicity classification.

11.5.4.1 Static Image-Based Approach

Given a target face video sequence, a straightforward approach to extract facial soft biometrics is to analyze each frame in the video and then combine the results through majority voting which consists of determining the gender (or age or identity) in every frame and then fusing the results. Basically, for efficient representation, each facial image (frame) is divided into several local regions from which LBP histograms are extracted and concatenated into an enhanced feature histogram. Then, the results are presented to an SVM classifier for recognition. Finally, the recognition scores over the face sequence are fused using majority voting. In such an approach, only static information is used while the facial dynamics are discarded.

11.5.4.2 Spatiotemporal-Based Approach

For spatiotemporal representation, volume LBP (VLBP) operator has been introduced in [52] and successfully used for combining appearance and motion for face and facial expression recognition [15] and for dynamic texture recognition [52]. The idea behind VLBP is very simple. It consists of looking at a face sequence as a rectangular prism (or volume) and defining the neighborhood of each pixel in three-dimensional space (X, Y, T) where X and Y denote the spatial coordinates and T denotes the frame index (time). Then, similarly to LBP in spatial domain, volume textons can be defined and extracted into histograms. Therefore, VLBP combines structure and motion together to describe the moving faces.

Each face sequence is divided into several overlapping rectangular prisms of different sizes, from which local histograms of VLBP code occurrences are extracted. To combine facial structure and dynamics, VLBP features are first extracted from the face sequences and feature selection is performed using AdaBoost. The result is then fed to an SVM for classification. In such an approach, both static facial information and facial dynamics are used.

11.5.4.3 Experiments on Gender Recognition

The static image-based and the spatiotemporal-based approaches are first applied to the problem of gender recognition from videos. Three different publicly available video face databases (namely CRIM (http://www.crim.ca/), VidTIMIT [46] and Kanade et al. [25]) are considered. They contain a balanced number of male's and female's sequences and include several subjects moving their facial features by uttering phrases, reading broadcast news or expressing emotions. The datasets are randomly segmented to extract over 4,000 video shots of 15–300 frames each. From each shot or sequence, the eye positions are automatically detected from the first frame. The determined eye positions are then used to crop the facial area in the whole sequence. Finally, the resulted images are scaled into 40 × 40 pixels. For evaluation, a fivefold cross-validation test scheme is adopted by dividing the 4,000 sequences into five groups and using the data from four groups for training and the left group for testing. This process is repeated five times and we report the average classification rates. When dividing the data into training and test sets, we explicitly considered two scenarios. In the first one, a same person may appear in both training and test sets with face sequences completely different in the two sets due to facial expression, lighting, facial pose, etc. The goal of this scenario is to analyze the performance of the methods in determining the gender of familiar persons seen under different conditions. In the second scenario, the test set consists only of persons who are not included in the training sets. This is equivalent to train the system on one or more databases and then do evaluation on other (different) databases. The goal of this scenario is to test the generalization ability of the methods to determine the gender of unseen persons. Table 11.1 summarizes the gender classification results using the two approaches (static image based and spatiotemporal based) in both scenarios (familiar and unfamiliar). We can notice that both methods gave better results with familiar faces than unfamiliar ones. This is not surprising and can be explained by the fact that perhaps the methods did not rely only on gender features for classification but may also exploited information about face identity. For familiar faces, the combination of facial structure and dynamics yielded in perfect classification rate of 100%. This proves that the system succeeded in learning and recognizing the facial behaviors of the subjects even under different conditions of facial expression, lighting and facial pose. For unfamiliar faces, the combination of facial structure and dynamics yielded in classification rate of about 83% which is still encouraging although the best result for unfamiliar faces is obtained using the static image-based approach (without facial dynamics). This may indicate that incorporating motion information with facial appearance was useful for only familiar faces but not with unfamiliar ones. More detailed experiments and results can be found in [16].

Table 11.1 Gender classification results on test videos of familiar and unfamiliar subjects using static image-based and spatiotemporal-based methods

Method	Gender classification rates	
	Familiar subjects (%)	Unfamiliar subjects (%)
Static image-based	94.4	90.6
Spatiotemporal-based	100	82.9

11.5.4.4 Experiments on Age Estimation

To study whether facial dynamics may enhance the automatic age estimation performance, a set of experiments using the static image-based and spatiotemporal-based approaches is performed. Five age classes are considered as follows: child = 0–9 years old; youth = 10–19; adult = 20–39; middle age = 40–59 and elderly = above 60. Then, a novel classification scheme based on a tree of four SVM classifiers is built. The first SVM classifier is trained to learn the discrimination between child class and the rest. If the target face is assigned into the child category, then the classification is completed. Otherwise, the second SVM classifier is examined to decide whether the face belongs to the Youth category or not. If not, the third SVM is examined and so on. The static image-based and spatiotemporal-based approaches are applied to age estimation from videos. For evaluation, a set of video sequences (mainly showing celebrities giving speeches in TV programs and News) is collected from Internet. The videos of unknown individuals (especially children), are manually labeled using our (human) perception of age. Then, the videos are randomly segmented to extract about 2,000 video shots of about 300 frames each. In the experiments, we adopted a tenfold cross-validation test scheme by dividing the 2,000 sequences into 10 groups and using the data from nine groups for training and the left group for testing. We repeated this process 10 times and we report the average classification rates. The performances of both static image-based and spatiotemporal-based approaches are shown in Table 11.2. From the results, we can notice that both methods did not perform very well and this somehow confirms the difficulty of the age estimation problem. Interestingly, the static information-based method significantly outperformed the spatiotemporal-based method (i.e., combination of face structure and dynamics). This might be an indication that facial dynamics is not useful for age estimation. However, due to the challenging nature of the age estimation problem, it is perhaps too early to make such a conclusion and more investigations are needed to study the integration of facial dynamics and facial structure for age estimation.

11.5.4.5 Experiments on Ethnicity Classification (Asian Versus Non-Asian)

Similarly to the previous experiments on gender recognition, the two experimental approaches are also applied to ethnicity classification from videos. Because of lack of ground truth data for training, only two ethnic classes (namely Asian and non-Asian) are considered. The same set of 2,000 video shots previously used in the experiments on age estimation is also considered here for ethnicity classification

Table 11.2 Average age classification rates

Method	Average age classification rates (%)
Static image-based	77.4
Spatiotemporal-based	69.2

Table 11.3 Average ethnicity classification rates using static image-based and spatiotemporal-based methods

Method	Ethnicity classification rates (%)
Static image-based	97.0
Spatiotemporal-based	99.2

tests. A manual labeling yielded in 81% of non-Asian and 19% of Asian data samples (i.e., video shots). For evaluation, we also adopted a fivefold cross-validation test scheme. The performances of both static image-based and spatiotemporal-based approaches are shown in Table 11.3. From the results, we can notice that both approaches perform quite very well but the spatiotemporal-based method (i.e., combination of face structure and dynamics) slightly outperforms the static image-based method (using only facial structure). This is somehow surprising because one may not expect better results using spatiotemporal methods for ethnicity classification.

11.5.4.6 Discussion

To gain insight into the use facial dynamics in extracting face soft biometric traits, we considered two approaches to face analysis from videos using LBP features and SVMs, and reported experimental results on gender classification, age estimation and ethnicity determination. The experiments on age estimation pointed out that combining face structure and dynamics does not enhance the performance of static image-based automatic systems. Our experiments also showed that incorporating motion information with facial appearance for gender classification might be only useful for familiar faces but not with unfamiliar ones (while the psychological and neural studies indicated that facial movements do contribute to gender classification in the human visual system). Finally, our experiments on the ethnicity classification problem yielded in quite surprising results indicating some relative usefulness of facial dynamics in ethnicity classification.

The primary goal of the above experiments is to provide the reader with clear case studies and examples on using facial dynamics for extracting facial soft biometric traits from videos. Note that the reported results may be specific to the methods and test material used in the experiments. Therefore, it is perhaps early to make final conclusions on the role of facial dynamics in extracting facial soft biometrics.

While many other works on extracting facial soft biometrics reported accuracy of above 90%, most of these studies have utilized face images captured in rather controlled sensing and cooperative subject scenarios [17]. However, in many real-word applications such as video surveillance, the available face images of a person of interest are most likely to be captured under unconstrained and un-cooperative scenarios. Most of the proposed techniques have been evaluated on general face databases, which are not intentionally designed for the problem in hands. Thus, there is clear lack of benchmark databases and protocols to evaluate the progress in extracting soft biometric traits. Recently, efforts have been made within the BeFIT project (http://www.fipa.cs.kit.edu/befit/) by proposing standardized datasets and protocols for evaluating different face analysis tasks. We approve this valuable initiative, which allows a fair comparison and an easy reproduction of research results.

11.6 Conclusions

Today, biometric measurements in CCTV are used in a limited number of cases compared to the number of cameras installed in urban environments, despite the methods being known for decades and the resulting evidences being fully usable in court. The limited applications partly rely on a high resource demand of skilled experts and partly on the typically limited image quality and the challenging perspectives, which reduce the strength of evidence [5, 32, 31].

To meet these challenges in future, the research community has developed a new software platform which makes various video analysis tools and photogrammetric tools easier to apply in a user-friendly manner. Furthermore, a study on applying 3D imaging for analysis of human gait has been conducted, which showed that gait recognition can be conducted with high reliability by using only six carefully selected kinematic parameters. Therefore, the current research of the community focuses on developing new 3D imaging methods suitable for CCTV in the fields. Finally, whenever faces are visible in surveillance videos, this information should be taken into account in the recognition process. In unconstrained scenarios, using low resolution unaligned images, traditional face recognition algorithms may not be used, but several soft biometrics may still be considered, for instance exploring facial dynamics.

References

1. Ariyanto G, Nixon M (2012) Marionette mass-spring model for 3D gait biometrics. In: Proceedings of the International Conference on Biometrics (ICB), pp 354–359
2. Baluja S, Rowley H (2007) Boosting sex identification performance. Int J Comput Vision 71:111–119
3. Baumgart BG (1974) Geometric modeling for computer vision. Stanford University
4. Biber K (2009) Visual jurisprudence: the dangers of photographic identification evidence. CJM 78:35–37
5. Bouchrika I, Goffredo M, Carter J, Nixon M (2011) On using gait in forensic biometrics. J Forensic Sci 56(4):882–889
6. Bouguet J-Y (2011) MATLAB calibration tool. http://www.vision.caltech.edu/bouguetj/calib_doc/. Accessed 26 Mar 2015
7. Breiman L (2001) Random forests. Mach Learn 45:5–32

8. Dantcheva A, Velardo C , D'angelo A, Dugelay JL (2011) Bag of soft biometrics for person identification: new trends and challenges. Multimed Tools Appl 51(2):739–777
9. Fu Y, Guo G, Huang TS (2010) Age synthesis and estimation via faces: a survey. IEEE Trans Pattern Anal Mach Intell (T-PAMI), 32(11):1955–1976
10. Fu S, He H, Hou Z (2014) Learning race from face: a survey. IEEE Trans Pattern Anal Mach Intell (TPAMI)
11. Furukawa Y, Ponce J (2010) Accurate, dense and robust multi-view stereopsis, vol 32
12. Gallagher AC, Chen T (2009) Understanding images of groups of people. In: Proceedings of IEEE CVPR
13. Guan Y, Li C-T (2013) A robust speed-invariant gait recognition system for walker and runner identification. In: The 6th IAPR international conference on biometrics: IAPR, pp 1–8
14. Guo G, Mu G, Fu Y, Huang T (2009) Human age estimation using bio-inspired features. In: CVPR'09, pp 112–119
15. Hadid A, Pietikäinen M, Li SZ (2007) Learning personal specific facial dynamics for face recognition from videos. In: IEEE international workshop on analysis and modeling of faces and gestures (in conjunction with ICCV 2007), pp 1–15
16. Hadid A, Pietikäinen M (2008) Combining motion and appearance for gender classification from video sequences. In: 19th international conference on pattern recognition (ICPR 2008), p 4
17. Han H, Jain AK (2014) Age, Gender and Race Estimation from Unconstrained Face Images, MSU Technical report (2014): MSU-CSE-14-5
18. Harris C, Stephens M (1988) A combined corner and edge detector. In: Alvey vision conference: Manchester, UK, p 50
19. Hartley R, Zisserman A (2003) Multiple view geometry in computer vision, 2nd edn. Cambridge University Press
20. Hautamaki S (2011) Forevid: an open source software for forensic video analysis. MSc Thesis, Tampere University of Technology
21. Horn BKP (1970) Shape from shading: a method for obtaining the shape of a smooth opaque object from one view
22. Iwama H, Muramatsu D, Makihara Y, Yagi Y (2012) Gait-based person-verification system for forensics. In: 2012 IEEE 5th international conference on biometrics: theory, applications and systems (BTAS), Sept 2012, pp 113–120
23. Jain A, Dass S, Nandakumar K (2004) Soft biometric traits for personal recognition systems. In: Proceedings of the international conference on biometric authentication, ICBA, LNCS 3072, pp 731–738
24. Jain A, Russ A (2015) Bridging the gap: from biometrics to forensics. Philos Trans Roy Soc B
25. Kanade T, Cohn JF, Tian Y (2000) Comprehensive database for facial expression analysis. In: IEEE international conference on automatic face and gesture recognition, pp 46–53
26. Klare B, Klum S, Klontz J, Taborsky E, Akgul T, Jain AK (2014) Suspect identification based on descriptive facial attributes. In: Proceedings of the international joint conference on biometrics
27. Klontz JaC, Jain AK (2013) A case study of automated face recognition: the Boston marathon bombings suspects. IEEE Comput 46(11):91–94
28. Kwon YH, da Vitoria Lobo N (1994) Age classification from facial images. In: CVPR'94, pp 762–767
29. Lanitis A, Taylor C, Cootes T (2002) Toward automatic simulation of aging effects on face images. TPAMI 24(4):442–455
30. Larsen PK, Hansen L, Simonsen EB, Lynnerup N (2008) Variability of bodily measures of normally dressed people using PhotoModeler® Pro 5. J Forensic Sci 53:1393–1399
31. Larsen PK, Lynnerup N, Henriksen M, Alkjær T, Simonsen EB (2010) Gait recognition using joint moments, joint angles, and segment angles. J Forensic Biomech 1:7
32. Larsen PK, Simonsen EB, Lynnerup N (2008) Gait analysis in forensic medicine. J Forensic Sci 53:1149–1153

33. Lienhart R, Maydt J (2002) An extended set of haarlike features for rapid object detection. In: Proceedings of the international conference on image processing, Rochester, USA
34. Lucy D (2005) Introduction to statistics for forensic scientists. Wiley
35. Makinen E, Raisamo R (2008) An experimental comparison of gender classification methods. Pattern Recogn Lett 29(10):1544–1556
36. Marr D, Hildreth E (1980) Theory of Edge Detection. Proc Roy Soc B: Biol Sci 207:31
37. Moghaddam B, Yang M-H (2002) Learning gender with support faces. IEEE Trans Pattern Anal Mach Intell 24(5):707–711
38. Ng CB, Tay YH, Goi B-M (2012) Recognizing human gender in computer vision: a survey. PRICAI 335–346
39. Ocean Systems (2015) Ocean systems forensic video and image analysis solutions. http://www.oceansystems.com. Accessed 26 Mar 2015
40. Ojala T, Pietikäinen M, Mäenpää T (2002) Multiresolution gray-scale and rotation invariant texture classification with local binary patterns. IEEE Trans Pattern Anal Mach Intell 24:971–987
41. OpenCV (2015) Open source computer vision and machine learning software library. http://www.opencv.org. Accessed 26 Mar 2015
42. Panis G, Lanitis A (2014) An overview of research activities in facial age estimation using the FG-NET aging database. In: International ECCV workshop on soft biometrics
43. Qt (2015) Cross-platform application and UI framework. http://www.qt.io/, Accessed 26 Mar 2015
44. Reid DA, Nixon MS, Stevenage SV (2013) Soft biometrics; human identification using comparative descriptions. IEEE Trans Biom Compend Pattern Anal Mach intell. 36(6)
45. Ricanek K, Tesafaye T (2006) MORPH: a longitudinal image database of normal adult age-progression. In: Proceedings of FG
46. Sanderson C, Paliwal KK (2003) Noise compensation in a person verification system using face and multiple speech feature. Pattern Recogn 36(2):293–302
47. Thornton J, Peterson J (2002) The general assumptions and rationale of forensic identification. In: Modern scientific evidence: the law and science of expert testimony, vol 3. West Publishing Company
48. Viola P, Jones M (2001) Rapid object detection using a boosted cascade of simple features. In: Proceedings of the 2001 IEEE computer society conference on computer vision and pattern recognition, 2001. CVPR 2001, vol 1, pp I–511–I–518
49. Will PM, Pennington KS (1971) Grid coding: a preprocessing technique for robot and machine vision. Artif Intell 2:319–329
50. Xu Z, Schwarte R, Heinol H-G, Buxbaum B, Ringbeck T (1998) Smart pixel: photonic mixer device (PMD); new system concept of a 3D-imaging camera-on-a-chip. In: Eheung EHM (ed) Proceedings: M2VIP '98; Nanjing, China, 10–12 Sept 1998, Hong Kong. pp 259–64
51. Zhang Z (2000) A flexible new technique for camera calibration. IEEE Trans Pattern Anal Mach Intell 22(11):1330–1334
52. Zhao G, Pietikäinen M (2007) Dynamic texture recognition using local binary patterns with an application to facial expressions. IEEE Trans Pattern Anal Mach Intell 29(6):915–928
53. Zivkovic Z (2004) Improved adaptive Gaussian mixture model for background subtraction. In: Proceedings of the 17th international conference on pattern recognition, 2004. ICPR 2004, Aug 2004, vol 2, pp 28–31

Chapter 12
Locating People in Surveillance Video Using Soft Biometric Traits

Simon Denman, Michael Halstead, Clinton Fookes and Sridha Sridharan

Abstract Semantic descriptions are a commonly used and very natural way for people to describe one another. Descriptions comprising details of clothing types and colours, skin and hair colour, gender and build are very effective ways to communicating an approximate appearance; however such descriptions are not easily utilised within intelligent video surveillance systems, as they are difficult to transform into a representation that can be utilised by computer vision algorithms. In this chapter, we will investigate two recent approaches to using these semantic, soft biometric descriptions to automatically locate people in surveillance imagery. We present the strengths and weaknesses of each, and discuss their suitability for real-world deployment and how they may be further improved.

12.1 Introduction

When describing the appearance of a person, we commonly use a set of semantic traits. This includes the use of details such as the colour of clothing, skin or hair, the type and pattern (or lack of pattern) of the clothing being worn, and the gender, build or stature of the person being described. Traits such as these can be viewed as a set of soft biometrics, and are widely used in soft biometric systems [6, 17].

In law enforcement and security situations, soft biometrics such as these are commonly used to describe a suspect or person of interest (i.e. 'a tall, middle aged male

---

S. Denman (✉) · M. Halstead · C. Fookes · S. Sridharan
Image and Video Research Laboratory, Queensland University of Technology,
2 George Street, Brisbane 4000, Australia
e-mail: s.denman@qut.edu.au

M. Halstead
e-mail: m.halstead@qut.edu.au

C. Fookes
e-mail: c.fookes@qut.edu.au

S. Sridharan
e-mail: s.sridharan@qut.edu.au

M. Tistarelli and C. Champod (eds.), *Handbook of Biometrics for Forensic Science*, Advances in Computer Vision and Pattern Recognition,
DOI 10.1007/978-3-319-50673-9_12

Fig. 12.1 A closed circuit television image of the London bombing suspects taken from [3]. The low resolution of the image and small size of the suspects faces makes identification using traditional biometrics such as face recognition extremely challenging

wearing a red hoodie and black jeans'). Due to the ease and speed in which these descriptions can be relayed and understood by human operators, soft biometrics are part of a shifting focus in the surveillance community.

However locating a person from such a description is still a significant challenge. Typically, it is a manual task that involves either combing through hours of CCTV footage, or having officers on the ground looking. The recent Boston Marathon bombing provides an example of how challenging this task is, as it took the FBI 3 days to search CCTV footage based on eye-witness reports and release suspect photographs to the public [19].

State-of-the-art identification currently still relies heavily on classical biometric systems like facial recognition, however these may fail in a surveillance environment due to factors including low-resolution cameras and relative distance from the camera, deliberate and accidental target occlusions, and various lighting conditions. Although carrying the limitations of a lack of permanence and limited individual discriminability, soft biometrics remain detectable at distance from low-resolution cameras (commonly seen in CCTV networks) where classical biometrics may fail, as witnessed in Fig. 12.1, depicting the London bombers.

Anthropometric measurements can be viewed as a forerunner to soft biometrics. Lucas and Henneberg [18] compared Anthropometric methods of body measurement to facial recognition, and demonstrated their effectiveness as a means of subject identification. When identifying or redetecting a subject of interest in real-world surveillance, the outward appearance is generally dominated by the appearance of clothing, as illustrated in Fig. 12.1. Jaha and Nixon [16] have shown the efficacy of these traits for subject identification, and Scoleri et al. [24] have shown that while clothing may distort body measurements, accurate data can still be obtained in their presence, further improving the ability for soft biometrics to perform identification tasks.

Recently, spurred on by developments in soft biometrics and attribute matching [29], a number of automated approaches to locate people in video from semantic descriptions have been proposed [8, 22]. The development of such techniques has the potential to greatly reduce the manual labour required to locate people, while also improving security. To date, approaches have operated in one of two ways, either as

1. a database indexing approach [14, 22, 27, 30], where people are first detected (i.e. using a person detection approach [4, 13, 21]) in a video feed, and their attributes are subsequently extracted and stored in a database for later search and retrieval;
2. a stimulus-driven approach [5, 8, 9, 15], where the image is searched directly using a template of model that describes the intended subject.

However, despite the growing interest in this area, existing approaches are limited in their utility. In particular, a reliance on person detection to first locate people in a scene limits a technique's ability to operate in crowded and complex scenes. While the use of person detection as a preprocessing step may initially seem intuitive, it was shown in [8] that the use of person detection actually reduces the performance of a semantic person search system. The complex surveillance environment in which the search takes place is also a challenging environment for person detection, and both false alarms and missed detections are highly common, complicating the search process. Indexing approaches are also limited by their design, which restricts their use to post-event analysis tasks as they are unable to search live data. Finally, the use of simplistic methods to represent the query limits the power of the search, and leads to a variety of matching errors including regions of the background being detected as the person of interest.

Other key considerations for any semantic search include the need to model uncertainty: both within the incoming video data and the provided semantic query. For instance, a shirt that is described by a witness are 'red' may actually be 'orange'; but due to local lighting conditions in the scene this same garment may actually appear to be 'brown' in CCTV footage. Similar concerns exist with other traits, including the type of clothes being worn, and the height or build of the person of interest.

In this chapter, we discuss two recent approaches to locate people in surveillance footage using soft biometric traits. The first uses a simplistic region-based representation to describe a person, and a particle filter to search and track them in video [15]. The second uses a channel representation to model the person's appearance [9], which is then incorporated into a single object tracking approach [12] to locate and track the target subject. Both of these approaches are stimulus driven (i.e., they do not require the use of person detection and are able to operate in a live setting), and both use dominant torso and leg colours, height and clothing type to describe a person's appearance. We compare the performance of these two approaches, and discuss their strengths, limitations and suitability for use in large surveillance installations.

The remainder of this chapter is structured as follows: Sect. 12.2 presents an overview of recent research in the area; Sect. 12.3 discusses the traits used by the two systems and how they are represented; Sects. 12.4 and 12.5 outline the approaches of [15] and [9] respectively; Sect. 12.6 outlines the data and evaluation protocol used in this chapter; Sect. 12.7 presents experimental results and discussion; and Sect. 12.8 concludes this chapter.

12.2 Prior Work

In surveillance and security two distinct tracks of personal identification can be considered: person re-identification and person search (semantic search). In each case, the primary goal is to locate and tag each instance of a target subject's appearance in a video, based on the subject's soft biometric signature.

While the re-identification [1, 10] of a target is a common method of target search, in many law enforcement situations visual enrolement of the subject (i.e. enrolment based on an acquired image) is not possible and a description is required. Of primary concern in description-based target searches is limiting the impact of the 'semantic gap', Reid et al. [23] outline methods of achieving this in their study of comparative soft biometric labels, reducing the uncertainty and subjectiveness witnessed in categorical labelling.

While several approaches have been proposed to locate a person from a semantic query, the majority of these approaches are detection based [14, 22, 27, 30], in that they first require the person (or in the case of [14], the vehicle) to be detected using a computationally expensive object detection routine (such as [4, 13]). Following this detection, traits are extracted and stored in a database, allowing later processes to search for an entity within this index.

A variety of traits are used including clothing colour [22, 27, 30], gender and the presence of luggage [27], and facial attributes (i.e. bald, hair, hat) [30]; while [14] incorporates details on the vehicle size, its location and direction of travel. While promising results are obtained for all systems, the evaluations of these approaches are piecemeal, and a rigorous evaluation using a standard database is not performed. Furthermore, these approaches are all reliant on object detection, limiting utility in crowded environments. In an unconstrained surveillance environment, person detection remains a challenging problem with state-of-the-art approaches [21] still prone to false alarms and missed detections, while also being computationally expensive.

In contrast to detection and indexing-based approaches, the techniques proposed in [5, 8] are designed to work with a live video feed. Motivated by a desire to reduce confrontations between rival sporting fans, [5] developed a system to detect situations where supporters of one team are located near supporters of a second, based on known colour quantities (i.e. jersey colours) within a crowded scene. While not specific to a single individual, the system did have some success in accurately gauging when two possibly hostile groups were converging on each other.

Denman et al. [8] sought to interrogate the scene directly to locate people who matched a given description. This technique allowed for a query to be searched for within a live video feed without the use of detection routines. Colour (torso and leg) and height features are used to construct a simplistic avatar, which the system subsequently uses to search the video feed. A particle filter is used to detect and track the subject, with the avatar being compared to a region described by each particle to determine the similarity of the particle to the target. This approach [8], although moderately effective, also has several limitations, largely arising from the use of a small number of traits and the manner in which the avatar is constructed. The simplistic nature of the avatar, which effectively models the person as a series of regions which are assumed to be dominated by the target clothing colours, leads to the incorrect localisation of several subjects due to factors including incorrect trait attachment (torso as legs, and background as torso) and cases where the background is confused for an individual (i.e. the background is the same approximate colour as the target).

In this chapter, we examine two recent approaches to the problem of locating a person in a scene from a semantic query, both of which search the scene directly rather than using person detection to first localise targets. The approach of Halstead et al. [15] is an extension of [8], which overcomes some of the problems relating to incorrectly localising targets in background regions. We also discuss the approach of Denman et al. [9], who propose using a channel representation (CR) [11] to model the search query. In this approach the target query is represented by a multi-dimensional image, where each channel corresponds to a particular colour band, or texture type.

12.3 Modelling Traits

A variety of traits are available for use when searching for a person from a description. In theory, any trait that can be observed from CCTV footage is suitable, and the database of [15] used in this chapter includes traits that cover the primary and secondary torso and leg colours, clothing texture and type, age, height, build, skin and hair colour, gender and the presence of luggage.

The two systems presented in this chapter only use a subset of these traits

- Torso and leg primary colour, categorised into the 11 culture colours (black, blue, brown, gray, green, orange, pink, purple, red, yellow, white) [2];
- Clothing type, categorised into long sleeve and other for torso garments, and long pants and other for leg garments (note that [15] uses only the leg clothing type, while [9] uses both legs and torso);
- Height (in metres), incorporated as either a height range (i.e. average height: 1.7–1.9 m), or directly as a value (i.e. 1.76 m). The database of [15] defines 5 height ranges: very short, short, average, tall, very tall.

These five traits are denoted as T_{colour} and L_{colour} for the torso and leg colour; T_{type} and L_{type} for the torso and leg clothing type; and H for the subject height;

Colour models are trained for each of the target colours and skin (i.e. 12 colours in total) using the colour patches provided by [15]. GMMs with up to 12 components (determined using the BIC) are trained in the LAB colour space. A confusion matrix is also computed using the test patches provided in [15], which is used by the second system (see Sect. 12.5). No normalisation or illumination correction is made when training the models, and each model relies solely on the range of colour snippets available, and the expected illumination invariance achieved through using the LabCie colour space.

Height is catered for using camera calibration [28], allowing templates and/or regions of interest to be scaled to the appropriate real-world size.

12.4 Locating People Using a Region-Based Approach

The first approach we examine is the region-based approach of [15]. This approach builds on the earlier work of [8], including provision for leg clothing type and a method to model the uncertainty present in the colour traits. Like [8], the search process is driven by a particle filter.

12.4.1 Search Query Formulation

As outlined in Sect. 12.3, colour selection is categorised into the 11 culture colours while also incorporating skin, and a GMM is trained for each colour. A particle filter drives the search, and each particle describes a candidate location (x and y position, height and aspect ratio), and particle heights and aspect ratios are distributed within a range set according to the target query (i.e. when searching for a 'tall' person, the height will be uniformly distributed between 1.7 and 1.9 m).

The approach compares torso and leg colour similarity by comparing fixed regions within the bounding box described by each particle to the target colours (see [8]). Leg clothing type is incorporated by allowing the size of the lower region (i.e. the region that contains the legs) to vary according to type of clothing expected. However the region-based approach makes a similar consideration of torso clothing types difficult, and thus torso clothing is not considered.

12.4.2 Searching for a Target

The approach has four stages: particle filtering, trait similarity calculation, trait weight filtering and finally particle weighting. The particle filter is initialised with a

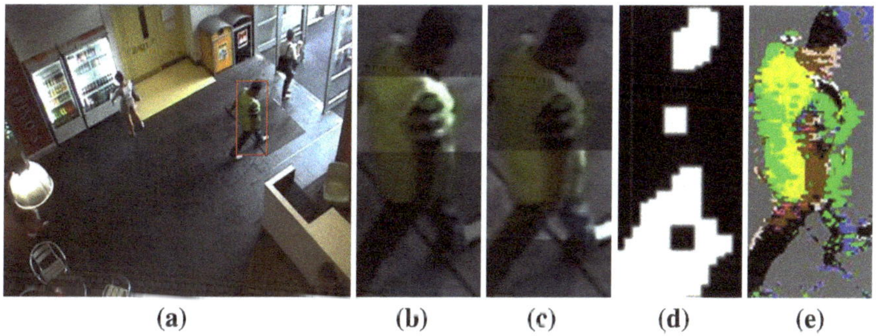

Fig. 12.2 An image to be searched, and a particle location (*red bounding box*) are shown in (**a**). Given this particle location, regions of interest for the torso (**b**) and legs (**c**) are defined. Within each of these regions, the motion (**d**) and colour (**e**) are considered and used to determine how well the candidate bounding box matches the query (note that when considering the colour, a soft decision approach is used rather than the hard decision indicated by (**e**))

randomly generated 500 particle set, and three iterations are performed per frame to avoid convergence on incorrect subjects.

The similarity of the primary torso colour and primary leg colour are computed using a method similar to that outlined in [8]. A similarity score (S_t for the torso, and S_l for the legs) is produced based on the normalised probability of the target colour appearing in the desired area, such that for the torso,

$$S_t = \frac{\sum_{x,y\in t} P_{x,y,c} \times Mo_{x,y}}{\sum_{x,y\in t} \times Mo_{x,y}}, \quad (12.1)$$

where the summation of the likelihood, $P_{x,y,c}$ of the target colour, c appearing at each pixel location, x, y, is completed over the limits of the torso region, t. $Mo_{x,y}$ indicates the presence of motion at x, y, and is set to $Mo_{x,y} = 1$ if motion is present, and $Mo_{x,y} = 0.5$ otherwise, resulting in regions that contain motion (and are thus more likely to contain the target) receiving a higher weight, and regions that are likely to correspond to the background (and are thus less likely to match the target colour) being diminished. S_l is calculated in a similar manner. Torso and leg regions are selected as in [8], such that areas likely to correspond to the head and feet (and thus likely to have a different colour) are discarded. Figure 12.2 displays an overview of the two primary regions of interest for which the torso and leg similarity scores are calculated.

A key consideration when comparing traits is their reliability. To incorporate this, the quality of each trait is incorporated such that observations that have a lower quality receive a diminished weight, helping the particle filter converge on areas of greater quality and confidence.

To model the quality of the trait, a combination of motion segmentation (the approach of [7]) and a pixel-wise histogram that captures the colour distribution at each pixel over time is used. The use of motion segmentation allows uncertainty around the location to be captured (confidence is reduced when there is little to no motion), while the colour history allows the confidence of the query to be assessed (a query colour that is the same as the dominant historic background colour has greater uncertainty).

The motion segmentation quality component, Q_{Mo}, is calculated in a two-step process. Initially the probability of motion within the bounded region is obtained Mo. If this probability is above 0.5,

$$Q_{Mo} = 1 - log_2(Mo), \tag{12.2}$$

is used to calculate the final quality score for motion segmentation. However if $Mo <$ 0.5, the quality of the motion segmentation component is set to zero.

A pixel-wise histogram model that captures individual pixel colour classification over a period of time is used to capture uncertainty associated with the colour query. Additional captured video sequences are classified using the trained GMM's to capture the distribution of colours at each individual location over time to create the histogram model, V_{PH}. The colour quality, Q_{vp}, is then calculated as follows:

$$Q_{PH} = \frac{\sum_{x,y \in r} 1.0 - V_{PH}(x, y, c)}{R}, \tag{12.3}$$

where r is the region of interest (i.e. the target torso or leg region), c is the target colour and R is the size of the region, r. Thus, Q_{PH} represents the proportion of the background that has historically been a different colour to the target colour.

The two quality components are then simply combined by calculating their geometric mean,

$$Q = \sqrt{Q_{Mo} * Q_{PH}}. \tag{12.4}$$

Quality measures are calculated for both the torso and leg regions (Q_t and Q_l respectively), and are subsequently used to scale the similarities (S_t and S_l for the torso and legs respectively). The similarities are then combined using the geometric mean.

12.4.3 Assessing Clothing Type

A limitation of the approach in Sect. 12.4.2 is that for torso and leg regions, when the subject is wearing clothing that does not cover the entire region (i.e. shorts rather than long trousers), a significant portion of the region will be skin colour which will falsely diminish the weight. To help alleviate this problem, the bounds of the target leg region are modified to remove areas that do not represent the article of clothing. Two categories of clothing are considered: 'long' clothes that will cover the bulk of the leg region, and all others.

The motivation behind this is to rebound the leg region by decreasing the total area, and in turn increasing the desired target colour presence in the target region. The asymmetry driven chromatic and spatial operators described in [10] are used (which were proposed to segment a body into head, torso and legs and find the dominant plane of symmetry in the head and leg regions), and applied to a skin mask, *Sk*, rather than a motion mask. The chromatic operator measures the difference in two adjoining colour patches, while the spatial operator measures the difference in two adjoining mask regions. The skin mask is computed as follows:

$$Sk_{x,y} = P_{x,y,c} \times Mo_{x,y}, \tag{12.5}$$

where $P_{x,y,c}$ is the probability of a given colour, c, in this case skin colour; and $Mo_{x,y}$ is a scaling factor based on the motion at pixel x, y, such that $Mo_{x,y} = 1$ if motion is present, otherwise $Mo_{x,y} = 0.5$. As with the region similarity computation in Eq. 12.1, pixels that contain motion are emphasised are they are less likely to represent background regions.

The chromatic, $C(i, \delta)$, and spatial, $S(i, \delta)$ operators from [10] are then applied as follows to rebound the region of interest,

$$A_i = argmin((1 - C(i, \delta)) + S(i, \delta)) \tag{12.6}$$

where A_i corresponds to the image index associated with the minimum score achieved through the summation of the spatial and chromatic operators resulting in a newly bounded leg region, and is intended to represent the lower boundary between the item of clothing (i.e. shorts) and skin.

12.5 Searching Using a Channel Representation

The recent single object tracking approaches of [12, 25] have demonstrated state-of-the-art performance using a simple distribution field [25] or channel representation [12]. Furthermore, the template used by these approaches is well suited to being generated from a description rather than an image patch. The nature of these template representations is such that they model an estimated appearance, incorporating uncertainty about the exact colour, or location. In this section, we outline a recent approach [9] that uses a channel representation to model a subjects appearance.

12.5.1 Generating an Avatar

An avatar is generated from a set of characteristics that describe the target subject. In this approach, the traits outlined in Sect. 12.3 are used. To generate an avatar, a set of learned components that relate to the selected traits are summed. The average appearances for different body regions and clothing types are learned using a set of manually annotated silhouettes (see Sect. 12.6 for details). Silhouettes are resized to the same height, and edges are zero padded to the same width. Following this, all examples belonging to a given class (i.e. torso regions for ‘long sleeve shirt’) are used to learn the appearance by simply averaging the examples,

$$A_c = \frac{1}{N}\sum_{n}^{N} a_c(n), \tag{12.7}$$

where A_c is the average appearance of component c; $a_c(n)$ is the nth example image; with N examples in total. This approach is used to learn the appearance of the two torso clothing types and corresponding torso skin regions; the two leg clothing types and leg skin regions; and the head skin regions.

The learned appearances and colour models are then used to generate an avatar that describes the target subject’s appearance. An occupancy mask that indicates the likelihood of a person being at a location is generated by combining the learned silhouettes for the target modes,

$$A_{skin} = A_{ts,T_{type}} + A_{ls,L_{type}} + A_h, \tag{12.8}$$

$$A_{torso} = A_{tc,T_{type}}, \tag{12.9}$$

$$A_{legs} = A_{lc,L_{type}}, \tag{12.10}$$

where $A_{ts,T_{type}}$ and $A_{tc,T_{type}}$ are the appearance of the torso skin (ts) and clothing (tc) regions for the selected torso type, T_{type}; $A_{ls,L_{type}}$ and $A_{lc,L_{type}}$ are the appearance of the leg skin (ls) and clothing (lc) regions for the selected leg type, L_{type}; and A_h is the average appearance of the head.

A set of colour masks, C_n, that correspond to a channel representation are then generated as follows:

$$c(x,y,n) = A_{torso}(x,y) \times P(n|T_{colour}) + A_{legs} \times P(n|L_{colour}) + A_{skin} \times P(n|S_{colour}), \tag{12.11}$$

$$C_n(x,y) = \frac{c(x,y,n)}{A_{torso}(x,y) + A_{legs}(x,y) + A_{skin}(x,y)}, \tag{12.12}$$

where $C_n(x,y)$ is a pixel, x, y, in the nth channel (i.e. representing the nth colour) of the channel representation; T_{colour}, L_{colour} and S_{colour} are the selected torso, leg and skin colours; $P(n|T_{colour})$ is the likelihood of colour n being the target colour, T_{colour}, and is estimated using the earlier computed confusion matrix. The channel representation is normalises using the sum of the masks (i.e. $A_{torso}(x,y) + A_{legs}(x,y) + A_{skin}(x,y)$) to ensure that it sums to 1. This process will generate a mask for each colour, with the mask’s content determined by the likelihood of the colour being

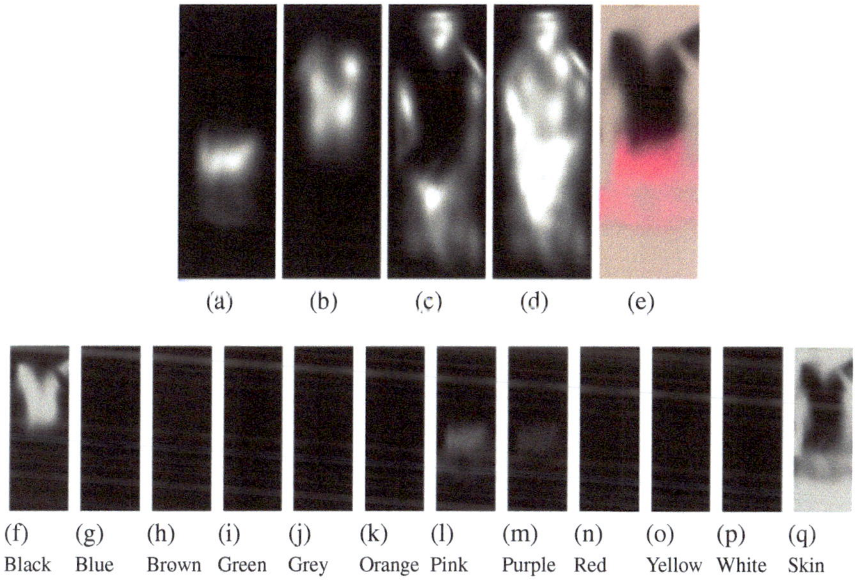

Fig. 12.3 An example avatar for the query 'Tall, pink shorts, black short sleeve shirt': **a–c** show the masks for the leg clothing, torso clothing and skin regions respectively. These masks are generated based on the type of clothing selected, and are combined to create (**d**) and (**e**). **d** shows the overall occupancy mask, and **e** shows the expected colour at each location. Note that the most likely colour for every pixel is given in (**e**), even though some pixels are very unlikely to belong to the person as shown by (**d**). The images in the *second row* show the channels for the 12 colours. The uncertainty that exists in the channel representations can be seen in the weights of the *pink* and *purple* channels

observed at each pixel. This likelihood is driven by two factors: the colour in the target query, and the confusability of that colour.

Finally, a combined mask that represents the likelihood of each pixel belonging to the person is created,

$$A_P = min(1.0, A_s + A_{tc,T_{type}} + A_{lc,L_{type}}), \tag{12.13}$$

where *min* is an operator that takes the minimum of two values. Importantly in this combined mask, normalised masks for the components are not used to ensure that pixels that are unlikely to contain the target have a low weight. This mask is used as an auxiliary channel in the CR to weight the contribution of each pixel to the overall similarity. An example avatar is shown in Fig. 12.3.

12.5.2 Searching for a Target

A particle filter-like approach is used to search for the target. A small number of particles are created at random locations within the field of view, and the single object tracking approach of [12] is used to refine the location of each. The similarity of each refined particle location to the target model and a stored background model is computed, based on which the particle set is refreshed and the current position of the target is estimated.

Input images are transformed into a channel representation where the channels are given by the culture colour space,

$$I_n(x, y) = P(n|I(x, y)), \tag{12.14}$$

where I_n is the nth channel of the channel representation; $P(n|I(x, y))$ is the likelihood of the pixel $I(x, y)$ being the nth colour, and is computed using a lookup table that contains the likelihoods for the whole colour space computed using the learned GMMs.[1] As per [12], each channel is then convolved with a Gaussian filter.

A gradient descent search is then performed to find the particle location (X_p, Y_p) within a local region that minimises

$$S_F = \sum_{n,x,y}^{N,X,Y} \left| C_n(X_p + x, Y_p + y) - I_n(x, y) \right| \times A_P(x, y), \tag{12.15}$$

where S_F is the similarity of the foreground to the template; $C_n(x, y)$ is the nth channel of the template (i.e. search query) and X and Y are the width and height of the template, and N is the number of channels. Note that A_P is used to weight the summation such that pixels that are more likely to belong to the person are given a greater weight. Although this search will converge on an optimal location, it is only guaranteed to be locally optimal [25]. To overcome this, multiple particles are refined using this search process, after-which particles are filtered in preparation for the next input frame.

As the particles move during the search process, a dense collection of particles is not needed. Following the updating of particle locations, a two-stage filtering process is applied, where first particles which record a poor match are removed, after-which particles which are located nearby another are removed.

One of the limitations observed in [8] is that locations in the background can be well matched to the target. To help overcome this, a universal background model style approach is used. An average channel representation for the background which is progressively updated every frame is stored,

$$B_n(x, y, t) = \alpha \times B_n(x, y, t - 1) + (1 - \alpha) \times I_n(x, y), \tag{12.16}$$

---

[1] The lookup table is pre-computed for computational efficiency.

where $B_n(x, y, t)$ is the n channel in the background channel representation at time t; and α is the learning rate. Using this stored background model, the similarity of the template to the target location in the background is computed,

$$S_B = \sum_{n,x,y}^{N,X,Y} \left| B_n(X_p + x, Y_p + y) - T_n(x, y) \right| \times A_P(x, y), \tag{12.17}$$

and used to determine if the particle is a better match to the background or the foreground,

$$S_R = S_B / S_F. \tag{12.18}$$

If $S_R \leq 1$, the particle is discarded, as it is more like the background than the foreground. Remaining particles are then filtered such that if two particles lie within a distance, d, the particle with the lower value of S_R is removed. The location of the target subject is given by the particle that yields the highest value of S_R.

12.5.3 Compensating for Scale

An additional parameter for the search query is the target height. This is incorporated using camera calibration information (Tsai's camera calibration [28], information is provided with the dataset of [15]). A resolution parameter, R, in pixels per meter, is used to generate the template and resized target patches when searching. The target template is set to a height (in pixels) of $R \times H$, where H is the target query height in metres. When comparing the template to an image, the local region around the initial estimated position (i.e. X_p, Y_p) is resized to the same resolution.

12.6 Database and Evaluation Protocol

12.6.1 Data

We use the database and evaluation protocol outlined in [15]. This database consists of 110 video clips with semantic queries and the correct match annotated at every frame. Example images from the database are shown in Fig. 12.4.

Avatar models are trained using a set of person images extracted from the background videos in [15] (i.e. they do not overlap with the queries), and are originally presented in [9]. In total, images of 103 people from the same 6 camera network are used. An example of the annotation is shown in Fig. 12.5.

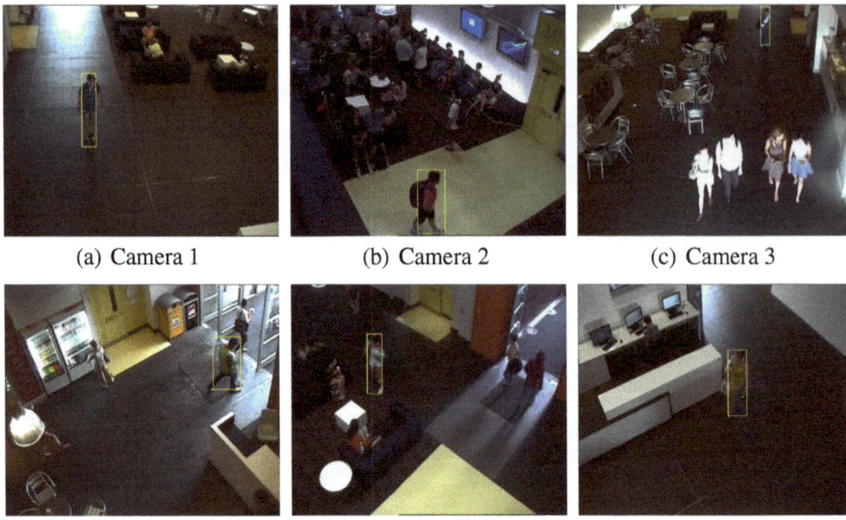

(a) Camera 1 (b) Camera 2 (c) Camera 3

(d) Camera 4 (e) Camera 5 (f) Camera 6

Fig. 12.4 A sample image from each camera, each showing an image from a different sequence. The target queries for the six images are: **a** Sequence *C1-BlackBlueStripe-BlueJeans*: 15–35-year-old short Caucasian male of average build with *brown hair*, wearing a *blue striped short sleeve shirt*, *plain blue shorts* and *brown shoes*, and carrying *luggage*; **b** Sequence *C2-RedShirt-BlackShorts*: 25–45-year-old very short Asian female of large build with *dark hair*, wearing a *red short sleeve shirt*, *plain black shorts* and *white shoes*, and carrying *luggage*; **c** Sequence *C3-DiagonalTop-HorizontalPants*: 15–35-year-old short Asian male of average build and height with *dark hair*, wearing a *green and white striped short sleeve shirt*, *blue and white striped trousers* and *white shoes*, and carrying *luggage*; **d** Sequence *C4-FluroYellowTop-BluePants*: a 15–35-year-old *dark skinned* and *dark haired* male of average height and large build, wearing a *yellow and grey striped sleeveless shirt*, *plain blue trousers and white shoes*; **e** Sequence *C5-LightGreenShirt-WhiteShorts*: a 15–35-year-old short Caucasian female of very slim build with *brown hair*, wearing *green sleeveless top*, *white shorts and white shoes*, and carrying *luggage*; **f** Sequence *C6-YellowWhiteSpotDress*: a 15–35-year-old short Caucasian female of slim build with *brown hair*, wearing a *yellow and white spotted dress*, and carrying *luggage*. Images also show the annotated *feet*, *waist*, *shoulder*, *neck* and *head positions*, and the *target bounding box* (*yellow*)

12.6.2 Evaluation Protocol

Performance is evaluated by computing the localisation accuracy for all frames with annotated ground truth. A ground truth bounding box is constructed from the annotated points. Left and right bounds are taken from the feet, shoulder, waist or neck annotations, while the head and feet provide the top and bottom bounds. If any of these bounds were not located then that frame is deemed to be un-annotated, and is not used in the evaluation.

The bounding box computed by the proposed algorithm is compared to the ground truth using,

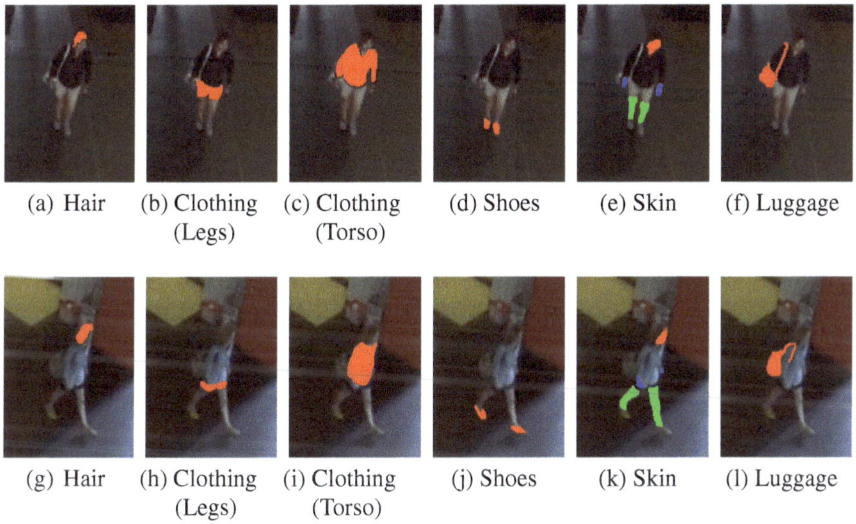

Fig. 12.5 Example of the annotation of two subjects into their constituent parts. Note that in the skin mask we annotate the head (*red*), arms (*blue*) and legs (*green*) separately

$$L_{x,i} = \frac{D_{x,i} \cap GT_{x,i}}{L_{x,i} \cup GT_{x,i}}, \tag{12.19}$$

where $D_{x,i}$ is the output of the algorithm for subject x, frame i, and $GT_{x,i}$ is the corresponding ground truth bounding box; to measure the localisation accuracy.

The accuracy over an entire sequence is given by the average accuracy for each frame in the sequence,

$$L_x = \frac{1}{N}\sum_{i=1}^{i=N} L_{x,i}, \tag{12.20}$$

where N is the total number of frames for subject x; and the overall performance is given by the average of each sequence accuracy,

$$L = \frac{1}{M}\sum_{x=1}^{x=M} L_x, \tag{12.21}$$

where M is the total number of subjects (110). Sequences are not weighted by their length when computing the average to ensure that all queries are given equal weight, and long sequences do not dominate the overall performance metric.

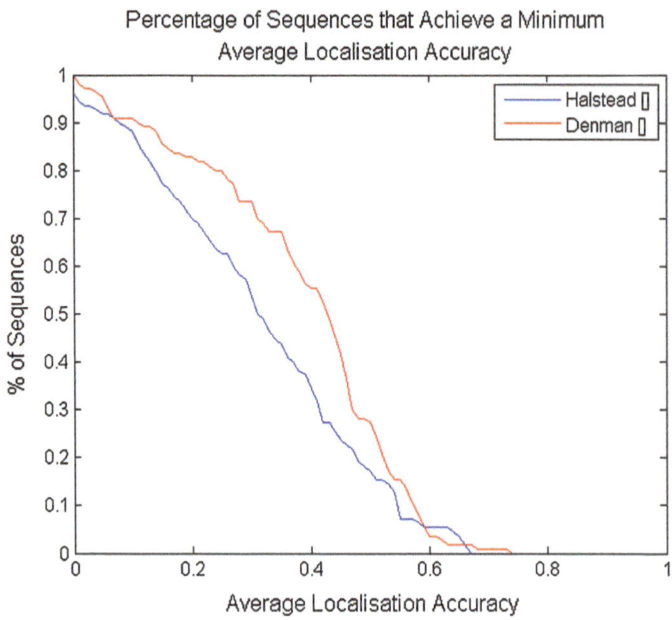

Fig. 12.6 The percentage of sequences above a given accuracy level

12.7 Results

Performance of the two approaches are evaluated on the dataset of [15]. For the approach of [15] (see Sect. 12.4 for details) we use the recommended parameters of 500 particles and 3 iterations of the particle filter. For the approach of [9] (see Sect. 12.5 for details) we use the suggested default parameters of 20 particles, $R = 20$ (i.e. 1 meter is scaled to 20 pixels), and Gaussian blur kernel width and standard deviation to 3 and 1.5 respectively.

Figure 12.6 shows the number of sequences that achieve above a given threshold and it can be clearly seen that [9] is able to better locate the majority of queries. For instance, 56% of queries are located with an average accuracy greater than 0.4 by [9], while only 37% can be located with the same level of accuracy for [15].

However, despite the approach of [9] performing better across the majority of sequences, there are a number of sequences for which [15] performs best, as shown by Fig. 12.7.

Figures 12.8 and 12.9 show example output for a variety of queries from the systems of [15] and [9] respectively. It can be seen that in the majority of cases, the approach of [9] outperforms that of [15], however there are some exceptions.

In Sequences 12 and 70, [15] confuses the target subject with the background. The use of a background model in a UBM-style configuration by [9] helps suppress matches to background regions, improving performance in situations such

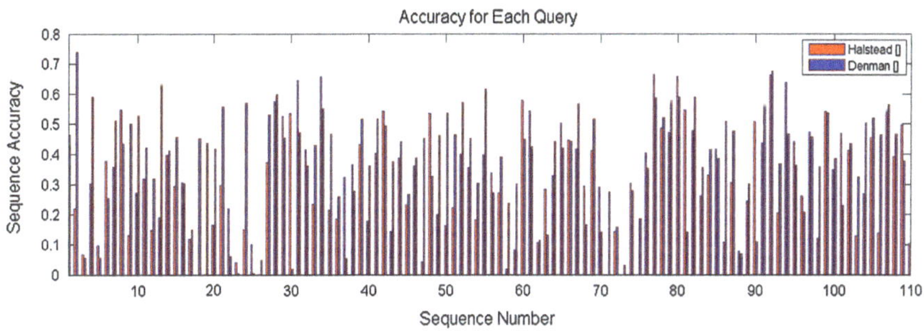

Fig. 12.7 The percentage of sequences above a given accuracy level

as this. In Sequence 17, [15] incorrectly detects a person of similar appearance as the target. In this case, the richer query used by [9] helps, as it better enforces the spatial constraints regarding the relative positions of the colours.

In Sequence 29, we observe that [15] achieves much better performance, with [9] only localising the subject towards the very end of the sequence. In this sequence, the subject's shirt is specified as being 'orange', however the shirt is predominately classified as being 'pink'. The CR used by [9] is intended to allow for this sort of mis-match, however it does so using a confusion matrix. In this case, the confusion matrix records that orange is predominately confused with red, and so there is very little expectation of observing pink; resulting in a poor match with the CR. This, combined with the prevalence of other grey regions (the targets shorts colour) leads to misclassification. Ultimately, the simpler matching method used by [15] is better able to deal with this form of ambiguity.

In the remaining two sequences (Sequences 85 and 94), both approaches manage to detect the target with a reasonable degree of success. In Sequence 85 [15] initially confuses the target with the background causing a drop in performance, while in Sequence 94 [9] does not localise the subject as accurately, although both systems occasionally switch tracking to the second person that the target is walking beside. In both these sequences (85 and 94), the target subject is wearing patterned clothing (a striped shirt in both cases), highlighting a weakness with the approaches. Each system is effectively searching for a single colour within both the torso and leg regions. In sequence 94, this leads to a second person wearing a similar coloured shirt (although one that does not contain the desired pattern) being detected by mistake.

Overall, the approach of [9] performs better for most sequences, however it is less flexible in the way that it manages ambiguous colour matches. This may in part be aided using more data to train the confusion matrix, however there are still likely to be situations that arise where colour mis-match occurs due to unusual lighting conditions, or similar environmental effects. Both approaches are also impacted by the presence of clothing textures (i.e. stripes or checks), which reduce matching accuracy. Ultimately, the use of more traits such that colour is less important is one way to address this.

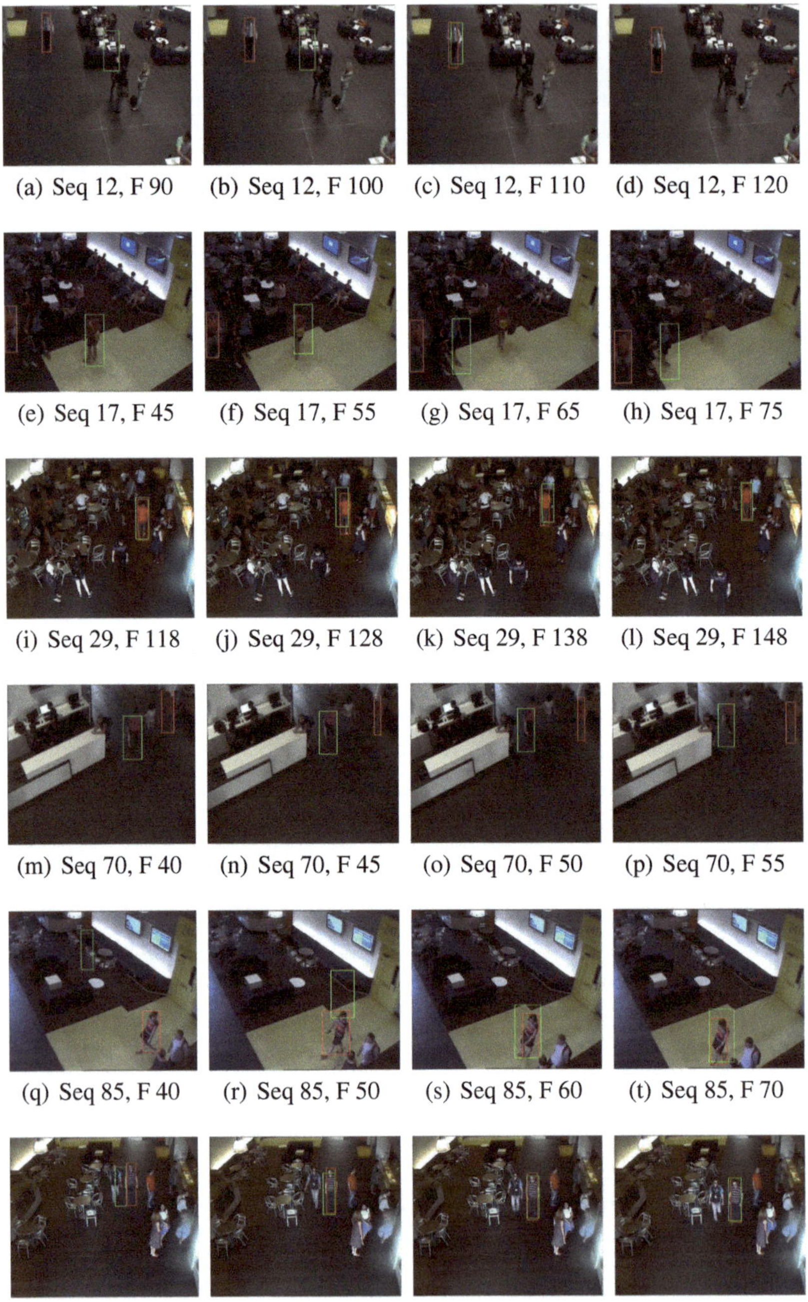

(a) Seq 12, F 90 (b) Seq 12, F 100 (c) Seq 12, F 110 (d) Seq 12, F 120

(e) Seq 17, F 45 (f) Seq 17, F 55 (g) Seq 17, F 65 (h) Seq 17, F 75

(i) Seq 29, F 118 (j) Seq 29, F 128 (k) Seq 29, F 138 (l) Seq 29, F 148

(m) Seq 70, F 40 (n) Seq 70, F 45 (o) Seq 70, F 50 (p) Seq 70, F 55

(q) Seq 85, F 40 (r) Seq 85, F 50 (s) Seq 85, F 60 (t) Seq 85, F 70

(u) Seq 94, F 65 (v) Seq 94, F 75 (w) Seq 94, F 85 (x) Seq 94, F 95

Fig. 12.8 Example frames from six sequences showing performance of [15]. Ground truth locations are marked with a *red bounding box*, while the estimated location is marked with a *green box*. For the 6 sequences, sequence accuracies of 0.1918, 0.0, 0.5356, 0.0, 0.1100 and 0.4411 are achieved

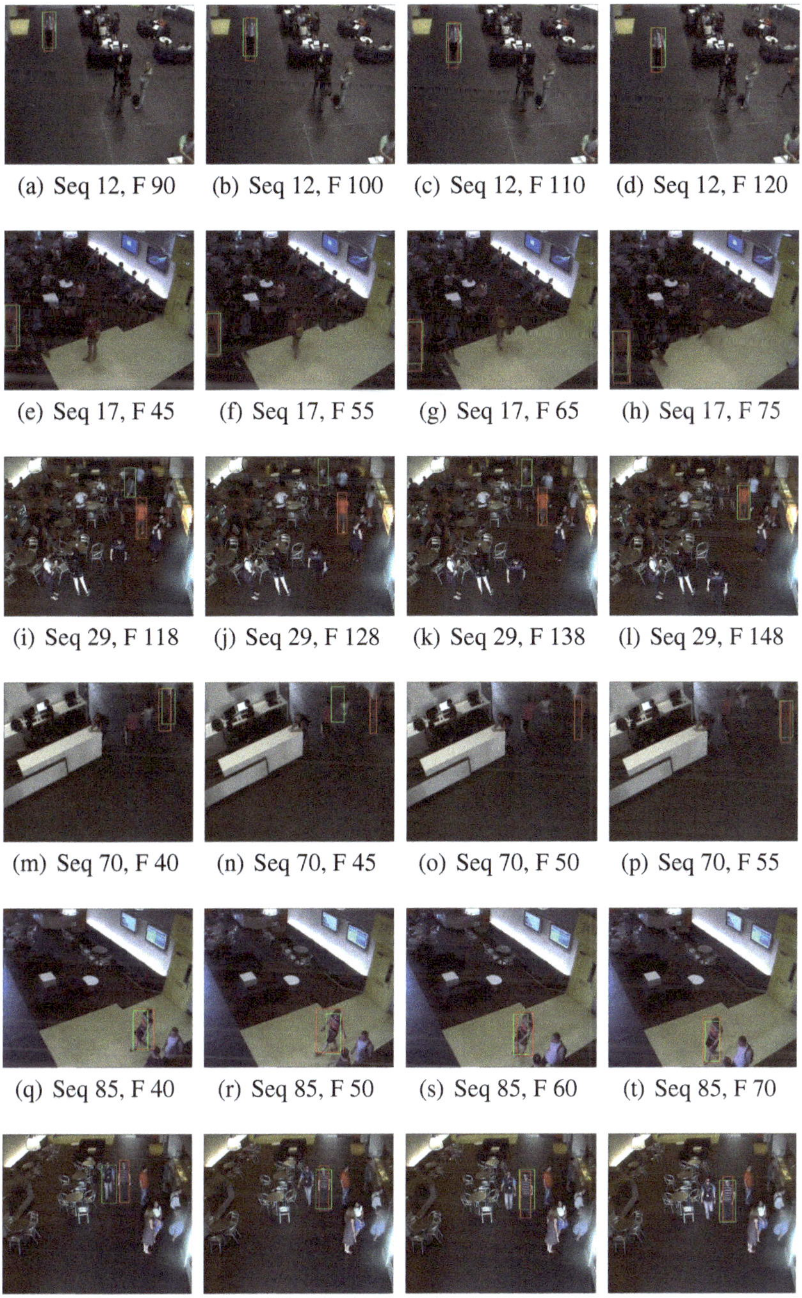

(a) Seq 12, F 90 (b) Seq 12, F 100 (c) Seq 12, F 110 (d) Seq 12, F 120

(e) Seq 17, F 45 (f) Seq 17, F 55 (g) Seq 17, F 65 (h) Seq 17, F 75

(i) Seq 29, F 118 (j) Seq 29, F 128 (k) Seq 29, F 138 (l) Seq 29, F 148

(m) Seq 70, F 40 (n) Seq 70, F 45 (o) Seq 70, F 50 (p) Seq 70, F 55

(q) Seq 85, F 40 (r) Seq 85, F 50 (s) Seq 85, F 60 (t) Seq 85, F 70

(u) Seq 94, F 65 (v) Seq 94, F 75 (w) Seq 94, F 85 (x) Seq 94, F 95

Fig. 12.9 Example frames from six sequences showing performance of [9]. Ground truth locations are marked with a *red bounding box*, while the estimated location is marked with a *green box*. For the six sequences, sequence accuracies of 0.6266, 0.4528, 0.0190, 0.2757, 0.5072 and 0.3633 are achieved

12.7.1 Computational Efficiency and Scalability

Comparing the runtimes of both approaches, [9] is able to execute faster running at 5.59 frames per second compared to 3.23 frames per second for [15] running on identical hardware.[2] It should be noted that neither approach has been optimised for speed, and performance gains are possible for both approaches.

The main computational process for both systems is the calculation of particle similarity. For [15], this process is greatly faster for each particle due to the simple nature of the comparison (a summation of likelihoods over a region). [9] doesn't compute a simple comparison, rather each particle is subject to a search process which itself involves several comparisons, and each comparison is the sum of a difference over a large number of channels, making the overall process for an individual particle much more demanding. However, the search process in [9] that allows particles to refine their own position means that an order of magnitude fewer particles are needed. This, combined with the fact that motion segmentation is not required leads to faster run times. For both approaches, parameters can be adjusted to further improve speed. Obviously particle numbers can be reduced in both approaches, and in the case of [9] the resolution parameter, R, can also have a significant impact on processing speed. By reducing R to 10, which as shown by [9] has only a slight impact on accuracy, throughput can be roughly increased by 25%. Similar gains could be made for [15] by simply reducing image resolution.

One key point of difference between the two system is the use of motion segmentation. While [15] could be run without motion segmentation, it does greatly benefit from it, and would further benefit from more accurate and reliable segmentation. This use of motion segmentation becomes potentially problematic when dealing with very large camera networks, as an up-to-date background model must be maintained for all cameras. Although [9] also maintains a background model of sorts, it simply requires an average frame which can be very quickly computed using a moving average. As such, while [15] may be faster for a single field of view, across a large network for 10s or even 100s of cameras, an approach such as [9] that does not require the continual update of a background model may be preferable.

12.8 Conclusions and Future Work

In this chapter, we have examined two approaches to locate a person in video from a semantic query. Both approaches use clothing colour and height information, and incorporate clothing type to varying degrees. The channel representation-based approach of [9] is shown to outperform the region-based approach of [15], however both approaches have their strengths and weaknesses.

A common limitation of the approaches is the small number of traits they consider, with other traits such as gender, clothing texture (or more sophisticated cloth-

[2]both approaches are running on a single core of an Intel Xeon E5-2670 processor.

ing type), hair and skin colour and the presence of luggage all traits that may warrant inclusion. For traits that impact upon the silhouette of the subject (i.e. gender, clothing types), it is clear how these could be easily incorporated into the channel representation approach of [9] by simply learning richer appearance models to guide the generation of the channel representation. The incorporation of such traits into [15] is less clear cut, however [15] is better suited to the addition of traits relating to clothing texture. Texture requires the analysis of a region (i.e. it cannot be determined from a single pixel), which is well aligned with [15]'s region-based approach. However within the CRs used by [9] it would require the use of a sliding window, which is potentially computationally demanding.

Ultimately, both approaches are limited in how they fuse data. [9] relies on the CR to model uncertainty, and thus the possible errors need to be first learnt; while [15] modifies trait weights based on motion segmentation data and the observed background colour. There is obvious scope to incorporate a more robust approach such as Dempster-Shafer theory [20, 26] into the approach of [15], which would better model the uncertainty observed and help improve performance.

References

1. Bak S, Charpiat G, Corvee E, Bremond F, Thonnat M (2012) Learning to match appearances by correlations in a covariance metric space. In: ECCV. Springer, pp 806–820
2. Berlin B, Kay P (1969) Basic color terms: their universality and evolution. University of California Press, Berkeley
3. CBC: London police investigation timeline. CBC News (2005)
4. Dalal N, Triggs B (2005) Histograms of oriented gradients for human detection. In: CVPR, pp 886–893
5. D'Angelo A, Dugelay JL (2010) Color based soft biometry for hooligans detection. In: ISCAS, pp 1691–1694
6. Dantcheva A, Velardo C, D'Angelo A, Dugelay JL (2011) Bag of soft biometrics for person identification: New trends and challenges. Multimedia Tools Appl 51(2):38
7. Denman S, Fookes C, Sridharan S (2009) Improved simultaneous computation of motion detection and optical flow for object tracking. In: DICTA, Melbourne, Australia
8. Denman S, Halstead M, Bialkowski A, Fookes C, Sridharan S (2012) Can you describe him for me? a technique for semantic person search in video. In: DICTA, pp 1–8
9. Denman S, Halstead M, Sridharan S, Fookes C (2015) Searching for semantic person queries using channel representations. In: IEEE international conference on acoustics, speech and signal processing (ICASSP). IEEE
10. Farenzena M, Bazzani L, Perina A, Murino V, Cristani M (2010) Person re-identification by symmetry-driven accumulation of local features. In: CVPR, pp 2360–2367
11. Felsberg M (2012) Adaptive filtering using channel representations. In: Mathematical methods for signal and image analysis and representation. Springer, London, pp 31–48
12. Felsberg M (2013) Enhanced distribution field tracking using channel representations. In: International conference computer vision workshops. IEEE, pp 121–128
13. Felzenszwalb P, McAllester D, Ramanan D (2008) A discriminatively trained, multiscale, deformable part model. In: CVPR
14. Feris R, Siddiquie B, Zhai Y, Petterson J, Brown L, Pankanti S (2011) Attribute-based vehicle search in crowded surveillance videos. In: ACM international conference on multimedia retrieval, p 18

15. Halstead M, Denman S, Fookes C, Sridharan S (2014) Locating people in video from semantic descriptions: a new database and approach. In: ICPR
16. Jaha E, Nixon M (2014) Soft biometrics for subject identification using clothing attributes. In: 2014 IEEE international joint conference on biometrics (IJCB), pp 1–6. doi:10.1109/BTAS.2014.6996278
17. Jain AK, Dass SC, Nandakumar K (2004) Soft biometric traits for personal recognition systems. In: International conference on biometric authentication, pp 717–738
18. Lucas T, Henneberg M (2015) Comparing the face to the body, which is better for identification? Int J Legal Med 1–8. doi:10.1007/s00414-015-1158-6
19. McKelvey T, Dailey K (2013) Boston marathon bombings: how notorious bombers got caught. BBC News Mag
20. Nguyen Thanh K, Denman S, Sridharan S, Fookes C (2014) Score-level multibiometric fusion based on dempster-shafer theory incorporating uncertainty factors. IEEE Trans Hum Mach Syst
21. Paisitkriangkrai S, Shen C, Hengel AVD (2013) Efficient pedestrian detection by directly optimize the partial area under the roc curve. In: ICCV, pp 1057–1064
22. Park U, Jain A, Kitahara I, Kogure K, Hagita N (2006) Vise: Visual search engine using multiple networked cameras. ICPR 3:1204–1207
23. Reid D, Nixon M, Stevenage S (2014) Soft biometrics; human identification using comparative descriptions. IEEE Trans Pattern Anal Mach Intell 36(6):1216–1228. doi:10.1109/TPAMI.2013.219
24. Scoleri T, Lucas T, Henneberg M (2014) Effects of garments on photoanthropometry of body parts: application to stature estimation. Forensic Sci Int 237(0):148.e1–148.e12. doi:10.1016/j.forsciint.2013.12.038. http://www.sciencedirect.com/science/article/pii/S0379073814000073
25. Sevilla-Lara L, Learned-Miller E (2012) Distribution fields for tracking. In: CVPR. IEEE, pp 1910–1917
26. Shafer G (1976) Mathematical theory of evidence. Princeton University Press
27. Thornton J, Baran-Gale J, Butler D, Chan M, Zwahlen H (2011) Person attribute search for large-area video surveillance. In: IEEE international conference on technologies for homeland security (HST), pp 55–61
28. Tsai RY (1986) An efficient and accurate camera calibration technique for 3d machine vision. In: CVPR, pp 364–374
29. Turakhia N, Parikh D (2013) Attribute dominance: what pops out. In: ICCV. IEEE, pp 1225–1232
30. Vaquero DA, Feris RS, Tran D, Brown L, Hampapur A, Turk M (2009) Attribute-based people search in surveillance environments. In: WACV

Chapter 13
Contact-Free Heartbeat Signal for Human Identification and Forensics

Kamal Nasrollahi, Mohammad A. Haque, Ramin Irani and Thomas B. Moeslund

Abstract The heartbeat signal, which is one of the physiological signals, is of great importance in many real-world applications, for example, in patient monitoring and biometric recognition. The traditional methods for measuring such this signal use contact-based sensors that need to be installed on the subject's body. Though it might be possible to use touch-based sensors in applications like patient monitoring, it will not be that easy to use them in identification and forensics applications, especially if subjects are not cooperative. To deal with this problem, recently computer vision techniques have been developed for contact-free extraction of the heartbeat signal. We have recently used the contact-free measured heartbeat signal, for biometric recognition, and have obtained promising results, indicating the importance of these signals for biometrics recognition and also for forensics applications. The importance of heartbeat signal, its contact-based and contact-free extraction methods, and the results of its employment for identification purposes, including our very recent achievements, are reviewed in this chapter.

13.1 Introduction

Forensic science deals with collecting and analyzing information from a crime scene for the purpose of answering questions related to the crime in a court of law. The main goal of answering such questions is identifying criminal(s) committing the crime. Therefore, any information that can help identifying criminals can be

K. Nasrollahi · M.A. Haque (✉) · R. Irani · T.B. Moeslund
Visual Analysis of People (VAP) Laboratory, Aalborg University, Aalborg, Denmark
e-mail: mah@create.aau.dk

K. Nasrollahi
e-mail: kn@create.aau.dk

R. Irani
e-mail: ri@create.aau.dk

T.B. Moeslund
e-mail: tbm@create.aau.dk

M. Tistarelli and C. Champod (eds.), *Handbook of Biometrics for Forensic Science*, Advances in Computer Vision and Pattern Recognition,
DOI 10.1007/978-3-319-50673-9_13

useful. Such information can be collected from different sources. One such a source, which has a long history in forensics, is based on human biometrics, i.e., human body or behavioral characteristics that can identify a person, for example, DNA [1], fingerprints [2, 3], and facial images [4]. Besides human biometrics, there is another closely related group of human features/characteristics that cannot identify a person, but can help the identification process. These are known as soft biometrics, for instance, gender, weight, height, gait, race, and tattoo.

The human face, which is of interest of this chapter, is not only used as a biometric, but also as a source for many soft biometrics, such as gender, ethnicity, and facial marks and scars [5, 6, 7]. These soft biometrics have proven great values for forensics applications in identification scenarios in unconstrained environments wherein commercial face recognition systems are challenged by wild imaging conditions, such as off frontal face pose and occluded/covered face images [8, 7]. The mentioned facial soft-biometrics are mostly based on the physical features/characteristics of the human. In this chapter, we look into heartbeat signal which is a physiological feature/characteristic of the human that similar to the mentioned physical ones can be extracted from facial images in a contact-free way, thanks to the recent advances in computer vision algorithms. The heartbeat signal is one of the physiological signals that is generated by the cardiovascular system of the human body. The physiological signals have been used for different purposes in computer vision applications. For example, in [9] electromyogram, electrocardiogram, skin conductivity and respiration changes and in [10] electrocardiogram, skin temperature, skin conductivity, and respiration have been used for emotion recognition in different scenarios. In [11] physiological signals have been used for improving communication skills of children suffering from Autism Spectrum Disorder in a virtual reality environment. In [12–14] these signals have been used for stress monitoring. Based on the results of our recent work, which are reviewed here, the heartbeat signal shows promising results to be used as a soft biometric.

The rest of this chapter is organized as follows: first, the measurements of heartbeat signal using both contact-based and contact-free methods are explained in the next section. Then, employing these signals for identification purposes is discussed in Sect. 13.3. Finally, the chapter is concluded in Sect. 13.4.

13.2 Measurement of Heartbeat Signal

The heartbeat signal can be measured in two different ways: contact-based and contact-free. These methods are explained in the following subsections.

13.2.1 Contact-Based Measurement of Heartbeat Signal

The heartbeat signal can be recorded in two different ways using the contact-based sensors:

- By monitoring electrical changes of muscles during heart functioning, by a method that is known as Electrocardiogram which records ECG signals.
- By listening to the heart sounds during its functioning, by a method that is known as Phonocardiogram which records PCG signals.

The main problem of the above-mentioned methods is obviously the need for the sensors to be in contact (touch) with the subject's body. Depending on the application of the measured heartbeat signal, this requirement may have different consequences, for example, for

- Constant monitoring of patient, having such sensors on the body may cause some skin irritation.
- Biometric recognition, the subjects might not be cooperative to wear the sensors properly.

Therefore, contact-free measurement of heartbeat signals can be of great advantage in many applications. Thanks to the recent advances in computer vision techniques, this has been possible recently to measure heartbeat signals using a simple webcam. Methods developed for this purpose are reviewed in the following subsection.

13.2.2 Contact-Free Measurement of Heartbeat Signal

The computer vision techniques developed for heartbeat measurement mostly utilize facial images. The reason for this goes back to this fact that heart pulses generate some periodic changes on the face, as well as other parts of the human body. However, since the human face is mostly visible, it is usually this part of the body that has been chosen by the researchers to extract the heartbeats from. The periodic changes that are caused by the heartbeat on the face are of two types:

- Changes in head motion which is a result of periodic flow of the blood through the arteries and the veins for delivering oxygenated blood to the body cells.
- Changes in skin color which is a result of having a specific amount of blood under the skin in specific periods of time.

None of these two types of changes are visible to the human eyes, but they can be revealed by computer vision techniques, like Eulerian magnification of [15, 16]. The computer vision techniques developed for heartbeat measurement are divided into two groups, depending on the source (motion or color) they utilize for the measurement. These two types of methods are reviewed in the following subsections.

13.2.2.1 Motion for Contact-Free Extraction of Heartbeat Signal

The first motion-based contract-free computer vision method was just recently released by [17]. This system utilizes the fact that periodic heart pules, through aorta and carotid arteries, produce periodic subtle motions on the head/face which can be detected from a facial video. To do that, in [17] some stable facial points, known as good features to track, are detected and tracked over time. The features they track are located on the forehead area and the region between the mouth and then nose are as these areas are less affected by internal facial expressions and their moments should thus be from another source, i.e., heart pules. Tracking these facial points' results in a set of trajectories, which are first filtered by a Butterworth filter to remove the irrelevant frequencies. The periodic components of these trajectories are then extracted by PCA and considered as the heartbeat rate. Their system has been tested on video sequences of 18 subjects. Each video was of resolution of 1280 × 720 pixels, at a frame rate of 30 with duration of 70–90 s.

To obtain the periodicity of the results of the PCA (applied to the trajectories), in [17] a Fast Fourier Transform (FFT) has been applied to the obtained trajectories from the good features to track points. Then, a percentage of the total spectral power of the signal accounted for by the frequency with the maximal power and its first harmonic is used to define the heartbeat rate of the subject [17]. Though this produces reasonable results when the subjects are facing the camera, it fails when there are other sources of motion on the face. Such sources of motion can be for instance, changes in facial expressions and involuntary head motion. It is shown in [18] that such motions makes the results of [17] far from correct. The main reason is because the system in [17] uses the frequency with the maximal power as the first harmonic when it estimates the heartbeat rate. However, such an assumption may not always be true, specifically when the facial expression is changing [18]. To deal with these problems [18] has detected good features to track Fig. 13.1 (right) from the facial regions shown in Fig. 13.1 (left).

Then, [18] tracks the good features to track to generate motion trajectories of these features. Then, it replaces the FFT with a Discrete Cosine Transform (DCT), and has employed a moving average filter before the Butterworth filter of [17]. Figure 13.2 shows the effect of the moving average filter employed in [18] for

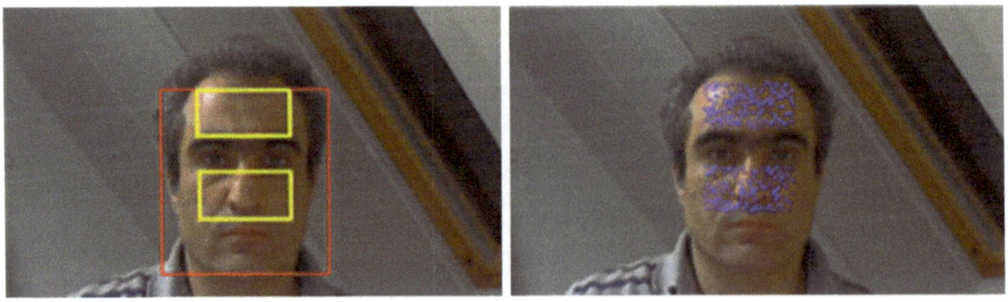

Fig. 13.1 The facial regions (*yellow* areas in the *left* image) that have been used for detecting good feature to track (*blue dots* in the *right* image) for generating motion trajectories in [18]

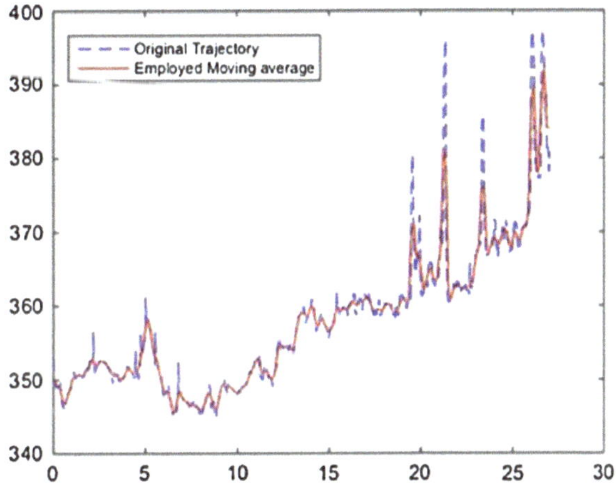

Fig. 13.2 The original signal (*red*) versus the moving averaged one (*blue*) used in [18] for estimating the heartbeat rate. On x and y-axis are the time (in seconds) and the amplitude of a facial point (from (good features to track)) that has been tracked, respectively

reducing the noise (resulting from different sources, e.g., motion of the head due to facial expression) in the signal that has been used for estimating the heartbeat rate.

Experimental results in [18] show that the above-mentioned simple changes have improved the performance of [18] compared to [17] in estimating the heartbeat signal, specifically, when there are changes in facial expressions of the subjects. The system in [18] has been tested on 32 video sequences of five subjects in different facial expressions and poses with duration about 60 s.

To the best of our knowledge, the above two motion-based systems are the only two methods available in the literature for contact-free measurement of the heartbeat rate using motion of the facial features. It should be noted that these systems do not report their performance/accuracy on estimating the heartbeat signal, but do so only for the heartbeat rate. The estimation of heartbeat signals are mostly reported in the color-based systems which are reported in the next subsection.

13.2.2.2 Color for Contact-Free Extraction of Heartbeat Signal

Using expensive imaging techniques for utilizing color of facial (generally skin) regions for the purpose of estimating physiological signal has been around for decades. However, the interest in this field was boosted when the system of [19] reported its results on video sequences captured by simple webcams. In this work, [19], Independent Component Analysis (ICA) has been applied to the RGB separated color channels of facial images, which are tracked over time, to extract the periodic components of these channels. The assumption here is that periodic blood circulation makes subtle periodic changes to the skin color, which can be revealed by Eulerian magnification of [15]. Having included a tracker in their system, they have measured heartbeat signals of multiple people at the same time [19]. Furthermore, it has been discussed in [19] that this method is tolerant towards motion of the subject during the experiment as it is based on the color of the skin. They have reported the results of their systems on 12 subjects facing a webcam that was about 0.5 m away in an indoor environment. Shortly after in [20] it was shown that besides heartbeat, the methods of [19] can be used for measuring other physiological signals, like respiratory rate.

The interesting results of the above systems motivated others to work on the weakness of those systems, which had been tested only in constrained conditions. Specifically,

- In [21], it has been discussed the methods of [19, 20] are not that efficient when the subject is moving (questioning the claimed motion tolerance of [19, 20]) or when the lightning is changing, like in an outdoor environment. To compensate for these they have performed a registration prior to calculating the heartbeat signals. They have tested their system in an outdoor environment in which the heartbeat signals are computed for subjects driving their vehicles.
- In [22] auto-regressive modeling and pole cancelation have been used to reduce the effect of the aliased frequency components that may worsen the performance of a contact-free color-based system for measuring physiological signals. They have reported their experimental results on patients that are under monitor in a hospital.
- In [23] normalized least mean square adaptive filtering has been used to reduce effect of changes in the illumination in a system that tracks changes in color values of 66 facial landmarks. They reported their experimental results on the large facial database of MAHNOB-HCI [24] which is publicly available. The reported results show that the system of [23] outperforms the previously published contact-free methods for heartbeat measurement including the color-based methods of [19, 20] and the motion based of [17].

13.3 Using Heartbeat Signal for Identification Purposes

Considering the fact the heartbeat signals can be obtained using the two different methods explained in the previous section, different identification methods have been developed. These are reviewed in the following subsections.

13.3.1 Human Identification Using Contact-Based Heartbeat Signal

The heartbeat signals obtained by contact-based sensors (in both ECG and PCG forms) have been used for identification purposes for more than a decade. Here we only review those methods that have used ECG signals as they are more common than PCG ones for identification.

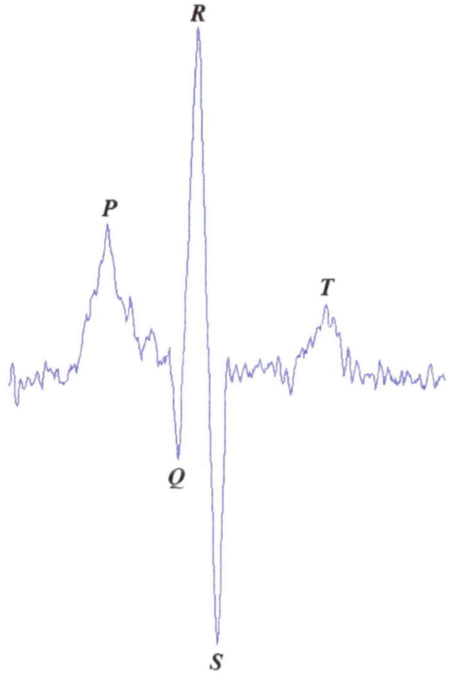

Fig. 13.3 A typical ECG signal in which the important key points of the signal are labeled

There are many different methods for human identification using ECG signals: [25–42], to mention a few. These systems have either extracted some features from the heart signal or have used the signal directly for identification. For example, it has been discussed in [25] that the heart signal (in an ECG form) composes of three parts: a P wave, a QRS complex, and a T wave (Fig. 13.3). These three parts and their related key points (P, Q, R, S, and T, known as fiducial points) are then found and used to calculate features that are used for identification, like the amplitude of the peaks or valleys of these point, the onsets and offsets of the waves, and the duration of each part of the signal from each point to the next. Similar features have been combined in [27] with radius curvature of different parts of the signal. It is discussed in [36] that one could ultimately extract many fiducial points from an ECG signal, but not all of them are equally efficient for identification.

In [28, 29, 33, 35, 37] it has been discussed that fiducial points detection based methods are very sensitive to the proper detection of the signal boundaries, which is not always possible. To deal with this, in

- [28] the ECG signals have directly been used for identification in a Principal Component Analysis (PCA) algorithm.
- [29] the ECG signal has been first divided into some segments and then the coefficients of the Discrete Cosine Transform (DCT) of the autocorrelation of these segments have been obtained for the identification.

- [33] a ZivMerhav cross parsing method based on the entropy of the ECG signal has been used.
- [35, 38, 41] the shape and morphology of the heartbeat signal have been directly used as feature for identification.
- [37] sparse representation of the ECG signal has been used for identification.
- [31, 32, 34] frequency analysis methods have been applied to ECG signals for identification purposes. For example, in [31, 34] wavelet transformation has been used and it is discussed that it is more effective against noise and outliers.

13.3.2 Human Identification Using Contact-Free Heartbeat Signal

The above-mentioned systems use contact-based (touch-based) sensors for measuring heartbeat signals. These sensors provide accurate, however sensitive to noise, measurements. Furthermore, they suffer from a major problem: these sensors need to be in contact with the body of the subject of interest. As mentioned before, this is not always practical, especially in identification context if subjects are not cooperative. To deal with this, we in [43] have developed an identification system that uses the heartbeat signals that are extracted using the contact-free technique of [20]. To the best of our knowledge, this is the first system that uses the contact-free heartbeat signals for identification purposes. In this section, we review the details of this system and its findings.

Having obtained the heartbeat signals, in form of RGB traces, from facial images using the method of [20] in [43] first a denoising filter is employed to reduce the effect of the external sources of noise, like changes in the lightning and head motions. To do that, the peak of the measured heartbeat signal is found and used to discard the outlying RGB traces. Then, the features that are used for the identification are extracted from this denoised signal. Following [44] the features that are used for identification in [43] are based on Radon images obtained from the RGB traces. To produce such images from the RGB traces, in [43] first the tracked RGB traces are replicated to the same number as the number of the frames that is available in the video sequence that is used for the identification, to generate a waterfall diagram. Figure 13.4 shows an example of such a waterfall diagram obtained for a contact-free measured heartbeat signal.

The Radon image, which contains the features that are going to be used for the recognition in [43], is then generated from the waterfall by applying a Radon transform to the waterfall diagram. Figure 13.5 shows the obtained Radon image from the waterfall diagram of Fig. 13.4. The discriminative features that are used for identification purposes from such a Radon image are simply the distance between every two possible pixels of the image.

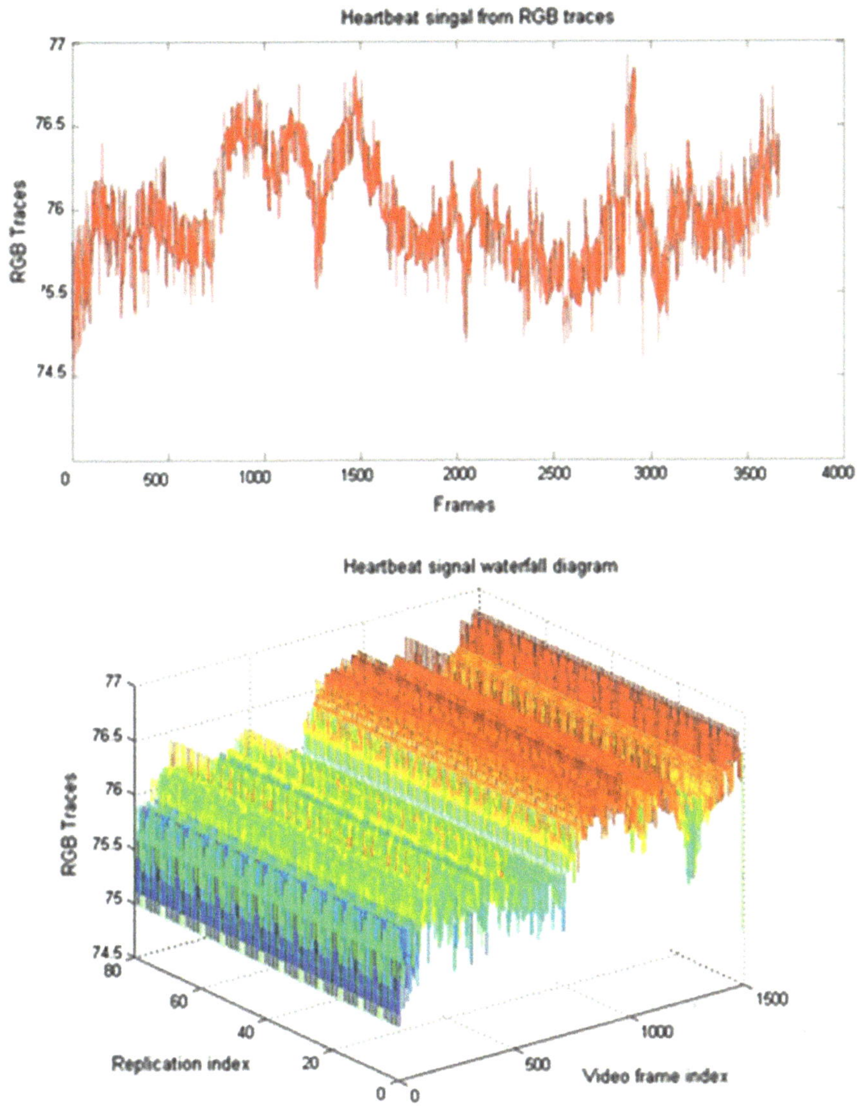

Fig. 13.4 A contact-free measured heartbeat signals (on the *top*) and its waterfall diagram (on the *bottom*)

The experimental results in [43] on a subset of the large facial database of MAHNOB-HCI [24] shown in Table 13.1 indicate that the features extracted from the Radon images of the heartbeat signals that were collected using a contact-free computer vision technique carries some distinctive properties.

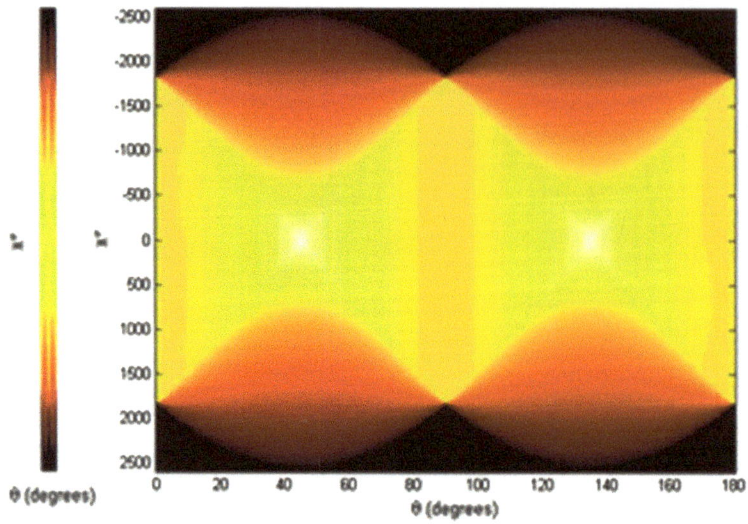

Fig. 13.5 The Radon image obtained from the waterfall diagram of Fig. 13.4. The discriminative features for the identification purposes are extracted from such Radon images [43]. The image on the *right* is the zoomed version of the one on the *left*

Table 13.1 The identification results using distance features obtained from Radon images of contact-free measured heartbeat signals from [43] on a subset of MAHNOB-HCI [24] containing 351 video sequences of 18 subjects

Measured parameter	Results (%)
False positive identification rate	1.28
False negative identification rate	1.30
True positive identification rate	98.70
Precision rate	80.86
Recall rate	80.63
Specificity	98.63
Sensitivity	97.42

13.4 Discussions and Conclusions

If the heartbeat signals are going to be used for identification purposes, they should serve as a biometric or a soft-biometric. A biometric signal should have some specific characteristics, among others, it needs to be

- Collectible, i.e., the signal should be extractable. The ECG-based heartbeat signal is obviously collectible, though one needs to install ECG sensors on the body of subjects, which is not always easy, especially when subjects are not cooperative.

- Universal, i.e., everyone should have an instance of this signal. An ECG heartbeat signal is also universal as every living human has a beating heart. This also highlights another advantage of heartbeat signal which liveness. Many of the other biometrics, like face, iris, and fingerprints, can be spoofed by printed versions of the signal, and thus need to be accompanied by a liveness detection algorithm. Heartbeat signal however does not need liveness detection methods [33] and is difficult to disguise [27].
- Unique, i.e., instances of the signal should be different from one subject to another.
- Permanent, i.e., the signal should not change over time [45].

Regardless of the method used for obtaining the heartbeat signal (contact-free or contact-based), such a signal is collectible (according to the discussions in the previous sections) and obviously universal. The identification systems that have used the contact-based sensors (like ECG), [25–42] have almost all reported recognition accuracies that are more than 90% on datasets of different sizes from 20 people in [25] to about 100 subjects in the others. The lowest recognition rate, 76.9%, has been reported in [32]. The results here are however reported on a dataset of 269 subjects for which the ECG signals have been collected in different sessions. Some of the sessions are from the same day and some are from different days. If both the training and the testing samples are from the same day (but still different sessions), the system report 99% recognition rate, but when the training and testing data is coming from different sessions recorded in different days, the recognition rate drops to 76.9% for the rank-1 recognition, but still as high as 93.5% for rank-15 recognition. This indicates that an ECG-based heartbeat signal might be considered as a biometric, though there is not that much study on the permanent dimensions of such signals for the identification purposes, reporting their results on very large databases.

On the other hand, due to the measurement techniques that contact-free methods provide for obtaining the heartbeat signals, the discriminative properties of contact-free obtained heartbeat signals is not as high as their peer contact-based ones. However, it is evident from the results of our recent work, which was reviewed in the previous section, that such signals have some discriminative properties that can be utilized for helping identification systems. In another words, a contact-free obtained heartbeat signal has the potential to be used as soft-biometric.

To conclude, the contact-free heartbeat signals seem to have promising applications in forensics scenarios. First of all, because according to the above discussions they seem to carry some distinguishing features, which can be used for identification purposes. Furthermore, according to the discussion presented in [17] the motion-based methods, which do not necessarily need to extract these signals from a skin region, can extract the heartbeat data from the hairs of the head, or even from a masked face. This will be of great help in many forensics scenarios, if one could extract a biometric or even a soft-biometric from a masked face because in many such scenarios the criminals are wearing a mask to hide their identity from, among others, surveillance cameras.

References

1. Ehrlich D, Carey L, Chiou J, Desmarais S, El-Difrawy S, Koutny L, Lam R, Matsu-daira P, Mckenna B, Mitnik-Gankin L, ONeil T, Novotny M, Srivastava A, Streechon P, Timp W (2002) MEMS-based systems for DNA sequencing and forensics. In: Proceedings of IEEE Sensors, vol 1, pp 448–449
2. Lin WS, Tjoa SK, Zhao HV, Liu KJR (2009) Digital image source coder forensics via intrinsic fingerprints. IEEE Trans Inf Forensics Secur 4(3):460–475
3. Roussev V (2009) Hashing and data fingerprinting in digital forensics. IEEE Secur Priv 8 (2):49–55
4. Peacock C, Goode A, Brett A (2004) Automatic forensic face recognition from digital images. Sci Justice 44(1):29–34
5. Jain AK, Unsang P (2009) Facial marks: soft biometric for face recognition. In: 16th IEEE international conference on image processing (ICIP), pp 37–40
6. Unsang P, Jain AK (2010) Face matching and retrieval uses soft biometrics. IEEE Trans Inf Forensics Secur 3:406–415
7. Han H, Otto C, Liu X, Jain A (2014) Demographic estimation from face images: human versus machine performance. IEEE Trans Pattern Anal Mach Intell 99
8. Jain AK, Klare B, Unsang P (2011) Face recognition: some challenges in forensics. In: 2011 IEEE international confer-ence on automatic face gesture recognition and workshops (FG 2011), pp 726–733
9. Wagner J, Jonghwa K, Andre E (2005) From physiological signals to emotions: implementing and comparing selected methods for feature extraction and classification. In: IEEE international conference on multimedia and expo, pp 940–943
10. Li L, Chen J (2006) Emotion recognition using physiological signals. Adv Artif Reality Tele-Existence Lect Notes Comput Sci Springer 4282:437–446
11. Kuriakose S, Sarkar N, Lahiri U (2012) A step towards an intelligent Human Computer Interaction: Physiology-based affect-recognizer. In: 4th international conference on intelligent human computer interaction (IHCI), pp 1–6
12. Liao W, Zhang W, Zhu Z, Ji Q (2005) A real-time human stress monitoring system using dynamic Bayesian network. In: IEEE computer society conference on computer vision and pattern recognition—workshops
13. Zhai J, Barreto A (2006) Stress detection in computer users through non-invasive monitoring of physiological signals. Biomed Sci Instrum 42:495–500
14. Barreto A, Zhai J, Adjouadi M (2007) Non-intrusive physiological monitoring for automated stress detection in human-computer interaction. Human-Comput Interact Lect Notes Comput Sci Springer 4796:29–38
15. Liu C, Torralba A, Freeman WT, Durand F, Adelson EH (2005) Motion magnification. ACM Trans Graph 24(3):519–526
16. Wu HY, Rubinstein M, Shih E, Guttag J, Durand F, William TF (2012) Eulerian video magnification for revealing subtle changes in the world. In: Proceedings of SIGGRAPHACM transactions on graphics, vol 31, no 4
17. Balakrishnan G, Durand F, Guttag J (2013) Detecting pulse from head motions in video. In: IEEE Conference on Computer Vision and Pattern Recognition (CVPR), pp 3430–3437
18. Irani R, Nasrollahi K, Moeslund TB (2014) Improved pulse detection from head motions using DCT. In: 9th International Conference on Computer Vision Theory and Applications, vol 3, pp 118–124
19. Poh MZ, McDuff DJ, Picard R (2010) Non-contact, automated cardiac pulse measurements using video imaging and blind source separation. Opt Express 18:10762–10774
20. Poh MZ, McDuff DJ, Picard R (2011) Advancements in noncontact, multiparameter physiological measurements using a webcam. IEEE Trans Biomed Eng 58:7–11

21. Sarkar A, Abbott AL, Doerzaph Z (2014) Assessment of psychophysiological characteristics using heart rate from naturalistic face video data. In: IEEE interna-tional joint conference on biometrics (IJCB)
22. Tarassenko L, Villarroel M, Guazzi A, Jorge J, Clifton DA, Pugh C (2014) Non-contact video-based vital sign monitoring using ambient light and autoregressive models. Physiol Meas 35:807–831
23. Li X, Chen J, Zhao G, Pietikainen M (2014) Remote heart rate measurement from face videos under realistic situations. In: IEEE conference on computer vision and pattern recognition (CVPR), pp 4264–4271
24. Soleymani M, Lichtenauer J, Pun T, Pantic M (2012) A multimodal database for affect recognition and implicit tagging. IEEE Trans Affect Comput 3(1):42–55
25. Biel L, Pettersson O, Philipson L, Wide P (2001) ECG analysis: a new approach in human identification. IEEE Trans Instrum Measur 50(3):808–812
26. Hoekema R, Uijen GJH, van Oosterom A (2001) Geometrical aspects of the interindividual variability of multilead ECG recordings. IEEE Trans Biomed Eng 48(5):551–559
27. Israel SA, Irvine JM, Cheng A, Wiederhold MD, Wiederhold BK (2005) ECG to identify individuals. Pattern Recogn 38(1):133–142
28. Wang Y, Plataniotis KN, Hatzinakos D (2006) Integrating analytic and appearance attributes for human identification from ECG signals, In: Biometrics symposium: special session on research at the biometric consortium conference
29. Plataniotis KN, Hatzinakos D, Lee JKM (2006) ECG biometric recognition without fiducial detection. In: Biometrics symposium: special session on research at the biometric consortium conference
30. Singh YN, Gupta P (2008) ECG to individual identification. In: 2nd IEEE international conference on biometrics: theory, applications and systems
31. Fatemian SZ, Hatzinakos D (2009) A new ECG feature extractor for biometric recognition. In: 2009 16th international conference on digital signal processing
32. Odinaka I, Po-Hsiang L, Kaplan AD, O'Sullivan JA, Sirevaag EJ, Kristjansson SD, Sheffield AK, Rohrbaugh JW (2010) ECG biometrics: a robust short-time frequency analysis. In: IEEE international workshop on information forensics and security (WIFS)
33. Coutinho DP, Fred ALN, Figueiredo MAT (2010) One-lead ECG-based personal identification using Ziv-Merhav cross parsing. In: 20th international conference on pattern recognition (ICPR), pp 3858–3861
34. Can Y, Coimbra MT, Kumar BVKV (2010) Investigation of human identification using two-lead Electrocardiogram (ECG) signals. In: Fourth IEEE international conference on biometrics: theory applications and systems (BTAS)
35. Islam MS, Alajlan N, Bazi Y, Hichri HS (2012) HBS: A novel biometric feature based on heartbeat morphology. IEEE Trans Inf Technol Biomed 16(3):445–453
36. Tantawi M, Revett K, Tolba MF, Salem A (2012) A novel feature set for deployment in ECG based biometrics. In: 7th international conference on computer engineering systems (ICCES), pp 186–191
37. Wang J, She M, Nahavandi S, Kouzani A (2013) Human identification from ECG signals via sparse representation of local segments. IEEE Sign Proces Lett 20(10):937–940
38. Fratini A, Sansone M, Bifulco P, Romano M, Pepino A, Cesarelli M, D'Addio G (2013) Individual identification using electrocardiogram morphology. In: 2013 IEEE international symposium on medical measurements and applications proceedings (MeMeA), pp 107–110
39. Rabhi E, Lachiri Z (2013) Biometric personal identification system using the ECG signal. In: Computing in cardiology conference (CinC), pp 507–510
40. Ming L, Xin L (2014) Verification based ECG biometrics with cardiac irregular conditions using heartbeat level and segment level information fusion. In: IEEE international conference on acoustics, speech and signal processing (ICASSP), pp 3769–3773
41. Lourenco A, Carreiras C, Silva H, Fred A (2014) ECG biometrics: A template selection approach. In: IEEE international symposium on medical measurements and applications (MeMeA)

42. Nomura R, Ishikawa Y, Umeda T, Takata M, Kamo H, Joe K (2014) Biometrics authentication based on chaotic heartbeat waveform, In: Biomedical engineering international conference (BMEiCON)
43. Haque MA, Nasrollahi K, Moeslund TB (2015) Heartbeat signal from facial video for biometric recognition. In: Proceedings of 19th Scandinavian conference on image analysis
44. Hegde C, Prabhu HR, Sagar DS, Shenoy PD, Venugopal KR, Patnaik LM (2011) Heartbeat biometrics for human authentication. SIViP 5(4):485–493
45. Van de Haar H, Van Greunen D, Pottas D (2013) The characteristics of a biometric. In: Information security for South Africa

Part IV
Statistical Analysis of Forensic Biometric Data

Chapter 14
From Biometric Scores to Forensic Likelihood Ratios

Daniel Ramos, Ram P. Krish, Julian Fierrez and Didier Meuwly

Abstract In this chapter, we describe the issue of the interpretation of forensic evidence from scores computed by a biometric system. This is one of the most important topics into the so-called area of forensic biometrics. We will show the importance of the topic, introducing some of the key concepts of forensic science with respect to the interpretation of results prior to their presentation in court, which is increasingly addressed by the computation of likelihood ratios (LR). We will describe the LR methodology, and will illustrate it with an example of the evaluation of fingerprint evidence in forensic conditions, by means of a fingerprint biometric system.

14.1 Likelihood Ratio Framework for Evidence Evaluation

The evaluation of the relationship between two pieces of evidence at judicial trials has been the subject of discussion in the past years [1]. Here, the problem is to give a value to a comparison of a trace specimen of unknown origin (for instance a fingermark revealed in a crime scene, or a wire tapping involving an incriminating conver-

---

D. Ramos (✉) · R.P. Krish · J. Fierrez
ATVS - Biometric Recognition Group, Escuela Politecnica Superior,
Universidad Autonoma de Madrid, Calle Francisco Tomas y Valiente 11,
28049 Madrid, Spain
e-mail: daniel.ramos@uam.es

R.P. Krish
e-mail: ram.krish@uam.es

J. Fierrez
e-mail: julian.fierrez@uam.es

D. Meuwly
Netherlands Forensic Institute, Laan van Ypenburg 6, 2497GB
The Hague, The Netherlands
e-mail: d.meuwly@utwente.nl

D. Meuwly
University of Twente, Drienerlolaan 5, 7522NB Enschede, The Netherlands
e-mail: d.meuwly@utwente.nl

M. Tistarelli and C. Champod (eds.), *Handbook of Biometrics for Forensic Science*, Advances in Computer Vision and Pattern Recognition,
DOI 10.1007/978-3-319-50673-9_14

sation) with a reference specimen of known origin (for instance, a fingerprint from a suspect, or some recordings of a known individual). From a formal logical perspective [2], the given value should represent the degree of support of the comparison to any of the *propositions* (also called *hypotheses*) involved in the trial. Examples of simple hypotheses might be "the trace and the reference specimens originated from the same source" or "the trace and the reference specimens originated from different sources", but more complex hypotheses can be considered [2]. In some sense, the value of the evidence represents the strength of the link between the trace and the reference specimen in the context of the propositions considered.

Evidence evaluation using a Bayesian probabilistic framework has been proposed in recent years as a logical and appropriate way to report evidence to a court of law [3]. In Europe, there have been initiatives to foster this approach, some of them in response of notorious reluctance to the use of statistics in courts [4]. These have been the main reason leading to the release of a Guideline [5] for the expression of conclusions in evaluative forensic reports. This Guideline is proposed by the European Network of Forensic Science Institutes (ENFSI), an organization that includes almost all the main forensic laboratories in Europe.[1] According to this Guideline, a Bayesian framework for forensic evaluative reports is recommended for all disciplines and laboratories within ENFSI. Under this Bayesian approach, a likelihood ratio (LR) is computed to represent the value of the evidence, and to be reported to a court of law (mainly in the form of a verbal equivalent). This framework clearly complies with the requirements of evidence-based forensic science [1]: it is scientifically sound (transparent procedures, testability, formal correctness), and clearly separates the responsibilities of the forensic examiner and the court.

The increasing establishment of this Bayesian evaluative framework has motivated the convergence of pattern recognition and machine-learning approaches to yield probabilistic outputs in the form of likelihood ratios. A common architecture for this considers two steps: first, the computation of a discriminating score between two specimens, trace and reference (e.g., a fingermark in the crime scene and an exemplar fingerprint from a known suspect), which can be obtained from a standard biometric system; and second, the transformation of the score into a likelihood ratio [6–9]. This architecture is especially suited for biometric systems, where the output of a conventional biometric system is typically expressed as a score, even though it is used as *black-box* technology. Therefore, the score is most of the times a necessary intermediate step to the likelihood ratio.

14.1.1 Challenges in LR-Based Evidence Evaluation

Despite its advantages, the computation of likelihood ratios still presents important challenges. We enumerate the most important as follows.

---

[1] http://www.enfsi.eu/.

First, the typical scenario in forensic science involves data presenting diverse and unfavorable conditions, which means that automatic comparisons between the specimens will result in a challenging problem. Efforts to model or compensate the effects of these adverse conditions in likelihood ratio computation should be improved. Some works such as [10] have contributed to evaluate the impact of this problem. Moreover, integration of advanced machine-learning algorithms (like in [11, 12]) for the compensation of adverse conditions into forensic evaluation helps in this direction. However, adverse condition compensation still remains a challenge.

Second, in forensic science the databases are difficult to obtain and to use, even for research purposes. This is because, although there is plenty of forensic data in some disciplines (e.g., large fingerprint databases), there are legal, privacy and interoperability issues that hamper the use of this data by academic and research institutions. This leads to two opposite situations: either the databases are big when there is access to the data, and therefore big-data solutions are a challenge to face; or the databases are highly scarce, and the use of robust models is necessary. Data scarcity has been tackled by different techniques as in [13, 14]. However, to our knowledge, evidence evaluation models have not been adapted to big-data scenarios to handle big databases when possible, which represents a loss of information in these scenarios. Other lines of research have proposed the use of simulated forensic data in order to prevent the problem of data scarcity [15]. The involvement of simulated data is a big improvement against data scarcity situations, but the testing of the validity of simulated databases for the operational use of systems in a real setup is still controversial.

Third, although likelihood ratio computation methods are becoming more and more popular, the validation of those methods for its use in forensic casework is still not standardized. Even if likelihood ratios are computed to evaluate the links between evidential materials, this does not guarantee that they will be able to be integrated into a Bayesian decision framework to ultimately allow a fact finder to do optimal decisions. In this sense, the measurement of the performance characteristics that a likelihood ratio model should manifest is of paramount importance. Recent work has shown that one of the most important characteristic that forensic likelihood ratios should present is the so-called calibration [9]. This is a property of a set of likelihood ratios, by which the LR is itself a measure of evidential weight. This leads to the property that "The LR of the LR is the LR", meaning that the LR is interpreting the evidence with the best possible probabilistic meaning in terms of Bayes decisions [16]. Therefore, computing likelihood ratios is not enough, they should also be the best calibrated as possible. There are current efforts of the forensic community in order to establish formal frameworks for the validation of likelihood ratio models [9, 17, 18], but research is still needed. Also, a framework for the validation of likelihood ratio methods has been recently published [19].

Fourth, evidence evaluation in complex cases is still problematic. Probabilistic graphical models, particularly Bayesian networks [20], have been proposed to address those situations. However, this emerging field is an active area of research in forensic science. More efforts are needed in order to provide forensic examiners with appropriate tools in operational scenarios, especially if those models are to be learned from data.

14.2 Case Assessment and Interpretation Methodology

A milestone in the use of the LR methodology in Europe was the Case Assessment and Interpretation (CAI) methodology developed by the Forensic Science Service (FSS) in the late 1990s [2]. This was the result of the efforts of the now closed Forensic Science Service of the United Kingdom, in order to homogenize and make more agile the relationship between courts and forensic service providers (e.g., police forces or other public or private forensic laboratories). An ultimate aim is the use of a logical methodology to avoid pitfalls of reasoning and fallacies. The methodology has been described in several papers during the end of the twentieth century, remarkably [2, 21, 22], and serves as the core of likelihood ratio-based evidence interpretation.

There are several characteristic features of the CAI methodology, which we summarize below.

- Full integration of the LR methodology into the forensic evidence evaluation process. In this sense, all the elements typical from LR evidence evaluation are present, namely the evidence, propositions, probabilistic reasoning, etc.
- A particular emphasis is put in the definition of the propositions in a given case, which have to be informed by the circumstances of the case themselves. Thus, the relationship between the court and the forensic science provider should be essential in order to define the propositions. Issues like the definition of the population considered to model the alternative proposition, the specificity of the propositions with respect to the population, the suspect and the trace, or the selection of the most appropriate database to address the propositions [23], are of particular importance.
- A hierarchy of propositions [21] is introduced in order to address the forensic casework in the most appropriate manner with respect to the information in the case. In this sense, there are three basic levels in the hierarchy: *source level*, where the source which originated the trace(s) is considered; *activity level*, where the activities from which originate the traces are under discussion; and *offence level*, that focuses on the question whether the activity from which originate the traces is an infraction. Depending on the question asked by the requester/fact finder and on the information in the case available to the forensic scientist, it is possible to escalate the inference a to higher level, but in most cases the forensic examiner is requested to report at source level, reason for which most of the effort to produce increasingly robust models has been focused on source level. Nevertheless,

nowadays there is a push towards the use of activity-level propositions in casework (even in the ENFSI Guideline for evaluative reports [5]), although LR models for activity or offence levels are mostly in a research stage.

- Case pre-assessment is encouraged by the model. Under this concept, a preliminary LR value is reported prior to the case itself, in order to indicate what would be the expected outcome of the forensic analysis by the examiner. This helps to focus the expectations of the fact finder, and has important implications regarding the efficiency of resources in a case.

14.3 Evidence Evaluation with Likelihood Ratios

The LR framework for interpretation of the evidence represents a mathematical and logical tool in order to aid in the inference process derived from the analysis of the evidence. In this methodology, the objective of the forensic scientist is computing the likelihood ratio (LR) as a degree of support of one proposition versus its alternative [3, 24].

The LR framework is stated as follows. Consider a forensic case. There is a forensic evidence E, which contains the specimens to compare in a forensic case, namely, in a fingerprint case, a *recovered* fingermark of unknown origin and a *reference* fingerprint (namely the *exemplar*) whose origin is known to be a given suspect involved in the case. In this context, the unobserved variable of interest is the true proposition H with values $\{H_p, H_d\}$, where H_p and H_d are the possible relevant propositions defined in the case, according to the CAI methodology. As mentioned before, the definition of H_p and H_d varies in each case. A possible definition at the source level could be as follows:

H_p: The origin of the fingermark (trace) and the fingerprint (reference) is the same finger of one single donor.

H_d: The origin of the fingermark (trace) and the fingerprint (reference) are fingers from two different donors.

H_p is typically called *prosecution* proposition, whereas H_d is referred to as *defense* proposition. This is due to the fact that alternative, and mutually exclusive propositions arise naturally in an adversarial trial system like in the UK, where the CAI methodology was developed. Other propositions can be addressed, and variation of their statement can lead to a radically different selection of databases for LR computation [23], and even to different likelihood ratio models [25]. Therefore, care should be taken in order to clearly and appropriately define the propositions in a case.

In Bayesian decision theory, decisions are made considering the probability distribution of the variable of interest (in this case, the proposition variable H), given all the observed information. In a forensic case, this can be represented as $P(H = H_p \mid E, I)$ and $P(H = H_d \mid E, I)$, or simply $P(H_p \mid E, I)$ and $P(H_d \mid E, I)$, where I is the background information available in the case not related to the evidence E, as defined by the CAI methodology. H_p and H_d are in most cases mutually exclusive. Then, Bayes' theorem [3] relates probabilities before and after evidence analysis.

$$P\left(H_p \mid E,I\right) = \frac{P\left(E \mid H_p,I\right) \cdot P\left(H_p \mid I\right)}{P(E \mid I)} \tag{14.1}$$

In terms of interpretation, it is useful to use ratios of probabilities. Then, Eq. 14.1 becomes

$$\frac{P\left(H_p \mid E,I\right)}{P\left(H_d \mid E,I\right)} = LR \cdot \frac{P\left(H_p \mid I\right)}{P\left(H_d \mid I\right)} \tag{14.2}$$

$$LR = \frac{P\left(E \mid H_p,I\right)}{P\left(E \mid H_d,I\right)} \tag{14.3}$$

In Eq. 14.2, we can distinguish the following:

1. The prior probabilities $P\left(H_p \mid I\right)$ and $P\left(H_d \mid I\right)$, which are province of the fact finder and should be stated assuming only the background information (I) in the case [24].
2. The LR (Eq. 14.3), assigned or computed by the forensic practitioner [3].

A critical point in the application of the LR methodology is the selection of proper databases to address the propositions and also the trace material, for example the language of the trace will determine the language of the speech databases used in the case, but also from the definition of the propositions themselves. We will address this issue in the example below, but many works in the literature give recommendations on how to select these databases, both in fingerprints [26] or in forensic science in general [23].

This LR-based framework for interpretation presents many advantages

- It allows forensic practitioners to evaluate and report a meaningful value for the weight of the evidence to the court, with a universal interpretation, allowing for the combination of results across disciplines when the same propositions are considered [5, 24].
- The role of the examiner is clearly defined, leaving to the court the task of using prior judgments or costs in the decision process.
- Probabilities can be interpreted as degrees of belief [27], allowing the incorporation of subjective opinions as probabilities in the inference process in a clear and scientific way.

The LR value has an interpretation as a *support* to a previously stated opinion, due to the analysis of the evidence E. In other words

- If the LR > 1 the evidence will support that $H = H_p$, i.e., the prosecutor proposition.

- If the LR < 1 the evidence will support that $H = H_d$, i.e., the defense proposition.

Moreover, the value of the LR represents the *degree of support* of the evidence to one value of H against the other. For instance, LR = 3 means that "the evidence supports $H = H_p$ against $H = H_d$ with a degree of 3 versus 1". Therefore, a single LR value has a *meaning* by itself, as opposed to a biometric score, that may have only meaning if compared to a reference threshold or another set of scores.

It is important to note that the LR *supports* an opinion about H, but the LR *is not* an opinion about H. Opinions about H are represented as probabilities of propositions, or in our binary case, their ratios. Therefore, it is not possible to make a decision about the value of H based solely on the value of the LR, because decisions will be taken from posterior probabilities, not only from degrees of support.

14.4 Interpreting Biometric System Scores with Likelihood Ratios

According to [6, 7], in biometrics all the information that the systems yield about the propositions after observing E is in most cases condensed into a so-called *score*, a single number which is an observation of a random variable S, and must contain as much information as possible about H. Therefore, the interpretation of the evidence using biometric systems requires that the score will be first computed by the system, yielding the particular value $S = s$, and then the score is interpreted using a likelihood ratio. This leads to the following expression:

$$LR = \frac{P\left(E|\,H_p, I\right)}{P\left(E|\,H_d, I\right)} = \frac{P\left(s|\,H_p, I\right)}{P\left(s|\,H_d, I\right)} \tag{14.4}$$

Moreover, most biometric scores are continuous, and in that case the ratio of probabilities becomes a ratio of probability density functions, yielding

$$LR = \frac{P\left(s|\,H_p, I\right)}{P\left(s|\,H_d, I\right)} = \frac{p\left(s|\,H_p, I\right)}{p\left(s|\,H_d, I\right)} \tag{14.5}$$

Thus, the LR value (Eq. 14.5) is the quotient of two probability densities. On the one hand, the probability density function (pdf) $p\left(S|\,H_p, I\right)$ in the numerator in Eq. 14.3 is known as the intra-variability distribution. Its evaluation in the particular value of the score $S = s$ gives a measure of the probability density of observing the evidence under H_p. On the other hand, the pdf $p\left(S|\,H_d, I\right)$ in the denominator is known as the inter-variability distribution, and its evaluation in the particular value of the score $S = s$ gives a measure of the probability density of observing the evidence under H_d.[2]

The aim of LR methods with biometric score-based systems is to provide a model that transforms scores into LR values in a case. Moreover, the resulting LR values should present adequate performance in order to correctly aid the decisions of fact finders.

14.5 LR Computation Methods from Biometric Scores

In this section, some of the most common algorithms for LR computation from biometric scores are described.

14.5.1 Generating Training Scores

The main commonality of all the methods described in this section is that they need two proposition-dependent sets of *training* scores, namely $\mathbf{S_p}$ and $\mathbf{S_d}$. These sets and some of the issues associated to them are described as follows.

- The set $\mathbf{S_p} = \left\{ s_p^{(1)}, \ldots, s_p^{(N_{pt})} \right\}$ consists of N_{pt} scores computed assuming that $H = H_p$. Therefore, the selection of data to compute the scores in $\mathbf{S_p}$ has to be done accordingly to the definition of the propositions. As H_p proposition typically assumes that the trace and reference specimens in the case come from the same person, the $\mathbf{S_p}$ consists of *same-source* scores.[3] However, the rest of information in H_p can be determinant in order to select the database to generate those same-source scores. For instance, if the particular suspect in the case is included in the propositions (e.g., "the trace was left by Mr. Dean Keaton"), then the propositions will be *person-specific* or *source-specific*, and the database to generate $\mathbf{S_p}$ should include specimens coming from the particular donor, because in many biometric traits each person has a particular behavior regarding their score distribution [28]. On the other hand, *person-generic* or *source-generic* propositions (e.g., "the trace and the reference samples come from the same source") would allow the use of any same-source score from other people, since there is not knowledge of a particular subject. Another example of the influence of propositions in the model for LR computation is related to the definition of suspect-based or finger-based proposition for fingerprint interpretation [25].

---

[2]The background information about the case I will be eliminated from the notation for the sake of simplicity hereafter. It will be assumed that all the probabilities defined are conditioned to I.

[3]Here we work at the source level, and therefore *same-source* scores refer to scores generated from two biometric specimens coming from the same source. They are what in biometric authentication terminology are called *genuine* scores.

- The set $\mathbf{S_d} = \left\{ s_d^{(1)}, \ldots, s_d^{(N_{dt})} \right\}$ consists of N_{dt} scores computed assuming that $H = H_{dt}$. For the computation of these scores, several things should be taken into account. First, H_d typically assumes that the questioned materials were not generated by the suspect in the case, but other person. Therefore, the scores in $\mathbf{S_d}$ will essentially be *different-source* scores,[4] since the case always considers the donor reference specimens as part of the evidence. Second, the way in which these scores are generated is critical, since the selection of different strategies to obtain $\mathbf{S_d}$ might lead to different LR values. Also, theoretical issues should be taken into account regarding these strategies (for a discussion about this, see [29]). Last, but not least, the determination of the population of sources of the test specimen must be handled with care. The key point is that the population must be seen as the set of potential donors of the test specimen, considering the definition of the proposition and the information about the case that is relevant and available to the forensic examiner.

An important remark is in order here. The aim of the $\mathbf{S_p}$ and $\mathbf{S_d}$ score sets is to represent the variation of S conditioned to the propositions. As S is the variable representing the score to be obtained from the evidence in the case, the conditions in the forensic case should be preserved for all comparisons in $\mathbf{S_p}$ and $\mathbf{S_d}$. For instance, if the evidence consists of a degraded, partial fingermark and a fingerprint from a ten-print card of a known suspect, all the scores in $\mathbf{S_p}$ and $\mathbf{S_d}$ should be generated from comparisons of degraded fingermarks and fingerprints from ten-print cards, in the conditions as similar as possible to those in the case. An exception would be if the conditions do not affect the behavior of the scores at all, but this rarely happens in real forensic scenarios.

Moreover, the scores in $\mathbf{S_p}$ and $\mathbf{S_d}$ should represent all possible sources of variability in S. Therefore, the use of models of variability is essential in order compute better likelihood ratios. Good examples exist in the literature of the use of variability models to compute the LR [26], or to compensate this variability at the level of the biometric score [11, 12].

14.5.2 Common Methods for Score-Based LR Computation

14.5.2.1 Generative Assignment of Probability Densities

LR computation in forensic biometrics has been classically performed by the use of generative techniques modeling the hypotheses-conditional distribution of the scores variable S. This is the approach already presented in [30], and has been followed in subsequent works in the literature. Under this approach, the objective is assigning

[4] Here we work at the source level, and therefore *different-source* scores refer to scores generated from two biometric specimens coming from different sources. They are what in biometric authentication terminology are called *impostor* scores.

the likelihoods $p\left(S|H_p\right)$ to the training scores $\mathbf{S_p}$, and $p\left(S|H_d\right)$ to $\mathbf{S_d}$. Then, the ratio of the particular value of these densities at $S = s$ will be the LR value.

Assigning $p\left(S|H_p\right)$ and $p\left(S|H_d\right)$ implies the selection of a proper model. The most straightforward choice for biometric scores could be the Gaussian distribution, obtained via Maximum Likelihood from the training set of scores. However, this requires the distributions involved to present a good fitting with Gaussian probability density functions, which is not typically the case. Fortunately, some score normalization techniques such as T-Norm tend to generate Gaussian distributions for scores when H_d is true [31]. Other approaches for generative ML fitting includes the use of Kernel Density Functions [30, 32], Gaussian Mixture Models [32] and other parametric distributions [18, 42].

14.5.2.2 Logistic Regression

Logistic regression is a well-known pattern recognition technique widely used for many problems including fusion [33, 34] and more recently likelihood ratio computation [7, 35]. The aim of logistic regression is obtaining an affine transformation (i.e., shifting and scaling) of an input dataset in order to optimize an objective function. Let $\mathbf{S_f} = \left\{s_f^{(1)}, s_f^{(2)}, \ldots, s_f^{(K)}\right\}$ be a set of scores from K different biometric systems. The affine transformation performed by the logistic regression model can be defined as

$$f_{lr} = \log\left(\frac{P\left(H_p\middle|\mathbf{S_f}, I\right)}{P\left(H_d\middle|\mathbf{S_f}, I\right)}\right) = a_0 + a_1 \cdot s_f^{(1)} + a_2 \cdot s_f^{(2)} + \cdots + a_K \cdot s_f^{(K)} \tag{14.6}$$

This leads to the following *logistic regression model*:

$$P\left(H_p\middle|\mathbf{S_f}, I\right) = \frac{1}{1 + e^{-f_{lr}}} = \frac{1}{1 + e^{-\log(LR)-\log(O(H_p))}} \tag{14.7}$$

where $O(H_p)$ determines the prior odds in favor of H_p.

The weighting terms $\{a_0, a_1, a_2, \ldots, a_K\}$ can be obtained from a set of training data with optimization procedures found in the literature.[5] Moreover, by training the weights for some given simulated value of the prior odds, and removing the influence of that value of the prior odds after computing f_{lr}, likelihood ratios are obtained.

Notice that logistic regression can be used for computing likelihood ratios from a single biometric score ($K = 1$), but also to perform fusion and LR computation simultaneously (when $K > 1$) [34]. This fact, joined to the good behavior that logistic

[5] Typical implementations used in biometrics include toolkits like FoCal or BOSARIS, which can be found in http://niko.brummer.googlepages.com.

regression presents in most situations, have made this LR computation algorithm one of the most popular ones.

14.5.2.3 Pool Adjacent Violators (PAV)

Another approach to score-to-LR transformation has been proposed by the use of the Pool Adjacent Violators (PAV) algorithm [7]. The PAV algorithm transforms a set of scores into a set of LR values presenting optimal calibration. However, it is only possible to apply an optimal PAV transformation if the ground-truth labels of the propositions for each score in the set are known. As suggested in [8], a PAV transformation can be trained on the set of training scores $\mathbf{S_p}$ and $\mathbf{S_d}$, and then apply the trained transformation to a score in a forensic case. Although a straightforward use of PAV leads to a non-invertible transformation, several *smoothing* techniques can be applied to PAV in order to keep it monotonically increasing. For instance, adding a small slope to the function defining the PAV transformation will lead to an invertible transformation. Interpolating with linear, quadratic or splines approaches are also possible smoothing schemes.

14.6 Performance Measurement of LR Methods

As it was previously stated, the issue of performance measurement of LR methods is paramount in order to achieve validation of forensic interpretation prior to its use in casework [18]. In this section, we describe some of the performance metrics adequate for LR-based forensic interpretation.

At the source level, performance measurement is typically carried out in an empirical way. In order to measure the performance of a LR method, a test set of LR values should be generated by comparisons of specimens from a biometric database using that LR method. These comparisons should be in fact simulated cases, where the conditions of specimens should be similar to the conditions of the case scenario whose performance is to be measured. This would lead to N_p LR values computed when H_p is true and N_d LR values computed when H_p is true.

A solution to measure the performance of likelihood ratio values has been proposed in [7] for speaker recognition, and has been dubbed *log-likelihood-ratio cost* (C_{llr}). Later, it has been used in many other fields in forensic sciences [14, 17, 36, 37]. C_{llr} is defined as follows:

$$C_{llr} = \frac{1}{2 \cdot N_p} \sum_{i_p} \log_2 \left(1 + \frac{1}{LR_{i_p}} \right) + \frac{1}{2 \cdot N_d} \sum_{j_d} \log_2 \left(1 + LR_{j_d} \right) \tag{14.8}$$

The indices i_p and j_d respectively denote summing over the LR values of the simulated cases where each proposition is respectively true.

An important result is derived in [7], where it is demonstrated that minimizing the value of C_{llr} also encourages to obtain reduced Bayes decision costs for all possible decision costs and prior probabilities [38]. This property has been highlighted as extremely important in forensic science [9]. Moreover, in [7], the Pool Adjacent Violators algorithm is used in order to decompose C_{llr} as follows:

$$C_{llr} = C_{llr}^{min} + C_{llr}^{cal} \tag{14.9}$$

where

- C_{llr}^{min} represents the *discrimination cost* of the LR method, and it is due to non-perfect discriminating power.
- C_{llr}^{cal} represents the *calibration cost* of the system.

C_{llr} is a scalar measure of performance of LR values, the lower its value the better the performance. Another useful measure of performance, with interpretation in terms of information loss, is the Empirical Cross-Entropy (ECE), which is a generalization of C_{llr}, as follows:

$$\begin{aligned} ECE = & -\frac{P(H_p|I)}{N_p}\sum_{i_p} log_2 P\left(H_p|s_{i_p}, I\right) \\ & -\frac{P(H_d|I)}{N_d}\sum_{j_d} log_2 P\left(H_d|s_{j_d}, I\right), \end{aligned} \tag{14.10}$$

where s_{i_p} and s_{j_d} denote the scores from trace and reference specimens in each of the simulated cases, where either H_p or H_d is respectively true.

As it happens with C_{llr}, ECE can be additively decomposed also using the PAV algorithm into $\text{ECE} = \text{ECE}^{min} + \text{ECE}^{cal}$. This leads to ECE^{min} measuring information loss due to bad discriminating power, and ECE^{cal} measuring information loss due to miscalibration.

As it can be seen, ECE is dependent of the prior probabilities both explicitly and through $P\left(H_p|s_{i_p}, I\right)$ and $P\left(H_d|s_{i_d}, I\right)$. Thus, ECE can be represented in a prior-dependent way. This has been proposed to be done by a so-called ECE plot [17], which shows three comparative performance curves together (Fig. 14.1)

- solid, red curve: accuracy. This curve is the ECE of the LR values in the validation set, as a function of the prior log-odds. The lower this curve, the more accurate the method. This curve shows the overall performance of the LR method;
- dashed, blue curve: ECE^{min}. This curve is the ECE of the validation set of LR values after the application of the PAV algorithm. This shows the best possible ECE in terms of calibration, and it is a measure of discriminating power;

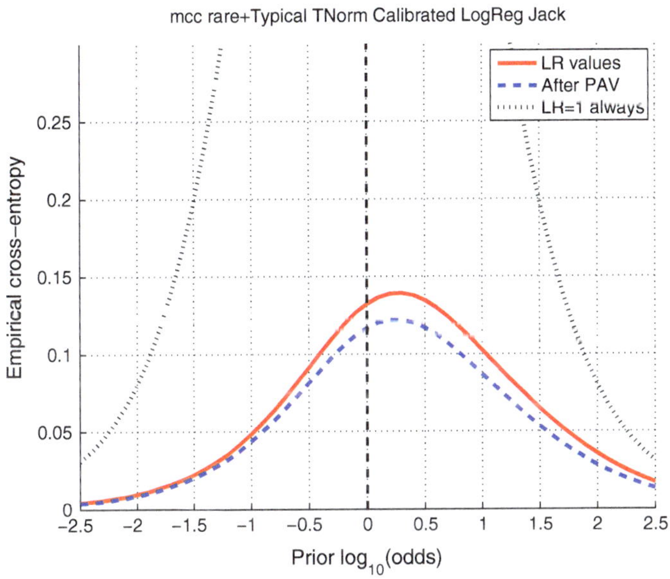

Fig. 14.1 Example of ECE plot

- dotted curve: neutral reference. It represents the comparative performance of a so-called *neutral LR method*, defined as the one which always delivers LR = 1 for each forensic case simulated in the set of LR values. This neutral method is taken as a *floor of performance*: the accuracy should always be better than the neutral reference. Therefore, the solid curve in an ECE plot should be always lower than the dotted curve, for all represented values of the prior log-odds (the names *floor* and *ceiling* are the opposite of the usual physical connotations but are chosen to represent the lowest and highest levels of performance).

A free Matlab™ software package to draw ECE plots can be found in the following webpage: http://arantxa.ii.uam.es/~dramos/software.html.

14.7 Computing LR Values from Biometric Scores: An Example with Forensic Fingerprint Recognition

In this section, we illustrate the process of computing forensic LR values from biometric fingerprint scores. We use a database collected from real cases, and in collaboration with Spanish Guardia Civil. Also, we use a state-of-the-art fingerprint system based on Minutiae Cylinder Code [39–41].

Evidence evaluation in fingerprints by the use of LR has been recently proposed in remarkable works like in [26] for minutiae configurations extracted manually from forensic examiners. However, other models based on the use of AFIS scores to compute likelihood ratio values can be found in [42], and more recently [18]. The reasons of modeling AFIS scores are diverse. On the other hand, it may give a complementary information to other methods more based on the direct statistical modeling of the minutiae extracted by the examiners. On the other hand, it allows the use of powerful systems to extract the information of identity, after which a likelihood ratio model performs the interpretation with the less loss of information possible [6].

14.7.1 Database and Statistics

The database used in this work was obtained from Guardia Civil, the Spanish law enforcement agency. The Guardia Civil database (GCDB) is a realistic forensic fingerprint casework database. Apart from having typical minutiae feature types (*ridge-endings, bifurcations*), GCDB also comprises rare minutiae types like *fragments, enclosures, dots, interruptions, etc.* [43]. A comprehensive list of rare minutia features used by Guardia Civil are shown in Fig. 14.2 and the corresponding minutiae type names are listed in Table 14.1.

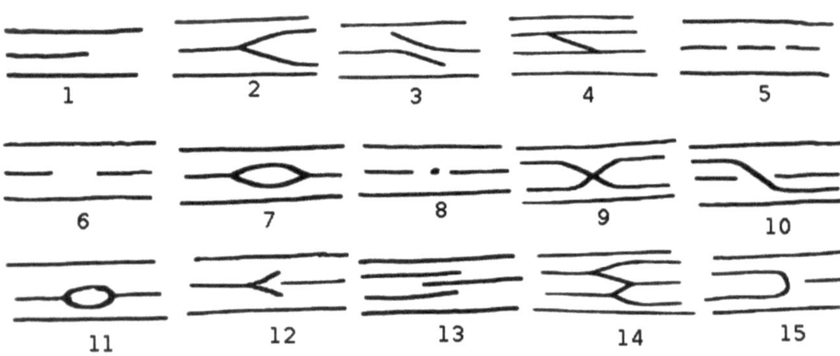

Fig. 14.2 Minutia types used by Guardia Civil. Names corresponding to individual minutia type numbers can be found in Table 14.1

Table 14.1 List of minutia types used by Guardia Civil. Numbering with respect to Fig. 14.2

No	Minutiae type	No	Minutiae type	No	Minutiae type
1	Ridge ending	6	Interruption	11	Circle
2	Bifurcation	7	Enclosure	12	Delta
3	Deviation	8	Point	13	Assemble
4	Bridge	9	Ridge crossing	14	M-structure
5	Fragment	10	Transversal	15	Return

Table 14.2 The probability of occurrence and the entropy-based weights for the minutia types present in the 268 fingermarks of GCDB. The numbers correspond to minutia types in Fig. 14.2

No	Minutiae type	Probability (p_i)	Weight ($w_i = -\log_{10} p_i$)
1	Ridge-ending	0.5634	0.2492
2	Bifurcation	0.3620	0.4413
3	Deviation	0.0015	2.8294
4	Bridge	0.0024	2.6253
5	Fragment	0.0444	1.3523
6	Interruption	0.0021	2.6833
7	Enclosure	0.0204	1.6896
8	Point	0.0036	2.4492
10	Transversal	0.0003	3.5284

GCDB used in this work consists of 268 fingermark and reference fingerprint images and minutia sets. All the minutiae in the fingermark images were manually extracted by forensic examiners of Guardia Civil. The corresponding mated minutiae in the reference fingerprints were also manually established. This includes the typical (ridge-endings and bifurcations) minutiae and the rare minutiae. The minutiae in the reference fingerprints were combined with the minutiae extracted by Neurotechnology Verifinger algorithm, in order to generate a complete set of minutiae for the reference fingerprint. For the fingermark, the minutiae will be the ones marked by the examiners. The average number of minutiae in the fingermarks was 13 and that of tenprints was 125.

The original fingermark minutia sets provided by Guardia Civil and the post-processed VeriFinger generated minutia sets are used in all our experiments. To represent some rare minutiae, multiple points were needed. For example, to represent a *deviation* two points are needed (see type 3 in Fig. 14.2), and to represent an *assemble* three points are needed (see type 13 in Fig. 14.2). Whenever multiple points are needed to represent a rare minutia, we mapped them to a single point representation by taking the average of locations and orientations of all points.

From the 268 fingermark minutia sets, we estimated the probability of occurrence (p_i) of various minutia types. The probability (p_i) and the entropy-based weights ($w_i = -\log_{10} p_i$) for each minutia type present in GCDB are listed in Table 14.2. In the 268 fingermarks of GCDB, we noticed only seven types of rare minutia features. They are listed in Table 14.2. Other rare minutia types are not found in the current database used in this study, because they did not appear in the whole database.

14.7.2 Biometric System

The system used to compare the minutiae was based on Minutiae Cylinder Code (MCC) representation, also extensively presented in another chapter of this book, deeply described in [39–41].[6] It is not the aim to deeply describe the score computation system in this chapter, because we aim at the likelihood ratio computation process. Details about the algorithm can be found in the relevant references [39–41].

In order to exploit the information in the rare minutiae features in the GCDB, the minutiae included in those rare points are part of the features directly added to the ridge endings and bifurcations. Thus, everything together has been used to feed the MCC system. Therefore, the scores obtained by the system include information from both typical and rare minutiae.

Finally, a T-Norm stage has been performed in order to align and normalize the output different-source scores of the system. Test-Normalization, or T-Norm [44] has been used to perform score normalization. In order to do that, a set of different-source fingerprints, namely a *cohort* of different sources, is needed. From those so-called T-Norm scores, the mean and the standard deviation μ_{Tnorm} and σ_{Tnorm} are computed. The T-Norm technique is then applied to a particular score computed form a given fingermark query as follows:

$$s_{Tnorm} = \frac{s_{raw} - \mu_{Tnorm}}{\sigma_{Tnorm}} \tag{14.11}$$

Thus, T-Norm performs query-dependent score normalization, and the result is the alignment of the query-dependent different-source score distributions for all comparisons in the particular set of scores.

Thus, this normalization technique compensates variability in the scores due to the recovered fingermark. The T-Norm cohort in this experiment has been selected from the same Guardia Civil database that has been used to simulate real forensic fingermark-reference fingerprint comparisons, and therefore the results may be overstated in terms of performance. However, for the sake of illustration on the computation of likelihood ratios, this is not a problem.

It has been reported that the different-source scores of a biometric system tend to be more Gaussian after the application of T-Norm [31]. Therefore, we will assume that a Gaussian model will be appropriate for the MCC scores after T-Norm is applied.

[6] We have used the implementation of this score computation system provided by the authors.

14.7.3 Methodology and Proposed LR Methods

This section proposes several methods for likelihood ratio computation using scores from the MCC algorithm with the Guardia Civil database (GCDB) described in Sect. 14.7.1.

14.7.3.1 Definition of Propositions

According to the methodology of CAI, the first step to compute likelihood ratios is to establish the propositions considering the information present in the case. The *simulated cases* that we are going to conduct here consist of the comparison of one fingermark and one reference fingerprint. Both fingermark and reference fingerprint come from GCDB. The scores used to train the models for the LR computation are the rest of scores in the GCDB generated from individuals different from the donors of the fingermark and the reference fingerprint. In this way, the models are trained with scores not used in the case, and the data handling is honest in the sense of the performance measurement.

According to this setup, there are several observation that are in order:

- The information in the case is almost non-existent. We only have the images of the fingermark and the reference fingerprint, and therefore no assumption can be done about the donors of fingermark and reference (e.g. ethnicity, gender, etc.). This only allows generic propositions about the populations involved.
- The trace and reference specimens are pseudonymised because the metadata of the donors are not necessary.
- We only have a single same-source comparison for each subject in the database. Therefore, it is impossible for us to focus in source-specific models, because there are no additional data available to model the particular behavior of their scores in comparison to the whole population of scores.
- There is no information whatsoever about the relevance of the donor of fingermark and reference fingerprint with respect to the action in the crime scene, or even more with respect to any offense. Therefore, only propositions at source level can be addressed.
- Because of the way it was built, we assume that all fingermarks in the GCDB dubbed as different in the ground-truth labels are generated by different people. It is assumed also in the corresponding reference fingerprint. Therefore, in this database it will be equivalent to talk about donors as about fingers, since different fingerprints will definitely belong to different donors (and not to different fingers of the same donor).

Under these premises, we decide to state source level, person-generic and general-population propositions for this case. Therefore, we have the following propositions:

H_p: The origin of the fingermark (trace) and the fingerprint (reference) is the same finger of the donor.

H_d: The origin of the fingermark (trace) and the fingerprint (reference) are fingers from two different donors.

This definition of the propositions implies that, for a forensic case involving the comparison of a fingermark and its corresponding reference fingerprint, the scores needed to train the LR model should be generated with comparisons of fingermarks and reference fingerprints without the constrain of belonging to a particular individual. This implies that more scores will be typically available to train the models, therefore improving their statistical robustness. On the other hand, the use of person-generic propositions inevitably implies an important loss of information in cases where the identity of the individual is known, as it is typical in court. However, for this example we will consider this person-specific scenario because of the limitations of the GCDB, as explained above.

14.7.4 Likelihood Ratio Models

As example in this chapter, we will compare the performance of the following common models for likelihood ratio computation.

- Pool Adjacent Violators.
- Gaussian-ML.
- Logistic regression.

14.7.5 Experimental Results

14.7.5.1 Experimental Protocol

The experimental protocol has been designed in order to simulate a real forensic scenario where fingermarks are compared with reference fingerprints using typical minutia features and also rare minutia features.

In our experiments, we used the Guardia Civil database (as described in Sect. 14.7.1), because it is the only forensic fingerprint database which contains rare minutiae, as it has been previously described. Since the GCDB is limited in size, a cross-validation strategy has been followed in order to optimally use the data without using the same dataset to train and test the LR models proposed. This cross-validation strategy is described as follows: for each same-source comparison of a fingermark and a reference fingerprint, the scores to train the LR model for that particular comparison will consist of all the scores generated with the GCDB, except those generated with either the fingermark or the reference fingerprint involved in the case. Therefore, the separation between the fingermark and reference fingerprint and the individuals in the training database is guaranteed.

This cross-validation strategy has many advantages in the sense of the optimal usage of the available database. However, it also presents the disadvantage that the conditions of the training scores matches the conditions of the fingermark and reference fingerprint under comparison to a higher degree than in a potential real case. Thus, the results presented here could be overstated in terms of performance. However, due to the limitation of the database, and also because the aim of the work is to show how to apply the methodology, we consider it appropriate to use this protocol.

Notice that this cross-validation strategy does not only guarantee that the data used to train and test the models are different. Moreover, it also guarantees that the T-Norm scores generated with the cohort are not present in the training database. This is because the T-Norm cohort scores must be generated with the scores of the query fingermark, which will be not present in the training database. Therefore, the situation is realistic in the sense of the data handling to normalize the scores and also to train the LR models.

14.7.6 Results on the Comparison of LR Computation Methods

In this section, we compare all the proposed LR computation methods not only from the perspective of the discriminating power, but also with respect to the calibration loss. Thus, accuracy as the sum of both performance measures will allow us to select the best choice for LR computation. From Fig. 14.3, it is seen that the logistic regression model presents the best accuracy (red solid curve), and therefore is the best of the three methods proposed.

We now analyze calibration (separation between red and blue curves) more deeply. It is generally seen in Fig. 14.3 that the calibration loss is better for PAV and logistic regression methods rather than for the Gaussian method. Thus, both methods are apparent good options for LR computation. Regarding the Gaussian-ML method, it is seen that the calibration performance is worse than for PAV or logistic regression, especially in the region of low prior odds. As a possible explanation, although T-Norm different-source scores tend to be Gaussian when they are pooled among all queries, it is not the case for the same-source scores, and this makes the same-source distribution to seriously diverge from Gaussianity even after T-Norm is applied.

An additional warning is in order here. The cross-validation procedure to train LR models and to select T-Norm scores implies a scenario with low dataset shift between training and testing data. In a forensically realistic setup, where dataset shift between training and testing data can be severe, the performance of LR methods that excessively fits the training data can seriously degrade. On the other hand, it is known in pattern recognition that models with lower complexity are more robust to this effect to avoid overfitting. Therefore, the much lower complexity of logistic regression with respect to PAV indicates that the former can be potentially more robust to overfitting and dataset shift than the latter in forensically realistic conditions. Due to this reason, logistic regression is more preferable to PAV computation method in this scenario.

As a conclusion of this section, the calibration loss represents a low percentage of all the loss of accuracy for logistic regression and PAV LR computation methods, in this order. This makes the overall performance of logistic regression superior, which among other reasons makes it the best choice. On the other hand, Gaussian-ML presents poorer calibration loss, sometimes presenting worse performance than the neutral reference, which makes it less recommendable for the score computation systems proposed in this chapter.

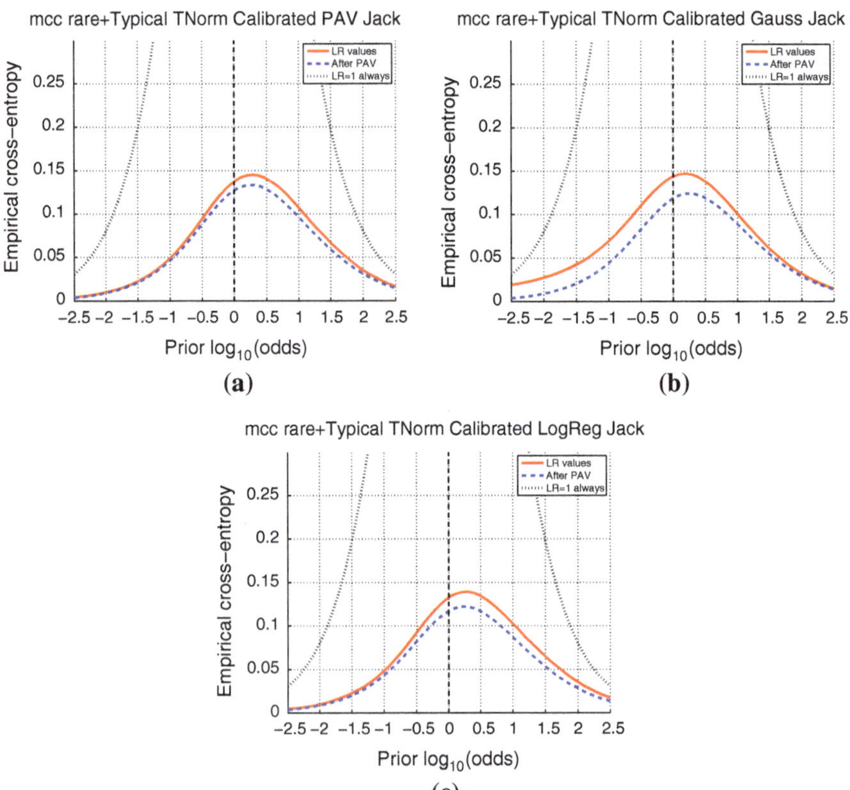

Fig. 14.3 ECE plots showing performance of LR methods with T-Normed MCC scores. The different LR methods are PAV (**a**), Guassian-ML (**b**) and Logistic regression (**c**)

14.8 Conclusions

In this chapter, we have described the methodology for computing likelihood ratios from biometric scores, with an example of fingerprint recognition in forensic conditions using rare minutiae. This has allowed the interpretation of the evidence from the fingermark-to-reference-fingerprint comparisons simulating a real forensic case by the use of a cross-validation strategy with the GCDB. Several LR methods have been proposed and compared in terms of discriminating power and calibration performance. These results clearly show that the proposed methods present far better performance than the neutral reference and therefore are useful for forensic interpretation.

References

1. Saks MJ, Koehler JJ (2005) The coming paradigm shift in forensic identification science. Science 309(5736):892–895
2. Cook R, Evett IW, Jackson G, Jones PJ, Lambert JA (1998) A model for case assessment and interpretation. Sci Justice 38:151–156
3. Aitken CGG, Taroni F (2004) Statistics and the evaluation of evidence for forensic scientists. Wiley, Chichester
4. Berger CA, Champod JS, Curran C, Dawid J, Kloosterman AP (2011) Expressing evaluative opinions: a position statement. Sci Justice 51:1–2. Several signatories
5. Willis S (2015) ENFSI guideline for the formulation of evaluative reports in forensic science. Monopoly Project MP2010: the development and implementation of an ENFSI standard for reporting evaluative forensic evidence. Technical report, European Network of Forensic Science Institutes
6. Ramos D (2007) Forensic evaluation of the evidence using automatic speaker recognition systems. PhD thesis, Depto. de Ingenieria Informatica, Escuela Politecnica Superior, Universidad Autonoma de Madrid, Madrid, Spain. http://atvs.ii.uam.es
7. Brümmer N, du Preez J (2006) Application independent evaluation of speaker detection. Comput Speech Lang 20(2–3):230–275
8. van Leeuwen D, Brümmer N (2007) An introduction to application-independent evaluation of speaker recognition systems. In: Müller C (ed) Speaker classification. Lecture notes in computer science/Artificial intelligence, vol 4343. Springer, Heidelberg, Berlin, New York
9. Ramos D, Gonzalez-Rodriguez J (2013) Reliable support: measuring calibration of likelihood ratios. Forensic Sci Int 230:156–169
10. Zadora G, Ramos D (2010) Evaluation of glass samples for forensic purposes–an application of likelihood ratio model and information-theoretical approach. Chemometr Intell Lab Syst 102:62–63
11. Li P, Fu Y, Mohammed U, Elder J, Prince SJD (2010) Probabilistic models for inference about identity. IEEE Trans Pattern Anal Mach Intell (PAMI) 34(1):144–157
12. Dehak N, Kenny P, Dehak R, Dumouchel P, Ouellet P (2010) Front-end factor analysis for speaker verification. IEEE Trans Audio Speech Lang Process 19(4):788–798
13. Villalba J, Brümmer N (2011) Towards fully Bayesian speaker recognition: integrating out the between-speaker covariance. Proceedings of the 12th annual conference of the international speech communication association, Interspeech 2011. Florence, Italy, pp 505–508
14. Zadora G, Martyna A, Ramos D, Aitken C (2014) Statistical analysis in forensic science: evidential values of multivariate physicochemical data. Wiley

15. Rodriguez CM, de Jongh A, Meuwly D (2013) Introducing a semiautomatic method to simulate large numbers of forensic fingermarks for research on fingerprint identification. J Forensic Sci 57(2):334–342
16. van Leeuwen DA, Brümmer N (2013) The distribution of calibrated likelihood-ratios in speaker recognition. arXiv preprint
17. Ramos D, Gonzalez-Rodriguez J, Zadora G, Aitken C (2013) Information-theoretical assessment of the performance of likelihood ratio models. J Forensic Sci 58:1503–1518
18. Haraksim R, Ramos D, Meuwly D, Berger CE (2015) Measuring coherence of computer-assisted likelihood ratio methods. Forensic Sci Int 249:123–132
19. Meuwly D, Ramos D, Haraksim R (in press) A guideline for the validation of likelihood ratio methods used for forensic evidence evaluation. Forensic Sci Int. 10.1016/j.forsciint.2016.03.048
20. Taroni F, Aitken C, Garbolino P, Biedermann A (2006) Bayesian networks and probabilistic inference in forensic science. Wiley
21. Cook R, Evett IW, Jackson G, Jones PJ, Lambert JA (1998) A hierarchy of propositions: deciding which level to address in casework. Sci Justice 38(4):231–239
22. Evett IW, Jackson G, Lambert JA (2000) More on the hierarchy of propositions: exploring the distinction between explanations and propositions. Sci Justice 401(1):3–10
23. Champod C, Evett IW, Jackson G (2004) Establishing the most appropriate databases for addressing source level propositions. Sci Justice 44(3):153–164
24. Evett IW (1998) Towards a uniform framework for reporting opinions in forensic science casework. Sci Justice 38(3):198–202
25. Neumann C, Evett IW, Skerrett JE, Mateos-Garcia I (2011) Quantitative assessment of evidential weight for a fingerprint comparison I: generalisation to the comparison of a mark with set of ten prints from a suspect. Forensic Sci Int 207:101–105
26. Neumann C, Evett I, Skerret JE (2012) Quantifying the weight of evidence from a forensic fingerprint comparison: a new paradigm. J R Stat Soc Ser A: Stat Soc 175(2):371–415
27. Taroni F, Aitken CGG, Garbolino P (2001) De Finetti's subjectivism, the assessment of probabilities and the evaluation of evidence: a commentary for forensic scientists. Sci Justice 41(3):145–150
28. Doddington G, Liggett W, Martin A, Przybocki M, Reynolds DA (1998) Sheeps, goats, lambs and wolves: a statistical analysis of speaker performance in the NIST 1998 speaker recognition evaluation. In: Proceedings of ICSLP
29. Hepler AB, Saunders CP, Davis LJ, Buscaglia J (2011) Score-based likelihood ratios for handwriting evidence. Foresic Sci Int 219(1–3):129–140
30. Meuwly D (2001) Reconaissance de Locuteurs en Sciences Forensiques: L'apport d'une Approache Automatique. PhD thesis, IPSC-Universite de Lausanne
31. Navratil J, Ramaswamy G (2003) The awe and mystery of T-Norm. In: Proceedings of ESCA European conference on speech, communication and technology, EuroSpeech, pp 2009–2012
32. Gonzalez-Rodriguez J, Fierrez-Aguilar J, Ramos-Castro D, Ortega-Garcia J (2005) Bayesian analysis of fingerprint, face and signature evidences with automatic biometric systems. Forensic Sci Int 155(2–3):126–140
33. Pigeon S, Druyts P, Verlinde P (2000) Applying logistic regression to the fusion of the NIST'99 1-speaker submissions. Digit Signal Process 10(1):237–248
34. Brümmer N, Burget L, Cernocky J, Glembek O, Grezl F, Karafiat M, van Leeuwen DA, Matejka P, Scwartz P, Strasheim A (2007) Fusion of heterogeneous speaker recognition systems in the STBU submission for the NIST speaker recognition evaluation 2006. IEEE Trans Audio Speech Signal Process 15(7):2072–2084
35. Gonzalez-Rodriguez J, Rose P, Ramos D, Toledano DT, Ortega-Garcia J (2007) Emulating DNA: rigorous quantification of evidential weight in transparent and testable forensic speaker recognition. IEEE Trans Audio Speech Signal Process 15(7):2072–2084
36. Vergeer P, Bolck A, Peschier LJ, Berger CE, Hendriks JN (2014) Likelihood ratio methods for forensic comparison of evaporated gasoline residues. Sci Justice 56(6):401–411

37. Morrison GS (2009) Likelihood-ratio-based forensic speaker comparison using parametric representations of vowel formant trajectories. J Acoust Soc Am 125:2387–2397
38. Duda RO, Hart PE, Stork DG (2001) Pattern classification. Wiley
39. Cappelli R, Ferrara M, Maltoni D (2010) Minutia cylinder code: a new representation and matching technique for fingerprint recognition. IEEE Trans Pattern Anal Mach Intell 32:2128–2141
40. Cappelli R, Ferrara M, Maltoni D (2010) Fingerprint indexing based on minutia cylinder code. IEEE Trans Pattern Anal Mach Intell 33:1051–1057
41. Ferrara M, Maltoni D, Cappelli R (2012) Noninvertible minutia cylinder-code representation. IEEE Trans Inf Forensics Secur 7:1727–1737
42. Egli N (2009) Interpretation of partial fingermarks using an automated fingerprint identification system. PhD thesis, Institute de Police Scientifique, Ecole de Sciences Criminelles
43. Santamaria F (1955) A new method of evaluating ridge characteristics. Fingerprint Ident Mag
44. Auckenthaler R, Carey M, Lloyd-Tomas H (2000) Score normalization for text-independent speaker verification systems. Digit Signal Process 10:42–54

Chapter 15
Dynamic Signatures as Forensic Evidence: A New Expert Tool Including Population Statistics

Ruben Vera-Rodriguez, Julian Fierrez and Javier Ortega-Garcia

Abstract This chapter presents a new tool specifically designed to carry out dynamic signature forensic analysis and give scientific support to forensic handwriting examiners (FHEs). Traditionally FHEs have performed forensic analysis of paper-based signatures for court cases, but with the rapid evolution of the technology, nowadays they are being asked to carry out analysis based on signatures acquired by digitizing tablets more and more often. In some cases, an option followed has been to obtain a paper impression of these signatures and carry out a traditional analysis, but there are many deficiencies in this approach regarding the low spatial resolution of some devices compared to original offline signatures and also the fact that the dynamic information, which has been proved to be very discriminative by the biometric community, is lost and not taken into account at all. The tool we present in this chapter allows the FHEs to carry out a forensic analysis taking into account both the traditional offline information normally used in paper-based signature analysis, and also the dynamic information of the signatures. Additionally, the tool incorporates two important functionalities, the first is the provision of statistical support to the analysis by including population statistics for genuine and forged signatures for some selected features, and the second is the incorporation of an automatic dynamic signature matcher, from which a likelihood ratio (LR) can be obtained from the matching comparison between the known and questioned signatures under analysis. An example case is also reported showing how the tool can be used to carry out a forensic analysis of dynamic signatures.

R. Vera-Rodriguez (✉) · J. Fierrez · J. Ortega-Garcia
ATVS - Biometric Recognition Group, Escuela Politecnica Superior, Universidad Autonoma de Madrid, Calle Francisco Tomas y Valiente 11, 28049 Madrid, Spain
e-mail: ruben.vera@uam.es

J. Fierrez
e-mail: julian.fierrez@uam.es

J. Ortega-Garcia
e-mail: javier.ortega@uam.es

M. Tistarelli and C. Champod (eds.), *Handbook of Biometrics for Forensic Science*, Advances in Computer Vision and Pattern Recognition,
DOI 10.1007/978-3-319-50673-9_15

15.1 Introduction

Forensic handwriting examiners (FHEs) have been carrying out studies about the authorship of handwritten signatures for court cases for over a century [1]. The great majority of works in the forensic field relates to offline signature analysis [2–7]. With the rapid evolution of technology, which allows the acquisition of dynamic signatures from tablets and smartphones, applications are spreading in the commercial sector to facilitate payments and also in banking to facilitate the digital storage of all the signed paperwork. Therefore, FHEs are being required to provide forensic evidence to determine the authenticity of handwritten signatures written on digitizing tablets [8], which can provide a static image of the signature but also, and most importantly, contain the dynamic information of at least the X and Y spatial coordinates over time.

Signature dynamics can be further processed to provide features such as the signing velocity, acceleration, and other stroke information along the signing trajectory. However, there are very few research works in the field of dynamic signature for forensic examinations [9–11]. The majority of relevant literature regarding dynamic signature analysis is in the field of biometric recognition [12], which make use of algorithms such as Hidden Markov Models [13, 14] or Dynamic Time Warping [15, 16].

In the last years there have been competitions on forensic signature verification for both offline and on-line signatures for automatic systems organized within the International Conference on Document Analysis and Recognition and (ICDAR) and the International Conference on Frontiers in Handwriting Recognition (ICFHR) from 2009 to date. It is interesting to note that in ICFHR 2010 offline signature competition, results of FHEs were also given allowing a comparison of performance of both automatic systems and FHEs [17]. It is also worth noting that in real practice FHEs carry out a multi-class problem classifying the signatures under analysis into genuine, forged, disguised (written by the authentic reference author, where he has deliberately tried to make the signatures look like a forgery, normally with the purpose of denying the signature at a later stage) or as inconclusive. On the other hand, automatic systems normally perform a two class problem deciding whether or not the given signature belongs to a referenced author. Results showed that different FHEs perform very differently, with some FHEs having very little opinion errors while some others many, and no correlation was observed with the experience in years of the FHEs or with the time (hours) they took to carry out the analysis (proficiency tests). Also, a significant percentage of FHEs decisions were inconclusive (between 30–50% of the datasets considered).

There are some commercially available tools for dynamic signature analysis (e.g., TOPAZ SigCompare[1] or KOFAX FraudOne[2]), which provide very limited functionalities to carry out a forensic analysis. This paper introduces e-BioSign, a new tool specifically designed to carry out forensic analysis of dynamic handwritten sig-

[1] http://www.topazsystems.com/sigcompare.html, accessed April 2015.

[2] http://www.kofax.com/products/kofax-signature-solutions/kofax-fraudone, accessed April 2015.

natures in order to facilitate the work of FHEs and give scientific support to their conclusions. In this sense, a survey of the methodology employed by the FHEs has been conducted and included in the functionalities of the tool. Together with these functionalities, e-BioSign tool also allows the measurement of dynamic information contained in the signatures, not taken into account normally by FHEs. With the use of dynamic signatures there is additional information available which can be used to carry out a more comprehensive and reliable forensic analysis.

Additionally, e-BioSign tool includes two important functionalities. On the one hand, it gives statistical support to the FHEs for some selected parameters such as the duration, fluency or level of tremor of the signatures. Population distributions for these parameters were computed for genuine and forged signatures allowing to position the questioned and known signatures under analysis on these distributions and extract some conclusions with statistical support. On the other hand, a dynamic signature verification system is included, from which a Likelihood Ratio (LR) can be obtained from the matching comparison between the signatures under analysis which is complementary to the analysis carried out by the FHE.

The remainder of the paper is organized as follows. Section 15.2 describes the traditional forensic practice followed to carry out the analysis of dynamic signatures. Section 15.3 describes e-BioSign tool with all its functionalities including the description of the statistical analysis carried out on a set of selected features in order to give statistical support to this forensic tool. Section 15.4 reports a Case Study using the tool for some genuine and forged dynamic signatures, and finally, Sect. 15.5 draws the final conclusions. This chapter is based on an extension of the previous work [18].

15.2 Forensic Practice for Signature Analysis

As mentioned, traditionally the practice of FHEs has been mainly concerned with the analysis of paper-based (offline) signatures. In order to carry out an analysis regarding the authorship of a questioned signature FHEs normally use some kind of variant of the following protocol.[3]

The first requirement is to have an appropriate set of signatures to perform the analysis, otherwise it wouldn't be possible to obtain convincing conclusions. Therefore, FHEs can ask the person whose signature is being investigated to provide a set of signatures (around 20) in order to have some samples produced with natural fluency. If the questioned signature was produced a considerable time before, then FHEs try to find some examples of contemporary genuine signatures.

Then, the analysis is performed taking into account aspects such as the **composition** of the signature (with or without name, surname, if legible, presence of flourish, etc.), **location** regarding other text or box (if it is close to the text or box on

[3]Based on published documentation from the Spanish Guardia Civil [4], the Netherland Forensic Institute [7] and the Victoria Police Forensic Services Centre (Australia) [3].

the right, left, etc.), **direction** (inclination of the written part regarding the horizontal, also the flourish), **written part** (FHEs carry out a comparison letter by letter), **flourish** (initial and final points and their direction), **fluency** and **pressure**. Even if in offline signature analysis fluency and pressure can not be measured as accurate as with dynamic signatures, this dynamic information is considered as an important and discriminative factor and it is estimated by analyzing the width of the stroke or the groove left in the paper.

Some important aspects taken into account by FHEs to detect forged signatures are the following: in general the forger is only able to focus in one of the two main aspects required to obtain a good quality forgery: (i) precision in the production of the signature (size, proportion and shape), or (ii) written fluently. Therefore, in general the forgeries can be precise regarding the appearance but not fluent, or written fluently but imprecise. Other signs to detect forgeries are changes in velocity in different strokes, tremors, monotonous pressure, traces of practice or guiding lines, unnatural pen lifts, corrections, etc. Also, the complexity of the signature is an important aspect to take into account as complex signatures are much harder to be forged.

15.3 e-BioSign Tool

This section describes the main functionalities of e-BioSign tool, which is a tool designed to be used by FHEs to carry out the analysis of dynamic signatures and give scientific support to their forensic reports. This first version of the tool has been developed under Matlab GUI interface, but a second version of the tool as an independent application is under development. The most important functionalities of this tool are:

- Several signatures can be loaded and visualized simultaneously (i.e., reference signatures and the signature under analysis).
- Signatures can be normalized in the spatial and time domains.
- Strokes can be manually selected for further analysis (to measure dimensions, angles, etc.).
- Statistical analysis of a selection of parameters can be conducted positioning the signatures under analysis in a population distribution.
- Automatic signature verification provides a matching score to complement the analysis of the FHE.

Next, the functionalities of e-BioSign Tool are described. We have divided these functionalities in four main modules.

15.3.1 Module 1: Signatures Loading and Normalization

Module 1 allows to load several signatures for further analysis. The signatures can be visualized simultaneously, i.e., both the spatial image of the signature and the dynamic information of the X and Y coordinates and pressure. This is very useful as questioned and known signatures can be visualized at the same time allowing to analyze similarities and dissimilarities. Figure 15.1 shows a screenshot of Module 1 of e-BioSign tool with three signatures loaded, two of them genuine and one forgery.

When loading the signatures the information regarding frequency sampling (in Hz) and spatial resolution (pixel per inch) needs to be entered in a pop up window. In the example shown in Fig. 15.1a it is interesting to see how the two genuine signatures (orange and blue) have similar time duration, while the forgery (black) has a longer duration. In Module 1, it is also possible to normalize the loaded signatures both in the spatial domain and in the time domain. In the spatial domain, three position normalizations are possible considering different reference points: (i) center of mass, (ii) geometric center, or (iii) beginning of the signatures. A size normalization can be also applied maintaining the aspect ratio of input signatures. In the time domain, the signatures can be resampled to have the same time length. Figure 15.1b shows the same three example signatures shown in Fig. 15.1a after time normalization. In this case, it is possible to see how the two genuine signatures provide a good match in X, Y and pressure values, while there are more dissimilarities (especially in the pressure) regarding the forged signature.

15.3.2 Module 2: Individual Signature Analysis and Stroke Selection

Module 2 allows to analyze the input signatures independently, and also to select strokes from each signature for further analysis. In order to analyze each signature, it is possible to reproduce the realization of the dynamic information of the signature, both in the spatial and time domains, with or without considering the pen-up dynamics. The pen-up dynamic information can be also visualized in the spatial representation. This is very interesting as this information can be very discriminative. Also, the pressure level information of each point can be incorporated in the visualization through a color map. Figure 15.2 shows a screenshot of Module 2 with one signature, in which the signature is represented with a color map based on the pressure values, and also the pen-up information is visible (in pink).

This module also allows to select strokes from the signature for a more detailed analysis. The strokes can be selected both by choosing initial and final points in the spatial representation of the signature, or using sliding bars in the time representation.

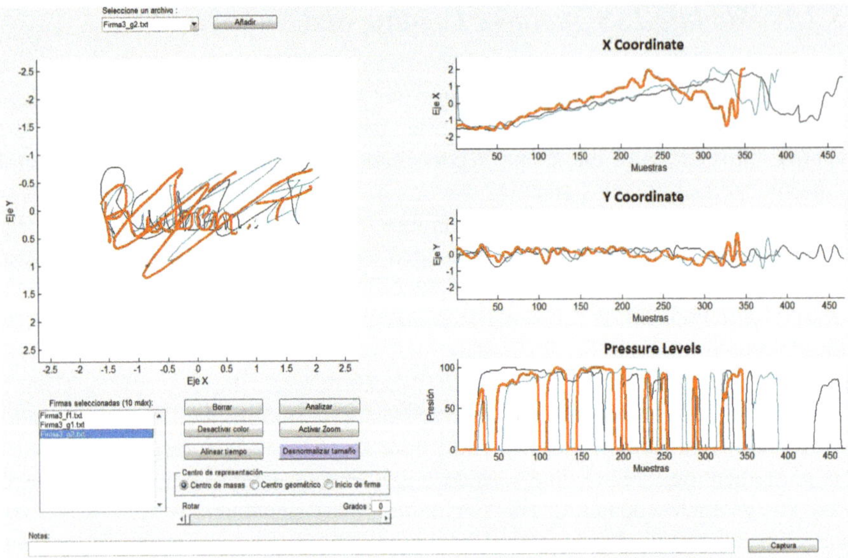

(a)

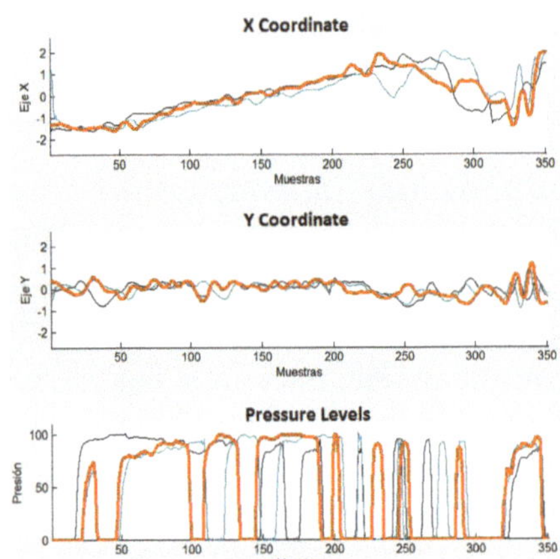

(b)

Fig. 15.1 **a** Screenshot of e-BioSign tool Module 1, which allows to load several signatures and carry out a joint analysis. **b** Same signals normalized in time

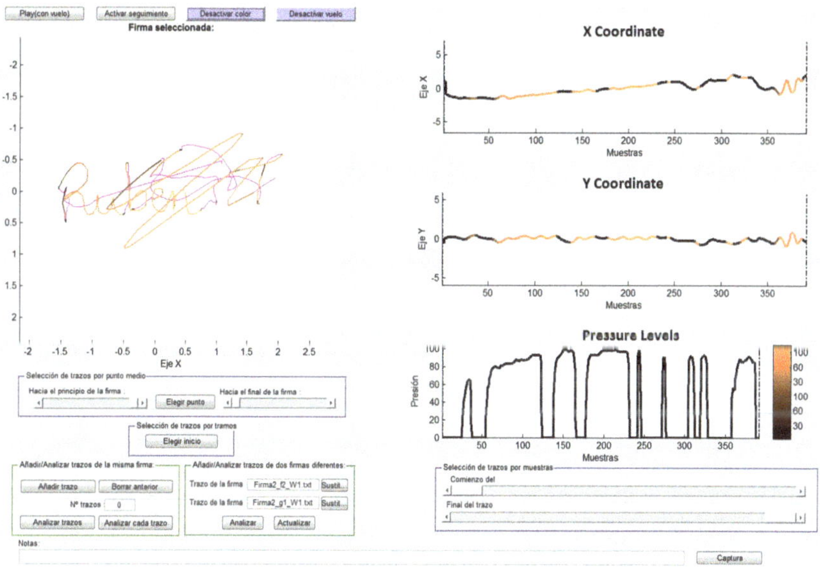

Fig. 15.2 Screenshot of e-BioSign tool Module 2, which allows to analyse signatures individually reproducing the dynamic of the signature and showing the pen-up information. Strokes can be selected for further analysis

15.3.3 Module 3: Strokes Analysis

Module 3 allows to carry out a more detailed analysis of the selected strokes from the signatures. It is worth noting that the whole signature can be also selected as one stroke. Figure 15.3 shows a screenshot of Module 3. On the left part, it is possible to visualize the dynamics of the velocity and acceleration, and below again the X and Y coordinates and pressure. The analysis here can be conducted on single or multiple strokes at the same time, from one or more different signatures.

In the middle part of Fig. 15.3 there are some additional functionalities: it is possible to rotate the stroke regarding the center of representation chosen (geometric center, center of mass or any other fixed points), the stroke thickness can also be selected, it is possible to zoom in and out the stroke and also the real sample points of the signature can be visualized. Moreover, this module allows to take measurements of the length (both in pixels and cm) and the angle of any segment with respect to the horizontal line (in degrees).

Module 3 also allows to carry out a statistical analysis of some features automatically extracted from the signatures, as can be seen on the right part of Fig. 15.3. The idea is to provide the forensic expert with a population distribution of genuine and forged signatures for a selection of features together with the actual value of these features for the signatures at hand. For the initial release of e-BioSign Tool five global features have been selected. Three of them are common in feature based

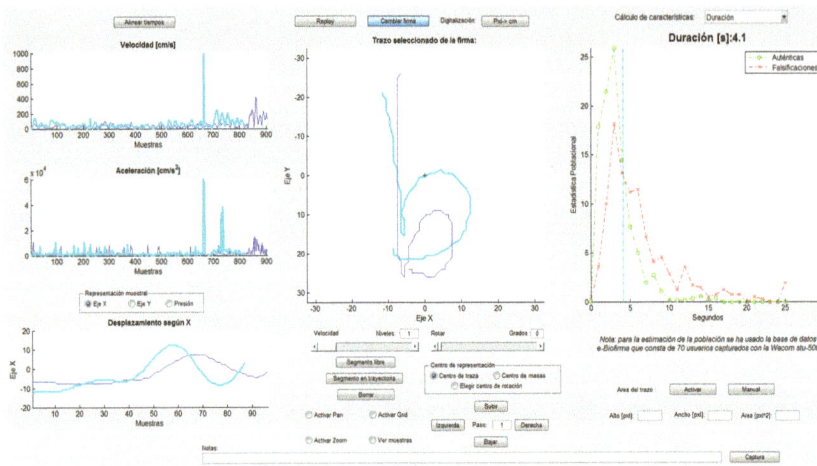

Fig. 15.3 Screenshot of e-BioSign tool Module 3. This module allows to carry out a detailed analysis of the selected strokes, it also allows to position the selected strokes (or signatures) in a population distribution of genuine and forged signatures for five selected features

dynamic signature recognition systems [14, 19]: total duration of the signature, average velocity and average acceleration. The other two parameters are commonly used in offline signature forensic analysis [2–6]: time fluency and spatial tremor. These two parameters are normally considered as good indicators to discriminate between genuine and forged signatures.

The **time fluency** of the signature is related to the number of samples with very low velocity in X and Y coordinates. Therefore, the time fluency was calculated following Eq. 15.1.

$$Fluency = \frac{-(N_{Vx} + N_{Vy})}{N} \tag{15.1}$$

where N_{Vx}, N_{Vy} and N correspond respectively to the number of samples with velocity in X or Y (*Vx* or *Vy*) equal or less than a threshold, which was set empirically to value 1 for obtaining Fig. 15.4, and N is the total number of time samples. The fluency is finally normalized in the range [0, 10] using an hyperbolic tangent normalization [20]:

$$Fluency' = \frac{10}{2}\{\tanh(1.5(\frac{Fluency - \mu}{\sigma})) + 1\} \tag{15.2}$$

where μ and σ are the mean and standard deviation of a set of signatures used exclusively to carry out the data normalization.

The **spatial tremor** present in the signatures can be due to low confidence in the realization of the (possibly forged) signature. The level of tremor of a signature was obtained using the Euclidean distance between the X and Y time functions of

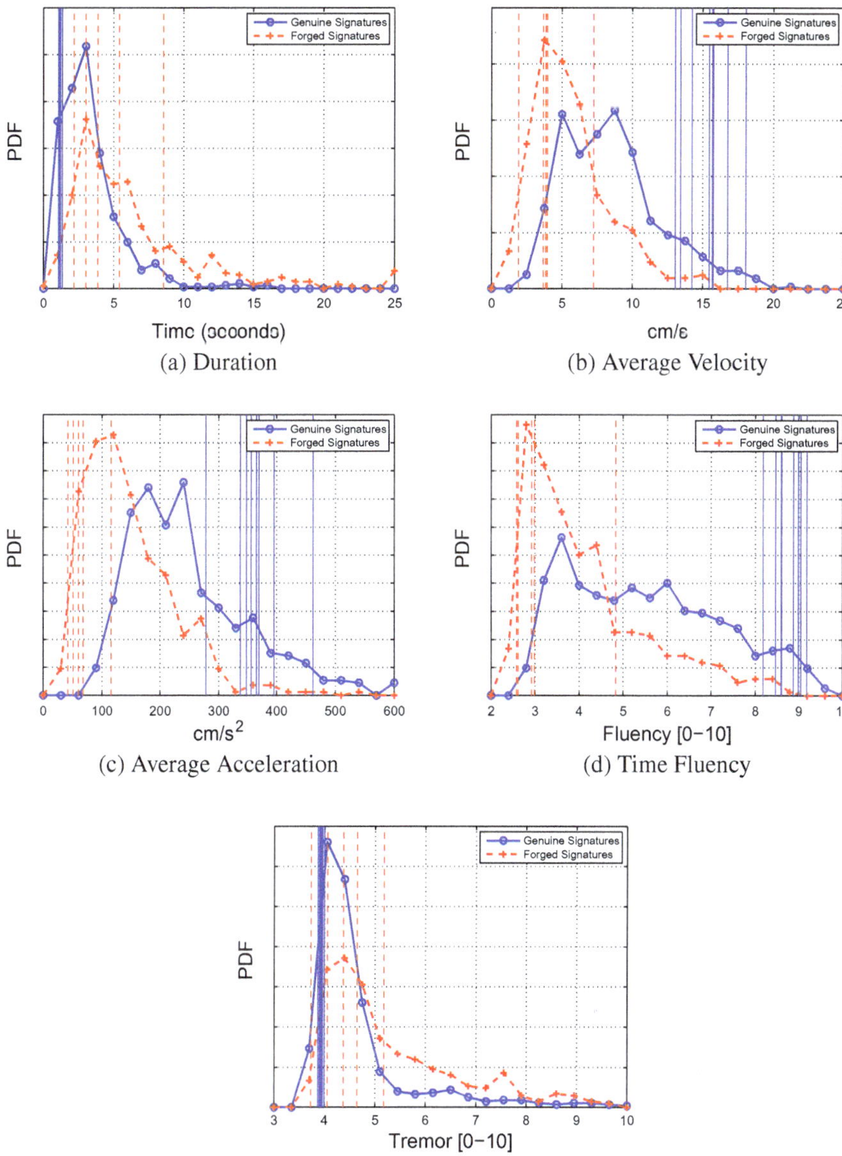

(a) Duration (b) Average Velocity

(c) Average Acceleration (d) Time Fluency

(e) Spatial Tremor

Fig. 15.4 Frequency histograms for genuine and forged signatures for the five selected parameters: **a** signature duration, **b** average velocity, **c** average acceleration, **d** time fluency, and **e** spatial tremor. *Vertical lines* show the positioning of the genuine and forgery signatures for a given user of the database

the signature to analyse and a smoothed version of them. This smoothed signature is obtained using a low pass Gaussian filter. Finally, these distance values for the tremor were also normalized to the [0, 10] range using the hyperbolic tangent method similar as before, adjusting the values of μ and σ accordingly for this case.

Figure 15.4 shows the population statistics for the five selected features. These distributions were obtained for a subset of e-BioSign database [21] which is comprised of 70 users signing on a Wacom STU-530 tablet. This database was comprised of eight genuine signatures per user and six skilled forgeries collected in two different sessions with a time gap of at least three weeks. The skilled forgeries signatures were performed in two different ways, in the first session forgers were allowed to visualize a recording of the dynamic realization of the signature to forge for a few times, while in the second session, a paper with the image of the signatures to forge was placed over the device and they can trace the lines to perform the forgery.

For each of the graphs shown in Fig. 15.4 we also show the position of the eight genuine and 6 forgery signatures with vertical lines for one of the users (as an example of use) inside the population distribution. This can help the FHEs to analyze if the questioned signatures are within the distribution of genuine signatures in general and for that user in particular. In the examples shown, it can be seen that for that particular user genuine and forgery signatures are well separated, especially for the average velocity, average acceleration and time fluency.

In a future release of e-BioSign Tool, in order to provide the FHEs with statistical support for these five parameters, apart from plotting population distributions, a Likelihood Ratio (LR) will be also provided for each parameter, which would be calculated from a matching score using the signatures under analysis, and using a LR model trained on a reference database (or a subset of it).

15.3.4 Module 4: Automatic Signature Verification

An additional functionality of e-BioSign Tool is Module 4, which is an automatic signature matcher. With this matcher, a questioned signature can be compared to a number of known or reference signatures to obtain a matching score.

The automatic signature matcher is based on a selection of time functions extracted from the signature such as the X and Y coordinates, the pressure, velocity, etc. Then, Dynamic Time Warping (DTW) is used to compare the similarity between the selected time functions extracted from the signatures [22]. The matching scores are then converted to likelihood ratios (LR) as commonly done in the forensic community [23–25]. In this case, e-BioSign database is used to train a likelihood ratio model following a logistic regression approach. As stated in [26], the aim of logistic regression is to obtain an affine transformation of an input dataset to generate an output value which optimizes an objective function. It may be demonstrated that logistic regression leads to LR values with low calibration loss from a training score set. In our case, Bosaris Toolkit [27] has been used.

In a first release of this tool, a person-generic LR model is considered, therefore obtaining same-source scores and different-source scores (in this last case comparing genuine signatures with skilled forgeries signatures). In future releases, functionalities to select a group of specific users by age, hand they use to sign, complexity of the signature, etc., will be provided in order to obtain more meaningful LR models for the particular case to study.

15.4 Case Study

In this section we describe a case study for e-BioSign Tool. In this example, we analyze two genuine signatures from a given user and two skilled forgeries. Signatures are acquired using a Wacom STU-530 device. The two skilled forgeries are performed in different ways, for the first one the forger places a printed copy with the signature to forge on top of the device and traces the lines to perform the forgery (for the remaining of the analysis we refer to it as *traced forgery*). For the second one, the forger carries out the forgery directly on the device after practicing a few times on a paper (we refer to it as *natural forgery*). In both cases, the forger is allowed to visualize a recording of the dynamic realization of the signature to forge for a few times in order to obtain good quality forgeries.

This case example is not meant to be an exhaustive forensic analysis of the signatures as the one that would be done by a FHE. The purpose is to show with real examples how the functionalities of e-BioSign Tool can be used to analyze and measure the similarities and dissimilarities of dynamic signatures.

First, signatures are loaded for their analysis on e-BioSign Tool. Figure 15.5 shows the two genuine signatures (Module 1). They are both normalized in the spatial domain by the center of mass. Both signatures have a similar time duration and a striking similar shape of their X, Y and pressure temporal values, even not being aligned in time. This shows that this user is very consistent performing his signature. There are some parts (beginning and end) with some time misalignments which can be better analyzed with functionalities present in Module 3 of the tool.

Figure 15.6 shows the same two genuine signatures and the traced forgery signature. As can be seen, the traced forgery has a much longer time duration with more than double number of samples (almost 2,000 samples which correspond to 10 s as the Wacom STU-530 was configured to sample at 200 Hz, compared to less than 700 samples for both genuine signatures), which can be a sign that the signature has been performed by a forger. Figure 15.7 shows the three signatures aligned in time, with the forgery having longer strokes in general (particularly at the flourish) and also shorter duration pen-ups.

Figure 15.8 shows the same two genuine signatures as previously and the natural forgery signature. As can be seen, this forgery contains a similar number of time samples compared to the two genuine and in general shows a similar shape. We will describe the subsequent analysis steps using these three signatures with the remaining modules of the tool.

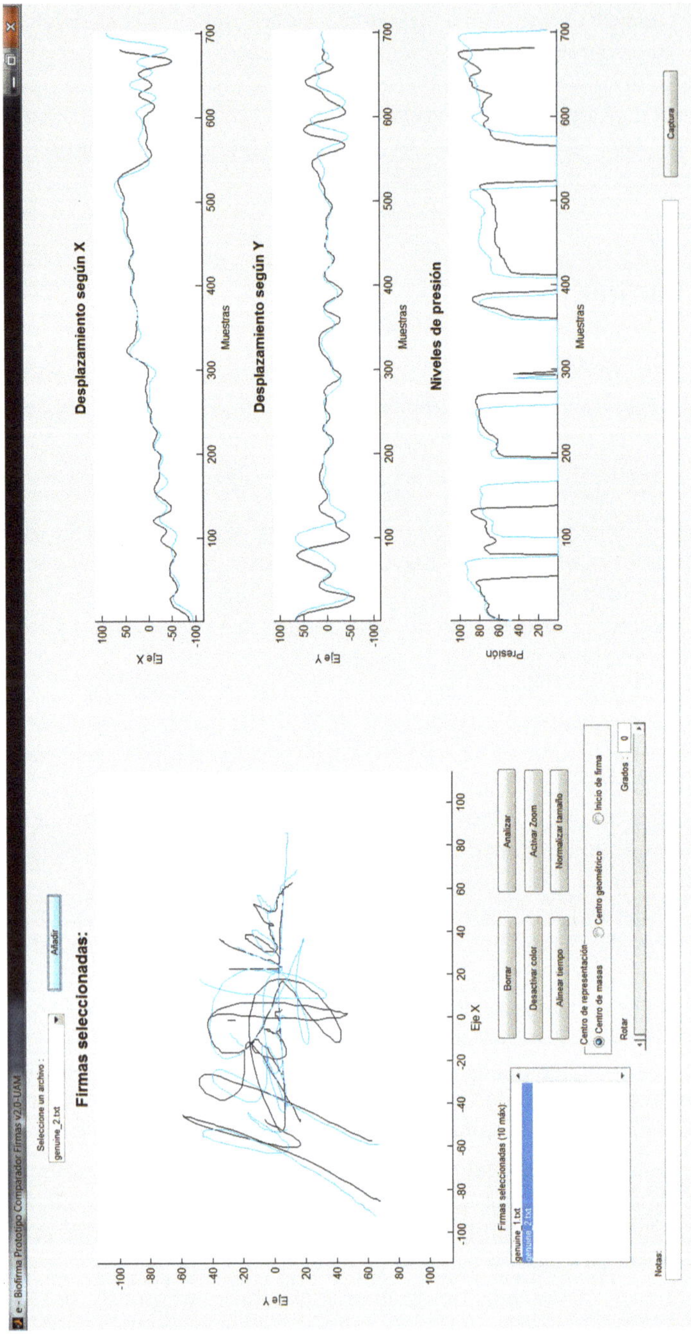

Fig. 15.5 Examples of two genuine signatures from the same user (reference known samples)

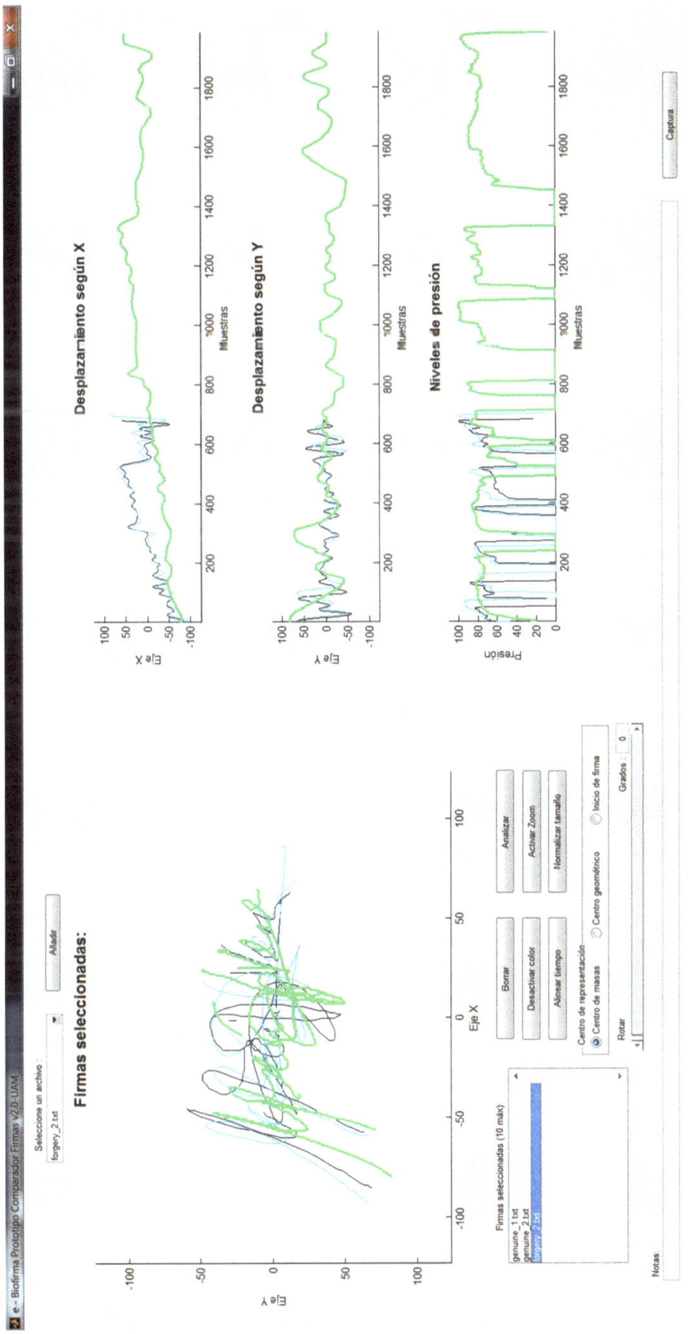

Fig. 15.6 Examples of two genuine signatures and one traced forgery signature

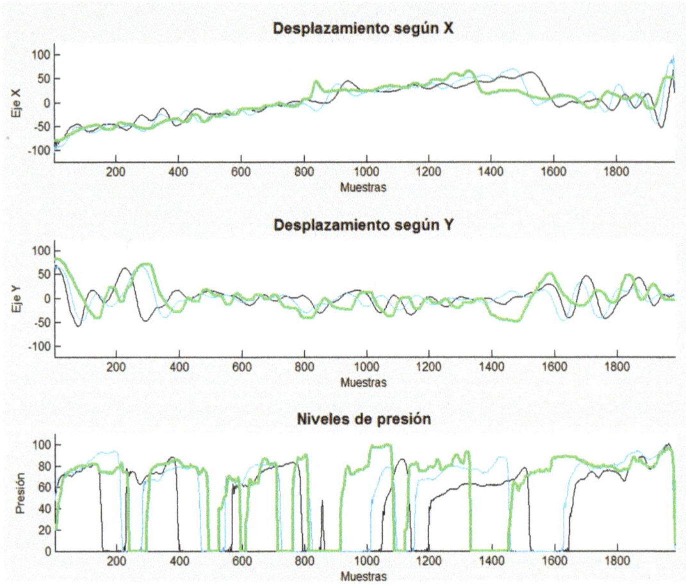

Fig. 15.7 Same signals as Fig. 15.6 but normalized in time

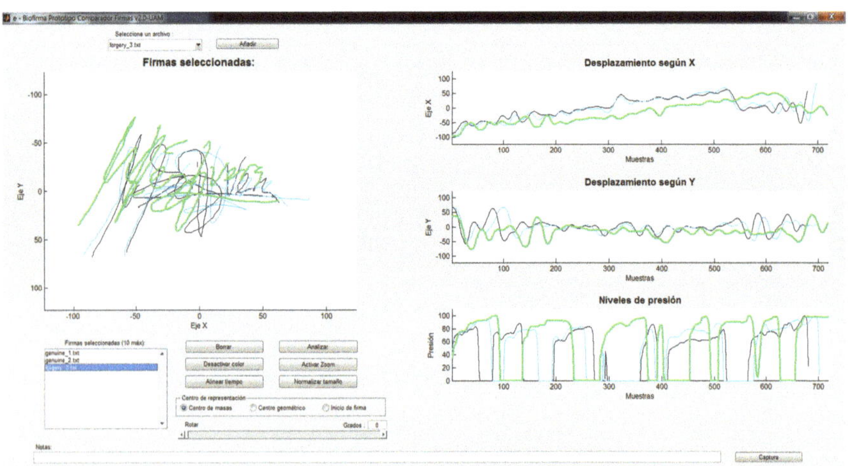

Fig. 15.8 Examples of two genuine signatures and one natural forgery

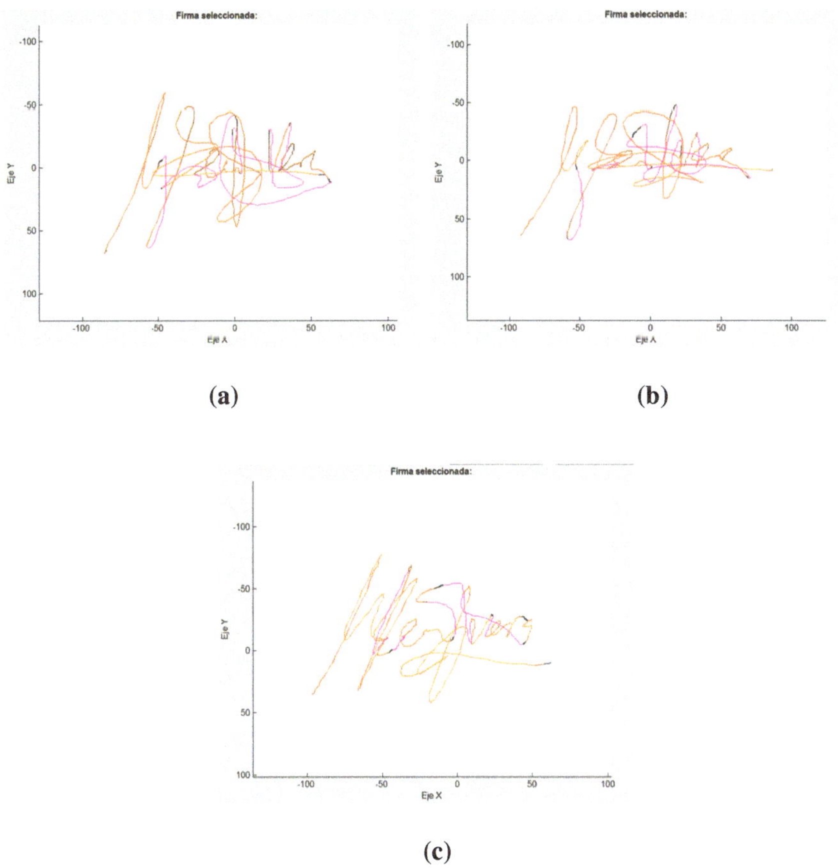

Fig. 15.9 Module 2. Spatial information (X and Y coordinates) also showing the pen-up information for **a** and **b** genuine signatures, and **c** forged signature

Module 2 of e-bioSign Tool is used to carry out a comparative general analysis of the signatures and to select some strokes for further analysis. Figure 15.9 shows the spatial information (X and Y coordinates) for the three signatures under analysis (the two genuine and the natural forgery). Also, the pen-up information is shown in pink color. Having a general look at the three signatures, there are some features quite different between the two genuine signatures and the forgery. For example, some letters have different shapes, or the last line of the flourish is placed just below the name letters for the genuine signatures, while it is placed much lower for the forgery. Additionally, Module 2 allows to visualize the direction of the trajectory of the signatures, indicating the beginning and end and connecting the different strokes as can be visualized in Fig. 15.10. With this functionality is easy to check that the signatures under analysis follow the same trajectory pattern.

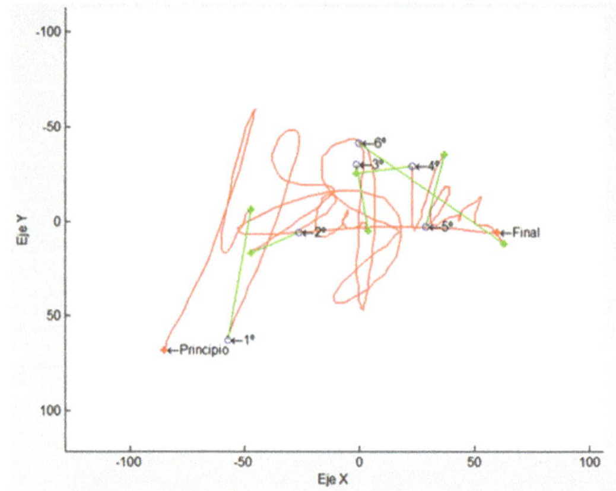

Fig. 15.10 Module 2. Trajectory information for one of the genuine signatures

Figure 15.11 shows the X and Y coordinates and pressure information along the time axis for the same three signatures. Having a close analysis to Fig. 15.11a, b, the two genuine signatures have very similar temporal information, following the same pattern for the X, Y and pressure axes. However, although there are some general similarities with the remaining signature (c), a close analysis reveals many differences, such as: the accent mark (samples around 300 for the two genuine and around 400 for the forgery) has a longer duration and higher pressure value compared to the two genuine; in general the pressure information presents higher values (for example see the last stroke). Also, the last part of the forged signature (Fig. 15.11c) (samples between 500 and 650) presents a completely different pressure pattern compared to the two genuine. Moreover, the are some strokes with very different pattern for the X and Y coordinates (the second stroke, for example). Some of these strokes of the signatures are selected for further analysis using Module 3 of the tool.

Module 3 of e-bioSign Tool is now used to carry out a more detailed analysis for some of the strokes selected with Module 2. Figure 15.12 shows the spatial and temporal information (X, Y, pressure, velocity and acceleration) that can be visualized in Module 3 for a comparison of the flourish stroke for the two genuine signatures (a) and one of the genuines and the forgery (b). These strokes have been aligned spatially for a better comparison with a shift in X and Y coordinates and rotation (for which the tool incorporates semi-automatic functionalities).

Figure 15.12a shows that even though the two flourish strokes do not have exactly the same spatial shape, the time functions follow a very similar pattern, with only a small difference in Y coordinates for samples between 60 and 90. It is possible to see how the velocity and acceleration functions follow a very similar pattern with just small time misalignments. On the other hand, Fig. 15.12b shows the same for one genuine signature and the forgery under analysis. In this case the differences between the two signatures are very significant both in spatial shape and for all the time functions.

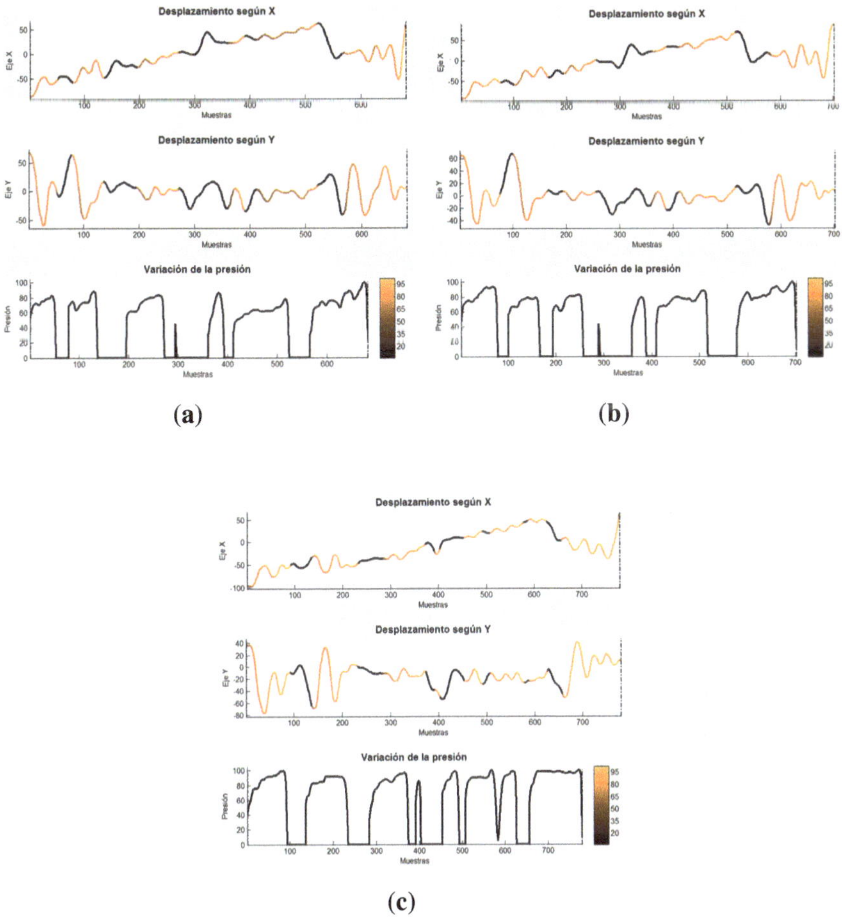

Fig. 15.11 Module 2. Temporal X, Y and pressure coordinates information for **a** and **b** genuine signatures, and **c** forged signature

For completeness, we also show in Fig. 15.13 the pen-up information that can be visualized (in red) with Module 3. In the case shown, following the trajectory of the pen-up information we can observe that the accent mark can be seen that is performed following a different trajectory for the genuine signature (a) and the forgery. This difference, although small, can be very significant for a FHE to give an opinion on these signatures.

Module 3 also allows to carry out a statistical analysis of five parameters extracted automatically. The values of these parameters for the four signatures considered in this case example are shown in Table 15.1. It is worth noting that in a real case analysis carried out by a FHE, a larger number of reference or known signatures should be considered (if possible) in order to carry out the analysis with higher statistical

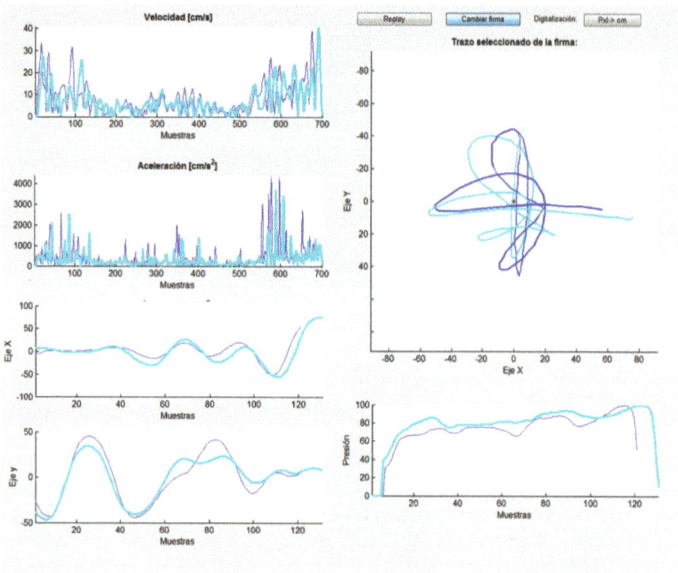

(a)

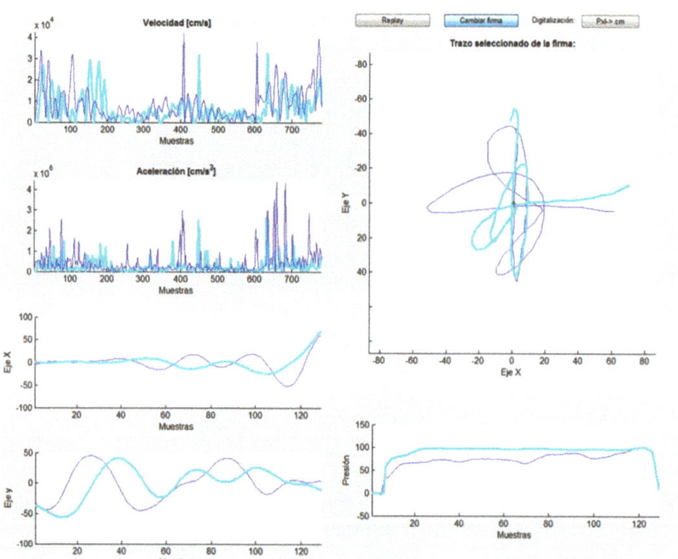

(b)

Fig. 15.12 Module 3. Comparison of the flourish stroke with their spatial and time information (X, Y, pressure, velocity and acceleration). **a** Genuine-genuine comparison and **b** genuine-forgery comparison

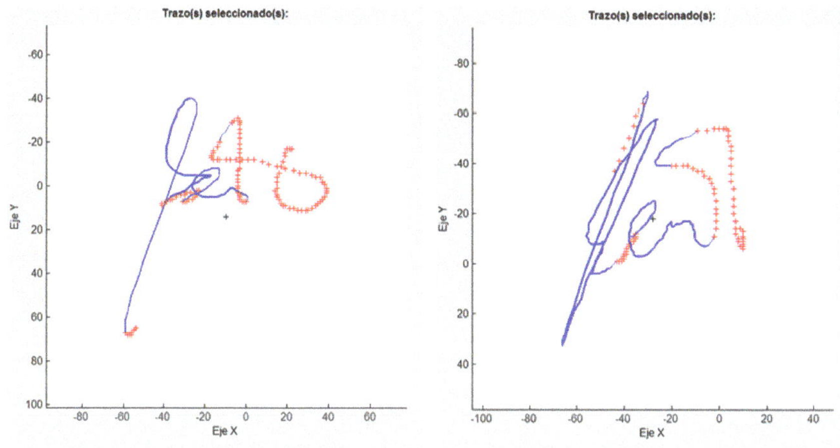

(a) (b)

Fig. 15.13 Module 3. Comparison of a stroke for one **a** genuine and **b** the natural forgery signatures with their spatial information. Also pen-up samples are shown for a more complete analysis

Table 15.1 Values of the five statistical parameters obtained for the four signatures under analysis. Time fluency and spatial tremor are normalized to the range [0–10]

	Genuine 1	Genuine 2	Traced forgery	Natural forgery
Duration (s)	3,4	3,5	9,9	3,9
Average velocity (cm/s)	8,4	7,7	2,6	6,4
Average acceleration (cm/s^2)	302,9	273,6	64,7	228,4
Time fluency	6,3	5,8	2,8	5,2
Spatial tremor	3,8	3,7	5,2	3,8

significance. The values shown in Table 15.1 can be visualized on top of the population distributions as per Fig. 15.4. As can be seen in the table, the two genuine signatures obtain similar values for the five parameters considered. Also, the natural forgery obtains similar values for these five parameters with just a bit longer duration, lower velocity, lower acceleration, lower fluency value and similar tremor value, but not very significant difference with just two reference signatures to compare. On the other hand, the traced forgery obtains very different values for the five parameters, which would indicate with a higher confidence this signature was produced by a different person.

15.5 Conclusions

This paper has described a new tool e-BioSign specifically designed to carry out dynamic signature forensic analysis and give scientific support to FHEs. This tool allows to analyse the traditional information taken into account by FHEs to carry out the analysis for paper-based signatures, and also permits to exploit the dynamic information contained in signatures acquired from digitizing tablets which can be very discriminative. As mentioned in Sect. 15.2 it is very difficult to perfectly forge a signature, good forgeries normally either have a similar appearance and shape but are not written fluently, or the opposite. With the analysis of both spatial and time information for dynamic signatures using e-BioSign, we believe it will be easier for FHEs to detect forged signatures. Additionally, the tool incorporates two important functionalities, the first is the provision of statistical support to the analysis by including population statistics for genuine and forged signatures for some selected features (signature duration, average velocity and speed, time fluency, and spatial tremor), and the second is the incorporation of an automatic signature matcher which can provide a matching score between the known and questioned signatures under analysis.

For future work, this tool will be provided to FHEs for testing and a new version will be released based on their suggestions. Also, LR values will be provided for the signatures under analysis for the five statistical parameters considered. FHEs will be able to select a particular subset of the reference dataset (based on the gender, hand used for writing, age, etc.) in order to obtain more meaningful LR values for the particular cases under analysis.

Acknowledgements This work has been supported by project CogniMetrics TEC2015-70627-R (MINECO/FEDER) and in part by Cecabank e-BioFirma2 Contract.

References

1. Huber RA, Headrick AM (1999) Handwriting identification: facts and fundamentals. CRC Press
2. Found B, Dick D, Rogers D (1994) The structure of forensic handwriting and signature comparisons. Int J Speech Lang Law Forensic Linguist 1:183–196
3. Found B, Rogers D (1999) Documentation of forensic handwriting comparison and identification method: a modular approach. J Forensic Doc Examination 12:1–68
4. de la Uz Jimenez J (2013) Manual de Grafistica. Tirant Lo Blanch
5. Vinals F (2008) Boletin Electronico num. 8, tech. rep., Instituto de Ciencias del Grafismo
6. Galende-Diaz JC, Gomez-Barajas C (2008) En busca de la falsedad documental: La figura del perito caligrafico. In: Proceedings of the VII Jornadas Cientificas Sobre Documentacion Contemporanea (1868–2008), pp 193–231, Univ. Complutense de Madrid
7. Alewijnse L (2013) Forensic signature examination. In: Tutorial at international workshop on automated forensic handwriting analysis (AFHA)
8. Harralson HH (2012) Forensic document examination of electronically captured signatures. Digit Evid Elec Signat L Rev 9:67–73

9. Ahmad SMS, Ling LY, Anwar RM, Faudzi MA, Shakil A (2013) Analysis of the effects and relationship of perceived handwritten signature's size, graphical complexity, and legibility with dynamic parameters for forged and genuine samples. J Forensic Sci 58(3):724–731
10. Mohammed MCLA, Found B, Rogers D (2011) The dynamic character of disguise behavior for text-based, mixed, and stylized signatures. J Forensic Sci 56
11. Franke K (2009) Analysis of authentic signatures and forgeries. In: Geradts Z, Franke K, Veenman C (eds) Computational forensics. Lecture notes in computer science, vol 5718. Springer, Berlin, pp 150–164
12. Fierrez J, Ortega-Garcia J (2008) Handbook of biometrics, ch. On-line signature verification. Springer, pp 189–209
13. Fierrez J, Ortega-Garcia J, Ramos D, Gonzalez-Rodriguez J (2007) HMM-based on-line signature verification: feature extraction and signature modeling. Pattern Recognit Lett 28:2325–2334
14. Martinez-Diaz M, Fierrez J, Krish RP, Galbally J (2014) Mobile signature verification: feature robustness and performance comparison. IET Biometrics 3:267–277
15. Houmani N, Mayoue A, Garcia-Salicetti S, Dorizzi B, Khalil M, Moustafa M, Abbas H, Muramatsu D, Yanikoglu B, Kholmatov A, Martinez-Diaz M, Fierrez J, Ortega-Garcia J, Alcob JR, Fabregas J, Faundez-Zanuy M, Pascual-Gaspar J, Cardeoso-Payo V, Vivaracho-Pascual C (2012) Biosecure signature evaluation campaign (BSEC2009): evaluating online signature algorithms depending on the quality of signatures. Pattern Recognit 45:993–1003
16. Martinez-Diaz M, Fierrez J, Hangai S (2009) Encyclopedia of biometrics, ch. Signature matching. Springer
17. Malik M, Liwicki M, Dengel A, Found B (2013) Man vs. machine: a comparative analysis for forensic signature verification. In: Proceedings of the biennial conference of the international graphonomics society
18. Vera-Rodriguez R, Fierrez J, Ortega-Garcia J, Acien A, Tolosana R (2015) e-BioSign tool: towards scientific assessment of dynamic signatures under forensic conditions. In: Proceedings of the IEEE international conference on biometrics: theory, applications and systems (BTAS), (Washington), Sept 2015
19. Richiardi J, Ketabdar H, Drygajlo A (2005) Local and global feature selection for on-line signature verification. In: Proceedings of the eighth international conference on document analysis and recognition, vol 2, pp 625–629, Aug 2005
20. Jain A, Nandakumar K, Ross A (2005) Score normalization in multimodal biometric systems. Pattern Recognit 38(12):2270–2285
21. Vera-Rodriguez R, Tolosana R, Ortega-Garcia J, Fierrez J (2015) e-BioSign: stylus- and finger-input multi-device database for dynamic signature recognition. In: Proceedings of the 3rd international workshop on biometrics and forensics (IWBF), (Norway). IEEE Press, March 2015
22. Tolosana R, Vera-Rodriguez R, Ortega-Garcia J, Fierrez J (2015) Preprocessing and feature selection for improved sensor interoperability in online biometric signature verification. IEEE Access 3:478–489
23. Gonzalez-Rodriguez J, Fierrez-Aguilar J, Ramos-Castro D, Ortega-Garcia J (2005) Bayesian analysis of fingerprint, face and signature evidences with automatic biometric systems. Forensic Sci Int 155:126–140
24. Morrison GS (2011) Measuring the validity and reliability of forensic likelihood-ratio systems. Sci Justice 51(3):91–98
25. Ramos D, Gonzalez-Rodriguez J, Zadora G, Aitken C (2013) Information-theoretical assessment of the performance of likelihood ratio computation methods. J Forensic Sci 58(6):1503–1518
26. Gonzalez-Rodriguez J, Rose P, Ramos D, Toledano DT, Ortega-Garcia J (2007) Emulating DNA: rigorous quantification of evidential weight in transparent and testable forensic speaker recognition. IEEE Trans Audio Speech Lang Process 15:2104–2115
27. Brummer N, de Villiers E (2011) The BOSARIS toolkit user guide: theory, algorithms and code for binary classifier score processing. Tech. Rep, Agnitio

Part V
Ethical and Legal Issues

Chapter 16
Ethics and Policy of Forensic Biometrics

Emilio Mordini

Abstract Ethical issues raised by forensic biometrics partly overlap with general ethical implications of biometrics. They include issues related to collecting, processing, and storing, personal data, privacy, medical information, and respect for body integrity, risks of misuse and subversive use, and respect for human dignity. There are, however, also ethical issues specifically raised by forensic biometrics. One of them is particularly intriguing. It concerns the nature of biometric evidence and to what extent biometric findings could be accepted as an evidence in court. At a first glance, this problem could seem purely legal, without major ethical implications. Yet, at a deeper analysis, it turns out to have significant ethical components. I will focus on them and on some recent policy developments in this field.

Ethical issues raised by forensic biometrics partly overlap with general ethical implications of biometrics [1]. They include issues related to collecting, processing, and storing, personal data [2], privacy [3], medical information and respect for body integrity [4], risks of misuse and subversive use [5], respect for human dignity [6]. There are, however, also ethical issues specifically raised by forensic biometrics. One of them is particularly intriguing. It concerns the nature of biometric evidence and to what extent biometric findings could be accepted as an evidence in court. At a first glance, this problem could seem purely legal, without major ethical implications. Yet, at a deeper analysis, it turns out having significant ethical components. I will focus on them and on some recent policy developments in this field.

E. Mordini (✉)
Responsible Technology SAS, 12 rue de la Chaussee d'Antin, 75009 Paris, France
e-mail: emilio.mordini@rtexpert.com

M. Tistarelli and C. Champod (eds.), *Handbook of Biometrics for Forensic Science*, Advances in Computer Vision and Pattern Recognition,
DOI 10.1007/978-3-319-50673-9_16

16.1 Biometric Evidence in Law Enforcement and Criminal Justice

The history of biometrics largely coincides with the history of its forensic applications, which include applications used for crime prevention, crime investigation, and administration of justice. Also prejudicial scientific discourses applied to criminology, such as physiognomy and phrenology, owed mostly to biometrics their temporary good scientific reputation (incidentally, this is likely to be one the reasons why biometrics have had later on such a bad press among human rights advocates and ethicists).

In early 1900s, law enforcement agencies started collecting fingerprints from convicted criminals and suspected individuals, and rather soon, they created vast fingerprint libraries. In parallel, the refinement of methods for latent fingerprints retrieval made biometric identification a fundamental tool for investigation at the crime scene. Finally, fingerprints (and later on, palm prints and impressions of bare soles) were accepted as admissible evidence into courts in most jurisdictions. Since then, biometrics (chiefly fingerprint) have been increasingly used for revealing or confirming the identity of people involved in the criminal investigation or in the judicial process (including victims); for establishing whether an accused person was at the scene of a crime or used an item that was used in perpetration of the crime; whether other person was at the scene of the crime or touched an item that was used in perpetration of the crime; whether an alleged victim was at some place that was consistent with the prosecution; whether a witness was at a place it is claimed he was. Biometrics have been also used to impeach the credibility or integrity of a suspect or a witness or a victim, based upon criminal records that show his prior history. Into courts, biometrics provided also a certain, additional, "scientific objectivity" to "traditional" (e.g., eyewitness) circumstantial evidence.

The way of assessing of biometric findings varies among jurisdictions, notably between common law and civil law systems. There are, however, also important similarities. As it happens with most scientific evidences,[1] usually biometric findings are not considered immediate evidence, but they have to be presented in court by one or more qualified experts who provide their testimony. Their opinions are assessed by the judge, who takes the final decision about whether biometric findings are admissible as an evidence in that specific case. In some jurisdictions (especially in the civil law area) the law establishes the minimum number of biometric details that should be analyzed in order to produce a positive identification; in other jurisdictions (especially in the common law area), the judge simply assesses experts' qualification and credibility. In both cases, the judge asks the expert to state whether a given biometric finding allows recognizing an individual, say, whether it matches with any recorded biometrics collected in the past, or with biometrics

[1]"Scientific evidence" in court is an evidence that is inferred from a known fact by using the scientific method.

gathered from any relevant individual involved in the judicial procedure. Experts are expected to answer yes or no.

In conclusion, the main events occurring under the heading of forensic biometrics include (1) the preventive activity of police and other law enforcement agencies, which collect biometrics from convicted criminals and suspected individuals in order to monitor them and prevent crime; (2) if a crime occurs, biometrics could be collected on the crime scene and in other relevant contexts, in order to ascertain the identify of supposed victims, suspected criminals, and alleged witnesses; (3) finally biometric findings are usually brought into court where the judge (after hearing experts and parties) decides whether, and to what extent, these findings could be considered an evidence and will contribute to form the judicial decision.

16.2 Digital Biometrics

This scenario is changing with the arrival of new digital biometrics. New digital biometrics (automated biometrics) entered into the market in the late 1970s, chiefly thanks to the development of new sensors, capable of capturing a vast array of different inputs. Sensors are devices that turn various inputs—generated by the interaction between them and physical object—into electrical outputs, whose electrical magnitude is proportional to the magnitude of the initial signal. Through the repetitive measurement of the electric output at certain intervals of time, the magnitude of the voltage is turned into a proportional number, which is further encoded into a binary number, or a gray code, or still in other ways. This allows representing bodily attributes (including those that were traditionally considered qualitative, such a skin color, or walking style) as measurable physical properties.[2] Two or more individuals could be subsequently compared in quantitative terms to ascertain whether they share the same properties as far as specific bodily attributes are concerned. From such a comparison, one could deduce whether two (apparent) individuals are actually the same individual, whose attributes were captured in different fractions of time, say, one could identify the individual (in the literally sense of assessing whether there is only one individual, considered under different accounts, instead of two or more distinct individuals). The main conceptual differences between pre-digital and digital biometrics is that digitalization allows performing the comparison (1) always in quantitative terms, avoiding qualitative assessment; (2) automatically, by exploiting ad hoc computer algorithms; (3) on a huge number of bodily attributes, unthinkable in the pre-digital era.

---

[2]Physical properties are discrete elements that can be put in bi-univocal correspondence with a set of numbers. There are seven base physical properties, Length, Mass, Time, Electric Current, Temperature, Amount of Substance, and Luminous Intensity. Biometric sensors measure one or more of these properties.

Absolute identity is logically and practically impossible. It does not take a Heraclitus, to realize that all bodily attributes, even the most stable and persistent, change (maybe slightly) over time, and conditions of data collection change, as well as sensor sensitivity. In other words, biometric features vary, sometime degrade by themselves; moreover, they also vary in the way in which they are presented to sensors. Finally, sensor precision is limited and may vary at different sites and according to different conditions of usage. This implies that it is impossible that two or more data sets captured by a sensor and turned into digits might exactly match, digit by digit. In other words, digital biometric recognition is always by approximation, and it inevitably implies some errors. This could be mitigated by creating, storing and comparing normalized biometric samples, called "templates". Yet errors cannot be eliminated because of their systematic nature. Accordingly, one of the main features to be considered in any given biometric system is always its error rate. One speaks of "false rejection", or "false negative", when the system fails to recognize someone; and "false acceptation", or "false positive", when the system recognizes someone erroneously. The ratio between false negatives and the total examined population is called "specificity"; the ratio between false positives and the total examined population is called "sensitivity". Specificity indicates the system ability to discriminate between different individuals; sensitivity indicates the system ability to detect all searched individuals. In principle, sensitivity and specificity are independent, in practice; there is a tradeoff, such that they are almost inversely proportional to one another. Also pre-digital biometrics could not avoid systematic errors, but their degree of uncertainty have been never studied in rigorous probabilistic terms, as it is today with new digital biometrics.

If only biometric features perfectly matching, point by point, led to recognition, the system would never recognize anyone because such a perfect identity can never be obtained. Consequently, the system tolerance level must be tuned, that is to say, the system must be "told" within what confidence interval it should consider two different biometric sets as though they were identical. In practice, this means that engineers have to decide when the gap between two biometric series can be considered negligible. Rather intuitively, the narrower the confidence interval is, the higher are the probabilities that the recognition is accurate, say, there will be less false positive. Yet, with a too narrow confidence interval, the system would increase the risk of failing to recognize the same individual presented twice, because the gap between his biometric features, taken in different moments and circumstances, could fall outside the confidence interval. Larger confidence intervals would mitigate this risk, but they would increase false acceptation (someone confused with someone else). It is important to emphasize that there is not a "right" confidence interval, but it depends on the specific context and application. Ultimately, the decision on the confidence interval depends on the policy adopted by system administrators.

16.3 Probabilistic Biometrics in Court

Past debates on forensic biometrics chiefly focused on conditions of admissibility of biometric evidence and qualifications of expert witnesses [7]. Today, legal experts, jurists, and scholars find increasingly problematic the probabilistic nature of biometric identification. I will only hint at the main terms of this debate, which is richer and full of nuances, because it is not the focus of my article, although it is a necessary premise to my argument.

Current debate on probabilistic biometrics in court is driven by two main facts. The first is a 1993 decision of the US Supreme Court,[3] which introduced new standards for scientific evidence. Although this decision was directly relevant only to the US legal system, its philosophy is considered a benchmark and has deeply influenced many other legal systems, including those belonging to the civil law area. In this sentence the Supreme Court ruled that a scientific evidence could be admitted into court only if it respects the following five criteria: (1) the evidence "can be (and has been) tested" using a scientific method; (2) such a method has "been subjected to peer review and publication"; (3) it is known the "potential rate of error" of the method in question; (4) the "existence and maintenance of standards controlling the technique's operation"; (5) the "general acceptance" of the technique within the relevant scientific community. Would biometric evidence survive *Daubert* criteria? This has been the core discussion, developed first within the US forensic community and then among scholars and legal experts belonging to other jurisdictions and legal schools. In particular, some scholars [8, 9] have argued that the scientific soundness and reliability of expert-testimony-based biometrics is definitely suboptimal. This was emphasized also by a few clamorous cases of error, for instance the one that occurred in the wake of Madrid terrorist attack [10].

The second driver of the current debate is a technological driver. With the rapid development of new digital biometrics (and a vast array of new biometric applications, exploiting modalities whose existence were not even imaginable in the pre-digital era) the issue of probabilistic identification has become paramount. Scholars [11, 12] have advocated a more mindful, and scientifically refined, approach to forensic biometric by adopting a probabilistic mindset. For instance, Champod et al. [13] have suggested that, instead of posing the naïf question whether a biometric feature is ***identical*** to another, a biometric examiner should ask to himself "*Given the detail that has been revealed and the comparison that has been made, what inference might be drawn in relation to the propositions that I have set out to consider?*' (p. 25).

The two discussions are clearly intertwined, as *Daubert* criteria should be applied to new digital biometrics, and digital biometrics should come to terms to more stringent legal criteria for admissibility of scientific evidence [14]. The interplay between the notion of forensic evidence and the probabilistic nature of

---

[3]Daubert v. Merrell Dow Pharm. Inc., 727 F. Supp. 570, 575 (S.D. Cal. 1989).

biometrics is the core of the next chapters, in which I will present my central argument.

16.4 Law Enforcement and Administration of Justice: Two Different Missions

In the first chapter of this paper, I listed the main activities included under the heading of forensic biometrics, say, anticipation of crime, criminal investigation, and administration of justice. Although practically and theoretically distinct, these three main activities belong to a unique cycle, whose languages must be interoperable if the cycle works. Two of these activities (anticipation of crime and criminal investigation) are carried out by law enforcement agencies; the third (administration of justice) is up to the judicial system. Law enforcement and judicial systems are thus distinct but interoperable. Their missions are different, yet in democratic and liberal societies, they have been developed rather harmonically in order to compensate each other.

Law enforcement's overarching mission is to prevent, and, in case, repress crime. To be sure, crime prevention includes many other activities, which are not up to law enforcement agencies, such as education, social policies, urban management, and so. Yet, there is an important aspect of crime prevention that is up to law enforcement authorities, that is to say, pre-crime (anticipative) investigation. Anticipative investigation [15] aims to prevent crime by identifying potential criminals and future criminal events, and by taking action accordingly. Ultimately, anticipative investigation is based on the assessment and management of risks, its goal is to prevent risks or, at least, to mitigate them. While anticipative investigation is proactive, criminal investigation is reactive, it follows crime and it aims to ascertain facts, identify, and prove the guilt of one or more suspects. Ultimately, its goal is to repress crime by bringing the suspects into the judicial system. Overall, anticipative and criminal investigations do not aim to discover truth, to pursue justice, or to achieve fairness—at least as their primary goal—rather they simply aim to reduce the rate of crimes in society. Unpleasant though it may sound, law enforcement must be ruled by the "principle of suspicion" (of course opportunely mitigated), that is to say, anybody could be in principle suspected.

The judicial system aims instead to administer the justice. What is "justice"? Lay citizens often think that making justice means to discover factual truth about a crime or a civil case. Yet legal scholars know that in court factual truth is hardly at stake. Actually, the business of a court of justice is not to discover the truth, as Oxford professor and distinguished English legal scholar, Sir Frederick Pollock (1845–1937) put it,

> Its real business is to pronounce upon the justice of particular claims, and incidentally to test the truth of assertions of fact made in support of the claim in law, provided that those assertions are relevant in law to the establishment of the desired conclusions [16]

In other words, the goal of the judicial procedure is not to ascertain the "truth" in trivial sense, rather to identify the "legal truth". The "legal truth" is the truth as it emerges from the judicial hearing [17]. It may or may not corresponds to the totality of facts. Even when it does not correspond to facts, the "legal truth" is still practically effective, say, it produces effects, as it is showed, for instance, by the principle that a defendant cannot be tried twice on the same charge following a legitimate court decision. The notion of "legal truth" is better understood by considering it in parallel with another notion, which is foundational for the whole Western legal system, the principle of presumption of innocence. Presumption of innocence is a legal principle adopted in criminal cases. In criminal cases, the gap between "factual" and "legal" truths could produce inacceptable outcomes; presumption of innocence mitigates this risk. Its original formulation dates back to Roman law and reads "*Ei incumbit probatio qui dicit, non qui negat*" (the burden of proof is on he who declares, not on he who denies), also "*in dubio pro reo*" (when in doubt, for the accused).[4]

In modern terms, presumption of innocence is usually expressed by saying that a defendant is innocent until proven guilty,

> In a criminal case the truth of facts against the accused must be established "beyond a reasonable doubt," and in certain civil cases, e.g., where punitive damages may be awarded for fraud, the truth of facts against the defendant must usually be shown by "a clear and convincing preponderance of the evidence". The more that is at stake, e.g., criminal blame, or punitive damages, the higher the standard of proof. In an ordinary civil case involving an ordinary claim for damages, the facts against the defendant need only be shown by a "balance of probabilities", a significantly lower standard of truth. Thus, depending on the relevant standard of truth, the very same evidence would warrant a finding of truth in one type of case but not in another. Thus, truth varies with standards of proof, and standards of proof vary with what is at stake. Yet, as indicated, there are good reasons for these variations in standards of truth. In criminal cases for example, we accept a higher risk of erroneous acquittals in order to minimize the risk of erroneous convictions. Moreover, this may have the effect of increasing the total number of erroneous verdicts. Our tolerance for the risk of divergence, here, goes up the more that is at stake [17]

Presumption of innocence, which was initially a legal procedural rule, has become one of the main principles of Western legal systems, a constitutional principle in many democracies,[5] and a fundamental human right. The Universal Declaration of Human Rights, Article 11, reads

> Everyone charged with a penal offence has the right to be presumed innocent until proved guilty according to law in a public trial at which he has had all the guarantees necessary for his defense

Similarly Article 6.2 of the Convention for the Protection of Human Rights and Fundamental Freedoms of the Council of Europe reads

---

[4]"*Digesta seu Pandectae* 22.3.2" (http://webu2.upmf-grenoble.fr/Haiti/Cours/Ak/Corpus/d-22.htm).

[5]Presumption of innocence is mentioned for instance by Italian, French, German, Brazilian, Canadian, Russian constitutions. It is not explicitly mentioned by the US Constitution, yet there is a consensus that it follows from the 5th, 6th, and 14th amendments.

> Everyone charged with a criminal offence shall be presumed innocent until proved guilty according to law

Finally, the same principle is iterated by Article 48 of the Charter of Fundamental Rights of the European Union, which reads

> Everyone who has been charged shall be presumed innocent until proved guilty according to law

In conclusion, law enforcement and administration of justice have different (although congruent) missions and follow two distinct logics; the former is ruled by the *principle of suspicion*, while the latter is governed by the *presumption of innocence*. In democracies, these two different perspectives are mutually consistent, because systematic errors made by the former are compensated by systematic errors made by the latter. In other words, the law enforcement system shows a natural tendency to minimize false negative (no criminal should get off scot-free), although this could rise false positive (an innocent could be unjustly accused); the judicial system shows the opposite behavior, say, it aims to keep false positive as lower as possible (no innocent should be wrongly condemned), although it could increase false negative (it could happen that a guilty individual is acquitted). If the two systems work properly, and each one of them respects its mission, the overall cycle functions rather well because opposite errors mutually compensate. The law enforcement tight mesh net may capture also innocents, but they will be eventually released by the judicial wider mesh net (of course, it is always possible that a criminal escapes and an innocent is condemned, I am just arguing that the two systems are theoretically complementary).

16.5 Probabilistic Biometrics and Presumption of Innocence

I have illustrated the probabilistic nature of biometric recognition and the way in which biometric applications deal with it, by tuning the tolerance of the system according to different user requirements. I would like now to pose a question: could law enforcement and judicial systems adopt the same degree of tolerance? Say, are user requirements the same in the two systems, which jointly form the forensic cycle? This question could seem purely technical; on the contrary, I argue that it is the main ethical question raised by forensic biometrics.

Suppose that positive identification is the critical element to determine who committed a crime (e.g., detecting and identifying terrorists who attacked a metro station). Suppose that positive identification should rely on biometrics (e.g., face recognition carried out on a videotape recorded on the crime scene) and suppose that the biometric matching system is based on a similarity score[6], which range from 0.0

[6]Beyond similarity scores, there are also other mathematical tools used for comparing two biometrics, but this would not change the sense of my example.

(no match at all) to 1.0 (exact match digit by digit). As I have previously explained, a perfect match is theoretically and practically impossible, consequently the similarity score should be set by administrators at any value lower than 1.0. For instance, if one sets the system at a similarity score of 0.95, it means that only biometrics which have a score beyond this threshold will match. Now, suppose that we know (from previous performance tests) that a 0.95 score implies a very low—suppose 0.1%—risk of false recognition (that is to say, almost all recognitions are right). Yet from the same tests, we also know that the score 0.95 implies 20% failed recognition (20% guilty individuals who escape from our biometric fishnet). If we lower the score to 0.75, the failed recognition rate will decrease dramatically to 1% (only 1% guilty individuals would escape recognition). Unfortunately, such a lower score would also provoke a hike of false recognitions, which would increase to 10%, say, our fishnet will wrongly fish also 10% innocent people. What should system administrators do? In the investigation phase, they would be plenty legitimate to set the system at the lowest similarity score compatible with its correct use. This would respect the logic behind criminal investigation, which aims to avoid that a criminal gets off scot-free. This might imply that some 10% innocent people are unjustly accused of being terrorists. In an ideal world, these people would be discharged by the judicial system. What happens if probabilistic digital biometrics is admitted as an evidence in court? It happens that the 10 % innocent people of our example are burdened by a "positive identification", notwithstanding the doubt that they could be "false positive". The principle of presumption of innocence is de facto bypassed, because its foundation, *in dubio pro reo*, could not put up with an evidence obtained through a system whose initial aim was to detect the highest number of suspects.

I argue that if a biometric system is tuned in order to meet law enforcement requirements, its results should not be transferred, as they stand, into the judicial system, which has different, even opposite, user requirements. Also pre-digital biometrics were somehow probabilistic, at least in very rough terms, but today one can set the degree of confidence of the system. In other words, differently from the past, probabilities of recognition can be tuned. If biometrics in law enforcement were tuned to minimize the risk of false recognition, I would not see any ethical problem in being their results transferred in court as well. Yet, would law enforcement agencies ever accept to purchase (and use) a system burdened by a higher failed recognition rate when that system could be tuned in order to minimize it?[7] I doubt.

If a system fulfills law enforcement requirements, it cannot also fulfill judicial requirements, and vice versa. Both requirements are fully legitimate, but they should work in parallel. If one of them "takes the leadership" (notably, law enforcement requirements) this becomes a serious ethical and democratic problem.

---

[7]The biometric performance at different thresholds is expressed through the "Detection Error Tradeoff" (DET) curve.

16.6 Solutions and Trends

The ideal technical solution to this ethical challenge would be to develop more robust, accurate, and sensitive, biometric applications, with negligible false rejection and false acceptance rates. If false rejection and false acceptance rates were truly negligible, the contradiction between law enforcement and judicial system requirements would be eliminated and one could transfer results from one system to the other, without major ethical issues. This is the illusion that has ruled forensic biometrics till almost today. This illusion is no longer tenable and there are not current applications which are contemporarily—in real life (not in labs)—as specific and sensitive as to consider negligible both their false rejection and false acceptance rates. In principle, a strategy exists that could increase contemporarily both specificity and sensitivity. This strategy is based on tighten requirements on the quality of biometric input data. Unfortunately, this would imply that a larger number of people could not be enrolled in the system, because of their poor biometric features, due to various causes, including the way in which in real life conditions biometric features are presented to sensors. Notably, this solution would not be applicable to biometrics extracted from materials, which were not originally designed for collecting biometrics. This is the case of latent fingerprints, but also of other "biometric traces" (e.g., recorded images, voices, pictures, etc.) that we are increasingly able to detect and collect for forensic reasons.

This leads to the problem posed by biometrics extracted from outside the forensic context, and brought into the legal cycle only at a later stage. Recorded faces, images, and voices, found online, in the Internet, are the largest (accidental) biometric library ever created (it is enough to think of the number of freely available pictures of Facebook users). Searching these huge, dispersed, online, databases is becoming one of the main activities, not only in criminal investigations, but also in crime prevention and judicial decisions.[8]

Online face and voice recognition—often coupled with soft biometrics[9] and geolocalization—are increasingly used for searching and recognizing people. This is destined to become still more pervasive with the arrival of new and emerging biometrics. New behavioral biometrics (also including electrophysiological biometrics) and cognitive biometrics will be able not only to extract biometric features from recorded online materials, but also to elicit meaningful biometric information from online behaviors and human-machine interaction patterns. New biometrics are extremely promising for law enforcement purposes. Will these biometrics be ever

---

[8]To give an idea of the magnitude and pervasiveness of this phenomenon, it is enough to mention that the Internet is today the main source of evidence on marriage validity or nullity in Catholic ecclesiastic courts.

[9]Sex, ethnicity, age, body shape, skin color, and so.

admissible in court? I doubt if presumption of innocence still rules criminal proceedings. Yet, trends seems to go toward an opposite direction.[10]

In November 2013, the European Commission presented a package of proposals to strengthen procedural safeguards for citizens in criminal proceedings. *Inter alia*, these proposals included a proposal of "*Directive on the strengthening of certain aspects of the presumption of innocence and of the right to be present at trial in criminal proceedings*",[11] aiming at harmonizing this principle (considered chiefly in its dimension of procedural right instead of human right) in different EU jurisdictions. When legislators feel the need to rule on great principles, it is often because they aim to mitigate them. Indeed, after a long preamble and four initial, generic, articles, Art.5 of the proposal directive focuses on *Burden of proof and standard of proof required.* Par.1 reaffirms the principle that

> Member States shall ensure that the burden of proof in establishing the guilt of suspects or accused persons is on the prosecution. This is without prejudice to any ex officio fact finding powers of the trial court

But Par.2 seriously mitigates it, by allowing Member States to shift the burden of proof on the defendant for any "*sufficient important*" (!) reason

> Member States shall ensure that any presumption, which shifts the burden of proof to the suspects or accused persons, is of sufficient importance to justify overriding that principle and is rebuttable.
> In order to rebut such a presumption it suffices that the defense adduces enough evidence as to raise a reasonable doubt regarding the suspect or accused person's guilt.

The Commission explained the rationale behind Art.5 Par.2 in an accompanying Communication on Making progress on the European Union Agenda on Procedural Safeguards for Suspects or Accused Persons—Strengthening the Foundation of the European Area of Criminal Justice,[12] which reads,

> In criminal proceedings, the burden of proof should be on the prosecution and any doubt should benefit the suspect or accused person, without prejudice to the independence of the judiciary when assessing the suspect or accused's guilt. A judgment must be based on the evidence put before it and not on allegations or assumptions. However, the ECtHR[13] has accepted that in specific and limited cases, the burden of proof may be shifted to the defense, and the Directive will reflect this standard, striking a balance between the public interest in effective prosecution and the rights of the defense.

---

[10]In his 2003 paper on Evaluation of Forensic Science [18], Arizona State University Professor of Law, Michael J. Saks, raised the issue of reversal of the burden of proof related to biometric evidence. His argument is different from mine, because he focuses on the fact that some courts are asking the defendant to demonstrate that biometric evidence ***does not*** fulfill *Daubert* criteria, instead of assessing by themselves whether it does. However, it is interesting to note that trends move in the same direction.

[11]COM(2013) 821 final, Brussels, 27.11.2013.

[12]COM(2013) 820 final, Brussels, 27.11.2013.

[13]European Court of Human Rights.

The initial formulation of COM (2013) 821 has raised many perplexities in the LIBE[14] (main) and in the JURI[15] (opinion) Committees of the European Parliament. More recently, the Council[16] has proposed to modify Art.5 Par.2 by eliminating the expression "*sufficient importance*" in its place listing cases in which it would be possible to shift the burden of proof on the defendant, say,

> (…) in two situations:
>
> (a) in case of certain minor offences, notably traffic offences (see recital 15a);
> (b) in case of certain other types of offences, when two conditions have been complied with:
>
> (i) the shifting of the burden of proof must be strictly necessary in the interest of the criminal proceedings; and
> (ii) the shifting of the burden of proof must be justified to override the principle that the burden of proof is on the prosecution (see also recital 15b);

It is definitely out of scope of this article to discuss this important debate, and its potential consequences on the European legal system. I think that the reader has probably understood that the issue at stake is something more important than "minor traffic offences".[17] This is also suggested by the web page of the *Justice Directorate of the European Commission*, which is not, of course, a Commission official statement or a policy document, but it is expected to represent the Commission's point of view,

> When designing and implementing measures in this field, it is important for the EU to get the balance right between measures that protect such rights and those that *facilitate*[18] the investigation and prosecution of crime [19]

This is why the current debate is likely to be so relevant also to ethics of forensic biometrics, because it finally concerns the delicate balance between pursue of the common good, and respect for individual liberty.

References

1. Mordini E, Tzovaras D (2012) Second generation biometrics: the ethical and social context. Springer, Berlin
2. Mordini E, Massari S (2008) Body, biometrics, and identity. Bioethics 22(9):488–498
3. Mordini E (2008) Nothing to hide. biometric privacy and private sphere. In: Tistarelli M, Juul N, Drygajlo A, Schouten B (eds) BIOID 2008 Biometrics and identity management, Springer, Berlin, Heidelberg, pp 247–57

[14]European Parliament Committee on Civil Liberties, Justice and Home Affairs.

[15]European Parliament Committee on Legal Affairs.

[16]Council of the European Union, 12196/14, Brussels, 29 July 2014.

[17]It is worth recalling that the issue of presumption of innocence has been one of the main issues at stake in the US legal, political, and ethical debate on war on terrorism and terrorists' detention.

[18]My italics.

4. Mordini E, Rebera AP (2013). The biometric fetish. In: About I, Brown J, Lonergan G (eds) People, papers, and practices: identification and registration in: transnational perspective, 1500–2010 London, Palgrave, pp 98–111
5. Mordini E (2009) Ethics and policy of biometrics. In: Tistarelli M, Stan ZL, Chellappa R (eds) Handbook of remote biometrics for surveillance and security. Springer, Berlin Heidelberg, pp 293–309
6. Mordini E, Rebera AP (2011) No identification without representation: constraints on the use of biometric identification systems. Rev Policy Res 29(1):5–20
7. Moenssens AA (1963) Admissibility of fingerprint evidence and constitutional objections to fingerprinting raised in criminal and civil cases. Chicago-Kent Law Rev 40(2):85–124
8. Kaye DH (2003) Questioning a courtroom proof of the uniqueness of fingerprints. Int Stat Rev 71:521–533
9. Haber L, Haber RN (2004) Error rates for human latent print examiners. In: Bolle R, Natalini R (eds) Advances in automatic fingerprint recognition. Springer, New York, pp 339–360
10. Stacey R (2004) Report on the erroneous fingerprint individualization in the madrid train bombing case. J Forensic Ident. 6(54):706–718
11. Champod, C. (2000). Standards of proof. In: Siegel J(ed) Encyclopaedia of forensic sciences, Academic Press p 890
12. Egli NM, Champod C, Margot P (2007) Evidence evaluation in fingerprint comparison and automated fingerprint identification system—Modelling within finger variability. Forensic Sci Int 167:189–195
13. Champod C, Lennard C, Margot P, Stoilovic M (2004) Fingerprints and other ridge skin impressions. CRC Press—Taylor & Francis, London
14. Cole S (2008) Comment on 'scientific validation of fingerprint evidence' under Daubert'. Law Probab Risk 7:120–132
15. Hirsch Ballin MF (2012) Anticipative criminal investigation. Springer, Berlin
16. Pollock F (1922) Essays in the law. Oxford University Press, Oxford
17. Summers RS (1999) Formal legal truth and substantive truth in judicial fact-finding—their justified divergence in some particular cases. Cornell Law Faculty Publications, Paper 1186
18. Saks MJ (2003) The legal and scientific evaluation of forensic science (especially fingerprint expert testimony). Seton Hall Law Rev 1167–87
19. European Commission (2014) Rights of suspects and accused. http://ec.europa.eu/justice/criminal/criminal-rights/index_en.htm. Accessed 2 June 2015

Index

M. Tistarelli and C. Champod (eds.), *Handbook of Biometrics for Forensic Science*, Advances in Computer Vision and Pattern Recognition,
DOI 10.1007/978-3-319-50673-9

FSC
www.fsc.org
MIX
Papier | Fördert gute Waldnutzung
FSC® C083411

Kolibri 360 GmbH
Ferdinand-Jühlke-Straße 7
99095 Erfurt, Deutschland
produktsicherheit@kolibri360.de